THE LAST MUSLIM CONQUEST

The Last Muslim Conquest

THE OTTOMAN EMPIRE AND
ITS WARS IN EUROPE

GÁBOR ÁGOSTON

PRINCETON UNIVERSITY PRESS

PRINCETON & OXFORD

Published by Princeton University Press
41 William Street, Princeton, New Jersey 08540
6 Oxford Street, Woodstock, Oxfordshire OX20 1TR

press.princeton.edu

All Rights Reserved

Library of Congress Cataloging-in-Publication Data

Names: Ágoston, Gábor, author.
Title: The last Muslim conquest : the Ottoman Empire and its wars
    in Europe / Gábor Ágoston.
Description: Princeton : Princeton University Press, [2021] | Includes bibliographical
    references and index.
Identifiers: LCCN 2020046919 (print) | LCCN 2020046920 (ebook) |
    ISBN 9780691159324 (hardcover) | ISBN 9780691205380 (ebook)
Subjects: LCSH: Turkey—History—Ottoman Empire, 1288–1918. |
    Turkey—Civilization—1288–1918. | Turkey—History, Military. |
    Turkey—Foreign relations—Europe. | Europe—Foreign relations—Turkey.
Classification: LCC DR486 .A376 2021 (print) | LCC DR486 (ebook) |
    DDC 956 / .015—dc23
LC record available at https://lccn.loc.gov/2020046919
LC ebook record available at https://lccn.loc.gov/2020046920

British Library Cataloging-in-Publication Data is available

Editorial: Priya Nelson, Thalia Leaf
Jacket Design: Jason Anscomb
Production: Danielle Amatucci
Publicity: Kate Hensley, Kathryn Stevens

Jacket art: (top) "The Dragoman of the Porte at the reception of a European ambassador and a Bukharan envoy, with the Reis ül-küttab seated in the middle." (middle left) "A Dance for the Pleasure of Sultan Ahmet III (1673–1736)," from the *Surname-i Hümayun*, 1720. Gouache on paper / Bridgeman (middle right) Sultan Mehmet II (1432–1481), 1480. Oil on canvas / Bridgeman (bottom) View of the capture of Constantinople by the Crusades, 1203–1204. Miniature from *Chroniques abrégées*, by David Aubert, 15th century, Paris (Bibliotheque de l'Arsenal). Background photo: "View from bridge in Constantinople," c. 1895, photochrome / Granger Historical Picture Archive

This book has been composed in Arno

Printed on acid-free paper. ∞

Printed in the United States of America

10 9 8 7 6 5 4 3 2 1

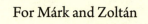

For Márk and Zoltán

CONTENTS

vii

NOTE ON CONVENTIONS

ATTAINING AGREEMENT on terms, personal names, and place-names related to a vast region once ruled by the Ottomans and their Habsburg rivals is impossible. People in those lands spoke many languages, including Turkish, Greek, Armenian, Kurdish, Arabic, Persian, Bulgarian, Serbian, Croatian, Romanian, Hungarian, Slovak, Polish, Ukrainian, German, Italian, and Latin. They used different names for the same places. For Ottoman terms, which are written in the Arabic script, I have opted for the post-1928 modern Turkish transliteration system that uses Latin script. Unfamiliar terms and names will challenge many English-speaking readers. I tried to minimize their challenge by using accepted English forms of Turkish and Arabic terms whenever possible (such as agha, beg, pasha, sharia, vizier). I kept these forms even if the term had become part of the name of individuals (Osman Agha, Osman Beg, Osman Pasha). Because these foreign terms have entered English, they are not italicized. I opted for the modern Turkish forms of bey in composite words, such as *sancakbeyi* and *beylerbeyi*, meaning "district governor" and "provincial governor-general." For simplicity, I do not indicate lengthened vowels, except when it is essential to avoid confusion—for example, to differentiate Âli, meaning "exalted" or "sublime," from the commonly used name Ali. I do not generally use the Turkish capitalized dotted "i" (İ) for place-names and personal names that entered English (Istanbul, Izmir, Ismail), whereas lesser-known names are given in their Turkish orthography. For Serbian and Bulgarian names, written in Cyrillic, I use the Croatian orthography rather than any of the more complex scholarly transliteration systems. To help English-speaking readers, I have Anglicized the first names of historical figures (John Hunyadi instead of János Hunyadi and George Branković instead of Đurad/Djuradj

xiii

Branković), providing the original first name when they first appear in the book. In the Kingdom of Hungary and the Habsburg monarchy, many aristocratic and noble families were multilingual and used various name forms. I opted for the one most commonly used in the sources and literature I am familiar with.

Place-names are generally transcribed according to their modern name forms, with the following exceptions. Serbian and Bulgarian place-names are transliterated according to the Croatian orthography. Where established English forms exist, these are preferred. For the place-names in the Kingdom of Hungary that are situated since the end of World War I in Romania and Slovakia, the Hungarian name forms are preferred, as the modern Slovakian or Romanian name forms would represent anachronism. For the same reason, and for the sake of simplicity, I use the Polish name forms for place-names that belonged to the Polish-Lithuanian Commonwealth—hence, Kamieniec Podolski instead of its Ukrainian name, which has too many transliterations (Kamianets Podilsky, Kamjanec' Podil'skyj, Kam'yanets' Podil'skyy, Kamenets Podil'skiy). A glossary of place-names at the end of the book lists the various name forms of frequently discussed places.

Throughout the book, I use Constantinople and Istanbul interchangeably. By doing so, I intend to dispel a common misconception that the Ottomans renamed the Byzantine capital Constantinople as Istanbul after they conquered it in 1453. In fact, the Ottomans called their new capital city Kostantiniyye (after the Arabic name form of Constantinople) on coins and in official documents until the end of the empire, especially when they referred to the court, where official documents were issued. At the same time, Istanbul (a distortion from the Greek phrase "to the city") was also used in official documents and by the common people. The following pronunciation guide might be useful.

For Croatian: c = as *ts* in waits, ć = soft *ch*, č = hard *ch* as in church, j = as *y* in yes, š = as *sh* in should, ž = as *s* in leisure.

For Hungarian: á = as *a* in father, c = as *ts* in waits, cs = as *ch* in church, é = as in café, gy = as in duke, í = as *ee* in see, j = as *y* in yes, ny = as in new, ó = as *o* in go, s = as *sh* in should, sz = as *s* in sound, ty = as in stew, zs = as *s* in leisure, ú = as *oo* in root

For Romanian: j = as *s* in leisure, ş = as *sh* in should, ţ = as *ts* in waits.

For Turkish: c = as *j* in jet, ç = as *ch* in church, ğ = soft *g* (lengthens preceding vowel), ı = undotted i (similar to the vowel sound in the word "cousin"), i = as *ee* in see, ö = as *ö* in German (similar to the vowel sound in the word "bird"), ş = as *sh* in should, ü = as *ü* in German.

THE LAST MUSLIM CONQUEST

Prologue

"EITHER I TAKE THIS CITY, or the city will take me, dead or alive," announced the Ottoman sultan Mehmed II to the Byzantine emperor Constantine XI before the final assault of Constantinople (modern Istanbul). On 29 May 1453, the capital of the thousand-year-old Eastern Roman or Byzantine Empire fell to Mehmed, who is remembered as Fatih or the Conqueror. Three generations later, on 29 August 1526, at the battle of Mohács in southwestern Hungary, Mehmed's great-grandson, Süleyman I, annihilated the army of the Kingdom of Hungary, which had halted Ottoman advance in Europe for more than 150 years. Three years later, in 1529, Süleyman stood at the gate of Vienna. The siege failed, but the Ottomans would rule over central Hungary for 150 years from Buda (modern Budapest), just 250 kilometers (150 miles) from Vienna.

Since Voltaire and Edward Gibbon, many historians considered the Byzantine Empire's fall to the Ottoman Turks in 1453 as a watershed in European and world history that signaled the beginning of the modern era. Some saw the ensuing exodus of Greek scholars to Italy and the Ottomans' control of the trade routes between Asia and Europe as stimuli for the European Renaissance and geographical explorations. While the extent to which the Ottomans influenced the European Renaissance and the geographical explorations remains disputed, the conquest's effects on European geopolitics are clear and manifest. Possession of Constantinople enabled the Ottomans to cement their rule in southeastern Europe, Asia Minor, the Mediterranean, and the Black Sea littoral and build the most potent contiguous empire since ancient Rome.

The consequences of the battle of Mohács were equally profound. After the death of the young King Louis II of Hungary in the battle, Archduke Ferdinand of Habsburg acquired the long-coveted thrones of Hungary and Bohemia. Together with Austria, the two kingdoms became part of the Habsburg dynasty's Danubian monarchy in central Europe. With the Holy Crown of St. Stephen of Hungary, the Habsburgs inherited from the medieval Kingdom of Hungary the burden of defending Christian Europe against the Muslim Ottomans. Hungary became the principal continental battleground between the Ottomans and the Habsburgs. The other frontier was the Mediterranean, where the Ottomans fought Ferdinand's brother, Charles of Spain, the emperor of the Holy Roman Empire of the German Nation. This was a dramatic turn of events, as Charles's grandparents—Isabella the Catholic, queen of Castile, and Ferdinand the Catholic, king of Aragon—had conquered the last Muslim state of the Iberian peninsula, the Kingdom of Granada, completing the Reconquista by 1492. *The Last Muslim Conquest* narrates the emergence of the Ottoman Empire and the epic rivalry between the Muslim Ottomans and the Catholic Habsburgs.

The Ottoman Turks emerged in the late thirteenth century in northwestern Asia Minor, which the Turks, Persians, and Arabs called Rum (Rome), the land of the Eastern Roman Empire. Named after its eponymous founder, Osman I (d. 1324), the small Ottoman principality was but one among the many chiefdoms that the Turkic and Muslim semi-nomads of Central Asian origin established in Asia Minor. The Ottoman polity was ruled throughout its existence by the House of Osman, the descendants of Osman. While Europeans saw them as a Turkish empire, the followers of Osman called themselves *Osmanlı* in Turkish—which in English came to be rendered as Ottoman. The Ottomans called their polity the Realms of the House of Osman (*memalik-i Osmaniye*), emphasizing the importance of the dynasty of Osman (*âl-i Osman*). Likewise, Ottoman chroniclers titled their histories "Annals of the House of Osman" (*Tevarih-i Âl-i Osman*), whereas compilations of laws enacted in the name of the ruler were titled the "Laws/Law Code of the House of Osman" (*Kavanin/Kanunname-i Âl-i Osman*). The dynastic empire that Osman's successors built was multiethnic and multiconfessional. It was the longest-lived such empire of its kind in Eurasia, which collapsed during World War I, along with its longtime rivals, the similarly multi-ethnic empires of the Houses of the Habsburgs and Romanovs, the Austro-Hungarian and Russian Empires, respectively.

The Ottoman dynasty and the ruling elite remained distinctly Muslim. However, for centuries the rulers married across ethnic lines, and the ruling elite and bureaucracy incorporated recent converts to Islam both at the center of power and in the provinces. The empire's subjects spoke dozens of languages. They worshiped according to the teachings of Sunni and Shiite Islam, various Christian churches, and Judaism, to name but the most important religious communities. To rule over such a diverse population required flexibility, negotiation, and adaptability to local customs in governance. As this book demonstrates, Ottoman strategies of conquest and incorporation went beyond sheer military might, which has often been singled out in the general literature when explaining the "rise" of the Ottomans. Eclectic pragmatism that incorporated Turco-Mongolian, Byzantine-Slav, Persian, and Arab traditions and institutions of governance characterized Ottoman rule from the time of their earliest conquests in the fourteenth century. Strategic adaptability and negotiation remained the hallmark of Ottoman governance throughout the period covered in this book.

After the conquest of Constantinople, Mehmed II subdued the Turco-Muslim emirates in Asia Minor and the Christian Slavic states of Bulgaria, Serbia, and Bosnia. Mehmed's successors extended Ottoman rule to Hungary in the north and to Yemen in the south, to Algeria in the west and to Iraq in the east. In its heyday in the sixteenth century, the Ottoman Empire was among the militarily most formidable and bureaucratically best-administered empires that impacted the lives of millions across three continents. The Ottomans were a crucial player in European power politics too. They were a constant military threat to their Venetian, Hungarian, Polish-Lithuanian, Spanish, and Austrian Habsburg neighbors, besieging, albeit unsuccessfully, the latter's capital city Vienna twice, in 1529 and 1683.

At the end of the seventeenth century, an international coalition of the papacy, the Habsburg monarchy, the Polish-Lithuanian Commonwealth,

The growth of the Ottoman Empire (Drawn by Béla Nagy.)

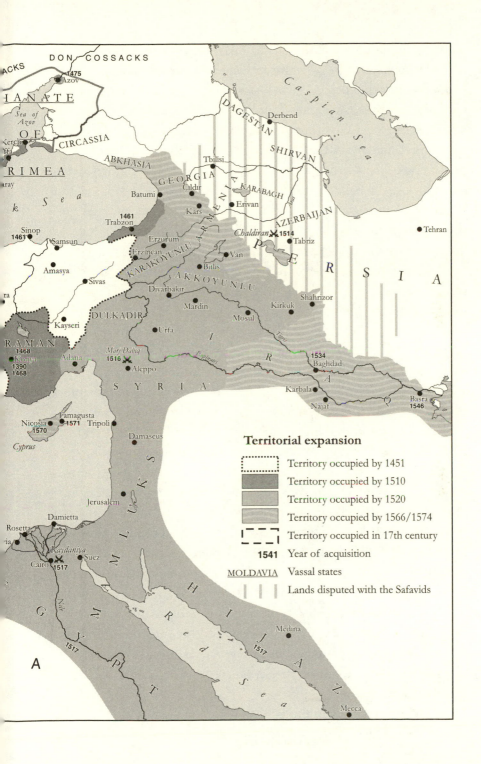

DON COSSACKS
ACKS
1475
Azov
IANATE
Sea of
Azov
O F
Kerch
CIRCASSIA
Ha
RIMEA
ABKHASIA
aray
k Sea
Batumi
GEORGIA
Çıldır
Tbilisi
ARMENIA
KARABAGH
DAGESTAN
Derbend
SHIRVAN
Caspian Sea
Kars
Erivan
AZERBAIJAN
1461
Sinop
Trabzon
1461
Samsun
Erzurum
Erzincan
KARAKOYUNLU
Chaldıran 1514
Tabriz
Tehran
P
E
R
S
I
A
Amasya
Sivas
AKKOYUNLU
Van
Bitlis
Diyarbakır
Shahrizor
ra
Mardin
Kirkuk
DULKADIR
Urfa
Mosul
Tigris
Kayseri
I
RAMAN
1468
Adana
Marj Dabiq
1516
Euphrates
1534
Baghdad
R
Konya
1390
1468
Aleppo
A
SYRIA
Karbala
Basra
1546
Najaf
Famagusta
Nicosia 1571 Tripoli
1570
Damascus
Cyprus
M
A
M
L
U
K
S
Jerusalem
Damietta
Rosetta
ia
Raydaniya
Cairo 1517
Suez
H
I
J
A
Z
G
Nile
E
G
Y
P
T
Red
Sea
Medina
1517
A
1517
Mecca

Territorial expansion

Territory occupied by 1451

Territory occupied by 1510

Territory occupied by 1520

Territory occupied by 1566/1574

Territory occupied in 17th century

1541 Year of acquisition

MOLDAVIA Vassal states

Lands disputed with the Safavids

Venice, and Muscovy conquered most of the Ottoman domains north of the Danube River. In the eighteenth century, the Ottomans' military might continued to decline vis-à-vis the Habsburg monarchy and Romanov Russia. The fate of the Ottoman Empire—its possible partition by the European "Great Powers" or among the emerging nation-states—became one of the crucial issues in European politics, known in its day as the "Eastern Question." Yet, the Ottomans continued to rule over much of the Balkan Peninsula and the Middle East until 1878 and World War I, respectively. It is a formidable accomplishment, even considering that Ottoman control over provinces far from the capital was often nominal in the eighteenth and nineteenth centuries.

The Last Muslim Conquest contributes to four overarching histories. First, chapters in part 1, "Emergence," examine how the small principality of Osman had, by the early sixteenth century, evolved into the most powerful empire in the region by conquering and incorporating the neighboring polities. These chapters illustrate how the Ottoman conquest shaped European history, especially that of southeastern and central Europe, the main theaters of Ottoman expansion. Second, chapters in part 2, "Clash of Empires," examine the entanglement of Ottoman and European politics in the context of Ottoman-Habsburg competition, one of the defining imperial rivalries of the age. These chapters demonstrate the impact of this rivalry on both European and Ottoman policy-making and diplomacy. Third, chapters in part 3, "Sinews of Empire," examine the shifting military and soft power of the Ottomans and their regional rivals. Finally, two chapters in part 4, "Frontiers and Wars of Exhaustion," and segments of other chapters examine the history of the empire's Danubian frontier provinces. It was here that the Ottoman Empire and the Habsburg monarchy deployed their military might, resulting in the heaviest concentration of forts and garrison soldiers on both sides of the Muslim-Christian divide. This contested borderland is examined from several angles, including Habsburg and Ottoman military commitments, administrative strategies, and the use of diplomacy and intelligence gathering.

When I first envisioned this project some ten years ago, chapters in part 1 were meant to be a much shorter introduction to a book whose primary focus was to be on Ottoman and Habsburg power and their contested borderlands. However, I soon realized that to understand how the Ottoman-Habsburg imperial rivalry unfolded, one should first examine how the Ottoman conquest in southeastern and central Europe shaped the Ottoman Empire and affected the emergence of the Habsburgs' Danubian monarchy. My goal was to explore the Ottoman conquest as an integral part of European history by putting the respective source material and specialized historiographies into dialogue. These chapters serve as a synthetic narrative of the emergence of the Ottoman Empire in its European context.

In our global twenty-first century, we often emphasize multiculturalism, varied ethnic and religious contexts, cultural exchange, and connected histories. Such an approach is a welcome corrective to earlier studies that privileged religious antagonisms. Yet, the emergence of the Ottomans shows the continued significance of religion. Although the Ottomans emerged in a multireligious milieu, Islam and holy war— termed *ghaza* by the Ottomans—played a useful role in rallying support for the Ottoman enterprise. *Ghaza* became an increasingly important part of Ottoman loyalty creation and dynastic legitimation. This was especially true from the mid-fourteenth century onward when the Ottomans fought against Bulgarians, Serbs, Hungarians, and Crusaders from central and western Europe. The use of religion for legitimation was not unique to the Ottomans. The Ottomans' Muslim neighbors also employed similar strategies of religious legitimation. Examples include the Sunni Akkoyunlu Turkmen Confederation of Uzun Hasan, the Mamluks of Syria and Egypt, the Shaybanid Uzbeks of Central Asia, and the Shiite Safavids of Persia. However, since the Ottomans fought against their Christian neighbors in Europe for centuries, they could claim to be the true *ghazis*, fighters in the way of God (*mujahid*), and defenders of Islam.

Along with the ideology of holy war, historical contingency and accidents, and longer-term Ottoman strategies of conquest and incorporation (dynastic marriages, forced resettlement, and the co-optation of the defeated elites into the Ottoman military and bureaucracy) were significant factors that contributed to the emergence of the House of

Osman. Of the historical contingencies, I use the Byzantine civil wars in the middle of the fourteenth century to illustrate how the policies of Emperors Andronikos III and John VI Kantakouzenos of soliciting military help from the neighboring Turkish emirs of Saruhan, Aydın, and Ottoman created opportunities for the latter to extend their influence into Byzantine domains. The alliance between Kantakouzenos and Orhan, the son of Osman and the second Ottoman ruler—who married Kantakouzenos's daughter, Theodora—is especially illuminating. It demonstrates that the Ottomans (unlike their Turkish neighbors, who were contented with war spoils) used these temporary alliances to occupy strategic sites and gain territory. These alliances created a pattern. The Ottomans later masterfully exploited the civil wars of their neighbors, as the conquests of Serbia and the Morea (the Peloponnese) demonstrate.

Despite temporary alliances with their Muslim and Turkish neighbors, the Byzantine emperors were busy organizing crusades against the Ottomans and routinely exploited domestic disturbances and civil wars in the Ottoman domains. They sought military help from the papacy and the Catholic monarchs of Europe. Their clergy and political elite were willing to accept the union of the Orthodox and Latin churches in return for Western military aid against the "Turks," presented in Byzantine chronicles as the "natural enemies" of Byzantium and Christendom. As the Ottomans reached the borders of the medieval Kingdom of Hungary, Hungarian monarchs styled themselves as "Champion of Christ" (*athleta Christi*)—such as King Louis I of Hungary and Poland, the first king who had to deal with Ottoman incursions into his domains. His successors assumed the titles of "shield and rampart" (*scutum atque murus*) of Christendom. Sigismund of Luxemburg led the Crusade of Nikopol in 1396 and established the first effective defense system against the Ottomans along Hungary's southern Danubian borders (as discussed in chapters 1 and 2). Threatened by Ottoman conquests, statesmen and intellectuals in Hungary, Croatia, and Poland formulated their self-image as "bulwark of Christendom" (*antemurale, propugnaculum Christianitatis*) against the new religious "other," the "infidel Turk" (*infideles turcos*). The images of self and the Turkish other were then disseminated through political propaganda, influencing thinking about Turks and Muslims to this day.

The details in the book may try the patience of the reader. But the details are necessary if one wants to go beyond superficial generalizations. Detailed narratives give agency to lesser-known actors. Traditional histories of the Ottoman Empire—following Ottoman court chroniclers—have privileged the rulers of the dynasty as the most important actors in the Ottoman story. The first ten sultans undoubtedly brought stability and shaped Ottoman policy in the long term: six sultans ruled for between twenty-five and thirty-seven years, and Süleyman ruled for forty-six years. However, other actors played important roles too. Marcher lords and their raiders, viziers, advisers, provincial governors, soldiers, surveyors of revenues, tax collectors, interpreters, and spies shaped Ottoman policies, as did their counterparts in the Byzantine Empire, and the polities in southeastern and central Europe.

I discuss selected Ottoman sieges and battles to demonstrate how the Ottomans overcame their rivals by using military might and diplomatic skills. Historians, with the benefit of hindsight, habitually single out battles and sieges that they deem decisive in shaping history. Few battles in the early modern era shaped geopolitics so profoundly as did the Ottoman conquest of Constantinople (1453) and the Ottoman battlefield victories at Chaldiran (1514), Marj Dabiq (1516), Raydaniyya (1517), and Mohács (1526). The conquest of Constantinople marked the end of the Byzantine Empire. It reconfigured the power balance in the Mediterranean and the Black Sea littoral. It also empowered Sultan Mehmed II to transform the nascent Ottoman frontier polity into a more centralized patrimonial empire. The battle of Chaldiran secured Ottoman rule over most of eastern and southeastern Asia Minor and Azerbaijan, the traditional base of Turkmen confederations and the homeland of pro–Safavid Qizilbash tribes who had long challenged Sunni Ottoman rule. Chaldiran also pushed the Safavid state, originally a Turkmen confederation, to assume a more pronounced Persian and Shiite character and to position itself as the main counterweight to its two Sunni Muslim neighbors: the Ottomans to the west and the Timurids (Mughals) of India to the east. During two centuries of

Ottoman-Safavid rivalry, Shiism solidified in Persia and the adjacent territories in Iraq, as did the split between Sunni and Shiite Islam (with consequences to this day). Marj Dabiq and Raydaniyya marked the end of the Mamluk sultanate, which had ruled Greater Syria and Egypt for more than 250 years between 1250 and 1517. These victories heralded the introduction of Ottoman rule in the Arab heartlands of Islam, with significant consequences for the development of both the region and the Ottoman Empire. The conquest of Egypt also acquainted the Ottomans with the Red Sea and the Indian Ocean. It offered the Ottoman padishah an opportunity to dislodge the Portuguese from the Indian Ocean and control the spice trade, a chance that the Sublime Porte, as the Ottoman government was known in Europe, missed. However, the Porte achieved its more limited goals. It secured the Holy Cities of Mecca and Medina and restored the spice trade routes in the Red Sea and the Mediterranean. Some Ottoman governors in Egypt and naval commanders in Suez may have entertained a more ambitious strategy. Nonetheless, Ottoman policy in the Red Sea, the Persian Gulf, and the Indian Ocean remained limited in scope and objectives owing to Ottoman strategic priorities that focused on the Mediterranean and central Europe and the modest size and restricted radius of action of the Ottoman oarpowered galley fleets.

Ottoman conquests energized the papacy and the European monarchs to devise new crusading plans to halt further Ottoman advances in the Mediterranean and central Europe. Yet, the Habsburg-Valois rivalry, which unfolded after the election of Charles of Spain as Holy Roman emperor in 1519, and the religious division in Christendom (following Martin Luther's movement) divided Europe and diverted attention from the "Turkish menace." As examined in chapters 5 and 6, European political and religious discord coincided with the shift in Ottoman strategy under Süleyman. After his father's decade-long war against the Safavids and Mamluks, Süleyman targeted central and Mediterranean Europe. The ensuing Ottoman-Habsburg rivalry and wars profoundly influenced the fates of both the Ottoman Empire and Habsburg central Europe.

The focus on imperial rivalry and wars underlines the important role that war played in shaping Ottoman history, Ottoman-European relations, and the evolution of governmental, military, and financial institutions in the Ottoman Empire and in the countries neighboring the Ottoman domains—issues discussed in part 3, "Sinews of Empire." Wars influenced domestic policies too, as they forced the competing imperial governments in Constantinople and Vienna to negotiate with their respective elites. The interdependence of Ottoman and Habsburg imperial governments and their elites shaped imperial policies, military capabilities, and strategies not only vis-à-vis their imperial opponents but also concerning domestic opposition.

Recent trends in the scholarly literature privilege European-Ottoman encounters, alliances, and cultural exchange.[1] While these works are useful, as they balance the one-sided "clash of civilizations" approach, one should be careful not to overstate their importance. The fact that European contemporaries felt the need to justify their alliances with the "infidel Turk" suggests that alliances across the Muslim-Christian religious-cultural divide were considered the exception instead of the norm. When King Francis I of France, King John Szapolyai of Hungary, and the Protestant princes of central Europe sought Ottoman help, their propagandists were keen to convince their Christian brethren that they did this in desperation, and only because the Habsburgs attacked them. Their opponents, on the other hand, assailed them as heretics. Ottoman jurists, for their part, argued that peace with the infidel would be temporary, and only if it benefited the Muslims.

By all accounts, the Ottoman leadership was practical. Chapters 10 and 11 ("Lawfare and Diplomacy" and "Embassies, Dragomans, and Intelligence") illustrate how the Ottomans manipulated truces and commercial treaties with selected European monarchs to their advantage, making lawfare and intelligence gathering an integral part of Ottoman grand strategy. Unlike the more centralized Venetian and Habsburg secret services, Ottoman intelligence gathering remained ad hoc and personal. Rivalries and factionalism among the various power groups in Constantinople and the provinces had a negative effect on Ottoman efforts to seek information. As a consequence, the Ottoman intelligence-gathering function was less efficient than that of the Venetians and Habsburgs and failed to translate the gathered information into systematized knowledge about the Porte's

European rivals. Lack of such knowledge about their enemies weakened the Ottomans' soft power at a time when their military might was also waning.

In the sixteenth century, the Ottomans were feared and admired by Europeans from Niccolò Machiavelli to the Russian soldier and social critic Ivan Peresvetov. Having served as a professional soldier in Poland-Lithuania, Hungary, and Moldavia, Peresvetov knew the Ottomans and regarded Sultan Mehmed II's just governance and orderly army as models to be emulated by his ruler, Ivan IV (r. 1547–84) "the Terrible" of Muscovy. Venetian diplomats regarded the Ottoman sultans as "the most powerful" monarchs. The Flemish Ogier Ghiselin Busbecq, Habsburg ambassador sent to the Ottoman court in the mid-sixteenth century, noted the Ottomans' military superiority over the Habsburgs. Yet, at the beginning of the Long Ottoman-Habsburg War of 1593–1606, fought in Hungary, the Hungarians and Habsburgs realized that the once formidable Ottoman Empire no longer constituted a deadly threat to them. Writing in 1596, Hasan Kafi, an eyewitness Ottoman jurist from Bosnia, noted the Habsburg troops' superiority over the Ottoman cavalry. Four generations later, Ibrahim Müteferrika—a Hungarian convert to Islam and the founder of the Arabic-letter printing press in Constantinople—considered the military reforms of Peter the Great (r. 1682/96–1725) of Russia as an example worthy of imitation in his advice literature, written in 1732 for Sultan Mahmud I. Ottoman military setbacks and the contrasting views of Peresvetov and Busbecq, on the one hand, and Hasan Kafi and Ibrahim Müteferrika, on the other, reflected significant shifts in Ottoman, Habsburg, and Russian military fortunes.

Contemporaneous Ottoman thinkers and later historians found the causes of Ottoman military defeats in the corruption of the institutions of the idealized "old order" (*nizam-i kadim*). The paradigm of "Ottoman decline" was created. It has been echoed by the Ottomans' European contemporaries and in the works of historians. The latter blamed "Islamic conservatism" and "military despotism" for the Ottomans' decline. Some scholarship has questioned the traditional "rise–golden age–decline" periodization of Ottoman history. This scholarship disproved almost all the major arguments of the traditional decline schools, demonstrated the resurgence of the Ottoman Empire in the seventeenth century, and declared the decline paradigm a myth.[2] However, none of these studies was able to satisfactorily explain the eclipse of Ottoman military capabilities by the Ottomans' two major regional rivals, Habsburg Austria and Romanov Russia.

Comparing and contrasting military developments in the Ottoman Empire, the Habsburg monarchy, and Muscovy/Russia helps us better understand the divergent paths that the Ottomans, Habsburgs, and Romanovs took, and thus the nature of their respective empires. *The Last Muslim Conquest* uses new evidence from the Ottoman archives to examine Ottoman military capabilities vis-à-vis their immediate rivals, demonstrating that such an approach yields a more realistic assessment of Ottoman strengths and weaknesses and the shifting military balance. The book also shows the long-unappreciated role that the Ottomans played in catalyzing military transformations, and related fiscal and institutional developments, across a vast terrain from Habsburg central Europe to Safavid Persia and beyond.

While the empire experienced significant military and socioeconomic transformations from the late sixteenth century onward, these did not constitute such a break with the past as to mark the beginning of a "second Ottoman Empire," as one study argued.[3] After all, the empire remained an ancien régime. While recruitment strategies, resource management, taxation, and central and provincial administration had all been adjusted to meet new challenges, these changes did not trigger a radical overhaul of the Ottoman Empire and its military, finances, and administration. The legal system established in the fifteenth and sixteenth centuries remained in use until the nineteenth-century legal reforms. The same can be said of the frameworks within which the empire's peoples lived and interacted with one another and with representatives of the government. Although new geopolitical realities at the end of the seventeenth century forced the Ottomans to accept international principles of respecting the sovereignty and territorial integrity of foreign states, Ottoman diplomacy, too, followed traditional patterns. It was not until the late eighteenth century that the overhaul of the Ottoman ancien régime started in earnest during Selim III's reign, labeled "new order." It continued with the *Tanzimat* reforms (1839–76), resulting in the emergence of a "second" Ottoman Empire, which increasingly looked and acted like the other nineteenth-century European empires. This is not to say that the empire of Mehmed IV (r. 1648–87) was the same as that of Mehmed II, the Conqueror of Constantinople. To the contrary, I have attempted throughout the book to demonstrate how successive generations of the Ottoman elite tried to adjust their policies and institutions to new challenges, both domestic and external, and how these adjustments affected the relations of the Porte with its European neighbors from the fifteenth through the early eighteenth centuries.

PART I

Emergence

1

The Early Ottomans

Turks and the Byzantine World

The ancestors of Osman, the eponymous founder of the Ottoman dynasty, arrived in northwestern Asia Minor and settled in the former Byzantine province of Bithynia shortly before 1300. By that time, the Byzantine emperor of Constantinople had long lost control over much of Asia Minor. After the victory of the Seljuk Turks over the Byzantine army in 1071 at Manzikert, a branch of the Great Seljuks of Iran gradually extended its rule in eastern and central Asia Minor, which the newcomers called Rum, the land of the Romans or Greeks. Under the Seljuks and the rival Turkmen dynasty of the Danishmendids (whom the Seljuks eliminated only a century after Manzikert), large numbers of nomadic Turks from Transoxania arrived in Rum, whose upland pasturelands and warm coastlands offered ideal conditions for the pastoralists' way of life.

Conversion to Islam, the religion of the winning party, seems to have been widespread from the eleventh century onward. Despite conversion and the Turkification of the population, the Seljuk sultanate of Rum remained a multiethnic and polyglot polity. Turks were living mainly along the border zones, which they called *uc*, while Greeks and Armenians were partly rural and partly urban, as were the Persians (Tajik) and Arabs. Relations between Greeks and Turks were close and intermarriages relatively common. Some Byzantine aristocratic families—the Komnenoi, Tornikoi, Gabrades, and Mavrozomai—became members of the Seljuk nobility. Greeks worked in the Seljuk administration, while the Byzantine emperors hired Turkish troops. The emperors also launched joint military campaigns with the Seljuks against other rivals. Fleeing Seljuk rulers and rebel princes sought refuge in Byzantium as often as they did among their Muslim brethren in Asia Minor, Syria, Mesopotamia, and Iran. At the same time, rebel Byzantine lords escaped to the Seljuk capital Konya. Despite raids and punitive campaigns, there existed a long-lasting, if uneasy, political cooperation between Byzantium and the Seljuk sultanate of Rum from 1160 until 1261. This amicable relationship was based on the friendship between the Byzantine emperors and Seljuk sultans and their respective political elites, as well as on the influence of the Orthodox Church in Seljuk domains.

The Seljuk sultanate acted as the chief guarantor of the Nicene Empire after the Latin crusaders captured Constantinople in 1204 during the Fourth Crusade, established a Latin empire in Constantinople, divided the former Byzantine lands among themselves, and forced the Byzantine emperors into exile in Nicaea (modern Iznik). During the Nicene era, the Seljuk sultans acknowledged the emperors in Nicaea. In contrast, the Seljuks considered the "Empire of Trebizond" in northeastern Asia Minor and the Despotate of Epirus in Albania and northwestern Greece (the other Byzantine successor states after the Fourth Crusade) only as regional polities of nonimperial dignity. The peoples of Rum under Seljuk rule shared elements of each other's cultures. The beliefs of the Greeks in Seljuk Rum differed from those living under the Byzantine emperors. They also dressed like Turks, used Turkish weapons, and spoke a vernacular with Turkish and Persian loan words. Many Turks, Greeks, Armenians, and Persians in Rum spoke at least two languages. Jelaleddin Rumi (1207–73)—the founder of the *mevlevi* order of dervishes, originally from Balkh in Central Asia—wrote most of his works in Persian. But he also used Turkish and Greek vocabularies when addressing his poems to the townsfolk of Konya, his chosen new home.[1]

The influx of Turkish nomadic peoples—known as Turkmen or Turcoman—into western Asia Minor is closely related to the Mongol invasion of the Middle East in the 1240s and 1250s. A western army of the Mongols invaded and defeated the Seljuks of Rum in 1243 at

Kösedağ, northeast of Sivas. The Seljuks of Rum became the vassals of the Mongol Ilkhanids. The Ilkhanids established their empire in the vast area from present-day Afghanistan to Turkey after Hülegü Khan (r. 1256–65), the grandson of Chinggis Khan, had conquered and sacked Baghdad, ending the rule of the Abbasid caliphs (750–1258). As the Mongols occupied more and more grasslands for their horses in Asia Minor, the Turkmen tribes moved farther to the west and settled on the Seljuk-Byzantine marches. By the last decades of the thirteenth century, the Ilkhanids and their Seljuk vassals had lost control over much of Asia Minor. In the ensuing power vacuum many local Turkmen tribal chiefs, known as *beg* or *emir*, managed to establish themselves as rulers of small chiefdoms or principalities. The Ottomans, who were only one among the numerous Turco-Muslim emirates, settled in northwest Asia Minor, in the former Byzantine province of Bithynia.

The Ottomans benefited greatly from their new location. After the Byzantines recaptured Constantinople from the Latin crusaders in 1261, the emperors in Constantinople were primarily preoccupied with re-gaining control over southeastern Europe, while still managing their defenses in Asia Minor against Turkmen attacks. But because of Vene-tian threats, Emperor Andronikos II Palaiologos (r. 1282–1328) followed a more passive policy along the eastern borders. He also attempted to improve Byzantine finances by reducing the size of the army and dis-mantling the fleet.[2] In the words of the contemporary Byzantine chroni-cler Pachymeres, writing circa 1310, "the defenses of the eastern territory were weakened, whilst the Persians (Turks) were emboldened to invade lands which had no means of driving them off."[3]

Holy Warriors and Marcher Lords

Until the late 1970s, most scholars understood the Ottoman polity as a quintessential Islamic frontier warrior state, whose raison d'être was the holy war or jihad—termed *ghaza* in Ottoman sources—against the "in-fidels" and the continuous expansion of the Ottoman emirate's frontiers at the expense of its Christian neighbors. Formulated in the 1930s by the Austrian Ottomanist scholar Paul Wittek, the *ghaza* thesis served as an all-embracing elucidation of the rise, evolution, and fall of the Ottoman Empire. Wittek believed that the early Ottomans shared the chivalrous spirit of the *futuwwa* religious "corporations," whose understanding and practice of Islam differed from that of the religious establishment (*ulama*). Situated on the frontier of Byzantium, the Ottoman *ghazis* were strategically positioned to wage such "holy wars." Opportunities for glory served as a magnet for the warriors of the neighboring Turco-Muslim emirates. The ostensibly inexhaustible supply of zealous *ghazi* warriors under the banner of the early Ottoman rulers seemed to explain their military successes.[4]

Scholarship from the late 1970s began to question Wittek's thesis. Critics have argued that what Wittek termed as early Ottoman *ghazas* were more inclusive political enterprises. In the early fourteenth century, the Muslim Turkmen emirates of Aydın, Karasi, Saruhan, and Ottoman forged alliances and launched military ventures with Christian Catalans, Byzantines, and Genoese. Catalan mercenaries, whom the Byzantines hired to fight the Turkmens, fought both against and alongside the Turks.[5] The Byzantine emperors Andronikos III (r. 1328–41) and John VI Kantakouzenos (r. 1347–54) enlisted the help of the Muslim Turkmen emirs of Saruhan, Aydın, and Ottoman against their opponents both in the empire and beyond. Local Byzantine governors cooperated with the Ottomans, while dissatisfied Byzantine generals and soldiers joined the victorious Ottomans. In the late 1340s and early 1350s—during the war between Genoa, on the one hand, and Venice, Aragon, and Byzantium, on the other—the Genoese of Galata sought the assistance of the Ottomans. Galata was a suburb of Byzantine Constantinople north of the Golden Horn and home of a Genoese colony, established almost a century before. In the summer of 1351, the Ottomans supplied the Genoese with a thousand archers to fight against Genoa's Christian enemy.[6] The Genoese-Ottoman cooperation lasted until the Ottoman conquest of Constantinople in 1453. Genoese ships helped the Ottomans on multiple occasions to maintain communication between their lands in Asia Minor and southeastern Europe, sabotaging Byzantine and Western attempts to block the crossing of Ottoman troops from Asia to Europe.[7]

The fourteenth century witnessed Ottoman campaigns against fellow Muslim Turks. The Ottomans also annexed the neighboring Turkish emirates of Karasi, Saruhan, Germiyan, and Hamid. Fifteenth-century Ottoman chroniclers portrayed the early Ottomans as *ghazi* warriors, often ignoring these conflicts and the Ottomans' alliances with Christians. These chroniclers claimed that the Ottomans acquired the lands of the neighboring emirates via peaceful means, such as by purchasing it and by marriage. When they mentioned the wars between the Ottomans and their Turkish neighbors, Ottoman chroniclers tried to legitimize them by stating that the Ottomans acted in self-defense. Other chroniclers claimed that the Ottomans were forced to fight because the emirates' hostile policies hindered the Ottomans' holy wars against the Christians.[8]

The heterogeneous nature of the early Ottoman society was a rich source of military and administrative skills. Among the allies of Osman, the founder of the Ottoman dynasty, one finds Orthodox Greeks and recent Christian converts to Islam, such as Evrenos and Köse Mihal. Ghazi Evrenos was one of the most famous Ottoman marcher lords. Ottoman chronicles claimed that Evrenos was a Muslim Turk from the neighboring Karasi emirate. However, a recently discovered source suggests that he was of Serbian descent, the son of a certain Branko Lazar, who after his conversion to Islam was known as İsa Beg. Branko Lazar may have joined the Ottomans to extend his original patrimony at the expense of his local Christian rivals. His Serbian origin may explain why the Ottoman ruler Murad I entrusted Evrenos to lead the Ottoman army to the battlefield of Kosovo in 1389. Unlike the newcomer Ottomans, Evrenos had been familiar with the region's geography and politics.[9]

Köse (Beardless) Mihal, a Byzantine castellan of the small fort of Harmankaya in Bithynia, which controlled strategic communication arteries along the Sakarya River basin, first fought at the side of Osman as a Greek Christian by guiding Osman's troops against the Byzantines. Mihal later converted to Islam and mediated between the Ottomans and the local Byzantine lords. In 1326, as an Ottoman commander, Mihal negotiated the surrender of Prousa (Bursa) to the Ottomans. The latter allowed the town's Byzantine commander to leave for Constantinople, but his chief adviser with whom Mihal negotiated the surrender, a certain Saroz, decided to join the Ottoman conquerors.[10]

Ottoman chroniclers of the fifteenth century downplayed the role of the semi-independent warrior lords of the Ottoman marches in the early Ottoman conquests, giving agency to the House of Osman. Yet, these marcher lords played a crucial role in expanding the Ottoman domains and shaping Ottoman rule in southeastern Europe. Until his death in 1417, Ghazi Evrenos was an influential actor in the Ottoman conquests in Rumeli, capturing most of the lands between the Marica River and the Adriatic coast. His light cavalry raiders fought in the battles of Kosovo (1389) against the Serbs and their allies and of Nikopol (1396) against the crusaders. Three of the four most famous marcher lord dynasties—the Evrenosoğulları, Mihaloğulları, and Malkoçoğulları (the Sons of Evrenos, Mihal, and Malkoç/the Serbian Malković family)—were of Christian origin.[11]

These frontier lords possessed large hereditary estates and substantial armies of frontier raiders. The Turks called these raiders akıncı, "those who flow," from the Turkish verb akın, meaning "to flow." In the words of the fifteenth-century Byzantine chronicler Doukas (d. after 1462), when they heard "the herald's voice summoning them to the attack— which in their language is called akın—they descend like a flooding river."[12] The marcher lords often acted independently of the Ottoman rulers. They governed large areas of the southeastern European marches as fellow generals equal in status to the Ottoman sultan rather than military commanders subject to the latter's orders. The role the marcher lords played in the Ottoman succession struggles of 1402–13 illustrates their status and influence. By siding with the Ottoman prince, who seemed to have supported their raids and lifestyle, the marcher lords wielded substantial power. None of the warring Ottoman princes could hold on to their lands in southeastern Europe without their support.[13] Early Ottoman rulers were very much aware of the power of the marcher lords and were thus careful not to increase their status further. This may explain why no marcher lord appears to have ever been appointed to the highest administrative positions (provincial governors-general and vizier) of the Ottoman domains. Nor do they appear to have been given

Ottoman princesses in marriage, despite the Ottoman practice of dynastic marriages, whereby Ottoman rulers forged political alliances with local Turkmen emirs in Asia Minor and vassal Christian rulers in southeastern Europe.[14]

The extent to which the raids of the marcher lords and the campaigns of the early Ottomans were religiously inspired is subject to debate. These wars likely meant different things to different segments of the early Ottoman society. Some understood that they fought a religious war; others joined the campaigns for the booty.[15] While the early Ottomans emerged in "a largely multi-confessional context," the military and the ruling elite later adopted "both *ghazi* legitimation and a more exclusive religious posture. A conquest that did not start as a *ghaza* became one over the course of time."[16] Such an approach is a reminder that an emphasis on Ottoman pragmatism, flexibility, inclusiveness, and political shrewdness should not overshadow the importance of religious fervor in the early Ottoman society, especially after the mid-fourteenth century. In the first decades of their emergence, the Ottomans faced Byzantine Christians, with whom the Muslim Turks of Asia Minor had established relationships after living side by side for centuries. The relationships involved wars and rivalry as much as they did cooperation and occasional political alliances. After the Ottomans crossed into southeastern Europe, however, they fought against Bulgarians, Serbs, and European crusaders from Hungary and western Europe. Fighting against these new enemies meant that *ghaza* became an increasingly important part of Ottoman ideology and legitimation. The Turks of western Asia Minor went willingly to war against their Christian enemies, seeking both glory and booty.

Historical Contingency and Accidents

One problem with the *ghaza* thesis is that it is monocausal. Monocausal explanations tend to have great appeal among historians and social scientists in explaining "origins," especially in fields that lack major paradigms. Such explanations suggest inevitability to the way things evolved. However, the emergence of the Ottomans as a significant regional power by the sixteenth century was neither inevitable nor foreseeable in 1300. It involved, as did all complex processes of state formation, a good deal of historical contingency and accidents. Students of the early Ottoman enterprise have long pointed out the propitious location of Osman's small emirate, the power vacuum, and the wars among the Ottomans' neighbors, as well as various natural disasters that aided the emergence of the House of Osman. Historians have drawn attention to the possible relationship between a flood in the spring of 1302 and Osman's first major victory against the Byzantines in the summer of the same year on the plain of Bapheus near modern İzmit.[17] Others have pointed to the possible effects of the Black Death, which arrived in Asia Minor in 1347. Plagues affect urban and coastal populations to a greater extent than pastoral communities in the interior of Asia Minor. Therefore, it is plausible that the Turkish maritime principalities of Menteşe, Aydın, Saruhan, and Karasi suffered more severely from the plague than did the Ottomans, who lived farther from the coast, and whose sparsely populated pastoralist society was often on the move. The plague also could have weakened the military capabilities of the Byzantines, who then hired Turkish troops, including Ottoman mercenaries, a practice that had a long tradition well before the plague.[18]

While historical accidents and contingencies were important in the initial Ottoman conquest, the opportunities created by floods, earthquakes, civil wars, and the power vacuums within and among their neighbors were quickly exploited by the Ottomans. The early Ottomans were shrewd tacticians, and they established their first bridgehead in Europe as a direct consequence of such a policy. In 1347 Ottoman troops, profiting from yet another Byzantine domestic strife, crossed the Dardanelles Straits into Thrace as allies of John Kantakouzenos, commander in chief of the Byzantine army. Kantakouzenos challenged the rule of the underaged emperor John V Palaiologos (r. 1341–91), claiming the throne for himself. Kantakouzenos first enlisted the help of his old ally Umur, the emir of Aydın. But the emir faced a crusading army and thus was unable to assist him. Kantakouzenos then turned to Orhan (r. c. 1324–62), Osman's son and heir. He gave his daughter Theodora in marriage to Orhan in 1346 and with Ottoman help acquired the throne as coemperor in 1347. In 1352 war broke out between Emperor John V Palaiologos and Kantakouzenos's son Matthew, the governor in Edirne. John V Palaiologos enlisted the support of the Serbs and Bulgarians, while Kantakouzenos called on his Ottoman son-in-law. In the battle near modern Didymoteicho in northeastern Greece, Kantakouzenos's Ottoman mercenaries soundly defeated the emperor's Serbian and Bulgarian allies. The Ottomans then raided and plundered Thrace. Amid these raids, Orhan's son Süleyman, commander of the Ottoman forces, occupied the town of Tzympe near the Byzantine coastal fortress of Gallipoli on the European shore of the Dardanelles. Ottoman soldiers gradually extended their control over the north shore of the Marmara Sea from Gallipoli to Constantinople. Two years later, when an earthquake destroyed the walls of Gallipoli, Süleyman seized it. John Kantakouzenos lost support in Constantinople, primarily because he received blame for allowing the Ottomans to conquer Byzantine lands in Europe. When John V Palaiologos returned to Constantinople aboard Genoese ships, Kantakouzenos abdicated. But the damage had been done. Gallipoli became the Ottomans' European bridgehead for their raids into Europe. The attacks commenced shortly after Kantakouzenos's abdication, as Orhan had no allegiance or family ties to Emperor John V Palaiologos.[19]

The Ottomans turned Gallipoli into a maritime base and a naval arsenal, built on the existing Byzantine dockyards. Their use of Gallipoli as a springboard for raids in Europe demonstrated a significant difference between the Ottomans and the other Turkish emirs in Asia Minor. The latter were contented with pay and plunder and returned the conquered lands to the Byzantines. The Ottomans, by contrast, used their alliance with the Byzantines to acquire strategic sites and territory.

Ottoman-Byzantine relations and Gallipoli's fate illustrate how the Ottomans capitalized on the weakness of their Byzantine neighbors. In 1366, the Ottomans lost Gallipoli to Amadeo of Savoy, who restored it to Byzantium. Sultan Murad I (r. 1362–89) had demanded the restoration of Gallipoli since 1371. Still, he regained it only years later as a consequence of yet another Byzantine civil war. In 1373, while Emperor John V—by this time an Ottoman vassal—and Murad I were campaigning in Asia

Minor, their sons Andronikos IV and Savcı plotted against their fathers. The emperor and the sultan joined forces and defeated their rebellious sons. While Murad beheaded Savcı, the emperor spared his son's life. However, obeying Murad's demands, he had Andronikos partially blinded and transferred his right of succession to his younger brother, Manuel. In the summer of 1376, Andronikos IV seized the throne from his father with Genoese and Ottoman help, offering the Ottoman ruler his allegiance and an annual tribute. As a token of his subservience, Andronikos surrendered Gallipoli to Murad.[20]

Material Rewards and Religious Legitimation

A fourteenth-century text on *ghaza* demonstrates that Ottoman leaders encouraged fighting for both glory and booty, as the latter composed the material base of the warriors of the marches.[21] Booty was a significant source of revenue for raiders and soldiers. Narrating the attacks against Belgrade and the conquest of Smederevo (1439), the Ottoman chronicler Aşıkpaşazade, who was present during these campaigns, claimed that he purchased nine slave boys from the raiders, whom he later sold for between 200 and 300 *akçe* per slave.[22] These were significant sums in the mid-fifteenth century, when the elite janissaries of the sultan received a daily wage of three to five *akçe*. Booty and service land grants (*timar*) remained an essential tool for the Ottoman rulers to motivate their followers. As late as 1484 Sultan Bayezid II (r. 1481–1512) mobilized for war with the following words: "All those wishing to enjoy the pleasure of *ghaza* and jihad, and those who desire booty, those brave comrades who gain their bread by their sword, and those wishing to receive *timar* by comradeship, are requested to join me with their weapons and military equipment in this blessed *ghaza*."[23] As a further incentive, the sultan added that in this expedition, he would not claim one-fifth of the booty, which was the Muslim ruler's share.

While material rewards were an essential incentive for the soldiers, religion was a useful tool for loyalty creation and legitimation. From the mid-fourteenth century onward, the Ottomans increasingly thought of themselves and their religion as superior to that of the Byzantines. Gregory

Palamas—archbishop of Thessaloniki (1347–60) and a prisoner held in Orhan's summer camp outside Bursa in 1354—remarked that his captors considered the bishop's captivity "as a proof of the ineffectiveness" of the Christian religion, attributing their victories to Islam's superiority.[24] Recently converted Turkish marcher lords who sided with the Ottoman dynasty had become devout Muslims. Ghazi Evrenos's pilgrimage to Mecca, and his largesse toward the various Sufi brotherhoods—the spiritual guides of the marcher lords and their *akıncı* horsemen—is illustrative in this regard. The region that Evrenos conquered contained 267 dervish convents and 65 soup kitchens. These buildings were initially designed to provide lodging and food for the wandering Muslim dervishes. They also served the needs of traveling merchants, students, and the local poor, both Muslim and Christian, greatly facilitating the acceptance of Ottoman rule among the conquered peoples.[25]

The use of religion for legitimation was not unique to the Ottomans. Neither was the 1337 Bursa inscription, Wittek's primary source for his *ghazi* thesis, which titled Osman "the exalted great emir, mujāhid [the one striving in jihad] in the way of God, sultan of the *ghazis*, *ghazi*, son of the *ghazi*."[26] Other contemporary emirs of Asia Minor also used such titles. The ruler of Kastamonu, Yavlak Arslan of the Çobanoğlu dynasty (r. c. 1280–91), was titled "the mine of generosity and munificence to the *ghazis*, the eradicator of rebels and destroyer of infidels." On mosque inscriptions and coins, Mehmed Beg of Aydın (r. 1308–34) was "sultan of the *ghazis* and mujāhid." His successor, Umur Beg (r. 1334–48), was titled on his tombstone as *ghazi*. İshak Beg of Saruhan (r. 1362–68) was named "protector of the *ghazis* and mujāhid."[27] Whether these sources used the word *ghazi* to mean "holy warrior" or as an alternative to the pre-Islamic Turkish term *alp* (meaning simply "hero" or "warrior-adventurer") is subject to scholarly debate.[28]

The Ottoman sultans of the early fifteenth century routinely legitimized their rule by using normative Islamic titles on coins and mosque inscriptions, projecting their images as righteous rulers of Islam who fought for the expansion of Islam's domains. On the Arabic-language inscription of the Hamza Beg or Eski Cami (Old Mosque) of Stara Zagora in Bulgaria—built by Prince Süleyman's subordinate Hamza in

1409—Prince Süleyman is titled as "the mighty, righteous and conquering sultan, the sultan of Islam and Muslims, the shadow of God," "the lord (Persian *khudawandgar*) and commander Süleyman, son of Bayezid, son of Murad, the khan." On the inscription of the Eski Cami in Edirne, Sultan Mehmed I (r. 1413–21) legitimized his rule as a righteous sultan, mujāhid and murābit (that is, the one who guarded Islam's frontiers). The Ottoman ruler is also titled as "victorious (*mansūr*) with his flag, overwhelming the enemies, spreading justice and beneficence over the inhabitants of the earth, the sultan, son of the sultan, son of the sultan, helper of the earth and the religion." The titles mujāhid and murābit are "closely connected to the piously militant frontier spirit founded in the Salvation History of the first century of Islamic history."[29] The Ottoman rulers used religious legitimization against the neighboring Turco-Muslim emirs because the latter employed similar Islamic titles to justify their rule. Islamic legitimacy remained important in later years too, when Ottoman sultans sought religious rulings (fatwa) to justify their wars against Muslim neighbors and rivals.

Religious legitimation also remained paramount for the Byzantine imperial propaganda. John VI Kantakouzenos framed his wars against the Turkmen emirates as a struggle between the pious Byzantines and the evil "Ismaelites" and "barbarians," the "natural enemies" of Byzantium. Byzantine authors presented Byzantium's defensive wars against the Ottomans in a similar fashion, emphasizing Byzantine moral and cultural superiority. While this rhetoric aimed at attracting western European military aid, it also served to exonerate John VI Kantakouzenos from the charge that his hiring the Ottomans as mercenaries against his rivals contributed to the Ottoman expansion in southeastern Europe.[30]

Balkan Geopolitics

In the first half of the fourteenth century, three powers ruled over much of the Balkan Peninsula: the Byzantine Empire, Serbia, and Bulgaria. Serbia emerged as the most powerful of the three, controlling vast lands from the Danube in the north to the Gulf of Corinth in the south under Stephen Dušan (r. 1331–55). Dušan's brother-in-law, John Alexander

(r. 1331–71), ruled Bulgaria. However, by the time the Ottomans started their conquests in the peninsula in earnest, all three powers had been weakened. The Byzantine Empire had been engulfed in a civil war. Serbia broke up into competing principalities following disintegration under Dušan's son and heir Uroš (r. 1355–71), and the extinction of the Nemanjić dynasty (1371). Tsar Alexander partitioned Bulgaria between his two sons and lost northeastern Bulgaria to Dobrotica—a powerful lord of perhaps Turkish descent—after whom these lands came to be known as Dobrudja.[31]

King Louis I of Hungary (r. 1342–82) used the weakening of his southern neighbors to force them to accept Hungarian suzerainty. After the death of Dušan, two Serbian magnate families quarreled in the region of Braničevo in northern Serbia. By 1361, the region had seceded from Serbia and was ruled by the Hungarian king's Serbian vassal. The same year, Prince Lazar Hrebeljanović (r. 1371–89), who ruled parts of northern and eastern Serbia, accepted Hungarian suzerainty. King Louis also recovered the Bosnian territories that his father had lost, making Tvrtko I of Bosnia (ban 1353–77, and king 1377–91) his vassal.[32] The Hungarian king also arranged a marriage between Tvrtko and Dorothy, the daughter of John Stracimir of the Tsardom of Vidin. Since Stracimir was Louis's vassal, the marriage strengthened the Hungarian king's influence in both kingdoms.[33] His suzerainty over parts of Serbia, Bosnia, and Bulgaria brought Louis I closer to the Ottomans. Realizing the Ottoman threat, Louis signaled his intention to participate in a crusade against them. In 1366, the Byzantine emperor John V Palaiologos visited Louis's capital Buda. He pleaded for help against the Ottomans, promising to comply with papal instructions regarding church union. However, the pope soon suspended the crusade because the Greeks did "not appear to want union by choice alone and through religious zeal," but were "driven to it so as to get your help," wrote the pope to the Hungarian king.[34]

By about 1369, the Ottomans had conquered northern and central Thrace. By capturing Adrianople (Edirne)—located at the confluence of the Marica and Tundža Rivers—they gained access to Thrace and Bulgaria. That the sultan chose the city as the center of his court signaled

Ottoman plans to stay in Europe.[35] Having crushed the Serbian forces at the battle of Černomen (T. Çirmen, 26 September 1371), Ottoman raiders overran Macedonia, conquering the lowlands as far as Samakov by about 1375. These events forced the Serbian princes of Macedonia, the Bulgarian tsar John Šišman of Trnovo, and the Byzantine emperor John V Palaiologos to accept Ottoman suzerainty. The Ottoman victory in 1371 was more significant in opening the Balkan Peninsula to the Ottomans than the better-known battle of Kosovo in 1389.[36]

Following the Serbian princes' defeat in 1371, Pope Gregory XI urged Louis I to resist the Ottomans. However, two months later, the pope expressed his hopes that the Hungarian king would help him in his war against the Visconti. While King Louis demonstrated a genuine interest in leading a crusade against the Ottomans, he soon defaulted on his promise. However, when the rumor spread that Vaicu of Wallachia had sided with the Ottomans, Louis marched against him in 1375. In Wallachia, the Hungarians clashed with Ottoman troops who supported the Wallachians. To secure his realm's southeastern borders against Wallachian and Ottoman incursions, Louis built and reconstructed several forts. However, these could not stop Ottoman raids into Transylvania, which had traditionally played the role of Hungary's eastern frontier province. Despite his limited success against the Ottomans, King Louis gained a reputation as a devote son of Christ who campaigned against the pagan Lithuanians and the schismatics and heretics of Serbia, eliciting titles from the popes like "champion of Christ" (*athleta Christi*), "very devout prince and most illustrious son of God's holy Church," and "most Christian prince and heroic hammer of the infidels."[37]

Following the death of Louis I in 1382, Prince Lazar regained his independence by taking advantage of the succession struggles for the Hungarian crown between the Angevin claimants and Sigismund, son of Emperor Charles IV of Germany.[38] However, sometime before 1386, Lazar arranged the marriage of his daughter Theodora to Nicholas II Garai (Nikola Gorjanski). Ban of Croatia and Slavonia and leader of the pro-Sigismund baronial faction, Garai played an essential role in persuading his father-in-law to acknowledge King Sigismund's (r. 1387–1437) suzerainty in 1389.[39]

In 1386 Murad conquered Niš and thus gained access to the northern section of the Roman military road leading to Prince Lazar's Serbia in the Morava River valley. However, either before or shortly after the Ottoman conquest of Niš, Prince Lazar managed to temporarily stop the Ottomans near Pločnik, southwest of Niš.[40] Pločnik was an Ottoman setback, as was Şahin Pasha's defeat at the hands of the Bosnians of Tvrtko at Bileća before or on 27 August 1388. Şahin's defeat at Bileća provoked Murad to retaliate in the spring of 1389.[41]

The Ottoman chronicler Neşri believed that the troops of Prince Lazar fought with the Bosnians at Bileća. But Sultan Murad had good reasons to attack Lazar, as the latter's acknowledgment of Hungarian suzerainty threatened Ottoman interests.[42] The armies of Murad and Lazar met on 15 June 1389 at the battle of Kosovo Polje, near present-day Priština. While Lazar was captured and executed, the Serbian Miloš Obilić murdered the sultan. After the battle, Stephen Lazarević (c. 1377–1427), Lazar's son and successor, became the vassal of the new Ottoman ruler, Bayezid I (r. 1389–1402), while Stephen's sister, Olivera, married Bayezid. For more than a decade, Stephen Lazarević fought alongside his Ottoman overlord against Hungary, Wallachia, the European crusaders, and Timur (Tamerlane). The sultan rewarded his vassal's services by giving him the lands of his Serbian rival.[43]

As Sultan Bayezid I's vassal, Stephen Lazarević was compelled to allow Ottoman soldiers into his castles, including Golubac on the border river Danube. Ottoman and Serbian raids into Hungary's southern counties became yearly occurrences. For the first time since the Mongol invasion in 1241, Hungary's border regions suffered from regular foreign attacks, increasingly with devastating consequences. In retaliation, King Sigismund led his armies into Serbia annually between 1389 and 1392, when the sultan was fighting against the Karamans in Asia Minor. Sigismund's forces captured several Serbian forts and fought the Ottoman and Serbian troops in the district of Braničevo, southeast of Belgrade.[44]

In 1393, the Ottomans conquered Trnovo, annexing Danubian Bulgaria and sending Tsar Šišman to Nikopol on the Danube as Sultan Bayezid's vassal. In 1394 Bayezid invaded southern Hungary and Wallachia, and ousted the pro-Hungarian voivode Mircea the Elder (r. 1386–1418), replacing him with his own vassal, Vlad the Usurper (r. 1394–97). At the battle fought in the fall of 1394 at the mountain pass of Rovine, Mircea and his allies defeated the retreating Ottoman army, killing Ottoman begs and the Ottoman-vassal Serbian princes Marko "Kraljević" and Constantine Dejanović. Bayezid managed to cross the Danube at Nikopol aboard ships provided by Tsar Šišman. Back on Ottoman-controlled lands, the sultan—suspicious of the Bulgarian tsar's collusion with Mircea and King Sigismund—ordered Šišman's execution.[45] Most of modern Macedonia fell under Ottoman rule after Rovine. The better part of the region, however, was included in the frontier lands of the marcher lords Paşa Yiğit, his heir İshak Beg (1414–39), and İsa Beg (1439–63), İshak's son.[46]

Despite his defeat at the battle of Rovine, Bayezid managed to depose the pro-Hungarian Wallachian voivode and installed his own vassal. The deposed Mircea fled to Sigismund, and in March 1395 he and his boyars acknowledged Hungarian suzerainty, promising to participate in Sigismund's planned crusade. Sigismund restored Mircea into the voivodeship in the summer. By the fall, however, the Ottomans had their man back in Wallachia. Ottoman control over Wallachia, Bulgaria, and two strategic Danubian crossings at Nikopol and Vidin sped up the preparations for the crusade.[47]

The Crusade of Nikopol

Ottoman conquest in southeastern Europe reinvigorated the idea of the crusade, especially in Byzantium, whose monarchs and envoys had traveled in Europe from Buda to London, hoping to secure military and financial aid against the Ottomans. Owing to a four-year truce in the Hundred Years' War, French and English knights were available for the crusade. In the end, western European participation in the crusade remained rather limited. Although Pope Boniface IX supported the crusade, he called the peoples of Dalmatia, Bosnia, Croatia, and Slavonia into arms not against the "infidel Turks" but against his own rival, Benedict III, the pope in Avignon.[48]

Only a few thousand European knights—from France-Burgundy, England, Germany, and Bohemia—joined the crusade. The French-

Burgundian heavy cavalry of about a thousand men was the largest army. The backbone of the crusader army was the Hungarian troops, numbering perhaps ten thousand men. With a thousand Wallachian mounted archers and woodland fighters provided by Mircea, the crusader army could have reached fifteen thousand fighting men.[49] The majority of the troops consisted of heavy cavalry, but the Hungarians and Wallachians also fielded mounted archers. While these were better suited to fight the Ottoman light cavalry, Ottoman archers were superior owing to their outstanding composite reflex bows and better firing technique.[50]

Historians have criticized Sigismund for wasting time capturing Ottoman castles along the Danube. However, the crusaders' slow movement reflected a strategy aimed not at expelling the Ottomans from Europe but at expanding the Hungarian zone of influence in southeastern Europe so that the advance of the enemy could be halted beyond the borders of the kingdom.[51] Whatever Sigismund's goals may have been, the crusade ended in disaster. The defeat came as a result of the French knights' insistence to lead the charge despite their ignorance of the enemy's tactics. The Ottoman infantry's fortified positions stopped the French heavy cavalry's charge, and the knights' retreat swiftly degenerated into a rout.[52]

Barely escaping with his life, King Sigismund fled via the Black Sea to Constantinople and then to Hungary by sea. The rest of the Hungarian army, led by Sigismund's governor of Transylvania, returned home via Wallachia. In 1397, the Hungarians managed to unseat the Ottoman vassal Wallachian voivode, who had assaulted the crusaders on their return to Hungary. They restored Mircea to the voivodeship, this time for good.[53] However, having seized the territories of the Bulgarian tsardom of Vidin from his ruler in 1396, the Ottomans now were bordering Hungary and Wallachia along the Danube River.

Called "a *ghazi* river" by fifteenth- and sixteenth-century Ottoman chroniclers and "the mother of rivers" by the seventeenth-century Ottoman traveler Evliya Çelebi, the Danube henceforth defined the northern border of the sultan's domains. For the Ottomans on the frontier, the Danube separated the lands of Islam from those of the "infidel."[54]

The Ottomans organized the conquered territories to the south of the Danube into the districts (*sancak*) of Nikopol (T. Niğbolu), Vidin, and Silistra (T. Silistre). They conquered Silistra in 1388, appointing the marcher lord Mihaloğlu Firuz Beg as its first *sancak* governor. However, the voivode Mircea retook the border town several times until Mehmed I subdued him into vassalage in 1417 and reconquered Silistra in 1419. Silistra, Vidin, and Nikopol served as Ottoman springboards for cross-border raids into Hungary, Wallachia, and Moldavia until the conquest of Hungary in the middle of the sixteenth century.[55]

2

Defeat and Recovery

Timur and the Defeat at Ankara

When Bayezid extended his rule over eastern Asia Minor in the late 1390s, the clash with Timur, or Tamerlane (r. 1370–1405), the last of the great Mongol conquerors, became unavoidable. By the early 1400s, from his capital in Samarqand in Transoxania, Timur had overrun northern India, the territories of the Golden Horde, Persia, Syria, and eastern Asia Minor. Timur claimed suzerainty over all emirs in Asia Minor on account of his descent from Chinggis Khan, whose Ilkhanid successors had ruled Asia Minor in the second half of the thirteenth century. When Timur demanded submission from Bayezid, the Ottoman ruler rejected it.

Bayezid considered himself heir to the Seljuk Turks, who had governed Asia Minor from the late eleventh through the early fourteenth century. To strengthen Ottoman legitimacy in the face of competing Timurid and Mamluk claims over Asia Minor, historical narratives about the origins of the House of Osman were fabricated in Bayezid's court. These legends asserted that the Seljuk sultan delegated his authority—which he received from the Abbasid caliph in Baghdad—to Osman, the founder of the Ottoman dynasty, or his father, Ertuğrul. Another version of the legend maintained that the last Seljuk sultan appointed Osman the heir apparent. In open defiance of Timur, Bayezid turned to the shadow caliph, now residing in Mamluk Cairo, and in 1395 requested the title of "Sultan of Rum," which the Seljuks also used. Moreover, Bayezid signaled his pretensions to be a world-conquering ruler of the central Asian traditions, known as *sahib-kıran*, the "lord of the [auspicious] conjunction [of the planets]." On his silver and copper coins he placed clusters of three dots, sometimes surrounding a star, representing planetary bodies, a known cosmographic reference to world power.[1] In 1396, for the ransom of a Burgundian prince, captured at the battle of Nikopol, Bayezid obtained a series of tapestries from Arras in northern France, the famed center of the industry, illustrating the life of Alexander the Great, the sultan's hero and symbol of universal sovereignty. Bayezid also declared his intention to capture St. Peter's Basilica in Rome upon his planned conquest of Constantinople, as he was "born to rule the whole world."[2] However, his ambitions were soon checked.

In 1402 Timur marched into Asia Minor via Erzurum and Erzincan. Timur reached Ankara in July and laid siege to the town. He lifted the siege when scouts brought the news of the approaching Ottoman army. The battle took place at the Çubuk Plain northeast of Ankara on 28 July. Available figures regarding the sizes of the opposing armies are greatly exaggerated, but most sources agree that Timur's forces greatly outnumbered the Ottomans.[3] Apart from their low number and exhaustion, a lack of fresh water resources also weakened the Ottomans, for Timur had destroyed the nearby wells. Modern scholarship has also suggested that Timur had diverted the creek that flowed on the plain by constructing a diversion dam and an off-stream reservoir, thus denying drinking water to the Ottoman soldiers and their horses on the day of the battle.[4] Timur also called on the Turkmens, whom the Ottomans had recently subjugated. Emphasizing their common ancestry, Timur urged them to side with him against Bayezid:

> Your nobility is also mine, and your race joined with mine and our countries with yours; we have the same ancestors, we are all shoots and branches of the same tree; our fathers long ago in the past grew up in one nest and gradually occupied countless others; you are therefore truly a shoot from my stock. . . . How then have you let this shame come to you, for you have become subjugated. . . . And why should you be slaves of a man who is a son of slaves set free by Ali Saljuqi? . . . After conquering these provinces, I take my own way

therein . . . and make you possessors of villages, forts, cities and their plains, and establish each of you there according to his merit; if then it seems good to you not to give aid against us and you have an opportunity of going over to us, take your chance as a prize and take your share of it and so you will be in appearance and truth on our side.[5]

In the battle, the Turkmen and Tatar horsemen in Bayezid's camp deserted to their emirs, who fought in Timur's camp. Bayezid fought bravely with his janissaries and Serbian vassal cavalry under Stephen Lazarević, but quickly lost and was captured. Known as "Thunderbolt" for his swift conquests, the Ottoman sultan died in Timur's captivity, most likely by suicide.[6]

Timur restored Bayezid's recent conquests in eastern Asia Minor to their former lords and divided the remaining Ottoman domains among Bayezid's sons. The division of the ruler's domains among his sons was customary in the central Asian Turco-Mongol empires, but it contradicted Ottoman customs of dynastic succession. The Ottomans did not recognize the partition of the realm and introduced the practice of dynastic fratricide to avoid the breakup of the Ottoman patrimony. Historians have attributed the "law of fratricide" to the "Law Code of Mehmed II," which ordered that "to whichever of my sons the sultanate would pass from God's favor, it is proper that he should kill his brothers for the good order of the world."[7] The disputed origin of the "law of fratricide" notwithstanding,[8] the dynasty and the Ottoman ruling elite had already followed these rules by the time of the battle of Ankara and supported the notion of the indivisibility of the Ottoman domains.[9] After the division of the Ottoman lands by Timur, Bayezid's sons started a decade-long civil war—known in Ottoman history as the interregnum (1402–13)—to establish undivided sovereignty over the Ottoman domains. This was achieved by Prince Mehmed, who had established control over the Ottoman lands by the summer of 1413 as Sultan Mehmed I. In 1416 Shahrukh (r. 1405–47), Timur's son and successor, objected to the reunification of the Ottoman lands according to Ottoman custom (töre-i Osmani), noting that war between brothers was against the Ilkhanid Mongol custom (töre-i İlkhani). To this Mehmed I replied by quoting the famous Persian poet Saadi's *Gulistan* (Rose garden): "Ten dervishes can huddle together on a carpet, but two kings don't fit in the same clime."[10]

Sultan Mehmed I managed to restore Ottoman power in the former Ottoman lands, but his domains were smaller than those under his father, and his rule was challenged repeatedly. In 1415, Mehmed's missing brother Mustafa appeared first in Asia Minor and then in Wallachia and entered into negotiations with the Byzantines, Venetians, and Wallachians. Although Ottoman chroniclers considered him an impostor and dubbed him "False" Mustafa, it is plausible that he was Mehmed's brother, released by Shahrukh, who considered the consolidation of Ottoman power in the vicinity of his Persian lands undesirable. The trouble that Mustafa and his allies caused proved short-lived. They were defeated but found refuge with Emperor Manuel II Palaiologos (r. 1391–1425). To keep Mustafa and his supporter (the former emir of Aydın) in Byzantine custody, Sultan Mehmed agreed to pay Emperor Manuel an annual compensation of 10,000 gold ducats.[11]

In Dobrudja, southwest of the Danube delta in the Wild Forest (Deli Orman), a rebellion erupted against Mehmed's rule, led by the charismatic Muslim mystic and judge Sheikh Bedreddin. He was born to a Greek convert mother (the daughter of a Byzantine fortress commander) and a Muslim *ghazi* father near Edirne. Having immersed himself in religious studies in Konya (home of the Mevlevi dervishes), Cairo (capital of the Mamluk sultanate), and Ardabil in Iranian Azerbaijan (the center of the Safaviyya dervish order), Bedreddin propagated syncretic religious beliefs and common ownership of property. Prince Musa had appointed Bedreddin judge in Edirne, but his tenure ended with Mehmed's victory. When Bedreddin returned to Rumeli, he enjoyed the support of many of the marcher lords, who opposed Mehmed for having revoked the land grants that Bedreddin had given to them in the name of Prince Musa. Mehmed's troops swiftly apprehended Bedreddin. He was accused of disturbing the order of the sultanate by advocating for similarities between religions and their prophets. Although Bedreddin was publicly hanged in Serres in Macedonia (December 1416), his ideas remained popular among the Bektaşi order of dervishes and their supporters, the janissaries. Other similar rebellions led by a certain Börklüce Mustafa in southwestern Asia Minor were also suppressed.[12]

Having overcome his internal challengers, Mehmed turned against those who had supported the rebels. In 1417, the sultan defeated Mircea the Elder of Wallachia and subdued him into vassalage. Mircea agreed to pay a tribute and to send his sons as hostages to the sultan's court. To strengthen his hold over the Danube, Mehmed placed Ottoman garrisons at Turnu (opposite Nikopol) and Giurgiu (opposite Ruse) on the left bank of the river.[13] He soon recaptured Silistra on the right bank of the Danube (1419). Mehmed also managed to impose vassalage on the Turkmen emir of Karaman. Weakened by poor health, the sultan focused on securing the throne for his eldest son, Murad. According to his agreement with Emperor Manuel, Murad was to be acknowledged as Mehmed's successor; his other son Mustafa was to remain in Asia Minor, while the two youngest sons, Yusuf and Mahmud, aged eight and seven, were to be handed over to Manuel. The emperor was to keep them in custody in Constantinople, along with Mehmed I's brother Mustafa. However, upon the accession of Sultan Murad II in 1421, his viziers rejected the division of the Ottoman domains and the handover of the sultan's younger brothers to the Byzantine emperor. Emperor Manuel therefore released from his custody Murad's uncle and brother, dubbed "False" and "Little" Mustafa in Ottoman court chronicles, to incite revolt against the sultan. It was not until 1423 that Murad II managed to restore his authority by defeating and killing his challengers, who also enjoyed the support of the Rumelian marcher lords and the Turkish emirs in Asia Minor. The latter were punished promptly, as Murad II annexed the emirates of Aydın, Menteşe, Germiyan, and Teke in the following years, thus reconstituting Ottoman rule in southwestern Asia Minor. The Byzantines' use of "False" Mustafa to incite civil war in the Ottoman domains backfired. As a reprisal, Murad laid siege to both the Byzantine capital Constantinople and the empire's "second city" Thessaloniki in 1422. Constantinople was saved as Murad had to deal with his younger brother, "Little" Mustafa. Having been unable to defend Thessaloniki, the Byzantines handed the city over to Venice in

1423. The Venetian occupation of the city prompted another war with the Ottomans. Although the Venetians reinforced Thessaloniki's defense, it fell to the Ottomans in 1430. Recent Ottoman victories and the reconstitution of the Ottoman realms by Mehmed I and Murad II demonstrated growing Ottoman military strength.[14]

Pillars of Power: *Timars* and *Sancaks*

The military under the control of the House of Osman played an important role in reconstituting the Ottoman realms after the Ankara debacle. The army also helped the dynasty overpower the rival Turkish principalities in Asia Minor and the lords of the Rumelian marches. The most important pillars of the dynasty's military power were the Ottoman prebendal system and the standing household army under the direct control of the sultans. The prebendal system, based on the so-called *timar* revenue grants, had developed under the first Ottoman rulers, following preexisting Byzantine and Seljuk patterns of land tenure. These conditional revenue grants—similar to the Byzantine *pronoia* and the Seljuk *iqta*—financed thousands of mounted soldiers, called *sipahi*. The *timariot sipahis*, or military prebend holders, collected taxes and dues from their respective villages in return for military service, and played a crucial role in maintaining law and order in the countryside. The Ottoman *timar* system was the basis of not only the Ottoman military organization but also revenue management and provincial administration. Following Seljuk models, in the first part of the fourteenth century cavalrymen remunerated by *timar* were led into campaigns by their commanders. The latter received large *timars* and governed large territorial units, known under different terms. In the second part of the fourteenth century, larger military-administrative units called *sancaks* were created with the aim of counterbalancing the influence of the military leaders with tribal and familial bonds. The *sancak* (literally "flag," standard) originally designated an army unit, without territorial association, under a standard that the unit commander received from the ruler as a symbol of transferred authority. The *sancak* (also called *liva*) soon became the basic Ottoman territorial administrative unit. It was headed by a governor (*sancakbeyi* or *mir-liva*), who commanded the *timariot* cavalry troops in his respective *sancak*. The Ottoman rulers' intention to incorporate the conquered Turkmen emirates into the Ottoman domains may also have aided the creation of *sancaks*, as the existing administrative units were too small to accommodate these principalities.[15]

The proliferation of *sancaks* owing to territorial expansion necessitated their integration into larger military-administrative units. Therefore, Murad I appointed the first governor-general to command the *timariot* forces of all the *sancaks* in Rumeli. The Ottoman term for the governor-general of a province was *beylerbeyi*, literally "bey of [*sancak*] beys" or "lord of lords," whereas the provinces were known under various names (*beylerbeyilik*, *vilayet*, and from the late sixteenth century on, *eyalet*). In 1393 Sultan Bayezid I appointed the governor-general of Anadolu, who from his seat in Kütahya governed western Asia Minor. In 1413, after the conquest of Tokat and Sivas, the governorship of Rum was established to administer these newly conquered lands in north-central Asia Minor. This was followed in the second half of the fifteenth century by the appointment of the *beylerbeyi* of Karaman to govern the newly incorporated principality of Karaman in south-central Asia Minor. This new military-administrative system significantly strengthened the Ottoman dynasty's control over the provinces, revenue management, and the provincial military.[16]

In return for the right to collect revenues from his assigned villages, the Ottoman provincial cavalryman, or *sipahi*, had to provide for his arms (short sword and bows), armor, and horse and to report for military service along with his armed retainers when called on by the sultan. During campaigns, muster rolls were checked against *timar* registers to determine whether all the *timariot* cavalry had reported for military duty and brought the required share of retainers and equipment. If the cavalryman did not report for service or failed to bring the required number of retainers, he lost his *timar*, which was assigned to someone else. Numbering between ten thousand and fifteen thousand in Murad I's wars, the *timariot* provincial cavalry and the *timar* system played an important role in transforming the early Ottoman military, which had originally relied on the horsemen of the Turkish marcher lords, into a semipermanent army under the sultan's command.

Pillars of Power: The Child Levy and the Standing Army

From the earliest times, the Ottoman rulers could count on their military entourage, known as *kul* (literally "slave" or "servitor") and *nöker* (companion, client, retainer). These were the forerunners of the sultan's salaried household troops, known as *kapukulu*—that is, "slaves/servitors of the Sultan's gate." Under Murad I, the cavalrymen of the household troops, known also as *sipahis*, gradually replaced the volunteer peasant cavalry (*müsellem*; literally "exempt"), whereas the *azab* peasant infantry archers and the more famous janissaries took the place of the peasant footmen (*yaya*) of the early Ottoman military. The *müsellem* and *yaya* soldiers became auxiliary forces, charged with transporting weapons and ammunition and building roads and bridges during campaigns.[17]

Organized similarly to the janissaries, and armed with bows and swords, the infantry *azabs* were a kind of peasant militia, originally composed of unmarried (*azab*) young men. They received their military kits from a certain number of taxpaying families. The *azabs* were lower-quality troops who could be used as cannon fodder and who fought in the first ranks of the Ottoman battle formation, in front of the cannons and janissaries. Although their number was significant even in the early sixteenth century (some eighteen thousand in 1514 and ten thousand in 1521), the sultan's elite infantry, known as janissaries, gradually replaced them.[18] Either Orhan or Murad I established the janissary corps, whose name derives from the Turkish *yeniçeri,* or "new troops." As the ruler's elite slave guard, they initially comprised only a few hundred men.[19] The janissaries were the first standing infantry in European history that existed continuously for centuries, preceding similar permanent infantry formations in western Europe by some two centuries.

In battle, the janissaries' main function was to protect the sultan. Forming a square of several rows and positioned after the irregular forces, the janissaries engaged in the fight only if the enemy, having routed the provincial cavalry on the wings and the irregular infantry *azabs* before them, reached their ranks and threatened the sultan. Accounts of mid-fifteenth-century battles such as Varna (1444) and Kosovo (1448) describe the janissaries as an impassable wall, protected by a trench and earth embankment behind it, strengthened with iron stakes and large shields. The Ottomans placed their camels laden with rich baggage and sacks of gold behind the janissaries. Should the enemy reach the embankment, these were to be used to distract the enemy to buy time. In siege warfare, the janissaries played an equally important role. Ordered to scale the walls of enemy fortresses during attacks, they regularly broke the resistance of defenders, leading to the capture of the fortress.[20]

At first, the sultan used prisoners of war to create his independent military guard. In the 1380s, a forced levy of Christian boys, known as *devşirme,* or "collection," was introduced to recruit soldiers for the sultan's household army of slaves. Military slavery was a known practice in the Islamic world from the 830s onward, when the Abbasid caliphs began to recruit Turkish-speaking mounted archers from Central Asia, predominantly as slave soldiers (*ghulam, mamluk*). Though only a couple of thousand in number, the caliphs' Turkish slave soldiers significantly enhanced the Muslim armies' speed, maneuverability, and firepower. These improvements were due to the Turkish soldiers' new military technique (mounted archery) and tactics (feigned retreat), along with their skills in horsemanship and the endurance of their horses. Soon, Turkish soldiers dominated most Muslim armies. The Ottoman "slave army" of the janissaries differed from the slave soldiers of the Islamic heartlands in one important respect. Unlike the Abbasids and later the Mamluks of Syria and Egypt, who purchased their slave soldiers from outside the lands of Islam, the Ottoman sultans collected their own Christian subjects, contradicting the sharia or Islamic law.[21] The *devşirme* may have originated in the Balkan frontiers, where Evrenos Beg and his frontier warriors collected "booty fifth or tribute children" in central Macedonia in the 1380s or earlier. If this was indeed the case, the Ottoman sultans only followed the practice of their marcher lords.[22] In 1395, Isidore Glabas, metropolitan of Thessaloniki, lamented "the seizure of the children by the decree of the emir." An Italian source from 1397 claimed that the Ottomans took boys of ten to twelve years old for their army. Both sources suggest that by the late 1390s the Ottoman rulers regularly practiced the *devşirme* levy.[23]

Under the *devşirme* levy, Christian boys—preferably between twelve and fourteen years of age—were periodically collected. In the 1490s, the average age of levied boys was 13.5 years. The recruiting officers gathered one boy per forty households. The collection occurred haphazardly in the fifteenth century and more regularly in the sixteenth century, when frequent and prolonged wars decimated the ranks of the janissaries. Reports recording the number of levied boys varied from as low as one thousand to as high as twelve thousand per collection. The latter figure is an exaggeration. The number of janissary novices recorded in the Ottoman pay lists and treasury account books in the 1510s and 1520s was in the order of three thousand, rising to above seven thousand only in the 1560s. Extensive regulations governed the collection of boys on the basis of their social status and physical and mental condition. These regulations are recorded in the *Laws of the Janissaries*, written in 1606 by a former janissary, reflecting both early practices and changes that had occurred until the early seventeenth century. The officials charged with collecting the boys could not take the only child of a family, because the head of the household needed his help to cultivate his land and pay the taxes to the *timariot* provincial cavalryman. Similarly, they were not supposed to collect the sons of the village elders, "as they were vile and so were their children"; the children of shepherds and herdsmen, "as they had been brought up in the mountains so they were uneducated"; the boys of craftsmen, because they did not fulfill their duties for soldier's pay; and the married boys, because their "eyes had been opened, and those would not become padishah's household slave (*kul*)." Also excluded from the child levy were orphans and those who spoke Turkish or were circumcised (for they could have been Turks and Muslims— that is, people originally excluded from the sultan's household army); those who were too tall or too short (they were considered stupid and troublemakers, respectively); and those who had visited Constantino-

ple but returned to their province ("for they were shameless"). The
Turks were excluded from the levy to avoid the situation in which their
relatives would demand tax exemptions, a privilege that the members
of the sultan's household army enjoyed. Certain ethnic groups, like the
Hungarians and Croatians beyond Belgrade, or Christians who lived in
the regions between Karaman and Erzurum, were also excluded from
the collection. The Hungarians and Croatians were considered unreliable, while those belonging to the second group were suspicious
because they lived among Georgians, Turkmens, and Kurds.[24] Ottoman
administrators compiled two copies of a detailed register for each group
of one hundred to two hundred boys, called "the flock." The registers
listed the boy's name, the name of his father, and that of his *sipahi* and
his village. It also gave a physical description of the boy.[25] The "flock"
then traveled on foot to the capital. Many perished during the long journey of hundreds of kilometers, while others ran away. Still others escaped the levy because their families bribed the recruiting officers. Despite the cruelty of the system, Ottoman and European sources indicate
that some Christian families volunteered their boys, "who flock in to
enjoy the imaginary honor and privilege of a *Turk*,"[26] because the levy
provided them with opportunities for upward social mobility.

Those who made it to the imperial capital were inspected, converted
to Islam, and circumcised. The smartest ones were singled out for education in the Palace School or for service in the padishah's gardens.
Others were given to Ottoman dignitaries. The ones selected for the
Palace School were the most fortunate. They were looked after and
given the best education of the time. In due course, these lads could
achieve the highest offices within the empire. The majority of the levied
boys, however, were hired out to Turkish farmers for seven to eight
years. During this time they became "accustomed to hardship" and
learned the rudiments of the Turkish language and Islamic customs. All
the boys were "delivered by name and written down in a book" so that
the padishah could "have them returned again" when vacancies in the
janissary corps occurred. Government officials inspected the boys every
year, and in the sixteenth century collected an 80 *akçe* "inspection-fee"
from the families on whose farm the lad was working. After seven or

eight years of hard work in the fields, the boys were recalled to the Ottoman capital and Gallipoli. There, they joined the ranks of janissary novices and lived in their barracks under strict military discipline. They also served as a cheap workforce for public construction. Others worked in the imperial gardens or in the dockyards as blacksmiths, caulkers, carpenters, oar makers, and so on. Yet others started their apprenticeship in the Imperial Cannon Foundry or the Imperial Naval Arsenal. Only after several years of such service did the novices become janissaries or fill vacancies in the corps of artillery gunners, gun carriage drivers, armorers, and bombardiers.[27]

To keep records of revenues, military prebends, and troops—both *timariot* cavalrymen and stipendiary soldiers of the sultan's household—the Ottomans instituted a bureaucratic surveillance system through cadastral surveys, registers of *timars*, and salary pay lists. By the early fifteenth century a range of institutions and bureaucratic mechanisms had emerged to mobilize resources and troops and to administer conquered lands. The beneficiaries of these institutions had vested interests in restoring the power of the House of Osman after the debacle of Ankara. While supporters of the future sultan Mehmed I, the winner of the succession wars of 1402–13, profited the most, those who subsequently accepted his authority and proved ready to serve him also benefited. The Ottoman *timar* and *devşirme-kul* systems strengthened the Ottoman ruler's position vis-à-vis the marcher lords and helped consolidate the rule of the House of Osman after the debacle of Ankara.

Strategies of Conquest

The marriage of Orhan to Theodora established a pattern of Ottoman dynastic marriages as a tool of subjugation and conquest. Dynastic marriages were not unique to the Ottomans. Other contemporary ruling dynasties, both Christian and Muslim, used them to forge marital alliances, further diplomatic goals, and acquire crowns and lands. The Habsburg dynasty—the Ottomans' main rival in early modern Europe—turned its modest patrimonial territories into a world empire through marital alliances. Rulers of the Empire of Trebizond arranged

the marriages of their daughters to the emirs of Sinop, Erzincan, Kara-
man, and the Karakoyunlu and Akkoyunlu Turkmen confederations,
hoping to gain allies in the fight against the Ottomans. The Akkoyunlu
Turkmens and the Safavids—the Ottomans' main Muslim rivals in the
East—also used dynastic marriage to forge alliances. In 1458, Uzun
Hasan of Akkoyunlu, the adversary of the Ottoman sultan Mehmed II,
married Princess Theodora Comnena of Trebizond, the daughter of
John IV of Trebizond (r. 1429–58/60). The two rulers formed an anti-
Ottoman alliance. According to the marriage agreement, Theodora kept
her Orthodox faith and maintained a chaplain and a Trapezuntine
household. She was the ruler's chief wife (*ulu hatun*) and the protector of
local Christians. She also influenced Akkoyunlu foreign policy, such as
Uzun Hasan's diplomatic overtures to Venice in 1465–66 and to Buda,
Moldavia, Cracow, and Rome in 1472–75. Their daughter Martha/Mara
(Halima) married Haydar (d. 1488), the head of the Safaviyya order and the
father of Shah Ismail (r. 1501–24), the founder of the Safavid Empire.[28]
The Safavids contracted marriage alliances with influential Qizilbash
tribal leaders and local dynasties such as the Shirvanshahs of Azerbaijan.[29]
Dynastic marriages were commonly used in Hungary and the medieval
Slavic kingdoms of southeastern Europe. We will see how the Serbian,
Bosnian, and Bulgarian ruling dynasties intermarried with each other
and with members of the Hungarian aristocracy to counterbalance their
ties to the House of Osman. The medieval Hungarian kings used marriage
policy to tie the ruling dynasties in southeastern Europe to the Hungarian
crown, thus countering Ottoman influence in the region.

Some distinctive features define Ottoman marriage strategy. First
and foremost, it was used to subjugate, and eventually annex, both
Christian and Muslim neighboring polities. At the same time, the sultans were careful not to produce children by these marriages, denying
the wives' families an opportunity to claim Ottoman patrimony, the
basis of the power of the House of Osman. Except for Murad I's and
Selim I's mothers, the Ottomans procreated with slave concubines.[30]

Through their marriage alliances with the Byzantine, Serbian, and
Bulgarian royal houses and with the Turkmen principalities of Germiyan, İsfendiyaroğlu, Aydın, Saruhan, Çandar, Karaman, and Dulkadır,

the Ottomans acquired new territories, gained useful alliances, and re-ceived tax and military help via the auxiliary troops that their vassals provided. When, sometime between 1371 and 1376, Murad I married Thamara, the sister of the Bulgarian tsar John Šišman of Trnovo, the latter became an Ottoman vassal. And in the late 1370s, when Murad I arranged the marriage of his son Bayezid to the daughter of Yakub of the neighboring Turkmen emirate of Germiyan, the Ottomans acquired part of that emirate, including its capital Kütahya. Bayezid I's marriage in 1392 to Olivera Lazarević, the sister of Despot Stephen (Stefan) Lazarević (r. 1389–1427) of Serbia, and Murad II's marriage in 1436 to Mara Branković, the daughter of Despot George (Djuradj) Branković of Serbia (r. 1427–56), reinforced the two Serbian rulers' vassal status. İsfendiyaroğlu, the defeated lord of Kastamonu in eastern Asia Minor, became an Ottoman vassal when he gave his daughter to Sultan Murad II in marriage in 1423.[31]

Mehmed II ended the policy of dynastic marriages, for it would have been below the sultan's dignity to marry his sons and daughters to petty princesses and princes of southeastern Europe and Asia Minor. The Ot-toman armies soon conquered most of these lands, thus leaving no viable candidates for such marriages anyhow.[32] The marriage strategy of the first sultans is a reminder that Ottoman conquest went beyond the use of sheer military force.

Establishing Ottoman influence and rule entailed a host of other policies. Traditional histories of the Ottomans usually overlooked them, as it proved difficult to square these policies with the supposed milita-ristic nature of the Ottomans. One such policy was the Ottoman prac-tice of accommodation (*istimalet*), which the Ottoman elite found use-ful for ruling in their newly conquered lands. Through this policy, the Ottomans preserved and absorbed local administrative practices and institutions, including the Byzantine ecclesiastical hierarchy. To ease the transition to Ottoman rule, the Ottomans often adopted elements of pre-Ottoman tax regulations. Consequently, the conquered subjects often paid about the same amount of taxes to the Ottomans that they had paid before the conquest. Adjusting Ottoman taxation regimes to match that of the pre-Ottoman system in a given locality, protecting the taxpaying subjects from unjust levies through an efficient provincial administration that kept law and order, and providing for the poor through a network of soup kitchens and dervish lodges were all methods in accordance with the Islamic principle of *istimalet*, but also indications of Ottoman governmental pragmatism.[33]

By integrating the pre-Ottoman administrative divisions into the Ottoman provincial organization, the Ottomans demonstrated pragmatism in governing their newly conquered lands. The Ottoman *sancaks* (subprovinces) of Nikopol and Vidin, for instance, incorporated the lands of the last Bulgarian tsars of Trnovo and Vidin. The *sancaks* of Küstendil in Bulgaria, Karlıeli in Epiros, and Dukakin in Albania were named after these regions' former Christian lords, as were three of the five subdivisions of the *sancak* of Bosnia after its establishment in 1463. In similar fashion, the *sancaks* of Karasi, Saruhan, Aydın, Menteşe, Germiyan, Hamid, and Teke in western Asia Minor preserved the names of the preconquest dynasties. To maintain law and order and secure the steady flow of revenues to the imperial center, the Ottomans allowed pre-Ottoman local communal organizations and their leaders (*knezes* and *primikürs*) to continue to function in conquered Serbia, Bulgaria, and Greece.[34]

This pragmatism remained the hallmark of Ottoman provincial administration and revenue management in the sixteenth century. The Ottomans often retained old forms of property ownership and taxation, accommodated the previous systems of agriculture and mining regulations, and adopted local coinage. The first Ottoman provincial tax regulations in eastern Asia Minor were often copies or variations of the tax codes that the former Akkoyunlu, Dulkadır, and Mamluk sovereigns had used. In Hungary and Iraq, the Ottomans honored and adapted the tax regulations of their Hungarian and Safavid enemies, as the law codes of the newly created provinces of Buda and Baghdad demonstrate. We will also see that in border areas, the Ottoman administration shared taxation and jurisdiction with the local elite. When conducting daily business, Ottoman administrators often relied on local village headmen, elders, and notables.[35]

While the Ottomans usually eliminated the royal dynasties and aristocracies of the conquered lands after a victory, they tried to win over the lesser nobility by granting them military prebends. They enlisted thousands of local Christians in the Ottoman *timar*-holding provincial cavalry, frontier garrisons, and auxiliary military organizations. In doing so, the conquerors eased their shortage of fighting men and integrated layers of the local elite and former military into their provincial military-administrative system, which facilitated the acceptance of Ottoman rule among the conquered. In return for their cooperation with and service to the conquerors, Christian *timariot* cavalrymen preserved portions of their hereditary estates (*baština*) and pronoia lands. The latter had initially been military prebends conditional on state service but had become hereditary too. Christian *timariots* also succeeded in conserving their privileged status within the indigenous society. In 1431 in Albania, 17 percent of the 335 *timar* holders were Christian. In 1467–68 in northern Serbia (Braničevo region), 59 of the 91 *timar* holders (65 percent) were Christians.[36] The share of Christian *timariots* was 48 percent in Smederevo in 1476. Within a generation or two, many Christian *sipahis* disappeared from the registers of *timar* holders, indicating their gradual conversion to Islam and the consolidation of Ottoman rule through fuller integration. In the *sancak* of Tırhala (Trikala in Thessaly), conquered in 1395–96, only 36 of the 182 *timar* holders (20 percent) were Christians in 1455. In the *sancak* of Vidin, established in 1396, the share of Christian *timariots* by the time of Mehmed II was as low as 3.5 percent. The proportion of Christian *timariots* in the *sancak* of Smederevo decreased from 48 percent in 1476 to 21 percent in 1516. While the number of Christian *timar* holders sharply declined by the late fifteenth century, Muslim sons of Christian fathers received *timars* in significant numbers. In the mid and late sixteenth century they represented between 3 and 18 percent of *timar* holders, and occasionally more.[37]

By converting to Islam, the sons and grandsons of the original Christian lords who sided with the conquering Ottomans achieved higher offices, occasionally becoming *sancak* governors. A scion of the Albanian Muzaki family, for instance, governed the Albanian *sancak* of Arnavut-ili ("the land of Arnavut/Albania") in 1441, and died during the 1442 Ottoman campaign against Hungary. Yet, these men also had to give up part of their patrimony and feudal privileges. The wealthier their family had been, the greater loss they sustained. This occasionally led to resistance and insurrection. Of these revolts, the uprising led by George (Gjergj) Kastrioti (1405–68)—who is also called Skanderbeg—is best known. A member of the Albanian Kastrioti noble family, George Kastrioti had been sent to Murad II's court in Edirne as a hostage in 1423 after his father was forced to accept Ottoman suzerainty. Having been educated in the sultan's court, he served the Ottomans for some twenty years, including as *sancak* governor of Debar in northern Albania. When the sultan ordered his *sancak* governor at Kroja to take control of the Kastrioti family's forts, Skanderbeg deserted the Ottoman army that was marching against the crusaders in 1443. He led a protracted rebellion against the Ottomans for the next twenty-five years.[38]

In addition to the co-opted Christian nobility and *timariots*, the Ottomans also integrated the conquered lands' military men into their *voynuk* and *martolos* organizations. Established in the 1370s or 1380s, *voynuks*—from the Slavic *vojnik*, meaning "fighting man" or "soldier"— retained part of their hereditary *baština* estates as *timars* in lieu of military service. They were found in significant numbers in Bulgaria, Serbia, Macedonia, Thessaly, and Albania, especially along strategic routes and border regions. Large numbers of Christian nomads in Rumeli, called *vlachs*, were also incorporated into the ranks of *voynuks*. Around the 1420s, the Ottomans also incorporated into their military system the Christian *martoloses*, from the Greek *armatolos*, meaning "armed men." Guarding border forts, and often composing a substantial part of border garrison troops in Rumeli, *martoloses* also served on river flotillas. They habitually raided enemy territory, terrorizing and kidnapping their fellow Christians on the other side of the border. They also guided Ottoman soldiers into enemy territory and were regularly charged with reconnaissance missions. Performing military service in return for tax exemptions, these Christian military men soon became part of the Ottoman privileged military class, receiving regular pay and a share of the booty. Christian *timariot sipahis*, *voynuks*, and *martoloses* significantly augmented the Ottomans' military potential in southeastern Europe, while also contributing valuable tactical diversity and geographical knowledge of enemy lands.[39]

Besides pragmatism, the policy of accommodation also reflected the manpower shortage of a polity, whose conquering soldiers and administrators remained a minority in comparison with the indigenous Christian population.[40] The Ottomans addressed this shortage in part by state-organized resettlement or forced population transfer (*sürgün*). This method helped to achieve a number of goals. First, by transferring Turkmen nomads from Asia Minor to southeastern Europe, Murad I and his successors increased the number of their Turkic-speaking Muslim subjects in a hostile, Slavic-speaking Christian environment. The transfer of Christian populations, occasionally whole communities, from southeastern Europe to Asia Minor served similar purposes. When this policy joined with the voluntary Turkmen migration from Asia Minor to the Balkan Peninsula, encouraged by the Ottoman government, it resulted in massive Turkification of the population of Thrace and the eastern Balkan Peninsula. Migration expanded Ottoman colonization far beyond garrisons and urban centers. Second, the Ottomans used deportation to increase the Ottoman military presence in the newly conquered lands. The Turkmens transferred to Europe often belonged to the early Ottoman military formations, such as the *yaya* infantrymen in Asia Minor. By granting them farm plots (*çiftlik*) in their new lands, the Ottoman government financed them locally, using the resources of the conquered territories. Third, forced migration proved instrumental in establishing or restoring Ottoman control in Asia Minor among the unruly and rebellious Turkmen tribes by transferring them to the Balkan Peninsula, thereby uprooting them from their traditional base. Examples of this policy include the transfer of Turkmen nomads from the recently subdued Saruhan emirate to the vicinity of Skopje and Plovdiv in the 1380s and 1390s, the resettlement of the rebellious Çepni Turkmens from Canik on the Black Sea to Albania, and the transfer of the Tatars of the Amasya-Tokat region to the Marica valley. Fourth, forced resettlement under Murad II and Mehmed II helped the urban reconstruction projects of the former Byzantine cities of Thessaloniki, Constantinople, and Trabzon. To repopulate, rebuild, and Ottomanize them, the Ottoman government transferred Muslim, Christian, and Jewish peasants, craftsmen, and merchants into these cities from other urban centers such as Bursa, Edirne, Plovdiv, Gallipoli, and from regions as diverse as Asia Minor, Serbia, Albania, the Morea, the Aegean Islands, and the Crimea. Resettlement, voluntary migration, and conversion to Islam had reshaped the ethnic-religious landscape of the southeastern Balkan Peninsula. By the time the Ottoman conquest reached Serbia and Greece, there were not enough Turkmen tribes to be resettled. The lack of settlers explains the smaller proportion of the Muslim population in these lands. As a result, southeastern Europe remained largely Christian. In the 1520s, Christian households accounted for about 82 percent of the more than one million households that Ottoman officials surveyed and registered in the province of Rumeli.[41]

Halting the Ottoman Advance: King Sigismund's Buffer States

The failure of the Crusade of Nikopol made clear to King Sigismund that the country was unable to defeat the Ottomans in open battle even with western European military support. This realization led the king to abandon the preemptive offensive strategy in favor of a multilayer defensive one, which aimed at containing the Ottoman expansion before it reached his kingdom's borders. Earlier historiography on Sigismund had labeled the decade of the Ottoman civil wars as a period of "missed opportunities," accusing the king of neglecting the Ottoman threat and of squandering the country's resources by seeking the crown of the Holy Roman Empire and fighting the Hussites in Bohemia. By contrast, recent research has demonstrated how Sigismund used the early 1400s to strengthen his kingdom's defenses, despite his troubles in Hungary, Bohemia, and the empire. No other monarch had expended as much effort to ward off the Ottomans as Sigismund did.[42]

Sigismund was aware of the importance of his fight against the Ottomans. His role as "shield and rampart" (*scutum atque murus*) and "strong arm/rampart" (*fortitudinis brachium*) of the Christian faith was recognized in 1410 by John XXIII, one of the popes during the Western schism, who ironically was later deposed by the Council of Constance, headed by Sigismund.[43] While Louis I's crusading plans earned the king the honorific title of "champion of Christ," it was under Sigismund that Hungarian kings and their country had increasingly been perceived in Europe as the "bulwark of Christendom" (*antemurale, propugnaculum Christianitatis*) against the advancing Ottomans, an image that Hungarian monarchs shared and cultivated with other rulers in southeastern and central Europe. In Sigismund's case, the title came not so much from the king's anti-Ottoman wars but rather from his defensive policy. King Sigismund envisioned a multilayered defense system, consisting of a ring of buffer states between Hungary and the Ottomans, frontier dependences called banates, and two parallel lines of border forts relying on the Danube and Sava Rivers. The fourth element of this strategy was a strengthened field army whose primary function was to relieve the castles of the southern defense line besieged by the enemy and to launch punitive campaigns into the Ottoman domains and the Ottoman client states in the Balkan Peninsula. This army was also to be used as a last resort in case the Ottomans broke through the first three layers of defense.

Sigismund's attempts to extend his influence in the Balkan Peninsula predictably led to confrontation with the Ottomans, who also considered the Balkan rulers their vassals. Desperate, the Balkan rulers often changed sides or accepted double vassalage. Stephen Lazarević remained loyal to Sultan Bayezid, his brother-in-law, until Bayezid's debacle at Ankara, after which he freed himself from Ottoman vassalage. Having strengthened his legitimacy vis-à-vis his Serbian rivals by receiving the Byzantine title of despot of Serbia from Emperor Manuel II on his way home from Ankara, Stephen, upon his return, confiscated the lands of his nephew, George Branković. In part because of his conflict with his nephew, Stephen Lazarević swore loyalty to King Sigismund in 1404. Sigismund gave him large estates in Hungary, Belgrade, and part of the Banate of Mačva (Hun. Macsó). The despot made Belgrade his residence and a hub of regional trade; his rebuilding of the Byzantine-style castle led contemporaries to regard the city as "the key to Hungary." In December 1408, Sigismund made Stephen the founding member of the Order of the Dragon, which the king and his second wife, Barbara of Cilli

(1392–1451), founded from among their closest supporters. Fashioned after the crusading military orders, the members of the Order of the Dragon had to protect the king and fight against "pagans" and "schismatics"—that is, the Turks and such Christian "heretics" as the Bogomils of Bosnia and the Hussites of Bohemia. Listed right after the king and queen in the foundation charter of the order, Despot Stephen became one of Hungary's greatest lords, frequenting the royal court in Buda and attending the Hungarian diets and the meetings of the order.[44]

Like other Balkan rulers, Despot Stephen was active during the succession struggles among Bayezid's sons. Whereas his brother Vuk and his nephews George and Lazar Branković sided with Prince Süleyman, Stephen Lazarević supported Prince Musa. Thanks in part to the despot's support, Musa was able to defeat Süleyman, seizing the Ottoman throne in Edirne. While Musa eliminated the despot's Serbian rivals for supporting Süleyman, Musa's victory also brought about major changes in Muslim-Christian relations. Yielding to the demands of the akıncı raiders, his main power base, Musa renewed his father's policy of conquests, the first target of which was the despot's Serbia. Musa's aggressive policy also alienated George Branković, whom the Ottoman prince reportedly wanted to poison. This caused reconciliation between the two Serbian lords, who eventually made peace through the mediation of Mara Lazarević, Stephen's sister and George's mother. While George accepted Stephen's suzerainty, he also became his possible successor, as Stephen had no male successor and George was his closest male relative. In the face of Musa's aggressive policy, the Serbs now supported his brother, Mehmed, as did the Byzantine emperor. By the summer of 1413, Prince Mehmed had defeated Musa.[45] Mehmed's army consisted of Turkish frontier raiders from Rumeli, Turkmen troops from Asia Minor, and Serbian, Bosnian, and Hungarian troops under the command of Stephen Lazarević. This coalition of Christian and Muslim forces in Mehmed's camp is a reminder of how complex power relations and temporary alliances had been in southeastern Europe in the early fifteenth century. While the policy of the Hungarian king's Balkan vassals ironically helped the reunification of the Ottoman realms under Mehmed I, the new sultan repaid their services with a relatively peaceful policy.

This Ottoman policy, along with Despot Stephen's loyalty toward King Sigismund, spared Hungary's southern borders from Ottoman raids.[46]

In the Hungarian-Serbian treaty concluded in May 1426 in Tata in northwestern Hungary, Sigismund accepted the aging and childless despot's nephew, George Branković, as his heir. Branković, whose legitimate sons were to inherit the Despotate of Serbia, was to remain the vassal of the Hungarian king and of his descendants, serving his overlord with troops whenever called on. In return for his loyalty and service, Branković would keep his uncle's possessions, except for some strategically important castles such as Belgrade and Golubac.[47]

Sigismund had been in Transylvania, close to the southern borders, since December 1426, owing in part to renewed Ottoman raids in Bosnia and Serbia. Though details of these events are disputed, it is possible that these raids were the Ottoman response to the Treaty of Tata. The agreement changed power relations between the Ottomans and the Hungarians, as the Hungarians acquired key fortresses along the Danube River and reasserted their suzerainty over Serbia, which the sultan considered an Ottoman vassal. It is also possible that Sigismund did not trust Branković and wanted to make sure that Belgrade and Golubac reverted to him after Stephen Lazarević's expected death. The despot died on 19 July 1427. Sigismund took possession of Belgrade in late September, but only after George Branković ordered its handover to the Catholic Hungarians, which the Orthodox clergy opposed.[48] Belgrade controlled the Danubian waterways and the most important river crossing, and was the end point of the Niš-Belgrade military corridor. Belgrade's possession was imperative for the Hungarians if they wanted to halt Ottoman incursions into their country and maintain their influence in Serbia and Wallachia.

Golubac's castellan, however, ceded the fort to the Ottomans, causing a major gap in the Hungarian defense line. Despite King Sigismund's careful preparations, his attempt to recapture the fortress in the summer of 1428 was foiled by the arrival of an Ottoman relief force, with which the king signed a truce. The loss of Golubac was a major blow to the Hungarians, for the castle was a convenient crossing point through which Ottoman *akıncı* raiders crossed the Danube River into Hungary.[49] Once in possession of Golubac, the Ottomans placed a garrison in the fort and turned it into a naval base. In the spring of 1433, the Burgundian traveler Bertrandon de la Brocquière was in Belgrade and noted that in Golubac, "two days journey below Belgrade," the "Turk . . . keeps a hundred light galleys, having sixteen or eighteen oars on a side to pass over to Hungary at his pleasure."[50]

George Branković tried to balance his obligations between Hungary and the Ottomans, accepting double vassalage. The despot's marriage policy reflected his situation. In May 1428, he made peace with Murad II and promised to give his daughter Mara (1418?–78) in marriage to the sultan. The governor-general of Rumeli, Saruca Pasha, performed the betrothment ceremony in the name of Sultan Murad II. As Mara was only about ten years old, the marriage was postponed and took place in September 1436 in the Ottoman capital city Edirne. Mara was the second wedded wife of the sultan. She kept her Christian faith and lived most of the time in Bursa, where she had a small court. Although Mara had no children, she was very close to her stepson, the future Mehmed II. The despot's sons Stephen (d. 1476) and Gregory (d. 1459) accompanied Mara to Edirne, and it seems that Stephen remained in the Ottoman court as a hostage. Gregory returned to Serbia and got parts of southern Serbia as a fief from the sultan, following the Ottoman capture of Smederevo in 1439. In 1441 Gregory was accused of plotting against his Ottoman suzerain, and the Ottomans captured and blinded him, along with his brother Stephen.[51] To counterbalance his Ottoman vassalage, Despot George Barnković gave his older daughter Catherine (Katarina, ?–1492) in marriage to Ulrich II of Cilli (d. 1456) in April 1434. Ulrich II was one of the most influential barons of Hungary and the nephew of King Sigismund's second wife, Barbara of Cilli. In 1446, the matrimony between Barnković's third son, Lazar (d. 1458), and Helena Palaiologina—the daughter of Despot Thomas Palaiologos, Emperor Manuel II's youngest son, who since 1443 had ruled the Despotate of the Morea with his brother Constantine—strengthened Serbian ties to the Byzantine imperial family and political elite. Branković's own marriage to Princess Eirene Palaiologina Kantakouzene (c. 1400–1457), the sister of the last empress of Trebizond Helena Kantakouzene, served the same goal.[52]

Sigismund's policy vis-à-vis Wallachia and Bosnia—which were to play the role of buffer states along Hungary's southeastern and southwestern borders, respectively—was less successful. Sigismund supported Mircea, because "the Turks could reach the Danube from Edirne in five days," and if the Wallachians could not count on Hungary's support, "they would soon submit themselves to the Turkish yoke."[53] In the fall of 1401 Hungarian and Wallachian forces jointly defeated Evrenos Beg's troops, who had raided Wallachia and Transylvania. Using the collapse of Ottoman rule in Rumeli in the wake of the battle of Ankara, the Wallachian voivode recaptured his old Trans-Danubian possessions (Dobrudja-Deliorman), which Prince Süleyman acknowledged (1402) in exchange for Mircea's tribute. However, Dobrudja contained one of the largest groupings of Ottoman frontier fighters, who habitually raided the voivode's lands. Mircea repeatedly renewed his pledge of fealty to Sigismund, despite his treaties with the Ottoman princes during the Ottoman succession wars of 1402–13, in which the voivode played an active role.[54] After Mehmed reconstituted Ottoman authority in Rumeli, Mircea turned against the sultan and in 1416 supported both the Ottoman claimant "False" Mustafa and the rebel Şeyh Bedreddin, who found refuge in Wallachia. That same year, Sigismund dispatched an army under the command of his Transylvanian governor to join Mircea's troops in their failed attempt to help Mustafa claim the Ottoman throne. Following his victory over Mustafa and Bedreddin, Sultan Mehmed launched a punitive campaign against Mircea in 1417, capturing the Danubian fortresses of Giurgiu and Severin, which guarded the river crossings into Wallachia and Transylvania. The sultan reduced Mircea to a tribute-paying vassal, who also had to send his son to the Ottoman capital as a hostage.[55] Although Sigismund recaptured Severin in 1419, the Ottomans remained in control of the Danube crossings to the east of the fortress. Sigismund's Danube flotilla of twenty-two ships, established the previous year with the help of shipbuilders from Flanders, only partly frustrated the Ottomans' activity.[56]

The succession war among Mircea's sons threw Wallachia into anarchy. In the next fifteen years, the voivodeship changed hands about ten times between Dan II and Radu II, supported by, respectively, the

Hungarians and the Ottomans. As a result, incursions into Transylvania by Ottoman raiders and by Ottoman-vassal Wallachian forces became perennial, as did Hungarian raids into Wallachia in support of the pro-Hungarian voivode, Dan II. Relative calm returned only under Vlad II Dracul (r. 1436–47 with interruptions), a Hungarian vassal, who had been brought up in Sigismund's court. In 1431 Sigismund made him a member of his knightly Order of the Dragon—hence his nickname Dracul, the Dragon. However, after Sigismund's death in December 1537, Vlad accepted Ottoman vassalage and supported Murad II's campaign into Transylvania in the summer of 1438. Although he sent some four thousand Wallachian horsemen to Hunyadi in 1444, Vlad declined to participate in Hunyadi's campaigns against the Ottomans in 1443–44 so that he could protect his throne and his sons—Vlad III Țepeș (the Impaler), known as Dracula (Rom. Drăculea, "son of Dracul"), and Radu—who had been hostages in the Ottoman court since 1442. After the Crusade of Varna in 1444, he captured the returning Hunyadi in Wallachia. Although he later made peace with Hunyadi, the relationship deteriorated after Vlad again accepted Ottoman suzerainty. Given the questionable loyalty of the Wallachian voivodes, it was all the more crucial for Orșova and Severin along the southeastern section of Hungary's borders to remain in Hungarian hands.[57]

From the Hungarian point of view, the most problematic of the buffer states was Bosnia. Tvrtko I used the anarchy that followed the death of Louis I to reestablish his independence from Hungary. Tvrtko supported the Angevin party against Sigismund, and by 1390 his troops had occupied most of the Dalmatian castles and towns, held by Hungary since 1358, when these had exchanged Venetian suzerainty for Hungarian. After Tvrtko's death in 1391, the majority of the Bosnian magnates followed his policy; Sigismund and his commanders led numerous costly campaigns to force them to accept Hungarian suzerainty, which King Stephen Dabiša (r. 1391–95) did in 1393. However, the Orthodox peoples of Bosnia did not trust the proselytizing Catholic Hungarians, who in 1408 massacred some 120 Bosnian nobles. Hungarian campaigns achieved only temporary results in Bosnia, and Sigismund's rivalry with Ladislaus of Naples and Venice over Dalmatia further compromised the defense of the Hungarian kingdom's southwestern borders. Venice won Dalmatia in the wars of 1410–13 and 1418–20, except for the aristocratic republic of Ragusa (modern Dubrovnik in Croatia), which had flourished under nominal Hungarian suzerainty since 1358 owing to its extensive trade networks in the Balkans, the Adriatic, and the Mediterranean. Sigismund acknowledged Venetian rule in Dalmatia only in 1433. The Ottomans exploited the divisions among the Bosnian nobility, supporting one faction against the other. After the Bosnian and Ottoman forces jointly defeated Sigismund's army in 1415 in Bosnia, the Ottomans gained more influence over Bosnian politics and imposed heavy tribute on the Bosnian rulers.[58]

King Stephen Tvrtko II (r. 1404–9, 1421–43), the longest-reigning king of the House of Kotromanić, also tried to play his more powerful neighbors off against one another. He first concluded a treaty with Venice, but later accepted Ottoman suzerainty, after the Ottomans launched punitive raids into Bosnia. Realizing that Venice was in no position to aid Bosnia against the Ottomans, Tvrtko II acknowledged Sigismund's suzerainty. In 1427 Tvrtko II, who had no children, accepted the Hungarian demand making Count Hermann II of Cilli (Celje)—son of Catherine of Bosnia (Katarina Kotromanić)—his heir presumptive. However, Tvrtko II's Bosnian rivals opposed the deal, as Hermann II belonged to King Sigismund's inner circle of powerful barons and was the monarch's father-in-law and closest confidant. Nothing would come of the arrangement, because Tvrtko outlived Hermann, who died in 1435. In 1428, Tvrtko II further strengthened his relations with Hungary by marrying Dorothy Garai. She was the daughter of the deceased John Garai, another of Sigismund's influential loyal barons of the Garai noble family, who also intermarried with the Cillis. However, Sigismund failed to protect Tvrtko II against his pro-Ottoman Bosnian rivals. Sigismund's failure was, to an extent, counterbalanced by the Hungarian conquest of Srebrenik (1404) and Jajce (1434), which became centers of two frontier administrative units called banates. This meant that the Hungarians could engage Ottoman raiders in territories beyond the Sava River in northern Bosnia, before they reached the kingdom's borders. However, these Hungarian outposts were unable to stop Ottoman incursions into southwestern Hungary. Therefore, the building of an efficient border defense system was inevitable.[59]

Danubian Border Defense

In the 1390s, recurring Ottoman raids exposed the weakness of the Hungarian kingdom's southeastern borders. Whereas before 1390 there were only four castles between Severin and Belgrade, by 1429 fourteen castles guarded this section of the border, thanks largely to Sigismund's Florentine soldier-baron Pipo of Ozora (Filippo Scolari), who governed the border between 1404 and 1426.[60] To strengthen the kingdom's defenses, Sigismund gradually withdrew royal castles and the accompanying estates from under the influence of the barons, and governed them with the help of royal officers subordinated to him and his soldier-barons, such as Pipo of Ozora and the Ragusan Talovac brothers. The king's attempt in 1429 to settle the Teutonic Knights along the southern borders, an idea first discussed with the Estates in 1397, quickly faltered. The knights were unable to defend the twelve castles entrusted to them in the Banate of Severin with the planned 1,370 infantrymen, 550 horsemen, 328 crossbowmen, and 1,400 boatmen. When the Ottomans renewed their attacks in 1432, after the expiration of a three-year truce, the Teutonic Knights suffered a serious defeat and left Hungary.[61]

The new defense line that the king established in the 1420s required a permanent military force in the border castles, which entailed hitherto unknown financial burdens for the treasury. A calculation from 1429 estimated the costs of maintaining the border garrisons at 100,000 florins annually, amounting to about one-third of Sigismund's annual ordinary revenues.[62] To finance the border defense, Sigismund collected extraordinary taxes at least nine times during his reign. In addition, from 1397 onward the monarch kept half of the ecclesiastical revenues for himself to finance his Turkish wars. The king also left archbishoprics and bishoprics vacant for years, allowing his frontier commanders to use revenues from these estates to pay the garrisons under their command.[63]

The failure at Nikopol prompted reforms in the field army. Traditionally, the backbone of the Hungarian army had been the armored cavalry, consisting of the servitor-soldiers of the king and the queen, as well as those of the prelates and barons holding state offices. Barons went to war under banners (*banderia*) bearing their own coat of arms and were called "lords with banners." Their baronial armies, consisting of their retainers, were known as banderia. According to the Golden Bull of King Andrew II (1222), which contained the obligations and privileges of the nobility, this force could be mobilized only for defensive wars within the borders of the realm, and only for a limited time period. Upon his return to Hungary from the failed crusade of Nikopol, Sigismund convoked a diet in 1397 to enact a series of military reforms. The diet not only renewed the nobility's privileges but also imposed new military obligations on them. Nobles were now obliged to take up arms and join the king personally when called on by the monarch—or pay a penalty if they failed to perform their duties. The diet also decreed that landowners equip and bring to war one mounted archer for every twenty peasant plots they possessed. The new troops, first raised in 1398, later became known as *militia portalis*, after the Latin name of the peasant plot (*porta*), which was the basis of their mobilization. Considering that in the fifteenth century Hungary had about four hundred thousand peasant plots, the militia troops could have numbered some twenty thousand mounted archers, if fully mobilized. Assembled in emergency for general campaigns, this overwhelmingly light cavalry, equipped with bow, quiver, and sword and lance, was an important auxiliary force, well suited to fight the Ottoman light cavalry, which was similarly equipped.[64]

These reforms reflected Sigismund's plans to put the burden of warfare on the shoulders of the county nobility. Whereas traditionally nobles went to war in person, they now had to mobilize additional cavalry archers, proportionate to their wealth. With the militia portalis, Sigismund laid down the nucleus of the future county-based banderia forces, which eventually were to replace the increasingly ineffective personal military service of the nobility. In his lifetime, however, the king was unable to force his plan on the county nobility, who insisted on fighting in person, fearing that with the abandonment of their personal military service they would also lose their privileges.[65]

Sigismund also experimented with establishing mercenary troops, but his treasury's revenues were insufficient to cover their costs. Ever resourceful in raising funds, the king opted for a different solution. He authorized his court soldiers (*milites aulici*) to secure a specified number of horsemen. He advanced part of the pay of such soldiers from the treasury, while paying for the rest by mortgaging royal estates. Mortgages and loans that the king took from his subjects benefited the barons, and the exercise gave rise to a group of soldier-barons, such as the Rozgonyi, Maróti, Losonci, and Pongrác families, the Ragusan Talovac brothers, the Polish Stibor, the Florentine Pipo of Ozora, and the most famous of all, John Hunyadi, future governor and regent of Hungary.[66]

Sigismund's military reforms and his truces with the Ottomans in 1419 and 1424 temporarily relieved the Ottoman pressure. However, using the collapse of royal authority in Hungary after Sigismund's death (9 December 1437) and the election of his son-in-law—Albert V of Habsburg, duke of Austria—as king of Hungary (1437–39), the Ottomans renewed their attacks. Ottoman troops ravaged Transylvania in 1438, and by 1439 had conquered the lands of George Branković, Sigismund's former vassal. The Ottomans took Novo Brdo and its rich silver mines, along with the Serbian princely residence Smederevo. With the capture of Golubac, Thessaloniki, and Smederevo, Sultan Murad II had reestablished the Balkan possessions of his grandfather, Bayezid I.

Doukas claimed that Murad II conquered Smederevo to gain access into Hungary. In the summer of 1440 the sultan attacked Belgrade, the key fortress of the southern Hungarian defense line since 1427, defended by the Talovac brothers. The siege failed, largely because of the besiegers' lack of gunpowder artillery and the defenders' expert use of guns and countermining. However, the six-month siege prompted a change in Hungarian defense strategy, which thereafter had become more active, with preemptive attacks against the Ottomans.[67]

The Habsburg-Jagiellonian Rivalry

Hungary, which suffered recurring Ottoman attacks from 1438 onward, led the anti-Ottoman coalition under the command of the country's new hero John Hunyadi. John's father, Woyk, a lesser Romanian nobleman from Wallachia, served King Sigismund, and in 1409 was awarded the estates of Hunedoara, from which the family's name originates. Hunyadi learned the basics of contemporary warfare in the service of Stephen Újlaki, ban of Mačva. He later served as King Sigismund's court knight, and served briefly in the court of Filippo Maria Visconti, duke of Milan. Participating in Sigismund's campaign against the Hussites in Bohemia in 1436–37, Hunyadi observed the Hussites' tactics and their use of armed wagons. He later deployed these tactics effectively against the Ottomans. King Albert (r. 1437–39), the first Habsburg on the Hungarian throne, who had married King Sigismund's daughter Elizabeth, appointed Hunyadi ban of Severin, charging him with the defense of the border. After King Albert's death (27 October 1439), a civil war over the succession broke out in Hungary between the supporters of Władysław III (r. 1424–44) Jagiellon, the fifteen-year-old king of Poland-Lithuania, whom the Hungarian diet invited to the throne, and those of the queen dowager Elizabeth and her infant son Ladislaus the Posthumous, born in February 1440. In early January, at their assembly in Buda, the Hungarian Estates rejected the deceased king's testament that was to give the throne to his son under the guardianship of Albert's cousin, Frederick III, king of the Romans (r. 1440–93) and after 1452 Holy Roman emperor. Resenting Habsburg influence and fearing Ottoman advance, the Estates argued that in the face of imminent Ottoman threat the country needed a warrior king, not an infant, and thus decided to offer the Hungarian throne to Władysław. At the negotiations in Cracow, Władysław accepted the Estates' conditions, promising to uphold Hungary's ancient laws and privileges, and defend the country against foreign enemies. On 8 March, authorized by the Hungarian diet, the delegation elected Władysław as king of Hungary, who henceforth was known in Hungary as King Wladislas I (Hun. Ulászló, r. 1440–44).[68] However, Queen Elizabeth rejected the election. On 15 May, she had her infant son crowned with the Holy Crown of St. Stephen, which one of Elizabeth's ladies-in-waiting had stolen from safekeeping in the citadel of Visegrád.[69]

Although the coronation of Ladislaus V (r. 1440–57) met all the constitutional requirements, since he had not been elected by the diet, the supporters of Wladislas declared the coronation invalid. They justified their act by the new idea that "the crowning of kings is always dependent on the will of the kingdom's inhabitants, in whose consent both the effective-ness and the force of the crown reside."[70] This was a momentous act, for the Estates declared for the first time in Hungarian history their preemi-nence over royal authority and "the priority of the principle of election over that of legitimacy."[71] Since the country was in danger and needed a king capable of defending the kingdom against the advancing Ottomans, the partisans of Wladislas crowned him on 17 July. For the coronation, they used another crown from the reliquary "of the most blessed King Stephen, apostle and patron of this kingdom," upon which the Estates transferred "all the force, and all the efficacy of the previous crown."[72] This is but one example of how the Ottoman threat could be used to justify crucial constitutional changes in countries neighboring the Ottomans.

Owing in large part to Hunyadi's military campaigns against Eliza-beth's partisans, Wladislas established his rule over the majority of the country. The king in turn rewarded Hunyadi's services with enormous estates, appointing him and Nicholas Újlaki jointly as royal governors (*voivode*) of Transylvania, counts of the Székelys, and castellans of Temesvár, Belgrade, and the border castles along the Danube.[73] These appointments made Hunyadi the uncontested strongman of the king-dom's eastern territories. However, the Habsburg party remained strong and controlled most of northern Hungary under Elizabeth's Bohemian warlord, John (Jan) Jiškra of Brandýsa, while key castles and towns in western Hungary were in the hands of Elizabeth's supporters. These included the counts of Cilli (the family of Elizabeth's mother), the in-fluential Garai family, and the Serbian despot George Branković, whose daughter Catherine (as mentioned) was the wife of Ulrich II of Cilli. Elizabeth's strongest supporter was her uncle, Frederick III, the head of the Habsburg dynasty. The queen appointed Frederick as her son's guardian and entrusted the crown of St. Stephen to his care.[74]

Europe's Last Offensive Crusade: Varna 1444

The civil war in Hungary, which lasted through 1445, considerably weak-ened the country's defense potentials. The successful defense of Belgrade in the summer of 1440 and Hunyadi's victories in the early 1440s against the Ottomans should be evaluated in light of these circumstances.

Having launched several campaigns into Serbia and Wallachia, Hunyadi defeated the Ottoman *sancak* governor of Smederevo in 1441. In March 1442 he destroyed an Ottoman force that had ravaged Transylvania, killing the Ottoman commander, the marcher lord of Nikopol, Mezid Beg, and his son. When the sultan sent the governor-general of Rumeli, Şehabeddin Pasha, to avenge Mezid's defeat, Hunyadi met him in early September near the Upper Ialomiţa River in Wallachia. In a battle that lasted several hours, Hunyadi used his heavy cavalry and war wagons to rout the enemy, a tactic Hunyadi had learned from the Hussites. Although these victories did not affect Ottoman strategic positions in the Balkan Peninsula, the killing of Mezid and his son, and the capture of Ottoman soldiers was a major humiliation for the sultan. Hunyadi's patrons celebrated him as the champion of the anti-Turkish wars. In October 1443, the Hungarian army, led by Hunyadi and King Wladislas, launched the first major offensive campaign against the Ottomans since the fateful Crusade of Nikopol in 1396. The Hungarians moved deep into the sultan's domain, defeating the governor-general of Rumeli and forcing him to flee to Sofia. The Hungarians took Pirot and Sofia, as the Ottomans seemed unprepared to fight during the winter months, when most of the *timariot* cavalry retired to their villages. Hunyadi's use of the Hussite Wagenburg tactic and the deployment of some six hundred taborite war wagons also proved a major advantage for the crusaders. Murad II's forces only stopped the enemy at the narrow gorges of the Balkan Mountains near Zlatica that guarded the passage to Edirne, the Ottoman capital. Although horse plague and logistical difficulties during the cold winter forced the Hungarians to withdraw and give up their recent conquests, the swift victories well inside the sultan's domains forced Murad II to seek peace.[75]

Through the mediation of his Serbian Byzantine wife, Mara Branković, Murad II concluded a peace treaty with the Hungarians and George Branković. The sultan communicated his peace initiative first in January 1444 and later in April via an Orthodox monk, whom Mara sent to her father. The Ottomans used the captivity of Çandarlı Mahmud Çelebi—brother of the grand vizier Çandarlı Halil Pasha and brother-in-law of the sultan—as a pretext for the negotiations. These early contacts quickly led to the Ottoman-Hungarian-Serbian peace treaty, concluded in Edirne for ten years on 12 June 1444 between the plenipotentiary envoys of Wladislas, Hunyadi, and Branković, on the one hand, and Sultan Murad II, on the other. In the treaty, the sultan agreed to return Ottoman-conquered Serbia (including Smederevo and Novo Brdo) to Branković, along with his two blinded sons, and pay an indemnity of 100,000 florins to the Hungarian king.[76]

The Treaty of Edirne, and its confirmation and later violation by the Hungarians, has produced a vast literature both at its time and later. Historians, depending on their national and religious biases, have interpreted it differently, trying to exonerate their respective protagonists—the Polish king, the Hungarian national hero Hunyadi, or Pope Eugene IV, whose legate lobbied for violation of the treaty and for the crusade against the Turks.[77] The despot knew that without Hunyadi no treaty could be confirmed, so he promised his vast estates in Hungary to Hunyadi if he could persuade the king to accept the Ottoman peace offer. On 4 August in Szeged in southern Hungary, King Wladislas and his barons swore in public in front of the papal legate, Cardinal Giuliano Cesarini, that they would proceed with the crusade against the Ottomans, "regardless of any treaty that had been or would be concluded with the sultan." However, the negotiations with the Ottoman envoys continued—not in Szeged, where the crusaders were gathering, but in Várad (modern Oradea in Romania). After Branković and Hunyadi (in lieu of the king) confirmed the treaty by their oaths, the Ottomans returned the promised castles and the despot's blinded sons within eight days, as stipulated in the treaty.[78] Sultan Murad II now turned against the Karamans, who attacked the Ottomans in Asia Minor as the sultan's troops were fighting against the Hungarians. Seeing that Murad II now could deploy all of his fighting men in Asia Minor, the Karaman emir accepted the status quo ante. Soon after his victory, Murad II abdicated and retired to Manisa, leaving the government to his twelve-year-old son Mehmed II.

The Ottomans faced simultaneous threats from the Albanians, Byzantines, and European crusaders led by the Hungarians. In Albania, Skanderbeg—a local Christian lord by the name of George (Gjergj) Kastrioti who had been brought up as a Muslim in Murad II's court and

sent back to Albania to represent Ottoman authority—rose up against
the House of Osman in 1443. Meanwhile, the despot of the Morea had
rebuilt the Hexamilion ("six mile") wall that defended the Corinth isthmus and the Peloponnese against attacks from the north by the spring
of 1444. In the summer of 1444, the Byzantine emperor released another pretender to the Ottoman throne. Most dangerously for the Ottomans, on 22 September a European crusading army led by King
Wladislas I and Hunyadi crossed the Ottoman-Hungarian border. At
this critical moment, Grand Vizier Çandarlı Halil Pasha recalled Sultan
Murad II. Arriving in Edirne, Murad II assumed command of the Ottoman troops while Mehmed II remained the sultan. At Varna on the
Black Sea coast, the Ottomans scored a major victory against Europe's
last crusader army on 10 November 1444. King Wladislas I was dead and
Hunyadi, the hero of the Turkish wars, barely escaped with his life.[79] In
addition to Ottoman numerical superiority, their victory can be attributed to Murad's unwavering leadership and to his janissaries' steadfast-
ness at critical moments of the battle. Georgius de Hungaria, who was
held captive by the Ottomans between 1438 and 1458, seconded this
widespread contemporary opinion about the importance of the janissaries at Varna. He heard that in the battle "the enemy completely
crushed and nearly defeated the [sultan's] army, but in the end the sultan proved victorious because of these troops."[80]

Bows, Firearms, and Military Acculturation

The janissaries were famed archers. Most Ottoman soldiers used swords
and bows. The Ottomans made their reflex and recurved composite
bows of wood, horn, sinew, and glue. The typical Ottoman bow mea-
sured only 102 to 110 centimeters in length and was the shortest among
its relatives. Making such a bow required great skill and could take one
to three years because its organic materials had to be sufficiently dried.
Ottoman composite bows had formidable range and armor-piercing
capability. Historical records suggest that Ottoman master archers
could shoot their light arrows at distances of more than 800 meters.

Modern velocity tests performed with bows and arrows similar to historical Ottoman bows and arrows have validated these records, set in the sixteenth through nineteenth centuries. While flight archery had little military applicability, target shooting was important in military training. Ottoman archers practiced target shooting from a distance of 165 to 250 meters, thought to be the optimal distance for making aimed shots. Ottoman archers owed their superiority to their archery technique: drawing and releasing the string with the thumb, using a ring to protect the thumb, and having a shorter draw, which allowed the archer to shoot from horseback. Compared with the three-finger technique, the thumb-release technique resulted in faster release and better stability of the arrow. Since the string hand of the archer could hold several extra arrows, this technique also resulted in faster shot sequence.[81]

Ottoman cavalrymen wore mail shirts or mail-and-plate armor, constructed of large spring rings and steel plates. The latter provided extra protection for the chest, underarms, and the back, although there are extant Ottoman mail shirts from the fourteenth and fifteenth centuries that have no plates. Under the mail-and-plate armor the Ottomans wore undershirts made of cotton and linen, inscribed with quotations from the Qur'an. Mail shirts could also be covered by cotton or linen. Iron arm guards or greave and vambrace protected the arms, whereas mail-and-plate cuisse guarded the knee and leg. Ottoman *sipahis* protected their heads with helmets made of steel, which had cheek and neck guards also of chain mail. The earliest extant helmets in Turkish collections date from the first decades of the Ottoman emirate. From the sixteenth century onward, under Mamluk influence, the conical form of Ottoman helmets became more accentuated. Helmets for sultans and dignitaries were decorated in gold with quotations from the Qur'an and were often worn as parade helmets. Before the introduction of firearms, shields—usually round in form and made of leather, bound cane, iron, copper, and brass—provided effective protection. Since the *timariot sipahis* were responsible for their own equipment, usually made in local workshops near their places of residence, they employed a great variety of weapons of uneven quality.

The mass use of firearms in warfare was one of the most significant developments of the late Middle Ages. Gunpowder—a mixture of saltpeter, sulfur, and charcoal—was first made in China in the seventh or eighth century, and the first proper firearms were manufactured there from the 1280s onward. The long transition from the Yuan dynasty (1279–1368) to the Ming dynasty (1368–1644), which lasted for a century from around 1350 to around 1450, witnessed the proliferation of firearms in China; the percentage of soldiers fighting with guns rose from 10 percent to 30 percent from the early Ming era to the last third of the 1400s. Within decades of its introduction in China, gunpowder weapons had reached both the Muslim world and Christian Europe. By the first decades of the fourteenth century, firearms were being used on European battlefields and in sieges, although their proportion did not reach that of China until the mid-1500s.[82]

By midcentury, firearms had reached the Balkan Peninsula, and by the 1380s, the Ottomans were also acquainted with the new weapon, as they faced enemies already in possession of firearms—Byzantines, Venetians, and Hungarians. More importantly, the Ottomans established a separate artillery corps as part of the sultan's standing army in the early fifteenth century, well before their opponents in Europe and Asia. In the time of Sultan Bayezid I (r. 1389–1402), the Ottomans had artillery gunners paid with military prebends, and a generation later began to employ salaried cannoneers. From the mid-fifteenth century onward, a separate unit of armorers (sing. *cebeci*) within the sultan's household troops looked after and carried the infantry janissaries' weapons. By the second half of the same century, the army had its gun carriage drivers (sing. *top arabacı*), whose job was to manufacture, repair, and operate war wagons in campaigns, including the setting up of the Ottoman wagon laager or *tabur*. The corps of bombardiers (sing. *humbaracı*) was established in the late fifteenth century. All this was in sharp contrast to most of the Ottomans' European adversaries, in whose realms the gunner remained a master craftsman, who had a special relationship with his weapon. In Europe, individual artillery pieces were often named and cannons were elaborately decorated.[83] Western sources mention the Mahometa, Mehmed II's giant cannon manufactured by the Hungarian renegade Orban before the siege of Constantinople (1453). However, such specialized names for artillery pieces are absent from Ottoman chronicles and fortress inventories, which suggests that the business of the Ottoman gunner was more mundane. While his profession required specialized knowledge and brought him prestige, he was first and fore-most a professional soldier of the sultan's standing household army.[84]

From the middle of the fifteenth century onward, Ottoman artillery gunners and arquebusiers, both Muslim and Christian, served in Ottoman-held forts in Rumeli, including Novo Brdo, Nikopol, Sme-derevo, Vidin, and Zvornik. While most of these specialized troops were Christians or recent converts, in strategically located castles—such as the recently conquered Kilia and Akkareman at the mouth of the Dan-ube and Dniester Rivers, and Modon on the southwestern edge of the Peloponnese—all of the artillerymen were Muslims. Muslim cannon-eers gradually outnumbered their Christian peers in other Ottoman castles as well.[85] Ottoman soldiers used cannons in their sieges of Byz-antine Constantinople (between 1394 and 1402, 1422 and 1453), Thes-saloniki (1422 and 1430), Antalya (1424), Novo Brdo (1427 and 1441), Smederevo (1439), and Belgrade (1440). Considering that cannons became common in European sieges only from the 1420s on, the above examples suggest that the Ottomans were on par with developments occurring elsewhere in Europe. In addition to siege warfare, by 1444 the Ottomans had started to use cannons aboard their river flotillas and in battles. They employed cannons against both fixed and moving targets, such as castles and enemy ships. By this time, they also used matchlock arquebuses (*tüfek*).[86] The matchlock is named after its simple firing mechanism. When the soldier pulled his gun's trigger, a smoldering match was brought down to ignite the priming powder in the flash pan, which in turn ignited the main powder charge in the barrel, forcing the projectile out of the barrel.

The Hungarian-Ottoman wars of the 1440s catalyzed the spread of firearms technology among the Ottomans. In the wars, the Ottomans acquainted themselves with the Hussite Wagenburg tactic. The Wagen-burg, or wagon laager, perfected by the Hussites in Bohemia during the Hussite wars (1419–36), was a defensive arrangement of hundreds of war wagons chained together and staffed by crossbowmen and hand-gunners. The Hungarian general John Hunyadi had learned the tactic in Bohemia while fighting against the Hussites in the service of King Sigismund of Hungary. When preparing to fight against the Ottomans in March 1443, Hunyadi ordered the artisans of the Saxon town of Kronstadt (Braşov in modern Rumania) to send him "war wagons furnished with guns, arquebuses and other war-machines," made according to the instructions of a certain Bohemian artisan. In his winter campaign of 1443–44, Hunyadi deployed some six hundred war wagons, whereas in the 1444 Varna campaign the crusaders had some two thousand wagons, most of which the Ottomans captured in the battle. The Ottomans quickly realized the usefulness of the Wagenburg and also determined how to overcome it. They surrounded the wagon laager out of range of the guns, forcing the enemy to give up its positions, a tactic they successfully employed at the battles of Varna (1444) and Kosovo (1448). It is not known when the Ottomans first used their wagon laager, known as *tabur*, after the term *szekér tábor*, the Hungarian name of the Wagenburg. In the battle of Kosovo in 1448, John Hunyadi, the commander of the Hungarian army, used the wagons as Wagenburg. In contrast, the Ottomans did not employ the Hungarian-style wagon laager but rather a type of defensive embankment that served them so well at Varna in 1444. It was a deep trench, with a dirt embankment strengthened with iron stakes and large shields, behind which stood janissary archers, arquebusiers, and light artillery pieces. By the second half of the fifteenth century, however, the combined use of field artillery, arquebus infantry, and the *tabur* had become a decisive factor in Ottoman battlefield victories.[87]

3

Constantinople

The Conquest of Constantinople

Threatened by Ottoman expansion, the Byzantine leadership was willing to pay the price for western European military assistance against the Ottomans. Emperor John VIII Palaiologos (r. 1425–48) led a Byzantine delegation to the Council of Ferrara–Florence in 1438 to accept papal supremacy and the union of the Catholic and Orthodox churches. After long negotiations Patriarch Joseph II of Constantinople and all Orthodox bishops but one signed the Decree of Union in June 1439 in Florence, where the council had been relocated in early 1439. Many in Byzantium feared that the union would arouse the sultan's suspicions and provoke Ottoman retaliation. Indeed, once informed about the union, Sultan Murad II demanded an explanation from Emperor John VIII Palaiologos. The emperor assured the sultan that the union was not aimed at the Ottomans, but Murad did not believe him. It is also likely that the sultan knew that the majority of the Byzantine lower clergy rejected the union. The Byzantine chronicler George Sphrantzes, friend and confidant of the last Byzantine emperor Constantine XI Palaiologos (r. 1449–53), recorded in retrospect that the council and the union of the Catholic and Orthodox churches were the most potent causes of the Ottoman siege of Constantinople in 1453.[1]

The crises of 1443–44 revealed the vulnerability of the young Ottoman polity and the friction between the old and new political and military elite, represented respectively by viziers from the old Turkish aristocracy and by statesmen who were either renegades or products of the Ottoman child-levy system. The first group pursued a cautious policy, whereas the new elite advocated for a more belligerent strategy against the Ottomans' European enemies and Byzantium. To avoid a disaster that such aggressive policy might cause, Grand Vizier Halil Pasha, the leader of the old elite, recalled Murad II from his retirement for the second time, using as a pretext the 1446 janissary rebellion in Edirne. The rebellion erupted partly because of Mehmed II's debasement of the Ottoman silver coinage in which the janissaries received their salaries. Although deposed, as the heir to his father, Mehmed periodically participated in Ottoman campaigns on his father's side, including the second battle of Kosovo (October 1448), against another crusading army led by John Hunyadi. When Murad II died in 1451, Mehmed ascended to the throne, poised to resume his belligerent policy against Byzantium and its European allies.

Emperor Constantine XI adhered to the Union of the Catholic and Orthodox churches, hoping that he could get military aid from the Catholic monarchs in Europe against the Turks. On 12 December 1452, the union was formally celebrated in the Hagia Sophia, but most in Constantinople rejected it. Many shared the sentiment of the last Byzantine first minister and perhaps the wealthiest man of the land, the Grand Duke Lucas Notaras (1449–53), who on the eve of the fall of Constantinople reportedly declared that "it would be better to see the turban of the Turks reigning in the center of the city than the Latin miter."[2] However, in return for military help, many were willing to cooperate with the papacy and the Western Catholic kingdoms, including Notaras himself. Some Europeans may have been misled by the first political acts of the young sultan, who, upon his accession to the throne, renewed the existing truces with his neighbors, including Serbia, Venice, and Hungary. If some interpreted Mehmed II's move as a sign of peaceful policy, they soon realized the sultan's true intentions. Mehmed used the renewal of truces to prepare for the siege of Constantinople, his ultimate political goal.

Sultan Mehmed carefully planned the siege of the Byzantine capital. Constantinople was known as an impregnable city. The Sea of Marmara protected the city from the south and east, and the Golden Horn from the north. Mehmed spent 1452 and the spring of 1453 preparing for war. With the construction of Rumeli Hisarı (Rumelian Castle) completed in just over three months in 1452 on the European shore of the Bosporus Straits opposite Güzelcehisar (today Anadolu Hisarı) on the Asian side, the young sultan signaled his intentions to the world. The Ottomans called the new fortress Boğazkesen, meaning "cutter of the throat/channel." The sultan's navy and the cannons deployed in the twin fortresses on the Bosporus Straits' opposite shores sealed off the Byzantine capital.

Before the siege, the sultan's Muslim and Christian gun founders cast some sixty cannons of various calibers in Edirne, the Ottoman capital. Some of these cannons threw stone balls weighing between 240 and 400 kilograms (530 and 880 pounds), such as the one cast by Sarıca, the chief Turkish artillery gunner. These were similar to the few still existing Ottoman large bronze cannons, which are about 420 centimeters long with bore diameters between 63 and 68 centimeters. Even these, however, were surpassed by the sultan's largest bombard, cast by the Hungarian master Orban, which fired stone balls weighing between 400 and 600 kilograms (880 and 1,300 pounds).[3]

Emperor Constantine XI did all that he could to prepare for the siege. He sent envoys to Venice, Genoa, the pope, the Holy Roman emperor, and the kings of Hungary and Aragon with the message that, unless immediate military help was provided, the days of Constantinople were numbered. The response was unimpressive. Some Italians, embarrassed by their government's impotence, came as volunteers. One of them was Giovanni Guglielmo Longo Giustiniani, a young Genoese condottiere and the Genoese consul of Caffa, who had previously been engaged in piracy. He came from Chios, as the Ottoman construction of Rumeli Hisarı prevented his return to his consulship. The emperor charged this able man of fortune with the command of the defense. His several hundred men and the two hundred soldiers who came with Cardinal Isidore formed the core of the defense.[4] The Venetian colony in Constantinople and many citizens in Pera, opposite Constantinople, also stayed, as did Orhan, a pretender to the Ottoman throne who had been kept in Byzantine custody. All in all, Emperor Constantine XI had some eight thousand

A large Ottoman cast bronze cannon displayed outside the walls of the Rumeli Hisarı fortress in Istanbul. While in the fifteenth and sixteenth centuries the Ottomans used several such large cannons, most of their artillery pieces were small- and medium-caliber cannons. (Photo courtesy of the author.)

Greek and two thousand foreign soldiers at his disposal, along with some thirty thousand to forty thousand civilians. The civilians were divided among many minorities and factions: Greeks, Venetians, Genoese, Jews, pro-Western and pro-Turkish, pro-unionist and anti-unionists. Still, they rendered valuable service by repairing the walls of the city before and during the siege.

Sultan Mehmed II, who laid siege to the city on 6 April, concentrated his forces along the city's western land walls.[5] Ottoman artillery gunners and miners were on the cutting edge of their art. The artillerymen bombarded the walls from several batteries, each consisting of a large bombard and several smaller pieces. They fired at the wall so that the shots formed the shape of a triangle, a known firing technique in Renaissance Europe.[6] To destroy the Byzantine and allied ships sheltering in the harbor and guarded by the walls of Galata, Sultan Mehmed, a keen student of contemporaneous military technology, urged his cannon makers to experiment with a "different sort of gun with a slightly changed design that could fire the stone to a great height, so that when it came down, it would hit the ships amidships and sink them."[7] Although not unknown to contemporaries, historians credit the Ottomans with developing the mortar—a shorter cannon that fired projectiles with parabolic trajectories, usually against targets protected by walls.[8] Whatever the damage of Ottoman mortars, their constant operation at the port area further stretched the Byzantine defense, already diminishing in numbers. The same was true for the continuous Ottoman bombardment of the massive Theodosian land walls, whose protection and repair required a lot of defenders.[9]

In the end, it took an unexpected maneuver on the part of the young sultan to bring the siege to a successful close. On the morning of 23 April, the Byzantines noticed with terror that the Ottomans had portaged some seventy smaller ships overland from the Bosporus into the Golden Horn, whose entrance the Byzantines had blocked with a stretched chain before the siege. Using sheep and ox tallow as lubricants, the Ottomans portaged their ships on rollers possibly along the longer (twelve to thirteen kilometers) land route that runs from the Double Columns (Beşiktaş-Kabataş) to where the third bridge over the Golden Horn is located today (opposite Eyüb), rather than along the shorter (two to three kilometers) Tophane-Taksım-Kasımpaşa route, which the Byzantines would have detected.[10] The maneuver was a severe blow to the Byzantines, who now had to allocate men and resources to defend the sea walls along the Golden Horn. This further stretched the already overwhelmed defense.

Ottoman assaults and bombardment continued. Food supplies and ammunition in the besieged city were running short. When the defenders learned that neither relief forces nor the promised Venetian armada would arrive, they lost hope and felt abandoned. The sultan's messengers urged the citizens to surrender or face slaughter and slavery. The emperor offered the sultan as much annual tribute as he wanted. But the victory was in sight. Replied Mehmed: "If you will admit defeat and withdraw in peace, I shall give you the Peloponnese and other provinces for your brothers and we shall be friends. If you persist in denying me peaceful entry into the city, I shall force my way in and I shall slay you and all your nobles; and I shall slaughter all the survivors and allow my troops to plunder at will. The city is all I want, even if it is empty."[11]

Peculiar natural phenomena preceding the fall of the city affected both sides. Some scholars attribute the lunar eclipse, the unseasonably chilly weather, the violent thunderstorm and thick dry fog, and the infernal lights on the roof of the church of the Hagia Sophia to the massive volcanic explosion on the South Pacific island of Kuwae that spread clouds of volcanic ash throughout the upper atmosphere worldwide.[12] Unaware of such explanations, Constantinople's defenders took these natural occurrences as signs of divine displeasure and omens that foretold the looming fall of their city. To the besiegers, though, these were signs of hope and imminent victory. On 29 May, Constantinople succumbed to the final assault.

Historians have cited the Ottoman conquest of Byzantine Constantinople as one of the most dramatic examples of the "gunpowder revolution" and the decisiveness of cannons. While cutting-edge military technology, which enabled the Ottomans to deploy the largest bombards known to date, played an essential role in breaching Constantinople's walls in 1453, it was but one element in the Ottoman success. Other factors included careful planning, resourceful leadership (portaging ships, soldiers, and weaponry into the Golden Horn, where the Byzantine defense was the weakest), prowess in siege warfare (mining, "triangle" firing technique, and the use of mortars), numerical superiority (seventy thousand Ottomans versus ten thousand defenders), better logistics (abundant supplies in weaponry and food), and the lack of relief forces.[13]

Last seen near the Gate of Saint Romanos, Constantine XI Palaiologos, the last emperor of the Romans (who ironically bore the name of the founder of the Byzantine capital), died as a common soldier, fighting the enemy. His body was never found, though Ottoman chroniclers and Konstantin Mihailović of Ostrovica reported that a janissary severed the emperor's already lifeless head and brought it before the sultan, saying: "There you have the head of your cruelest enemy."[14] Sultan Mehmed II entered the city on horseback through the Gate of Saint Romanos, later known to the Ottomans as Topkapı ("Cannon Gate"). He granted a three-day plunder to his troops.[15] After the pillage, the sultan entrusted the newly appointed Ottoman governor of Constantinople with the reconstruction and repopulation of the city.

Claiming Universal Sovereignty

The consequences of the Ottoman conquest of Constantinople were paramount both domestically and internationally. The conquest gave the young Mehmed II unparalleled prestige and legitimacy, and dramatically reshaped the Ottoman political worldview. Mehmed was now the "Conqueror" (*Fatih*), the first Muslim ruler to accomplish the old objective of the Muslims, who first besieged the city under the Umayyad caliph Muawiyya (r. 661–80). Constantinople had long been the target of the Turks, as it was the home of the "red apple" (*kızıl elma*), the symbol of universal sovereignty. The resplendent metal ball, held in the hand of Emperor Justinian's statute standing before the Church of Hagia Sophia, was the lucky charm of the Byzantine Empire. Its capture by Mehmed symbolized the fulfillment of the Ottomans' destiny, the defeat of Christendom, and the realization of their dream of world domination. After the conquest of Constantinople, the red apple referred to other royal capitals, including Rome, Buda, and Vienna, which the Ottomans intended to conquer. More generally, it signified world domination.[16]

Europeans believed that following the conquest of Constantinople Mehmed wanted to revive the Roman Empire by conquering Rome and uniting the Mediterranean under his rule. The fact that in 1480 Mehmed sent Gedik Ahmed Pasha, his grand admiral and former grand vizier, against southern Italy suggests that the sultan entertained this ambitious goal throughout his life. Conscious of the importance of his 1453 success, Sultan Mehmed II dispatched an envoy to the Mamluk sultan Sayf al-Din Inal (r. 1453–61) with a victory announcement. Two slightly different versions of the document have survived: one in an Ottoman collection of documents, and the other in both a Mamluk chronicle and a Mamluk collection of letters. In the version preserved in the Ottoman collection, the twenty-one-year-old Ottoman sovereign conveyed his respect for the seventy-two-year-old Mamluk sultan, in accordance with reverence for seniority in Islamic societies; but he also made an important distinction between the two rulers, displaying the young conqueror's escalating ambitions. "Now this is the time," read Mehmed II's victory proclamation, "to reconnect between the person who shouldered the responsibility of enabling the pilgrimage for the pilgrims and pious people and the person who shouldered the responsibility of preparing and equipping the people of *ghaza* and jihad, as he inherited this task from his fathers and ancestors."[17] Mehmed II not only disregarded the Mamluk sultans' fight against the Mongols and crusaders, a role at the core of the Mamluks' self-image and legitimacy, but also alluded to the fact that his was a dynastic empire, whereas the Mamluk sultans were of slave origin. The fact that the author of Mehmed's victory proclamation, Molla Gürani, once worked for the Mamluk sultans but now served Mehmed and tutored him in youth contained an implicit message as to the importance of the Ottoman court as patron of Muslim scholars. On the other hand, it is not surprising that the passage cited above is missing from the version preserved in Mamluk sources, suggesting that the Mamluk sultan, who was also the protector of the caliphate, did not wish to accept Mehmed II's pretensions. Sultan Inal's letters to Mehmed II were also reserved, but recognized Mehmed II's achievement. While Inal did not title Mehmed II as "sultan," he acknowledged the Ottoman ruler's role in jihad and—in a novel gesture—included the titular "victorious" (*mansur*) among Mehmed's titles. The splendid reception and festivities organized for the Ottoman envoy in Cairo also conveyed respect.[18]

By adopting the Roman-Byzantine titles Kayser-i Rum (Caesar of Rome) and *basileus*, Mehmed II announced his claim to be the heir to the Roman emperors. He enthroned George Scholarios as the new patriarch, known henceforth as Gennadios, with all the ceremonial attributes known in the fallen Byzantine Empire. By reconstituting the patriarchate, Mehmed II acted in his role as basileus, establishing control over the Orthodox church. Byzantine scholars such as Georgios Trapezuntinos also accepted Mehmed's claim, calling him basileus. The titles kayser and basileus would be used by Mehmed II's successors as well, thus challenging the claims that Muscovy was the "Third Rome," an idea that appeared in the early 1520s.[19] Serbian-language documents issued by the Ottoman chancery in the name of Sultans Mehmed II, Bayezid II, and Selim I used the Slavic variant of Caesar (*tsar*), calling the Ottoman sultans "great and mighty *tsars*." These Byzantine titles,

along with the old Turkish and Islamic titles of *kaghan* and sultan, signaled Mehmed II's claim to universal sovereignty.[20] Mehmed's claim of
lordship over "two lands" (Rumeli and Rum/Asia Minor) and "two
seas" (the Aegean and the Black Seas) demonstrated his realization of
Constantinople's geostrategic importance, but also suggested that the
sultan regarded his empire as firmly rooted in both Europe and Asia.

A New Imperial Capital

Before 1453, the Ottoman domains lacked a suitable capital city and
logistical base, for neither southeast Europe nor Asia Minor has a natural
geographical center. Constantinople provided the Ottomans with such
a center, an ideally located imperial capital city with a thousand-year-old
imperial pedigree. Mehmed II and his successors rapidly rebuilt and re-
populated Constantinople, whose pre-conquest population (circa
40,000) doubled by 1477 and reached perhaps 250,000 inhabitants by
the late sixteenth century, making it the most populous city in contemporaneous Europe. Owing to the Ottomans' tolerant policy toward the
city's former inhabitants (Byzantine Greeks, Jews, and Genoese and Venetian resident merchants) as well as to Bayezid II's welcoming of the
Sephardic Jews expelled from Iberia, by the late fifteenth century the
population of Ottoman Constantinople was 60 percent Muslim and
40 percent Christian and Jewish. The Ottoman imperial capital retained
this multiethnic and multiconfessional character, with similar population
distribution, throughout the sixteenth century, an era when monarchs
in Europe imposed their religions on their subjects.[21]

The two castles of Rumeli Hisarı and Anadolu Hisarı on the shores
of the Bosporus defended the capital from the Black Sea. To guard his
capital from the Aegean, in 1462 Mehmed ordered the construction of
Kale-i Sultaniyye (the Sultan's Castle) on the Asian side of the Dardanelles, near ancient Abydos, and Kilid al-Bahr (Key of the Sea, or Kilid
al-Bahreyn / Key of the Two Seas) on the European shore.[22] According
to the *Turkish History* of Giovanni Maria Angiolello of Vicenza (who
was taken prisoner by the Ottomans in 1470 at the siege of Negroponte
[Chalkis] and served in the courts of Prince Mustafa and Sultan

Mehmed II until 1481), the four castles and the artillery placed on their walls made the city so impregnable that not even a bird could pass without permission.[23] Mehmed also had new commercial and residential quarters built in the city, grouped around mosques and markets, of which the Conqueror's mosque complex and the Covered Bazaar remain landmarks of modern Istanbul to this day. The Hagia Sophia was turned into the sultan's mosque of Aya Sofya by adding two minarets, a marble niche (*mihrab*) in the wall indicating the direction of Mecca (the direction Muslims face while praying), and a pulpit (*minbar*), where the prayer leader stood to deliver his sermon. Ottoman masons also covered the mosaics with stucco. The Church of the Holy Apostles was razed to make space for Mehmed's foundation complex. Newly built mosques, religious colleges, libraries, dervish lodges, bathhouses, hospitals, soup kitchens, and caravanserais gradually transformed the urban landscape of the city, giving it a markedly Islamic character.[24] The Covered Bazaar not only housed merchants' shops and provided safe storage for valuable goods and money, but also made supervising, regulating, and taxing mercantile activity in the imperial capital easier, in accordance with the economic policy of an increasingly centralized state. The construction boom, initiated by the sultan and duly followed by the elite, invited capital investment and provided employment for thousands of skilled workers and day laborers in both the city and its hinterlands. Thousands of newcomers—who arrived in the city via either forced population transfers or voluntary immigration, encouraged by economic incentives—provided the bulk of the workforce.[25] The Ottoman capital offered boundless opportunities for political, military, economic, and cultural advancement. These openings invited talent from all corners of the empire and beyond, thus affording the empire with a large pool of talented people whom the government employed in its army, administration, and economy.

Constantinople's control over the road networks and maritime lines of communication made Constantinople an ideal logistical center for Ottoman campaigns in Europe, Asia Minor, and beyond. The city soon developed into a naval base of a formidable armada. Constantinople was one of three port cities in the Mediterranean (along with Venice and

Barcelona) capable of serving a large galley fleet, thanks to its natural harbor, the Golden Horn, and wealthy hinterland, rich in timber. When these fortunate conditions were paired with the Ottomans' inexhaustible resources and organizational skills, the Ottoman Empire evolved into a Mediterranean naval power. By the early sixteenth century, Ottoman naval capabilities had eclipsed those of Venice; and for most of the sixteenth century, the sultans' fleets competed with those of Spain for dominance in the Mediterranean.[26]

Constantinople soon became the center of Ottoman armament and ammunition production, owing to the activities of the Imperial Cannon Foundry (founded by Mehmed II), gunpowder and saltpeter works, and workshops that manufactured hand firearms and cold weapons. With its Turkish and Persian artisans and blacksmiths, Armenian and Greek miners and sappers, and Bosnian, Serbian, Turkish, Italian, German, and later French, English, and Dutch gun founders and military engineers, as well as Venetian, Dalmatian, and Greek shipwrights and sailors, the Ottoman capital proved to be an ideal place for technological dialogue and helped the Ottomans keep pace with the latest innovations in military and naval technology.[27]

A New Cadre of Viziers

Using the prestige that the conquest of Constantinople afforded him, Mehmed II dismissed and ordered the execution of his seasoned grand vizier, Çandarlı Halil Pasha, who had been responsible for deposing the boy sultan in 1446 and opposed the siege of Constantinople. According to contemporaries, Halil Pasha had exerted disproportionate authority under Sultan Murad II. His long tenure as grand vizier symbolized both the power of the old Turkish aristocracy and a different style of governing, in an age when the sultan shared power with his viziers and advisers.[28] Mehmed II, however, considered himself an absolute sovereign and did not want his sovereignty restricted by his viziers. Çandarlı Halil Pasha's downfall signaled major transformations in the Ottoman governing elite. To transform his father's *ghazi* frontier state into a centralized empire with claims to universal rulership, Mehmed needed statesmen of a

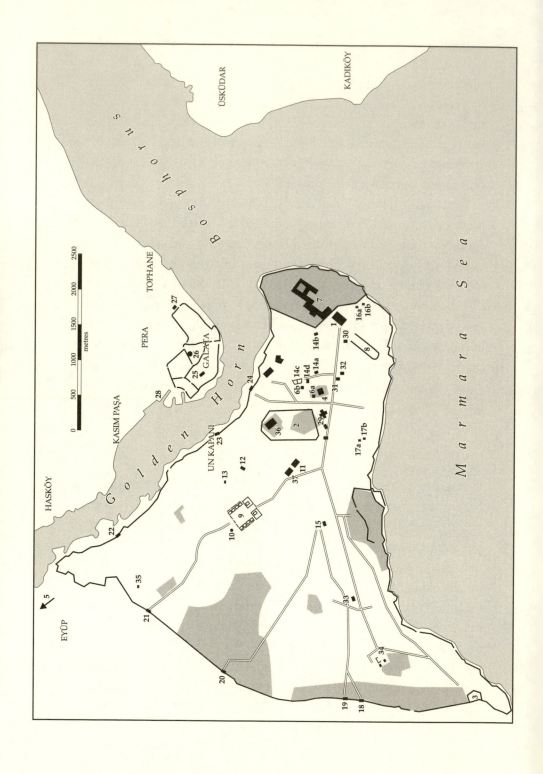

Major buildings and sites in Constantinople and Galata from the reign of Mehmed II through Süleyman I. Under Mehmed II: 1–28; under Bayezid II through Süleyman I: 29–37. Based on Kafescioğlu 2009, maps 1, 2, and 3.

1	Hagia Sophia	19	Silivri Gate
2	Old Palace	20	Cannon Gate
3	Citadel / Seven Towers	21	Edirne Gate
4	Bedestan / market complex	22	Balat Gate
5	Ayyub al-Ansari funerary complex	23	Un Kapısı
6a 6b	Caravanserais (hypothetical location)	24	Vasiliko Gate
7	Topkapı Palace	25	St. Paolo Church / Friday mosque of Galata (Arap Cami)
8	Hippodrome	26	Galata Tower
9	Mehmed II Mosque Complex	27	Tophane / Cannon Foundry
10	Sultan Bazarı markets	28	Arsenal
11	Janissary barracks (hypothetical location)	29	Bayezid II complex
12	Pantocrator monastery / Zeyrek mosque and madrasa	30	Firuz Agha mosque
13	Eski Imaret and soup kitchen	31	Atik Ali Pasha complex
14a,b,c,d	Mahmud Pasha convent-mosque, palace, caravanserai, and bath	32	Elçi Hanı
15	Has Murad Pasha complex	33	Davud Pasha complex
16a,b	İshak Pasha mosque and bath, and palace (hypothetical location)	34	Koca Mustafa Pasha complex
17a,b	Nişancı Mehmed Pasha mosque and bath	35	Chora monastery / Kariye mosque
18	Kalagru Gate	36	Süleymaniye
		37	Şehzade mosque

Ottoman Constantinople/Istanbul in the fifteenth and sixteenth centuries. (Drawn by Béla Nagy, based on Kafescioğlu 2009, maps 1, 2, and 3.)

different mold. He recruited and promoted men from among his household slaves (*kul*), who owed their power to the sultan. These new statesmen replaced the old Turkish aristocracy, who had dominated Ottoman politics and military leadership before 1453.

After Çandarlı Halil Pasha's execution, Sultan Mehmed II chose his grand viziers from his slaves of Christian origin, except for Karamani Mehmed Pasha (1477–81), his last grand vizier of freeborn Muslims. Halil Pasha's successor was Zağanos Pasha, Halil's rival and the young sultan's tutor (*lala*) and father-in-law. A recent convert from Christianity and member of the "war party," Zağanos Pasha played a key role in the siege, especially in portaging the Ottoman ships into the Golden Horn and thus lifting the spirit of the besiegers. After the conquest, he asserted an aggressive policy—advocated from 1444 onward—that was more in line with that of the ambitious young sultan.

Under Bayezid II, the old Turkish aristocracy briefly regained its prestige, including the Çandarlıs. Çandarlı Ibrahim, the son of Halil Pasha, served as chief judge of Anatolia and Rumeli, third and second vizier, and for a short time before his death, as grand vizier. Bayezid II's policy was more in line with the old Ottoman customs and Islamic law. However, the course of policy established by Mehmed II, which envisioned both a centralized government based on the *kuls* and a more aggressive foreign policy aimed at world supremacy, could not be derailed. According to one tally, of the seventy-one grand viziers in office during the two-hundred-year period between 1453 and 1654, only nine were born as Muslim Turks, and their aggregate time of tenure was only sixteen years.[29] The rest were scions of noble Serbian, Byzantine, Bosnian, and Albanian families or had more modest Christian backgrounds from the Balkan Peninsula, Italy, and the Caucasus. These latter servants of the state arrived into the Ottoman palace as prisoners of war or hostages or through the periodic levies of Christian boys.[30]

Employing Christian converts from Rumeli in high offices helped integrate the subdued Rumelian aristocracies into the Ottoman political elite and solidify Ottoman rule in newly conquered, overwhelmingly Christian lands. Mehmed II's longest-serving grand vizier was Mahmud Pasha Angelović, who held the empire's highest office in 1456–68 and again in 1472–74 and was grand admiral of the Ottoman fleet in 1469–72. A descendant of the great Byzantine families of Angeloi and Palaiologi, Mahmud Pasha came from a noble Byzantino-Serbian family. Ottoman frontier raiders had captured him and his mother in Serbia, probably in 1427, when he was about seven years old. He was raised and educated in the palace school of Sultan Murad II in Edirne and rose to prominence under Sultan Mehmed II. As we will see later in this chapter, in 1459 he conquered Serbia with the help of his brother, Michael Angelović, member of the regency council in Serbia and leader of the pro-Ottoman party; two years later, he negotiated the surrender of Trebizond with his cousin George Amiroutzes, chief minister of the last ruler of the "Empire of Trebizond."[31]

Members of the Rumelian aristocracy served future Ottoman sultans. Three times governor-general of the province of Anatolia (1486, 1489, 1493–96), three times grand admiral of the Ottoman navy (1488, 1500–1501, 1506–11), and five times grand vizier between 1497 and 1516, Hersekzade ("the Duke's Son") Ahmed Pasha (d. 1517) was the youngest son of Stephen (Stefan) Vukčić Kosača. Ruling over a duchy in southwestern Bosnia on the Adriatic coast called Hum, this Bosnian lord declared his separation from Bosnia in 1449 by dropping his title, voivode of Bosnia, and taking instead the title of herceg (duke) of Saint Sava, after the famous Serbian saint, whose relics lay in a monastery in his principality. It is his new title from which both Ahmed Pasha and modern Herzegovina (the land of Herceg) took their names.[32]

Born in 1459 in Herceg Novi in modern Montenegro and named as Stephen (Stefan), the future Ahmed Pasha was educated partly in Ragusa (Dubrovnik in Croatia), a flourishing merchant republic, which since 1458 had been an Ottoman tributary. He left his hometown for Ottoman Constantinople in 1472, after a falling-out with his elder brother, Duke Vladislav, who had seized his inheritance. In the Ottoman capital, the young Stephen converted to Islam, took the name Ahmed, entered palace service, and began his meteoric rise. Later he married the daughter of Sultan Bayezid II and was appointed as *sancak* governor of Hüdavendigar (Bursa). Five years later, he earned the title of governor-general of Anadolu province in western Asia Minor, and subsequently served as grand vizier three times under Bayezid II (1497–98, 1502–6, 1511). During the fight among Bayezid's sons for the Ottoman throne, Ahmed Pasha supported Prince Selim. Following Selim's accession to the throne, Ahmed Pasha served two more times as grand vizier (1512–14, 1515–16). In addition to his services during the Ottoman conquest of the Moldavian fortress of Kilia in 1484, and in the wars against the Mamluks (1485–91) and Safavids (1514), Ahmed Pasha proved instrumental in concluding the peace treaty with Venice, which ended the Ottoman-Venetian war of 1499–1503. Ahmed Pasha negotiated the treaty with his "beloved brother" Andrea Gritti (1455–1538), the unofficial Venetian ambassador-consul, who had been living in Pera—the Latin quarter of Constantinople at the promontory on the north side of the Golden Horn—since 1479 as a wealthy grain merchant. During the talks, the two men conversed in Gritti's native tongue, Italian, although Gritti knew Turkish.[33]

Both Mahmud and Ahmed were educated in the Ottoman palace and related by marriage to the imperial dynasty. Mahmud Pasha was Mehmed II's brother-in-law, as both men married the daughters of Zağanos Pasha, Mehmed II's grand vizier.[34] Ahmed Pasha married Hundi Hatun in 1481, shortly after her father, Bayezid II, acceded to the throne. With the matrimony, Bayezid II initiated a marriage policy whereby viziers and high-ranking Ottoman statesmen became *damad*, son-in-law or brother-in-law of the sultan, marrying Ottoman princesses. While the *damads* under Bayezid II usually did not rise to the rank of vizier, most of Selim I's *damads* did. Süleyman's reign is known as the age of the *damad*. Three of Süleyman's most trusted grand viziers—Ibrahim, Rüstem, and Sokollu Mehmed—were all *damads*. This marriage policy, through which the sultans tied their viziers to the dynasty, remained an important feature of Ottoman governing until the end of the empire.[35]

Controlling the Military

Changes in the structure of the armed forces and related fiscal and economic systems also aimed at strengthening imperial sovereignty. Mehmed II tried to counterbalance the power of the marcher lords and their *akıncı* raiders by expanding the standing salaried *kapukulu* troops and by bringing the marcher lords under the sultan's control. Following the rebellion of the janissaries upon Mehmed's accession in 1451, the sultan purged the corps, replacing the dismissed units with new ones from the keepers of the sultan's hounds (*sekban* or *seymen*) and raising the total number of the corps from 3,000 to 5,000 men. Increased revenues from territorial expansion and trade enabled Mehmed to enlarge his standing household army. By the end of his rule, the number of janissaries had doubled, reaching 10,000 men according to Ottoman chronicles, although an official Ottoman pay register listed only 7,841 janissaries in 1484.[36] These elite troops—along with the more specialized units of artillery gunners, armorers, and the six salaried palace cavalry divisions—afforded Mehmed II and his son a strong professional standing army, numbering 12,000 to 13,000 men, and 16,000 to 17,000 men including janissary novices.[37] Mehmed II deployed janissaries in strategically important garrisons, strengthening central control over the frontier lands and their marcher lords.

Mehmed II also transformed the *akıncı* forces from freelance cavalry under the command of the marcher lords to peasant soldiers and integrated them into the Ottoman military and provincial administration. The *akıncıs* now worked on the plots that they received from the state, and fought for the dynasty as light cavalry in return for tax exemptions. Government officials surveyed and recorded the *akıncıs* into registers that contained their numbers, privileges, and obligations. One such register was drawn up in 1472–73, in preparation for the sultan's 1473 campaign against Uzun Hasan, the ruler of the Akkoyunlu or White Sheep Turkmen confederation. Mehmed ordered his judges in Rumeli to conscript "from every thirty households of unbelievers and Muslims" one mounted *akıncı*, while the remaining households, called helper (*yamak*), paid 33 *akçe* each to cover the expense of their fighting peer. Mehmed's intention was clearly to weaken the corps' traditional Turkmen and Muslim character, as he ordered his judges to levy Muslims only if they could not find persons "among the unbelievers."[38]

In the late fifteenth and early sixteenth centuries, the *yürüks* or seminomadic Turkish soldiers had also been organized similarly. In the subprovince (*sancak*) of Silistra, which guarded the lower Danube and the northwestern Black Sea, about 80 percent of the population consisted of Muslim Turks. Of these Turks, *yürüks* performing military duties composed 55 percent. The Ottoman authorities organized them into units (*ocak*) of twenty-five men and gave them plots of land—similar in size to the pre-Ottoman *baštinas*—as well as exempted them from taxes. In return for their land and tax exemption, five men in each unit had to participate in the sultan's campaigns, while the remaining twenty men served as reserves, obliged to equip and finance their fighting peers.[39]

Mehmed II and his government also used the conquest of Serbia in 1459 and Bosnia in 1464, and the creation of new administrative units to tighten the ruler's control over the marcher lords by appointing them *sancak* governors. Following the conquest of Serbia, the Ottomans organized their new acquisitions into the *sancak* of Smederevo, appointing Minnetoğlu Mehmed Beg as its first governor (1459–63). The most important *sancakbeyi* of Smederevo, however, was Ali Beg of the Mihaloğlu dynasty of marcher lords, who had previously served in a similar position in Vidin. Ali Beg was the longest-serving *sancak* governor of Smederevo, directing this frontier *sancak* and its *akıncı* raiders for more than twenty-five years in the latter part of the fifteenth century.[40] The conquest of Bosnia provided Mehmed II an opportunity to dismantle yet another semi-independent frontier (*uc*), that of Skopje, by appointing its marcher lord, İsa Beg, as the first *sancak* governor of Bosnia in 1463 and integrating most of his marches into the new *sancak*.[41] The gradual incorporation of the marcher lords and their *akıncı* raiders into the Ottoman military and provincial administration was also reflected in the terminology used in contemporaneous Ottoman sources. The *uc* of the marcher lords gradually became *serhad*—that is, a frontier province governed by *sancak* governors, appointed by the government. Changing terminology in turn reflected the gradual transformation of the Ottoman frontier polity into a territorial empire, increasingly under the control of the sultan and his government.

A New Palace and the Imperial Council

Mehmed's vision of empire is reflected in the ways he and his new elite recast the urban landscape of Constantinople. Having spent a month in the ruined city after its conquest, Mehmed returned to his recently completed New Palace in Edirne. However, he had already made plans to restore Constantinople to its former splendor and make the city his empire's new capital. When he returned the next year, he had a strong fortress built near the city's Golden Gate, the stronghold that later became known as Yedikule or Seven Towers. He also ordered the construction of a palace, which was completed by 1458. The contemporary Ottoman chronicler Tursun Beg described residential buildings and kiosks for the sultan and his pages, a well-guarded harem, a council hall, and royal hunting preserves. However, Mehmed soon ordered the construction of another palace. Known today as the Topkapı Palace, Ottoman sources until the nineteenth century called it the New Imperial Palace. The basic structure of the palace complex had been completed between 1459 and 1478. Its location between the Golden Horn and the Sea of Marmara on the Seraglio Point offered the palace complex an unmatched defensive position and spectacular views. The palace's deliberate use of Byzantine, Timurid, Mamluk, and Italian architectural references reflected Mehmed's universalist vision of empire and the imperial ideology of a centralized, patrimonial empire. Admired by foreign diplomats, the New Imperial Palace was divided into three courts. The third, innermost, court housed the private quarters of the sultan and his family and was divided into male and female sections. Initially only about 150 women were relocated to the new harem, while the rest stayed in the Old Palace. The second court housed the imperial council, the empire's highest governing body. An outer wall and the monumental Imperial Gate, facing Hagia Sophia, were added by 1478 according to the gate's inscription. Mehmed's successors added new structures transforming the palatial complex into three successive courts with three gates, surrounded by an outer garden and kiosks.[42]

From the earliest times an informal advisory body of lords and state officials assisted the Ottoman rulers. Out of this body, a formal government organ or state council emerged, which the Ottomans called *divan*, following earlier Islamic empires. The Ottoman *divan* was originally a court of justice and appeals and performed the most important task of a Muslim ruler, that of dispensing justice. The *divan* also acted as the supreme organ of government, and in wartime as high command. Until

Mehmed II, the sultans personally presided at the *divan's* meetings, which usually took place near the gate (Turkish *kapı*, Arabic *bâb*, and Persian *dergâh*) of the sultan's palace. The phrase Sublime or High Porte—from the Latin *porta*, meaning "gate"—was the translation of the relevant Ottoman phrases *Dergâh-i 'Âli* or *Bâb-i 'Âli* and referred to the meeting place of the council, and by extension the Ottoman government.

The members of the *divan* represented the three major groups of the Ottoman ruling class (*askeri*) and the three major branches of the empire's administrative apparatus: the "men of the sword" or the military (*seyfiye*), "the men of the religious sciences" (*ilmiye*) or the religious establishment (*ulama*), and "the men of the pen" (*kalemiye*) or bureaucrats. Each of these groups was responsible for a distinct branch of government: matters related to politics and the military, the judiciary, and finances, although these branches had evolved into distinct bureaucratic tracks with specialized training and knowledge only by the 1570s. The representatives of these branches acted independently in their departments. The grand vizier, in his capacity as the supreme deputy of the sultan, had supervision over the various office holders. In important decisions, the heads of the individual departments needed the consent of their colleagues.[43]

In the council, the grand vizier, other viziers, and the governor-general of Rumeli represented the military. Acknowledging the increasing importance of the imperial navy, starting under Süleyman the Magnificent in the mid-sixteenth century, the *kapudan* pasha, or the grand admiral of the Ottoman navy, also had the right to attend the *divan*. From the latter half of the sixteenth century, the commander of the sultan's elite infantry, the agha of the janissaries, was also allowed to take part in the council's meetings.

The *kadıasker*, or military judge, spoke for the religious establishment in the council. Unlike most viziers from Mehmed II onward, they were free-born Muslims and graduates of the religious colleges. As heads of the Ottoman judiciary, they assisted the sultan and the grand vizier in matters related to jurisdiction. Murad I appointed the first military judge, who was joined by a second judge in the last years of Mehmed II's reign. Besides being the supreme judges of Rumeli and Anadolu, the two *kadıaskers* also supervised all judges and college professors. The chief jurisconsult (*mufti* or *şeyhülislam*) was not a member of the council, but his written opinion (*fatwa*) was sought if the two supreme judges disagreed. These were his subordinates. By the latter part of the sixteenth century, the chief *mufti* had acquired the right to appoint and dismiss the *kadıaskers*, high-ranking judges, college professors, and heads of religious brotherhoods. By turning scholars into scholar-bureaucrats with clear carrier paths, Mehmed II and his successors further strengthened the power of the imperial dynasty and gradually transformed the frontier polity of their ancestors into a dynastic empire.[44]

The chief treasurer (*defterdar*) and the chancellor (*nişancı*) represented the bureaucracy in the council. The number of treasurers grew from one under Mehmed II to four by the late sixteenth century. They were responsible for royal revenues in Rumeli, Asia Minor, Constantinople, and the Danube region. However, between the mid-1540s and 1583 more than a dozen provincial treasurers (in Diyarbakır, Baghdad, Buda, Damascus, Erzurum, Trablusşam, Basra, Egypt, Algiers, Dulkadır, Yemen, Aleppo, Rum, Karaman, Van, Maraş, and Kars) had been appointed to administer the central treasury's revenues in these provinces far from the capital.[45] The rising number of treasurers reflected the growing importance of the treasury in an empire that faced repeated financial crises from the end of the sixteenth century.

The *nişancı*, head of the Ottoman chancery, was responsible for authenticating all imperial documents by affixing the sultan's monogram (*tuğra*). This ensured that all orders and letters issued from the council conformed to Ottoman laws and chancery practice. The chief chancellor also supervised the council's archives (*defterhane*), which housed the provincial cadastral or revenue surveys and tax registers, classified in alphabetical order by province, as well as other official documents regarding *timars* and lands of religious endowments. Clerks in the defterhane stood ready during the council's meetings so that registers could be consulted when needed. The clerks of the council—some 110 of them in the 1530s—worked under the supervision of "the chief of the clerks" (*reisülküttab*). The latter's position grew over time and gradually overshadowed the chief chancellor. In the seventeenth century, foreign diplomats referred to the *reisülküttab* as "foreign minister." By this time, the council—as it was shaped by Mehmed II—had lost its importance to the office of the grand vizier. Called *Bâb-i Âsafi* and later *Bâb-i 'Âli*, "the gate of the grand vizier" was known to Europeans as the Sublime Porte and referred to the Ottoman government.

The scope of administrative capabilities of the various bureaus of the council is impressive. The central Ottoman archives contain some 400,000 register books (*defter*) and 150 million documents. Among these, there are more than 320 volumes of the so-called important affairs (*mühimme*) from the mid-sixteenth century to the late eighteenth century that contain copies of hundreds of thousands of outgoing imperial orders issued by the *divan* in the name of the padishah. The number of revenue survey books in the same archives is close to 2,000, the vast majority of which concerns the sixteenth and seventeenth centuries.[46]

Following his policy of royal seclusion, Mehmed II is said to have stopped attending the meetings of the council around 1475. While Bayezid II seems to have attended the *divan* meetings, later sultans kept to the practice introduced by Mehmed. However, a French traveler in the mid-sixteenth century noted that after the council meetings, the grand vizier would "report to the sultan all the truth: what had been discussed and matters of importance. At this time, lying is mortal, because often the sultan is listening at a window overlooking the said chamber without being seen or noticed. And even if he were never there, one always thinks that he is."[47]

Ottoman Constantinople and Europe

Mehmed's conquest eliminated Byzantium, which had been the heart of anti-Ottoman diplomacy and crusades. It also separated the Ottomans' European and Asian provinces, and often hindered the crossing of Ottoman troops from one continent to the other. The conquest also reshaped Mediterranean power politics. Girolamo Minotto, Venice's resident ambassador-consul in Constantinople (*bailo*)—an office that the Republic of Venice had maintained since 1268 in the Byzantine

The domed chamber (*Divanhane* or *Kubbealtı*, literally "under the dome") of the imperial council in the Topkapı Palace. Notice the window overlooking the room—from here the sultans could follow the discussions of the council members "without being seen or noticed." (Photo courtesy of the author.)

capital—fought alongside the Byzantines against the Ottomans during the siege. After the conquest, he, along with one of his sons, was executed by the Ottomans.[48] Once the news of Mehmed II's conquest arrived in the Most Serene Republic of Venice (*Serenissima Repubblica di Venezia*), the government swiftly dispatched its ambassador, Bartolomeo Marcello, to congratulate the sultan on his victory and to secure the republic's trading rights with the Ottomans.

The Venetian elite must have remembered how Genoa, Venice's maritime rival, outmaneuvered them in the spring of 1261, in the Byzantine-Genoese treaty drawn up at Nymphaion, the favorite winter residence of the Byzantine emperors during the Nicene period. In return for fifty Genoese ships that were to help the emperor reconquer Constantinople from the Venetians, the Genoese received the privilege of free trade in the Byzantine Empire. They also obtained the right to establish

The Tower of Justice in the Topkapı Palace, next to the *Divanhane*, was
visible from the city. It reminded the council members and the sultan's
subjects of the importance of justice in Ottoman governance.
(Photo courtesy of the author.)

self-governing quarters in the empire—including Pera, a suburb of Constantinople on the European side of the Golden Horn—thus ending Venetian dominance of the Bosporus and the Black Sea, which the Serenissima
had enjoyed during the Latin Empire of Constantinople (1204–61).[49]

In 1453, Venice took its turn at outmaneuvering the Genoese by concluding a treaty with the new master of Constantinople. Finalized on 18
April 1454, the Ottoman-Venetian treaty granted the Venetians the right
to maintain a colony in Ottoman Constantinople with a *bailo*, a perma-

nent ambassador-consul, at their head. The republic's merchants were allowed to trade freely in the sultan's domains, paying a mere 2 percent customs duty.[50] Then, on 16 August 1454, the Venetian Signoria, the republic's governing body, appointed Bartolomeo Marcello as the republic's first *bailo* (1454–56) at the Sublime Porte.[51] By delegating a permanent representative to the Sublime Porte, soon to become the most important position in the republic's diplomatic corps, the Venetians established a practice that other European states would follow. Ottoman Constantinople soon became one of the most critical diplomatic capitals of early modern Europe, a focal point of European imperial rivalry and espionage.[52] In the sixteenth century, the Porte would conclude treaties with, and issue charters of privileges to, other favored nations, whose merchants and diplomats would enjoy privileges and a sort of extraterritorial status in the empire. Known as *ahdname* in Ottoman chancery language, these documents are called capitulations in European usage. The regime they describe is known as the capitulatory system.[53]

The Ottoman-Venetian treaty and the granting of diplomatic and commercial privileges to the Venetians must have surprised some contemporaries. Unlike the Venetians, whose *bailo* fought on the side of the Byzantines, the Genoese of Pera aided the besieging Turks by allowing them to set up artillery positions near Pera or by informing the besiegers of the defenders' plans.[54] But the Ottoman decision was hardly surprising for the keen observer, as it revealed a well-tried Ottoman strategy of appeasing the stronger rival at the expense of the weaker. The Ottomans already controlled Genoa's maritime possessions and trade from the Black Sea to the Mediterranean, as it had to pass through the Bosporus and Dardanelles Straits. Venice, on the other hand, was a naval power with trade interests and colonies in the Aegean and Mediterranean, over which the Ottomans had limited control in the mid-fifteenth century.

Constantinople's commanding position over trade routes in Asia and Europe turned the city into a commercial and financial hub of the eastern Mediterranean region under Ottoman control. The Ottoman Empire thus became a desirable trading partner for Europeans. Favorable trade agreements with the Sublime Porte played an essential role in reshaping trade and power relations in the Mediterranean. Although Mehmed II renewed the trading privileges of Genoa as well, in the long run his policies of favoring the Venetians led to the ascendancy of Venice and the decline of Genoa as a Mediterranean maritime power.[55]

Venice occasionally went to war with the Ottomans, often as a member of alliances of Christian states, called the Holy League by contemporaries. However, the Serenissima's goal was to protect its maritime empire and trade interests. Periods of armed conflict between the republic and the Ottoman Empire in the sixteenth century (1499–1503, 1537–40, 1570–73) were relatively brief as both parties intended to maintain the uneasy peace in the interest of trade, from which both Ottoman and Venetian elites profited. Apart from the benefits of trade, the Ottomans were interested in maintaining peaceful relations with Venice to neutralize one of the most potent Mediterranean naval powers. Mehmed knew well that without the Venetian navy, no Holy League or crusade could succeed against his empire.[56]

To keep the Venetians out of anti-Ottoman leagues, the sultans extended trade privileges to the merchants of the Serenissima. As noted, these privileges were issued in the form of trade documents, called *ahdname* in Turkish and "capitulation" in English, from the Latin *capitula*, meaning the articles of a treaty. Following peace talks, the Ottoman sultans issued similar *ahdnames* containing the articles of the peace treaty (It. *capitoli de la pace*) that the parties had negotiated and approved.[57] As we will see, the peace treaties and *ahdnames* had to be renewed after the death of the Ottoman sultans. So long as Ottoman naval and military power could be used as a credible deterrent, the peace treaties and *ahdnames* were a potent and effective weapon of Ottoman "lawfare," capable of influencing power relations in the Mediterranean.

Calling himself "Lord of Two Seas and Two Lands," Mehmed indicated that he was aware of the connectedness of the Black Sea and the Mediterranean and the lands bordering these seas in Asia Minor and the Balkan Peninsula, regions that historians too have considered as one geopolitical unit. Mehmed also realized these regions' importance for his empire's economy and its new capital's provisioning. Now that he was in control of the Straits, the passage between the Mediterranean and the Black Sea, Mehmed attempted to dislodge the Genoese from the Black Sea right after his victory. The sultan allied himself with the new lord of the northern Black Sea region, Haci Giray of the Crimean Tatar khanate—a recently emerged polity and the most energetic successor state of the Golden Horde. A joint Ottoman-Tatar campaign in 1454 against Caffa—the Genoese colony and the center of their trade in the Crimea—failed. But it was just a matter of time before the Ottomans assumed control over the northern Black Sea, the area that provisioned the growing Ottoman capital with wheat, meat, and salt. For the time being, Mehmed was contented with the Genoese paying him a yearly tribute of 3,000 gold coins, not least because the sultan did not want to challenge the Crimean khan, the successor of Chinggis Khan and a fellow Muslim ruler, who claimed suzerainty over the Crimea and Genoese Caffa.[58]

As noted, many saw the exodus of Greek scholars to Italy as an important stimulus for the European Renaissance. Byzantine specialists have demonstrated the role that a handful of high-profile Byzantine political emigrés and scholars and the more numerous Greek scribes and copyists played in spreading the knowledge of ancient Greek history, literature, and philosophy, especially the works of Aristotle and Plato, in Italy and beyond.[59] Competing Greek and Turkish historiographies perceived 1453 as a significant breaking point. However, new research has qualified these traditional narratives by demonstrating continuities and connectivity between Byzantine and Ottoman cultures. Mehmed II's monumental urban project of rebuilding, repopulating, and representing Constantinople demonstrates how the Ottomans appropriated (rather than suppressed) the city's Byzantine legacy, and how the sultan's projects were products of the city's complex cultural environment. For example, the sultan's Yedikule fortress incorporated, and thus rendered obsolete, the Golden Gate, Byzantium's ceremonial entrance to the city. The Yedikule was also one of the first star-shaped fortresses in Renaissance Europe, and an example of the Ottomans' use of contemporary Italian architectural designs. It not only housed the sultan's treasury but also had royal residential quarters, where the ruling dynasty could find refuge if threatened.[60]

The city's various names also reflected continuity rather than a break between the cultures. In official documents and on coinage it was known as Kostantiniyye, an Arabic/Ottoman redaction of Constantinople, which referred to the center of the sultanate rather than the city proper.[61] The inhabitants of the city called the Ottoman capital by various names. For Turkish speakers, it was known as Istanbul, a corruption from a Greek phrase meaning "to the city." Turkish speakers also referred to it as Islambol (literally "abounding with Islam"), a result of folk etymology that reflected the desire of the common people to make the city's name meaningful. The sultan's Slav subjects in Rumeli continued to refer to the city as Carigrad, "the city of the Tsar/Caesar." Carigrad was also the end point of the main military corridor and trade route of the Balkan Peninsula, known to the Romans as *via militaris* or *via publica*—leading from Belgrade to Constantinople. The Serbs called the road *Carigradski put* or *drum* (the Carigrad road), and the Ottomans *şah-rah* (the shah's road).[62]

Sultan Mehmed II himself promoted continuity rather than a break with Byzantium. His interest in ancient Greek learning and European culture and his patronage of scholars and artists were well known to his contemporaries. In his Topkapı Palace, the sultan surrounded himself with dozens of Muslim and Christian scholars, artists, and courtiers, many of whom were polyglots. These included the great Muslim astronomer Ali Kuşçu, Venice's Gentile Bellini, the humanist Ciriaco of Ancona, and George Amiroutzes of Trebizond, Grand Vizier Mahmud Pasha's cousin. Bellini painted the sultan's portrait, identifying him as "Conqueror of the World." Ciriaco of Ancona read to the conqueror daily from the works of Livy and Herodotus. George Amiroutzes translated Ptolemy's *Geography* to Arabic and compiled a large world map or wall chart so that Mehmed could spatially visualize his expanding empire. In addition to Arabic, Persian, and Turkish manuscripts in Mehmed's palace library, scholars and scribes in his Greek scriptorium also wrote works for the sultan. These included Arrian's *Anabasis Alexandri* (*The Campaigns of Alexander*)—the standard classical history of the conquests of Alexander the Great, Mehmed II's hero—prepared by the sultan's Greek historian and eulogist, Kritoboulos of Imbros. Kritoboulos's history of Mehmed II is full of references to Arrian's history, including the sultan's speech to his soldiers before the siege of Constantinople, the model of which is Alexander's speech before the battle of Gaugamela in Arrian's *Anabasis*.[63] Mehmed's Greek secretaries tutored the sultan and members of his court in Greek learning and served as the sultan's diplomats to Italy. They were also instrumental in Mehmed II's decision to restore the Orthodox patriarchate. By appointing as patriarch George Scholarios (Patriarch Gennadios), well known to his contemporaries for his uncompromising anti-Western views, Mehmed hoped that any future attempt to unite the Western and Eastern churches would fail.[64]

These examples remind us that while the conquest of Constantinople was an important step in the transformation of the early Ottoman frontier polity into a patrimonial empire, Ottoman policies and institutions continued to be shaped by a Byzantine-Slav milieu. This culture and policy were represented and promoted by a handful of Byzantino-Slavic-Ottoman statesmen, such as Grand Vizier Mahmud Pasha Angelović, Mehmed Pasha the Greek, Hass Murad Pasha, and Mesih Pasha, the latter two hailing from the Byzantine imperial dynasty.[65] They were joined by a small but indispensable group of bilingual and polyglot chancery secretaries and translators. Greek continued to be used as a medium of communication and language of diplomacy well into the sixteenth century. In this regard, Mehmed and his successors followed the practice of the Seljuk Turks, of the Turkish principalities of Menteşe, Aydın, and Karaman, and of earlier Ottoman sultans, all of whom had used Greek as a language of diplomacy, issuing trade agreements and other documents in Greek to the Genoese, Venetians, and the Christian kings of Cyprus.[66] More importantly, in the fifteenth through eighteenth centuries, documents written in Greek and the Serbian/Bulgarian language (in Cyrillic script) and issued by the church chancery or local authorities were used, and accepted as authentic legal documents, in the Ottoman sharia courts. These were medieval charters or contemporary contracts and documents concerning agreements, debts, payments, sureties, and other issues, involving mainly non-Muslim subjects. Such documents were used not just in recently conquered border regions but in lands that had been under Ottoman rule for generations or centuries. In these lands, the non-Muslim subjects of the Sublime Porte had been familiar with the Ottoman administration of justice. They decided to turn to the *kadı* courts even in cases when the issue could have been settled with the help of their church and lay authorities—yet another example of Ottoman administrative flexibility and pragmatism.[67]

This emphasis on continuity and connectivity should not deceive us into equating the Ottoman sultans with the European Renaissance princes, as some proponents of the "global" Renaissance and the "connected" early modern Mediterranean have tried to do rather superficially. While acknowledging the role that Turks, Arabs, and Islamic culture in general played in the Renaissance and the Mediterranean is a welcome corrective to earlier Eurocentric historiography, it is crucial not to lose sight of the differences that distinguished Mehmed II from his European rivals.[68] The Ottomans were part of Europe not because they were just like other European empires. To the contrary: while Mehmed II considered himself heir to Rome, he did it as a Turco-Muslim ruler, whose goal was to build a universal monarchy shaped by Turco-Iranian and Islamic models. The rich literature about the Turks penned by Christian captives, European diplomats and merchants, humanist scholars, theological writers, counselors, and propagandists for European monarchs all suggests that in Europe the Ottomans were perceived as the antithesis of Christian and Renaissance Europe. To be sure, the "image of the Turk" was complex and has changed considerably over time. It exhibited many layers and nuances, reflecting the authors' biases, cultural dispositions, and political aims. But for most writers and their targeted audiences, the "infidel Turk" was the cultural "other" and the natural enemy (*hostis naturalis*), against which Christian Europe defined itself, waged its late medieval crusades, and formed its many "holy leagues," even if some European monarchs in an increasingly divided Europe concluded temporary alliances with the "Grand Turk."[69]

4

Conquests

Belgrade 1456: European Crusade—Ottoman Defeat

After the fall of Constantinople, the papacy proclaimed a new crusade in September 1453 against the Ottomans. For assistance, it called on the European rulers, including Venice and King Ladislaus V of Hungary, who had recently been released from the custody of Emperor Frederick III (r. 1452–93) and started his effective rule in Hungary. As noted, Venice had concluded its treaty with the Ottomans by the spring of 1454 and thus was not interested in the crusade. Since rumor had it that the sultan was preparing his forces to invade Hungary the next year, King Ladislaus V ordered John Hunyadi to prepare the country's defense. Upon the king's arrival in Hungary, Hunyadi resigned from the governorship of the kingdom. However, in light of the Ottoman threat, he promptly assumed the position of captain-general of Hungary with wide authority, including managing the royal revenues. To boost the country's defense capabilities, the Hungarian diet ordered a general levy in January 1454: the insurrection of all nobles (*insurrectio generalis*) and the mobilization of the peasant militia (*militia portalis*).[1]

The rumor about Mehmed II's plans proved correct. In the spring of 1454, the sultan attacked Smederevo, the seat of Despot George Branković of Serbia and an important passage to Hungary. Perhaps at the news that a relief army under the command of Hunyadi was approaching, the sultan withdrew to Sofia, leaving behind his besieging troops at Smederevo. By early August, Hunyadi was in Belgrade, and the

Ottomans soon lifted the siege of Smederevo. Marching in the Morava River valley, along the route of his victorious winter campaign of 1443–44, Hunyadi neared Kruševac by early October, where he defeated an Ottoman army. He continued his march via Pirot toward Sofia. However, not wanting to risk an open battle with the sultan's main forces, Hunyadi returned to Hungary via Vidin, which he burned down. Hunyadi's 1454 campaign was celebrated in Hungary and beyond as a major victory, but it thwarted the Ottoman advance only temporarily.[2] Having failed in northern Serbia, Mehmed invaded southern Serbia the next year. He conquered Prizren, Peć, and the important silver-mining and commercial town of Novo Brdo, the "mother of cities."[3] "From then on," noted the Ottoman chronicler Tursun Beg, "the production of the mines belonged to the Ottoman treasury."[4] During the siege of Novo Brdo the Ottomans captured a young Serbian boy, Konstantin Mihailović of Ostrovica. Having been converted to Islam by force, Konstantin was recruited to the janissary corps. Nine years later he would surrender to King Matthias Corvinus, John Hunyadi's son, return to Christianity, and settle in Poland. There he would pen his memoirs, a valuable source on the Ottomans, especially their military and conquest.[5]

At the end of 1455, news about Mehmed II's impending campaign against Belgrade, which the Ottoman chronicler called "the key to the conquest of Hungary,"[6] reached the Hungarian court in Buda through Ragusa. King Ladislaus V fled to Vienna under the guise of a royal hunt. Hunyadi rushed to Belgrade with ten thousand soldiers. A crusader army of eighteen thousand men was also marching toward Belgrade. The crusaders were recruited in Hungary on the authorization of Pope Callixtus III. Giovanni da Capistrano, the almost seventy-year-old Franciscan friar, was their leader. To boost the crusaders' morale, the pope issued a bull ordering the church bells to be tolled every day throughout Christendom. Although popular belief later connected the custom of the noon bell-ringing, observed to this day in central Europe, with the crusaders' victory at Belgrade, the tradition originated in the papal bull.[7]

Belgrade lay at the confluence of the Danube and Sava Rivers on a hill, and was protected from the north and the west by the two rivers. The fortress had been integrated into Hungary's defense systems since its takeover in 1427 from George Branković. In 1456, Michael Szilágyi, Hunyadi's brother-in-law, guarded the fortress with a few thousand defenders and crusaders. Before the siege, Mehmed II had sent his Danube flotilla to Zemun, northwest of Belgrade, and set up a river blockade to prevent Hunyadi's approaching relief force from reaching the fortress. The sultan's army arrived at Belgrade on 3 July. The besieging army could have numbered up to fifty thousand fighters, including five thousand janissaries, according to Capistrano's secretary Giovanni da Tagliacozzo.[8] Referencing accounts of escaped Christians from the sultan's camp, Tagliacozzo also reported that Mehmed believed that he would take the castle in two weeks and be in the Hungarian capital Buda in two months.[9]

A double wall and a deep moat guarded Belgrade's southern landward side, adjacent to which lay the fortified town. The Ottomans concentrated their attack on this most vulnerable side of the fortress, positioning their cannons in three batteries that were protected by earth-filled gabions. Mehmed II again deployed some of the most powerful artillery of his time, consisting of 7 mortars, 22 large bombards, and between 140 and 200 field pieces. Many of the latter had been captured from the Hungarians at the battle of Varna in 1444.[10] Some of the large bombards were cast in Kruševac near the Morava River and shipped to Belgrade from there. The largest cannons are said to have been 32 palms (224–288 centimeters) in length and 7 palms (49–63 centimeters) in width. Although shorter, these pieces were similar in caliber to the largest bombards that the sultan used in 1453 against the Byzantine capital.[11]

Heavy bombardment by the sultan's Turkish, German, Italian, Bosnian, and Dalmatian artillery gunners crumbled sections of the castle's walls. On 14 July, Hunyadi managed to break through the blockade of the Ottoman ships in a fierce five-hour fight, sinking many of the enemy galleys and capturing their crews. The next day, Hunyadi entered Belgrade with part of his army and fresh supplies. He deployed the crusaders on the island across the Sava River, opposite Belgrade, which the sultan had failed to occupy despite his commanders' advice.[12]

On 21 July, the sultan ordered a general assault. But before it began, Hunyadi managed to bring four thousand crusaders (selected by

Capistrano) into the castle to compensate for the loss suffered earlier during the siege.[13] The overwhelming force of the besiegers soon broke the defenders' resistance, and the Ottomans entered the outer bailey. Hunyadi repelled them with his heavy cavalry. The sultan ordered the final assault at around midnight, but by the morning of 22 July the defenders had prevailed. Thrilled with their victory, the defenders sallied forth from the outer bailey in the early afternoon and attacked the Ottoman left flank. Encouraged by this development, the crusaders waiting on the far bank of the Sava crossed the river on Capistrano's orders and attacked the Ottomans. The sultan sent reinforcements to his left flank, but at the cost of weakening the guard of his cannons. The crusaders and Hunyadi took this opportunity to capture the Ottoman cannons left unguarded and turn them against the besiegers. The defenders of the castle also fired their cannons, killing the Ottoman attackers in large numbers and destroying their tents. Having suffered heavy losses in the assaults and from the plague, Mehmed II lifted the siege.[14] The Ottomans would not attack Belgrade again until 1521. This was partly due to the psychological effects of 1456 and to the policy and military reforms of King Matthias Hunyadi (r. 1458–90), John Hunyadi's son. Known also as Matthias Corvinus, his crown was secured by the fame that his father achieved in his wars against the Ottomans.

Manipulating Internal Strife:
From the Morea to the Crimea

John Hunyadi's victory at Belgrade could not stop the Ottoman conquests in southeastern Europe. The Morea, Serbia, and Bosnia fell in short order. These conquests occurred amid domestic civil wars in which one party invited the Ottomans against its rival. The Ottomans masterfully manipulated these domestic disputes, which became a hallmark of their conquest strategy. The first to fall was the Despotate of Morea. Emperor John VI Kantakouzenos created the despotate in 1349 as an autonomous province for his son Manuel. After Manuel's death in 1380, the rival Palaiologos imperial family took over the despotate and ruled it from its capital Mistra via its junior members. The competition between the despots gave the Ottomans ample opportunity to interfere. After the news of the fall of Constantinople reached the peninsula, most of its Albanian subjects revolted, followed by many Greeks. The quarreling despots Thomas and Demetrios called on the Ottomans to restore order. When civil war erupted between the brothers and they failed to send the tribute to the Ottoman capital, Sultan Mehmed II himself led his armies against them, capturing half of the despotate and Corinth, which the Ottoman chronicler Tursun Beg called the "key to the conquest of the gateway of that land."[15] In 1459, civil war again erupted between the brothers. While Despot Demetrios was pro-Ottoman, his brother Thomas hoped that the new pope, Pius II—who had proclaimed a new crusade against the Ottomans in Mantua—would assist him. However, only a few hundred soldiers arrived from the pope. Mehmed conquered most of the peninsula in 1460, save for a few port cities. Modon (Gr. Methoni) welcomed the sultan with lavish gifts and was spared. Monemvasia withstood the Ottoman siege and in 1464 was acquired by Venice.[16]

In Serbia, the political elite were torn between Hungary and the Ottomans after the death of Despot George Branković on 24 December 1456 in the fortress of Smederevo. For a short while the despot's oldest son, the blind Gregory, ruled under the tutelage of his mother. However, internecine struggle within the Branković family presented the Ottomans with an opportunity to conquer the country. Lazar Branković (r. 1456–58), who poisoned his mother and forced his siblings to flee the country, took over the government. His brother Stephen first escaped to Hungary, then to Albania. Gregory and his sister, Mara—who had regained her freedom and returned to Serbia after the death of Murad II in 1451—fled to the Ottomans.[17] The Ottomans invaded and conquered northern Serbia, including Resava and Golubac, reducing the country to Smederevo and its environs.

When Despot Lazar died in January 1458, two factions—a pro-Hungarian and a pro-Ottoman—started yet another fight for power. The pro-Hungarian faction deposed and imprisoned Michael Angelović, the leader of the pro-Ottoman faction and head of the regency council, delivering him to King Matthias. For a short time, the blind Stephen Branković ruled, but in the spring of 1459 he too lost the throne. Under Hungarian and Bosnian influence, the Serbs brought into Smederevo Stephen Tomašević, the son of the Bosnian king Tomaš (r. 1444–61), to marry the deceased despot's daughter and follow him in the despotate. Since these events threatened recent Ottoman conquests, Mehmed II ordered his army under the command of Grand Vizier Mahmud Pasha Angelović, brother of Michael Angelović, to complete the subjugation of Serbia. Smederevo, the seat of the Serbian despots, fell in June 1459, as King Matthias of Hungary—who was fighting for his own throne against the Habsburg party—could not defend his protégé. At the conquest of Serbia the Ottomans also abolished the Serbian Orthodox Patriarchate of Peć (in Kosovo), which Tsar Dušan had established in 1346.[18] The Ottomans organized the conquered territory into the *sancak* of Smederevo. Its governors played a leading role in launching raids into Hungary. A Hungarian attempt to recapture Smederevo in 1460 failed. King Matthias and his uncle, Michael Szilágyi, one of the heroes of 1456 and ex-governor of the kingdom, disagreed as to what policy they should pursue concerning the Ottomans. Following recent Ottoman attacks against the Lower Parts of the kingdom, King Matthias appointed Szilágyi ban of Mačva and Slavonia and captain of the Lower Parts in the summer of 1460 and sent him against the Ottomans. Having learned in early November that Mihaloğlu Ali Beg launched yet another campaign against Hungary, Szilágyi marched against the *sancak* governor but was defeated, captured, and taken to Constantinople. He was later executed in the Ottoman capital after Mehmed II returned from his Trabzon campaign.[19]

After the conquest of Serbia, the Ottomans made Bosnia their next target. The Bosnian kings had repeatedly offered their kingdom to and sought military and financial aid from the Republic of St. Mark (1442, 1444, 1460). But Venice responded with empty words, stressing the amicable relations that existed between the republic and the sultan. King Stephen Tomašević, who followed his father on the Bosnian throne in 1461, alerted both the Venetians and the papacy of the looming Ottoman onslaught. The last of these warnings reached Venice and the papacy in early 1463. The king informed them that he had received news from his informants in the sultan's court in Constantinople that the Ottoman assault on Bosnia was imminent. He added that after the conquest of Bosnia, the sultan's next targets were Venetian Dalmatia, Hungary, Carniola, Istria, and Rome, for Mehmed "aspired to rule" all these lands. Yet again, Venice offered only words and some war matériel, but no soldiers or crusade that the Bosnians were hoping for. As a result, the Bosnian castles fell swiftly, including Jajce. The Ottomans apprehended and beheaded the last Bosnian king after the fall of Ključ.[20] As mentioned, the Ottomans organized the conquered lands into the *sancak* of Bosnia. Mehmed used the establishment of the new *sancak* to dismantle yet another *uc*, the marches of İsa Beg. To ease the transition from Bosnian to Ottoman rule, three of the five subdivisions of the new *sancak* followed the pre-Ottoman Bosnian administrative division and preserved the names of their former lords.[21] Until the conquest of Buda in 1541, the *sancak* of Bosnia was one of the most important Ottoman frontier provinces. Its governor, based in Sarajevo until 1554 and then in Banja Luka, was under the command of the governor-general of Rumeli until 1580, when the Ottomans established the independent province of Bosnia. The *sancak* governor of Bosnia, along with that of Smederevo, directed Ottoman raids into Croatia, Slavonia, and Hungary. In 1463, the Ottomans also conquered parts of Herzegovina, to the south of Bosnia. However, when Ottoman troops left the region, Duke Stephen Vukčić Kosača regained his realm. The Ottomans returned in 1465–66 and attached the conquered territories to the *sancak* of Bosnia. In 1470, they established the independent *sancak* of Hersek. Its governor, residing in Foča until 1552 and then in Mostar, answered to the governor-general of Rumeli until 1580, when the *sancak* was attached to the newly created province of Bosnia.[22]

Having annexed Amasra on the southern shores of the Black Sea in 1459–60, Mehmed turned to the "Empire" of Trebizond of the Grand Komneni, whose rulers sought help from European rulers against the Ottomans. John IV of Trebizond (r. 1429–59/60?) sent to the Council of Ferrara-Florence his chief minister and humanist scholar George Amiroutzes, who signed the proclamation of the Union of the Catholic and

Orthodox churches. Successive emperors of Trebizond also sought help from the neighboring Turkmen emirs and gave their daughters in marriage to the emirs of Sinop, Erzincan, Karaman, and the Karakoyunlu and Akkoyunlu Turkmen confederations. As mentioned, John IV gave his daughter Theodora (Despina Hatun) in marriage to Uzun Hasan of Akkoyunlu, Mehmed II's Turkmen rival, who promised to defend Trebizond. However, when John IV died, his brother and successor David provoked the Ottoman sultan by seeking allies against the Ottomans and requesting that Mehmed remit the tribute that the sultan had imposed on his brother. Mehmed decided to complete his conquest of the Byzantine Empire by taking its last outpost. The Ottomans attacked Trebizond in the summer of 1461. Following a monthlong siege, David, the last emperor of Trebizond, surrendered. Later Greek sources claimed that George Amiroutzes not only persuaded Emperor David to surrender to Sultan Mehmed II but also negotiated the terms of surrender with his cousin, Grand Vizier Mahmud Pasha Angelović. While some modern historians have questioned this latter information, in light of Mahmud Pasha's role in the conquest of Serbia, this presentation of the surrender is not that improbable.[23]

Having secured the southern shores of the Black Sea, Mehmed turned to the sea's northern shores. In late October 1469, an Ottoman fleet under the command of Yakub Beg, the admiral of the navy during the Trabzon campaign, attacked the Crimea. He set two towns ablaze, unsuccessfully besieged the Genoese colony of Caffa, and took a significant number of captives. Since the Crimean khan claimed suzerainty over the Crimea and Caffa, the attack created tension between Sultan Mehmed and Mengli Giray Khan. The Ottomans presented their campaign as a punitive response to Genoese attacks on Ottoman subjects. However, the attack signaled a change in the relations among the Ottomans, Genoese, and the Crimean Tatars. Disturbed by Genoese interference in Crimean affairs and wary of Genoese-Crimean rapprochement, Mehmed decided to resolve the problem by conquering the Crimea. An opportunity presented itself in 1475 when a civil war in the Crimean Tatar khanate broke out. One of the displaced Tatar leaders from the junior Shirin clan (Eminek) stirred a civil war. He invited the

Ottomans against his rival, Mengli Giray, who found refuge in Genoese Caffa. In June 1475, Ottoman troops aboard 300 to 380 ships commanded by Grand Vizier Gedik Ahmed Pasha captured Caffa. Kerch and Tana (Azov in Russia) soon followed. Having left their soldiers in the castle of Caffa, the Ottomans transported Mengli Giray and the wealthier inhabitants of the town to Constantinople. Mengli Giray returned to the Crimean in 1478 to rule the khanate as Sultan Mehmed II's vassal.[24]

Bayezid II completed Mehmed II's conquests in 1484 by capturing Kilia and Akkerman at the mouths of the Danube and Dniester Rivers, respectively. Other important fortresses that defended Ottoman interests near the Danube delta included Brăila, Isaccea, Izmajil, and Tulçea. Ottoman chroniclers reflect a common understanding of the geostrategic importance of Kilia and Akkerman by calling them "keys to those realms," whose conquest "opened" Moldavia to the Ottomans.[25] With these conquests, the Ottomans also blocked the access of Poland-Lithuania, the strongest Christian kingdom in the north, to the Black Sea. The Ottoman-Moldavian treaty in April 1486 recognized Sultan Bayezid's new conquests and made Moldavia—whose voivodes had been paying tribute to the Ottoman sultan since 1455—an Ottoman tributary. The border between the two states was demarcated in a separate boundary document (sınırname).[26] However, it was not until Süleyman I's campaign in 1538 that the Porte secured its rule over the region known as Budjak—southern Bessarabia between the Lower Dniester and the Lower Prut-Danube—and the coastline between the Dniester and Dnieper Rivers.

The near contemporary Ottoman chronicler Ibn Kemal or Kemalpaşazade (1468–1534) thought that as a consequence of the Ottoman conquest of Caffa, "the Black Sea coast, which is a flourishing land, was annexed to the abode of Islam . . . and the Black Sea became fully controlled [by the Ottomans] and evil people of sedition no longer inhabited these parts."[27] Historians have seconded his observation, declaring the Black Sea an "Ottoman lake." While research has shown that piracy disappeared from the region after these conquests, it has also emphasized the detrimental consequences of the arrival of the Cossack raiders in the early seventeenth century. Moreover, Ottoman authority waned in the "Wild Fields," where the nomadic Little Nogay Horde and the sedentary Zaporozhian Cossacks challenged both Ottoman and Polish-Lithuanian authority.[28]

With their conquests, the Ottomans inherited a flourishing trade network from the region's previous merchant empires of the Genoese and the Venetians. Under the Ottomans, the Black Sea littoral and its trading centers—such as Caffa in the Crimea and Azak on the Don River—preserved their position for both long-distance and regional trade, now serving the expanding Ottoman market and its capital city Constantinople. Caffa remained the principal trading and administrative center of the region. The Black Sea provided the empire and Constantinople with wheat, horses, and slaves. The slave trade continued to flourish. In 1578, the Ottoman treasury collected 4.5 million *akçe* from the slave trade in Caffa. Since the highest tax paid for any one slave was 255 *akçe*, at least 17,500 slaves were sold at the slave markets of Caffa in that year.[29] Other tax revenue figures from Caffa suggest that between 1500 and 1650, over 10,000 slaves were brought annually to the Ottoman slave markets from Poland-Lithuania, Muscovy, and Circassia. Taking into consideration those slaves who perished while being transported, other scholars estimate the population losses to Poland-Lithuania and Muscovy from slave trading at 2 million people in the sixteenth and seventeenth centuries. These numbers are comparable to the population losses experienced by African societies owing to the Atlantic slave trade (about 1.8 to 2.1 million until about 1700) and by Mediterranean countries owing to slave taking by the Barbary corsairs (1.25 million between 1530 and 1780).[30]

Ottoman Threat and Dynastic
Rivalry in Central Europe

The belief among the central European political elite that no single country could withstand Ottoman assaults justified the creation of dynastic unions in the region by which two or more of the crowns of Austria,

Hungary, Bohemia, and Poland were united for periods of time. The House of Luxemburg held the crowns of Bohemia (1310–1437), the Holy Roman Empire (1347–1437), and Hungary (1387–1437). Hungary and Poland had joined in dynastic unions under Louis I of Anjou, who was king of Hungary (r. 1342–82) and Poland (1370–82). As noted, the Hungarian Estates justified the election of Władysław Jagiellon of Poland to the Hungarian throne in 1440 with the looming "Turkish threat." From 1386 through 1569 the Jagiellons ruled the Grand Duchy of Lithuania and the Kingdom of Poland in personal union. After the Union of Lublin (1569) the two countries were united in the Polish-Lithuanian Commonwealth, ruled until 1572 by the last Jagiellonian king, Sigismund II Augustus. Between 1471 and 1526 the Jagiellons also held the crowns of Bohemia, and from 1490 through 1526 that of Hungary. King Matthias of Hungary (r. 1458–90)—who owed his throne partly to the fame of his father, John Hunyadi, the champion of the Turkish wars— also tried to establish the House of Hunyadi among the leading dynasties of central Europe by portraying his country as a bulwark of Christendom against the Ottomans. Matthias was elected king of Bohemia in 1469 but was never crowned. From 1479 onward, he ruled over only Moravia, Silesia, and Lusatia. In 1485 he occupied Austria and Styria, ruling from Vienna as duke of Austria.

With the Ottoman conquest of Serbia and Bosnia, Matthias's Hungary lost two crucial buffer states, which had halted the Ottoman advance since the reign of King Sigismund. Many shared Pope Callixtus's hope that King Matthias would use his power against the Ottomans.[31] However, in the early years of his reign, Matthias could not react to the Ottoman conquests of Serbia and Bosnia, for the king was fighting for his crown. Regent and soon-to-be king of Bohemia George Podiebrady held the fifteen-year-old Matthias captive in Prague at the time of his election. George Podiebrady released Matthias upon a written pledge to marry his daughter, Catherine, which Matthias fulfilled three years later in May 1461. More dangerously, a group of Hungarian aristocrats— led by palatine Ladislaus Garai and Nicholas Újlaki, voivode of Transylvania and ban of Slavonia and Mačva—rebelled against Matthias and elected Emperor Frederick III as their king in February 1459. The emperor was crowned as king of Hungary with the Holy Crown of St. Stephen, which had been in Frederick's possession since 1440. At the same time, the Hussite mercenary soldier John Jiškra of Brandys controlled most of Upper Hungary. During the wars between Matthias and Emperor Frederick III, Jiškra fought on the latter's side. Matthias only managed to win him over in 1462 in return for large estates, after which he served his sovereign faithfully, his soldiers providing the foundations of Matthias's mercenary army. During Matthias's Bohemian wars (1468–78), the king controlled Moravia and Silesia, two important markets for mercenaries. Matthias recruited most of his soldiers for his army from these markets. His army's maximum strength is said to have been twelve thousand cavalry and eight thousand infantry.[32]

In light of the looming Ottoman threat, the representatives of King Matthias and Emperor Frederick agreed on a peace in Graz in April 1462. According to the agreement, finalized in the summer of 1463 in Wiener Neustadt, the emperor would return the Holy Crown but was allowed to use the title of king of Hungary and to keep most of the towns that his forces had occupied in western Hungary. Under the treaty's terms, if Matthias died without a legitimate heir, the emperor or his son Maximilian would inherit the Hungarian crown. Since at the time of the agreement a married twenty-year-old Matthias expected to produce a legitimate heir, no one considered how the agreement could be used in the future to support Habsburg claims to the Hungarian crown.[33]

After the fall of Bosnia, King Matthias waited until Sultan Mehmed returned to his capital before attacking. With financial help from Venice—whose Dalmatian possessions were threatened by Ottoman troops in Bosnia—Hungarian forces moved into northern Bosnia in the fall of 1463. The ban of Slavonia, Jan Vitovec, pledged allegiance to King Matthias and assisted the attack on Ottoman Bosnia. On 26 December, the Hungarians recaptured Jajce on the Vrbas, a tributary of the Sava.[34] Most of the garrison, who fought heroically against the besiegers, now accepted the king's sovereignty. Several smaller forts in northern Bosnia also surrendered, including the captain (*dizdar*) of Zvečaj, Konstantin Mihailović. As mentioned, Konstantin had been captured by the Ottomans at the conquest of Novo Brdo in 1455. Now he returned to his

Christian faith and joined the king's army. Later he settled in Poland and wrote his memoirs.[35] In 1464, Mehmed II personally tried to recapture Jajce, using six large stone-throwing cannons, which the Turks cast in situ. However, the siege (20 July to 24 August) failed.[36] Matthias drove off the Ottoman troops and captured Srebrenica, the main Bosnian silver-mining town. The king's successes, especially the reconquest of Jajce, boosted his reputation as a worthy successor to his father.[37] However, occupied in the Bohemian wars from the late 1460s, Matthias could not confront the Ottomans. Sources mention several Ottoman and Hungarian embassies in the fall of 1467 and in 1468, suggesting that a two- or three-year truce was concluded. Either a formal or a tacit agreement must have existed between the king and the sultan, because for a couple of years there were no major clashes between their forces. It was despite the attempts of Uzun Hasan of Akkoyunlu, who sought help against the Ottomans in Buda, Rome, and Cracow, proposing coordinated attacks against Mehmed II. Uzun Hasan's envoys negotiated with Matthias in 1472, 1474, and 1475. In the end, nothing came of these missions.[38]

However, it proved impossible to control the Ottoman frontier raiders. In February 1474, the Ottoman frontier governor of Smederevo plundered Hungary as far as Várad (Rom. Oradea). Then, in late 1474, the Ottomans invaded Moldavia, whose voivode, Stephen the Great, turned to Matthias for help. With Transylvanian and Polish military assistance, Stephen defeated the Ottomans. The next year, the Ottomans were victorious. Matthias retaliated for Ottoman incursions in the winter of 1475–76 by attacking Šabac (Tr. Böğürdelen), which the *sancak* governor of Bosnia, İshakoğlu İsa Beg, had built in 1471 on the right bank of the Sava River. Since Matthias was unable to frustrate its construction, he built a fortress on the opposite side of the river. After long and careful preparations, Matthias set out for the siege of Šabac in mid-October 1475. The Ottoman defenders of Šabac capitulated in mid-February 1476. Matthias's diplomats presented his capture of this Ottoman fort as a major military feat. However, the king—who himself had almost been captured under the walls of Šabac—realized that it was a modest success of his costly military investment. The same lessons were learned from Paul Kinizsi's victory against the Ottomans at Kenyérmező in 1479.[39]

The king's policy of strengthening his country's southern border defenses produced longer-lasting effects. In the 1470s Matthias reorganized the border defense from the Adriatic through the eastern Carpathians under three military officials, integrating the garrison forces with the noble troops of the counties under their command. The offices of the bans of Croatia, Dalmatia, and Slavonia were united under one person, and this ban commanded all the military forces of the counties in Croatia and Slavonia up to the Lower Danube. To direct the defenses of the Lower Danube region, the king created the office of captain-general of the Lower Parts of Hungary (*supremus capitaneus partium regni Hungariae inferiorum*), usually held by the *comes* of Temes, who commanded the garrisons and military forces of fifteen counties, including those between the Drava and Sava Rivers. The easternmost territories came under the command of the voivode of Transylvania, with similar authority. The border forts under the command of these three military officials formed two parallel lines. The southern chain of forts stretched from Klis in the Adriatic through Knin, Jajce, Srebrenik, Šabac, Zemun, Belgrade, Szentlászló (Pescari), and Orşova to Severin; the northern one from Senj on the Dalmatian coast to Bihać, Krupa, Petrovaradin, Temesvár, Lugos, and Karánsebes.[40] King Matthias financed the defense system from his increased revenues, which amounted to about 612,000 to 678,000 gold florins annually from the mid-1470s to the mid-1480s. The bulk of the treasury's income (49%–61%) came from the war tax, collected from the peasants. The rest came from salt (13%), mines and mints (10%), crown estates (8%), free royal cities (3.5%), and Saxon towns (4%). The modest revenue from towns was an indication of underdeveloped urbanization.[41]

After the death of King Matthias (6 April 1490), the Habsburgs laid claim to the Hungarian crown with reference to the Treaty of Wiener Neustadt (1463). However, other pretenders competed for the Hungarian throne: Władysław Jagiellon, king of Bohemia (r. 1471–1516); his brother John Albert, soon to be king of Poland (r. 1492–1501); and John Corvinus, Matthias's natural son. The Hungarian Estates wanted a ruler who could marshal resources against the looming Ottoman threat, but one weaker than the Habsburgs. The Estates thus elected Władysław after receiving assurances that he would reside in the castle of Buda and rule in consultation with the Hungarian Estates. The supporters of the new king—known henceforth in Hungary as King Wladislas II (Ulászló, r. 1490–1516)—sought to appease John Corvinus by allowing him to keep the vast Hunyadi estates, appointing him ban of Croatia, and giving him the empty title of duke of Slavonia. Having invaded Hungary several times, John Albert gave up his claim to the Hungarian throne only after his forces were routed in late December 1491.

The Habsburgs emerged as the most dangerous rival to Wladislas II. Exploiting the "Turkish threat," Emperor Frederick III and Maximilian warned the imperial Estates that should Maximilian not be crowned king of Hungary, the Turks could conquer the kingdom. Maximilian hoped that with the Estates' help he could attach Hungary to the Holy Roman Empire and also make peace with the Turks. To the Hungarians, Maximilian communicated a different message. Should the Hungarians choose him as their king, he would defend their country against the "Turks" with the help of the empire. At the same time, Hungary could keep Moravia, Silesia, and Lusatia, which King Matthias had conquered.[42] Having failed to persuade the Hungarian Estates with these promises, Maximilian invaded the kingdom. By mid-November Habsburg forces occupied most of western Hungary, including Székesfehérvár, where King Wladislas had been crowned only a month earlier. By late November, Maximilian controlled some sixty castles and major towns in western Hungary and Croatia and was poised to conquer the Hungarian capital Buda. But Maximilian quickly depleted his limited funds and was unable to pay his mercenaries. Unpaid, the mercenaries refused to fight, forcing Maximilian to abort his campaign. By Christmas Eve, Maximilian was in Wiener Neustadt. His unpaid mercenaries withdrew from Hungary, though not before they pillaged and burned the countryside. After the enemy left the country, the supporters of King Wladislas swiftly recaptured it. However, Wladislas too lacked funds and still faced a challenge from his brother. As a result, the parties concluded a treaty on 7 November 1491. In it, Wladislas acknowledged

Maximilian's and his sons' hereditary rights to the Hungarian throne in case Wladislas or his sons left no lawful male heir. Should Maximilian have more than one son, the Hungarian Estates would choose which son to elect as king. In his letter to the Estates, Wladislas used the Turkish threat and John Albert's attacks to justify the treaty. He could not fight against "so many and so powerful enemies at the same time," wrote the king. He strove for peace with his fellow Christian monarchs so that he could use his power against the "Turks," who were "constantly thirsting for Christian blood." Maximilian, too, explained the treaty and his failure to conquer Hungary with the need to focus on the Turkish threat, promising Wladislas that he would intervene with the pope and the imperial Estates for help against the Turks.[43]

Hungary was important for Austria as a buffer against the advancing Ottomans. Ottoman raiders attacked Carniola and Styria repeatedly in the 1470s and 1480s. Using the turmoil of the succession wars, they raided the southwestern borders of Hungary around Jajce. Time was pressing for the Habsburgs, as the Hungarian Estates rejected the treaty. In their assembly at Rákos in 1505, the Estates declared that in the event of the death of Wladislas without a male heir, the diet would not elect another foreign king. The Estates also rejected the principle of female royal inheritance, a reference to Wladislas's daughter Anna, born two years earlier. Several influential barons and prelates—including the palatine, the archbishop of Esztergom, and the country's wealthiest baron, Count John (János) Szapolyai—concluded a pact to block Maximilian's claims to the Hungarian throne. The Rákos Resolutions favored Szapolyai and threatened Habsburg interests. To counter the resolution, in March 1506 Emperor Maximilian I (r. 1493–1519) signed a family contract with Wladislas, according to which the emperor's grandson Ferdinand was to marry Princess Anna. The contract was renewed in 1515 in Vienna at the meeting of the three monarchs: Emperor Maximilian, King Wladislas, and his brother King Sigismund I (r. 1506–48) of Poland. The treaty, which shaped the history of central Europe for centuries, stipulated that whichever dynasty died out, the other would inherit its lands. The agreement gained strength from the Habsburg-Jagiellonian double betrothal, which engaged Emperor Maximilian's granddaughter, Archduchess Mary, to Prince Louis, King Wladislas's son and heir, and Princess Anna to one of the emperor's two grandsons, Archduke Charles (1500–58) or Archduke Ferdinand (1503–64). The marriage of Ferdinand and Anna took place in Linz in 1521, and that of Mary and Louis in 1522 in Buda. In 1521, to make him a suitable match for Anna, Ferdinand got the Habsburg duchies of Tyrol, Styria, Carinthia, Carniola, and Austria.

Challenge from the East: Akkoyunlus and Safavids

In Asia Minor, Mehmed II defeated his most stubborn rival, the Karamans, in 1468, but he only succeeded in re-annexing their lands after overcoming the Karamans' eastern neighbor and ally, the Akkoyunlus ("White Sheep") in 1473. Uzun Hasan (r. 1453–78) transformed this Turkmen confederation into an empire. Having defeated the rival Karakoyunlu ("Black Sheep") Turkmen confederation, Uzun Hasan controlled a vast territory from eastern Asia Minor, through Azerbaijan, Iraq, and Iran, and as far as Kirman. Uzun Hasan posed an especially serious challenge to Ottoman sovereignty, for he and his supporters engaged in a religious discourse similar to that employed by the Ottoman sultans to legitimize their rule. The Akkoyunlu ruler also became a committed patron of dervishes of various Sunni and Shiite Sufi orders. The Persian Naqshbandi mystic and poet Abd al-Rahman Jami (d. 1492) hailed Uzun Hasan as the "Sultan of the *Ghazis*," owing to his *ghazas* against the Georgians in the late 1450s, while the theologian and philosopher Jalal al-Din Davani (d. 1503) saluted him as "*Ghazi* in the Path of God" and "the envoy of the Islamic ninth century," in reference to the Prophet's statement that Allah would send a renewer of the faith in every century.[44] Abu Bakr-i Tihrani, a close personal associate of Uzun Hasan's, titled his ruler "helper of the caliphate," "inheritor of the kingship and the caliphate," and world conqueror (*sahib-kıran*, literally "lord of the happy conjunction [of the stars"]). Uzun Hasan used building inscriptions placed on mosques that he restored in Iran to project his image as "the most lawful sultan," "the most exalted sultan," "father of victory," "the just imam," and "Emperor of Islam, shadow of God over mankind." These titles also appeared on coins issued in Uzun Hasan's name.[45] Mehmed's victory over Uzun Hasan at the battle of Otlukbeli in eastern Asia Minor in 1473 demonstrated the superiority of the Ottoman standing forces over the traditional Turkmen tribal military organization. Although the Akkoyunlus continued to challenge the Ottomans until Selim I incorporated their lands into his empire in the early sixteenth century, the Ottomans successfully reintegrated most of Asia Minor into their realms by the time of Mehmed II's death in 1481.

Mehmed's successor, Bayezid II, further consolidated Ottoman rule in Asia Minor. However, he failed to annex the lands southeast and east of the Taurus Mountains. Controlled by the Ramazan and Dulkadır emirs, these lands formed a buffer zone between the Ottomans and the Mamluks of Syria and Egypt. The escape to Europe of Bayezid II's brother, Prince Cem, after his defeat in the contest for the throne, seriously curtailed Ottoman strategic options in the 1480s and early 1490s. Having escaped to Rhodes in late July 1482, Cem spent a year in the Duchy of Savoy and five years in France, while both Pope Innocent VIII (r. 1484–92) and King Matthias of Hungary desired to use him for their planned anti-Ottoman crusades. So did the Mamluk sultan Qayitbay (r. 1468–96), who went to war with the Ottomans from 1485 through 1491 over the Cilician Plain and the lands of the Turkmen emir of Dulkadır. By the spring of 1489, Cem had arrived in Rome and Pope Innocent VIII started a new round of negotiations with proponents of a crusade. However, the Mamluks concluded their own treaty with Bayezid II (1491), and key figures of the plan died in short order: King Matthias in 1490, Pope Innocent in 1492, and Cem in 1495.[46]

The Ottomans faced their most formidable challenge in the early 1500s from Ismail, Uzun Hasan's grandson and the leader of the militant Safaviyya religious movement, named after the order's founder, Sheikh Safi al-Din (d. 1334). In 1501, Ismail routed the Akkoyunlus, took Tabriz (the seat of his grandfather), and declared himself shah of Persia and Twelver Shiism the official religion of his realm. Many believed Ismail to be the reincarnation of Imam Ali, Prophet Muhammad's cousin and son-in-law and the founder of the minority Shiite branch of Islam. Others hoped that Ismail was the long-awaited Hidden

Imam, who disappeared in 940 and was to return and establish the kingdom of God on earth.

Shah Ismail's belligerent policy and persecution of Sunni Muslims, along with his propagandists' proselytization among his adherents in the eastern lands of the empire, undermined Ottoman sovereignty among the Turkmen and Kurdish tribes. Many felt that Sultan Bayezid II's policy vis-à-vis Shah Ismail and his followers in eastern Asia Minor was ineffective. Ismail's followers in Asia Minor were known as Qizilbash or "Red-head" after their twelve tasseled red hats that symbolized the Twelver Shiism. While the majority of the Qizilbash in Asia Minor followed Shiism, others were closer to Sunni Islam. Historians often described the beliefs of the Qizilbash as heterodox, although methadoxy (being beyond "doxies") is probably a better way to characterize them.[47] Writing under the pen name "The Sinner" (Khatai), Ismail in his poems declared himself successor of and one with the chief figures of (1) the Safaviyya movement ("Know truly that I am Haydar's son"), (2) the Tajik-Persian culture ("I am Faridun, Khusraw, Jamshid, and Zohak. I am Zal's son [Rustam] and Alexander"), (3) Shiism ("The mystery of Anal-Haqq [literally 'I am The Truth'] is hidden in this my heart. I am the Absolute Truth [or 'Allah'] and what I say is Truth. I belong to the religion of the 'Adherent of the Vali [Ali]'), (4) Christianity ("I am the living Khidr and Jesus, son of Mary"), and (5) the region's messianic, Sufi movements when addressing his followers as *ghazi*, sufi, and brother (*akhi*) and himself "the leader of all these *ghazi*s."[48]

In 1507 Shah Ismail raided the neighboring Turkmen emirate of Dulkadıroğlu Alaüddevle. While he may have done this with Bayezid's tacit blessing, it was a violation of Ottoman sovereignty, as the shah marched through Ottoman lands and recruited into his army Turkmen fighters, who were Ottoman subjects. It was also a humiliation, as Alaüddevle's daughter, Ayşe/Gülbahar Sultan, was Bayezid's wife and mother of Prince Selim. While Bayezid did not retaliate, Selim—prince-governor in Trabzon, closer to the Safavid frontier—attacked Safavid-held Erzincan and defeated a Safavid army sent against him by the shah. Shah Ismail also eliminated the remnants of the Akkoyunlu Turkmen emirate and conquered Baghdad in 1508.

The turmoil created by the rise of the Safavids and Shah Ismail's Qizilbash followers in Asia Minor reshaped the balance of power among the elderly sultan's sons. Frustrated by his father's inactivity against the Safavids, and—with Bayezid being about sixty years old—concerned about a possible succession fight with his two elder brothers (Princes Ahmed, the sultan's favorite, and Korkud), Selim decided to act pre-emptively. Since both Ahmed's and Korkud's seats in Amasya and Antalya, respectively, were closer to Constantinople than his court in Trabzon, Selim demanded a new governorship closer to the capital. When rumor spread that Bayezid was about to abdicate in favor of Prince Ahmed, Selim traveled to Caffa, governed by his own son, the future Süleyman I the Magnificent (r. 1520–66). Thence Selim crossed into the Balkans and in March 1511 reached the former Ottoman capital Edirne, where Bayezid had been residing since the 1509 earthquake in Constantinople. In the meantime, a major Qizilbash revolt broke out in Teke in southwestern Anatolia, led by a holy man, known in Ottoman sources as Shah Kulu (Şahkulu, the Slave of the Shah), whom his supporters hailed as Messiah. Shah Kulu declared himself sultan in Antalya, capital of Teke *sancak* and a Qizilbash stronghold. When the rebels defeated the Ottoman imperial forces, sent against them under the command of Prince Korkud, and were marching against Bursa, Bayezid yielded to Selim's demands, appointing him prince-governor of the Danubian province of Smederevo. However, Selim did not trust his father. When he learned that the grand vizier planned to bring Prince Ahmed to the throne, Selim decided to take the throne. He eventually managed to do so in 1512, with the help of the janissaries and his supporters in Rumeli. When in the midst of the royal princes' succession struggle another Qizilbash rebellion broke out around Tokat in Anatolia, Bayezid yielded to the janissaries' pressure and invited Selim to the capital, appointing him commander in chief of the army. Selim arrived in Constantinople in April 1512, and with the support of the janissaries he deposed his father. He was proclaimed sultan on 24 April. It was the first time that the janissaries orchestrated the abdication of a sultan. The deposed sultan died on 10 June, on his way to Dimetoka, his birthplace in Thrace.[49]

The news of the change of ruler in Constantinople soon reached Venice, the Curia Romana, and the European courts. A letter from the rector and council of Ragusa, dated 10 May, informed the Signoria of Venice about how Selim, with the support of the janissaries (*praetoriani milites*), forced his father to surrender the throne. Other news about Selim's fight with his brothers, and Price Ahmed's alleged ties to Shah Ismail—the Sophi, as he was known in Europe—continued to arrive from the Bosporus. The news of Bayezid's death reached Venice by mid-July, and suspicions regarding his poisoning spread quickly in Europe. The Venetian *bailo* in Constantinople promptly informed the Serenissima about Selim's fight with his brothers, which the contemporary Venetian historian and diarist Marino Sanuto recorded in his *Diarii*. News about the sultan's building a fleet of galleys especially alarmed the Venetians. Their anxiety was allayed when Sultan Selim's envoy arrived in Venice on 23 July, bringing a letter from the new monarch. In the letter, dated 4 May and written in Greek, Selim informed the Venetians about his father's voluntary abdication and expressed his peaceful intentions. The Venetians congratulated Selim on his accession, but the departure of the Venetian ambassador, Antonio Giustinian, was delayed until the spring of 1513 because of the arrival of winter. The long delay annoyed the pashas in Constantinople, who were pressing the *bailo* to expedite the mission. It was not until the following October that the Venetian-Ottoman truce was renewed.[50]

Shah Ismail could not exploit the turmoil in the Ottoman lands as he faced a challenger in the northeast, the Shaybanid Uzbeks. By the early sixteenth century, the Persianized descendants of Shiban, the grandson of Chinggis Khan, had replaced the Timurids and Chagatays in Transoxiana. Exploiting the turmoil in the Timurid lands after the death of the Timurid ruler Abu Said (r. 1451–69 Samarkand, 1459–69 Herat), the Uzbek khan Muhammad Shaybani (r. 1500–1510) conquered Bukhara (1499), Samarkand (1500, 1501, 1505), Balkh (1505), and Herat (1507). To mark his rule in the Timurid lands, Muhammad Shaybani adopted the titles Imam of the Age (*Imam al-Zaman*) and Caliph of God (*Khalifat al-Rahman*), and ordered that the *khutba* be read and coins be struck in his name. However, several Timurid princes and *amirs* were still alive,

most important of whom was Zahir al-Din Muhammad Babur (1483–
1530). Although Babur briefly restored Timurid rule in Samarkand
(1500–1501), he was forced to retreat to Kabul (r. 1504–26).[51] During
Muhammad Shaybani's conquests, the Uzbek-Kazak relations deteriorated. In 1508, the Kazaks, who under Shaybani's grandfather had established one *ulus,* or "nation," with the Uzbeks, attacked the Uzbek khan's
Bukhara and Samarkand provinces. The next year, Muhammad Shaybani declared *ghaza* against the Kazaks, forcing the religious establishment of Samarkand and Khurasan to legitimize his war.[52] Muhammad
Shaybani's recent conquests and his encroachments into Safavid-
controlled Kirman alarmed Shah Ismail. The fact that the ousted
Timurid ruler of Herat, Badi al-Zaman ("Wonder of the Age," d. 1514),
found refuge in Shah Ismail's court did not help either. The Uzbek and
Safavid rulers mutually insulted each other in letters, demanding submission from each other. Muhammad Shaybani declared *ghaza* against
the Safavids, whom Uzbek sources depicted as "unfaithful" and "enemies of the faith." In October 1510, Shah Ismail ordered his troops and
governors in the two Iraqs, Fars, Kirman, Kurdistan, Luristan, Aran, and
Azerbaijan to join his campaign against the Uzbeks. He defeated the
Uzbeks at the battle of Merv, owing in part to the Safavid troops' use of
firearms, killing the fleeing Shaybanid ruler. However, Shah Ismail was
unprepared against Sultan Selim, who now wanted to resolve the
Safavid-Qizilbash challenge for good. Selim's wars against the Safavids
and Mamluks required adjustment in Ottoman ideology, propaganda,
and self-presentation. Ottoman propaganda justified the war against the
Safavids by portraying them as "heretics" and even "infidels," whose
revolts hindered the Ottomans' struggle against the infidel Europeans,
the main task of a *ghazi* sultan according to Ottoman chroniclers and
authors of advice for princes.[53]

Before he set out against Shah Ismail, Selim wanted to secure his
empire's European borders. With a new Ottoman sultan, previous treaties required renewal. Following his father's tactic, Selim exploited the
division among the European monarchs. The sultan concluded a four-
month truce with the Hungarians, asking for "an honorable Hungarian
envoy" to conclude a longer truce. However, the envoy, Barnabas

Bélay—the ban of Severin and an experienced diplomat—infuriated Selim when he suggested that Emperor Maximilian, King Sigismund I of Poland, and the voivodes of Wallachia and Moldavia all be party to the truce. The sultan's letter to the Hungarian king signaled a change in Ottoman attitudes. Selim informed Wladislas that only the Hungarians were part of the sultan's peace plan. Including other rulers indeed "had been" the practice, Selim conceded. However, "those times have passed," and "the mentioned Christian rulers shall by no means be included in the peace. . . . If they would like to have peace and alliance with our imperial majesty, they should send their envoys to our Porte, and when they arrive, we shall do as we see fit."[54]

Bélay was confined to his residence for forty days, and when Selim learned that his own envoy had been kept in "honorable detention" in the Hungarian capital, the sultan took Bélay along on his Iranian campaign. To put pressure on Wladislas, Selim ordered his troops against Knin, the residence of the ban of Croatia. This attack and the fiasco of the planned crusade against the Ottomans, which shortly after its announcement in March 1514 turned into Hungary's largest peasant uprising, persuaded King Wladislas to accept the Ottoman peace. The Hungarian-Ottoman peace was concluded with Selim's envoy in Buda for the duration of three years. Around the same time, in May 1514, while already en route against Shah Ismail, Selim succeeded in reaching another three-year truce with Wladislas's brother, King Sigismund I of Poland, once the Polish envoy caught up with the sultan at Akşehir in the province of Karaman.

Because of his commitment to the eastern campaign, and because he "found it difficult to maintain troops in Rumeli to defend it against the Hungarians," Selim had already gone back on his word concerning the planned joint Venetian-Ottoman military venture against Emperor Maximilian. According to the plan, the Ottomans would have supported the Venetians against the Holy Roman emperor by sending ten thousand horsemen from Bosnia to Friuli and a fleet from Valona (Avlonya) to Apulia. Selim's reference to the Hungarian threat soon proved to be no mere excuse, as John Szapolyai, voivode of Transylvania, raided northern Bulgaria. However, the peasant uprising forced Szapolyai to return home. News of the uprising quickly reached the Ottoman leadership. By this time, Prince Süleyman had arrived in Edirne to protect the Ottomans' Rumelian frontier. Selim could now continue his march against the Safavids, confident in the security of his European borders.[55]

Selim confronted Shah Ismail at the battle of Chaldiran on 23 August 1514, northeast of Lake Van, in present-day northwestern Iran. The Ottomans significantly outnumbered the Safavids, though modern estimates of 100,000 Ottoman troops versus 40,000 Safavid fighters seem exaggerated on both sides. While contemporaries put the number of janissaries between 12,000 and 20,000, a recently discovered roll call listed only 10,065 janissaries before the battle, and gave the total number of the sultan's household troops as 16,332 men.[56] The 293 artillery gunners and the 334 gun carriage drivers listed in the document could have served about 100 to 150 field pieces, and not 300 to 500 cannons as suggested by modern historians. However, even this more modest firepower provided a substantial advantage against the Safavids, who had no arquebusiers and cannons in the battle. This is puzzling, because the Safavids—like their predecessors, the Akkoyunlu Turkmens—had been familiar with gunpowder weapons. As mentioned, Shah Ismail himself put his guns and arquebuses to good use against the Uzbeks in late 1510 at the siege of Merv.

At the battle, Sultan Selim, "as was the Anatolian manner, surrounded his encampment with shields and caissons, linking the caissons together with chains. The twelve thousand matchlockmen he always had with him were stationed in front of the lines."[57] When the Safavid cavalry pushed the Ottomans back, they retired to their wagon laager (*tabur*). From behind the defensive wagon laager, janissary gunners drove back multiple charges of the Qizilbash cavalry, the backbone of the Safavid army.

Bringing their matchlockmen to the fore, they took the offensive once again. Since it was patently clear to the shah that to persist in battle would result only in losses of his own troops, he decided to implement the dictum "war is deception" and pull back several stages to the rear so that the Anatolians would be drawn out from behind their caissons and shields in pursuit, as Muhammad Khan Shaybani had done, and then he would attack them and wipe them off the face of the earth. Therefore, he sounded a retreat and proceeded to Tabriz and from there to Dargazin, dispatching heralds and messengers to all directions of his realm to order more troops gathered.[58]

However, this tactic did not work against the well-disciplined Ottomans. In addition to superior firepower and the wagon laager, the Ottomans also enjoyed numerical superiority, as the fifty thousand to sixty thousand Ottoman soldiers outnumbered the Safavids two to one. Ismail's tactical errors—enabling the Ottomans to set up their wagon laager, and the Safavids' frontal attack against the fortified Ottoman camp—also played a role in the Ottoman victory.[59]

Selim failed to exploit his triumph. Although the Ottomans pursued Ismail as far as the Safavid capital Tabriz, the shah managed to retreat to Dargazin, farther to the south. Selim's troops undermined the Ottoman ruler's strategic pursuit by refusing to winter in Persia, forcing the padishah to return to Asia Minor and abandon his plan to continue his campaign in the spring. Kwandamir noted that Selim had been able to stay in Tabriz "no more than eight days." He explained the Ottoman retreat by Selim's fear of the news "that the shah was assembling fresh troops and headed back in his direction," adding that "no matter how brave a deer may be, it cannot dwell in the lion's forest."[60] Nonetheless, the battle of Chaldiran was one of the most significant battles in world history. It secured Ottoman rule over most of eastern and southeastern Asia Minor and deprived Shah Ismail of a fertile recruiting ground for his Turkmen army, shaping the spheres of influence between Sunni and Shiite Islam for centuries to come.

The battle had immediate consequences for the development of the Safavid military too. Ottoman firepower impressed the Safavids and served as a stimulus for the widespread adoption of gunpowder weapons in Safavid Persia. According to an anonymous Ottoman intelligence report, by 1516, under the supervision of the chief gunner the Safavids had manufactured two thousand handguns. However, except for twenty defected Ottoman janissaries, Shah Ismail's troops did not know how to use the weapon. The Safavids also made fifty cannons (*top*) and caissons (*araba*), modeled after an Ottoman gun and its caisson, which the Safavids recovered from the Aras River after Chaldiran.[61] In 1516 the Safavids captured seventy pieces of artillery, and by the next year, the shah reportedly had some one hundred artillery pieces mounted on caissons. The number of gunners or *tufangchis* fluctuated in the years to come, but the high numbers of eight thousand gunners in 1517 and fifteen thousand to twenty thousand in 1521, mentioned in Venetian sources, are likely to be inflated. While most such gunners were infantry gunners, they were also able to fight on horseback when needed. Ottoman deserters helped train the shah's gunners. In 1518 and 1519, seven hundred and fifteen hundred Ottoman janissaries, respectively, are said to have defected to Safavid Iran.[62]

Shah Ismail's eldest son and successor, Shah Tahmasb I (r. 1524–76), continued to use firearms both in fortresses and in battles. In 1528 the shah successfully deployed his light cannons (*zarbzan*), matchlockmen, and the Ottoman-style wagon laager against the Shaybanid Uzbeks. Responding to Ubayd Khan's aggression against Khurasan, Shah Tahmasb confronted the Uzbeks at the battle of Jam on 24 September 1528. Although outnumbered and defeated on the wings at the early stage of the battle, the Safavids ended the battle as victors, owing to the firepower of the shah's six thousand infantry gunners and filed cannons. The cannons were mounted on some two thousand carts and arranged in the Ottoman fashion (*Rum dasturi*).[63] Despite the usefulness of firearms in 1528, Shah Tahmasb's army remained largely cavalry, based on the Qizilbash horsemen, which, however, was no match for the Ottoman army.

Selim's victory in 1514 engendered anxiety in Europe. Pope Leo X received the news of Selim's victory at Rome in late October through Ragusa. Cardinal Giovanni de' Medici, second son of Lorenzo the Magnificent and effective ruler of Florence at the time of his election as Pope Leo X in 1513, was an astute polititian. His election capitulations provided for the defense against the "perfidious Turk." He gained a reputation for his commitment to the crusade against the Turks. Memoranda and orations by envoys from Hungary, Dalmatia, and Poland-Lithuania, most affected by the Ottoman conquest, reminded the pope of the Turkish threat. Having received the news of Selim's victory, the pope summoned all resident diplomats at the Holy See. He announced Selim's victory proclamation to rally the diplomats and their Christian princes for another crusade against the Turks.[64] However, the idea of a crusade had little traction because European monarchs were consumed with their own, more immediate interests. Pope Leo X's attention, too, was diverted by the reform of the church during the Fifth Lateran Council (1512–17)—the last ecumenical council before the Protestant reformation—Italian politics, and the contest for European dominance between the French and the Spanish. Even Hungary, whose self-image was closely tied to the idea of *antemurale Christianitatis*, joined the ranks of European states wary of yet another crusade, especially after the last such attempt in the summer of 1514 led to a disastrous peasant uprising.

The Conquest of the Mamluk Sultanate

Selim's next move was to annex the Dulkadır emirate, whose ruler, Selim's maternal grandfather, Alaüddevle, refused to join the Ottoman campaign against Shah Ismail, attacked the Ottoman supplies, and cooperated with both the Safavids and the Mamluks. Following well-tried Ottoman tactics of manipulating internal division, Selim used Şehsüvaroğlu Ali Beg to guide his troops into Dulkadır territory. Ali Beg was the son of Şehsüvar Beg, the former Dulkadır emir under Mehmed II and nephew of the current ruler. Selim had appointed Ali Beg governor of the Ottoman *sancaks* of Kayseri and Bozok, adjacent to the Dulkadır emirate. Led by Şehsüvaroğlu Ali and the governor-general of Rumeli, Sinan Pasha, in June 1515 the Ottomans defeated and killed Alaüddevle in a battle, where some of the Dulkadır cavalry deserted Alaüddevle for Ali Beg. Selim's sending Alaüddevle's severed head to the Mamluk sultan Qansuh al-Ghawri (r. 1501–16), who considered himself the overlord of the emirate of Dulkadır, was a clear warning.[65]

To justify his attack against the Mamluks, Selim advanced several pretexts and secured a religious opinion or fatwa from the Ottoman religious establishment. Ottoman propagandists argued that the Sunni

Mamluks' cooperation with the "heretic" Safavids justified the war. They claimed that Selim needed to pacify these rebel Muslims before he could attack his Christian enemies.[66] Just like in 1513–14 before his Safavid campaign, Selim aimed to prevent a Hungarian attack on his European provinces. As a general principle, Ottoman strategy tried to avoid war on more than one theater at a time by concluding truces for the duration of the planned campaign. This time Selim's move was warranted caution on account of the recent Habsburg-Jagiellonian alliance (1515) and the reinvigorated crusading plans of Pope Leo X. To thwart a possible Hungarian attack, Selim dispatched his envoy to Hungary to prolong the expiring three-year truce with King Wladislas II for three more years. Pope Leo X, whom the Hungarians consulted regarding the Ottoman offer, urged the Hungarians to reject the truce. King Louis II (r. 1516–26), who succeeded his deceased father as a ten-year-old boy in March 1516, ultimately concluded a one-year truce with the Ottoman envoy.[67]

By this time, Selim had entered Syria. He confronted the Mamluk armies north of Aleppo at Marj Dabiq on 24 August 1516. The Mamluks faced multifront threats from the Portuguese, Safavids, and Ottomans that strained Mamluk resources. Rivalries between the Mamluk troops and the insubordination of some forces further weakened the Mamluks. Unlike the Safavids in 1514, the Mamluks deployed dozens of field guns and trained arquebusiers at Marj Dabiq. But these capabilities still could not match Ottoman firepower and numbers of troops, who outnumbered their enemies two to one. Like the Safavids, the Mamluks charged in vain against the Ottoman wagon laager, described by a contemporary Damascene chronicler as a fortified wall. The desertion of the Mamluk governor of Aleppo, who changed sides with his troops during the battle, sealed the Mamluk army's fate. When Sultan Qansuh al-Ghawri died halfway through the battle, apparently of a heart attack, the remnants of his troops fled.[68] Both Aleppo and Damascus surrendered without a fight. Selim attended the next Friday prayer in the Great Mosque of Aleppo together with the last shadow Abbasid caliph. Selim's name was mentioned in the *khutba* as "Servant of the Two Noble Sanctuaries" (*Khadim al-Haramayn al-Sharifayn*).[69]

The Ottomans pursued the fleeing Mamluk army to Egypt. They delivered a second crushing defeat on 23 January 1517 at Raydaniyya, outside Cairo. Through their spies, the Mamluks knew that Selim's forces numbered only about twenty thousand men and were exhausted from the more than four-month-long march across the Sinai desert and the continuous harassment by the Bedouins. Al-Ghawri's successor, Sultan Tuman Bay (r. 1516–17), also learned the lessons of Marj Dabiq and decided to use entrenched positions, firearms, and wagon laager against the invading enemy. With their entrenched positions and cannons, the Mamluks, whose troops may have numbered about twenty thousand men, hoped to surprise the Ottomans. However, Selim learned about Tuman Bay's plans from Ottoman spies and captured Mamluk soldiers. Before reaching the Mamluk cannons' range of fire, the Ottomans turned to the side and outflanked the enemy's gun emplacement. On the flanks, cavalry charges continued for some time with severe losses in both armies. Eventually the Mamluk right wing and center collapsed under the coordinated attack of the Ottoman artillery, arquebusiers, and cavalry. Mamluk resistance followed into the spring under the leadership of their escaped sultan. However, betrayed by the Bedouin chieftain and apprehended by Ottoman soldiers, Tuman Bay was executed on 13 April.[70]

With Tuman Bay dead, the Mamluk sultanate, which had ruled for more than 250 years in Egypt and Greater Syria, ceased to exist. Selim incorporated the former Mamluk territories into his empire as the new Arab province (*vilayet-i Arab*) and ordered the survey of its revenues. The first survey books of several *sancaks* had been completed by 1518. The Arab province was later divided into the provinces of Egypt and Damascus. The latter in the 1520s and 1530s was also named alternatively as Arab province. Its governor-general in 1523, Ferhad Pasha, was remunerated with rich *hass* estates yielding an annual revenue of 2 million *akçe*. To document the territorial changes brought about by conquests and administrative reorganizations, more extensive surveys of the province of Damascus were carried out in 1526, 1528, 1535, and 1548.[71]

As a consequence of his conquests, Selim became the master of Damascus and Cairo, former seats of the caliphs, and of Mecca and

Medina. The sharif of Mecca, Abu al-Barakat II bin Muhammad (r. 1473–1525), sent his son and co-ruler Abu Numayy II ibn Barakat (r. 1512–66) to the victorious Ottoman sovereign in Cairo to pledge loyalty to Selim. He also asked the Ottoman ruler to confirm him as *amir* of the Hijaz. Abu Numayy handed the keys to the Kaaba to Selim on 6 July at a meeting of the imperial council. Selim confirmed the sharif on his post and sent 200,000 gold coins and plenty of grain to the Holy Cities. He also released some of the nobles of Mecca, whom the Mamluks had imprisoned in Cairo.[72] The possession of the Islamic Holy Cities of Mecca, Medina, Jerusalem (whence the Prophet was believed to have ascended to heaven), and Hebron (the burial place of the patriarch Abraham) gave the House of Osman unparalleled prestige and legitimacy in the Muslim world. So did the title of "Servant of the Two Noble Sanctuaries" and the responsibility of protecting and organizing the annual pilgrimage to Mecca. With the unification of Islam's historical heartlands under Selim I and Süleyman I—who added Arab Iraq to the empire—the Ottomans commanded a large and versatile cadre of scholars, reflecting the rich Turkish, Persianate, and Arabic scholarly and cultural traditions. This, in turn, enabled the Ottomans to complete their incorporation of the legitimation apparatus of the preceding Muslim empires and to craft an imperial ideology based on the caliphate, which would also redefine their understanding, presentation, and use of political authority.[73]

Selim's conquests almost doubled the area of the Ottoman domains to 1.5 million square kilometers. Vast wealth accompanied impressive territorial gains. The incomes of the Ottoman central treasury from the imperial domains rose from 72.9 million *akçe* (1.4 million Venetian gold ducats) in 1509 to 116.9 million *akçe* (2.2 million gold ducats) in 1523, and to 141 million *akçe* (2.6 million gold ducats) in 1524, primarily due to revenues from Syria and Egypt. By 1527 the incomes of the imperial treasury had reached 277 million *akçe* (5 million gold ducats), excluding revenues from *timar* lands. Of these revenues, 42 percent came from the province of Egypt, and 9 percent from Syria. In other words, in 1527, Egypt and Syria accounted for about 51 percent of the treasury's revenues.[74] As late as the early 1580s, revenues from Egypt and Syria still accounted for 22 to 28 percent of the central treasury's annual income.[75] After the Ottomans consolidated their rule, following Ahmed Pasha's rebellion in 1524, the provincial treasury of Egypt was able to send substantial remittances to the imperial treasury in Constantinople.[76]

Missed Opportunity: The Indian Ocean

Threatened by the Portuguese expansion in the Indian Ocean, the sultanate of Gujarat (1407–1573)—a regional Muslim power that seceded from the Delhi sultanate of the Lodi dynasty in northern India and developed strong naval capabilities with ports such as Surat and Diu—sought help from the Mamluk sultan Qansuh al-Ghawri, whose revenues the Portuguese had endangered by diverting the spice trade from the Red Sea and Mediterranean to a new maritime route around the Cape of Good Hope. The Mamluk sultan in turn requested naval and military aid from the Ottomans. In 1507, the Ottoman sultan Bayezid II (r. 1481–1512) sent his commander Kemal Reis—known among the Mamluks as a famous *ghazi* corsair and warrior of Islam who engaged in jihad (*mujahid*)—to Egypt with a fleet that carried fifty cannons as well as copper to cast more ordnance in Suez.[77] In 1508, a Mamluk fleet commanded by Amir Husain al-Kurdi ("the Kurd"), the governor of Jeddah, joined the Gujarati fleet under Malik Ayaz, governor of Diu. At the battle of Chaul, south of present-day Bombay, the allied fleet defeated the Portuguese, killing the Portuguese commander D. Lourenço de Almeida, son of the viceroy of the Estado da India. However, at another battle near Diu the next year, the Portuguese, commanded by the viceroy Francisco de Almeida, destroyed the allied navy.[78]

Writing about the 1508 Mamluk-Gujarati victory three generations later, the chronicler Muhammad Kasim Firishta (d. 1623), who completed his Persian-language history at the request of Ibrahim Adil Shah II (r. 1580–1627) of Bijapur, recorded that the "Sultan of Rum [Sultan Bayezid II], who was the enemy of the European unbelievers, sent many ships to the coast of Hind for a holy war (*ghaza*) and protection, and many ships arrived near Gujarat. . . . Ten large ships of the Rumis [Ottomans from Asia Minor], who were come from the Khunkar of Rum

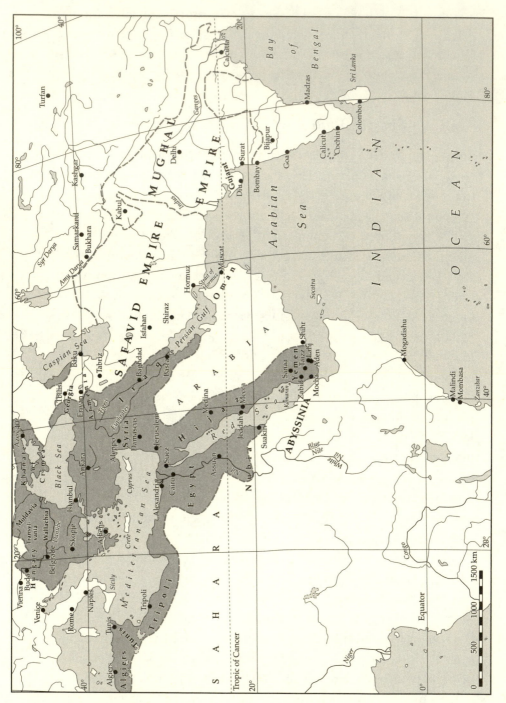

The Ottoman Empire and the Indian Ocean. (Drawn by Béla Nagy.)

[the Ottoman sovereign] for purposes of holy war, accompanied Ayyaz, and Ayyaz, having gone to Chewal (Chaul), fought with the Christians . . . and Ayyaz was victorious and slew very many."[79]

By 1514, the experienced Ottoman sea captain Selman Reis was supervising the construction of a naval arsenal in Suez and a Mamluk fleet at the Red Sea. The contemporary Mamluk chronicler Ibn Iyas claimed that Selman had some two thousand Ottomans assisting him, and that the Mamluk sultan Qansuh al-Ghawri—who inspected the construction of vessels—was so pleased with Selman's services that he "dressed him in a red robe lined with sable and gave him a gift of one thousand dinars."[80] The construction of the Mamluk fleet and the planned campaign was a response to the Portuguese attack in the spring and summer of 1513. In search of a Rumi (Ottoman) fleet, the Portuguese governor Afonso de Albuquerque (1509–15) entered the Red Sea. He unsuccessfully besieged Aden at the mouth of the Red Sea and destroyed the port of the Yemeni island of Kamaran. Albuquerque had plans to conquer Aden, for which he thought "4,000 or 5,000 men will be required." After Aden, he wanted to take Jeddah, Mecca, and Suez.[81]

The Mamluks also wanted to help Muzaffar Shah II of Gujarat (r. 1511–26), but the Mamluk fleet never reached the Gujarati coast. The fleet of some twenty ships and six thousand troops of Mamluks, Turks, Maghribis, and Arabs left Suez in August 1515 under the command of Selman Reis. It stopped at Jeddah, where the governor of Jeddah, Amir Husain "the Kurd," joined the expedition. In December, they took and reinforced Kamaran Island and called on the sultan of Yemen to join them against the Portuguese. Since the Yemenis refused to cooperate, Selman Reis and Amir Husain, who commanded the land forces, attacked the Yemeni coast and in July 1516 took Zabid. However, having unsuccessfully besieged Aden, the fleet returned to Jeddah by early August.[82] Although Selim I ordered Selman Reis to join him in Cairo, Selman stayed in Jeddah, citing the request of the sharif of Mecca for help against an expected Portuguese attack on the town, the gateway to Mecca.[83]

Thirty to thirty-six Portuguese sailing ships and galleys commanded by Lopo Suárez entered the Red Sea and attacked Jeddah in April 1517.

Selman Reis met them with his twenty-six galleys and sailing ships and three thousand fighting men. He also had several large Ottoman basilisks, firing cut stone balls of about a thousand pounds, placed on the earthworks of the reinforced town walls of Jeddah. Operated by experienced Ottoman artillery gunners, this coastal artillery dominated the S-shaped channel, the only entry into the town's port, making it suicidal for the Portuguese sailing ships to enter the narrow channel and attack the town. Lopo Suárez could not engage the earthworks with the heavy bow guns of his galleys either, as it would have exposed his galleys to the flank attack of the Ottoman galleys. Selman, on his part, could not directly attack the stronger Portuguese ships. But he masterfully exploited the maneuverability of his lighter galleys and constantly harassed the Portuguese, knowing that in case of an attack he could retire to the channel under the protection of the Ottoman basilisks of the seaside fortress. Selman's combined use of coastal artillery and Mediterranean war galleys repulsed the Portuguese attack on Jeddah in 1517, proving the defensive capabilities of the Mediterranean system of sea warfare on its home ground.[84]

Selim was lucky that Selman Reis defeated the Portuguese and saved Mecca and Medina for the Ottomans. However, Selman received little thanks from the Ottoman padishah. Upon arriving in Cairo, he was arrested and imprisoned in the citadel. The next spring, he was sent in chains to Constantinople. No known source explains the reason for Selim's harsh treatment of Selman, one of the finest Ottoman sea captains with knowledge of the Red Sea, the Indian Ocean, and the Portuguese. Historians have speculated about the Ottoman sultan's irritation over Selman's service to the recently defeated Mamluk enemy. Although Selim's son and successor, Süleyman, exonerated Selman Reis, the Ottomans missed an opportunity to confront the Portuguese in the Indian Ocean after the conquest of Egypt.[85]

Selim had shown little interest in another experienced Ottoman sea captain, Piri Reis. From the 1480s, Piri Reis had fought in the Mediterranean under the command of his uncle, the famed Ottoman sea *ghazi* and corsair Kemal Reis, who died in 1510 while he was on his way to Cairo with more Ottoman military aid for the resistance against the

Portuguese.[86] At Kemal Reis's side, Piri Reis had accumulated a great deal of nautical and cartographic knowledge regarding the Mediterranean and beyond. In 1513, at the Ottoman naval base in Gallipoli, Piri Reis produced a world map, a combination of portolan charts and *mappamundis*. He based his map on Arab and Portuguese maps, and a now-lost early map of the New World, made by Columbus, that he and his uncle had found on captured Christian ships.[87] During Selim I's campaign against the Mamluks in 1516–17, Piri Reis traveled with the Ottoman navy, and in Egypt he offered the map to Selim I. Alas, the map had been torn apart, and two-thirds of it are still missing; the other third, showing parts of south and west Africa and Europe, was discovered only in 1929 in the Topkapı Palace Library. There is no evidence to suggest that Selim showed any particular interest in Piri Reis's map,[88] let alone that he intentionally separated and kept the now-missing part of the map, which showed the Eastern Hemisphere, so that he could use it for his Indian Ocean strategy.[89]

Selim had no such strategy. After the conquest of Egypt, with Selman Reis, Piri Reis, and hundreds of Turkish and Arab marines with knowledge of the Red Sea and the Indian Ocean under his command, Selim had an opportunity to continue the Mamluks' struggle against the Portuguese. However, Selim did no such thing. Instead of charging Selman Reis with such a task, the padishah had him thrown in jail.[90] Selim and his successors were contented with defending the Holy Cities of Mecca and Medina and the Red Sea. Throughout the period examined in this book, Ottoman strategic priorities concerned the Safavids in Azerbaijan and Arab Iraq and the Habsburgs in the Mediterranean and central Europe. This is where the Ottomans invested most of their human and economic resources and where the sultans, grand viziers, and military commanders led their campaigns. The Indian Ocean could never compete with the strategic priorities of the Habsburg and Safavid theaters of war, and, from the latter part of the seventeenth century, with that of the northern Black Sea frontier.

After the conquest of Mamluk Syria and Egypt, Selim's immediate concern was the Safavids. In September and November 1517, Selim was still in Gaza and Damascus, where he received intelligence about Safavid war preparations. Now Selim wanted to eliminate the Safavids. When the Safavid envoy arrived in Damascus in mid-February 1518—requesting peace in return for an annual tribute, which the shah promised to pay for the places he possessed—Selim ordered the envoy arrested, suspecting deceit. On 5 May 1518, the padishah issued orders for his impending "eastern campaign." Two weeks later, however, Selim changed his mind. Having left Grand Vizier Piri Pasha in the region to continue the war preparations, Selim left Aleppo for Constantinople. Arriving at the Topkapı Palace on 25 July, he soon left for Edirne, never to return to the eastern frontier. Not even another Qizilbash rebellion near Tokat, led by a certain Sheikh Celal, a follower of Shah Ismail, would make Selim return to the Safavid frontier. By this time, Selim was occupied with planning a war against the European infidels, perhaps as a reaction to news arriving from Europe about the making of a new anti-Turkish crusade. [91]

European Reactions and Ottoman Naval Preparations

Europeans instantly recognized the significance of Selim's recent victories. The conquest of Egypt and Syria reshaped power relations in the Mediterranean. It threatened European (especially Venetian) access to the Asian markets, upon which the economies of Europe's countries depended for raw materials. Fear of the Ottomans energized European politics. Convening the members of the Sacred College and the European ambassadors accredited to the Holy See in early November 1517, Pope Leo X expressed the urgency to counter the "Tyrant of the Turks" (*Turcarum tyrannus*), as Selim and the Ottoman sultans were often called in Europe. The pope believed that after his recent conquests Selim aspired not just to conquer Italy but also to dominate the whole world. In his *Diarii*, Marino Sanuto preserved a contemporary text, reflecting the sentiment in Europe. The text claimed that Selim hoped to become the master of the world by uniting Africa, Asia, and Europe under his rule, imitating his hero, Alexander the Great, whose life Selim read about daily.[92] Contemporary Ottoman sources supported European fears. In the prologue of the law code of the *sancak* of Nikopol, composed immediately after the conquest of Egypt, Selim is described as "succored by God," "Shadow of Allah," and world conqueror (*sahib-kıran*). While other Muslim rulers also claimed these titles, their concurrent use in an official Ottoman document suggests that Selim aspired to world dominance. Later Ottoman sources from the mid-sixteenth century also testify to Selim's "apocalyptic pretensions."[93]

Pope Leo X believed that Selim planned to build the most massive armada in history. Echoing the sentiment in the Curia Romana, a letter sent in mid-November added that the Ottoman emperor paid "attention to nothing but collecting artillery, building ships, and surveying all these seas and the shores of Europe." The pope wrote to Francis I of France that Selim had "daily at hand a description and a painted map of the shores of Italy."[94] Venetian reports explained the large-scale shipbuilding activity in the Ottoman naval arsenal in Constantinople in 1518–19 with a planned overall Ottoman assault against Christian Europe, purportedly against Rhodes.[95] Ottoman sources also noted that Selim ordered the enlargement of the Imperial Arsenal in Constantinople as part of his "preparation for a campaign against the infidels." Soon, a navy of some 250 ships was ready to "conquer the infidels," in which 60,000 soldiers from Asia Minor were recruited. Most Europeans suspected that Selim's target was Rhodes.[96]

The news of Selim's recent victories energized Pope Leo X to declare a crusade. A report of mid-November 1517—prepared by a special crusading commission of cardinals charged by the pope—examined Selim's military and naval resources and the feasibility of a crusade. It found that Selim already had 300 galleys, with more being built. For the planned crusade, the report suggested recruiting 60,000 infantrymen from among the Swiss, German Landsknechte (who successfully imitated the Swiss pikemen), Spanish, and Czechs; 4,000 heavy-armed cavalry from France and Italy; and 12,000 light cavalry from among the Spanish, Italians, Albanians, and Greeks. The report calculated an armada of 110 galleys—20 galleys from France, Spain, and Genoa each, 40 from Venice, and 10 from the papacy—noting that large ships, called *carracas* and *galleones*, could be obtained from France, England, Spain, and Portugal. The commission considered three main directions of attack: through Germany and Hungary, through Dalmatia and Illyria, and through Italy. Above all, the cardinals pointed out the need for peace in Europe. Francis I, one of the intended leaders of the projected crusade, enthusiastically embraced the plans and seconded the need for peace within Europe. However, he also underscored the enormous costs and logistical difficulties of the enterprise, warning that such a large crusading army would suffer from "disorder and discord." He therefore suggested that the crusaders attack in three theaters: the French through Brindisi; the Germans, Hungarians, and Poles through Hungary and the Balkan Peninsula; and the English, Spanish, and Portuguese in the Mediterranean. Upset that the pope assigned such a prominent role to the king of France, Emperor Maximilian warned that such a large enterprise needed more time to organize. The emperor offered his own grandiose plan for a three-year crusade.[97]

The general European anxiety regarding the Turkish crusade can also be seen in a pamphlet, written by an anonymous Franciscan friar. While the friar's calculations—which claimed that with the help of a special tax, supposedly yielding 18,468,000 Hungarian gulden in a single year, an army of 124,800 horsemen and as many foot soldiers could be set up— were unrealistic, the plan contained interesting ideas. Unlike other plans, this pamphlet underscored the need to defend Christendom's southeastern borders against the Turks. It proposed that the military force be divided into five smaller armies of about 50,000 men each, which then would guard Christendom's eastern frontiers. These armies were to make regular inroads into Turkish territory, occupying smaller areas along the borders. In case of Turkish attacks, the engagement would take place near the Christians' home bases, where the latter could marshal reinforcements. Subsequent editions in 1522, 1532, 1541, and 1542 helped rally support for anti-Ottoman policies in times that coincided with the Ottoman campaigns against Rhodes (1522), Vienna (1532), and Buda (1541), and the Habsburgs' attempt at reconquering Buda (1542), all major events in the fight between Christendom and the Ottomans.[98]

Ottoman chroniclers seem to support the rumor about Selim's plans to attack Europe,[99] and the Mediterranean soon became an Ottoman priority. It was largely due to the need to secure the maritime lanes of communication between the Ottoman capital and the empire's wealthiest provinces of Egypt and Syria. This not only necessitated the strengthening of the Ottoman navy but also led to a more active Mediterranean policy. Confrontation with Venice and Spain, as well as alliances with France—Spain's main rival—would define Ottoman policy in the Mediterranean in the coming decades.

The Ottomans were fortunate to rely on the services of experienced Turkish sea *ghazis*. Against the Spanish Habsburgs and their allies in the Mediterranean, the Turkish Barbarossa brothers rendered invaluable services. The Barbarossas (İshak, Oruç, Hızır, and İlyas) hailed from Ottoman-ruled Midilli (Gr. Lesbos), where their father, Yakub, settled after the conquest of the island in 1462. Initially earning their livelihood from coastal trade, Oruç, İlyas, and Hızır (the future Hayreddin) soon became *ghazi* corsairs, fighting against the Knights Hospitaller and ravaging the Christian shores in the Aegean and the eastern Mediterranean with the support of the Ottoman prince Korkud, governor of the coastal *sancaks* of Antalya and Manisa.[100] By 1513 the Barbarossas had relocated to North Africa, as they lost their patron, Prince Korkud, whom Sultan Selim I executed. The Barbarossas made the island of Djerba, and later Tunis and then Algiers, their base. The brothers preyed on Christian shipping and ravaged Christian coastal towns, relying on their light galleys, which were faster than the galleys of their opponents. After the death of his elder brother Oruç in 1518, Hızır became the most important corsair in the western Mediterranean and the North African coast, which contemporary Europeans called the Barbary Coast or Barbary. Hızır assumed the honorific Hayreddin and the title of sultan, naming himself on the 1520 Arabic inscription of a mosque he had built in Algiers "the sultan, warrior in the Path of God the Lord of the World."[101] However, threatened by the Spanish, Hayreddin sought help from, and offered his services to, Sultan Selim I already in October 1519. The Ottoman ruler accepted Hayreddin's submission and appointed him governor of Algiers. Selim also sent Hayreddin two thousand janissaries and some artillery, authorizing him to recruit volunteers for his sea *ghazas*. These volunteers would enjoy the same privileges as the Ottoman janissaries.[102] Although Kâtib Çelebi claimed that the province (*vilayet*) of Algiers became that of the Ottoman padishah,[103] for the time being this meant only the nominal extension of Ottoman influence in the western Mediterranean, as Hayreddin's weakened position in the 1520s and his withdrawal from Algiers to Djidjel in 1520 offered little tangible advantages for the Ottomans.[104]

Selim's departure for Edirne in the summer 1518 caused anxiety in Hungary. To force the Hungarians to make peace with him while he was in Syria and Egypt, Selim had instructed his *sancak* governors in Bosnia and Zvornik to attack the Hungarian border castles, especially Belgrade and Jajce. On 2 September 1518, the Hungarian chancellor Ladislaus Szalkai told the Venetian envoy to Hungary that Selim was preparing for his campaign against Hungary. At least this is how the envoy from the voivode of Wallachia (who arrived a day before in the Hungarian court) interpreted Selim's departure from Constantinople, adding that the voivode feared that the sultan wanted to capture Wallachia. The Hungarian chancellor also told the Venetian diplomat that they convened yet another diet at Bács for Saint Michael's day (29 September) to strengthen the defenses of the southern border in light of the expected Ottoman attack and to deliberate the pope's crusade plan, which the papal envoy shared with King Louis in early January 1518. But a crusade seemed unfeasible. Most European states experienced war fatigue after the War of the League of Cambrai (1509–17), fought between Venice and its allied foes—France, the empire, Spain, the papacy, Ferrara, and Mantua. Suffering defeat after defeat on its mainland, Venice renewed its treaty with the Ottomans in September 1517, agreeing to pay the Ottoman padishah an annual tribute of 8,000 ducats, an amount that the Serenissima had previously paid to the Mamluk sultan for the possession of Cyprus.[105]

By 1518, the imperial Estates shifted their concern away from the Turkish question and toward the theses of the Augustinian monk Martin Luther (1483–1546). Luther's ninety-five theses that protested against the indulgences spread like wildfire—although the famous act of nailing his theses on the door of the castle church of Wittenberg (31 October 1517) perhaps never happened.[106] One of the objectives of the jubilee indulgencies was to raise funds against the Turks, whom the papacy considered not just a political but also a religious threat. But Luther rejected the fight against the Turk. In Luther's words, to resist the Turk meant to "resist the will of God, who chastises us through them."[107] Having listened to Emperor Maximilian I's elaborate plan to conquer the Ottoman capital, the imperial diet at Augsburg denied military aid against the Turks in July 1518, declaring that Christianity had "more to fear from the pope than from the Turks. Much as we may dread the ravages of the infidel, they can hardly drain Christendom more effectually than it is now drained by the exactions of the Church."[108]

Using the term "Turk" to mean tyranny in general, Luther wrote in 1520 that "if we want to fight against the Turks, let us begin here where they are worst of all." He condemned the pope's servants as his "lackeys and whores," declaring the pope not only a "tyrant" of Christianity but also the "Antichrist," a term used for the Prophet Muhammad. Pope Leo X first condemned Luther in the bull *Exsurge Domine* (arise, O Lord), published in June 1520, threatening him with excommunication if he did not retract his teachings in sixty days. After Luther publicly burned the papal bull in Wittenberg, Leo X excommunicated him in January 1521 in the bull *Decet Romanum pontificem* (It pleases the Roman pontiff).[109]

People who were closest to the Ottoman frontline had firsthand information about Selim's recent victories and the looming Ottoman threat. Barnabas Bélay finally returned to Buda in 1519. Selim had taken the Hungarian envoy on his campaign against the Mamluks, parading Bélay as the king of Hungary and his retinue as his Hungarian auxiliaries. Under Bélay, there were "some six thousand Bosnians and Serbians, dressed in Hungarian fashion with Hungarian banners to show that the King of Hungary was on his side and had come to aid him." After his return, the experienced soldier-diplomat Bélay shared his observations "about the customs and history of the Turks and Mamluks, known otherwise as Circassians," with the king and other dignitaries.[110] Reports on Selim's military power revealed for everyone that the balance between the Hungarians and Ottomans had tilted in the padishah's favor.

Changing Balance of Power along the Danube

For most of the time between the death of King Matthias in 1490 and the Ottoman conquest of Belgrade in 1521, Hungary and the Ottoman Empire were in peace. King Matthias and Sultan Bayezid II concluded a five-year truce in 1483, followed by a two-year truce in 1488.[111] The latter stipulated that both monarchs keep whatever castles they had in their possession along the border, but did not name the castles. It also stated that if the sultan were to attack a third party, his armies would not march through Hungary without King Matthias's knowledge. The treaty allowed the merchants of the two monarchs to freely trade in one another's country and stated that attacks against merchants would not be considered violations of the pact. To deal with such attacks and the merchants' grievances, the sultan was to appoint a suitable man in Smederevo, and the king in Belgrade.[112] However, the truce of 1488 became void with the death of the Hungarian king in 1490. Attempts to renew it in 1491 failed as the Ottomans used the change in Hungary's government to raid the Temes region. After Paul Kinizsi had relieved Severin and repulsed the Ottomans, Bayezid II accepted the truce in 1495. The Hungarians and Ottomans renewed the truce in 1498, 1503, 1509, and 1510. King Wladislas II and Sultan Bayezid II concluded the 1503 truce for seven years. Like earlier treaties, it ensured that merchants could freely trade in the contracting monarchs' domains and resolved that joint commissions should investigate attacks against merchants. The 1503 treaty also listed the border castles in possession of the king and the sultan, thus marking the borders between their respective domains.[113] King Wladislas II concluded another truce in 1514 with Sultan Selim I, which the newly elected Louis II of Hungary and Bohemia renewed in 1516. The Turkish envoy Kemal and Barnabas Bélay, who had returned from his long Turkish embassy and captivity, concluded the last known treaty between the medieval Hungarian Kingdom and the Ottoman Empire in Buda in 1519. Like the 1503 treaty, the treaty in 1519 also stipulated the borders between the two countries, listing all the major border fortresses and forts in the contracting monarchs' possessions. The treaty also acknowledged the former Banate of Srebrenik—which the Ottomans conquered in 1512—as Ottoman land. However, this pact became void with the death of Selim I in the fall of 1520.[114]

These accords with the sultan did not protect Hungary's southern counties against perennial Turkish raids. Except for the short periods of declared war—such as the years of 1490–91, 1501–2, and 1512–13—neighboring Ottoman frontier troops raided Hungary during periods of official truce. In 1492, the Ottomans attacked Belgrade and Šabac. Two years later, only the military prowess of Paul Kinizsi saved Belgrade. Jajce, the center of Hungary's southwestern defense line, fell under siege in 1479, 1492, and 1502. Other key strongholds of the southwestern defense line were also under continuous assault. The Ottomans besieged Knin, the center of Croatia and the residence of the ban, in 1511 and 1514. In 1513 both Skradin and Klis fell under siege. In the fall of 1512, the Ottoman border troops conquered the fortresses of the Banat of Srebrenik. In the late summer of 1513, Peter (Petar) Berislavić, bishop of Veszprém and ban of Dalmatia, Croatia, and Slavonia, defeated the *sancak* governor of Bosnia at Dubica, whereas the Transylvanian voivode John Szapolyai besieged Smederevo in late summer.[115] However, in July 1515 Szapolyai and his fellow commanders of the southern defense failed to capture Ottoman Hisarcık—between Ottoman Smederevo and Hungarian Belgrade. The Ottoman *sancak* governor of Smederevo, Yahyapaşazade Bali, routed the Hungarians. Jajce endured siege for most of 1517. Berislavić eventually rescued the fortress. But he died in battle in May 1520.[116]

By the 1510s, the balance of power between the Ottomans and Hungary had clearly shifted toward the former. Already in 1481, the area of the Ottoman Empire (868,000 square kilometers) tripled that of Hungary's (300,000 square kilometers). With Selim I's conquests, the Ottoman realms grew five times larger than Hungary. In the 1520s, the Ottoman Empire contained a population of 12–13 million. Only 3.1–3.5 million lived in Hungary. An Ottoman account gave the Ottoman treasury's annual revenues for the fiscal year 1494–95 at 1,259,000 ducats.[117] As noted, the Ottoman central treasury's annual revenues from the royal domains (that is, excluding military prebends) rose from 1.3 million ducats in 1509 to 2 million ducats in 1523. By comparison, annual revenues of the

Hungarian Kingdom even at their climax in the 1470s and 1480s under King Matthias amounted to 612,000 to 678,000 gold florins, the value of which in the late fifteenth and early sixteenth centuries was about the same as that of the Venetian ducat. After the death of King Matthias, revenues shrank to 310,000 gold florins in 1494–95. This amount was less than one-fourth of Sultan Bayezid II's revenues in 1494–95. The king's direct revenues in 1522 are estimated at 281,000 florins, and those of his kingdom at 441,000 florins.[118] Yet, even the kingdom's total revenues in 1522 were little more than one-fifth of Süleyman's direct revenues of 2.1 million ducats in 1523. However, this latter figure did not include the Ottoman Empire's revenues from *timar* prebends, which maintained the bulk of the padishah's military force. In the early sixteenth century, Hungary stood no chance against such a wealthy and militarily powerful enemy.[119]

Comparison of military potentials along the Ottoman-Hungarian border indicates similar Ottoman superiority. As noted, the Hungarian border defense along the Danube–Sava line was organized into two units. The captain-general of the Lower Parts, usually based in Temesvár, guarded the southeastern border forts between Severin and Belgrade. The ban of Croatia and Slavonia, based in Bihać, protected the western section of the border and guarded the castles of the Croatian Banate and northern Bosnia. In 1513–14 the Hungarian treasury paid 7,818 soldiers in the castles of the southern defense line. Of these, 5,090 served in the castles of the Lower Parts, while 2,427 soldiers were stationed in the castles of Croatia. Of the 5,090 soldiers serving in the Lower Parts, 2,100 men (700 cavalry, 400 footmen, and 1,000 boatmen of the Danube flotilla) guarded Belgrade, the key fortress of the eastern section of the defense line. Cavalry dominated the defense in the Lower Parts, accounting for 70 percent of the soldiers, followed by the boatmen of the Danube flotilla (22 percent) and the infantry (a mere 8 percent). While this force distribution indicated a more active defense in Lower Hungary that relied on cross-border cavalry skirmishes, one should remember that 83 percent of the soldiery were peasant soldiers, the majority of whom served only for a couple of months in the summer and fall, the period of most frequent enemy attacks. By contrast, the

TABLE 4-1. Ottoman and Hungarian Resources and Military Potential

	Ottoman Empire	Kingdom of Hungary
Area (in km²)		
1481	868,000	300,000
1520	1,500,000	300,000
Population (in millions)		
1489–90	8.6–9	3.1–3.5
1520	12–13	3.1–3.5
Annual revenue (in ducats): treasury account books		
1470s–1480s		600,000–680,000
1493–94	1,020,000	
1494–95	1,259,000	310,000
1509	1,300,000	
1522		280,000
1523	2,125,000	
Annual revenue (in ducats): Venetian estimates		
1475	1,500,000	
1496	3,300,000	
1500		350,000
1503	5,000,000	220,000
1510	3,600,000	
1512–20	3,130,000	
1516		140,000
Military potential in the 1520s	125,000	40,000
Military force along the Ottoman-Hungarian border (1510s–1520s)	15,000–20,000	7,000–8,000
Mobilized troops in 1526	60,000–70,000	26,000

Sources: Hungary: I. Balogh 1929; C. Tóth 2016; Pálosfalvi 2018: 455. Ottoman Empire: Çakır 2016; İnalcık (1994) 1997: 78; Genç and Özvar 2006.

Notes: Modern estimates of Hungarian revenues (1494–95 and 1522) are based on contemporary account books and are in Hungarian florins. The Venetian ambassadors' estimates of Hungarian and Ottoman revenues are given in Venetian ducats. Revenues given in Ottoman treasury account books (1493–94, 1494–95, 1509, 1523, and 1527–28) are given in silver *akçe*. These accounts did not include revenues administered as military fiefs (*timar*).

Croatian-Bosnian frontier cavalry accounted for merely 32 percent of the troops. This suggests a more defensive posture, as does the fact that the defense in Croatia and northern Bosnia was entrusted to professional mercenaries, who served year-round.[120] The two frontier *sancak* governors of Bosnia and Smederevo could jointly mobilize an army that was twice the size of the Hungarian defense forces.[121]

The comparison of Hungarian and Ottoman resources and military potential presented in Table 4-1 proves what contemporaries knew too well: with Hungary's modest financial resources and limited military potential, its garrisons along the Danube defense line could not withstand a sizable Ottoman army for long. Any successful defense depended on the timely arrival of a relief army. But as events in 1521 demonstrated, logistical limitations often prevented this. Hungary sought military and financial help from abroad. We have seen how Selim's recent conquests and the fear of an imminent Turkish invasion against Europe energized Pope Leo X, who declared a crusade in 1518. A fury of diplomatic negotiations to end the war in Europe and unite Christendom led to the Treaty of London (October 1518), announcing a five-year peace among the Christian monarchs. However, the death of Emperor Maximilian in January 1519 and the resultant rivalry and war between the Habsburgs and the French consumed European military resources and again diverted attention away from the Turks. There were two main candidates to the throne of the Holy Roman Empire: Maximilian's grandson, Charles I of Spain, and Francis I of France. Following fierce campaigning for the imperial office, Charles won the contest and was elected emperor at Frankfurt am Main on 28 June 1519, assisted by the staggering 850,000 gulden his supporters invested in him. Two-thirds of this money came from Jacob Fugger, who later reminded the emperor that "it is well known and obvious that your Majesty would not have acquired the Roman crown without my help."[122] By the time the war broke out between Charles and Francis, a new ambitious ruler had ascended to the Ottoman throne in Constantinople.

PART II

Clash of Empires

5

Süleyman in Hungary

Süleyman and the Collapse of the Danubian Defense

Europeans believed Selim's son and successor Süleyman I (r. 1520–66) to be a peaceful ruler from whom Christendom had little to fear. In reality, the new padishah's accession to the Ottoman throne initiated a significant change in Ottoman strategy and foreign policy: attacking the empire's European rivals instead of fighting against the Safavids in the east. Perpetual warfare since 1511 exhausted the empire's eastern provinces. Distance and an inhospitable climate with early winters and snow, combined with Shah Ismail's avoidance of pitched battles and scorched-earth policy, created severe problems for the otherwise well-organized Ottoman provisioning system. The wars exhausted the Ottoman imperial treasury, which covered the regular salaries of the standing troops and bonuses and pay increases meted out to the soldiers during campaigns. Selim's eastern wars fatigued the soldiers, too. During the march from Syria to Egypt in 1517, the provincial cavalry from Rumeli exhausted its money supply and borrowed from the central treasury.[1]

During their encounters with Shah Ismail's Qizilbash followers, the Ottoman troops often deserted and many allied with the enemy. According to a Venetian report from March 1519, the soldiers did not want to fight against the Safavids. Instead, they preferred to wage war against the weaker Hungarians. By sending exaggerated reports to Constantinople regarding the wealth of the Hungarian Kingdom and the weakness of its military, the Ottoman soldiery in Rumeli likewise lobbied for

Known as "the Magnificent" in Europe and "the Lawgiver" to his subjects, Sultan Süleyman challenged Charles V in the Mediterranean and Ferdinand I in Hungary. His conquests triggered an imperial rivalry in the Mediterranean and Hungary with the Habsburgs that affected European power politics for the next 150 years. (Unknown artist. Courtesy of the Hungarian National Museum, Budapest, TKCs 438.)

the renewal of European campaigns, from which they hoped to profit financially.[2] In 1521, the Ottoman *sancak* governor of Bosnia, Yahyapaşazade Bali Beg, assured the Porte that "the damned Hungarians had no strength" to oppose the Ottomans. Before 1521, Bali had spent almost a decade along the Hungarian frontier as *sancak* governor of Smederevo, lending credibility to his assessment of the Hungarians' military capabilities.[3]

Bali's father, Yahya Pasha, was the patriarch of this eminent frontier warrior family. A man of probably Albanian origin, he had been raised in the court of Mehmed II and later served as *sancak* governor of Bosnia. But his career flourished under Bayezid II (r. 1481–1512). He was twice governor-general of Anatolia, and three times that of Rumeli, and became second vizier in 1505. Yahya married one of Bayezid's daughters, making him a son-in-law and tying the pasha to the dynasty.[4] As the oldest of Yahya Pasha's seven sons, Bali soon became a powerful and famed leader of the frontier *ghazi* warriors in his own right.[5] In 1521, Bali wrote a letter in response to the Porte's order instructing him to gather his forces in Bosnia and Herzegovina as Süleyman was "going to set out against the damned Hungarians." Bali had to let the Porte know how many soldiers had gathered around him, and what his opinion and plan were. Bali's response demonstrates that he knew the conditions of the frontier well:

> One must come to Smederevo . . . then cross the Sava [River] into Srem, from where one can get to the stream of the Drava in two days. After crossing the Drava, it takes five days to get to Buda, the Hungarian king's seat. . . . It is up to the noble decision of our illustrious padishah whether his servants, the *akıncı* raiders, shall cross over at Požažin and destroy the province of Temesvár. To comply with the noble command—in addition to the troops from the *sancak* of Hersek—3,000 horsemen and some 7,000 footmen have been gathered from the *sancak* of Bosna and are with this humble servant. We are ready and equipped and waiting for the high order.[6]

Shortly after his ascension to the throne on 30 September 1520, Süleyman ordered the preparations for next year's campaign. It was the first major military undertaking of the young padishah and signaled a new course in Ottoman strategy: attacks against the Hungarians, who for more than a century had halted Ottoman advance in Europe. The humiliation of the Ottoman envoys sent by the late sultan Selim to the Hungarian king, and the "honorable detention" of Süleyman's envoy Behram Çavuş—who arrived at Buda in December 1520 to renew the truce of 1519—angered the proud Süleyman. Both served as a pretext for his attack against Hungary. According to his letter of victory, issued to the judges of his empire after his conquest of Belgrade, Süleyman's goal in 1521 "was to humiliate and crush the haughty king."[7]

Preparations for the campaign started in the fall of 1520. They continued despite the plague in the Ottoman capital and the revolt of the Ottoman turned Mamluk governor of Damascus, Janbirdi al-Ghazali. By late January 1521, Ottoman troops had killed al-Ghazali and restored Ottoman rule.[8]

King Louis II of Hungary had little hope for help from his Habsburg brothers-in-law. French troops invaded Milan in March. The French threat and the war—which officially started in August 1521—diverted attention from the Danubian frontier. When Queen Mary, Louis's newly wedded Habsburg wife, asked for help from his emperor-brother, Charles made his priorities clear to the Hungarian envoy. In reference to the king of France, the emperor explained: "We have a bad neighbor. First, we have to defend ourselves against him, and only after that shall we go against the Turks."[9] The imperial diet (*Reichstag*) at Worms, where the Hungarian envoys submitted their request for help against the Turks in early April, agreed to help the emperor with twenty thousand foot soldiers and four thousand cavalry against the king of France. The diet offered no help to the Hungarians against the Turks.[10] This was all the more surprising because the imperial diet heard from Venetian sources about Süleyman's suppression of the revolt in Syria and the Ottoman war preparations against Hungary. In January 1521, Venice also rejected the Hungarians' plea for help, telling the Hungarian envoy that the Signoria had just accepted the new sultan's offer for peace.[11]

Celebrated as a splendid victory once the troops returned to Constantinople, the 1521 campaign revealed the young Süleyman's inexperience and the factionalism among the Ottoman leadership. The padishah set out for the campaign rather late, on 18 May. He probably took with him most of the 15,825 standing stipendiary army, of whom 8,349 men were janissaries. They were joined by some 20,000 *akıncı* raiders. The bulk of the army, however, consisted of provincial *timariot* cavalry, although governors of Anadolu, Karaman, Rum, Dulkadır, Aleppo Diyarbakır,

Damascus, and Egypt were ordered to guard the eastern borders against a possible Safavid attack.[12]

Nobody knew the exact target of the campaign. The Ottoman command usually revealed the target to the troops en route, but in 1521 not even Süleyman seemed to have a clear target. At a council meeting on 19 June in Sofia, the Ottoman statesmen disagreed as to the campaign's target. Ahmed Pasha, governor-general of Rumeli, wanted to move against Šabac, then cross the Sava River into Srem, and strike against the Hungarian capital, Buda. Grand Vizier Piri Mehmed Pasha—Ahmed's rival— suggested laying siege to Belgrade. He argued that if the Ottomans marched against Buda without taking Belgrade, the Hungarians could cut off the Ottomans' return at Belgrade. Süleyman agreed with Ahmed. However, he permitted his grand vizier to lay siege to Belgrade. Šabac's small garrison of one hundred surrendered on 8 July, but the Turks slaughtered the defenders. Süleyman inspected the castle the next day, proudly noting: "This is the first castle I conquered." The padishah ordered his grand vizier to lift the siege of Belgrade and join the main army. Back in Šabac, the Ottomans started building a bridge over the Sava River. But they did not have the required number of boats for the planned pontoon bridge, a rare oversight for the well-oiled Ottoman logistics. On 19 July, Süleyman's campaign diary noted: "Today the bridge was completed. It was supposed to be built on boats, but since there were not enough boats, it was built according to the old custom. The Sava flooded, and its level was as high as the bridge." The next day the diary added: "The Sava flooded so much that it was impossible to cross over to the other bank."[13] Lutfi Pasha's chronicle added: "The rushing water tore most of the mills off and cast them onto the bridge, crushing the bridge to pieces."[14] To Süleyman's luck, his grand vizier had not lifted the siege of Belgrade. After the collapse of the bridge over the Sava, Süleyman informed his grand vizier that he would soon join him with the main army. Once the padishah arrived in Belgrade, the siege commenced in earnest. The fortress succumbed on 29 August, after a two-month-long siege. Of the seven hundred defenders, only seventy-two men remained alive. Süleyman let the small party leave, but the Ottomans deported most of the town's Serbian inhabitants to Constantinople.[15]

Belgrade and its environs were attached to the *sancak* of Smederevo. On 15 September, the town was declared the center of the *sancak*. Its newly appointed governor, Bali Beg, moved to Belgrade.[16] For the defense of the conquered castle, Süleyman left a strong garrison, including 485 janissaries.[17] A Christian spy reported in 1529 that there were 1,850 garrison soldiers in Belgrade, including 400 janissaries. This was rather good intelligence. A year later, an Ottoman revenue survey listed 1,479 garrison soldiers in Belgrade, excluding janissaries of the Porte.[18]

The fall of Belgrade, Zemun, and Šabac opened a large hole in the Hungarian defense system. "Our country is now open to the Turk both on land and water," wrote the fifteen-year-old Louis II to his uncle, King Sigismund I of Poland. "It cannot be happy and safe so long as Šabac and Belgrade remain in the hands of the enemy."[19] Writing about the fall of Belgrade in the mid-sixteenth century, Francis Zay (1505–70)—soldier, diplomat, and captain-general of Upper Hungary—also mourned the fall of this "principal fortress," the "gate of the entire Christendom."[20] Of the key fortresses of the southern defense line, only Orşova and Severin in the eastern edge, and Jajce and Klis in the western edge remained under Hungarian control. Alas, the Ottomans conquered Orşova in 1522 and Severin in 1524, thus assuming control over the lower Danube valley. In 1522, they also captured Skradin and Knin. By contrast, Klis's defenders and the Uskoks under the able leadership of Peter (Petar) Kružić repelled numerous attacks between 1515 and 1537, when the castle finally succumbed to overwhelming Ottoman power.[21]

Before 1521, Venice had been willing to assist the Hungarian forts of Klis and Skradin, provided the Turks would not learn about it. After the padishah's victory at Belgrade, however, the Signoria avoided even the appearance of any assistance to the Hungarians.[22] To its Christian allies, the Venetian Senate lamented the fall of Belgrade, "the main fortress and bulwark of the kingdom of Hungary."[23] But in November, the Signoria congratulated Süleyman for his recent conquest and secured the renewal of the 1517 treaty a month later. The Venetian government remained on alert, fearing Ottoman assaults against its possessions in Dalmatia, Cyprus, and Crete, and a possible invasion of Italy.[24]

Süleyman's next target in 1522 was Rhodes of the Knights Hospitaller, who had preyed on Ottoman shipping in the eastern Mediterranean for some time and threatened Constantinople's communication with Syria and Egypt. Süleyman's letter to the grand master, announcing his victory at Belgrade, was perceived by the Knights as a veiled threat. However, just like the Hungarians in 1521, the Knights sought in vain help from their European coreligionists. Francis I of France was preparing to fight Charles V in Italy. With the renewal of their treaty with Venice, the Porte made sure that the republic remained neutral during the Rhodes campaign.

On 26 June, an Ottoman fleet of three hundred sail arrived at Rhodes with soldiers who started the siege of the island's fortresses. By early December the island was more than half lost, and on 20 December the Knights accepted Süleyman's terms to surrender: the churches on the islands would be respected, the inhabitants would not be taken in the child levy, no one would be forced to convert to Islam, the inhabitants had three years to decide whether to leave or stay, and they would be free of tribute for five years. The Knights Hospitaller had to leave in ten to twelve days with their arms and movable goods. On 1 January 1523, the grand master left Rhodes for Crete.[25] The padishah's generosity soon backfired. In 1530, the Knights established their new base in Malta, from whence they continued to harass Ottoman shipping in the eastern Mediterranean.[26]

In two short years, Süleyman accomplished two major conquests, that of Belgrade and Rhodes. In light of previous Ottoman failures under his great-grandfather Mehmed II (Belgrade in 1456 and Rhodes in 1480), these conquests established Süleyman's prestige both at home and in Europe. He was also poised to continue his conquests in central Europe. However, rebellions in Egypt and the reorganization of Ottoman administration there occupied the Porte for the next four years, giving the Hungarians and central Europe temporary respite.

In May 1523, two Mamluk emirs and provincial governors rebelled. Despite support from many Mamluks and Arabs, the rebellion was quickly crushed. The next year the province's governor-general, Ahmed Pasha, rebelled. Ahmed resented that Süleyman appointed his favorite,

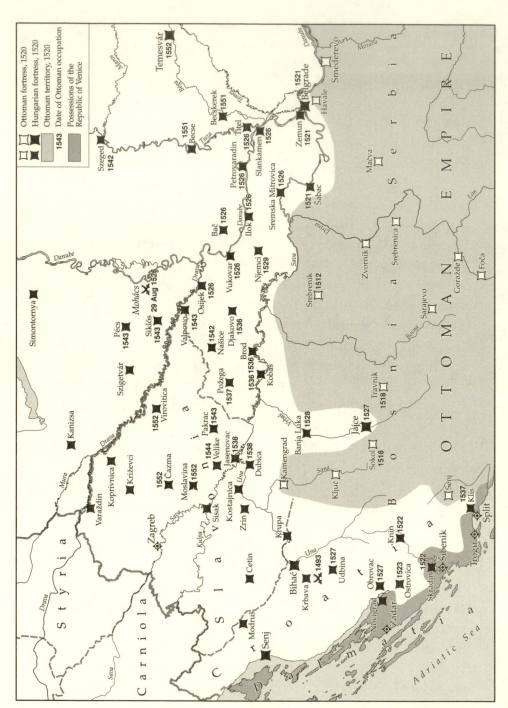

The collapse of the Hungarian-Croatian defense system. (Drawn by Béla Nagy.)

Ibrahim Pasha, to the grand vizierate, skipping Ahmed, then second vizier and next in line for that position. Frustrated, Ahmed requested the governorship of Egypt. Süleyman complied so as to distance Ahmed from Constantinople. Upon his arrival in Cairo, Ahmed replaced the citadel's garrison with troops loyal to him. When he learned that Ibrahim sent secret orders to the officials in Egypt to execute him, Ahmed rebelled and declared himself sultan. He was captured and beheaded (6 March 1524). His head was displayed for a day on Cairo's famous Zuwayla Gate and then sent to Constantinople. To solidify Ottoman rule and revenue management in Egypt, Süleyman sent Ibrahim to Cairo. Arriving on 2 April 1525, the grand vizier quickly restored order. He successfully reformed the province's military and civilian administration and taxation by issuing a new provincial law code, which adjusted Ottoman revenue management to that of the old Mamluk system. Ibrahim's activities were cut short as the padishah recalled him because of disturbances in the capital by janissaries and armed lads. Ibrahim left Cairo on 14 June, arriving in Constantinople with the annual tax yield of Egypt on 16 September 1525, a year after his departure.[27]

Mohács: 1526

In the spring of 1524, King Louis II of Hungary was expecting Süleyman to attack the next year. He dispatched his envoys to the European monarchs for help. The king urged Pope Clement VII to arrange peace among the Christian princes so that they could focus on the Turkish threat. Louis reminded the pope that the Hungarians had rejected Süleyman's latest peace offer at the request of the papacy. In 1525 the Hungarians clashed with Bali Beg's forces, and the following spring they were closely monitoring Ottoman war preparations. Ten days before Süleyman left his capital for the Hungarian campaign in 1526, Louis informed the pope that this time Süleyman planned to conquer the Hungarian capital.[28]

The Hungarians had little hope for help. Fearing Ottoman and Tatar attacks, Sigismund I of Poland—the Hungarian king's uncle—asked for a six-year truce in the Ottoman capital in 1525. He got a three-year

Louis II of Jagiellon, king of Hungary and Bohemia, was killed in the battle of Mohács in 1526 against Sultan Süleyman I. (Unknown seventeenth-century artist. Courtesy of the Hungarian National Museum, Budapest, TKCs 1391.)

truce.[29] Although Sigismund tried to include Hungary in the truce as well, Süleyman rejected this request. This was a clear indication that the padishah was preparing against the Hungarians. The Ottoman-Polish truce reflected the tried-and-true Ottoman policy of isolating the potential target by concluding truces with its allies. When Louis requested

Sigismund's help, the latter declined, referring to the recently concluded truce with Süleyman.[30]

Louis could not get help from Emperor Charles V either. When Archduke Ferdinand asked Charles to send urgent military aid to their brother-in-law against the Ottomans, the emperor replied, "I already have a tiresome Turk to deal with: the king of France." Defeated and captured in the battle of Pavia (24 February 1525) and taken to Madrid as Charles's captive, King Francis I signed the humiliating Treaty of Madrid (14 January 1526). In the treaty, he agreed that in exchange for his freedom, he would surrender all claims to Italy and the Netherlands (modern Belgium and Holland), evacuate Burgundy, and join Charles in fighting the Lutherans and the Turks. He also gave two of his older sons to the emperor as hostages. However, upon his return to France, Francis reneged on his promises; on 22 May 1526 he concluded an anti-Habsburg alliance with Venice, the pope, Florence, and Francesco Sforza (the deposed duke of Milan)—called by the signatories the Holy League of Cognac (1526–29).[31]

Süleyman left Constantinople on 23 April 1526. The troops followed the Roman military corridor in the Marica and Morava River valleys through Edirne, Plovdiv, Sofia, Niš, and Kruševac. Frequent rains, occasional hailstorms, and floods swept away bridges and made the roads difficult to traverse. Süleyman reached Belgrade on 30 June. Two weeks earlier, on 17 June, while camping near Kruševac, Süleyman dispatched Ibrahim Pasha against Petrovaradin, the only significant remaining Hungarian fortress on the Danube. The defenders of Petrovaradin, numbering about a thousand, put up an intense fight. However, on 27 July, the Ottomans captured the fortress after a two-week siege, thanks mainly to efficient mining. The smaller forts in the Srem fell quickly, many surrendering without a fight. On 23 August Süleyman crossed the Drava River at Osijek. By this time, King Louis II and the Hungarian army had arrived at Mohács, after a monthlong march from Buda. The two armies met south of Mohács; the Ottomans annihilated the Hungarian army in just a few hours.[32]

Contrary to received wisdom, the Ottoman victory at Mohács was not about the superiority of the Ottoman artillery over an obsolete

Hungarian heavy cavalry. An eyewitness report suggests that the army that reached Mohács with King Louis II was a mixed army of cavalry and infantry (about sixteen thousand and ten thousand men, respectively) armed with handguns, pikes, and large shields of the Bohemian type. The Hungarian artillery consisted of eighty-five cannons and six hundred smaller Praguer hook-guns, and was accompanied by five thousand wagons that could be used as wagon laager. Light horsemen, ideally suited to fight the Ottoman *sipahis*, composed much of the Hungarian cavalry.[33] However, this army numbered only about twenty-six thousand men, as contingents from Bohemia, Croatia, and Transylvania were still on their way to the battlefield. Because of uncertain intelligence regarding the primary target of the Ottoman campaign, the voivode of Transylvania, John Szapolyai, had initially been ordered to stay in Transylvania to guard the kingdom's eastern borders.[34] Szapolyai received a definitive order to hurry to his monarch only in late July. Facing the same problems of slow mobilization as his king, Szapolyai did not fully mobilize the Transylvanian troops until 15 August. He realized that he would not be able to reach the king's army in time with his army, so he hurried to his king alone. He also advised Louis II not to engage the enemy before his arrival.[35] In Szapolyai's absence, his younger brother, George, assumed the role as one of the two commanders in chief. The other commander was Archbishop Paul (Pál) Tomori of Kalocsa. Tomori had distinguished himself in the defense of the southern borders, defeating an Ottoman invasion in 1523. Even the Ottoman chroniclers acknowledged Tomori's bravery and valor.[36] However, he never commanded a large army.

The Ottomans greatly outnumbered the Hungarians. Süleyman commanded a mixed force of *timariot* provincial cavalry and a much smaller standing army, paid from the imperial treasury. The Ottomans had a potential provincial cavalry of seventy thousand strong, although some historians estimate the strength of the provincial cavalry as high as one hundred thousand men.[37] One out of ten cavalrymen stayed behind to attend his comrades' *timars* during campaigns, which coincided with the harvest season. Others farther from the theaters of war also stayed home to guard their provinces and maintain law and order. In 1526

Süleyman mobilized only about forty-five thousand provincial horsemen, most of which came from the Balkan Peninsula and western Asia Minor. In other words, Süleyman deployed only about 65 percent of his potential *timariot* cavalry in 1526.[38]

The standing army mobilized at a higher rate. In 1524–25 the imperial treasury paid 17,063 salaried household troops, including 9,390 janissaries. This latter figure was 10 percent higher than that of the previous fiscal year, indicating that the government increased the number of janissaries before the Mohács campaign. While the number of salaried troops mobilized in 1526 is unknown, it is likely that Süleyman took most of them to Hungary. With infantry *azabs* and *akıncı* raiders, the Ottoman combat forces in the 1526 campaign could have numbered seventy thousand men or more. These numbers are close to the estimates of Paul Tomori, the Hungarian commander in chief, who put the strength of Süleyman's professional forces at sixty thousand men, with eleven thousand janissaries.[39]

In addition to the numerical advantage of deployed troops, the Ottomans enjoyed clear firepower superiority, especially in artillery. Süleyman's army brought to the 1526 campaign about 150 to 200 field pieces and some more massive cannons, along with 30,000 shots. On the other hand, a register of 4,060 handguns and 3,000,000 projectiles indicates that only about half of the janissaries carried firearms. The rest of them, along with the household cavalrymen, used bows and arrows.[40] The eyewitness Ottoman chronicler Celalzade Mustafa confirmed that the Ottomans deployed only four thousand janissaries with handguns. Even more critical is the chronicler's note that these janissary gunners "were deployed in nine consecutive rows" behind the field pieces chained together, and "were firing their handguns row after row."[41] A miniature of the battle from 1558 shows the janissaries firing in two rows. The soldiers in the first row are in a kneeling position reloading their weapons, while those standing behind them in the second row are firing their guns. The janissaries are depicted as being behind light field pieces that are chained together. The question of whether these accounts refer to volleys known from western European examples from the latter part of the sixteenth century, and presented by historians as one of the hallmarks of the "European military revolution," requires further study.[42]

The Hungarian command planned to charge against the much larger Ottoman army in increments as the Ottoman soldiers were descending from a steep, thirty-meter-high plateau, made slippery by heavy rains in the previous days. At the start of the battle, the king's artillery opened fire at the Rumelian army on the Ottoman left wing. But this did little damage, for the enemy was out of range of the weapons. Next, the Croatian and Slavonian light cavalry charged on the right flank. This broke the resistance of the Rumelian cavalry, which fled—according to Ottoman tradition, retreated—and sought shelter behind the chained-together cannons. In their pursuit, the Hungarian light cavalry set out to loot. At this point, the Hungarian heavy cavalry and infantry also charged but were unable to penetrate the chained cannons. Behind the cannons stood the janissaries. The Hungarian infantry in the middle and the left wing fought bravely, but was unable to break the obstacles erected in front of the Ottoman cannons and were slaughtered by janissary volleys. Initially, the Ottoman cannons did little damage, likely because the uneven terrain caused the gun barrels to shoot beyond the attacking Hungarians. However, cannon fire caused disorder among the looting and fleeing Hungarian light cavalry. In the end, the janissaries' discipline and volleys sealed the fate of the Hungarians. The fact that the Ottoman cavalry outnumbered its Hungarian counterpart by four to one, and that Süleyman had vast reserves at his disposal, also played an essential role in the Ottoman victory.[43]

The medieval Kingdom of Hungary died at Mohács. The Ottomans eliminated the king's army. Chancellor Stephen Brodarics, the eyewitness and subsequent chronicler of the battle, claimed that most of the ten thousand infantry and some three thousand to four thousand cavalry were killed, as were the two commanders in chief. The king fled the battlefield but drowned when crossing the flooding Csele creek. Although palatine Stephen Báthory survived the battle, the death of twenty barons decimated the kingdom's political leadership. Many of the dead barons had held key governmental offices. As royal appointees, they headed the county government in their capacity as the king's representatives or high lords (*comes supremus, főispán*). Everyday administration of the counties fell into the hands of the deputy lord of the county (*vicecomes* or *alispán*), whom the high lords appointed from among their trusted noble clients. Since several of the five hundred nobles who died in the battle also functioned as *vicecomes*, their deaths created a vacuum in the provincial governance and county-level judiciary. Half of the high clergy, the archbishops of Esztergom and Kalocsa, and the bishops of Várad, Pécs, Győr, Csanád, and Bosnia also died in the battle.

Remaining on horseback for hours after the battle, Süleyman retired to his tent after midnight. All soldiers continued "holding onto the rein of their horses," fearing a possible attack from the Hungarians, as the Ottomans could not believe that they had destroyed the entire Hungarian army. Two days later, seated on a golden throne, Süleyman received the homage of his viziers at the meeting of the imperial council. The captives—about two thousand according to the campaign diary—were all executed. The severed heads of Tomori and the other magnates were brought into the *divan*.[44] Having stayed at the battlefield for three days as a measure of precaution against possible enemy attacks, Ottoman *akıncı* raiders now received permission to ravage the countryside. They raided with shocking cruelty, wreaking havoc as far as Komárom in northwestern Hungary. The main army set the town of Mohács ablaze and departed for Buda. Fearing a similar fate, the neighboring episcopal town of Pécs opened its gate to the conquerors, but the raiders nonetheless pillaged and set fire to the town. Only the castle and the bishop's cathedral survived. Most towns and villages on the right bank of the Danube between Mohács and Buda suffered the same fate. A handful of walled cities with stronger defenses—such as Visegrád, Esztergom, Székesfehérvár, Tata, and Komárom—protected themselves against the marauding enemy.[45]

Arriving at the Hungarian capital on 11 September, the Ottomans found a mostly deserted city. The news of the crushing defeat at Mohács reached Queen Mary in Buda in the evening hours of 30 August. Shocked by the news and fearing enmity of her Hungarian subjects, the queen and the royal court, accompanied by the papal nuncio Antonio da Burgio, hurriedly fled the capital for Pozsony (modern Bratislava in Slovakia). They took with them whatever treasure they could salvage— codices from King Matthias's famous library, furniture from the royal palace, jewelry, and cash. Buda's wealthy German and Hungarian bur- ghers, nobles and clerics, and a few wealthy Jewish families followed their queen, rescuing whatever assets they could.[46] The eyewitness George Szerémi, the court chaplain of the late king, gave a vivid descrip- tion of the flight in his *Letter on the Downfall of Hungary* (*Epistola de perditione regni Hungarorum*), written some twenty years later. Only the poor, who had no horses and carts, remained in the town, along with some artisans, merchants, and the Jewish community.[47]

A delegation representing the remaining inhabitants of the town sur- rendered Buda's keys to Süleyman in Dunaföldvár, a village about ninety kilometers south of Buda, asking for mercy. Based on Ottoman and Jewish sources, later literature perpetuated the story that it was the Jews of Buda who delivered the keys of the Hungarian capital to Süleyman.[48] Ottoman documents from the seventeenth through the nineteenth cen- turies echoed the event, identifying the leader of the Jewish delegation in 1526 under various names—Israil son of Yasef (Joseph), Yasef son of Salomon. These sources survived as his descendants eagerly sought con- firmation, generation after generation, of the tax exemptions they en- joyed in return for their ancestor's purported service in 1526. However, most contemporary sources mentioned neither the name of the leader of the Jewish delegation nor the fact that the keys of the town were delivered to Süleyman by the Buda Jews.[49] A recent study, therefore, suggested that the story must have originated later and that the initiator of the tradition could have been a seventeenth-century influential Jew in the Ottoman capital who wanted to legalize the privileges his family enjoyed by claiming that his grandfather led the Buda Jews in 1526 to Süleyman.[50] While this is possible, some contemporaries knew the story. The Ottoman chronicler Bostan Çelebi—the author of one of the best historical sources of the era covering Süleyman's reign from 1520 through 1542—claimed that when Süleyman arrived at Buda, the Jews of the town greeted him and asked for mercy.[51] The story is also re- corded in Joseph ben Joshua ha-Kohen's (1496–after 1577) *Chronicle of the Kings of France and the Kings of the Dynasty of Osman the Turk*, completed in 1553.[52] Whatever role the Jews played in the Ottoman takeover of Buda, they enjoyed their privileges elsewhere. Süleyman resettled Buda's Jewish community—2,000 to 2,500 people, according to Turkish, Hungarian, and Jewish sources—to Constantinople and other towns in southeastern Europe. Later Ottoman sources mention the Buda Jews in Sofia, Thessaloniki, Vidin, Plevna, Kavala, and Monastir.[53] This was an old practice. The Ottoman government resettled skilled artisans, craftsmen, and merchants of conquered towns into the capital or other major cities of the empire to alleviate economic life.

Süleyman spent ten days in the Hungarian capital. He visited the palaces and churches, invited his viziers to the palace of King Matthias Corvinus for a feast, and hunted in the king's game preserve, retiring to his tent outside the town every night. Despite Süleyman's orders, his soldiers set Buda ablaze. Two years later Ibrahim Pasha confessed to King Ferdinand's envoys that although Süleyman and Ibrahim ordered the troops not to destroy the town, such a large army could not be controlled. Still, Ibrahim insisted that Süleyman preserve the Hungarian king's palace unharmed, as he intended to return there soon.[54]

Before his soldiers sacked and set the Hungarian capital on fire, Süleyman ordered his soldiers to gather and ship the treasures to Belgrade. These included two monster cannons, which John Hunyadi had captured from Mehmed II in 1456 at Belgrade. Süleyman also took with him several codices from King Matthias's renowned library, church bells to cast cannons, and two candlesticks from the Church of the Assumption; from the king's palace he took three bronze statues, including that of Hercules, which King Matthias had commissioned to commemorate his older brother Ladislaus, executed by the rival faction.[55]

A generation later (1552), Paolo Giovio identified the two other statues as those of the pagan gods Venus (or Diana) and Apollo. While the candlesticks were transported to the Hagia Sophia in Constantinople, Ibrahim Pasha displayed the statues as trophies in front of his palace. The statues, which faced the Roman-era Hippodrome (At Meydanı) in the Ottoman capital, caused quite a scandal because their public display ran against Islamic customs. The poet Figani echoed the disapproving

Ibrahim Pasha's palace in Istanbul now houses the Museum of Turkish and Islamic Art. Ibrahim Pasha was Sultan Süleyman's childhood friend and grand vizier from 1523 to 1536. His palace faces the Byzantine Hippodrome, known as At Meydanı or "Horse Square" in Ottoman times. The square was a site of numerous festivals, which the grand vizier and the sultan watched from the balcony. The grand vizier and his successors also received foreign ambassadors here. (Photo courtesy of the author.)

sentiment of Constantinople's inhabitants in a satiric couplet: "There descended to this world two Ibrahims; one smashed the idols; the other revived them." The satiric verse cost Figani his life as the offended grand vizier ordered Figani's execution in 1530. The bronze statues were soon destroyed by an angry mob, who rioted in the capital upon the execution of Ibrahim Pasha in 1536.[56]

The "Greatest Victory"?

Historians have debated the causes of the 1526 Ottoman campaign and advanced different theories about Süleyman's policy. One historian detected no coherent strategy under Süleyman's rule and called his era "a crisis of orientation."[57] By contrast, others endowed the padishah with long-term strategic thinking, suggesting that Süleyman did not want to conquer Hungary but wished to transform it into a pro-Ottoman vassal state, a buffer zone between his empire and that of the Habsburgs. The reason for such a policy was, so the argument goes, Süleyman's realization that Hungary was situated beyond his army's radius of action, or the furthest limit of Ottoman military operations, constrained by distance and seasonal campaigning. The defense of such a distant province would have been too costly.[58]

Most historians have found the reasoning based on the Ottoman army's radius of action too mechanical. They argued that the conquest of Hungary had been Süleyman's primary objective from the beginning of his reign. In conquering Hungary, the padishah allegedly followed the Ottomans' proven method of "gradual conquest."[59] The idea of "step-by-step" Ottoman conquest and "gradual incorporation" emerged in Hungarian historiography in the late nineteenth century and was rediscovered in the late 1970s.[60]

Others have drawn attention to the fact that the financial burden of maintaining Ottoman Hungary did not discourage the Ottoman government from conquering Hungary. In 1527, Ibrahim Pasha acknowledged that maintaining Ottoman rule in the Srem region, occupied in 1526, cost the Ottoman treasury 56,000 ducats annually. Still, the grand vizier made it clear to the envoys of King John Szapolyai, who requested the return of the Srem to Hungarian rule, that Süleyman would not give up this strategic region even if it cost ten times as much.[61] Considering that the amount the Ottomans spent on the Srem was a mere 2 percent of the treasury's annual revenue, we should assume that the grand vizier meant what he said.[62] More importantly, Ibrahim's statement clearly indicated that in matters of conquest, financial considerations were not of primary importance at the Porte.

Süleyman's campaign diary recorded the destruction of the Hungarian capital as one of the goals of the 1526 expedition.[63] The victory proclamation (*fethname*)—penned by Celalzade Mustafa, soon to be Süleyman's chancellor and one of his more influential image makers—justified the padishah's campaign with reference to the Qur'anic obligation of Muslim rulers to fight against the infidels. Trusting in the help of Allah, says the *fethname*, Süleyman launched his jihad against the Hungarians, who rejected his offer of a truce.[64] Considering Süleyman's often reactive policy and the Porte's constraints and multiple commitments, it is reasonable not to overstate the importance of religious-political imperatives or any time-honored methods of conquest, as reconstructed by historians. Such a cautious approach is warranted, as the Ottoman grand strategy and decision-making processes are still not sufficiently understood.

Celebrated in Constantinople as "Islam's greatest" victory, the battle of Mohács became a turning point in the history of both the Ottoman Empire and central Europe. Süleyman's victory helped the Porte's archenemy, the Habsburgs, acquire the long-coveted Hungarian and Bohemian crowns. After 1526, the Porte faced not the weakened medieval Hungarian Kingdom but Europe's emerging Habsburg superpower: Charles V's Mediterranean empire and Ferdinand I's nascent Danubian monarchy. Mohács thus inaugurated the battle for European supremacy between the Ottomans and the Habsburgs, a contest that played out primarily in the Hungarian and Mediterranean theaters of war.

Contested Accessions

King Louis II of Hungary and Bohemia perished in the battle of Mohács along with most of the country's magnates and prelates. On 30 August, Queen Mary received the news of her husband's death from the late king's chamberlain, who fought with Louis in the battle. Archduke Ferdinand learned the sad news from his sister on 9 September. Charles V received Ferdinand's letter of 22 September only on 13 November.[65] Having visited and ransacked the Hungarian capital Buda after his victory, Süleyman had withdrawn from Hungary by the autumn of 1526. In

late September, Grand Vizier Ibrahim Pasha dispatched three chamber-
lains of Louis II, captured in the battle, to the king, whom the Ottomans
believed to be alive. In his message, Ibrahim offered an alliance to the
Hungarian king, demanding the handover of the Srem. After leaving
Hungary, the Ottomans occupied this historic region between the Sava
and Danube Rivers. The death of the childless Louis II in the battle led
to civil war in Hungary, as the competing Hungarian noble factions
could not agree on the successor to the late king. There were two claimants to the throne: John Szapolyai, Hungary's wealthiest aristocrat and
voivode of Transylvania, and Ferdinand of Habsburg, archduke of Austria and brother of Queen Mary and Emperor Charles V.

The Szapolyais were the most prominent family in Hungary in the
Jagiellonian era. Emeric Szapolyai (d. 1487)—John Szapolyai's uncle,
and son of a Slavonian nobleman with estates in Požega county—had
built the family's fortune and political influence. Under King Matthias,
Emeric served as treasurer (1459–64); ban of Dalmatia, Croatia, and
Slavonia and governor of Bosnia (1464–65); and palatine of Hungary
(1486–87). At the time of his death, Emeric had built a more considerable fortune than any other baron in the kingdom, other than John Corvinus, the illegitimate son of King Matthias. John Szapolyai's father, Stephen (d. 1499), was the younger brother and heir of the childless Emeric.
A venerated military commander, Stephen held high offices, including
locumtenens of Silesia in the 1470s, captain-general of Austria in the 1480s,
and palatine of Hungary (1492–99). In the mid-1490s he possessed over
eleven thousand peasant plots and more wealth than any other lord in
the country. The Szapolyais further enhanced their prestige and political
leverage by royal marriages. In 1486, Stephen married the Polish Duchess
Hedwig of Cieszyn (Ger. Teschen), a member of the House of Piast.
Since Hedwig was a second cousin of Emperor Maximilian I, their son
John was related, albeit distantly, to the Habsburgs and other European
royal families. From the early 1500s, Princess Hedwig started a marriage
policy to elevate the power of her family. She wanted her sons, John and
George, to marry, respectively, Princess Anna, daughter of King Wladis-
las II of Hungary and Bohemia, and Elizabeth Corvinus, daughter of
John Corvinus and Beatrice Frankopan. Elizabeth, the granddaughter of

King Matthias Hunyadi, was the sole heir of the vast Hunyadi estates after the death of her father, John Corvinus (1504), and her brother, Christopher (1505). Already in 1497, the assembly of the nobles of the kingdom had accused Stephen Szapolyai of plotting to make his son John, born some seven years earlier, king of Hungary.[66] Another royal marriage further enhanced the prestige of the Szapolyai family. In 1512, John's sister Barbara married King Sigismund I of Poland, brother of Wladislas II. The marriage established closer ties with the Jagiellons, who ruled Poland-Lithuania, Hungary, and Bohemia. But Barbara died in 1515, and the war between Poland-Lithuania and Muscovy forced King Sigismund to ally himself with Emperor Maximilian.[67]

As the voivode of Transylvania since 1510, John Szapolyai wielded significant power in Hungary. His fight against the Turks along the country's southern borders and his leadership in the suppression of the peasant rising of 1514 gained him much appreciation among the nobility. Beginning in the summer of 1525, Szapolyai led the middle nobility against the magnates' pro-Habsburg faction. After Mohács, his followers justified John's claim to the Hungarian throne with the Rákos Resolutions of 1505. At the diet in Rákos, the Estates had declared that they could not elect a king of foreign descent should their Jagiellonian king die without a male heir. Led by the legal expert Stephen Werbőczy, on 10 November 1526, at the diet at Székesfehérvár, the Estates elected John Szapolyai king of Hungary. Since the archbishops of Esztergom and Kalocsa had died at the battle of Mohács, Stephen Podmaniczky, the bishop of Nyitra and the most senior prelate, crowned John Szapolyai the next day (11 November), according to the country's old customs: with the Holy Crown of St. Stephen in Székesfehérvár.[68]

Ferdinand claimed the Bohemian and Hungarian thrones on the basis of his marriage to Anna Jagiellon and the treaties of 1463, 1491, and 1515. Since both countries were elective monarchies, neither the Bohemian nor the Hungarian Estates accepted Ferdinand's hereditary claims. Ferdinand faced difficulties in Austria, too. Because he was brought up in Spain, Ferdinand's rule in Austria had been challenged ever since he arrived there in 1521 by the opposition of the Estates, a peasant revolt in Tyrol (1525), and the Protestant Reformation, which began to take root in the Habsburg provinces. To these now were added the difficulties of acquiring the Bohemian and Hungarian crowns, long coveted by the House of Habsburgs. On 23 October 1526, however, he came closer to his goals when the Bohemian diet in Prague elected him king. Ferdinand quickly dispatched his envoys to the Hungarian diet, convened by his sister, Queen Mary, in December in Pozsony, to have himself elected king of Hungary. The instruction of his envoys and their speech at the Pozsony diet revealed the effectiveness of Habsburg propaganda.[69] The envoys described the events of the past couple of months according to Habsburg interests, employing many of the manipulations and distortions that are known from election campaigns today. They had two major tasks: to present Ferdinand as the sole legitimate heir and the only viable candidate to the Hungarian throne, and to discredit King John by using unfounded accusations, half-truths, and plain lies. The envoys emphasized Ferdinand's two main goals: to defend Hungary—called the "bulwark of Christendom" to flatter the Hungarian nobles' self-image—and to retake Belgrade and other castles that the Turks had captured recently. The envoys were to point out that Ferdinand, unlike Szapolyai, could count on the military and financial assistance of the emperor in the struggle against the Turks and that Ferdinand was willing to sacrifice his own life for the country. They also warned the Estates that should they refuse Ferdinand, Hungary would face not just the Turks as the enemy but also Ferdinand's "Bohemian, Moravian and Silesian subjects, along with Germany."[70] Despite his wars in Italy, the emperor sent Ferdinand 100,000 gold pieces in September, promising more money, soldiers, and artillery. Charles warned Ferdinand not to make peace with the Turks, a possibility Ferdinand himself raised should he fail to get sufficient help from the emperor and the imperial Estates.[71]

A month after King John's coronation, a small but influential group of pro-Habsburg Hungarian magnates, with whom Queen Mary surrounded herself, elected Ferdinand as their king at the rump diet in Pozsony on 17 December 1526.[72] The Estates of Slavonia and Croatia were missing from the diet. Two weeks after the battle of Mohács, Ferdinand charged the Croatian noblemen Nicholas (Nikola) Jurišić and Christoph (Krsto) Frankopan with persuading the Slavonian and Croatian Estates

Queen Mary of Hungary was the widow of King Louis II, sister of
Ferdinand I and Charles V, and regent of the Netherlands. She was
instrumental in organizing support in Hungary for the election and
coronation of Ferdinand. (Unknown artist, Low Countries, 1550–60.
Courtesy of the Rijksmuseum, Amsterdam, SK-A-4463.)

to elect him their king. In late December 1526, the Croatian Estates gathered in the Franciscan monastery in Cetin, which belonged to the estate
of the powerful House of Frankopan. Through his plenipotentiaries,
Ferdinand promised the Croatians that he would pay for one thousand
horsemen and two thousand foot soldiers to maintain a sizable army
along the borders between Croatia and his duchy of Carniola, and to
repair the border forts. Ferdinand also promised to respect the Croatians' ancient privileges and rights. Having studied Ferdinand's right to
the crown of St. Stephen and respecting the Hungarian Estates election
in Pozsony, the Croatian Estates confirmed their Hungarian peers' decision on 1 January 1527. They elected Ferdinand king of Croatia, and his
wife, Anna, queen of Croatia.[73] The election in Cetin altered the relations between Croatians and Hungarians little for the time being. Akin

Ferdinand I of Habsburg was elected king of Hungary and Bohemia after the
death of Louis II in 1526. He devoted most of his energies to building an
effective defense system against the Ottomans in Hungary. (Unknown artist.
Courtesy of the Hungarian National Museum, Budapest, TKCs 8.)

to his predecessors, Ferdinand governed Croatia through Hungarian
institutions: the Hungarian Chancery, Treasury, and Council. Still, the
election was a momentous act and had long-term consequences on the
relationship between the Hungarian and Croatian Estates.[74] Things
were different in Slavonia, where the Estates elected John Szapolyai as
their king.[75]

The decision of the Croatian and Slavonian Estates reflected differences with regard to their relations vis-à-vis the Habsburgs and their

peers in Hungary. Since 1522, Ferdinand had helped the Croatians defend their borders against the Ottomans. He appointed Nicholas Salm (Niklas Graf II zu Salm) commander in chief of the armies in the neighboring Habsburg hereditary duchies of Carniola, Carinthia, and Lower Austria. Croatian aristocrats entered in Ferdinand's service. After his election as king of Croatia, Ferdinand sent royal troops to Senj and Klis in 1527, and the following year Bihać came under royal control. The elections at the diets of Pozsony and Cetin were a significant victory for the House of Habsburgs. They tied Hungary and Croatia to the dynasty and shaped the history of central Europe for the next four hundred years. The Estates of Croatia and Slavonia merged in 1558, and the Croatian, Slavonian, and Hungarian Estates received substantial military and financial aid from their Habsburg sovereign, which proved crucial in their attempt to halt Ottoman advance in central Europe.[76]

For the time being, Ferdinand could not be crowned. The Holy Crown of St. Stephen remained in the possession of King John's Transylvanian voivode and guardian of the crown. Ferdinand had no military force to challenge King John either, as he had to assist his emperor-brother against the anti-Habsburg League of Cognac, an alliance of France, Pope Clement VII, the Republics of Venice and Florence (the Medici pope's home), England, and the Duchy of Milan. In the meantime, King John managed to restore his control over much of the country and was busy organizing his government and gaining international legitimacy. Except for a few pro-Ferdinand magnates, the majority of the nobles arrived at the diet of Buda in March 1527 to support their king by offering 10 percent of their wealth for the war against the Turks. King John's troops also defeated the pro-Habsburg Serbian "tsar," Jovan Nenad, "the Black (Černi)," whose mercenaries raided southern Transylvania and pillaged the estates of pro-Szapolyai nobles.[77]

King John enjoyed only moderate success in his foreign policy. Ferdinand rejected "the voivode's" offer to marry his widowed sister and to conclude an anti-Ottoman alliance with the Habsburgs. The members of the League of Cognac acknowledged King John as Hungary's legitimate ruler. His joining the league was announced in July 1527 in Buda, in the presence of the French envoy, Antonio Rincón. In Fontainebleau and Paris, King John's and Francis I's diplomats negotiated a treaty. Signed on 28 October 1528 by the two plenipotentiary negotiators in Paris, the agreement stated that there would be "everlasting brotherhood, union, confederation and friendship" between the two monarchs. However, Francis offered no military aid to his Hungarian ally. His vague promise stated that he would assist "to the best of his ability the King of Hungary in recovering and pacifying his country with both money and other necessary means so that the king might endure the burdens of war." The French king also promised 20,000 gold coins to King John "for sustaining the burden of war." Meanwhile, if Francis made peace with the emperor, the agreement stipulated King John's possible inclusion. By contrast, "the King of Hungary" must wage war "against Ferdinand, King of Bohemia . . . so long as the most Christian king recovers his sons, who are being held as hostage by Charles." King John could make no truce or peace with Ferdinand "without the expressed consent and agreement of the most Christian king," whom the Hungarian king had to aid with light cavalry and foot soldiers in Italy, even after he defeated Ferdinand and recovered Hungary.[78] In short, Francis crafted an uneven agreement to use the Hungarian king for diversionary military activities in his war against the Habsburgs without promising anything tangible in return, save for the 20,000 gold coins. The alliance did not help King John, who by the time of the agreement had been ousted from his kingdom.

In the spring of 1527, Charles repeatedly advised his brother to make peace with the "voivode of Transylvania," fearing that Szapolyai would ally himself with the Turks.[79] By the summer, however, Ferdinand could attack his rival, thanks to the emperor's recent victory against the League of Cognac. This culminated in the sack of Rome by the emperor's Lutheran Landsknechte and Spanish mercenaries, who pillaged the capital of the Papal States "with as much cruelty and wantonness as if it had been plundered by the Turks," wrote a Spanish eyewitness to Charles. An Italian poet and member of the Roman Academy seconded his opinion, noting that "no Turks, no Africans, no part of the human race, however remote or estranged from our religion, could ever have visited such carnage on us either with worse crimes or with wilder tortures."[80]

Freed on the Italian front, German mercenary troops invaded Hungary in July. With most of King John's troops still tied up in the south against the remnants of Jovan's forces, Ferdinand easily occupied Buda (20 August).[81]

Defeated near Tokaj in late September, King John fled to his home base of Transylvania. Yet the Saxon towns of Transylvania, inspired by the skillful propaganda of Ferdinand's agents, rose up against him. Meanwhile, Peter Perényi, King John's voivode in Transylvania and guardian of the Holy Crown, deserted his suzerain and handed the crown to Ferdinand. Having taken the solemn oath pledging to uphold Hungary's ancient laws and the nobles' privileges, Ferdinand was crowned with the Holy Crown of St. Stephen on 3 November 1527 at the diet at Székesfehérvár. Attended by the majority of barons and nobles, the ceremony was performed by Stephen Podmaniczky, the same bishop of Nyitra who just a year earlier had crowned King John.[82] After the coronation more barons and nobles switched their allegiance to Ferdinand, who left Hungary for Vienna in the spring of 1528. Having suffered yet another defeat in March 1528, King John fled to Poland. He soon returned, however, as his envoy concluded an alliance with Süleyman, who promised military help.[83]

Damage Control

Already in the fall of 1527, following his defeat near Tokaj and the loss of Transylvania, King John realized that if he was to reclaim Hungary, he had to strike a deal with the Ottomans. Closely following the events in Hungary, the Ottomans signaled their willingness to help Szapolyai against Ferdinand in November 1526 and April 1527. They also intensified their attacks against parts of the border that were under Ferdinand's control. In late June 1527, Ibrahim Pasha ordered the Ottoman border governors to assist King John against his Habsburg rival. Initially, the Ottoman frontier troops concentrated their offensive on Slavonia and Croatia, cutting the main land route between Croatia and Dalmatia. By early 1528, they conquered Jajce, the last Hungarian outpost in Bosnia, and raided Carniola.[84]

King Sigismund I of Poland advised King John against his plans to ally with Süleyman. However, both Venice and Francis I of France urged him to make a treaty with Süleyman. The Signoria also lobbied at the Porte on John's behalf.[85] In October 1527, King John dispatched to Constantinople Jerome (Hieronim) Łaski—nephew of John Łaski, the primate of Poland and a seasoned statesman and diplomat. He carried letters to Ibrahim Pasha and Lodovico (Alvise) Gritti.

Born in 1480 in Pera as one of four illegitimate sons of the Venetian nobleman, merchant, and diplomat Andrea Gritti and his Greek mistress, Lodovico had little hope for a political career in Venice. After his studies at the University of Padua, he returned to the Ottoman capital in 1506. As a banker and merchant, Lodovico supplied the sultan with jewels and armaments. He also maintained close personal and business contacts with his brothers, Lorenzo and Giorgio, who returned to Venice but visited Constantinople because of their business dealings and their work as the republic's diplomats. Lodovico helped the republic's merchants purchase wheat and other strategic commodities, whose export the Porte often prohibited, from the Ottoman domains. He gained influence at the Porte after his father, Andrea Gritti, became Venice's doge (1523–38). Henceforth, Lodovico was known at the Porte as Beyoğlu ("son of the lord"). Modern Istanbul's Beyoğlu neighborhood, where Lodovico's palace once stood, is named after him. Just as his father had good connections to Sultan Bayezid II's grand vizier, Lodovico befriended and became the confidant of Süleyman's grand vizier, Ibrahim Pasha. He used his wealth from commerce to build his political career, and his political connections to enrich himself. He lent money to merchants, ambassadors, and pashas alike. He maintained a splendid household, with a harem and some five hundred slaves. Fluent in Greek, Italian, and Turkish and knowledgeable in European matters, Lodovico Gritti was the grand vizier's adviser regarding European politics.[86]

Łaski presented himself to the grand vizier on 22 December 1527. Ibrahim knew about John's dire situation from the Venetian vice *bailo* and Gritti. The grand vizier and the pashas signaled their willingness to help, but they insisted on an annual tribute, a sign of vassalage, which Łaski rejected. Gritti, who mediated between the envoy and the pashas, signaled that Ibrahim Pasha might renounce his claim to the tribute if King John were to send a present of 10,000 florins every year. Łaski retorted: "To send a present at fixed intervals is tantamount to paying a tribute." Through Gritti, the envoy conveyed to the pashas "the harmful effects of offering a tribute," stating that "the Hungarians would certainly look upon it with disgust, while the Christian powers would abandon Hungary; in fact, even King Francis would be forced to withdraw his support on this account."[87] Łaski, who had requested the restoration of Srem, hinted that King John might pay a tribute if he received this strategically important region between the Sava and Danube Rivers, which traditionally had played a key role in the defense of the country. Gritti told him that Süleyman would never give up Srem as he had several mosques erected there. As the defender of Islam, he could not return it to the infidels. Gritti also added that the Drava River—which bordered Srem on the northwest—formed a perfect border between the two countries, an observation echoed in contemporary Ottoman sources. Łaski's perseverance paid off. On 23 January 1528, he informed his king that Süleyman would personally come to his aid and would send his grand vizier with janissaries in advance. Łaski himself would march to Transylvania with the troops of the *sancak* governor of Nikopol and the son of the Wallachian voivode.[88] By 27 January 1528, Łaski had succeeded in concluding a treaty of alliance without the tribute. "I gratefully accept your king's goodwill," said Süleyman to Łaski through his interpreter. "His country, conquered by war and sword, has hitherto belonged to me, not to him. Still, having heard about his intentions, I hereby not only return the country to him but shall also assist him against the Austrian Ferdinand."[89] Łaski attributed his success to Gritti, with whom he fostered a friendship. Gritti now wanted an official status at the Porte. He asked Łaski to present him to Süleyman as King John's representative and agent (*orator et rerum negotiorum procurator*). Thus started the career of this shrewd adventurer. As King John's royal councillor, treasurer, and governor, Gritti would play a crucial role in Ottoman-Hungarian relations in the coming years.[90]

Łaski, who had become ill, left Constantinople only on 29 February with the agreement. The whereabouts of Süleyman's actual letter of agreement (*ahdname*), which was to be the basis of the post-Mohács Hungarian-Ottoman relations, remain unknown. The document identified by Hungarian historians as the historic *ahdname* has recently been proved to be a forgery, prepared in 1530 by King John's statesmen and disseminated in Europe for propaganda purposes. However, the relationship between Süleyman and his Hungarian vassal king would become a model for the leaders of the anti-Habsburg insurrections in Hungary who sought Ottoman help against the Habsburgs in the seventeenth and early eighteenth centuries. To attain support and similar documents of agreement at the Porte, they would send to the Porte the *ahdname* that King John had purportedly received from Süleyman.[91]

From the Porte's point of view, the alliance with King John rectified the unintended consequences of Süleyman's victory at Mohács. On their part, King John and his supporters hoped to avoid the Ottoman occupation of their country with the alliance, which they justified in Europe with the following arguments. First, King John, Hungary's duly elected king, fell under attack from Archduke Ferdinand of Habsburg, from whom the Hungarians expected military aid against the "infidel" Turk. Second, despite his propaganda and promises, Ferdinand failed to protect the country against the Turks, and thus King John struck a deal with Süleyman to avoid Ottoman occupation. Third, the treaty that King John concluded with Süleyman was based on "good and Christian conditions" (*bonis et christianibus condicionibus*). Fourth, the treaty established peace in Hungary and protected the kingdom against future Turkish attacks, and therefore served the interests of Christendom at large. Fifth, Habsburg pretensions for world supremacy posed a threat to the whole of Christendom. Sixth, Ferdinand sought military aid against the Turks but used it against his fellow Christian monarch, while he himself also negotiated with Süleyman. King John's diplomats used these arguments to defend him abroad. At the same time, they advanced accusations against the "Germans" and Ferdinand, who, in their view, wanted to extirpate the Magyar nation and language (*gentem et linguam nostram extirpare*). These accusations were intended to court domestic allies by exploiting the anti-German sentiments of the Magyar nobility.[92]

By late 1528, most Hungarians recognized that Ferdinand had done very little to defend their country against the Ottomans and that he only wanted the Hungarian throne. Ferdinand left the Hungarian capital in the spring of 1528, leaving behind a regency council. But the council also left Buda, first in late 1528 and then in August 1529. Ferdinand received no military aid from his emperor-brother either. On the contrary, he had to help Charles against the king of France. When Ferdinand ousted his rival from Hungary and controlled the country, his mercenaries did not even attempt to challenge the Ottoman border forces. Instead, the unpaid mercenaries preyed on Hungarian villages. Frustrated, the unpaid boatmen (Hun. *naszádos*) of the Danube flotilla, who were supposed to defend the capital, threatened Ferdinand with defecting to King John or the Turk. Should the boatmen defect, warned the royal regency council in May 1529, the enemy could easily take Buda. Because Ferdinand did nothing, by mid-June most of the boatmen defected to King John.[93] Ferdinand's policies disappointed his supporters too. Thus, they returned to his rival, helping King John regain control of the country.

The news of Łaski's success soon reached the Habsburg brothers. The imperial ambassador in Venice reported to the emperor on 9 March 1528 that "the Turk has received with great solemnity and pomp the ambassador of the voivode . . . and promised to make his master [i.e., King John] King of Hungary. For this purpose, the Sultan has raised 50,000 cavalry and given the command to" Ibrahim Pasha.[94] Through its vice *bailo* and ambassador, Venice urged Ibrahim to send the promised Ottoman military aid to John promptly and to order the *sancak* governor of Bosnia to attack Ferdinand's possession in Carniola, Carinthia, and Styria.[95] Ibrahim assured the vice *bailo* in late April that Ottoman troops would soon be dispatched to help King John.[96] Orders were soon issued to the *sancak* governors along the border, commanding them to assist King John. Ottoman frontier governors had already stepped up their attacks against Ferdinand.[97]

Ferdinand hoped to outmaneuver his rival at the Porte. Although Habsburg propaganda accused Szapolyai of being in league with Süleyman, it was Ferdinand who first approached the Ottomans. In mid-February 1527, Ferdinand approached the Ottoman *sancak* governors of

Bosnia and Smederevo to get their support. He emphasized his rights to Hungary, arguing that "the Transylvanian voivode" had no claim to the country. Ferdinand even tried to bribe Bali Beg of Smederevo, offering him up to 6,000 gold ducats in an attempt to lure him away from King John. At about the same time, Ferdinand sent a messenger to Constantinople to collect a letter of safe passage (*salvus conductus*) for his envoy, and in May contacted Yahyapaşazade Mehmed, successor and younger brother of the recently deceased Bali Beg.[98]

Ferdinand's diplomatic overtures did not remain a secret. Ibrahim Pasha promptly informed the Venetian *bailo* about the arrival of Ferdinand's messenger. The Venetians obtained a copy of the letter, which Ferdinand's chancellor wrote to Ibrahim Pasha.[99] Meanwhile, King John's men intercepted Ferdinand's letter to Yahyapaşazade Mehmed and used it to prove to their European allies that Ferdinand had incited the Turks against the duly elected and crowned Hungarian king.[100]

The diplomatic fiasco did not deter Ferdinand. In July 1527, before he launched his Hungarian campaign, Ferdinand drafted instructions for his envoy to Süleyman. The envoy had to remind Süleyman that the Emperors Frederick and Maximilian enjoyed peaceful relations with Süleyman's ancestors. The envoy also had to inform the sultan about Ferdinand's election and coronation in Hungary and Bohemia and Charles's recent victories. He was also to offer a three-year truce on behalf of the Habsburg brothers.[101] When his troops defeated King John and conquered Hungary, Ferdinand postponed his envoy's trip. However, having received the news about King John's treaty with Süleyman, Ferdinand sent his ambassadors, John Habardanecz, a Hungarian-Slavonian aristocrat, and Siegmund Weichselberger, the king's courtier from Carniola to Süleyman. It was too late.

Ferdinand's ambassadors arrived in Constantinople on 29 May and were met by an angry grand vizier. During the negotiations, which lasted from 31 May to 28 June, Ibrahim accused Ferdinand of occupying Buda, which Süleyman had conquered with his sword and therefore considered part of his domains. The ambassadors replied in vain that Ferdinand took Buda not from the sultan but from Szapolyai. They also echoed the Habsburg propaganda that Szapolyai had himself elected king of Hungary illegally, whereas Ferdinand won a fair election. Well informed about the Hungarian and European affairs, Ibrahim mocked the ambassadors, interrogating them about Ferdinand's power, wealth, and allies. This pleased the Venetian *bailo*, who was determined to derail the Habsburg mission. The *bailo* enjoyed the support of Gritti, the Porte's interpreter Yunus, and Ibrahim Pasha, "a true friend of the Republic" in the *bailo's* words.[102] Things quickly escalated when the ambassadors proposed that Süleyman return the border castles of Belgrade, Šabac, Slankamen, Severin, Orşova, Jajce, Banjaluka, Knin, and Skradin for a substantial sum. Ibrahim mockingly remarked: "I am surprised that he [Ferdinand] did not ask Constantinople."[103] Ibrahim made clear that if Ferdinand wanted peace, he had to surrender Hungary. "After that, we can talk about Germany."[104] Süleyman's answer to Ferdinand's ambassadors, on 28 June 1528, amounted to a declaration of war. "Until now, your master did not experience what I am as a friend and neighbor . . . but he soon will. You can tell your master that I will personally come with all my power and might to return to him with my own hands the castles he requested. You better warn him so that he is prepared to receive us."[105] The ambassadors could not communicate Süleyman's answer to their monarch as they were held back in the Ottoman capital until early December. Habardanecz arrived in Innsbruck (Austria) on 18 February 1529 to report to Ferdinand about his mission. However, nobody knew Süleyman's response, because no translators were able to translate the padishah's letter from Turkish.[106]

On 10 May 1529, Süleyman set out from his capital for his third Hungarian campaign to settle the Hungarian issue by restoring King John to his throne and "ousting the cursed Ferdinand."[107] The victory proclamation in November noted Ferdinand's attack against King John and his conquest of Buda as justification for the campaign. Attacked by Ferdinand, John had "asked Süleyman's protection and support." The padishah "accepted [John's] submission" and decided "to take the banners of Islam" to Hungary. The victory proclamation presented the campaign "against the cursed infidels" as a holy war, a duty of all Muslims, but especially the padishah.[108] In a last, desperate attempt, Ferdinand tried in vain to deter Süleyman from his plan by offering the sultan an annual tribute of up to 100,000 gold coins for a truce.[109] But Süleyman continued his march to Hungary. He met King John on 18 August in the Ottoman camp near the battlefield of Mohács, a calculated move to remind the Hungarians of the fateful battle in 1526.

Fifteen years after the events, the eyewitness Hungarian chronicler and King John's court chaplain, George Szerémi, described the meeting in detail. Upon seeing King John, dressed in an opulent kaftan and escorted by Grand Vizier Ibrahim Pasha and his retinue of five hundred Ottoman soldiers, the padishah embraced his ally. Then the two men proceeded into Süleyman's lavishly decorated tent. At the audience, Süleyman promised to restore King John to the throne, protect him against his enemies, and return the Srem region, except for the castles of Belgrade and Šabac.[110] After the meeting, the two armies marched toward Buda on the opposite banks of the Danube. Ferdinand's castellan defended Buda with two thousand imperial mercenaries. After less than a week of halfhearted defense, the mercenaries surrendered the Hungarian capital to Süleyman on 8 September. Despite the agreement, the janissaries slaughtered the defenders and enslaved the children and women. Having restored Buda to King John, the sultan departed for Vienna on 14 September.[111]

After the sultan left for Vienna, his officials performed a strange "enthronement" of King John in Buda. Accompanied by ornately dressed Turkish horsemen and janissaries, King John was led into the dining room of his palace. He was made to sit upon a "high priest's chair." The Turks instructed him to "sit down on that seat, because just as the emperor [Süleyman] ordered us, so must we install Your majesty in your royal office. Then they grabbed him and had him sit on the imperial seat, telling him three times in Slavic, which King John would have understood as he knew both south Slavic and Czech: 'May the Lord Most High give you good luck and bravery in governing Hungary.'"[112]

Ferdinand lost Buda because he could not get help from his brother. Charles's imperial troops were busy besieging Florence, a member of the anti-Habsburg League of Cognac. The Peace of Cambrai

(3–5 August 1529) came too late to have any effect on the events in Hungary.[113] In their diet in Speyer, the imperial Estates promised to provide soldiers, as did the Estates of Bohemia, Moravia, Silesia, and Lusatia in their gathering in Budějovice (Budweis) in July, but on the condition that these troops only be used to defend Vienna. Now that Süleyman was marching against his capital, Ferdinand was able to send seventeen thousand infantrymen, fourteen hundred heavy cavalrymen, and twelve hundred light horsemen to Vienna's defense. Although still outnumbered five to one, the defenders put up a good fight. The siege commenced on 27 September, rather late in the campaign season, because Süleyman wasted precious time during the long march and in Hungary. The Ottomans relied on the sappers as they did not have siege artillery. However, the defenders disarmed most of the Ottoman mines. When the mines breached the walls, pikemen and arquebusiers repulsed the attackers. After less than three weeks of fighting, Süleyman lifted the siege on 15 October, succumbing to the pressure from his fatigued, sick, and demoralized troops. They suffered from the unusually cold and rainy weather, early snow, and shortage of food.[114]

Süleyman failed to capture Vienna, but he restored his client to the Hungarian throne, leaving some three thousand Ottoman troops for his defense and control. Ottoman chroniclers claimed that Süleyman had King John crowned and that the latter agreed to pay an annual tribute of 50,000 florins to the sultan's treasury as a sign of his vassalage. Yet, King John never paid tribute to Süleyman. Reports about the "coronation" are also confusing. Süleyman asked King John to show him the Holy Crown of St. Stephen. Once he was given the crown, the sultan decided to take it to Constantinople. Two days later he changed his mind and returned the crown to the king with Peter Perényi, the guardian of the crown, Archbishop Paul Várdai of Esztergom (1526–49), and Lodovico Gritti. The campaign diary and the chronicler Calalzede thought that the three men were sent to crown King John on behalf of the sultan.[115] An Ottoman miniature from about 1557 depicts Süleyman handing a crown to King John. It has been interpreted that Süleyman "invested his vassal John Zapolya with the Holy Crown of St. Stephen in 1529," after which the padishah "began to use the proud title 'Distributor of the Monarchs of the World' in his correspondence with European rulers."[116] This is unlikely. Szapolyai had been elected and crowned in 1526 according to old Hungarian custom. A new "coronation" on Süleyman's order would not have enhanced his legitimacy in the eyes of the Hungarians. The title of "Distributor of the Monarchs of the World" also goes back to an earlier tradition, and Süleyman himself had used it in 1525.[117]

6

Imperial Rivalries

Ottoman-Habsburg Rivalry

On 5 November 1529, three weeks after the Habsburg victory at Vienna, Charles entered Bologna, following his artillery and thousands of his troops, some "arrayed in the manner of a phalanx of Alexander the Great's soldiers." Charles rode on a white horse in full armor beneath a canopy, reminding spectators of the triumphal entries of the victorious Roman emperors. When he approached Pope Clement VII, he dismounted and fell to his knees before the pope. The two men made peace. On 24 February 1530, Pope Clement handed the emperor the sword, orb, and scepter and crowned him Holy Roman emperor. The day—the thirtieth birthday of the emperor and the fifth anniversary of his victory at Pavia—marked the last time that a pope crowned an emperor, ending the centuries-old ritual, which had started when Charlemagne received the imperial crown from Pope Leo III.[1] A year later, in January 1531, the emperor's brother, Ferdinand, was elected king of the Romans and heir to the empire.

Frustrated by his fiasco at Vienna in 1529, irritated by Charles's coronation and claim to universal monarchy, and threatened by the Habsburgs' fifty-day siege of Buda in the winter of 1530, Süleyman decided to attack Vienna once more in 1532. When news about the sultan's campaign reached the Habsburg brothers, they gathered a surprisingly large army. The imperial Estates—including the Lutherans, who had received assurances that the emperor would not implement the Edict of Worms—voted to mobilize 38,000 infantry, 6,000 heavy cavalry, and 6,000 light cavalry. With the Bohemian troops, the army numbered some 55,000 soldiers, though an official calculation of 16 August put the Reich's army at only 6,000 heavy cavalry and 30,000 infantry. The emperor had about 42,000 troops. Pope Clement sent money sufficient to hire 8,000 to 10,000 Hungarian and Croatian hussars. Ferdinand later claimed that Charles V's army altogether numbered 80,000 foot soldiers and 6,000 cavalrymen. He used over 400,000 ducats from the French ransom to pay his troops. In late August, Paolo Giovio, who was with the emperor in Regensburg, calculated that Charles's army would number 100,000 foot soldiers and 25,000 horsemen, with 75,000 camp followers. Ferdinand gathered 42,000 infantry, 6,000 heavy cavalry, 2,000 light horsemen, and 10,000 men of the Danube flotilla. The official estimate of 16 August put the combined military and auxiliary manpower of the Habsburg brothers and that of the Reich at 222,820 men.[2]

Whatever the actual size of the army, it was sufficiently strong to deter Süleyman. Fortune, again, helped Charles. The rains in June and July swelled the rivers, which, noted Charles, "allowed us time to repair and strengthen the fortification of Vienna." To stop the marching Ottoman army before it reached Vienna, Ferdinand dispatched his envoys to Süleyman. He requested peace and offered to surrender his Hungarian possessions, except for a few strategically essential fortresses that were vital for the defense of his Austrian hereditary lands.[3] The padishah rejected the offer and continued his march to Vienna. "The king of Spain—wrote Süleyman to Ferdinand from Osijek—has proclaimed for a long time that he wants to act against the Turks; and now, by the grace of God, I am advancing with my army against him. If he is a man who has balls and courage, let him come and draw up his army in the field ready to fight with my imperial host, and the issue will be whatever God wills. If, however, he does not want to meet me, let him send his tribute to my Imperial Majesty."[4]

Neither Charles nor Süleyman wanted to risk a battle. This reluctance explains why Süleyman spent three weeks with the siege of the small Hungarian fort Kőszeg in northwestern Hungary, some one hundred kilometers from Vienna. Commanded by Ferdinand's captain-general,

The young Charles V. This portrait shows Charles V around 1530,
when he was crowned Holy Roman emperor by Pope Clement VII,
the last emperor to be crowned by a pope, and was at the peak of his power.
(Low Countries, manner of Jan Cornelisz Vermeyen, c. 1530.
Courtesy of the Rijksmuseum, Amsterdam, SK-A-164.)

the Croatian Nikola Jurišić, the fort had only eight hundred defenders,
mainly burghers and peasants. In the end, Süleyman was contented with
Jurišić's symbolic surrender, arranged by Ibrahim Pasha, who knew
Jurišić from his 1530 embassy to Constantinople. Having "conquered"
Kőszeg symbolically (Jurišić kept the fort), Süleyman returned to
Constantinople.

Though militarily unsuccessful, the 1532 campaign allowed Ibrahim
Pasha to present his master as a world conqueror, directly responding

to Charles's coronation celebrations in Bologna. Süleyman's imperial entries to Niš and Belgrade—whose streets were decorated with triumphal arches "in the manner of ancient Roman triumphs"—reminded European observers of Emperor Charles's coronation. In the procession and during audiences, the padishah's pages displayed headpieces lavishly decorated with jewels and pearls. One of these headpieces was a four-tier ceremonial crown-helmet that Ibrahim and Lodovico Gritti had commissioned from and financed by a consortium of Venetian goldsmiths, merchants, nobles, and the sultan's chief treasurer. It had fifty diamonds, forty-seven rubies, twenty-seven emeralds, forty-nine pearls, and a large turquoise. It was valued at 144,400 Venetian ducats, a staggering sum comparable to the Ottoman treasury's annual revenue from the rich Damascus province. Süleyman's four-tier ceremonial crown-helmet bore "a striking resemblance to the papal tiara." It also purposefully imitated the crown that Charles wore during his coronation in Bologna. The crown-helmet intended to send a symbolic message to the padishah's European rivals: Süleyman challenged the authority of both the pope and the emperor.[5]

The parades orchestrated by Ibrahim Pasha demonstrated not only the Ottoman policy-makers' knowledge of Charles V's imperial ambitions but also the Ottomans' familiarity with the language and symbols of imperial aspirations in contemporary Europe. While these processions had a significant impact on the formation of Süleyman's image in Europe as "the Magnificent" emperor, they could hardly mask the campaign's failure. The padishah did not attempt to defeat his archenemy or to besiege his rival's capital.

The multiple commitments of the Habsburgs (northern Italy, Germany, the Netherlands, the Mediterranean, North Africa, and Hungary), as well as the divergent priorities of Charles and Ferdinand, led to a stalemate between Ferdinand and King John, with each controlling only parts of Hungary. Occupied with the war against the German Protestant electors and Estates, Charles instructed his brother to avoid confrontation with Süleyman. The emperor again urged his brother to conclude a peace with the sultan, for—as he had stated back in 1531—"the two of us alone are weak" against the Turks.[6] After the sultan returned

SVLIMAN·OTOMAN·REX·TVRC· X·

This engraving from 1535 shows Sultan Süleyman wearing his four-tier
ceremonial crown-helmet, which the sultan displayed during his 1532
Hungarian campaign and reminded contemporary European observers
of Charles V's crown and the papal tiara. (Agostino Veneziano [Musi].
Courtesy of the Hungarian National Museum, Budapest, TKCs 3915.)

home from the 1532 campaign, he accepted Ferdinand's request for
peace because he wanted to focus on the Safavids.

Ferdinand's ambassador, the Dalmatian Jerome of Zara, negotiated
the truce at the Porte.[7] Provided that King John remained unmarried,
Ferdinand was willing to return some castles and territory to his rival,
except for Komárom and other principal forts defending Vienna. Jerome

reached Constantinople on 10 January 1533. On 21 January he informed his sovereign that "by the Grace of God" he concluded the "much desired, honorable, glorious, useful, and long peace between the Invincible Emperor of the Turks and Your Sacred Royal Majesty."[8] He dispatched his son and secretary Vespasian to Vienna, while he remained in Constantinople to reassure Süleyman of the sincerity of Ferdinand's promises. In two separate letters, Süleyman informed Ferdinand and Charles about his decision. Although Süleyman had conquered the Kingdom of Hungary and given it to King John, the sultan was willing to recognize the partition of Hungary between the two kings. To delimit the borders between the Ottoman and Habsburg domains, Süleyman dispatched Lodovico Gritti to Hungary.[9] Despite Jerome's enthusiasm, the treaty remained a verbal promise, which, for the time being, Süleyman considered valid.

However, Gritti was not able to complete his mission of demarcating the borders. In September 1534 Gritti was murdered by the pro-Szapolyai Czibak clan.[10] The padishah dispatched Yunus Beg, the Porte's interpreter, to Hungary to investigate Gritti's death. Sending Yunus was a curious choice, as he hated Gritti. The investigation did not lead to imminent Ottoman retaliation. Süleyman was occupied with his campaign against the Safavids, and Ibrahim Pasha—Gritti's patron— was executed in 1536. Nevertheless, Yunus's hostility toward the Hungarians during the inquiry alerted King John to the dangers of his alliance with the Ottomans, pushing him closer to Ferdinand. Having successfully concluded his "campaign of the two Iraqs" (1534–35) against Shah Tahmasb (r. 1524–76) of Persia, Süleyman now considered the 1533 truce with Ferdinand void, citing, among others, the failure to demarcate the borders between his and Ferdinand's domains. The clash between the Ottomans and the Habsburgs on land was averted only because they confronted each other at sea.

Charles V's Mediterranean fleet was under the able leadership of Andrea Doria. The Genoese maritime condottiere had entered the emperor's service after his contract with Francis I of France expired in 1528. Doria's conquest of Koron and Patras in 1532 alerted the Ottomans to the danger in the Aegean. In 1533, Süleyman summoned the *ghazi* corsair

Hayreddin Barbarossa to Constantinople. In late September, the Ottomans received the corsair and his eighteen captains with great pomp in Constantinople. Having visited Ibrahim Pasha in Aleppo in early 1534, Hayreddin was appointed grand admiral of the Mediterranean fleet with the title of governor-general of the newly created province of the Archipelago.[11]

Hayreddin offered a bold plan for dislodging the Spanish Habsburgs from the Mediterranean and helping the Muslims in Spain. He noted that the western Mediterranean was too far from the Ottoman capital. He suggested that the Ottomans install in Tunis the brother of the Hafsid ruler al-Hasan (1526–34, 1535–43), Rashid. If Rashid were an Ottoman vassal and if "the harbor of Goletta were taken and protected by the [Ottoman] sovereign, the imperial fleet could be stationed in it most of the time. In that case, with the help of God the Sublime, it would be feasible to conquer and subdue Spain from there."[12] Hayreddin conquered Tunis in 1534. However, Charles V's campaign cut short the Ottoman attempts to extend Ottoman rule into Tunis.

While Süleyman was campaigning in Azerbaijan and Iraq, Charles scored his greatest victory against Islam. Under the emperor's command, the allied Christian navy captured La Goletta and Tunis. Painters, poets, and official chroniclers celebrated the emperor's Tunis campaign in 1535 as a victorious crusade against the enemies of the faith. The emperor's triumphal march in 1535–36 in Italy and his imperial entries into Palermo, Messina, Naples, Rome, and Florence, organized after similar triumphal entries of the Roman Caesars, presented a prolonged opportunity to propagate Charles's image as defender of Christendom, "Destroyer of the Turks," and "the Tamer of Africa." They were also a fitting answer to Süleyman's 1532 processions.[13]

Süleyman responded to Charles's Tunis campaign by raiding Italy near Brindisi and Otranto. In 1538, Hayreddin Barbarossa won a splendid victory at Preveza, off northwestern Greece, against the joint naval forces of the Holy League of Spain, Venice, Genoa, the papacy, Portugal, and the Knights of St. John, commanded by Doria. Historians have used Barbarossa's victory at Preveza to illustrate the defensive potency of the combined use of war galleys and shore batteries. The allied fleet had a clear superiority of fighting strength—130 war galleys and round ships carrying the artillery and 6,000 soldiers versus Barbarossa's 90 galleys and 50 galiots. Nevertheless, Barbarossa's decisiveness and the effectiveness of the Ottoman shore batteries, which dominated both sides of the entrance of the Gulf of Preveza, won the battle. Although Tunis remained in Spanish hands until 1569 (and again in 1573–74), the naval battle at Preveza proved to be more critical in the long run.[14]

Over the following decades, the Ottomans further strengthened their control in the Mediterranean. During the emperor's fatal expedition against Algiers in 1541, which contemporaries estimated to have cost him 4 million gold coins, Charles lost 130 ships and 17 galleys in a winter storm.[15] In 1551, under the command of Grand Admiral Sinan Pasha (1548–55), the Ottomans captured Tripoli. Sinan was succeeded by Piyale. A Croatian (or Hungarian) from the Hungarian town of Tolna, Piyale had been captured at the battle of Mohács in 1526. He was educated in the Topkapı Palace and appointed grand admiral of the navy in 1555. In 1560, Piyale Pasha, with some 120 galleys and other ships, took Djerba and defeated yet another Holy League aimed at retaking Tripoli.[16]

Meanwhile, Ottoman-Habsburg relations on land also deteriorated when Ottoman forces attacked Croatia and Slavonia. In the face of the Ottoman attacks, the Croatian and Slavonian nobles tried to survive by cooperating with the conquerors, moving to the north under Habsburg rule, or fighting the Turks. The Zrínyis tried all these options. From the 1530s onward they opted to fight the Ottomans. As early as 1534, Second Vizier Ayas Pasha complained to Ferdinand's envoy about the young Count Nicholas Zrínyi, "whose father was one of our tax-payers. But with him dead, his son has risen up against us, and not only does he not want to pay taxes, but he does much damage to the Sultan's subjects, robbing and massacring all those who cross his path. We want to punish him."[17] The Ottomans repeated their complaints in the coming years and in 1536 occupied both banks of the Sava.

Ferdinand authorized his general, Hans Katzianer, to regain control over the Drava and Sava Rivers by capturing Osijek, the Ottoman military base that guarded the padishah's famous bridge over the Drava into Hungary. But famine, epidemics, and quarrel among its leaders prevented the army from investing Osijek. They decided to withdraw but were bogged down in the nearby swamps, and were forced to leave behind their cannons and heavy armament. Katzianer fled, leaving his army of sixteen thousand infantry and eight thousand cavalry in the lurch. On 9 October 1537, the retreating Habsburg army suffered a humiliating defeat at Gorjan, near Osijek, at the hands of the *sancak* governor of Smederevo. Most of the troops were annihilated. Many of its leaders were killed, including Paul (Pavle) Bakić, who had served Ferdinand over the past ten years as captain of the Serbian hussars and was recently appointed as despot of the Serbs. Blaming Katzianer for the catastrophic defeat, Ferdinand imprisoned his general and appointed Nicholas Jurišić as commander of the Habsburg troops in Croatia. Katzianer later escaped from his Vienna prison (31 January 1538) and fled to Croatia, where he had good connections. He found refuge in Kostajnica on the Una River, the base of the Zrínyi family. Now Katzianer wanted to defect to King John, deliver Kostajnica to the Turks, and carve out an Ottoman-vassal principality. At least this is what Ferdinand thought and could not let happen. He ordered the Zrínyis to eliminate Katzianer, which they did on 31 January 1539.[18] In the meantime, the Ottomans integrated the newly conquered lands, most of what had been Požega county in the Kingdom of Hungary, into the Ottoman *sancak* of Požega, established in 1538.

King John showed little interest in Katzianer's plans. Recent Ottoman advances pushed the two Hungarian kings closer to each other. In late 1537, the parties resumed negotiations. They reached an agreement in early 1538, thanks to George Martinuzzi. The former Paulist monk was known to his contemporaries as Friar or Brother George (Frater Georgius), and Brata (Brother) to the Ottomans. As King John's leading statesman he played a crucial role in shaping Ottoman-Hungarian-Habsburg relations.[19] The Treaty of Várad, concluded on 24 February 1538, was his first significant diplomatic achievement. In it, Kings John and Ferdinand temporarily recognized the partition of Hungary, acknowledging each other's sovereignty over the lands they controlled. King John agreed that after his death his kingdom would revert to the House of Habsburg, even if he were to father a lawful heir. In this case—which few considered because John was fifty-one years of age and still unmarried—his heir would receive the (nonexistent) "Principality of Szepes" (Slov. Spiš). The parties agreed to keep the treaty secret in order to prevent a punitive Ottoman campaign, because they knew that Süleyman would not tolerate the Habsburg takeover of eastern Hungary. The Habsburgs were allowed to make the treaty public only if they were able to defend Hungary against the Ottomans.[20]

When informed about Süleyman's campaign in 1538, Friar George feared that the padishah's target was Hungary. Much to his relief, Süleyman turned against Moldavia. He wanted to depose the disloyal Moldavian voivode Petru Rareş. The voivode had concluded an anti-Ottoman treaty with the Habsburgs in 1535, disobeyed the padishah's orders to send soldiers against Ferdinand, and attacked both Transylvania (an Ottoman vassal) and Pokucie (Pokuttia in present-day western Ukraine). The latter act complicated Ottoman-Polish relations. In 1531, the Poles had reconquered this historic region, long disputed by the Poles and Moldavians. The Poles, who had signed an "eternal peace" with the Porte in 1533, protested against Rareş's attacks, requesting the Porte to remove him from Moldavia. Süleyman responded to his vassal's insubordination with the 1538 campaign, which he also used to cement his rule in the northern Black Sea littoral. The expedition, in alliance with the Poles and Crimean Tatars, resulted in the conquest of the strategic forts of Bender, upstream on the Dniester River, and Ochakiv at the mouth of the Dnieper River, along with southern Bessarabia (Budjak) and the Black Sea shoreline up to the Dnieper. Süleyman appointed Stephen (Ştefan) Lăcustă—who had spent years at the Porte—the new voivode of the territorially reduced Moldavian vassal principality. The voivode's coronation in the padishah's imperial *divan*, his appointment diploma, and the presence of an Ottoman military unit in the Moldavian capital signaled Moldavia's tightened vassalage, similar to that of Wallachia.[21]

Quest for Universal Kingship

As "Servant of the Two Holy Sanctuaries," Süleyman was responsible for the safety of the annual pilgrimage to Mecca. By sending the annual aid for the populations of the two Holy Cities, and by building and restoring mosques and other public buildings in Mecca and Medina, Süleyman cultivated his legitimacy among his Muslim subjects.[22]

Around 1540, Süleyman also assumed the title of caliph. The title was occasionally applied to earlier Ottoman rulers. But it was from 1540 onward that the caliphal title received particular emphasis, appearing more frequently in Ottoman documents, including the Venetian capitulation of 1540, and the Law Book of the newly established Buda province (1546). Şeyhülislam Ebussuud Efendi described Süleyman as "Caliph of the Messenger of the Lords of the Worlds . . . Possessor of the Supreme Imamate . . . Inheritor of the Great Caliphate." With such titles, Ebussuud intended to counterbalance the Safavid shah Tahmasb's claims for sovereignty over Ottoman subjects living in eastern Asia Minor and Azerbaijan. He also hoped to challenge Charles V's claims to universal Christian rule.[23]

One example of the propaganda war and clash of imperial ideologies between the Habsburgs and Ottomans was their competing titles.[24] Süleyman styled himself the ruler of the four Holy Cities of Islam—Mecca, Medina, Hebron, and Jerusalem—in his rather lengthy list of official titles. Moreover, he titled himself supreme emperor: "Sultan of Sultans," world conqueror, and padishah.[25] Süleyman's claim of being the sultan of Jerusalem conflicted with that of Charles. The Habsburg ruler included Jerusalem among his titles even in letters sent to Süleyman.[26]

Charles had his propagandists depict him as the emperor destined to recapture the Holy Land from the "infidels." Charles inherited both the Spanish and the Austrian/Germanic expectations of the coming of a universal monarch. His supporters viewed and presented Charles as the "Last World Emperor," under whose reign the Jews and pagans would be converted. It was suggested that this would be followed by the thousand-year reign of Christ and the Last Judgment. As early as 1515 portrayals of the then "Prince of Spain" depicted Charles as the future redeemer of Jerusalem. By 1519–20, Charles was the "King of the Romans, elected Emperor, always August, King of Spain, Sicily, Jerusalem, the Balearic Islands, Hungary, Dalmatia, Croatia, and the Indies." In 1519, Grand Chancellor Gattinara recognized divine inspiration in Charles's election as Holy Roman emperor, which signaled the "restoration of *sacrum*

Imperium" and predicted that Charles would recover the Holy Land.[27] An Augsburg armorer monogrammed Charles's suit of plate armor in 1525 "KD," standing for "Karolus Divus" (Charles the Divine). Charles and his councillors believed that Charles's victory over Francis and the capture of the French king at the battle of Pavia in 1525 came from God

> so that after the end of these civil wars (for that is what they should be called, since they are among Christians), he could seek out the Turks and Muslims in their own lands and, exalting our Holy Catholic faith as his ancestors had done, win the empire of Constantinople and the Holy City of Jerusalem, which are occupied because of our sins.[28]

As mentioned, Charles's coronation in Bologna in 1530 presented an opportunity to promote the image of the emperor as the defender of the Catholic faith who would defeat the Turks in a new crusade.

Millenarian prophecies and apocalyptic expectations were also current in the Ottoman Empire.[29] They influenced public opinion and the padishah's image makers—most notably Ibrahim Pasha and Lodovico Gritti. Ibrahim played an exceptional role in devising Ottoman imperial ideology and policy, publicizing Süleyman's image as the ruler of a new universal empire. He viewed Süleyman as the new world conqueror, the successor of Alexander the Great (his and his master's historical hero). Süleyman's European contemporaries knew of the padishah's imperial aspirations. In his speech before the Castilian Cortez in late 1527, Gattinara listed all the Ottoman conquests in Asia and Europe to remind his audience that Süleyman already ruled over a much larger empire than did Alexander the Great or the Caesars of Rome. He warned his Castilian listeners of Süleyman's intentions to build "a world empire."[30]

Gattinara did not exaggerate Süleyman's imperial ambitions. Ibrahim mentioned to a Venetian envoy how a book of prophecies, which he and Süleyman had read in their youth, predicted the rise of a man called Ibrahim and his master's triumph as the conqueror of the Roman Empire.[31] In December 1527, Second Vizier Mustafa Pasha reminded Jerome Łaski, the envoy of King John of Hungary, that Süleyman was second only to the Providence, and as there was only one sun on the horizon, there was only one ruler of the world: his master.[32] In February 1530,

Ibrahim Pasha registered his disappointment that the Venetians signed the Treaty of Bologna with Charles V and Ferdinand I. The grand vizier told the Venetian ambassador that "the faith of the Christians was writ in snow, that of the Sultan in marble." He added that "there must need be but one monarch in the world, either the emperor or his own lord."[33] In 1531 Erasmus noted that it was public knowledge that "the Turk will invade Germany with all his forces, in a contest for the greatest of prizes, to see whether Charles will be the monarch of the whole world or the Turk. For the world can no longer bear two suns in the sky."[34]

However, both emperors soon realized that universal kingship was beyond their reach and that they had to compromise. The result of this compromise was the partition of Hungary and the establishment of Ottoman and Habsburg military frontiers along the Danube, which guarded the delicate balance between the champions of Catholicism and those of Islam for the next 150 years.

Realpolitik and the Partition of Hungary

On 2 March 1539 at Székesfehérvár, King John married Isabella Jagiellon, daughter of Sigismund I of Poland. Isabella was duly crowned queen of Hungary the same day. A year later, on 7 July 1540, the queen gave birth to a boy, John Sigismund. King John died two weeks later. His death upset the military balance between the Habsburgs and the Ottomans in Hungary, leading to the partition of the country. Obeying his master's wishes, Friar George dispatched chancellor Stephen Werbőczy to Constantinople, asking Süleyman to acknowledge and protect his master's infant son. The friar hastily convened a diet at Rákos, which elected John Sigismund king of Hungary in September. The diet also appointed a regency council, consisting of Friar George, Peter Petrović, ban of Temes, and Valentine Török, captain-general of Transdanubia. On 17 October, the elderly chancellor reported from Constantinople Süleyman's favorable decision: "I can inform your lordships that after we had refuted our opponents' [Ferdinand's] arguments, with the Good Lord's help, we received from His Majesty [Süleyman] the desired response to all our proposals. His Majesty left the son of our master, born of happy memory, on his father's throne with all jurisdiction within the borders of Hungary and Transylvania."[35]

In the meantime, several of King John's former supporters who were sidelined after the king's death defected to Ferdinand. One of these men, voivode Stephen Maylád, wanted to seize power in Transylvania with the help of all interested parties—Queen Isabella, the Transylvanian Estates, Ferdinand, and Süleyman. He negotiated with all parties and played them against each other, unleashing a destructive civil war in Transylvania. However, when Maylád asked Süleyman to appoint him voivode of Transylvania, promising in return an annual tribute of 25,000 florins, Süleyman rejected him. The padishah ordered Maylád to serve "King Stephen" (Tr. Istefan)—as John Sigismund was known to the Ottomans—the same way he had served his deceased father.[36]

The fate of the House of Szapolyai and the Eastern Hungarian Kingdom was soon decided. By the autumn of 1540, Friar George and his men were in Buda to defend the capital city against Ferdinand's troops, who wanted to take possession of Buda under the Treaty of Várad. From October through early November, Habsburg troops conquered Visegrád, Székesfehérvár, and the poorly reinforced Pest, opposite Buda. But they failed to take the much better fortified Buda, vigorously defended by Friar George. Having left a garrison in Pest, they left.[37]

Ferdinand would not accept that Friar George outmaneuvered him. He was determined to secure Hungary at all costs. He revealed the secret Treaty of Várad to Süleyman, hoping that the padishah would abandon the friar and accept Habsburg rule in Hungary. Ferdinand commissioned his skillful diplomat, Jerome Łaski (who had deserted King John earlier), with the delicate task. In Constantinople, Łaski was arrested and Süleyman ordered his troops to prepare for next year's Hungarian campaign. Süleyman assured Friar George and Peter Petrović that he would protect the country against Ferdinand, for which he had made necessary preparations.[38] Ferdinand's generals were unable to wrest Buda from Friar George in the spring and summer of 1541. When they learned about the approaching Ottoman army, they lifted the siege and fled.

Arriving near Pest on 26 August, Süleyman pitched camp the next day north of Buda, as the Danube south of the city was full of corpses due to the long Habsburg siege. The next day, the sultan sent a letter to Queen Isabella, thanking her for the defense of Buda castle and announcing that he wanted to see the son of the late King John. In the imperial council held in the sultan's tent, the pashas disagreed as to what should happen to Isabella, her son, and their supporters. Yahyapaşazade Mehmed of Smederevo, known for his anti-Hungarian feelings, suggested killing the Hungarian magnates, sending the queen back to Poland to her parents, and taking her child to Constantinople to be raised there as a Muslim. He also proposed that Hungary should be occupied and turned into an Ottoman province to eliminate the need to help the queen with repeated and costly campaigns. However, Rüstem Pasha advocated for a peaceful transition so that the padishah could keep his promise to protect the queen and her son. Isabella's letter and presents, including her jewelry, which the queen sent to Rüstem and his wife Mihrimah, Süleyman's daughter, may have influenced Rüstem's more moderate views. Weeping and fearful, Isabella sent her son to Süleyman on 29 August, as requested. The sultan took the child in his hand, kissed him, then handed him to his sons, Selim and Bayezid, so that they could also kiss the child and consider him as their adopted brother. The occasion also enabled the padishah to inspect the child and refute the rumor—propagated either Mehmed Pasha or Jerome Łaski— that the boy was a girl. While the pro-Szapolyai magnates and politicians—Friar George, Valentine Török, Peter Petrović, and Stephen Werbőczy—paid their respect at Süleyman's military camp to discuss the future of their country, some three thousand Ottoman janissaries took possessions of the Hungarian capital, on the fifteenth anniversary of the battle of Mohács. In his message to Isabella, Süleyman told the dowager queen that he had to come to Hungary's defense many times in the past and that he could no longer do so, as other parts of his empire demanded his attention as well. Süleyman decided to take Buda under his control to defend it against the Germans, since, as he told Isabella, "as a womanly creature, and your son being still in the cradle and in the arms of his nurse" she was unable to defend and govern the country. However, Süleyman promised the queen that he would return Buda to her son when the king elect became of age. On Friday, 2 September,

This woodcut shows the siege of Buda in 1541 by Ferdinand I's troops.
Led by Wilhelm von Roggendorf, the Habsburg troops besieged the Hungarian
capital from 4 May through 21 August, hoping to capture it before Sultan Süleyman's
army reached it. Friar George defended Buda against the Habsburgs.
Sultan Süleyman took it on 29 August without a fight. (Woodcut by Erhard Schön.
Courtesy of the Hungarian National Museum, Budapest, TKCs 9129b.)

Süleyman entered Buda, and his name was mentioned during the prayer, performed in the Church of Assumption, which the Ottomans turned into a congregational mosque.[39]

Despite his promise to the Magyar nobility and Queen Isabella that he would return Buda to John Sigismund, the padishah's letter to his grand vizier, left behind in Constantinople, revealed his true intention: he decided to keep Buda for good. During King John's lifetime, Süleyman had maintained his influence in Hungary through his vassal. After King John's death, the padishah concluded that Queen Isabella could not defend Buda and that a possible Habsburg conquest of the Hungarian capital, which controlled the Danubian waterways, would compromise his strategic standing in Europe. Süleyman also distrusted the Hungarians, especially after he learned about the Treaty of Várad.

In his victory proclamation, Süleyman declared that he had conquered and attached Hungary to his empire, "with all its castles, provinces and inhabitants," ordered Muslim judges and garrison troops for its defense, and appointed Süleyman Pasha (apparently a Hungarian renegade) as the first governor-general of the newly established Ottoman province of Buda.[40] For the next 145 years, Buda was to function as the administrative center of Ottoman Hungary, known in Ottoman documents as the "strong bulwark of Islam."

Since eastern Hungary lay outside the main military corridor leading from Ottoman Belgrade to Habsburg Vienna, Süleyman did not consider its imminent conquest necessary. The padishah gave Transylvania and the Temes region—including the castles Lippa (Rom. Lipova), Solymos (Rom. Şoimoş), Karánsebes (Rom. Caransebeş) and Temesvár—as an Ottoman *sancak* to John Sigismund and Peter Petrović, a staunch supporter of the Szapolyai family. The sultan also appointed Friar George to govern the lands of John Sigismund until he came of age, and ordered Peter Petrović to be in charge of military affairs. If needed, Isabella could count on the military aid of the two Romanian voivodes and the pasha of Buda. Queen Isabella and his retinue left Buda on 5 September, arriving in Lippa by 18 September. Süleyman may have intended to integrate Transylvania into his empire. However, the stalemate with the Habsburgs and the partition of Hungary in the Habsburg-Ottoman treaty of 1547 allowed it to evolve into an autonomous country under the rule of Queen Isabella and John Sigismund, covering the eastern part of the Hungarian Kingdom and Transylvania.[41] Often described as an Ottoman vassal or tributary state, Transylvania had a complex and ever-changing legal status. At times it was under double Ottoman and Habsburg suzerainty with full privileges to handle domestic affairs and conduct foreign policy. At other times, it concluded international treaties without any interference from its nominal suzerains and was perceived and accepted by the European powers as a polity independent from both Vienna and Constantinople.[42]

The Ottoman conquest of Buda in 1541 shocked Europe. The imperial Estates offered their most effective military aid thus far to Ferdinand. In their assembly in Speyer in February 1542, they approved the hiring of twenty-four thousand infantrymen and four thousand cavalry mercenaries to recapture Buda.[43] Depressed by the destruction of his navy at the coast of Algiers in November 1541, Emperor Charles reneged on his promise to lead the expedition personally, citing the news about imminent Ottoman and French attacks. The emperor's fears were justified when the king of France declared war on him (May 1542), breaking the Truce of Nice, which had been concluded in 1538 for ten years.

Ferdinand's attempt in 1542 to expel the Ottomans from Buda ended in humiliation. The inept Joachim II, the elector of Brandenburg, proved to be a poor replacement for the emperor. Joachim had thirty thousand foot soldiers and seven thousand cavalry under his command, with fifteen thousand Hungarian cavalrymen joining them in Hungary. A flotilla of two hundred ships supported the expedition. The army proceeded along the Danube, using the river for transporting troops, weaponry, and food. Frustrated by late payments and hampered by disease, the mercenaries marched slowly, reaching Esztergom rather late, on 20 August. Süleyman got wind of the campaign preparations from France and his spies. He promptly ordered the Bosnian and Rumelian forces to help Buda.

Having reached Pest at the end of September 1542, the imperial army started to bombard the walls in earnest. The heavy bombardment destroyed a large enough section of the walls to attempt the attack. But the assault failed. Discouraged by the failed attack and fearing the Ottoman relief army, the German command lifted the siege of Pest on 8 October, after ten days of fighting. The German Empire's attempt to recapture Buda from the Ottomans failed even before the army shot a single cannonball at the Hungarian capital.[44] Insufficiently provisioned and decimated by disease, only about a fourth of the imperial mercenaries returned home. The soldiers brought with them a lethal illness, later identified as louse-borne typhus, a disease of war and famine. Although the disease was already known in Italy, Spain, and France, infected German mercenaries returning from the campaign of 1542 spread it throughout Europe, causing typhus fever outbreaks in Bohemia, Austria, and Germany. The disease would be known in Europe as the "Hungarian fever" or "Hungarian disease."[45]

By then, Charles had been fighting Francis, who invaded his domains on three different fronts: near Perpignan in southern France, Milan, and Antwerp. "I cannot do everything and be everywhere," Charles wrote to Ferdinand at the end of 1542. Therefore, "you must not count on my help, because I have enough problems—indeed, I fear, too many—of my own." Referring to Francis, he added, "I hope soon to reduce to reason our dear brother and friend, the most Christian King."[46] But the "most Christian King" allied himself with the sultan. Francis had viewed the Ottomans as a useful counterweight to Charles. "I cannot deny," said the French king to a Venetian envoy in March 1531, "that I keenly desire the Turk powerful and ready for war, not for himself, because he is an infidel and we are Christians, but to undermine the emperor's power, to force heavy expenses upon him and to reassure all other governments against so powerful an enemy."[47] In August 1543, a Franco-Ottoman fleet of 200 galleys, 16 large ships, and 2 galleasses under the command of Hayreddin Barbarossa besieged Nice, ruled by the emperor's ally the duke of Savoy. The French and the Turks jointly plundered and torched the lower town. However, their uncoordinated attack failed to take the citadel. Threatened by Andrea Doria's relief navy, they lifted the siege in early September. The French offered the port of Toulon as winter quarters for Barbarossa's 110 galleys and 30,000 men. Local authorities emptied the town, fearing the marauding Turks. However, contemporary accounts noted the discipline and order that Barbarossa kept in the vast Ottoman camp. In April 1544, the Ottoman navy was sent home. The French compensated the frustrated Barbarossa and his men with sacks of money, which thirty-two treasurers distributed for three days. Barbarossa took the Turkish and Barbary oarsmen from the French galleys and the French admiral to Constantinople.[48] The Franco-Ottoman military operations accomplished little strategically. Yet, the assaults impeded the emperor from helping Ferdinand in 1543, when Süleyman personally led his troops into Hungary, for the sixth time in just two decades.

Süleyman left Edirne on 23 April 1543. Following the Plovdiv (Filibe)–Sofia–Niš–Kruševac (Alacahisar) military road of his previous Hungarian campaigns, he arrived at Belgrade on 5 June. He crossed the border river Drava at Osijek on 22 June and arrived at Valpó (modern Valpovo) two days later. From Valpó the padishah marched against Siklós, which surrendered after eleven days of siege. Meanwhile, the *sancak* governors of Požega and Mohács captured Pécs, one of the largest towns in Hungary. Arriving in Buda on 23 July, the padishah and his pashas held a council meeting at which the leadership decided to attack Esztergom, the former seat of the primate-archbishop of Esztergom, the highest-ranking prelate in Hungary. Since 1530, Esztergom had been one of Ferdinand's key fortresses, which lay just fifty kilometers northwest of Ottoman Buda on the right bank of the Danube. Having repulsed several attacks, the castle's Spanish, Italian, and German mercenaries, some twenty-two hundred men, surrendered on 10 August. Süleyman celebrated his conquest by attending Friday prayer in the former cathedral, converted to a congregational mosque. The army then moved against Székesfehérvár, which controlled a large area in Transdanubia. It surrendered on 4 September. Meanwhile, the Crimean Tatars ravaged Transdanubia.[49]

Historians have long debated the goal of the campaign, some suggesting that Süleyman wanted to take Vienna. Süleyman informed the Venetian doge in mid-July that he would not stay long in Buda because he wanted to march against Vienna and then against Germany.[50] On the other hand, his victory proclamation—sent to the doge of Venice and issued at Smederevo on the way back to his capital in the middle of October—claimed the campaign was a response to the Habsburg attack on Buda the previous year, when the "Kings of Austria and Germany" invaded Hungary. Having conquered Esztergom and Székesfehérvár, "the burial place of the Hungarian kings," and unable to get news about the whereabouts of Ferdinand and Charles, Süleyman returned to "the seat of the Caliphate."[51] This may sound like a post-factum explanation, but other sources agree with it. The padishah cited Ferdinand's attack against Pest as the main reason for his campaign in February, when he informed Friar George about his impending expedition. On 8 May 1543, Friar George wrote Ferdinand that the padishah's targets were Pécs, Esztergom, and Székesfehérvár.[52]

The campaign cost the Porte more than a million Venetian ducats, about a fourth or a third of the empire's annual cash revenues.[53] But this expensive conquest established a defensive ring of forts around Buda, the administrative and logistical center of Ottoman Hungary. Chief among these forts was Esztergom, which for the next 140 years became the northwestern border stronghold of Ottoman Hungary. The conquest of Székesfehérvár, Siklós, and Pécs further extended the Ottoman province of Buda in Transdanubia and connected it with the Srem and Belgrade. In 1544, Yahyapaşazade Mehmed Pasha—the former *sancak* governor of Smederevo and governor-general of Buda since May 1543—conquered Visegrád in the Danube bend and other castles in Transdanubia. Over the next three years, the Ottomans organized the newly conquered lands into six newly established *sancaks*.[54] By 1545, the Ottomans had stationed 12,975 garrison soldiers in their twenty-nine forts in Hungary. With janissaries of the Porte (2,282 men in 1547), the occupying military force of the province of Buda numbered about 15,000 men. About two-thirds of them defended the four key fortresses of Buda, Pest, Esztergom, and Székesfehérvár.[55]

Recent Ottoman successes in Hungary convinced both the Transylvanians and the Habsburgs that the unification of the two remaining parts of the Hungarian Kingdom had to be postponed. The Transylvanians sent their first tribute of 10,000 coins to the padishah in 1543.[56] The nobles of the Trans-Tisza region realized that Ferdinand was unable

to defend them against further Ottoman conquests. Therefore, the nobles decided to seek protection from Friar George, who preserved Transylvania under the House of Szapolyai by accepting Ottoman vassalage.
In August 1544, the counties of the neighboring Temes and Maros-
Kőrös region sent their representatives to the diet of Transylvania, an
act that in due course resulted in the formation of a new region, the
"Parts" (Lat. *Partium*), whose fate would intimately blend with that of
the Eastern Hungarian Kingdom and its successor, the Principality of
Transylvania.[57]

Following Süleyman's conquests and the Bosnian *sancak* governor's
raids into Habsburg Slavonia, Ferdinand requested a cease-fire from
Mehmed Pasha of Buda in the fall of 1544. Meanwhile, Charles—
having marched through France with his forty-thousand-strong army
unopposed—made an advantageous peace with Francis's ministers in
the Treaty of Crépy (18–19 September 1544). In the treaty, Francis promised to end his alliance with Süleyman and committed to provide ten
thousand infantry and six hundred cavalry to fight the Turks in Hungary. But Francis had no intention of fighting Süleyman. Neither had
Charles. In a secret treaty that Francis signed the next day, the French
king promised to provide the Habsburg brothers "with our full assistance and favour in the reduction and pacification of religious discord
in Germany," and to use the "infantry and cavalry we have promised
against the Turks . . . against the said heretics."[58]

Francis now offered to mediate between Charles and Süleyman.
Charles accepted the offer and retracted his earlier promise to Ferdinand and the Hungarian Estates that he would personally attack the
Ottomans. When the Hungarian Estates—gathered to discuss the war
against the Turks at their diet—learned about the Habsburgs' peace
initiative, they were outraged. "Sire, at the diet of the Hungarians, I have
found the most terrible contention and heard the most licentious words
that have been spoken in my life . . . both against Your Majesty and the
King of the Romans [Ferdinand]," reported Charles's ambassador, Gerard
Veltwyck (Veltwijck) von Ravenstein.[59] In December, the emperor sent
Veltwyck to the Porte. He left the Imperial Court in Worms on 22 May
for Venice, where the French ambassador to Venice joined him. The two

diplomats arrived in Constantinople in late August 1545. Ferdinand had already dispatched his envoys to the Porte in late December 1544. He authorized them to make peace with Süleyman on the basis of the territorial division of Hungary and an annual present of 10,000 ducats to the sultan.[60] On 10 November 1545, the Habsburg envoys concluded a truce with Süleyman for one and a half years. The first Habsburg-Ottoman peace treaty soon followed.

The emperor again sent Veltwyck as his plenipotentiary to Süleyman. This time, the French tried to derail the negotiations. However, in April 1547 the news of the death of King Francis reached the Ottoman court in Edirne and the French envoy lost his leverage. In the meantime, Grand Vizier Rüstem Pasha and his fellow viziers grew anxious about the emperor's war in Germany. In June, the Ottoman court received news of the emperor's victory over the Lutheran princes of the Schmalkaldic League at the battle of Mühlberg (24 April 1547). Rüstem now feared that Charles might choose war over peace. Around the same time, Süleyman welcomed the Safavid prince Alqas Mirza, the brother of Shah Tahmasb and governor of Shirvan province. He offered his services to Süleyman against his brother. Süleyman refused the French proposal to attack the Habsburgs, with the excuse that the campaign "season was too far advanced." On 19 June the sultan concluded a peace with the Habsburgs and mobilized his troops for next year's campaign against the shah of Persia.[61]

The Habsburg-Ottoman treaty of 1547 committed Süleyman and the Habsburg brothers and their respective allies to peaceful relations. The Christian side included Venice, the French king, and the pope, despite the protest of Rüstem, who remarked that the pope should confine himself to matters of faith. On the Ottoman side, the treaty included the Barbary corsairs. The corsairs were prohibited from attacking Christian ships and coastal towns. In return, they were to be protected from attacks of the Christian signatories of the treaty. The peace treaty settled the territorial disputes in Hungary according to the status quo, except for villages that had been conquered or forced to pay taxes to the Turks since the signing of the truce in 1545. Süleyman considered Hungary his rightful possession, conquered by his sword, but dropped his claims on sev-

This portrait by an anonymous artist shows Charles V late in his life,
around fifty years of age. In 1547, Charles V and Ferdinand I made
peace with Sultan Süleyman. In 1555, Charles accepted defeat
against the Protestant princes and Estates of his empire, abdicated,
and withdrew to a monastery in Yuste, Spain, where he died in 1558.
Ferdinand followed his brother as Holy Roman emperor, using
the empire's resources to fight Süleyman in Hungary. (Courtesy of
the Rijksmuseum, Amsterdam, SK-A-979.)

eral disputed castles. All troops, except for those defending the borders,
had to be withdrawn. Violators of the peace were to be punished on both
sides. In return for the territories under his rule in Hungary, Ferdinand
agreed to pay an annual tribute of 30,000 Hungarian gold florins, to be
sent to the Porte by an embassy every year in March. The signatories
reached agreement on 13 June, and the Ottomans prepared a provisional
ahdname six days later, when the sultan confirmed the agreement. The
parties had three months to ratify the treaty. Süleyman sent two somewhat different charters to Charles and Ferdinand with their respective
ambassadors. The emperor signed the treaty on 1 August at Augsburg;

Ferdinand confirmed it on 26 August in Prague. A month later, on 29 September, Ferdinand's envoy arrived at the Ottoman court with the signed copies. Süleyman issued a new document ten days later, on 8 October. The Habsburg envoy soon left the Ottoman capital and returned there with the first tribute from Ferdinand in March 1548.[62]

Vienna interpreted the annual sum as "gifts of honor" (*munus honestum et honorarium*); the Ottomans saw it as an annual tribute (*harac*) and considered the Habsburg monarchs tribute-paying vassals.[63] However, the Ottoman governors-general in Buda—who had to ensure that the annual tribute from Vienna duly arrived in Constantinople every spring—also called the tribute "gifts of honor" (Hun. *tiztöségös aiándék*) in their Hungarian-language correspondence, and treated the emperor and the sultan as equals.[64] This was due in part to their Hungarian scribes, who followed the Habsburg chancery language. But it also reflected compromise along the Habsburg-Ottoman frontier, where the lofty titles of the padishah carried only as much weight as his viceroys in Buda could back up militarily. Moreover, nobody in Europe would have considered the kings of Hungary and the Holy Roman emperors as Ottoman vassals.

Ferdinand convened the Hungarian diet in Nagyszombat by late November 1547 to discuss the defense of the kingdom. In mid-December, the Estates at the diet received Ferdinand's letter regarding the Habsburg-Ottoman treaty; to this the king attached Süleyman's letter that summarized the main points of the agreement.[65] Ferdinand instructed his envoys to the diet not to reveal "certain secret points" of the treaty, including his acceptance of paying an annual tribute to the sultan. However, the Estates had learned enough to be frustrated, for the truce essentially acknowledged Süleyman's suzerainty over Ottoman-occupied Hungary. Declaring it a shameful act, the Estates asked both the emperor and Ferdinand not to ratify the treaty. Citing Süleyman's war with the Safavids and the emperor's recent victories in Germany, the Estates urged Charles to send military aid, which he had repeatedly promised in the past. They hoped that with such help, Ferdinand might liberate Hungary from the Turks. The protest of the Hungarian Estates came too late. Ferdinand's envoy had already delivered the first tribute in Constantinople. The Habsburg brothers felt unprepared to challenge Süleyman.

Ottoman-Safavid Struggle for Supremacy

The Safavids undermined Ottoman sovereignty among the Turkmen and Kurdish tribes in eastern Asia Minor, depriving the Ottoman government of valuable tax revenues, fighting men, and logistical support. In addition to having economic and strategic considerations, the lands of Mesopotamia, stretching southeast from Asia Minor into Iraq, also had religious and cultural significance to both the Ottomans and the Safavids. In addition to the old Abbasid capital Baghdad, once the center of Sunni Islam, Arab Iraq (*Iraq-i Arab*) also contained the sites of the sacred Shiite shrines of Imam Ali in Najaf and Imam Hussain in Karbala. Although the religious significance of the region had been invoked by both Ottoman and Safavid chroniclers, religion and the desire to control the respective Sunni and Shiite holy sites do not seem to have been the main motivation for the Ottoman-Safavid confrontation. While Arab Iraq figured prominently in Safavid sacred geography, its conquest by Ismail in 1508 and its reconquest by Shah Abbas in 1623 were motivated more by geopolitical concerns than by ideology. The Safavids ruled Arab Iraq only for 42 years during the dynasty's 220-year life span.[66]

Shah Ismail's death in 1524 temporarily removed the Safavid threat to the Ottoman domains. Moreover, the civil war that erupted in Persia among the various Turkmen Qizilbash tribes in the first decade of the reign of the ten-year-old Shah Tahmasb gave the Ottomans an opportunity to invade the Safavid domains. In 1532, some surviving Takkalu elements—who initially dominated the regency of the shah but were ousted and massacred by the rival Shamlu Turkmens—encouraged the Ottomans to intervene. Shifting loyalties of the commanders of various fortresses along the Safavid-Ottoman frontier also made the conflict predictable. Whereas the Safavid frontier governor sided with the Ottomans, the commander of Bitlis in eastern Asia Minor deserted to Shah Tahmasb, who appointed the deserter governor of Kurdistan (1533). Süleyman sent Grand Vizier Ibrahim Pasha against Bitlis and the Safavids. In 1533, Ibrahim captured Bitlis and the Safavid capital Tabriz. After he concluded a truce with the Habsburgs in 1533, Süleyman embarked on his first campaign against the Safavids, called in Ottoman sources the "campaign of the two Iraqs," to conquer both Arab Iraq and "Persian Iraq" (*Iraq-i Acem*)—that is, western Iran. Süleyman joined his grand vizier in Tabriz in September 1534 and held court in his rival's capital city. At the end of November, the padishah and his grand vizier entered Baghdad.[67]

Baghdad had a rich history for Muslims. In 749/50, the Abbasids toppled the Umayyad Caliphate (661–749/50), who ruled from Damascus. The Abbasids centered their power in Iraq, and the second Abbasid caliph, al-Mansur (r. 754–75), established Baghdad as the capital of the Abbasid caliphate (750–1258) in 962. The city quickly developed into a bustling metropolis of about a half million people, and it was five times larger than Constantinople of the Eastern Roman Empire. The reign of Caliph Harun al-Rashid (r. 786–809) witnessed the flourishing of Islamic learning and culture, and his court was the setting of the stories of the One Thousand and One Nights. The Abbasids lost political power first to the Shiite Buyid soldiers in 945 and then to the Seljuk Turks in 1055. In 1258, the Mongols destroyed Baghdad and the Abbasid caliphate. Still, the city remained in Muslim imagination as the capital of the Islamic golden age.[68]

In Baghdad, Süleyman "rediscovered" the tomb of Abu Hanifa, the eighth-century Muslim jurist, whose school of law the Ottomans favored. It had symbolic importance and was used to strengthen Süleyman's legitimacy within the Islamic world. The "campaign of the two Iraqs" secured Erzurum and Van in eastern Asia Minor, and Baghdad. The latter was of great strategic importance as it controlled communication and regional and international trade on the Tigris and Euphrates Rivers.

Confrontation with the Habsburgs in Hungary (campaigns of 1541 and 1543) and the Mediterranean (Preveza 1538), and the punitive campaign against the disobedient Moldavian voivode (1538), temporarily diverted Süleyman's attention from the eastern frontier. Meanwhile, Shah Tahmasb managed to retake the Van region. In 1546 Baghdad's Ottoman governor successfully dislodged the Safavid governor in Basra and established nominal control over the city. Süleyman could launch a new campaign against the shah only in 1548, after the conclusion of the 1547 treaty with the Habsburgs, using the opportunity created by the flight of the shah's brother, Alqas Mirza. The main objective of the campaign seems to have been eradicating the despised Qizilbash and punishing Shah Tahmasb, under whose reign the practice of cursing the second and third caliphs of Islam became institutionalized. Since Tahmasb escaped open battle and instead devastated Azerbaijan according to his tried-and-true scorched-earth tactics, Süleyman had to evacuate the region despite his taking the Safavid capital Tabriz again. Having incorporated Van and Kurdistan into his empire, Süleyman returned to Constantinople in late 1549.

The Ottomans integrated the conquered regions into two new border provinces: Erzurum and Baghdad. Iraq under Süleyman was organized into the five provinces of Mosul, Shahrizor, Baghdad, Basra, and Lahsa. This division took into consideration geographical, strategic, religious, and social realities on the ground. The provinces of Basra and Lahsa, for instance, guarded the Gulf of Basra against the Portuguese. Baghdad remained the center of the region. The Porte's hold over the other provinces depended on the power and influence of its governor in Baghdad.[69] As mentioned, the Ottomans also reorganized their administration in neighboring Syria. In 1549, they established the province of Aleppo with nine *sancaks*, whereas five *sancaks* belonged to the province of Dulkadır (Zülkadriye), which had existed since the 1520s.[70]

Once Süleyman's generals had secured the Ottoman possessions in Hungary in the 1551–52 campaigns, the padishah set off for his third and last campaign against the Safavids in late August 1553. Almost sixty years old and in ill health, Süleyman initially declined to lead the army personally. Instead, he wanted to send Grand Vizier Rüstem Pasha, his son-in-law who was married to Mihrimah, Süleyman's daughter from Hurrem. However, after receiving deceitful reports from his grand vizier that Prince Mustafa—Süleyman's eldest living son born from his first concubine Mahidevran/Gülbahar and the janissaries' preferred heir to the throne—wanted to dethrone him, the padishah changed his mind. Süleyman left for the campaign on 28 August. In early October, he invited the thirty-eight-year-old Mustafa to his military camp at Aktepe in central Asia Minor. Upon entering the tent of the imperial council, the prince was strangled by the sultan's executioners.[71]

With winter approaching, Süleyman moved to Aleppo. The campaign season of 1554 brought Nakhchivan in modern Azerbaijan and Erevan in Armenia under Ottoman rule. Distance, poor weather conditions, arid and sparsely vegetated terrain, Safavid guerilla warfare—which a contemporary Ottoman chronicler aptly dubbed as "dog fights"—and the shah's scorched-earth tactic caused supply problems for the Ottomans.[72] Negotiations with Shah Tahmasb's envoys in Erzurum and Amasya (21 May–1 June 1555) resulted in the Treaty of Amasya. For the Safavids, the treaty meant official recognition of their Shiite state, but at the expense of major territorial concessions and the promise that they end the cursing of the Sunni caliphs. For the Ottomans, the treaty guaranteed all their conquests, including eastern Asia Minor, Azerbaijan, Tabriz, Kars, Ardahan, and Arab Iraq, including Baghdad. Imperial orders commanded the Ottoman and Safavid border governors to comply with the treaty. While some communities on both sides showed no respect for the new territorial delimitation, both governments managed to maintain peace for the next twenty years.[73] The border established in 1555 served as a reference for later border demarcations in 1611–12 and 1639. It survived into the twentieth century with modifications.[74]

Both Süleyman and Tahmasb chose to maintain the peace and manage occasional conflicts arising from the shifting allegiances, defections, and raids of the Kurdish tribal leaders living along the Ottoman-Safavid border. Not even the flight of the rebellious Ottoman prince Bayezid to Safavid Iran (1559) led to war between the parties. While Shah Tahmasb considered the event an act of fitting revenge for Süleyman's use of Alqas Mirza's defection to the Ottomans, after lengthy negotiations the shah decided to hand over Bayezid and his four sons to the Ottoman envoys in 1562. However, Ottoman henchmen sent by Bayezid's brother, Prince Selim, murdered the fugitive prince and his sons in the Safavid capital Qazwin.[75]

Trouble in Transylvania

Ottoman imperial troops returned to Hungary in 1551 to retaliate for Transylvania's handover to the Habsburgs.[76] Ever since the fall of Buda to the Ottomans, Friar George—who governed Transylvania for the underage King John II (John Sigismund of Szapolyai) and his mother, Queen Isabella—tried to reunite the two Hungarian kingdoms under Ferdinand's rule. Encouraged by Emperor Charles V's victories against the Protestant princes in the Schmalkaldic War (1546–47), the friar sent his commissioners to the imperial diet in Augsburg. It took more than a year to finalize the negotiations, as the friar wanted to secure Habsburg military assistance to defend the country against Süleyman's retaliation. On 8 September 1549 at Nyírbátor in Hungary, Friar George signed the treaty with Ferdinand's general, the younger Nicholas Salm (Niklas Graf III von Salm). Similarly to the settlement in Gyalu (Gilău in Romania) in 1541, the Treaty of Nyírbátor surrendered Transylvania and the adjacent territories known as the "Parts" (Lat. *Partium*) to Ferdinand. As compensation, Queen Isabella and John Sigismund were to receive the Silesian duchy of Oppeln and Ratibor (Pol. Opole and Racibórz), and 100,000 gold florins. Friar George was to keep his offices as treasurer and lord-lieutenant of Transylvania, and continue governing the country in the name of Ferdinand. The friar, who was bishop of Várad Oradea, was also promised to receive the archbishopric of Esztergom and, with Habsburg mediation, a cardinal's hat.[77]

In early 1548, the Ottoman governor-general of Buda received secret intelligence and alerted the Porte that the friar's "envoy, together with Ferdinand, took part in talks with Charles," a clear reference to the talks in Augsburg. The spy heard that the friar kept his troops prepared "with the intension of helping the king and his brother, Charles, should they take up arms and start a campaign" against the Ottomans.[78] News kept coming to the Porte. Because the Treaty of Nyírbátor dispossessed her son of the kingdom, Queen Isabella opposed the agreement, which Friar George had concluded without her knowledge and consent. She rallied her supporters against the friar and reported the friar's treason to Süleyman. The French ambassador at the Porte also informed the padishah about the treaty. In March 1550, Süleyman dispatched his court interpreter, Mahmud, son of a Viennese merchant, to Vienna to investigate the matter. Having corroborated the reports, Mahmud traveled to Transylvania with the padishah's order to the Estates, convened by the queen. Süleyman reminded the Transylvanians that he had given the country to John Sigismund and Queen Isabella, leaving Friar George as governor and treasurer of the country. However, the friar did not honor his oath and made a pact with Ferdinand. Therefore, Süleyman ordered the Transylvanians to either kill the friar or hand him over to John Sigismund, "so that the country would not be lost on account of such a rogue person."[79]

In Transylvania, yet another civil war ensued. Friar George's troops twice besieged Gyulafehérvár (September 1550 and May 1551), the residence of Queen Isabella and John Sigismund. After long negotiations with Ferdinand's commissioners, Isabella abdicated in the name of John Sigismund, who was just eleven years of age, in the Treaty of Szászsebes (19 July 1551).[80] She was assured that Ferdinand would give his youngest daughter, Joanna, in marriage to John Sigismund. The Transylvanian Estates accepted the agreement at their diet. After they celebrated the engagement of John Sigismund and Joanna, Isabella handed Ferdinand's commissioners the country and the Holy Crown of St. Stephen, which the queen kept so that her son could be crowned when he came of age. Having entrusted Transylvania to Friar George and Ferdinand's general, Giovanni Battista Castaldo, in the middle of August, the queen and John Sigismund left for Kassa before continuing to the Silesian duchy that Ferdinand had granted her in the Treaty of Nyírbátor.[81]

By this time, Sokollu Mehmed Pasha, governor-general of Rumeli, had arrived in Slankamen with the Ottoman army.[82] The Porte knew about the Habsburg takeover of Transylvania from multiple sources— from the Ottoman governor-general of Buda, Queen Isabella, Peter Petrović, and a Frenchman who had been in Transylvania during the negotiations and related the news to the pashas in Constantinople. When confronted, Giovanni Maria Malvezzi, Ferdinand's resident diplomat in Constantinople, corroborated the reports. The padishah had Malvezzi imprisoned in the "Black Tower," confiscated his wealth, and sold the members of the Habsburg embassy into slavery.[83] To avoid an Ottoman attack on Transylvania, Friar George hastily dispatched the country's annual tribute to Constantinople. He assured Sokollu Mehmed Pasha of the Transylvanians' loyalty, blaming Peter Petrović—Isabella's faithful general and governor of the Temes region—for the surrender of the castles to the Habsburgs.

The maneuver seemed to work. In September 1551, Sokollu Mehmed targeted the castles in the Temes region, controlled by Petrović. Sokollu captured Becse, killing the defenders and their captains, who had been negotiating the surrender (19 September). From Becse, Sokollu proceeded southeast, taking Becskerek (25 September) on the Béga River. Even though the marshes surrounding the castle made it inaccessible, its small garrison of eighty men abandoned it. Sokollu also took the episcopal town and castle of Csanád, which guarded a crossing point on the Maros River. Csanád was Friar George's castle. The friar instructed its captain to surrender it to Sokollu, hoping that the Ottomans would withdraw for the winter. This would allow the friar to strengthen the country's defenses with Habsburg help. However, the inhabitants of the nearby castle of Lippa approached Sokollu and offered to surrender if their town was spared. Lippa's garrison had left before Sokollu's troops arrived. Thus, Sokollu took possession of Lippa (8 October) without obstruction, leaving Ulema Pasha with several thousands of troops in the castle.

The Serbs of the region offered their help to take Temesvár. Surrounded by marshes of the Temes and Bega Rivers, the castle of Temesvár was difficult to approach. It was well guarded by 2,020 horsemen and 1,550 foot soldiers. Temesvár's captain, Stephen (István) Losonczi, rejected Sokollu's call to surrender. Trusting his 3,500 soldiers, he declared that he "would fight to the last drop of his blood to the greater glory of his homeland and Christendom."[84] After ten days, food shortages and insubordination of his frustrated *timariot sipahis* forced Sokollu to lift the siege. He also feared the approaching Habsburg army of several tens of thousands of soldiers.

Castaldo suggested attacking and destroying Sokollu's army. However, Friar George wanted to avoid open confrontation with the Ottomans. He recommended an attack on Lippa, which the Transylvanian,

Hungarian, and Habsburg forces quickly retook. The Habsburg, Hungarian, and Transylvanian army, some fifty thousand strong, encircled Lippa on 3 November. After heated debate, the commanders accepted Friar George's suggestion and let Ulema Pasha and his Ottoman garrison withdraw. Having organized the newly conquered lands into the *sancak* of Becse-Besckerek, Sokollu retreated to Belgrade for the winter.[85]

Friar George claimed that he wanted the Ottoman garrison to leave Lippa in peace so as not to provoke retaliation from the padishah and save Transylvania for Ferdinand. He hoped that the Porte would renew the 1547 truce, due to expire in June 1552. He explained his constant communications with the Porte and his sending of the annual tribute to Constantinople by the same argument. But Ferdinand and his generals no longer trusted the friar. Even Palatine Thomas Nádasdy felt that they were all captives of the friar. Responding to Castaldo's constant complaints about the friar, Ferdinand authorized his general to do whatever he thought was in the monarchy's interest. To assist Castaldo, Ferdinand sent Sforza Pallavicini, another Italian mercenary captain, with additional imperial troops to Transylvania. On 17 December 1551, on Castaldo's orders, Pallavicini and his assassins killed Friar George, cardinal of the Roman Catholic Church, in the friar's favorite castle, Alvinc. Castaldo informed Ferdinand the same day that "it has pleased God to remove Brother George from the world."[86]

The Porte, too, had distrusted the friar. Sokollu warned him that the "Sultan will not always believe your tricks and the flatteries by which we have been beguiled and deceived."[87] Still, from the Porte's point of view, the Habsburg takeover of Transylvania and the assassination of Friar George amounted to a breach of the truce. Since Süleyman considered the war against the Safavids more pressing, he entrusted the reconquest of Transylvania to his second vizier Kara (Black) Ahmed Pasha, ordering Sokollu Mehmed and Hadım Ali of Buda to assist him.

The Ottomans surprised Ferdinand, who was unprepared for the assault in 1552. The Habsburg generals knew neither the direction of the main assault nor the strength of the attacking armies. Having retaken Szeged from the Hungarian hajduks (1 March), Hadım Ali captured Veszprém (1 June) with some ten thousand troops under his command.

He then turned against the defensive line of the mining towns. Ali captured the small castle of Drégely (9 July), whose captain, George (György) Szondi, refused the pasha's call to surrender and died with his soldiers. Most of the other forts in Nógrád county fell without a fight.[88]

Meanwhile, Kara Ahmed attacked the Temes and the Trans-Tisza region, the castles that guarded the main Habsburg river routes. At the end of July 1552, following a siege of more than a month, Captain Losonczi surrendered Temesvár to Kara Ahmed, as Castaldo and Bernardo de Aldana (the captain of Lippa) failed to answer the defenders' plea for help. Despite promises for safe withdrawal, the Ottomans massacred the defenders. Bernardo de Aldana deserted Lippa, "the gate of Transylvania." The Ottomans took Arad on the Maros River, opening the Maros valley toward Transylvania. In early September, the combined Ottoman army of Kara Ahmed, Hadım Ali, and Sokollu Mehmed conquered Szolnok, which controlled the confluence of the Tisza and Zagyva Rivers, and the only permanent bridge over the Tisza along the main military corridor leading to both Buda and Eger.[89]

From Szolnok, the Ottoman troops proceeded to Eger, a castle that guarded the route to the strategically important mining districts and Kassa, the seat of the Habsburg command in Upper (northeast) Hungary. By possessing Eger, the Ottomans could isolate Transylvania from Habsburg-controlled Hungary. In light of their numerical superiority (35,000–40,000 attackers against 2,300 defenders), the invaders predicted an easy conquest. But the defenders, under the command of Stephen (István) Dobó, repulsed the attackers. The siege was especially bloody as the defenders resorted to unconventional tactics. The women in the castle poured hot water and molten bitumen on the attackers. The defenders inflicted heavy casualties on the Ottomans with their sorties, countermines, firebombs, and "fire-wheels"—mill wheels stuffed with grenades and gun barrels filled with explosives. Heroic defense, a shortage of cannonballs and food in the Ottoman camp, and unusually cold and rainy autumn weather forced the attackers to lift the siege on 17 October, after five weeks of fighting.[90] The successful defense of Eger was celebrated across Europe. Sebastian (Sebestyén) Lantos Tinódi, a contemporary lyric poet, sung about Dobó's victory the same year. The victory quickly became the symbol of Hungarian patriotic heroism and Dobó part of the Hungarian national mythology.[91]

Despite the failure at Eger, the 1552 campaign further extended Ottoman rule in the Carpathian Basin, with Temesvár becoming the center of the second Ottoman province in Hungary. Yet, the Ottoman victory remained incomplete as Transylvania remained under Habsburg control. Luckily for Süleyman—who because of his war with the Safavids could not risk a major confrontation with Ferdinand over Transylvania—Habsburg rule in Transylvania soon collapsed. Ferdinand's military commander, financial administrators, and voivodes—whose job was to reorganize Transylvania's finances and administration under Habsburg rule—undercut each other. They also faced fierce opposition from the Transylvanian Estates, and thus subsequently resigned. In March 1553, Castaldo, the commander of the Habsburg forces in Transylvania, was forced out of the country. The Transylvanian Estates requested that if Ferdinand was unable to protect them against the Turks, he should let them recall Queen Isabella and John Sigismund from Poland.[92] The Porte also demanded the return of the Szapolyais to Transylvania but ordered its governor-general in Buda not to help the anti-Habsburg insurrection in the Trans-Tisza region. In the meantime, Ferdinand sent a tribute for Transylvania to Süleyman. He also offered a yearly tribute up to 140,000 florins, should Süleyman accept Habsburg rule in Transylvania and Hungary. Ferdinand's diplomatic maneuvering in Constantinople proved futile. Having concluded the Treaty of Amasya with the Safavids in 1555, Süleyman now ordered his governors in Hungary and Bosnia and his vassal voivodes in Wallachia and Moldavia to prepare for war, taking advantage of yet another insurrection against Ferdinand in eastern Hungary.

By this time, Ferdinand had lost Transylvania. In light of repeated Ottoman military threats, the Transylvanian diet sent word to Ferdinand in December 1555: "We were happy to be ruled by a Christian prince and to be affiliated with the Holy Roman Emperor, but God Almighty did not wish this to last for long. . . . Therefore, we ask Your Majesty for one of the two things: either to help us so that we can resist Süleyman, or to be so kind as to absolve us of our oath." They did not

IOANNES · SIGIS·M · HONG · REGIS · FILIVS · DVX · OPOLIENSIS ·

Ora SIGISMVNDI hæc qui conspicis Hungara JANI,
Cogeris Hvngaricis illachrimare malis.

John Sigismund Szapolyai, elected king of Hungary (as John II)
and prince of Transylvania. (Copper engraving by Custos Dominicus.
Courtesy of the Hungarian National Museum, Budapest, TKCs 4722.)

wait for an answer. In January 1556, at the diet of Torda, the Transylvanians recalled Queen Isabella and John Sigismund. In March, at the diet of Szászsebes, they swore allegiance to "the son of King John." Queen Isabella and John Sigismund arrived in Kolozsvár on 22 September. Pockets of Habsburg resistance lasted for years.[93] The Porte welcomed the return of its vassal to Transylvania. But two anchor fortresses, Szigetvár and Gyula, remained a thorn in the side of the Ottomans.

Having assumed control over Szigetvár in 1543, the Viennese government reinforced the castle's defenses in the 1540s and 1550s. Ferdinand's military commander in Hungary, the younger Nicholas Salm, dubbed it "the most important fortress of the kingdom," as it protected both southern Transdanubia and Slavonia. The Ottomans, too, recognized its strategic significance. In 1555, Toygun Pasha of Buda invested Szigetvár, but the fortress repelled the attackers. His successor, Ali Pasha, laid siege to the fortress in the summer of 1556. Led by Captain Mark (Marko) Horváth Stančić, the defenders withstood the forty-two-day siege. Szigetvár would have fallen, were it not for the timely arrival of a relief force. Assisted by imperial, Austrian, and Bohemian troops, Palatine Thomas Nádasdy—captain-general of Transdanubia and Horváth's patron—laid siege to the nearby Ottoman fortress of Babócsa, which the Ottomans had captured the previous year. The plan worked. Ali hurried to Babócsa but was defeated in a daylong battle, in which Nicholas (Miklós) Zrínyi, ban of Croatia and Slavonia, demonstrated his military prowess and knowledge of the enemy.

In the meantime, Archduke Ferdinand arrived with his army, and Ali decided to return to Buda. When Horváth died in 1561, Zrínyi requested and was granted the position of chief captain of Szigetvár and administrator (*provisor*) of the estates belonging to it. Two years later, Palatine Thomas Nádasdy, Zrínyi's lifelong friend and supporter, died. Ferdinand left the position of palatine vacant, but he filled Nádasdy's other position by appointing Zrínyi captain-general of Transdanubia.

Within years, Zrínyi asserted his power. To supply the castle and pay his soldiers, he reorganized the domains around Szigetvár. He collected feudal, state, and church taxes, demanding the uncompensated work of the peasantry (*robot*) from southern Transdanubia, including those under Ottoman rule. Supplied by thousands of tax-paying villages and surrounded by vast swamps and smaller forts that guarded the thoroughfares, Szigetvár had become a formidable fortress by the 1560s. It frustrated Ottoman taxation in Transdanubia and threatened Ottoman communication and shipping on the Drava and Danube Rivers. Along with Gyula in the east, Szigetvár projected Hungarian and Habsburg sovereignty into Ottoman-held Hungary by collecting taxes from the padishah's subjects. The castle became the target of Süleyman's last campaign, under whose walls the elderly padishah would die.[94]

Death at Szigetvár

In the spring of 1566, the seventy-two-year-old padishah set off for his last campaign. The onslaught took everyone by surprise. Ottoman imperial troops had not attacked Hungary since 1552, the sultan had not personally led his armies since 1555, and the Habsburg-Ottoman peace had recently been renewed. Contemporaries advanced various theories to explain the padishah's campaign.[95] Ottoman chroniclers claimed that the Porte wanted to capture Szigetvár, whose demolition and surrender the Ottomans had demanded in 1557 and 1562. Others thought that the campaign's target was Gyula in eastern Hungary. By the 1560s, Gyula had become the cornerstone of Habsburg defense in eastern Hungary. Its captain, Ladislas Kerecsényi (Szigetvár's captain in 1554–55), commanded vast resources as he was also captain-general of the Lower Parts of the kingdom in 1561–66 and the king's representative (*főispan, supremus comes*) of the neighboring Zaránd, Csanád, and Békés counties. Wedged in between the Ottoman-vassal Transylvania and Ottoman Hungary, Gyula also threatened the Temes region, home of the estates of the rising Sokollu clan. Yet others pointed to the troubles in Transylvania. After Queen Isabella's death in 1559, John Sigismund ruled as a loyal Ottoman vassal. However, at the end of 1561 Menyhért Balassa—one of John Sigismund's influential aristocrats and the lord of large estates around the anchor fortress of Szatmár—defected to Ferdinand. Habsburg troops took the castles of Tokaj, Szatmár, and Nagybánya (Rom. Baia Mare), which then belonged to John Sigismund. But the Habsburgs had miscalculated. The new leadership at the Porte could not allow Vienna to assert its power in the neighborhood of the sultan's vassal.

Upon the death of Grand Vizier Semiz ("the fat") Ali Pasha in June 1565, Second Vizier Sokollu Mehmed was promoted to the grand vizierate. European diplomats at the Porte considered the Bosnian-born Ali a voice for peace. In 1562, Ali had negotiated the renewal of the Habsburg-Ottoman peace for another eight years. When Emperor Ferdinand died in 1564, he proposed to renew the treaty for the remaining six years. In contrast to Ali, Sokollu was known as belligerent. The 1552 campaign resulted in the conquest of Temesvár and the establishment of a new Ottoman province, guarding the unreliable Ottoman-vassal Transylvania. Events in 1565, however, proved that Habsburg meddling in Transylvania remained a problem. Sokollu wanted to resolve the Transylvanian problem for good with a decisive campaign. Sokollu Mustafa—Mehmed's nephew and the *sancak* governor of Bosnia—also supported a more aggressive policy against the Hungarians and Habsburgs. With the help of Süleyman's spiritual adviser, the influential Halveti Sheikh Mustafa Musliheddin Nureddinzade, the grand vizier persuaded the padishah to join the campaign. In the run-up to the 1566 campaign, Nureddinzade paid an unexpected night visit to Süleyman to recount his dream in which the Prophet mandated the sultan to resume the holy war.[96] By having Süleyman on his side during the campaign, Sokullu made sure that if the aging sultan died, he could influence the succession, helping Prince Selim—Sokollu's father-in-law—succeed to the throne.[97]

The seventy-two-year-old padishah left Constantinople on 29 April.[98] Two months later, at his camp in Zemun near Belgrade, he received his vassal, John Sigismund. By this time, Second Vizier Pertev Pasha was in Gyula's vicinity. Built on an island in the Fehér-Körös River, Gyula had some two thousand Hungarian, Croatian, and German soldiers when Pertev and his army of thirty-thousand strong commenced the siege on 2 July. The Ottomans could not start their attacks until the water surrounding the castle was drained. Kerecsényi had fought heroically and withstood several assaults. The fortress fell on 2 September, after a brutal, sixty-three-day fight, the longest siege in Hungary in the sixteenth century.

While at Zemun, Süleyman received news about the battle of Siklós, in which Zrínyi annihilated the troops of the *sancak* governor of Tırhala. Some Ottoman chroniclers claimed that it was this news after which the padishah decided to march against Szigetvár. However, as a diversionary move, part of the army was sent to Petrovaradin, where the Ottomans were building a bridge, suggesting that the army would cross the river to Hungary there, possibly targeting Eger. The sultan ordered the building of another bridge near Vukovar, again to confuse his enemies. In the end, the army crossed the Drava River to southern Transdanubia at Osijek, on a bridge that the Ottomans built in seventeen days using 118 boats. The last troops crossed to Hungary on 19 July. The Ottomans shipped their cannons and heavy military equipment on the Danube to Mohács, whence they transported them to Szigetvár on carts. In the meantime, having been informed of Süleyman's campaign, Arslan Pasha of Buda wanted to secure his position by impressing the belligerent Ottoman leadership with his conquests. In early June, he invested Palota. Arslan failed to take the fortress. Having learned about an approaching relief army, he retreated. Capitalizing on his flight, Hungarian and Habsburg troops captured Veszprém and Tata, along with smaller forts in the region. When Arslan hurriedly arrived at the Ottoman camp at Nagyharsány to beg for forgiveness, Sokollu Mehmed had him executed. The grand vizier gave the governorship of Buda to his nephew, Sokollu Mustafa, who would govern this faraway province for the next twelve years.

Süleyman reached Szigetvár on 6 August. The fortress was surrounded by the waters of the Almás brook in the north, east, and west. The water was artificially raised and expanded for hundreds of meters around the castle by large dam banks. Szigetvár had three parts: the inner castle in the north (built of brick), the middle castle to the south and east, and the outer castle farther south and east. A broad moat separated the middle and outer castles. The outer castle was connected to the town by a wooden bridge, which was the only point one could enter the castle on dry land. At the time of the siege, some twenty-three hundred Hungarian, Croatian, and German troops guarded Szigetvár under the command of Zrínyi. Two thousand civilians lived in the town. All gathered in the inner castle and swore to fight the enemy to the death. Ali Portuk, who had been present at the unsuccessful siege of Malta the previous year, commanded the besieging force of some fifty thousand men. He quickly realized that to capture Szigetvár the water would need to be drained. By the time the town fell on 19 August, Zrínyi had lost more than half of his soldiers. Many were hunted down or captured as they tried to withdraw to the castle. The Ottomans impaled the captured. In response, Zrínyi executed his Turkish captives, some three hundred men, and displayed their heads on the castle wall. By this time, the number of defenders in the castle had been reduced to just eight hundred men. An imperial army of about fifty thousand stood in the vicinity of Győr. Since Emperor Maximilian II believed that the real target of the sultan's campaign was Vienna, he ordered his troops to protect the approaches to his capital and not to engage the besiegers. This sealed Szigetvár's fate. The defenders repelled several assaults, but on 5 September the Ottoman miners blew up the gunpowder that the defenders had buried behind the southern bastion. The outer castle was lost. The defenders withdrew to the inner castle. They had no gunpowder, food, or water. Around noon on 7 September, Zrínyi and the remaining defenders broke out of the inner castle, only to die. Süleyman did not see his soldiers' victory. The padishah had died in the early hours of 7 September in his tent, some four kilometers to the north of the castle on a small hill. Sokollu kept the padishah's death secret, fearing mutiny. The grand vizier also ordered the padishah's heart and inner organs to be buried in his tent. In 1575–76, the Ottomans erected a tomb over the burial site, which soon became a holy place and an object of Muslim pilgrimage.[99] Sokollu revealed the padishah's death to the troops only when Süleyman's son Selim arrived at the army camp near Belgrade and was declared the new ruler. Sultan Selim II's victory proclamation and Ottoman chroniclers celebrated the conquest of Szigetvár as a significant victory. However, the fact that Süleyman was still fighting the Hungarians forty years after he had annihilated their army at Mohács, and that he died just about eighty kilometers west of the site of his "greatest victory," demonstrated the failure of his grand strategy. Süleyman's formidable empire had reached its limits. It now faced the Habsburgs' Danubian monarchy, which was determined to halt the Ottoman advance in Hungary and Croatia, before it reached Vienna.

7

Overreach

The Red Sea and the Indian Ocean

Unlike Hungary (where Süleyman personally led seven of his thirteen campaigns) and the Mediterranean (the main theater of Ottoman-Habsburg rivalry at sea), the Red Sea and the Indian Ocean received low priority at the Porte. No padishah or grand vizier led campaigns in the Red Sea and the Indian Ocean. The Porte left these theaters to provincial governors, who received little support from Constantinople, or to Rumi and Levantine corsairs and soldiers of fortune. One of these adventurers was Selman Reis. By 1520, he had been exonerated and returned to Egypt. Selman set out for Jeddah upon the rebellion of the recently appointed governor-general of Egypt, Ahmed Pasha. In Jeddah, Selman persuaded the Ottoman governor, Hüseyin Rumi, to attack Yemen. They dislodged the Portuguese from the Kamaran Island and took Zabid. By the summer of 1524, Selman's situation in Yemen had become untenable as the people of Zabid rejected his tyrannical policies, choosing Hüseyin Rumi as their lord instead. Selman returned to Suez. He was soon in Cairo to meet Sultan Süleyman's grand vizier, Ibrahim Pasha. As mentioned, Ibrahim had arrived in Cairo to consolidate Ottoman power and reorganize the province's administration and finances after Ahmed Pasha's rebellion. One local chronicler claimed that Selman Reis's main motive in meeting the grand vizier was to wreak vengeance on Hüseyin Rumi, who had forced him out of Yemen. Having disparaged Hüseyin Rumi to the grand vizier, Selman asked Ibrahim

Pasha's permission to subdue Yemen and drive the Portuguese out of the Indian Ocean.[1]

A report (*Layiha*)—written on 2 June 1525 and attributed to Selman Reis—furnished further arguments for an attack on Yemen and the Portuguese. The report provided an overview of Ottoman and Portuguese naval and military resources in the Red Sea and the Indian Ocean and presented a plan for ousting the Portuguese.[2] The report listed eighteen ships and 298 guns of various types at the Ottomans' disposal at Jeddah, to be used against the "infidel Portuguese." It also listed the military and technical personnel needed for a fleet, with which "it is possible to capture and hold all the fortresses and ports in India which are under the Infidels." The report's author added that it was "the fear that these ships and guns might have been sent that [the Portuguese] have not entered the sea of Tur [the Gulf of Suez]. But if they hear that these ships are not operational and lack crews they will inevitably come with the big armada." Then the document reviewed the main Portuguese bases in Hormuz, Diu, Goa, Calicut, Cochin, the islands of Ceylon and Sumatra, and the port of Malacca. It noted their revenues, economic significance, and the size of their garrisons, concluding that the Portuguese held these bases with only two thousand men. "Therefore, when our ships are ready, and, God willing, move against them, their total destruction will be inevitable, for one fortress is unable to support another, and they are not able to put up [a] united opposition." A substantial part of the report deals with Yemen, which at the moment "has no lord—[it is] an empty province. It deserves to be a fine [Ottoman] *sancak*. It would be easy and possible to conquer. Should it be conquered, it would be possible to master the lands of India (*vilayet-i Hindustan*) and send every year a great amount of gold and jewels to the Sublime Port *Devlet-i Asitane*."[3]

Selman's lobbying paid off. Before leaving Cairo, the grand vizier sent a small fleet with four thousand undisciplined soldiers to Yemen to cement Ottoman authority. Ibrahim appointed Selman admiral of the fleet, but gave overall command of the expedition to Hayreddin Rumi, as the grand vizier did not trust the ambitious Selman. By the time they arrived in Yemen, Hüseyin Rumi was dead and had been replaced by another Rumi soldier of fortune. Selman and Hayreddin killed this soldier and then captured Zabid and Taizz. However, Selman and Hayreddin became rivals, and Hayreddin had Selman killed. Selman's nephew, Mustafa Bayram (Behram), avenged his uncle's death. These chaotic events resulted from the lack of a coordinated Ottoman policy in the Red Sea, which therefore achieved little in these early years. Ottoman presence in Yemen vanished for the next ten years.[4]

Selman Reis's report is found in the sultans' Topkapı Palace archives and may have been brought to Constantinople from Cairo by Ibrahim Pasha. As mentioned, the grand vizier had set out for Egypt on a ship whose pilot was none other than Piri Reis, who used this opportunity to show his *Book of Navigation* to Ibrahim, asking him to present it to Sultan Süleyman. Ibrahim promised to help but suggested that Piri produce a complete copy. By 1526, Piri had finished his expanded version, with a lengthy introduction that discussed the world's oceans and recent discoveries. Alas, neither Selman's memorandum nor Piri's portolan received much support from the padishah. Like his father after the conquest of Egypt, Süleyman too could have used the knowledge presented in Selman's and Piri's works to dislodge the Portuguese from the Indian Ocean. But Süleyman's priorities lay elsewhere.[5]

By the time Ibrahim Pasha returned to Constantinople, Süleyman was busy preparing for his campaign against the Hungarians, which ended with his victory at the battle of Mohács. Instead of the padishah, Rumi and Levantine corsairs and soldiers of fortune represented the Ottomans in the Indian Ocean. One such character was Mustafa Bayram. He briefly took control of the island of Kamaran, but the Portuguese expelled him. After an unsuccessful attempt to take the great entrepôt of Aden, whose ruler had accepted Portuguese vassalage, he retreated to the southern Yemeni port of Shihr. Mustafa Bayram witnessed the fate of his uncle and his fellow Rumi corsairs in Yemen, where the Shiite Zaidi imams and the Arab tribes rejected the Ottomans' claims for leadership in Islamdom and were hostile to the Ottomans. Therefore, he decided to try his luck in Gujarat, in western India, where his fellow Rumis had established a small colony. Another source claimed that his father in the Ottoman capital had informed him that he had been deprived of his office in Yemen, suggesting that he go to India before the arrival of the new Ottoman official. In 1531, Mustafa Bayram sailed to Diu, arriving just before its Portuguese siege commenced. Working together with Diu's Gujarati governor, Mustafa Bayram and his experienced Rumi artillery gunners repelled the Portuguese attack. Sultan Bahadur of Gujarat (r. 1526–35, 1536–37) rewarded Mustafa Bayram and made him head of the arsenal. But this soldier of fortune deserted to the Mughal emperor Humayun (r. 1530–40, 1555–56) after the latter defeated Sultan Bahadur.[6]

An attempt by Hadim Süleyman Pasha to launch a naval campaign against the Portuguese was aborted before it started in 1535. During his first tenure as governor-general of Egypt (1525–35), Süleyman Pasha had prepared eighty ships at the Suez arsenal, hoping to use them in his planned attack on the Portuguese. He had also started to dig a canal between Suez and the Nile. However, Sultan Süleyman ordered his governor to join the Iraq campaign against the Safavids.[7]

The Ottoman government invested limited resources in the Red Sea fleet. There were about 40 to 45 ships in the Suez arsenal in the sixteenth century. By contrast, the Ottoman fleet at the Gallipoli arsenal had as many as 181 ships in 1475 and 1518, including 93 galleys in both years.[8] Selman Reis had just 18 ships in 1525. The small Ottoman raiding expedition, which was launched in the summer of 1546 from Aden and sacked the Portuguese harbor of Muscat in Oman, counted only 4 ships.[9] By contrast, in the 1470s the Ottomans had already mobilized 250 to 380 galleys and light galleys in the Mediterranean and the Black Seas. In 1538, at the battle of Preveza, Hayreddin Barbarossa Pasha had 140 ships. During the Venetian-Ottoman war of 1537–40, the Ottomans launched their campaign against Herceg Novi (Castelnuovo) with 155 ships and 27,200 soldiers and crew. During the Ottoman-French naval campaign in 1543–44, Barbarossa commanded 110 galleys and 30,000 men.[10]

The only expedition in the Indian Ocean comparable to those in the Mediterranean took place in 1538. In response to Sultan Bahadur's request for a joint Ottoman-Gujarati attack on the Portuguese, Sultan Süleyman ordered Hadım Süleyman Pasha—who had returned to Cairo for a second term as governor-general (1537–38)—to gather his fleet in Suez and prepare for a holy war (jihad) against the Portuguese.

The padishah purportedly ordered his governor to capture the ports in India and expell the Portuguese, who had blocked the pilgrims' way to the Holy Cities.[11] In late June, an Ottoman fleet of seventy-six ships left Suez for Diu.[12] The fleet could have carried a crew of about ten to twenty thousand men, including about two to six thousand soldiers. Among the crew were a few hundred Venetians (rowers, gunners, and skilled artisans), whom Süleyman Pasha had forced to serve on his fleet, on account of the Venetian-Ottoman war that had started in 1537. After stopping at Jeddah and the Kamaran Island for water, the fleet arrived at Aden. In Aden, Süleyman Pasha tricked the local ruler onto his ship and executed him along with his viziers. Meanwhile, Turkish soldiers disembarked at the harbor and captured the fort of Aden. Leaving 415 soldiers in the fort, the pasha sent a letter to the Porte, requesting more troops, weapons, gunpowder, and provisions. Süleyman Pasha arrived near Diu in early October. He promptly besieged the city, which had been under Gujarati siege for more than three weeks. However, having seen the atrocities of the Ottoman janissaries, the Gujarati troops under Hoca Safar withdrew. Mahmud Shah III (r. 1537–54) of Gujarat—son and successor of Sultan Bahadur, whom the Portuguese had killed before the expedition—also refused to cooperate with the Ottomans, fearing that the Ottomans would establish permanent bases in India. Despite Ottoman numerical and firepower superiority, Süleyman Pasha failed to capture Diu. After twenty days of fighting, he lifted the siege and returned to Suez. The conquest of Aden, this vital trading port city of immense strategic value, greatly enhanced the Ottomans' ability to monitor the Indian Ocean maritime traffic and trade. It took until 1547 to capture Sanaa in Yemen. However, the Zaidi imam and his supporters refused to acknowledge the Ottomans and launched a protracted guerilla war.[13]

In 1552, an Ottoman expedition by Piri Reis, admiral of the Indian Ocean fleet, also failed. In April, Piri left Suez with twenty-five galleys, four galleons, and a larger ship with 850 soldiers onboard. Having captured and demolished the Portuguese base of Muscat in August, Piri laid siege to Hormuz on 19 September. Despite conquering most of the island, he failed to take the citadel. Fearful of an approaching Portuguese relief fleet, Piri lifted the siege on 9 October. In late October, he sailed for Basra. Warned by the captured Portuguese commander of Muscat that the Portuguese fleet at Hormuz could prevent his return to Suez, Piri left his fleet at Basra. He hurried to Suez with three galleys, laden with his expedition's spoils. From Suez, the Ottoman seaman went to Cairo, where the governor-general arrested him for abandoning the fleet. On the orders of Sultan Süleyman, Piri Reis was executed in late 1553. His wealth was confiscated and sent to the treasury in Aleppo, to be used in the ongoing campaign against the Safavids.[14]

The attempts to bring back Piri Reis's ships from Basra in 1553 and 1554 produced the same unfortunate end. In 1553, Murad Reis, the admiral of the Egyptian fleet, went overland to Basra. Taking with him fifteen galleys, one galleon, and one *barco*, he set sail from Basra in August, but the Portuguese defeated him at the Strait of Hormuz. The government next charged Seydi (Sidi) Ali Reis with the task of retrieving Piri Reis's ships. Seydi Ali was a veteran seaman of the Ottoman campaigns against Rhodes (1522), Preveza (1538), and Tripoli (1551) and the newly appointed admiral of the Indian Ocean fleet. He set sail from Basra on 2 July 1554 with his fifteen ships. But he never reached the Red Sea. In early August, he twice encountered a larger Portuguese fleet off the Omani coast. He claimed that he won the first encounter but lost the second. Then, a violent storm damaged and deflected his ships toward India. He disembarked at the Gujarati port of Surat in late September. Fearing Portuguese warships that patrolled the coast, Seydi Ali sold the remaining ships. In late November 1554, he embarked on a long and adventurous trip with some fifty companions to return to the Ottoman Empire overland. Passing through Ahmadabad, Lahore, Kabul, Samarkand, Bukhara, Rayy, and Qazwin, he arrived at the Ottoman frontier provincial capital of Baghdad in late February 1557.[15]

In 1561–62, Sultan al-Kahar of Aceh asked for Ottoman military aid against the Portuguese. Sultan Süleyman answered the plea with caution, reciprocating the mission by sending eight Ottoman gunners and his agent to Aceh. Süleyman hoped to reach an agreement with the Portuguese and did not want to risk his navy beyond Yemen. Things changed only slightly under Sultan Selim II, who wanted to assert his position in the Muslim world as a *ghazi* padishah. In peace with the

Safavids since 1555 and hoping to renew the peace with the Habsburgs, Selim II welcomed the request for help from the sultan of Aceh. In September 1567, he ordered seventeen Ottoman ships with guns to be sent to Aceh, but the fleet had to be diverted to quell a rebellion in Yemen.[16]

The idea to deploy part of the Ottoman Mediterranean fleet in the Indian Ocean via a canal at Suez reemerged in January 1568, when Selim II ordered the governor of Egypt to investigate the project's feasibility. The governor dispatched knowledgeable local architects and engineers, who studied the possibility of the construction of a canal between the Mediterranean and the Red Sea, reporting the length and width of the prospective canal. The plan was motivated by the threat that the Portuguese still posed to the Holy Cities and Muslim pilgrims coming from India. However, nothing came of it.[17]

The Ottoman Red Sea galley fleet did not permit long-range power projection and could not match the Portuguese oceangoing navy. Therefore, Ottoman strategy focused on containment rather than conquest. The Ottomans defended the Hijaz and the Red Sea, but attempts to dislodge the Portuguese from the Indian Ocean failed. The Ottomans' cooperation with the Indian Ocean Muslim sultanates did not lead to any tangible readjustment of Ottoman strategic priorities either. The empire's strategic focus remained the rivalries with the Habsburgs and Safavids. With no military success and no viable naval base beyond Yemen, Ottoman influence among the Indian Ocean Muslims remained modest.[18] But Ottoman efforts were not entirely futile. Despite Ottoman naval failures, the Muslim alliance helped restore the Islamic spice trade routes, bringing pepper from Aceh-ruled Pasai to the Red Sea. By the 1560s, the Islamic spice trade rivaled the Portuguese routes around Africa. Ottoman gunners and military advisers helped transmit firearms and naval technologies to the Indian Ocean.[19]

Muscovy and the Ottomans

The 1550s witnessed the emergence of Muscovy as a new rival. Until the 1550s, proxy conflicts typified engagement between the Ottoman Empire and Muscovy, in which the Crimean Tatars and the Don Cossacks, living upriver from Ottoman Azak (Ru. Azov), played the leading roles. The word *Cossack* comes from the Cuman (Kipchak Turkish) word *kazak*, meaning "free men" or "wanderer." The Cossacks may have originally been Tatar refugees hired as mercenaries by Muscovy. By the latter part of the sixteenth century, the majority of them had become Russians and Ruthenians (ancestors of the Ukrainians), with Tatars among them. They lived in the "wild fields" devoid of political authority along the Don, Donets, and Terek Rivers, and at the Dnieper bend, "beyond the rapids" (*Zaporozhe*). The relationship between Muscovy and the Don Cossacks was similar to that of the Ottoman Porte and the Crimean Tatars. As a client polity, but nominally independent until 1671, the Don Cossacks performed valuable military service for their Muscovite patron as a buffer against the Crimean Tatars and Ottomans, as auxiliaries and allied forces, and as gatherers of information. However, the various Cossack hosts routinely defied the authority of Muscovy and the Polish-Lithuanian Commonwealth and often switched sides. They habitually raided the Crimean khanate and the Ottoman Empire, causing much political disturbance in the Pontic steppe and igniting wars among Muscovy, the Commonwealth, and the Ottoman Empire.[20]

In the first part of the sixteenth century, Muscovy could mobilize some one hundred thousand soldiers, although deployed troop strengths were much smaller, ranging from about thirty thousand to thirty-six thousand men.[21] The potential strength of the Ottoman army exceeded one hundred thousand men, but in actuality, the size of mobilized troops for major Ottoman campaigns led personally by the padishah was closer to sixty thousand to seventy thousand soldiers. However, the Ottomans never led such campaigns against Muscovy, which in the mid-sixteenth century annexed the khanates of Kazan (1552) and Astrakhan (1554–56). These conquests under Tsar Ivan IV (r. 1547–84) changed the balance of power in the region. From the new fortress town of Astrakhan—built sixteen kilometers downstream from the old Tatar Astrakhan on the Volga River—Muscovy gradually expanded its influence among the peoples living in the Volga region and the northern Caucasus.

The chief outpost of Ottoman power in the region against Cossack raids and Muscovy's expansion was Azak on the Don estuary, conquered in 1475. A vital trading colony under the Venetians known as Tana, Ottoman Azak retained its significance as a trading center on the Don River for Muscovite, Ottoman, Italian, Polish-Lithuanian, Habsburg, Mamluk, and Persian merchants. In 1542, the town had about 3,380 overwhelmingly Muslim inhabitants. Armenian, Greek, Jewish, and Russian merchants represented the above states, according to Russian and European sources. Ottoman revenue surveys from 1520 and 1542 mentioned only "Rus," Circassian, and Greek inhabitants. Azak was one of the trading centers through which wheat, horses, and slaves from the region reached the Ottoman capital. In addition to its function as a trading center, Azak also served as a site of diplomatic contacts between the Ottomans and Muscovy. The latter stationed a representative in the town, charged with the task of assisting Muscovite diplomats. Azak was also a convenient place to gather information for the grand prince of Muscovy about events in the Crimea, the Ottoman Empire, the Caucasus, and Iran.[22]

From the middle of the sixteenth century onward, the Don Cossacks threatened Azak. They attacked the fort in 1559 in conjunction with the Dnieper Cossacks. The disintegration of the Nogays, a nomadic Turkic people and the remnants of the Golden Horde, further destabilized the region. While the Lesser Nogays, who settled between the Don River and the Caucasus, cooperated with the Ottomans and their Crimean vassals, the Great Nogay horde on the left bank of the Volga River recognized Moscow's authority. It was with Nogay support that the Muscovites conquered the khanates of Kazan and Astrakhan. The Russians also extended their influence into the Caucasus when the Kabardian prince Temrük asked for protection in 1558–59, gave his daughter to Ivan IV in marriage, and sent his son to Moscow, where he converted to Christianity.[23] Responding to threats of joint Muscovite, Don Cossack, and Nogay attacks against the Crimea and Azak, the Porte ordered the *sancak* governors of Caffa and Silistra to defend the Black Sea littoral. However, the ten forts of the *sancak* of Caffa had only about eleven hundred to twelve hundred garrison soldiers in the mid-sixteenth century. Therefore, the protection of the Ottoman Black Sea littoral depended on the Crimean khanate and the *timariot* cavalry of Rumeli, usually those serving in the *sancaks* of Silistra, Çirmen (Gr. Ormenio), Nikopol, and Vidin, but occasionally in regions as far west as Lepanto.[24] Azak was uniquely vulnerable when Ottoman ships sent there from Constantinople returned to the capital for the winter. Therefore, in the years after the 1559 Cossack attack, the Porte established a naval arsenal and a small flotilla at Azak.[25]

By 1563, Sokullu Mehmed Pasha had become receptive to the complaints that the Muscovite garrison in Astrakhan closed the pilgrimage and trade routes between Turkistan and Azak. Living in Constantinople as refugees, the last two khans of the Astrakhan Tatar khanate lobbied for Ottoman intervention. Sokollu's close associate Çerkes ("the Circassian") Kasım Pasha also supported the campaign and the plan to connect the Don and Volga Rivers with a canal. Kasım was the third treasurer of the empire and former *sancak* governor of Caffa with contacts among the Circassians and Nogays. When the plan of the canal was raised in the imperial council, Sokollu backed the project. The canal would have enabled the Ottomans to capture Astrakhan with the flotilla and Ottoman and Crimean Tatar land forces. The Porte hoped to transport Ottoman ships carrying siege cannons, arms, ammunition, and provisions from the Don River to the Volga River and thence to the Caspian Sea. This would have allowed the Ottomans to attack Safavid Persia from the north and conquer the province of Shirvan. Alas, Devlet Giray (r. 1551–77) of the Crimean khanate considered the region adjacent to his khanate his sphere of influence and objected to its control by the Ottomans. In the end, opposition at the Porte diverted Süleyman's attention from the Volga region to the Mediterranean.[26]

After the accession of Selim II in 1566, Sokollu Mehmed revived the plan of the Astrakhan campaign, despite opposition by some members of the imperial council. In addition to concerns raised in 1563, the Ottomans now were alarmed by reports about a new Muscovite fort on the Terek River. It increased Muscovy's influence in the North Caucasus and Persia by controlling the Astrakhan–Derbend–Tabriz route. The Ottomans also were concerned about a Muscovite mission to the Safavid court. The khan of Khiva also urged Sultan Selim to take Astrakhan, which obstructed the hajj route. His envoy may have intentionally exaggerated Astrakhan's revenues from trade ("more than a thousand gold coins a day") to make the campaign financially more attractive at the Porte. The Ottoman leadership also had heard from the Tatars and Azak Turks that the Don Cossacks had dragged their ships between the Don and Volga, which made the canal project seem feasible. In February 1568, the Porte ordered Devlet Giray and the *sancak* governor of Caffa to prepare for the campaign, planned for 1569.[27]

The 1569 Astrakhan campaign was a dismal failure. The Crimean khan, fearful of increased Ottoman influence in the region, did not allow the Ottoman troops coming from Rumeli to use the shorter route through the Crimea. The long march to Azak across the Kipchak steppes exhausted the soldiers and their food supplies. By the time Kasım Pasha of Caffa—the campaign's commander in chief—arrived at Azak, he had some fifteen thousand troops, including three thousand janissaries. Devlet Giray joined them in early July with the Tatar army of thirty thousand strong, including Nogay and Circassian contingents. The army soon left Azak, following the flotilla carrying cannons, ammunition, and provisions. They ascended the Don, reaching Perevolok by mid-August.

The plan was to dig a canal between the Don and Volga near the Tsaritsa River, a tributary of the Don. However, Kasım quickly realized that the topographical information he had been given was inaccurate. The distance between the rivers was about sixty kilometers, not ten as he had been told, and the terrain was hilly and challenging. Since building the canal was technically impossible, Kasım decided to haul the ships overland to the Volga. This too failed, because of insurmountable physical obstacles. Kasım abandoned the plan and sent the flotilla back to Azak with most of the siege artillery. He continued with the army to Astrakhan, where the plan was to winter in barracks built in Old Astrakhan. Ottoman and Tatar forces reached Astrakhan by mid-September. However, they failed to capture the fort with their light field artillery. The army ended the siege after just ten days and departed for Azak. They reached Azak after a devastating monthlong march, during which thousands died of hunger and thirst. Kasım wanted to renew the operation in the spring, but the government in Constantinople had already committed to the Cyprus campaign.[28] The Mediterranean still figured more prominently in Ottoman strategic thinking than the Volga and Caspian theaters.

A generation after the failure of the Astrakhan campaign, Cossacks from Zaporizhia and the Don region raided Ottoman towns in the Crimea and the Black Sea shores (1606–16) on many occasions, further complicating the relationships among the Ottomans, the Polish-Lithuanian Commonwealth, and Muscovy. In 1624, Cossack raiders even entered the Bosporus and ravaged the outskirts of the Ottoman capital.[29] Between 1574 and 1634, Akkerman, at the mouth of the Dniester River, suffered no fewer than fourteen raids. Caffa, the center of Ottoman administration in the Crimea, was sacked in 1616. The Cossacks raided Sinop on Asia Minor's Black Sea coast in 1614, and Trabzon on numerous occasions in the 1610s, followed by more severe attacks in the 1620s. In 1625, they again raided Trabzon and carried away its captured people as slaves. In 1637, the Cossacks even captured Azak, and it was not until 1642 that the Ottomans recovered it.[30]

Cyprus and the Battle of Lepanto

In the Mediterranean, the battle of Lepanto, on 7 October 1571, provoked by the Ottoman conquest of Cyprus, was the most dramatic confrontation between Muslim and Christian oar-powered navies. For Sokollu Mehmed Pasha, the conquest of Cyprus fulfilled a long-overdue task. This Venetian-held island stood as a nuisance in the Ottoman-controlled eastern Mediterranean. Cyprus offered a safe haven for Christian corsairs who preyed on Muslim merchant and pilgrim ships and endangered the Ottoman lines of maritime communication between Constantinople and Egypt, the richest province of the empire. The failure to eliminate Christian privateering raised the specter of severe economic losses and weakened Constantinople's legitimacy in the Muslim world. Cyprus's wealth and proximity to Ottoman logistical bases made it a desirable target. Moreover, a successful campaign against Cyprus would allow Sokollu to improve his standing, which had been compromised by the failure of the Don-Volga canal project and the Astrakhan campaign. The assertion of modern historians—following contemporary

Venetian sources—that Joseph Nassí, the influential Sephardic banker and agent, persuaded Sultan Selim II to attack Cyprus despite the opposition of his grand vizier is questionable.[31]

During the 1570 campaign against Cyprus, the Ottomans mobilized approximately 60,000 troops and somewhere between 200 and 360 vessels (if one includes transport ships for troops), horses, draft animals, food, and military supplies. A fleet of 25 ships sailed from Constantinople to Rhodes in March to gather information about the Venetian navy and to block potential Venetian assistance to the besieged island. A larger navy of 65 to 85 galleys and 30 galleons as transport ships under the command of Piyale Pasha left the Ottoman capital a month later on 26 April. Müezzinzade Ali Pasha, the admiral of the navy, left a few days after Piyale "with a goodly number of galleys" and a rough total of 160 ships. The two fleets joined in the Gulf of Antalya on 17 June. The last to leave the capital on 16 May was Lala Mustafa Pasha, commander in chief of the expedition. His fleet included 48 larger and smaller galleys, 8 mahones, and 80 transport ships.[32]

Despite its up-to-date fortifications, Nicosia, the capital of Cyprus, fell on 9 September, after forty-six days of siege. The Ottomans had shorter supply lines, and reinforcements resulted in a six to one advantage in personnel. The attackers excelled in siege warfare. Disunion in the allied Christian fleet and the dismal performance of the Venetian relief fleet, plagued by typhus and desertions, weakened the defense, as did the incompetence of Nicosia's commander. In addition, the Cypriots helped the Ottoman besiegers against their detested Venetian overlords. The ferocity of the three-day sack of Nicosia persuaded the other Venetian forts to surrender. The exception was the eastern port garrison of Famagusta, which the Ottomans captured a year later (1 August 1571), after it had resisted seven general assaults and seventy-four days of heavy bombardment. Although the conquerors agreed to generous terms of surrender, the massacre of Muslim pilgrims kept in the garrison provoked Ottoman retaliation. On 5 August, the Venetian officers were beheaded and Governor Marcantonio Bragadin was skinned alive for his order to kill the Muslims. The Ottomans stuffed Bragadin's hide with straw and paraded it along the Asian coast and in Constantinople.[33]

The Ottoman conquest of Cyprus provoked the formation of the anti-Ottoman Holy League of Spain, Venice, Genoa, Tuscany, Savoy, Urbino, Parma, and the Knights of Malta. Proclaimed in Rome on 25 May 1571, the league assigned itself the task of recapturing Cyprus and the Holy Land and fighting a perpetual war against the Ottomans and the Muslims of North Africa. The signatories agreed to provide two hundred galleys, one hundred transport ships (furnished with cannons), munitions, fifty thousand infantry, and forty-five hundred cavalry.[34] The league was the last major coalition of European Christian forces against the Ottomans in the Mediterranean. Still, divisions in Christendom undermined the possibility of the participation of all major powers. Shrewd Ottoman diplomacy also fostered disunity in Europe. In 1568, the Ottomans made peace with Emperor Maximilian II, who declined to join the league, hoping to maintain the precarious peace with the Ottomans in Hungary. The Porte also had extended trade privileges to France in the capitulation of 1569, and King Charles IX did not want to risk his merchants' most favored status in the vast Ottoman domains. The league also suffered from the competition over the command of the joint naval force.

Despite all difficulties and disagreements, the joint fleet—commanded by Don Juan de Austria, the twenty-three-year-old half brother of Philip II of Spain—achieved a resounding victory at the battle of Lepanto. The allied fleet assembled in Messina in early September and reached Corfu on 26 September. Here the alliance learned that the Ottoman navy, which had raided Crete and Venice's Adriatic possessions during the summer, had returned to Lepanto, a harbor town on the north side of the Gulf of Patras. On 4 October, the Christians became aware of the fall of Famagusta and Bragadino's torture. The news sparked desire for vengeance, giving the fragile alliance unity of purpose. Meanwhile, Ottoman scouts informed their commanders about the arrival of a Christian fleet off Caphalonia. At a war council held on 4 October, Pertev Pasha, commander in chief of the 1571 campaign, and Uluc Ali Pasha, governor-general of Algiers, believed that the Ottomans should take a defensive position in the Gulf of Lepanto, citing the undermanned nature and exhaustion of the navy. However, Müezzinzade Ali Pasha, admiral of the navy and a land commander with no experience in naval warfare, ultimately prevailed. He ordered his fleet to attack the Christians.

The opposing navies clashed on 7 October in the Gulf of Patras. The numbers of vessels recorded in various contemporary sources (202 to 219 galleys and 6 galleasses on the Christian side as opposed to 205 galleys and 35 to 68 *galiots* on the Ottoman side) are misleading. They exclude the smaller transport ships in both navies and the *galiots* and frigates in the Christian fleet. The Holy League slightly outnumbered the Ottomans in terms of combatants and auxiliaries (62,100 to 57,700). The league also had a substantial advantage in firepower (1,334 to 741 guns). Ottoman accounts also underline that their fleet suffered from a shortage of manpower. Many died during the 1571 campaign, and the soldiers aboard the coastal begs' ships had already returned home for the winter.[35]

At the beginning of the battle, the Venetian left wing lost several galleys and one of its commanders was mortally wounded. However, reinforcements sent from the rear guard soon turned the defeat into victory and destroyed the entire Ottoman right wing. Meanwhile, the Ottoman center collapsed. Don Juan's flagship (the *Real*) took the Ottoman flagship (the *Sultana*) in tow, following the death of its commander. Ottoman ships in the center were sunk or taken, and almost their entire crew mercilessly massacred. The clash between the seaward squadrons started later. Both Uluc Ali and Giovanni Andrea Doria— the most skilled sea captains on either side—tried to outmaneuver the other. Uluc Ali managed to inflict serious damage on Doria's galleys, which broke formation. To help the overwhelmed Ottoman center, Uluc Ali attacked the Christian center's right flank. But the maneuver came too late. Ali Pasha had already fallen in battle and Don Álvaro Bazán sent his remaining reserve against Uluc Ali. Realizing that he could not save the day, Uluc Ali escaped into the open sea with thirty galleys. The league's navy destroyed almost the entire Ottoman fleet with its crew and ordnance.[36]

After Lepanto

By next spring the Ottomans had rebuilt their navy. Under the supervision of the new grand admiral Uluc Ali—now known as Kılıç Ali—the arsenal in Constantinople constructed 150 new galleys and 8 galleasses, complete with artillery. The admiral initially regarded the task of rebuilding the fleet as impossible, complaining to Grand Vizier Sokollu Mehmed Pasha: "It is easy to construct the hulls, but to prepare five or six hundred anchors for two hundred ships and the matching amounts of cordage, sails and other equipment seems impossible." To this the grand vizier reportedly said: "The might and power of this Exalted State is such that if the order were given to provide anchors of silver, cordage of silk, and sails of satin for the whole fleet, it would be possible—whatsoever is lacking on any ship, just ask me for it."[37]

European observers confirmed the large-scale ship construction and its results. The French ambassador in Constantinople reported that

> in five months, they [the Ottomans] have built 150 vessels with all the artillery and equipment needed and, yes, they have resolved to continue at this pace for an entire year. . . . Already their general is prepared to set out to sea at the end of this month with two hundred galleys and one hundred *galiots*, of corsairs and others, without the Grand Seigneur's having used a single écu in his treasury for this huge expense. In short, I should never have believed the greatness of this monarchy, had I not seen it with my own eyes.[38]

When the rebuilt Ottoman navy of 180 to 230 ships emerged from Constantinople in July 1572, it appeared that Lepanto did very little to alter the balance of power in the Mediterranean.[39] But Lepanto ended Christendom's inferiority complex. It also demolished Ottoman maritime supremacy. Although the Ottomans quickly rebuilt their galleys, it took decades for them to replace the skilled Muslim marines, sailor-arquebusiers, and naval archers. The French ambassador noted that the fleet was "built of green timber, rowed by crews which had never held an oar, provided with artillery which had been cast in haste, several pieces being compounded of acidic and rotten material."[40] Ali Pasha knew too well the weakness of his navy. On 7 August 1572, he met a Christian armada of 145 galleys, 22 round ships, 6 galleasses, and 25 *galiots* and *fuste*. Instead of a head-on collision, he opted for hit-and-run tactics to break the enemy's formation. He followed the same tactics two days later, losing some 7 galleys. He suffered a tactical defeat, but won strategically, as the allied fleet left for Corfu.[41]

Pope Pius V, the driving force behind the league, died on 1 May 1572. Exhausted and under pressure from the mercantile elite to restore the lucrative trade with the Ottomans, the Serenissima was ready to reach a deal with the padishah. The Council of Ten secretly instructed the republic's imprisoned *bailo* in Constantinople to start negotiations. With the help of the French ambassador and Solomon (Shelomoh) Ashkenazi—Grand Vizier Sokollu Mehmed Pasha's Jewish doctor and confidant—Bailo Marc'Antonio Barbaro signed a "perpetual peace" with the Porte on 7 March 1573. Venice lost Cyprus and had to pay 300,000 ducats of war indemnity, but the republic recovered most of the lost territories in Albania and Dalmatia and saved Crete, Corfu, and Kotor.[42]

Disappointed by the Venetian-Ottoman treaty, the Spanish navy under the command of Don John of Austria attacked Tunis, which Uluc Ali had conquered in 1569. Tunis fell to the Spanish in October 1573. In response, in May 1574 an Ottoman fleet of some 240 galleys, 16 galleasses, 3 galleons, and other ships—an armada larger than those at Lepanto—left Constantinople to retake Tunis. Kılıç Ali Pasha commanded the fleet, while Koca (Great) Sinan Pasha led the land forces. They appeared at the Bay of Tunis on 12 July. After a monthlong siege, on 25 August they conquered La Goletta (Halk al-Wadi), which the Spanish had held since 1535. The Christian garrison of Tunis fell to the Ottomans on 13 September.[43] The victory—off the coast of Spanish Habsburg Sicily at such a great distance from Constantinople, the logistical center of Ottoman operations—demonstrated Ottoman naval resurgence and restored Ottoman military prestige on both sides of the religious divide.

Capitalizing on their recent victory, Ottoman janissaries and artillery gunners in 1576 helped unseat the Moroccan sultan Muhammad al-Mutawakkil, who challenged Ottoman sovereignty. They replaced him with an Ottoman client, Abd al-Malik, of the same Saadi dynasty. Threatened by recent Ottoman advance in North Africa, the Portuguese launched an attack on Morocco in 1578 under the command of their devout crusading king, Don Sebastian (r. 1557–78). The expedition resulted in the dramatic "Battle of the Three Kings" on 4 August 1578, near the Moroccan town al-Qasr al-Kabir (Port. Alcácer-Quibir). It left both Moroccan sultans and the Portuguese king dead. The battle was the last major confrontation between Christian and Muslim forces in the Mediterranean. Ottoman resurgence in the Mediterranean persuaded Philip II to reach out for a truce with the Ottomans. This was successfully negotiated by early February 1578 and renewed in March 1580 and the next year. The latter document stipulated the suspension of hostilities by the parties and their allies for three years. The conclusion of a truce allowed both parties to attend to more pressing concerns. The Ottomans had been waging a destructive war against the Safavids since 1578. Spain had been bogged down in the Dutch revolt since 1568. It fought the Protestant Northern Provinces in the Low Countries, which declared their independence in 1581. Spain also pursued the acquisition of its weakened Catholic neighbor Portugal (1581).[44] The grand admiral of the Ottoman navy set out each campaign season from Constantinople to make the "volta": the inspection tour in the Archipelago and along the principal maritime lanes in the eastern Mediterranean Sea. But lack of active campaigning soon resulted in the decline of the Ottoman fleet.[45]

By the time the Ottomans concluded the treaty with Spain, they were again at war with the Safavids. The Ottoman-Safavid war of 1578–90 broke out for a number of reasons. Tempted by the turmoil in Iran that followed the death of Shah Tahmasb in 1576 and confident of their military superiority, the war faction at the Porte hoped to conquer large swathes of territory from the Safavids in the Caucasus. The seasoned grand vizier, Sokollu Mehmed, advised Sultan Murad III (r. 1574–95) against the war, citing logistical and fiscal problems.[46] However, the anti-Sokollu faction at the court, assisted by Murad's Venetian-born queen mother, Nur Banu, swayed Murad into war. Deep-seated anti-Safavid and anti-Shiite sentiment among the Ottoman elite also played a role in launching the campaign against the vilified neighbor. The Porte accused the Safavids of spreading Shiite propaganda and inciting unrest in eastern Asia Minor, especially among the Kurds. At war with his other Sunni neighbor, the Shaibanid Uzbeks—who had seized Herat and attacked Mashhad—Shah Abbas I (r. 1587–1629) concluded a humiliating peace with the Ottomans in 1590. The treaty extended the Ottoman Empire's eastern borders, leaving in Ottoman hands Azerbaijan with the former Safavid capital Tabriz, parts of Armenia, Georgia, and Shirvan.[47]

Small Wars: The Bosnian-Croatian Frontier

The Ottomans could fight and win against the Safavids at the end of the sixteenth century partly because there was an official peace with the Habsburgs. In the Treaty of Edirne (1568), Emperor Maximilian II acknowledged the recent Ottoman conquests in Hungary and continued to pay the annual tribute to the padishah.[48] The Transylvanian issue, which had caused multiple wars between the Habsburgs and the Ottomans, was also settled. In the Treaty of Speyer, signed at the imperial diet in 1570, John Sigismund Szapolyai renounced his title of elected king of Hungary (*electus rex Hungariae*) and assumed the title of prince of Transylvania and of the adjacent parts of Hungary (*Princeps Transylvaniae et partium regni Hungariae eidem annexarum*), which Maximilian acknowledged. John Sigismund also accepted Maximilian's suzerainty over his principality, which remained part (*membrum*) of the Holy Crown of Hungary. At the same time, the Transylvanian prince remained an Ottoman vassal. In short, the Principality of Transylvania existed in a dual dependency, and its sovereignty was limited by both the padishah and Hungary's Habsburg kings.[49]

The Treaty of Edirne (1568) created mechanisms to settle anticipated border disputes by authorizing the Ottoman governor-general in Buda and his counterparts in Komárom and Vienna to handle conflicts. But mutual cross-border raids routinely disturbed the peace. Soldiers on both sides attacked enemy territories and collected taxes by force. They also took hostages, both soldiers and civilians. These captives were held for ransom, a flourishing frontier industry practice, while the less fortunate were sold at the Ottoman slave markets.[50] The parties acknowledged that it was impossible to stop cross-border raids and smaller clashes. Yet, for two decades they were able to manage local conflicts, renewing the 1568 treaty in 1574, 1576, 1583, and 1590.

In 1591 Sufi Sinan Pasha of Buda confessed that he was unable to stop smaller skirmishes but hoped to avoid major battles, which could lead to war between the two empires. So long as "cannons were not brought against castles" and the Habsburg monarch sent the annual tribute to Constantinople, the peace could be upheld.[51] Sinan and Archduke Ernst worked diligently to maintain the peace. When the latter complained that the *sancak* governor of Fülek had raided two villages and kidnapped peasants, Sinan promptly redressed the grievances. Once his investigation revealed that the complaints were legitimate, he searched for the abducted peasants as far south as Belgrade and returned them to their villages. Moreover, he achieved at the Porte the removal of the *sancak* governor of Fülek, assuring the archduke that from now on there "will be a good beg in his stead." Sinan promised that he would strive to maintain good neighborly relations.[52]

But problems were mounting along the Croatian-Bosnian border. The Ottoman chronicler Cafer İyani detailed several skirmishes.[53] The chronicler was privy to most of the events as he was from Pécs in southwestern Hungary and spent the 1580s and the early 1590s on the frontier. Most contemporaries blamed the escalation of hostilities on the recently appointed Bosnian governor, Telli or Derviş Hasan Pasha, a native of Herzegovina. Born as Nikola Predojević and taken in the *devşirme*, he became the protégé of Grand Vizier Siyavuş Pasha, a fellow south Slav from Croatia. After his arrival in Bosnia in 1591, Hasan launched cross-border raids into Croatia, unsuccessfully besieging Sisak in August. In early 1592, disregarding the Porte's order to avoid further conflicts, Hasan took Bihać (19 June). He also built a fortress, Yenihisar ("New Fortress," that is, Petrinja), on the Kupa River. The chronicler Selaniki Mustafa remarked that many praised the pasha at the Porte because his conquests "opened up the road to Vienna, and thus the victorious troops do not anymore need to go around Buda" when attacking the Habsburg capital.[54] A member of the Habsburg embassy in Constantinople later remembered the joyful celebrations with which the Ottomans greeted Hasan's victories. Hasan "brought, with great rejoicing, 300 Christian prisoners to Constantinople, each of whom was compelled to carry five or six stuffed heads of slaughtered Christians . . . [The Turks] were delighted at the victory, and lauded Hassan Pasha for having sent these Christians to Constantinople, as a conqueror."[55]

By tolerating Hasan Pasha's violations of the truce—which prohibited both sieges with cannons and the building of new forts—the Porte supported the escalation of hostilities. When in 1593 Hasan Pasha crossed the Kupa and besieged Sisak, the Viennese government sent a relief force to save the fortress that controlled the road to Zagreb and Austria along the Sava River. On 22 June 1593, Habsburg troops from Carniola, Carinthia, and Croatia routed the Ottomans at the battle of Sisak. An Ottoman eyewitness attributed the Ottoman defeat to the Christian forces' superior firepower and the Ottoman army's disorder. Since the beginning of the war at the Bosnian-Croatian border, the commanders had forcefully recruited peasants and artisans into the military. These individuals, however, lacked military skills and fled the battle.[56] Some eight thousand Ottoman soldiers were either killed or drowned in the river. Among the dead were Hasan, whose head was sent to Rudolf II, and seven of his *sancak* governors. The latter included two sons of Ayşe Sultan—Süleyman's granddaughter—Sultanzade Mehmed and Mustafa, the *sancak* governors of Hersek and Klis.[57]

Ottoman and European sources claimed that Grand Vizier Koca Sinan Pasha used the Sisak rout and the delayed Habsburg tribute to declare war against Vienna. The latter was indeed just an excuse, as it was not unusual that the tribute was delayed.[58] At the Ottoman court, there was strong support for a more belligerent policy vis-à-vis the Habsburgs. Known for his criticism of the Ottoman elite and his dislike of Sinan, the chronicler Mustafa Âli blamed the Ottoman governing elite for causing the war by not removing the Bosnian governor after he violated the truce. Âli also noted how Sinan—whom he described as arrogant, power-hungry, and cowardly—used the Sisak rout as a pretext for the war.[59] The same picture emerges from the chronicle of İbrahim Peçevi, who hailed from the southwestern Hungarian town Pécs, spent most of his life on the Hungarian frontier, participated in many battles of the Long War of 1593–1606, and personally knew many of the key players. Peçevi is the most explicit in pointing out factionalism at the Ottoman court and blaming Sinan for starting the war. Peçevi claimed that Sinan, who had been angry with Hasan over an older property dispute, denied military assistance to Hasan. Sinan transferred the former governor of Rumeli (whom Siyavuş Pasha had sent to assist Hasan) to Temesvár, appointing his own son, Sinanpaşazade Mehmed, to the governorship of Rumeli. However, Mehmed was still at the Porte when Hasan launched his fateful campaign in 1593 and thus could not help. Peçevi also asserted that by starting the war against the Habsburgs, Sinan hoped to outshine his rival Ferhad Pasha, the victorious commander in chief of the Ottoman-Safavid war of 1578–90.[60]

Contemporaries knew well the rivalry between Sinan and Ferhad Pashas. The latter not only scored victories against the Safavids but also concluded a favorable treaty with the Safavids in 1590. His rival, Sinan, commanded the Ottoman troops in the early phase (1579–80) of the Safavid-Ottoman war and was appointed grand vizier in 1580. However, his failure to conclude a truce with the Safavids led to his dismissal in 1582. Because of his substantial wealth and connections, Sinan was appointed grand vizier for the second time in 1589, but he was again dismissed and replaced by his rival Ferhad in 1591. A rebellion of the janissaries in the capital cost Ferhad his office in the spring of 1592. His successor, Siyavuş Pasha, the patron of the Bosnian governor Telli Hasan, also lost his office. In January 1593, the Porte gave the grand vizier's seal to Sinan for the third time.

At a council meeting hastily convened on 4 July 1593, a day after the news of the Sisak rout arrived in Constantinople, Sinan persuaded Sultan Murad III to declare war on the Habsburgs, disregarding the opposition of his rival Ferhad. The latter pointed out that the troops were exhausted from the long Safavid war and that it was too late in the campaign season to start a war.[61] The chief jurisconsult Zekeriya Efendi also opposed the war. Conveniently for the war party, Zekeriya died on 11 July, just days after his protest. Europeans believed that either Sinan or the padishah had Zekeriya poisoned.[62] The new chief jurisconsult sided with the war party by supporting the war. In addition to factionalism and Sinan's ambitions, the war party also received support from Ayşe Sultan, who hoped to avenge the deaths of her sons, who fell at Sisak.[63]

The Long War in Hungary

Grand Vizier Koca Sinan Pasha hoped for a short war. Ottoman propaganda claimed that the goal of the war was the conquest of the imperial capital Vienna, "the gate of Germany," and Prague, where the court moved under Emperor Rudolf II. In August 1593, Sinan wrote that the target of his campaign was "the German king and his country." In the fall, he told the Transylvanian envoy that he would besiege Vienna or Prague in the spring. Emperor Rudolf believed that Sinan wanted to conquer Vienna and then invade Germany. However, Sinan's immediate target was Royal Hungary. He would not touch Vienna, he declared, "so long as a single palisade existed in Hungary and Croatia."[64] To divide the Hungarians, Sinan tried a familiar Ottoman scheme. He offered some aristocrats vassal fiefdoms, including "the voivodeship of Kassa" (modern Košice in Slovakia). The latter would have replaced, as an Ottoman vassal mini-state, the Habsburgs' Upper Hungarian Border Fortress Captain Generalcy, demonstrating the Ottoman leadership's strategic thinking.[65]

Despite late mobilization and departure (29 July), in October 1593 Sinan captured Veszprém after only four days of siege and Palota after only two. But the Ottomans lost two field battles. At Székesfehérvár (3 November), Graf Ferdinand zu Hardegg defeated Sokolluzade Vizier Hasan Pasha, the Ottoman governor of Buda, son of the former grand vizier Sokollu Mehmed. At Romhány, the troops of Upper Hungary routed an Ottoman army sent by the governors of Buda and Temesvár to relieve Fülek (14 November). The Hungarian and Habsburg forces also retook several smaller forts in the counties of Hont and Nográd, which the Ottomans had conquered in 1552–54. The first year of the Long War saw smaller engagements, as neither party was prepared for a full-scale war. Strategically, the Ottoman conquests in Transdanubia were more important, but Hungarian and Habsburg gains in Upper

Hungary were more numerous. The Christian forces also won three field battles (Sisak, Székesfehérvár, and Romhány).[66]

The 1594 campaign season brought Ottoman successes. Sinan took Tata in July and Győr on 29 September, after just five days of siege. His siege of Komárom (4–24 October), however, was unsuccessful. The conquest of Győr—a modern fortified town (*Festungstadt*) and the seat of the Habsburg Border Fortress Captain Generalcy that protected Vienna—was a notable accomplishment. Győr's captain, Graf Ferdinand zu Hardegg, was sentenced to death and executed in June 1595 for the premature handover of the well-supplied fortress, defended by some six thousand Welsh and German mercenaries. Well aware of the strategic importance of the fortress, the Ottomans made Győr the center of a newly organized province. Ottoman conquests of 1593–94 pointed to a strategy that aimed at capturing key fortresses along the Danube military corridor leading to Vienna. The Habsburg conquest of Nógrád did not counterbalance their losses.

The campaign season of 1595 brought about a sudden reversal of Ottoman fortunes, as the Principality of Transylvania sided with the Habsburgs. Following his short-term abdication in July 1594, the Roman Catholic prince Sigismund Báthory returned to the throne with the help of his uncle, Stephen Bocskai, captain of Várad. The Transylvanian diet declared the principality's independence from the Porte on 27 August. Báthory's Spanish Jesuit confessor, Alfonso Carillo, and Stephen Bocskai traveled to Prague to negotiate the terms of a Transylvanian-Habsburg alliance. On 28 January 1595, the twenty-two-year-old prince joined the Christian coalition. A marriage treaty in March in Graz, and the wedding on 6 August in Gyulafehérvár between Sigismund Báthory and Maria Christina (daughter of Archduke Charles II of Habsburg) sealed the agreement. Báthory also formed an anti-Ottoman alliance with the Romanian voivodes—Michael of Wallachia and Stephen Razvan of Moldavia—who acknowledged Báthory's sovereignty. The alliance between the Habsburgs and the Ottoman vassal principalities jeopardized the Ottomans' supply lines along the Danube and the Black Sea. It also denied the Ottoman war effort much needed grain, meat, and transport animals and forced the Ottoman armies to fight on multiple fronts. The Transylvanian troops took Lippa (18 August) and Jenő (22 October), the seats of two Ottoman *sancaks*. Commanded by Báthory, the Transylvanian-Wallachian army took Tirgovişte and routed Sinan's army at the battle of Giorgiu.[67] Meanwhile, in September, Habsburg forces under the capable leadership of Karl Mansfeld captured Esztergom and Visegrád and then defeated an Ottoman army sent to relieve Esztergom. These conquests put Buda, the center of Ottoman Hungary, at risk. Unfortunately for the Habsburgs, Mansfeld died shortly after his victory. His successor, Archduke Maximilian, proved a less competent commander.

Thirty years after Sultan Süleyman's last campaign, the Hungarian theater saw another Ottoman padishah at the head of his army. On 23 September 1596, Sultan Mehmed III besieged Eger, the symbol of Hungarian resistance since its heroic defense in 1552. After the 1552 siege, the War Council strengthened the castle with the help of Italian military architects.[68] However, only four of the planned eight Italian bastions had been completed. Moreover, Eger was vulnerable because the besiegers' cannon fire reached the castle from the nearby hills, which stood thirty-five to fifty-five meters higher than the outer castle. In 1596, Eger had about thirty-four hundred defenders and stood no chance against the sultan's army of some eighty thousand men. Eger had only a handful of cannons and eight artillery gunners, five of whom were sick. After three weeks of siege and the promise to freely leave with their weapons, the defenders surrendered (12 October). The Turks let the Hungarians go but took the Walloons into captivity and let the Tatars massacre the Germans.[69]

Since Eger was damaged in the siege, Archduke Maximilian decided to attack it. But before the Habsburg-Transylvanian forces of about forty thousand to fifty thousand men could besiege Eger, they had to defeat the sultan's army of some eighty thousand men. The fight took place near (Mező)Keresztes, southeast of Eger, from 22 through 26 October. On the first day, the Habsburg-Transylvanian army defeated the sultan's Rumelian troops, capturing dozens of Ottoman cannons. Archduke Maximilian hoped that Sultan Mehmed III would withdraw, allowing him to retake Eger. However, the Ottomans continued the fight. The decisive battle took place on 26 October. The Christians again scored an initial victory, owing to their fortified positions and superior firepower. Pursuing the fleeing Ottoman army across the Csincse creek, they soon reached the Ottoman camp. At this point, the soldiers started to plunder the Ottoman tents, finding the treasury of the campaign. The Ottomans now capitalized on the disorder, regrouped, and led a counterattack. This surprised the Christians, whom the Ottomans routed.[70]

In the absence of a clear Ottoman strategy following Sinan's death (April 1596), the second phase of the war (1597–1604) proved inconclusive. This is illustrated by the failed Habsburg sieges of Buda (3 October–2 November 1598 and 2 October–14 November 1602) and the temporary conquest of Pest (7 October 1602–5 September 1604). The two significant developments of this phase of the war were the Christian reconquest of Győr (29 March 1598) and the Ottoman conquest of Kanizsa (22 October 1600). The realization that the war had reached an impasse led to the first attempts to end the war through negotiations.[71]

The Habsburg alliance with Transylvania proved an uncertain one. In March 1598, Sigismund Báthory abdicated in favor of Emperor Rudolph II, only to return to the throne in late August. Voivode Michael's invasion of Transylvania in 1599 and Moldavia in 1600 resulted in Hungarian resistance against Michael, Polish intervention in the principalities, and Michael's murder by the imperialists. Harsh Habsburg governance in Transylvania, Emperor Rudolph's cruel Counter-Reformation reforms in Upper Hungary, and his declaration that the Hungarian diet could not discuss complaints regarding the Habsburgs' religious policies provoked an armed insurrection. Stephen Bocskai, a Hungarian aristocrat and Báthory's ablest statesman, who previously supported Báthory's pro-Habsburg policy, led the insurrection. The Bocskai uprising changed the power relations between the two belligerent empires. After the uprising, the Habsburgs lost almost all of their recent conquests in a single year, including Pest (5 September 1604) and Esztergom (3 October 1605). The Hungarian and Transylvanian Estates elected Bocskai as their ruling prince. Grand Vizier Lala Mehmed Pasha confirmed him by an *ahdname*, issued in the name of Sultan Ahmed I. The Calvinist Prince Bocskai requested a crown from the Porte to legitimize his election as king of Hungary. On 11 November 1605, in the Ottoman camp on the Field of Rákos Lala Mehmed crowned Bocskai in the name of the padishah with an old crown jewel from the padishah's treasury, which Ottoman goldsmiths had refurbished for the occasion.[72] The choice of Rákos was not accidental: it had been the site of medieval Hungarian diets, where the Estates had elected Charles Robert (1307), Wladislas II of Jagiellonian (1490), and John II Szapolyai (1540) as their kings.

The news of the coronation and Bocskai's alliance with the Ottomans prompted distrust of the Hungarians in many European courts. The Dutch, however, saw similarities between the Dutch revolt against the Habsburgs in the Netherlands and Bocskai's insurrection. A history of the Dutch revolt published in 1608 devoted a great deal of attention to Bocskai and suggested that Ottoman rule was preferable to Habsburg Catholic tyranny. The book also asserted that the coronation legitimized Bocskai's rule.[73] Bocskai's propagandists—including his humanist court historian and diplomat, John (Johannes) Bocatius—claimed that the crown was sent to Bocskai on the Porte's initiative and that Bocskai accepted it only as a gift, not as a crown. Bocskai and his advisers hoped that this fictitious version of the coronation story would help them conclude a treaty with the Habsburg monarch and mediate between the Habsburgs and Ottomans to end the war. Losses against the Ottomans forced the Habsburg government to settle with Bocskai. The Peace of Vienna, on 23 June 1606, confirmed Bocskai's titles and the Estates' religious freedom and constitutional privileges, thus ending the anti-Habsburg insurrection.[74]

By this time, the Ottomans too were ready to end the war. A series of popular revolts had ravaged the Anatolian countryside since the late 1590s. Economic devastation, population pressure, wars, harsh climates, and natural disasters resulted in the collapse of the rural order in Asia Minor, depriving thousands of young peasants of home and country. Many of these lads obtained firearms, despite the government's efforts to ban the use of weapons among the subject population. These vagrants (*levend*) roamed the countryside, forming small groups of brigands. Others joined the household troops (*kapu halkı*) of provincial governors and local strongmen. Yet others sought employment in frontier garrisons or in the provincial mercenary troops—called *sekban* and *sarıca*—which the Porte established during its wars against the Safavids and Habsburgs. At the end of the campaign season, these mercenaries did not return to their villages but instead joined the rebel bands in Asia Minor. Ottoman chroniclers named the rebels Celali, after Sheikh Celal, who had raised a rebellion against the government in 1519. Led by local warlords and rebellious provincial governors, the Celali rebels devastated the Anatolian countryside from the late 1590s through about 1660.[75]

The first such rebellion was directly related to the wars in Hungary. The 1596 campaign saw a surprisingly large number of desertions. After the campaign, the Porte confiscated the *timar* prebends of those who failed to report for military duty or fled the battlefield at Mezőkeresztes. The acts of avoiding military service and deserting during campaigns were not new. But the Porte's harsh reaction in 1596 and the unjust punishment of those soldiers who had legitimate excuses—as they either served in garrisons or were ordered to the Wallachian front—provoked some *sipahis* to become bandits, prey on villagers, and attack government facilities. Some joined the rebellion that ravaged the countryside in Asia Minor. The outbreak of the Safavid-Ottoman war in 1603, on the heels of these rebellions, forced the Porte to redeploy experienced commanders and troops from Hungary to Asia Minor. It also pushed the Ottoman government to negotiate with the Habsburgs.

In December 1605, the Habsburg imperial interpreter, Caesar Gallo, had started the negotiations in Buda with the Ottoman governor-general Ali Pasha and judge (*kadı*) Habil Efendi. The parties agreed that they would continue the talks somewhere between Ottoman-held Esztergom and Habsburg-held Komárom. In January 1606, the Ottomans demanded that the Habsburgs send their representatives to Constantinople, according to ancient custom. The Habsburgs rejected the demand. With Bocskai's mediation, the Habsburg and Ottoman negotiators reached a compromise. The parties concluded their peace talks at "the mouth of the Zsitva" creek, where it joined the Danube River, some sixteen kilometers east of Komárom. It was the site where Bocskai set up his camp, and where the Habsburgs later joined him on the left bank of the Danube. Bocskai had about a thousand men, and five thousand Habsburg troops in Komárom guarded the Habsburg delegation. The Ottoman delegation's camp was near Almás on the right bank of the Danube, about five kilometers upstream from Esztergom. Ottoman troops in Esztergom and Buda guarded the negotiators. Bocskai's main task was to mediate between the parties. However, the Habsburgs refused to go to the Turkish camp, citing their "reputation." Persuaded by Bocskai, who guaranteed their safety, Ali Pasha and Habil Efendi arrived with their entourage on twenty-three boats to the Habsburg camp on 29 October. The parties signed the peace documents on 11 November 1606, ending the most destructive war thus far.[76]

The location of the peace talks, the Habsburg negotiators' camp in Habsburg-controlled Royal Hungary, signified a notable deviation from Ottoman diplomatic practice, according to which peace treaties had been concluded in Constantinople or Edirne. It was not the first treaty that deviated from this ancient practice. The Ottomans concluded a treaty with the Polish-Lithuanian Commonwealth in 1595 in Moldavian Țuțora (Pol. Cecora).[77] However, Moldavia was an Ottoman vassal and the treaty was temporary, confirmed two years later by the sultan. In Ottoman-Habsburg diplomatic relations, the Treaty of Zsitvatorok has been interpreted as a milestone, which signaled the weakening position of the Porte and the beginning of the Europeanization of Ottoman diplomatic conduct.[78]

The treaty ended the obligation of the Habsburg monarchs to pay an annual tribute of 30,000 florins to the padishah in return for the payment of a single "gift of honor" of 200,000 florins. Traditional scholarship has maintained that in the treaty Sultan Ahmed I (r. 1603–17) accepted Rudolf II as his equal, naming him emperor. Others argued that if Sultan Ahmed, who titled himself padishah in the treaty, had wanted to treat Rudolf as his equal, he would have used the title padishah and not "imperator" or "çasar," from the Hungarian császár, meaning "Caesar."[79] Yet, the term "imperator" was the title that the Habsburg emperors themselves used and that the Habsburgs routinely used in their Latin-language correspondence for the Ottoman monarchs. Regarding the much-debated issue of castles captured in the war, the parties accepted the status quo, keeping all forts they held at the time of the signing of the treaty. Debates concerning the tribute and castles continued for years. These issues became more difficult to sort out because the two versions of the treaty that the parties signed contained discrepancies.[80]

The Long War and the Treaty of Zsitvatorok reflected the Ottomans' weakening position vis-à-vis the Habsburgs. The war also changed how contemporaries saw the strengths and weaknesses of the belligerent parties. İbrahim Peçevi recorded how the imperialists' quick victories in 1595 shattered the perception of Ottoman invincibility. During the negotiations that led to the Ottoman surrender of Esztergom, Nicholas Pálffy reportedly told the following to the future grand vizier Koca/Kuyucu (Great/Well-digger) Murad Pasha:

> We used to compare the Muslims to a box that our ancestors did not dare to open. Anyone who asked what was in it received the reply that it was full of snakes, centipedes, and scorpions. If the box were to be opened, they would swarm all over our land, biting and killing people. As this story went the rounds, they came to believe it, and so became firm in their mistaken convictions. Each of our emperors and kings put a lock on it so that the box would not be opened and the world not be destroyed in his time. Now, out of necessity, we opened it, and it turns out that the box is empty. There is nothing at all inside. What a pity that up until now, we have lived our lives in this erroneous belief.[81]

Defeat and Consolidation: The Safavid Frontier

The weakening of Ottoman military capabilities is also observable in the Safavid frontier. With his western border secured through the Ottoman-Safavid peace of 1590, Shah Abbas turned against the Uzbek Turks. By 1603, through successive wars, the shah had reconquered the provinces of Khurasan and Sistan, stabilizing his eastern frontier. Turning his attention westward, Abbas now challenged the Ottomans, who were preoccupied with the Long War in Hungary and the Celali rebellions in Asia Minor and Syria. Abbas managed to retake substantial amounts of former Safavid territory, including Azerbaijan and Nakhchivan, but the 1612 Ottoman-Safavid treaty returned to the 1555 borders. In 1623–24, the Safavids managed to retake Kurdistan and Baghdad and occupied Diyarbakır. Led by Sultan Murad IV (r. 1623–40), the Ottomans reconquered Baghdad in 1638, profiting from both the internal disturbances in Safavid Persia and the Uzbek, Mughal, and Portuguese attacks that followed Shah Abbas's death and the accession of his successor, Shah Safi (r. 1629–42). The Ottoman-Safavid Treaty of Zuhab (Kasr-i Şirin) in 1639 ended the hostilities. It largely restored the borders established in 1555: the Ottomans kept Iraq with Baghdad and Basra, while the Safavids retained Erevan and their possessions in the Caucasus.[82]

Abbas's victories were partly due to his military, administrative, and financial reforms. From the outset, Qizilbash Turkmen tribes had composed the backbone of the Safavid army. A formidable cavalry famous for its speed, maneuverability, feigned retreat, shadowing, and ambush, these Turkmen light horsemen fought for booty and were compensated by their tribal chiefs' fiefs (*tiyul*). However, tribal allegiances and factionalism, lack of discipline, and the tendency to plunder and flee the battlefield compromised the reliability of the Turkmen cavalry. By setting up a standing army answerable to, and paid by, the ruler, Shah Abbas intended to curb the influence of the Qizilbash Turkmens and establish forces who could counter the Ottoman janissary infantry and artillery corps. As in the Ottoman Empire, Shah Abbas's new troops were based on military slaves, or *ghulams*, recruited from among Circassians, Armenians, and Georgians. *Ghulams* had existed under Shahs Ismail I and Tahmasb I, but Abbas created a corps of royal household slaves.

Abbas's household army of slaves is said to have had a personal bodyguard of three thousand *qurchis* (literally "quiver bearers"), a cavalry force of ten thousand men, and a corps of artillerymen twelve thousand strong with five hundred cannons, as well as twelve thousand musketeers (*tufangchi*), recruited mainly from Iranian peasants. The corps was created on the model of the Ottoman janissaries and with the aim of counterbalancing the latter. However, unlike the infantry janissaries, the *tufangchis* were "mounted infantry" who moved on horse and fought on foot. The shah called his *ghulams* "mounted janissaries." The *ghulams* did not foster an esprit de corps and did not develop into a "socio-political corporation," as did the janissaries barracked in Constantinople in the seventeenth century. Although the *ghulams* also participated in the power struggles in the Safavid court, they did it not as a separate political interest group but by joining forces with Tajiks and Turks/Qizilbash "and thus forming ethnically and socially mixed factions." They represented "a good (perhaps the best) instance of a hybrid and *ad hoc* Safavid answer to the new military challenges of the time."[83] Abbas's loyal chronicler and chancery secretary (*munshi*), Iskandar Beg Turkman, claimed that in the spring of 1602, when Abbas marched against Balkh, the last major Uzbek foothold in Khurasan, the shah mobilized three hundred cannons and mortars with carriages, and ten thousand infantry gunners and artillerymen, who composed about one-fifth of the fifty-thousand-strong army.[84] To pay his soldiers, the shah increased the royal revenues by converting the military fiefs of the Turkmen chieftains into crown lands. In so doing, Abbas further weakened the basis of the Qizilbash amirs. He also brought many of the autonomous and semiautonomous regions under direct royal control. By the end of Abbas's reign, eight of the fourteen key provinces of Persia, traditionally controlled by the Qizilbash chieftains, were administered by the military commanders of the new *ghulam*, answerable and loyal only to the shah. Still, tribal elements remained powerful, dominating key governmental offices and parts of the military.[85]

After the outbreak of the Ottoman-Venetian war in Dalmatia and Crete in 1645, the Republic of Venice tried in vain to incite the Safavids against the Ottomans. Shah Abbas II refused the Venetian proposal, as he was fighting against the Timurid/Mughal Empire. The peace with the Ottomans enabled the Safavids to reconquer Qandahar in 1649. Mughal attacks to recapture the city in 1650 and 1652 forced Shah Abbas II to personally lead his army against the Mughals in 1653. He therefore preferred to observe the peace with the Ottomans. The Porte also upheld the peace and refused the Mughal ambassador's suggestion in 1653 and 1656 that the Ottomans attack the Safavids.[86]

The Ottomans and Safavids maintained the peace despite numerous border incidents, such as the Basra affair of 1654–55. In 1654, the Porte dismissed the viceroy of the Ottoman hereditary dominion of Basra, Afrasiyaboğlu Hüseyin Beg. His uncles had complained about Hüseyin and offered to transfer part of the revenue from Basra to the Ottoman provincial treasury in Baghdad and the imperial treasury in Constantinople if one of them was appointed viceroy of Basra. The dismissed viceroy escaped to Safavid Iran seeking military aid. While Shah Abbas II rejected the plea, he allowed Hüseyin Beg to recruit soldiers in Iran. Alas, he was soon defeated by the Ottoman governor-general of Baghdad, Kara (Black) Murtaza Pasha. This could have ended the incident, but Kara Murtaza Pasha's greed and harsh treatment of the Basrans provoked opposition against the Ottoman governor-general. The Porte defused the tension by transferring Murtaza to Aleppo and reinstating Hüseyin Beg in Basra. The Ottoman government used the incident to strengthen its hold over Basra by converting it from a tributary dominion to a hereditary (*yurtluk-ocaklık*) province. Besides, the Porte detached the important fort of Kurna from Basra and turned it into a *salyaneli sancak* under the command of *sancak* governors directly appointed from Constantinople. Janissaries and artillerymen sent to Kurna solidified the Porte's control over the fort. Honoring the 1639 Ottoman-Safavid peace treaty and defusing border tensions profited both empires. It enabled the Ottomans to focus on their wars against Venice (in Crete and Dalmatia) and the Habsburgs (in Hungary), and the Safavids to recapture Qandahar from the Mughals. The 1657 Ottoman-Safavid trade agreement solidified the peace, benefiting the merchants of both empires.[87]

PART III

Sinews of Empire

8

Resources and Military Power

BY THE EARLY sixteenth century, the Ottoman Empire had emerged as a major military power in control of the Balkan Peninsula, Asia Minor, the Black Sea littoral, the eastern Mediterranean, and most of the Middle East. Modern sociologists do not consider the Ottoman Empire a world power, for it did not possess the "minimal threshold criteria for global and world power"; most importantly, it could not claim to be a seaborne empire, because its navy was not an oceangoing force.[1] However, in sixteenth-century Europe many shared the view of the Venetians, known for their knowledge of the Ottomans: the view that the Ottomans were "the most powerful" empire that threatened Western Christendom on its own territory. The Ottoman Empire projected this image by virtue of its geopolitical situation, its enormous territory and population, its wealth of economic resources, and a central and provincial administration capable of mobilizing these resources to serve the goals of the Ottoman dynasty and elite. The effective use of resources formed the base of an Ottoman army, feared and admired by its European contemporaries. Venetians and other Europeans penned hundreds of reports describing the wealth of the padishah and the power of his navy and army.[2]

But the Ottomans' main adversary was not the Venetians. In the middle of the sixteenth century one of the most important and most consequential imperial rivalries in Europe developed between the Ottomans and the Habsburgs. The first half of the sixteenth century saw both the Habsburgs and the Ottomans with multiple policy commitments:

the Habsburgs were preoccupied with France and German Protestant-
ism, and Safavid Shiism hit closer to home for the Ottomans than did
the Habsburg advance in the Mediterranean. But Habsburg-Ottoman
rivalry remained a major theme in international politics. Around the
middle of the sixteenth century the main theater of Habsburg-Ottoman
confrontation shifted from the Mediterranean to the Habsburg-
Ottoman frontier in Hungary and Croatia. Therefore, a comparative
examination of Ottoman and Habsburg resources, military capabilities,
and commitments will help us to better understand the sinews of power
and the history of Ottoman-Habsburg rivalry, as well as its impact on
the lands of the Danubian Habsburg monarchy.

Mapping Empires, Frontiers, and Resources

The sixteenth century witnessed an increased interest in mapping the
monarchs' domains, and the Ottoman conquest played an important
role in the birth of military cartography in Europe, especially in the
Habsburg monarchy. In 1559 Philip II of Spain (r. 1556–98) ordered a
"General Visitation" to gather information about his domains in Italy.
He also commissioned cityscapes and maps of the Iberian Peninsula.
On Philip's order, the Flemish court painter Anton van den Wyngaerde
traveled extensively in the 1560s in Spain and North Africa preparing a
series of topographical views of towns, of which sixty-two completed
ones survive. It seems that Philip planned to have them engraved and
published, but the cityscapes came to be scattered in Vienna, London,
and Oxford; they were rediscovered only in the nineteenth century. A
more ambitious project involved the mapping of the entire Iberian Peninsula. In the 1570s and 1580s, a team of cartographers surveyed the entire peninsula, some five hundred thousand square kilometers. They
presented their results in an atlas of twenty-one detailed and remarkably
accurate maps on a scale of 1:430,000. Known as the Escorial "Atlas of
Spain," these maps remained incomplete and unpublished, along with
the planned description of Spanish America.[3]

There was no such systematic mapping of the domains and resources
in the Habsburg monarchy or the Ottoman Empire. As we will see, the

Viennese government in the sixteenth century was more interested in mapping the border areas, commissioning sketches and colored maps. These maps were the earliest examples of what would, by the seventeenth century, become Habsburg military cartography. We have seen that the Ottoman sultans commissioned world maps as a means of visualizing their domains and presenting their ambitions for world supremacy. Mehmed II charged George Amiroutzes with the preparation of a world map; upon Selim I's conquest of Egypt, Piri Reis presented his monarch with such a map. In the early 1550s, Süleyman's three sons—Princes Selim, Bayezid, and Mustafa—each requested world maps from Venice.[4]

Ottoman sultans and grand viziers also showed interest in maps as tools of military reconnaissance and campaign planning. The archives of the Topkapı Palace contain military maps and siege plans, such as those of Kyiv (under Sultan Bayezid II [r. 1481–1512]), Belgrade (1521?), Malta (1556), Szigetvár (1566), Vienna (1683), and Van, Adakale (1738), and diagrams of the battles of Mezőkeresztes (1596) and Prut (1711). This trove evidences the employment of mapmakers during Ottoman campaigns and the use of cartographical representations in military communications. A map of the region to the north of the Black Sea (1768–69) shows Ottoman interest in locating waterways and roads for both commercial and military purposes.[5] Another map, shown here, recorded the major castles and smaller palisades along the Danube and its tributaries, as well as the hours of travel time between castles.

Until the end of the sixteenth century, the Ottoman padishahs often led their armies into wars and traversed their empires during campaigns, thus learning about the vast expanses and economic and social conditions of their empire. The Ottomans also prepared special campaign journals that recorded the day-to-day progress of the army, and compiled register books of posting or halting stations (*menzil*) that listed the sites where the army could stop for rest or where the official Ottoman couriers changed horses. The more elaborate ones—such as Murad IV's book of relay stations during his Baghdad campaign—give detailed information regarding the time it took for the padishah to travel from one station to the next, the condition of the roads, difficulties of the terrain,

This Ottoman map shows the following castles (*kale*) and palisades (*palanka*) along the Danube River from the north to the south on both sides of the river: Ciğerdelen (Hun. Párkány), Vişegrad (Hun. Visegrád), Vaç (Hun. Vác), Budun (Hun. Buda), Gürz İlyas (Hun. Gerllért-hegy), Peşte (Hun. Pest), Saray-ı Hamzabeğ (Hun. Érd), Erçin (Hun. Ercsi), Cankurtalan (Hun. Adony), Pentele, and Fedvar (Hun. Födvár). The map also indicates the distances in hours for a horseman to travel from one castle to the other. The maps of the Nile and the Tigris and Euphrates Rivers are similar. (Courtesy of the Military History Museum, Budapest, H III 20a.)

and the availability and quality of drinking water.[6] Some of these works include maps of major castles and stopping points, as well as the distance between them. The famous seventeenth-century Ottoman traveler Evliya Çelebi (1611–c. 1684?)included maps in his *Book of Travels* (*Seyahatname*). A detailed comparison of the relevant passages of the *Seyahatname* and the Qatar map of the Tigris and Euphrates Rivers— which charts the two rivers from their headwaters in eastern Asia Minor to the Persian Gulf and the Indian Ocean—indicates that either Evliya Çelebi himself or someone in his retinue drew the map. This impressive map on eight attached folios shows all major towns, castles, and roads along the rivers, suggesting that Evliya Çelebi saw these towns and castles as symbols of Ottoman rule.[7] The Vatican map of the Nile also belonged to Evliya Çelebi, though he did not draw it. This elaborate map, with its 475 entries, and Evliya Çelebi's travel account in the tenth volume of his *Seyahatname* are the most ambitious attempts before Napoleon Bonaparte to explore the Nile.[8] Ottoman corsairs and marines also gathered valuable information on ports and port cities. While many of the topographical illustrations in Piri Reis's *Book of Navigation* are schematic and inaccurate, it is clear that the careful portrayals of ports, harbors, and harbor fortifications are based on personal observation. As a former corsair, Piri Reis showed special interest in harbors. The depiction of the lagoon fortifications of Venice, along with those of the Venetian arsenal, may have been based on intelligence from a spy or renegade.[9]

Ottoman policy-makers used geography to their advantage. The systematic conquest of the Danube delta and the Black Sea coastline and the capture and construction of strategically essential fortifications along river routes also point to their understanding of geography. Other examples of Ottoman strategic thinking include Sultan Selim II's and Grand Vizier Sokullu Mehmed's Don-Volga and Suez Canal projects, discussed earlier. Another ambitious project was the Sakarya-İzmit canal plan. This would have connected the Black Sea with the Sea of Marmara. By building canals, the Ottomans could have brought timber from the forests of the *sancak* of Kocaeli to the Imperial Naval Arsenal in Constantinople, as well as firewood to the capital.[10] Although none of the canal projects materialized, they indicate strategic thinking on the part of the Ottoman leadership. On the other hand, they also reveal the lack of detailed knowledge with regard to the topography of remote lands, especially in the case of the Don-Volga canal project.

The Ottomans were also keen to map their new territorial acquisitions and the geographical extent of their empire. Matrakçı Nasuh's (d. 1564) two chronicles narrate and illustrate Süleyman's conquest during his Iraq and Hungarian campaigns in 1534–35 and 1543, respectively. Both works have been studied extensively, not least because of their splendid town views that, while resembling contemporary European bird's-eye views, represent a specifically Ottoman genre. However, it has only recently been noticed that all the prominently displayed towns— Tabriz and Sultaniye in western Iran, Baghdad in central Iraq, Najaf, Karbala, and Hilla in lower Mesopotamia—were newly conquered frontier towns that effectively defined the Ottoman-Safavid frontier in 1535. The same pattern is observable in Matrakçı Nasuh's other works, where the most prominently displayed towns are those on the empire's Hungarian frontier.[11]

Yet, historians of the Ottoman Empire have unearthed much fewer military maps than have their Europeanist colleagues. This can be explained in part by the fact that the Ottoman government collated and stored valuable information in land or revenue surveys. After a conquest, the Ottomans surveyed the land, village by village, to estimate its revenues. Ottoman officials recorded in these surveys the names of the household heads and the expected revenue from each village of a given *sancak*. They prepared new surveys in ten to thirty years to reflect changes in the size and economic capabilities of the population, which determined tax rates. The Ottomans surveyed strategically important frontier provinces more often, and the Ottoman archives possess dozens of survey books for the *sancaks* of Bosnia, Silistra, Buda, Erzerum, Diyarbakır, Aleppo, and Damascus.[12] One copy of the survey book remained in the provincial center, while another went to the imperial capital and was archived near the building of the imperial council so that it could be consulted whenever needed. These surveys and the registers that contained recordings of bestowals of military fiefs gave the Ottoman government and its provincial administrators a detailed database regarding the size, composition, and economic conditions of the population of the padishah's domains.

The vast empire of the Habsburgs possessed human and economic resources comparable to those of the Ottomans. However, unlike the padishah's territorially contiguous "well protected domains," the Spanish Habsburgs possessed a discontinuous empire with territories loosely arranged and scattered all over Europe and overseas.[13] Because of the Habsburgs' multiple foreign policy commitments, only a fraction of the available resources could be used against the Ottomans. For Emperor Charles V, the rivalry with France over European domination, his wars against the Protestant princes in the Holy Roman Empire, and the conflict with the Ottomans in the Mediterranean all were more important than the Ottoman advance in Hungary. Consequently, imperial resources were only partly committed to this latter front. This situation changed somewhat after the middle of the sixteenth century, following the Peace of Augsburg in 1555, which signaled the defeat of Charles's religious policy and the end of his quest for universal monarchy. Following the religious compromise between the Catholic Habsburgs and the Protestant princes of the Holy Roman Empire and the abdication of Charles, the "Turkish question" took center stage. It became the principal policy concern for Ferdinand I, who succeeded his brother on the imperial throne in 1558. However, the division of the Habsburg domains into a central European empire and a Spanish empire headed, respectively, by Charles's brother, Emperor Ferdinand I, and his son, Philip II of Spain (r. 1556–98), further diminished the resources available for the fight against the Ottomans. In Philip II's strategy, the Ottomans figured only as one of many policy concerns.[14]

Ferdinand, the Ottomans' main antagonist in central Europe, possessed only limited resources even after 1558. In the words of one scholar, Ferdinand's central European monarchy was "a complex and subtly-balanced organism, not a 'state' but a mildly centripetal agglutination of bewilderingly heterogeneous elements." Another scholar called the monarchy "a composite state of composite states."[15] Although geographically contiguous, the Austrian Habsburg lands were much smaller than the padishah's domains. The territories under the Austrian Habsburgs'

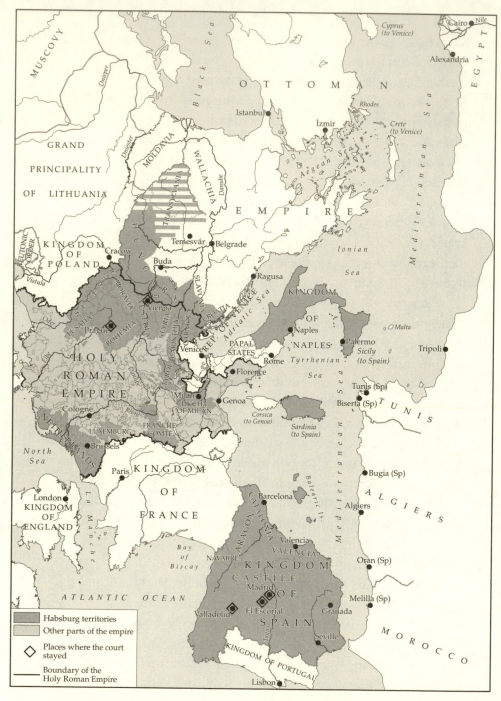

Charles V's empire as seen from Madrid. (Drawn by Béla Nagy.) This unusual perspective shows why the Mediterranean, France, Germany, and the Netherlands were more important for Charles than the Ottoman advance in Hungary.

direct rule had shrunk from about 450,000 square kilometers in the 1520s to about 350,000 square kilometers by the 1550s, owing to Süleyman's conquests in Hungary. Counting the territories of the Holy Roman Empire (estimated at 500,000 square kilometers), the geographical extent of the Austrian Habsburgs reached only about one-third of that of Süleyman, whose realm had grown to 2.3–2.5 million square kilometers by the end of his reign.[16] The Habsburg monarchy never enjoyed the sort of "ecological complementarity"[17] and self-sufficiency in raw materials and human resources that the Ottoman Empire did. Unlike the Spanish and Austrian Habsburgs, the Ottomans possessed ample deposits of saltpeter, sulfur, copper, and iron ore. These strategic raw materials were necessary for the production of gunpowder and firearms in an age when the possession of these weapons was essential to compete in an accelerating arms race successfully.[18]

The population of Ferdinand I's central European realms around 1550 is estimated to have been 6.5 million. The number of inhabitants of the same lands may have risen to 7.1–7.9 million by the beginning of the seventeenth century. Charles V's three wealthiest lands (Castile, the Kingdom of Naples, and the Low Countries' core provinces of Flanders, Holland, and Brabant) had a combined population of about 10 million inhabitants. Only by including some 14–16 million inhabitants of the Holy Roman Empire does one arrive at a population that was larger than that of the Ottoman Empire. In the early years of Süleyman's reign, about 12–13 million people inhabited the Ottoman domains. As a consequence of territorial expansion and population increase, this population reached 25–26 million people by the seventeenth century.[19]

The balance sheet of the Ottoman central treasury in 1527–28 recorded a total revenue of about 10 million gold ducats: 5 million in cash revenue for the treasury, 3.6 million from military prebends (*timar*), and an additional 1 million from pious foundations. By contrast, Charles V's combined revenue from Castile, the Kingdom of Naples, and the Low Countries' core provinces—realms that yielded the most income— amounted to about 2.8 million Spanish ducats in 1520 and 4.8 million Spanish ducats in 1540. Ferdinand's ordinary revenues amounted to only about 1.7–1.9 million Venetian ducats (2.15–2.5 million Rhine gulden or

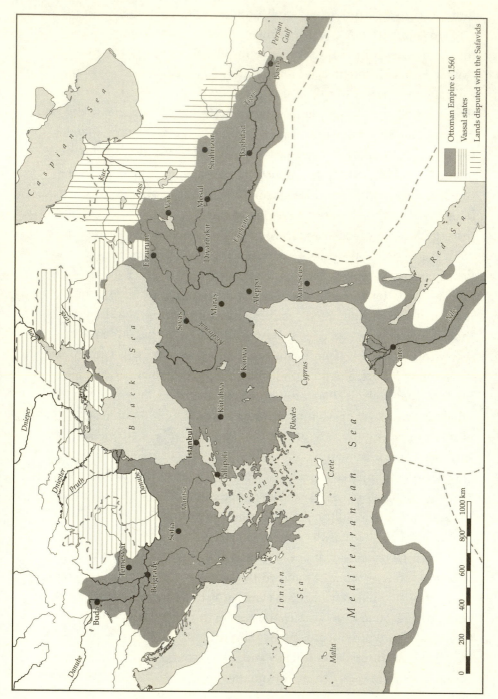

Sultan Süleyman's empire around 1560. (Drawn by Béla Nagy.)

florin).[20] Because of massive military and court expenditure, Ferdinand faced permanent deficits. By contrast, most of the available balance sheets of the Ottoman treasury show surpluses under Süleyman. The Ottoman treasury experienced persistent deficits only from 1592 onward.

These comparisons are useful only to an extent, and the recent tendency among economic historians to use revenues of the central treasuries to explain military capabilities is misleading.[21] Comparing treasury revenues in order to measure military capabilities is justified only if an army is financed from such revenues. This was not the case in either the Ottoman or the Habsburg realm. In the Ottoman Empire, *timar* revenues financed some 75 percent of the mobilized forces in the sixteenth century. The imperial treasury's income paid only for the wages of the standing household troops, which amounted to about 25 percent of Süleyman's mobilized armies. Except for the 1527–28 "budget," the balance sheets of the Ottoman imperial treasury record neither the revenues from *timars* nor the number of *timariot* provincial cavalry. Fiscal devolution and the complex system of credit, which paid Charles V's and Ferdinand I's mercenary troops, render Habsburg war finance too complicated to permit any meaningful connection between revenues and military potential.

The Ottoman Army

The Ottoman Empire derived its economic stability and military might from the prebendal system (*timar*), which managed revenue collection and maintained a sizable provincial cavalry army. While peasants retained the hereditary usufruct of the land and could pass their rights to their offspring, they paid taxes to the treasury and to the *timariot sipahi*—that is, the provincial cavalryman. On the surface, the European feudal regime and the Ottoman *timar* system may seem similar, but they had notable differences, crucial for their respective military potential and the quality of the troops they supplied. The Ottoman provincial cavalrymen differed significantly from the European feudal lords. Ottoman *sipahis* first and foremost were horsemen, who in return for their military service earned a military prebend or *timar*, usually a village. The cavalryman received an annual income of 3,000 *akçe*, about 50 Venetian gold ducats in the 1550s. Known as *dirlik* (living), this revenue was meant to cover his "living," horse, weapons, and armor. The *sipahi* resided in his village, collected taxes and fines according to regulations stipulated in his *sancak's* law code, and kept law and order among the villagers. When called on for military service, he presented himself to his *sancak* commander (*sancakbeyi*). The *sipahi* could increase his income through good military service and patronage. When he doubled his initial income, he had to maintain another fighting man. The more revenue he had, the larger his military retinue became. The *sancak* commander had a more substantial income. In the sixteenth century, those who served in the empire's European provinces usually started their service with revenue grants called *hass*, yielding annually 150,000 to 200,000 *akçe* (2,500 to 3,300 ducats). They, too, could increase their revenues. *Sancak* commanders in Ottoman Europe received grants in the first half of the century of as much as 500,000 to 600,000 *akçe* per annum (8,300 to 10,000 ducats). The most prominent of them, the *sancakbeyi* of Bosnia, collected a yearly revenue of 739,000 *akçe* (12,300 ducats) in the 1510s, at least on paper.[22] In return, *sancak* governors were expected to maintain a military retinue of 100 to 200 men, but they often had larger contingents of household troops. As noted, *sancaks* were organized into provinces, headed by provincial governors-general, or *beylerbeyis*. Governors-general resided in the chief town of the province. In the mid to late sixteenth century, they had revenue grants yielding annually 800,000 to 1,000,000 *akçe* (13,300 to 16,700 ducats). Governors-general maintained household troops numbering close to 1,000 men.[23]

When revenues administered by religious endowments (60 million *akçe*) are omitted, revenues from prebends (200 million *akçe*, or 3.6 million ducats) accounted for 42 percent of the empire's total revenues in 1527–28. The Ottoman prebendal system remained the basis of Ottoman military might through the mid-seventeenth century. As noted earlier in the context of the battle of Mohács, these conditional revenue grants, and the related bureaucratic surveillance system, provided the Ottoman sultans in the sixteenth century with a provincial cavalry potential of

70,000 men (27,888 *sipahis* and 41,800 estimated retainers), while relieving the central bureaucracy of the burden of raising revenue and paying military salaries.[24]

The most prosperous towns, with considerable revenues from customs and dues on artisanal production, were designated as imperial domains. Collected either through salaried tax officials or tax farmers, the annual revenue from the imperial domains amounted to 277 million *akçe*, or 5 million gold ducats, in 1527–28, 58 percent of the empire's total revenues, exclusive of religious endowments. This amount covered the salaries of the largest household of the empire, that of the padishah's servitors or *kuls*. In 1527–28, the imperial household numbered some 27,000 men, including 15,136 salaried soldiers, 3,553 janissary novices, 2,830 personnel of the imperial stables, and almost 3,000 servants of the inner palace. In terms of revenues and the size of his household, no vizier or provincial governor could come close to the padishah.[25]

Historians in the 1970s and 1980s maintained that the expansion of the Ottoman military, especially that of the musket-bearing janissary corps, started after the Long War of 1593–1606 in response to increased Habsburg firepower.[26] However, data summarized in table 8-1 demonstrate that the growth of the standing *kapukulu* troops started under Süleyman's reign. Whereas between 1520 and 1530 the padishah's standing troops averaged fewer than 16,000 men (19,000 men with janissary novices or *acemi oğlan*), by 1569 their number had risen to 19,390 men (26,621 men with janissary novices). Table 8-2 shows that the number of janissaries rose from 8,407 in 1530 to 12,131 in 1547 (that of the novices, from 3,640 to 5,840). From 1547 to 1564 the number of janissaries fluctuated between 12,300 and 13,500. After the death of Süleyman in 1566, the size of the janissary corps shrank, but, as will be discussed in chapter 9, the trend of military expansion continued, especially during the wars against the Safavids and Habsburgs.

The increased demand for military manpower under Süleyman and later might be explained in part by amphibious operations and long sieges of modernized artillery fortifications in the Mediterranean islands of Malta (1565) and Cyprus (1570–71), and in Hungary in the 1550s and 1566. The casualty rates of the protracted sieges of Malta (sixty-six days),

TABLE 8-1. Size and Composition of the Ottoman Standing (*kapukulu*) Army, 1484–1569

Date	Janissary	Janissary novice	Gunner	Armorer	Gun carriage driver	Sipahi	Silahdar	Four cavalry companies	Total
1484	7,841	—	—	—	—	1,401	1,446	1,459	12,147
1512	8,164	3,467	331	401	346	1,059	1,338	1,499	16,605
1514	10,065	—	353	451	378	1,951	2,064	2,187	17,449
1520a	7,780	2,668	394	518	305	1,771	1,664	2,232	17,332
1520b	8,361	3,190	396	522	308	2,090	1,904	2,386	19,157
1521	8,349	3,333	560	504	544	2,133	1,848	2,211	19,482
1522–23	7,010	3,002	688	484	543	2,228	1,782	2,012	17,749
1523	7,164	4,107	600	517	542	2,358	1,798	1,962	19,048
1523–24	8,641	3,514	594	568	543	2,274	1,734	1,874	19,742
1524–25	9,390	4,961	632	528	516	2,278	1,779	1,940	22,024
1527–28	7,886	3,553	695	524	943	1,993	1,593	1,502	18,689
1530	8,407	3,640	687	528	1,168	1,953	1,582	1,371	19,336
1567–68	12,798	7,745	1,204	789	678	3,124	2,785	5,135	34,258
1568–69	11,535	7,231	1,070	784	606	2,644	893	1,858	26,621

Source: 1484–1530: BOA, MAD 23, first published in Ágoston 2012a: 177–79; and in English in Ágoston 2014: 113; 1527–28 and 1567–68: Barkan 1953–54; and in English, Káldy-Nagy 1977b; 1568–69: BOA, KK.d 1767, published in Ágoston 2018: 966; and 2019a: 292–93.

A book published around 1580 shows Ottoman soldiers in sixteenth-century clothing. From left to right: a janissary with his matchlock handgun, an artillery officer with a fuse, an infantryman with an ax, and a bodyguard with an ax. (Courtesy of the Rijksmuseum, Amsterdam, RP-P-1896-A-19130.)

TABLE 8-2. Paper Strength of the Janissaries, 1484–1569

Date	Janissaries	Date	Janissaries
1484	7,841	1524–25	9,390
1512	8,164	1527–28	7,886
1514	10,065	1530	8,407
1520a	7,780	1547	12,131
1520b	8,361	1549	12,822
1521a	8,349	1549–50	12,285
1521b	7,422	1563–64	13,572
1522–23	7,010	1564	13,340
1523	7,164	1567	12,798
1523–24	8,641	1568–69	11,535

Source: 1484–1530: BOA, MAD 23, first published in Ágoston 2012a: 177–79;
and in English in Ágoston 2014: 113; 1527–28 and 1567–68: Barkan 1953–54;
and in English, Káldy-Nagy 1977b; 1568–69: BOA, KK.d 1767, published in
Ágoston 2018: 966; and 2019a: 292–93.

Note: 1520a = under Selim I; 1520b = under Süleyman I; 1521a = June–August;
1521b = September–November.

Gyula and Szigetvár in 1566 (sixty-three and thirty-three days), Nicosia
in 1570 (forty-six days), and Famagusta in 1571 (seventy-four days), and
that of the battle of Lepanto in 1571, were significantly higher than those
suffered in the early sixteenth century. At Szigetvár in 1566 the Porte lost
some 42 percent of its professional army and about 60 percent of its
janissaries. Another reason behind the expansion of Ottoman military
manpower was the need to garrison newly conquered frontier
provinces—Baghdad (1534), Erzurum (1535), Buda (1541), and Temesvár (1552). In general, military manpower needs in newly conquered
fortresses were largely met by local soldiers (neferat-i yerlüyan), often
redeployed from the empire's neighboring interior provinces and paid
from local provincial treasuries. However, central kapukulu troops, especially janissaries, were also sent to key fortresses in increasing numbers.[27] By 1547, 38 percent of the janissaries (4,648 men) were on garrison duty. The Porte deployed almost half of the latter (2,282 men) in
Hungary, demonstrating the significance of that frontier.[28] The Porte
also sent janissaries to the empire's eastern frontier in the thousands.[29]

Ottoman military expansion was also triggered by domestic developments unrelated to foreign wars. During the dynastic struggles of the

Ottoman princes under Bayezid II and Süleyman I, the prince who was unable to secure the support of the reigning sultan and the central standing troops recruited thousands of landless peasants, townsfolk, nomads, and vagrant irregular soldiers (*levend*), often armed with firearms. Known as "daily wagers" (*yevimlü*) because of their salaries, these militiamen were ordinary taxpaying subjects. They volunteered for military service in the hope of eventually joining the ranks of the padishah's salaried troops and thereby entering the privileged, tax-exempt military (*askeri*) class. The process reached its peak under Süleyman, when Prince Bayezid, whom Süleyman declared a rebel, reportedly recruited ten thousand such soldiers, pledging to enlist them in the janissary corps. With the support of Süleyman, Prince Selim also hired thousands of ordinary taxpayers with daily salaries. While about eight thousand soldiers perished in the battle of Konya between the competing armies, and the government persecuted Bayezid's men in the purges after the rebel prince's execution (1562), many of his *levend* soldiers escaped. Forming bands of fifty to sixty men, they roamed the countryside as bandits.[30] One undesirable consequence of these events was the spread of firearms among the taxpaying subjects, which Ottoman authorities tried, with little success, to prevent.[31] Since scores of the *timariot* cavalry also sided with the rebel prince, the government could not trust them to perform their traditional function of maintaining law and order in the countryside. To reestablish public order, the Ottoman government sent janissaries to towns and villages in increasing numbers. Settled in the countryside as guardians or law-enforcement officers (*yasakçı*), these janissaries helped the local authorities to fight crimes and arrest criminals. They supplemented their salaries by collecting penalty fees for transgressions (a function and privilege traditionally belonging to the *timariot* provincial cavalry), establishing businesses in towns, and acquiring farmland in villages. As public order further deteriorated during the Celali rebellions at the end of the sixteenth century, more and more cities and towns in Asia Minor requested janissaries from the government. The proliferation of janissaries and other *kapukulu* troops in the provinces created opportunities for ordinary taxpayers and *levend* soldiers to impersonate janissaries and janissary novices. How many of these pseudo janissaries managed to add their names to the official pay lists is unknown, but the practice was the first sign of the massive "civilianization" of the janissary corps, and it further exacerbated lawlessness and disorder in the countryside.[32]

The Ottoman *timar* and *kul* systems strengthened the Ottoman ruler's standing both domestically and internationally. Domestically, with the salaried and *timariot* forces, the padishah counterbalanced the traditional Turkish aristocracy, the frontier lords, and their armies of cavalry raiders. In the process, the Ottoman frontier polity evolved into a patrimonial empire, where resource management, administration, and the military fell under the control of the servitors of the ruler's household and the *timar*-holding military-administrative elite. The latter received their conditional revenue grants from the ruler, but only if they remained loyal and fulfilled their military-administrative service obligations to the ruler. Internationally, the *timar* revenue grants and the *devşirme* levy enabled the Ottomans to maintain the largest professional military in sixteenth-century Europe and western Asia, and an impressive navy. The combined military potential of the *timariot* cavalry, salaried standing army, and garrison forces in the 1520s is estimated at over 125,000 men (Table 8-3). While none of the Ottomans' neighbors could match Constantinople's military potential in the early sixteenth century, the size of the Ottoman military remained only about 1 percent of the empire's estimated thirteen million population, which is hardly a sign of "a near-perfect military society," as has been claimed.[33]

In addition to the professional standing troops and provincial cavalry, the Ottomans used peasant militia footmen (*azab*) and frontier raiders, the infamous *akıncıs*. As mentioned, Süleyman could still order some 10,000 *azab* archers to the Hungarian campaign in 1521. However, a generation later, most of the *azabs* were ordered to perform auxiliary services.[34] While in Süleyman's campaigns the *akıncı* raiders numbered 20,000 men, they were gradually incorporated into the frontier military. In 1595, the Transylvanian and Wallachian forces massacred most of them. They never regained their military significance. Writing in 1631, the Ottoman bureaucrat and author Koçi Beg put their number at only about 2,000 men.[35] Tatar horsemen of the vassal Crimean khanate took

TABLE 8-3. Potential Strength of the Ottoman Military in 1527–28

	Centrally stationed	Provincial	Total
Provincial *timariot* cavalry		27,888	27,888
Cebelü retainers (estimated)		41,832	41,832
Garrison soldiers paid via *timars*		9,653	9,653
Central *kapukulu* troops	15,136		15,136
Salaried garrison troops		27,617	27,617
Salaried troops in Egypt		3,761	3,761
Total *timariot* & salaried			**125,887**

Source: Barkan 1953–54.

their place as light cavalry raiders. While contemporary sources often exaggerated the number of the Tatars mobilized for Ottoman campaigns, at the end of the sixteenth century and the early seventeenth century about 10,000 to 30,000 Tatar horsemen fought in the Ottoman expeditionary armies in Hungary and the Safavid theaters of war.[36] The auxiliary peasant infantry and cavalry (*yaya*, *yürük*, and *müsellem*) mobilizable for war numbered about 12,500 in the early sixteenth century.[37] With the auxiliary peasant infantry and cavalry, the peasant militia, and raiders, Süleyman's military potential could have reached about 160,000 to 170,000 men.

Süleyman frequently deployed 60,000 troops (not counting the auxiliaries) for land campaigns, of whom about 45,000 men (or 75 percent) were provincial *timariot* cavalry and 12,000 to 15,000 were salaried foot soldiers and horsemen. These numbers matched those deployed in the Mohács campaign of 1526. The composition of the deployed troops varied according to the enemy and the challenge that the army had to overcome in the different theaters of war. We saw that in 1526 Süleyman mobilized only about 65 percent of his *timariot* manpower potential. When mobilizing the salaried troops, the Ottoman command adjusted the structure of the forces according to tasks and enemies. In 1514, the Ottomans expected field battles against the cavalry-dominated Safavid army. Therefore, Selim mobilized more salaried cavalry (5,262) and janissaries (10,065), but only about a thousand artillerymen, because the Safavids lacked fortified positions and therefore sieges were not anticipated. By contrast, in 1543 Süleyman brought with him fewer palace cavalry but more janissaries, artillery gunners, armorers, and gun carriage drivers to handle the cannons and siege equipment as he prepared to besiege a number of fortified positions along the Danube in Hungary. In 1549, most of the available janissaries (7,894 men), those who were not on garrison duty, accompanied the padishah to his campaign against Shah Tahmasb of Persia. The high number of elite janissaries in all these campaigns is understandable, as janissary firepower proved effective against both the Safavid cavalry and Hungarian castles.[38]

The Ottoman military developed gradually and continually adjusted to the needs of different tactical environments as the Ottomans waged wars against a variety of enemies: Turkic principalities and Turkmen confederations of Asia Minor and Iran, Byzantines and their Genoese and Catalan mercenaries, European crusaders, the Safavids of Persia and their Qizilbash partisans in Asia Minor, the Mamluks of Syria and Egypt and their allied Arab tribesmen, Georgians of the southern Caucasus, medieval Balkan states, Venice, Hungary, Poland-Lithuania, Cossacks, Muscovites/Russians, Spanish and Austrian Habsburgs, and the latter's Italian, Spanish, German, and French mercenaries. To effectively engage so many and so diverse an array of adversaries required constant adjustment and adaptation. It also offered opportunities for military acculturation. The high proportion of cavalry in the Ottoman military until the late seventeenth century can be explained not only by the persistence of military cultures and systems of recruitment and remuneration, but also by the continued effectiveness of the light horsemen against the Safavid light cavalry, Hungarian hussars, and the Cossack horsemen. Wars with the Hungarians in the 1440s acquainted the Ottomans with field artillery and catalyzed the integration of firearms technology into the Ottoman standing forces and the development of the old Turkic *tabur* along with the Hussite/Hungarian Wagenburg, or wagon fortress. Similarly, the combined use of Wagenburg and cavalry on the wings provided effective protection against enemy cavalry charges. This tactic explains the absence of pikes and the bayonet in the Ottoman arsenal, despite the Ottomans' exposure to Habsburg infantry armed with such weapons. To successfully besiege Byzantine and Balkan medieval castles, and later Italian bastioned fortresses in Hungary and Venetian-held Cyprus and Crete, required familiarity with the evolving art of siege warfare and the creation of a separate artillery corps within the standing salaried army as well as adequate weapon-manufacturing capabilities.

Ottoman Naval Power

Ottoman military history is too often equated with land warfare, and the importance of the fleet in Ottoman power projection seldom appreciated. Having lands in both southeastern Europe and Asia Minor, the Ottomans realized early on the need for a navy, which could maintain communication and ferry troops, weaponry, and supplies between the two parts of their domains. While the early Ottomans could occasionally rely on Genoese ships for such tasks, with the takeover of Byzantine Gallipoli in 1354, they acquired an important dockyard and naval base. They quickly turned Gallipoli into the basis of Ottoman naval construction and seafaring. By 1374 under Murad I, just two generations after the founding of their small frontier principality, the Ottomans possessed their own fleet. After the conquest of the maritime Turkish principalities of Aydın and Menteşe, Bayezid I fitted out sixty long warships and used this fleet to blockade Constantinople from 1394 to 1402. By the early 1410s, Ottoman vessels were plundering Venetian islands, which, in turn, forced the Venetians to challenge the Ottomans in an open battle. In the first such engagement between the two powers, in 1416, the Venetians soundly defeated the weak and inexperienced Ottoman fleet.[39]

In the sixteenth century, the Ottoman navy proved instrumental in the protection of the Ottoman imperial capital, the Levantine trade routes, and the maritime lanes of communication that connected Constantinople with Egypt and the Black Sea littoral—vital links for the provisioning of the capital, and for the Ottoman economy in general. The Mediterranean and Black Sea fleets, in cooperation with the riverine flotillas on the Danube, Tigris, and Euphrates Rivers and their tributaries, played a crucial role in Ottoman campaign logistics. These fleets transported troops and hundreds of tons of food, cannons, shots, and gunpowder to the theaters

of war in Hungary, eastern Europe, North Africa, the Mediterranean islands of Rhodes, Cyprus, and Crete, the Caucasus, and Iraq. Supply logistics required certain types of ships and crews, which were shared by the
Ottomans and their rivals in the two seas.[40]

The conquest of Kilia and Akkerman came as a result of coordinated land and naval operations. During the Venetian-Ottoman war
of 1499–1503, similar synchronized land and naval campaigns led to the
Ottoman conquest of Venice's naval bases of Lepanto, Navarino,
Modon, and Koron. While Sultan Bayezid commanded the land forces,
the famed Turkish *ghazi* sailors Kemal Reis (d. 1511) and Barak Reis (d.
1500) led the naval operations. The latter lost his life during the campaign. In the possessions of Koron and Modon, which Kemal Reis
called the "two eyes of Venice," the Ottomans could monitor the Venetian navy as it passed from the Adriatic into the Mediterranean.[41]

With the employment of Kemal Reis and his fellow Turkish *ghazi*
sailors, Bayezid II established a precedent for a mutually beneficial
relationship between the Ottoman government and Turkish (and later
Barbary) maritime corsairs. These sailors shared precious naval knowledge and personnel with the Ottomans. A prime example is Kemal's own
nephew, Piri Reis (d. 1553), who authored the *Book of Navigation* and the
first Ottoman map of the New World.[42] Under Selim I and Süleyman I, the
famed corsair Hayreddin Barbarossa (d. 1546) of Algiers and his seamen
extended Ottoman naval reach to North Africa. At the beginning of the
sixteenth century, apart from the Ottoman Empire, only Venice and the
Knights of Rhodes possessed regular fleets in the Mediterranean. The
Ottoman fleet conducted essential operations during the Ottoman conquest of Mamluk Egypt in 1516–17. The fleet was also instrumental in
halting Portuguese expansion in the Red Sea and the Persian Gulf, thus
protecting Islam's holy places, Mecca and Medina.[43]

The Ottoman navy possessed impressive capabilities by the late fifteenth century.[44] In their campaign against Belgrade in 1456, the Ottomans employed some 200 ships, including 64 galleys.[45] As noted,
Mehmed II mobilized 400 ships against the island of Negroponte
(1470) and 300 to 380 galleys for the Caffa campaign (1475). By this
time, the Ottomans could operate two large armadas independently. In

May 1480, an Ottoman fleet of 104 vessels (including 46 galleys) arrived at Rhodes under the command of Mesih Pasha, a member of the Byzantine Palaiologos family. Another Ottoman fleet of 28 galleys and 104 light galleys and transport vessels, under the command of Gedik Ahmed Pasha, landed at Otranto in July.[46] In 1492, Sultan Bayezid II sent 300 ships to the Albanian coast to suppress a rebellion, while the padishah himself marched from Edirne with the land forces.[47] The Venetian envoy claimed in 1496 that the Ottomans had a fleet of 250 ships, including 100 galleys and 10 large ships.[48] In the battles of Lepanto (1499) and Modon (1500), they had 260 and 230 ships.[49]

The Ottomans recruited oarsmen for their galleys via forced levies from western Asia Minor and the Balkan Peninsula in varying ratios according to demand: one oarsman for every four to twenty-three households in the mid-sixteenth century. They also used slaves captured by the Crimean Tatars and the Barbary corsairs. The Ottoman navy became the largest consumer of slaves and an important catalyst of slave raiding and slave trading in the empire. *Azab* infantrymen, the combatants of the galley crews, were recruited via forced levies. Janissaries and *timariot* cavalry supplemented these troops, resulting in about 60 fighting men per galley in the mid-sixteenth century. The number grew to 150 men per galley after the defeat at Lepanto in 1571.[50] Difficulty gathering *timariot* troops could delay naval operations. In June 1570, for instance, the navy that sailed against Venetian-held Cyprus waited twenty days in Finike for the provincial troops of Asia Minor.[51]

Gallipoli, the first naval arsenal (*Tersane*),[52] remained an important shipyard for the construction and repair of Ottoman ships. By the early sixteenth century, the arsenal in Constantinople on the shore of the Golden Horn had become the principal center of Ottoman shipbuilding and maintenance. Having inherited it from the Genoese of Galata, the Ottomans expanded the arsenal. By 1515 it had 160 docks. Between 1527 and 1531, the arsenal built 61 ships and repaired 146 vessels, including 44 and 32 galleys, respectively. In the 1550s the arsenal could construct and repair 250 ships at a time. Even in the mid-1580s, an era that saw a sharp decline in Ottoman shipbuilding and naval activity, the arsenal still constructed and repaired 114 ships.[53] In addition to Gallipoli and Constantinople, there were arsenals at İzmit on the Sea of Marmara, at Sinop and Samsun on the Black Sea, at Suez in the Red Sea, at Birecik on the Euphrates, and Basra on the Shatt al-Arab. If one includes the smaller shipyards, the number of sixteenth-century Ottoman shipbuilding sites is close to 70.[54]

The standard Ottoman galley carried a single mast with a lateen sail and had twenty-four to twenty-six banks of oars on both sides, with three oarsmen to a bench, all pulling separate oars. But beginning in the 1560s, the Ottomans, following their Mediterranean rivals, adopted the "al scaloccio" system, by which all oarsmen on the same bench pulled a single oar. This arrangement increased the number of oarsmen. Ottoman galleys usually carried a center-line cannon and two smaller flanking culverins. Impressed by the heavy Venetian galleys (*galleasses*), which played an important role in the Christians' victory at the battle of Lepanto, the Ottomans were quick to imitate these large and heavily armed galleys that could fire broadside, as opposed to the traditional galleys, which had guns only on the prow. During the rebuilding of their fleet after Lepanto, the Ottoman shipyards in Sinop and Constantinople constructed four or five galeasses. These vessels could carry as many as twenty-four guns and fire them from the stern, bow, and sides.[55]

The Mediterranean fleet under the command of the *kapudan* pasha, or grand admiral, was the core of the Ottoman navy. Smaller squadrons operated independently of this main fleet. The captain of Kavalla patrolled the northern Aegean, the *sancak* governors of Lesbos and Rhodes commanded the sea routes between Egypt and Constantinople, the admiral of Egypt controlled both the Egyptian fleet (based in Alexandria) and the Suez fleet, and the captain of Yemen guarded the entry to the Red Sea. In addition to the imperial navy, the Ottomans also mobilized the fleet of the so-called sea commanders (*derya beyi*), whose seaboard *sancaks* belonged to the province of the *kapudan* pasha. Established in 1533, the province of the *kapudan* pasha was known as the province of the Archipelago, the islands of the Aegean. It included the *sancaks* of Gallipoli—which served as its center—Rhodes, Lesbos, and Euboa. By the beginning of the seventeenth century, the number of *sancaks* had risen to thirteen. Unlike ordinary *sancak* governors, who commanded their respective *timariot* provincial horsemen, the governors of seaboard *sancaks* served at sea with their own galleys, which they had to build, maintain, and furnish with oarsmen, fighters, weapons, and all the necessary provisions from the revenues of their respective *sancaks*. Their duties included securing their respective coastlines and the maritime lanes of communication, above all the vital Alexandria–Constantinople route, against pirate and enemy ships. They also were expected to fight alongside the imperial fleet in naval campaigns and to provide logistical support to land campaigns by transporting troops, provisions, weapons, and munitions. In the sixteenth and seventeenth centuries these sea governors commanded some fifteen to twenty galleys and about 4,500 soldiers.[56]

Smaller flotillas operated on the Danube, Tigris, and Euphrates Rivers. The Ottomans used hundreds of light galleys on the Danube and its tributaries in their campaigns against Hungary in the fifteenth century.[57] In the sixteenth century, the Ottoman flotillas on the Danube—based in Vidin, Buda (since 1546), and Mohács (since 1560)—regularly assisted Süleyman's campaigns in Hungary. The Ottomans also operated flotillas on the rivers Sava, Drava, Mura, and Tisza, and the Lake Balaton. Emperor Maximilian believed in 1566 that the Ottoman flotilla on the Lake Balaton could ferry up to a thousand soldiers.[58]

The Gunpowder Revolution and the Ottomans

The mass adoption of firearms as a tool of warfare dramatically changed the nature of military conflicts from the mid-fifteenth century onward. Historians of early modern Europe have described the changes between 1550 and 1650, or more broadly between 1500 and 1800, as a "gunpowder revolution" or "military revolution"—a thesis that provoked a spirited scholarly debate in the 1990s. Scholars have argued that firearms helped central governments monopolize power. Only the monarchs possessed the necessary financial and organizational means to establish and maintain large artillery corps and cannon-proof fortifications. Cannons and artillery fortifications facilitated the strengthening of state power vis-à-vis the feudal lords and led to the emergence of the centralized sovereign state in Europe—and, on a global scale, to the "rise of the West."[59]

Many have embraced these ideas, but they have also provoked criticism, both conceptually and empirically. Some have suggested different chronologies for the military transformation in Europe, ascribing the revolutionary changes to periods other than the originally suggested 1560–1660 or 1500–1800 eras. Others have seen the changes as a more complicated process involving several interrelated revolutions, preceded by periods of incremental change.[60] Yet others have argued that "a wholly state-recruited and state-administered military force is an anomalous development," "a particular preoccupation of European states from roughly 1760 to 1960." Before that, "the characteristic pattern of European warfare" was "military organization on the basis of contracts with private suppliers." This view not only de-emphasized the role of military technology but also questioned the causal relationship between war and the rise of the centralized sovereign state through "military revolution," the very essence of the thesis.[61]

Students of non-Western history have started to add their voices to the discussion only recently.[62] The Ottomans typically appeared in the discussion as a counterpoint to their (supposedly) militarily more advanced European rivals. The Ottomans' successful participation in the artillery revolution of the fifteenth century has been acknowledged.[63] Some historians have even suggested that the Ottomans were a "gunpowder empire," implying that firearms played a crucial role in the formation and consolidation of their empire.[64] However, many historians of Europe have claimed that from the late sixteenth century onward, the Ottoman military lagged behind its western and central European rivals. The latter embraced the bastion fortifications and "a balanced mix of shock and shot infantry" of pikemen and arquebusiers, and thus established military superiority over the sultans' forces.[65] Others have suggested that the Ottoman military failed to keep pace with the "West" due to the "conservatism of Islam" and "military despotism, " which "militated against the borrowing of western techniques and against native inventiveness." Yet others have singled out the Ottomans' technological inferiority and insufficient manufacturing capacity, claiming that Ottoman technicians lacked the necessary knowledge to produce good-quality weapons. In short, the Ottomans' deficiencies ultimately sprung from their conservatism, fanaticism, and despotism, which in turn stemmed from their religion.[66]

These claims fly in the face of the evidence. The Ottomans successfully integrated firearms into their military in the fifteenth century. They established specialized corps to manufacture and handle cannons and mortars within the sultan's standing army before such corps appeared in Europe. In the fifteenth century, the Ottomans were capable of forging and casting some of the most massive guns known to contemporaries, a testament to their technological capabilities. But these large wrought-iron and bronze bombards were clumsy, were difficult to maneuver, and had a low rate of fire (a couple of shots per day). Therefore, they constituted only a small portion of the Ottoman ordnance. The Ottomans produced and employed all three main classes of guns used in early modern Europe: parabolic-trajectory mortars hurling large stone balls, bombs, and hand grenades; flat-trajectory large-caliber siege and fortress cannons; and medium- and small-caliber field pieces. Archival evidence regarding the production of cannons indicates that the overwhelming majority of the Ottoman artillery consisted of small- and medium-caliber cannons. Unlike their European opponents who used cheaper iron guns, the Ottomans cast their large- and medium-caliber pieces in bronze, which was more expensive but considered much safer and of better quality. Ottoman artillerymen used iron to cast small pieces, usually for river flotillas. Production data collected from the account books of the foundries and chemical analyses of extant gun barrels suggest that Ottoman cannon founders used the typical tin bronze, which contained 8.6–11.3 percent tin and 89.5–91.4 percent copper. In the 1520s, the Venetian *bailo* considered Ottoman cannons to be better than French and English ones. He also noted that the Ottomans had good gunners who made "basilischi" that shot huge cannonballs. Other Venetians disagreed and thought that Ottoman cannons were of inferior quality. They would melt down captured Ottoman cannons and use the recycled bronze to cast new cannons.[67]

The Porte gradually armed its janissaries with matchlock arquebuses and later with muskets. While numerical superiority, cavalry charge, better logistics, and tactics were significant in the Ottoman victories at

Chaldiran (1514), Marj Dabiq (1516), Raydaniyya (1517), and Mohács (1526) against the Safavids, Mamluks, and Hungarians, respectively, Ottoman firepower superiority also played a vital role. In siege warfare, firepower superiority and mining remained the Ottomans' strengths throughout the sixteenth and seventeenth centuries, resulting in their capture of a host of European artillery fortresses in Hungary, Cyprus, and Crete.[68] The janissaries used their matchlock muskets through the seventeenth century, although toward the end of the sixteenth century they also started to adapt flintlock muskets with the Spanish *patilla* or *miquelet* lock. When a soldier pulled the trigger, a piece of flint hit the steel pan near the touch hole, creating sparks that ignited the gunpowder in the pan. However, early flintlocks were not as reliable as the matchlock. The flint became worn, hit the pan at the wrong angle, or fell out of the finger piece, and failed to strike enough sparks to ignite the powder in the pan. Therefore, the Ottomans also used the combination of flint and match firing mechanisms, known in Europe as the Vauban-lock after about 1688.

Ottoman musket barrels were reliable. Gun manufacturers used flat sheets of steel, similar to that of the Damascus blades, that were coiled into a spiral, producing great strength in the barrel that could withstand higher explosive pressure. Musket barrels were less likely to burst than European barrels with longitudinal seams. In sieges and fortresses the janissaries used larger and heavier matchlock muskets. These eight-sided or cylinder-barreled trench guns had a 130 to 160 centimeter long barrel and bore diameters of 20 to 29 millimeters. They used muskets with larger bore diameters to fire shells. Yet, most janissaries used much smaller guns that were 115 to 140 centimeters long, weighed merely 3 to 4.5 kilograms, and had bore diameters of 11, 13, 14, or 16 millimeters. Muskets were manufactured in state-operated workshops in the capital. By the early seventeenth century, they were of inferior quality to those obtainable from private gun makers or from foreign (mainly English) imports.[69]

The mass employment of firearms in field and sea battles and sieges significantly changed the way states and empires waged wars. If states wanted to remain militarily competitive in the gunpowder age, they needed cannons, cannon-proof fortifications, and a sizable infantry armed with handguns, as well as navies with shipboard artillery. Organized violence between states and empires, geographical exploration, and overseas expansion led to an unprecedented arms race. If monarchs wanted to participate effectively in interstate rivalry, they had to create indigenous weapons industries or supply weaponry and ammunition. In the long run, the adequate and steady supply of weapons and military hardware proved to be more critical than technological or tactical advantages. Superiority in weapons technology and tactics may occasionally have determined the outcomes of battles and sieges, although weaponry in itself was hardly sufficient to win the day. Nevertheless, states and empires that wanted to achieve long-standing military prominence had to possess weaponry and military hardware in substantial quantities and of acceptable quality.

The Ottomans possessed vigorous weapons and munitions industries. Ottoman foundries and gunpowder works satisfied the demands of the Ottoman army, navy, and fortresses. In contrast, the Ottomans' Spanish and Austrian Habsburg rivals depended on imports. The Ottomans operated cannon foundries along the Adriatic (Vlorë in Albania and Preveza in Greece), in Hungary (Buda and Temesvár), southeastern Europe (Smederevo, Belgrade, Rudnik, Shkodër, Novo Brdo, and Eleftheroupoli, near Kavala), Asia Minor (Diyarbakır, Erzurum, Birecik, Mardin, and Van), Iraq (Baghdad and Basra), and Egypt (Cairo). The Imperial Cannon Foundry in Constantinople, established by Mehmed II, remained the center of cannon casting. It was one of the first arsenals in late medieval Europe that was built, operated, and financed by a central government during a time when most European monarchs acquired their cannons from smaller artisan workshops. While the foundry was capable of meeting the needs of the army and navy as late as the Russo-Ottoman war of 1768–74, contemporaries noted the poor quality of cannons. Reforms in the late eighteenth century improved both casting and artillery. Of the reforms, two were especially important: the introduction of a new casting technology by which the barrel of howitzers, light cannons, and medium cannons was cast solid and bored out with a suspension screw, and the establishment of quick-firing artillery. However, standardization and mobility remained significant problems.[70]

The Porte operated numerous gunpowder works in Constantinople, manufacturing between 150 and 300 metric tons of powder annually in the late sixteenth through the late seventeenth centuries. The Ottomans also produced gunpowder in their provincial centers, including Cairo, Baghdad, Aleppo, and Yemen in the Arab provinces; Buda, Esztergom, Pécs, Temesvár, Belgrade, Thessaloniki, and Gallipoli in the European provinces; and Izmir, Bor, Erzurum, Diyarbakır, Oltu, and Van in Asia Minor. At the end of the sixteenth century, Cairo supplied between 160 and 200 metric tons of powder to the Ottoman fleet, while the Baghdad powder works at its peak added about 270 metric tons of powder annually. Those in Hungary manufactured an additional 100 metric tons. Together, these gunpowder works met the empire's gunpowder needs well into the eighteenth century.[71] The manufacturing capacities of Ottoman cannon foundries and gunpowder works in Constantinople and the provinces, aided by their impressive logistical network and bureaucracy, enabled the Ottomans to establish long-lasting firepower superiority over the Porte's enemies.

There was no iron curtain between the Ottoman Empire and Christian Europe. The Ottomans and their European enemies constantly watched and learned from each other, copied and adopted their opponent's weapons, and participated in the early modern arms race. The sixteenth-century Ottoman Empire possessed all the characteristics to promote brain gain and had no difficulty attracting foreign experts into its employ. The empire's wealth and prosperity, the mobility of its multiethnic, multiconfessional, and polyglot population, and the pragmatism of its political elite made the empire, and especially its capital city Constantinople, just the sort of place where foreigners could sell their expertise, find new career opportunities, gain access to power, and advance the transmission, production, and dissemination of knowledge. And the best of them were generously rewarded. Frequent wars with the Venetians, Spaniards, Austrians, and Hungarians accelerated the transfer of military technology between the Ottomans and their rivals. Similarities in military and naval hardware were the result of illicit trade in weaponry and of common knowledge in weapons manufacturing and shipbuilding, shared by the Ottomans and their adversaries. This shared knowledge

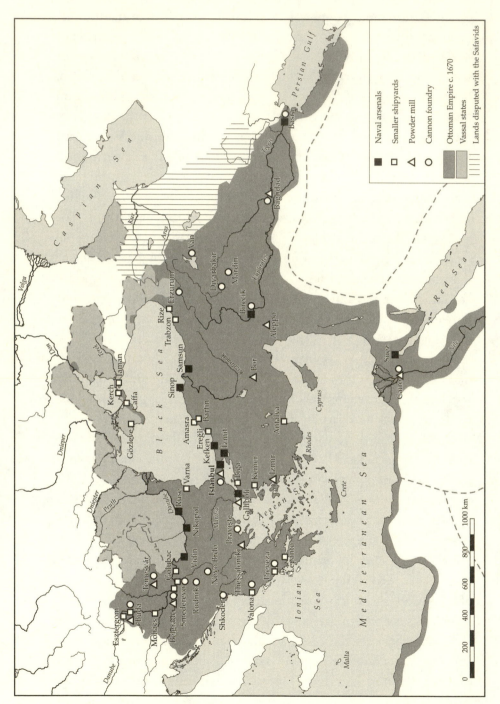

Ottoman cannon foundries, gunpowder mills, naval arsenals, and shipyards. (Drawn by Béla Nagy.)

was transmitted to the Ottomans by hundreds of cannon founders, blacksmiths, and shipwrights from Italy, Spain, southeastern Europe, Hungary, and Germany. Some of these people—Christians, Jews, and recent converts to Islam—offered their skills to the sultan voluntarily. Others were captured and forced against their will to work in the Ottoman cannon foundries, gunpowder works, and naval arsenals.[72]

One needs to be cautious not to overstate the importance of technology and science, and the European powers' advantages in these fields. Printed books on siege warfare and fortifications enjoyed wide circulation in early modern Europe, but what was useful in them was usually based on observation and had little to do with science. The same was true for inventions in metallurgy, such as bellows and furnaces. Improvements in the quality of gunpowder and guns and the various lock mechanisms of firearms were the products of trial and error or accidents and were introduced by specialized craftsmen such as gun founders, blacksmiths, and locksmiths. Improvements in weapons technology were slow and incremental, evolutionary rather than revolutionary. Their aim was economic, such as increased output and lower prices. Technical changes brought only negligible improvements concerning the ballistic performance of guns. Accuracy of the weapons was improved by rifling the barrel as early as the late fifteenth century, but it took much longer to reload these weapons than it did smoothbore muskets. Consequently, these "one-shot weapons" were used mainly as expensive hunting guns or as weapons of specialist troops such as snipers or skirmishers.[73] While mathematicians such as Niccolò Tartaglia, Galileo Galilei, and Evangelista Torricelli studied the old problem of projectile trajectory, they made little progress. The problem was solved only in the mid-eighteenth century with the publication in 1742 of Benjamin Robins's (1707–51) *New Principles in Gunnery*, a book based on his mathematical knowledge as much as on his extensive experiments. Galileo's and Torricelli's firing tables had little practical value for the gunner in an age when shooting remained irregular because of the unique casting of each cannon and the inconsistent quality of gunpowder—that is to say, before the mid-eighteenth century, when the first relatively standardized cannon appeared in France.[74] Even fortress design and the building of fortifications, a field where the usefulness of mathematics for the military engineer seems most obvious, required only "a minimum of geometry and a maximum of sound engineering common sense."[75] In an age when standardization of calibers and quality was only attempted but never achieved, and when there were no major technological breakthroughs in weapons design and manufacturing, the quality of weapons remained of secondary importance relative to that of their quantity. Firepower and military superiority were achieved through the sheer numbers of deployed weapons and troops. In battles and sieges, the party that outnumbered its opponent in terms of deployed weaponry and troops had a good chance of winning the engagement, provided that all other factors were equal. In this regard, the Ottomans were superior to their opponents until about the late seventeenth century. This was due to their military self-sufficiency in the production of weapons and ammunition and to their superior military provisioning and logistics.

Moving, feeding, and supplying troops with weapons and other necessary equipment in the early modern era was one of the greatest challenges statesmen and commanders faced. Ottoman administrators managed a sophisticated road network, partly inherited from Roman and Byzantine times. Roads, mountain passes, and bridges were repaired before the campaigns by specialized and auxiliary units operating locally in exchange for tax exemption. The administrators also had an elaborate and well-functioning provisioning system in which substantial quantities of wheat, barley, flour, and biscuits were stored in the depots along the campaign routes, and mobile bakeries baked bread. Military camps usually had an ample and cheap supply of grain, bread, and meat. The mobilization, storage, and distribution of food supplies to the fighting army remained the strength of the Ottomans until about the mid-eighteenth century, positively affecting discipline and moral. Owing to their supply and logistical system, Ottoman soldiers were usually better fed than their opponents.[76]

The availability of local cannon foundries, powder works, and major weapons and grain depots in Rumeli, Hungary, eastern Asia Minor, and Iraq greatly facilitated the deployment of military hardware and food supplies against the Austrian Habsburgs and Safavids. The Ottomans also utilized water transport. Heavy artillery, ammunition, and victuals were shipped from Constantinople via the Black Sea to Varna. There it was loaded onto carts, transported to Belgrade, and transferred onto hundreds of ships of the Ottoman Danube flotilla, bound for the Hungarian theater of war. Heavy cannons and stone cannonballs were transported on special ships, called gun ships and stone ships, respectively. The Ottomans used covered boats to transport gunpowder.[77]

Ottoman shipyards on the Danube and its tributaries built as many as 300 to 600 vessels of different sizes for major campaigns. In 1536–38, the shipbuilders in Smederevo and Zvornik had to construct 200 and 100 ships, respectively. In 1545, the *sancakbeyi* of Zvornik was ordered to construct 150 ships.[78] In preparation for Süleyman's last campaign in 1566, the imperial council ordered the *sancak* governor of Smederevo in November 1565 to construct 250 vessels. The *sancak* governor of Vidin had completed the construction of 140 ships by mid-April 1566, although he did not have enough oarsmen, who therefore were drafted from Wallachia. The government also instructed the *sancak* governor of Zvornik to build 200 vessels and 16 *şayka* boats on the Drina for the transportation of provisions. Shipbuilders in Ruse, Nikopol, Golubac, Požega, Kruševac, Mohács, Buda, and Esztergom also contributed. Most of the ships were transport ships that ferried troops and transported weapons, ammunition, and provisions.[79]

For campaigns against the Safavids, military hardware traveled to Trabzon on the Black Sea, where it was loaded onto camels and other draft animals and transported to the theater of war. When possible, the Ottoman river flotillas on the Tigris and Euphrates Rivers were also mobilized for transport and amphibious warfare.[80] The flotillas offered the Ottomans a great advantage. The absence of wheeled transportation and of navigable rivers, as well as the land-locked nature of the country, made it extremely difficult for the Safavids to move large artillery trains. The Safavids were also handicapped by the scarcity of raw materials needed for the casting of cannons and the manufacturing of gunpowder. These conditions, and not Islamic conservatism or any inherent cultural backwardness, were largely responsible for the dominance of traditional, non-gunpowder weapons in Safavid Persia.[81] The production and transportation capabilities of the Ottomans allowed them to accumulate large quantities of weapons and ammunition in their fortresses, often more than was needed or could be used.[82] It was not until the very end of the seventeenth century that the Austrian Habsburgs and their allies were capable of matching the Ottomans in terms of deployed troops and weaponry.

Habsburg Military Commitments and Border Defense

Neither Charles V nor Ferdinand I had a standing field army. Both had to raise armies anew for each new campaign and negotiate with the Estates of their respective kingdoms in order to get the troops and funds necessary to pay them. Ferdinand never had enough troops to match Süleyman's armies. The mobilization of Habsburg and imperial troops in 1532 proved that when not fighting against his Valois rival in Italy, Charles could assemble an army comparable in size to that of Süleyman. Owing to sustained modernization efforts and experimentation with weapons systems and tactics in the Italian wars, Charles's army, and especially his Spanish infantry, matched that of his Muslim antagonist. The proportion of arquebusiers in the Spanish infantry was about a quarter already in 1500. Just like the Ottoman janissaries at Mohács in 1526, they too discharged their weapons row after row in 1522 at Bicocca and in 1525 at Pavia, routing the famous Swiss infantry in both battles along with the French cavalry in the second. The maneuver by which these Spanish foot soldiers maintained a steady rate of fire in 1522 and 1525 is among the earliest known examples of the countermarch. Later in 1536, the Genoa Ordinances organized the Spanish infantry into three permanent *tercios*, or regiments, of pikemen and arquebusiers, each of about three thousand. One of Europe's most complex tactical and administrative formations, the *tercio* soon became early modern Europe's first standing force. Famous for their status as the empire's shock troops, *tercios* composed about 20 percent of the emperor's expeditionary armies, a percentage comparable with data regarding the 1532 mobilization. Just like the janissaries, they too stood firm in battles, often deciding the fate of the engagement. The reform of the artillery further enhanced Spanish firepower. By mid-century, it had evolved into a specialized artillery corps with cannons whose calibers the 1522 decree attempted to standardize.[83]

Without the help of his emperor-brother, Ferdinand was still able to guard Vienna by placing German Landsknecht and Spanish mercenaries in fortresses that protected his capital, such as Komárom, Győr, Esztergom, and Tata. His commanders in chief not only commanded the German and Spanish mercenaries serving in Habsburg-controlled Hungary and Croatia, but they also gradually assumed control over matters related to border defense. This created much resistance from the Hungarian and Croatian Estates. In the absence of the king, commanding the troops was the right of the Estates' leaders—the palatine (*palatinus*) and his proxy (*locumtenens*), and the ban of Croatia and Slavonia. However, since Ferdinand's Austrian lands (especially the Lower Austrian Estates) paid the troops serving in Hungary and Croatia, Ferdinand's Austrian commanders in chief, war councillors, and war secretaries gradually took over the management of the border defense in the 1530s. In the process, Vienna's military experts gained useful knowledge about border defense and the Turkish wars by consulting their Hungarian and Croatian counterparts experienced in these matters.[84] Consultations and military conferences resulted in lengthy reports and plans. A pamphlet from 1540 urged the rulers of Austria and Bavaria to recruit and maintain an army of one hundred thousand men, who

> would be permanently stationed on the frontiers of Hungary, Carniola and Styria. They would constantly harass the enemy. . . . There must be a careful planning to insure order and discipline among these troops, and to see that they have no lack of wages, foodstuff, equipment, and other necessities without which they could not survive or remain in existence [as a military force].[85]

But money was hard to come by. The Habsburg-Valois conflict consumed increasingly more resources. Charles's and Ferdinand's armies consisted of mercenaries whose wages grew by 55 percent from 1530 to 1552. The army that Charles led into Provence in 1536 cost him 1,500,000

Spanish ducats, but accomplished little. A somewhat larger army that the emperor used against Metz in 1552 cost him 3,276,000 Spanish ducats, and accomplished even less. The successful twelve-month campaign against the Schmalkaldic League in 1546–47 cost 3,000,000 Spanish ducats. This amounted to more than 60 percent of the combined revenues of Castile, Naples, and the Low Countries' core provinces.[86] Naval commitments against the Ottomans in the Mediterranean were even more expensive. Charles's Mediterranean fleet consisted of Andrea Doria's galleys, galley squadrons from Spain, Sicily, and Naples (Charles's Aragonese inheritance), and other hired galleys from Italy. Contemporaries estimated that the emperor's naval expedition against Algiers in the fall of 1541 cost him 4 million gold coins; a winter storm destroyed some 130 ships and 17 galleys of the fleet.[87] These costly wars made Charles even more reluctant to aid Ferdinand against the Turks in Hungary. Even if Charles wanted to help his brother, the parliamentary assemblies of the emperor's realms were unwilling to vote for subsidies spent outside their countries.

Facing imminent Ottoman conquest, members of the Hungarian nobility and their king used all possible structures to defend their borders, now situated in the middle of the kingdom, well beyond the collapsed medieval line of defense. They fortified castles, monasteries, watchtowers, and manor houses by building walls of compressed earth between rows of heavy logs. To prevent the Ottomans from using old structures, castles and forts that could not be fortified were demolished in accordance with the decrees of the Hungarian diets. The failure of the 1542 expedition and Ottoman conquests in Hungary in 1543–44 and 1551–52 demonstrated that the existing defense strategy needed readjustment. The hastily reinforced castles provided insufficient protection against the superior Ottoman art of siege warfare. A document that the Lower Austrian Estates presented at the imperial diet of Regensburg in 1556 listed 262 towns, castles, and manor houses that the Ottomans had captured between 1526 and 1556.[88] Between 1521 and 1566, only thirteen castles were able to resist Ottoman firepower for more than ten days, and only nine for more than twenty days. In the same period, only four castles managed to withstand Ottoman sieges: Kőszeg in 1532, Temesvár in 1551,

Eger in 1552, and Szigetvár in 1556. Yet, three of these forts enjoyed only temporary success, as the Ottomans captured Temesvár in 1552, Szigetvár in 1566, and Eger in 1596.[89]

In view of continued Ottoman advance, the Habsburg authorities in Vienna assumed a central role in organizing and financing the defense of their Hungarian and Croatian borders. Representatives of the Hungarian and Croatian Estates and the Habsburg authorities worked out a new defense strategy via proposals and military conferences. In early March 1556, King Ferdinand's Austrian, Hungarian, and Croatian councillors prepared a register of the royal castles stretching in crescent shape from the Adriatic Sea to Gyula in eastern Hungary. Another document listed the names of castles requiring additional garrisons of soldiers. They also discussed which castles needed to be rebuilt and supplied with weapons and ammunition so that they could withstand the attacks of "the eternal enemy."[90] These discussions led to the establishment of the Court War Council (Hofkriegsrat) in November 1556 in Vienna. As the central organ of military administration, the Court War Council had jurisdiction over the whole monarchy. However, in its first decades its main task was to organize and manage the anti-Ottoman border defense system in Hungary and Croatia. Since diplomatic relations with the Ottomans largely concerned war, the War Council also handled diplomacy with the Turks; this was an anomaly in Habsburg diplomacy, as the Imperial and Austrian Court Chanceries normally conducted diplomatic engagements. In 1578, the Inner Austrian Court War Council (Innerösterreichischer Hofkriegsrat) was established in Graz, the provincial capital, to assume organizational responsibility for the defense of the Croatian-Slavonian section of the military border. This was the consequence of the division of the Habsburg lands among Ferdinand I's three sons in 1564—Maximilian II, the future Holy Roman emperor, Archduke Ferdinand II, and Archduke Charles II Francis. Inner Austria obtained a great deal of independence under Archduke Charles II Francis. The archduke assumed command of the Croatian-Slavonian border and the Inner Austrian Court War Council, which was staffed by Inner Austrian nobles.[91] In addition to these two war councils, from the 1550s onward the Viennese authorities set up a host of other military-fiscal administrative offices to muster and pay the soldiers; to map, oversee, build, and modernize the forts; to construct ships and bridges and provision garrisons; and to supply fortresses with weapons and ammunition.[92] Although the establishment of these offices may seem haphazard, they were instrumental in managing and financing the anti-Ottoman defense system.

The birth of military cartography in the Habsburg monarchy is also closely related to the establishment of the anti-Ottoman defense system in Hungary and Croatia. Habsburg military cartography started in earnest only in the second half of the seventeenth century with the employment of specialized military cartographers. However, from the 1560s onward, the members of the Milanese Angielini family—Natale Angielini, his brother Nicolò, and son Paolo—had prepared several sketches and colored maps of the newly established Border Fortress Captain Generalcies (Grenzgeneralat) in Croatia and Hungary. The first such maps were prepared during the inspection tours of the frontiers ordered by the Viennese Court War Council. Natale Angielini's map of the Croatian-Slavonian frontier, which he drew during one such survey trip to the frontier in 1563, has not been located; however, the officials of the Court War Council and the Styrian Estates used its various versions, as did the humanist John Zsámboky (Johannes Sambucus) for his Illyricum map of 1573. In the 1560s Natale and Nicolò Angielini prepared the maps of the frontiers belonging to the Captain Generalcies of Kanizsa, Győr, the Mining Towns, and Upper Hungary and updated them in the early 1570s. In early 1574, Natale's son Paolo prepared an updated map of the Croatian-Slavonian frontier for the Viennese War Council, based on his father's sketches and other military surveys. The improved and colored maps made by Nicolò in 1573–75 survived in an atlas kept in Karlsruhe, whereas those made by Paolo in 1574 were found in a Viennese atlas. Around 1572, Nicolò and/or Natale also prepared a detailed colored map of Hungary. On the order of the Viennese War Council, Natale accompanied Lazarus Freiherr von Schwendi, captain-general of Upper Hungary (1565–68), to his campaign in 1565 against John Sigismund of Szapolyai, elected king of Hungary, and his Ottoman allies. Natale recorded the campaign's main events on a military map so that "His

Majesty [Emperor Maximilian II] could learn about these places." The emperor must have liked his map, as he allowed Natale to publish it. The Angielini maps and the dozens of fortress plans drawn in the 1560s and 1570s aided the Habsburg military administration in establishing the anti-Ottoman border defense system in Croatia and Hungary.[93]

After the Ottoman conquest of Szigetvár in 1566, the Habsburgs reorganized the defense around Kanizsa. Natale Angielini diligently recorded the changes, showing on his map the Habsburg and opposing Ottoman fortresses and castles (the latter are marked with a crescent), the villages belonging to the Kanizsa castle-estate, and the region's main roads. Mapmakers in 1580 and 1586 prepared updated maps of the Croatian-Slavonian frontier that reflected the conquests of the Bosnian *sancak* governor Sokollu Ferhad Pasha in 1577–78 and the Habsburg countermeasures. Of the latter, the most important was the construction of a new six-pointed, star-shaped fortress town at the confluence of the Kupa and Korana Rivers by the newly established Inner Austrian War Council in Graz. The fortress was later known as Karlstadt (modern Karlovac in Croatia), named after Archduke Charles II.[94]

When Ferdinand became king of Hungary in 1526, several of the castles slated to be modernized—including the key castles of Eger, Szigetvár, Kanizsa, Fülek, and Győr—were either mortgaged or in the hands of the members of the Hungarian aristocrats and members of the clergy. A similar situation existed in Croatia and Slavonia, where Ferdinand controlled only two of thirty-four castles in 1537. Between the mid-1540s and the late 1560s, the Habsburg administration not only redeemed several mortgaged estates but also obtained—through purchase and exchange—the important castles of Szigetvár, Eger, Gyula, and Kanizsa, along with their vast estates. The Hungarian magnates and nobility did not protest these exchanges, since the owners of these castles could not defend them against the Ottomans. Other castles and castle-estates, such as the ones in northeastern Hungary, were taken from their owners by military force in 1549 and 1565–66. Ferdinand controlled only 2 of the 280 castle-estates in Hungary in 1541. By 1560 the total number of castle-estates had been reduced to 150, of which Ferdinand controlled 35. Only a few decades later the treasury would mortgage or sell more than half of its castle-estates in Hungary. But in the 1560s these castles and estates played a crucial role in establishing the anti-Ottoman border defense system.[95]

After taking over these strategically important castles the Viennese government embarked on a major modernization project to rebuild and strengthen them according to the standards of the time. Italian architects and engineers supervised the modernization of the important castles of Szigetvár, Kanizsa, Győr, Komárom, Érsekújvár, Eger, and Temesvár. The most famous engineers—Pietro Ferabosco, Ottavio Baldigara, and Carlo Theti—planned the construction of the key fortresses that defended Vienna. The strategically vital towns of Győr, Komárom, Érsekújvár, Kassa, Nagyvárad, and Szatmár were turned into fortified towns of the type well known in Italy, France, and the Netherlands. In 1569, the Habsburgs established a new position to supervise these construction projects.[96]

The new crescent-shaped defense line stretched some 1,000 kilometers in length from the Adriatic Sea to northeast Hungary. In 1556, it comprised about 80 fortresses, forts, and smaller guardhouses, manned by 14,000 soldiers. The respective numbers rose to 170 and 22,700 by 1593, a result of systematic Habsburg and Hungarian efforts to strengthen the border defense. However, in the seventeenth century the Habsburgs managed to pay only 12,000 to 15,000 garrison soldiers. Of the 22,000 soldiers manning the border castles in the 1570s and 1580s, 15 percent were German, Italian, and Spanish mercenaries, stationed in key fortresses. The rest were Hungarians, Serbs, and Croats. The proportions of German and indigenous Hungarian, Croatian, and Serbian troops were similar in the seventeenth century. These numbers demonstrate that the Habsburg government was able to significantly strengthen the kingdom's defenses in just a few decades. However, figures for the seventeenth century indicate that the Viennese government was unable to maintain a similar robust defense.[97]

Such a concentration of fortresses and garrison soldiers was notable in the broader European context too. On the territory of the Hungarian Kingdom under Habsburg rule there were 7 forts in every 100 kilometer section of the defense line. The comparable numbers were 8 in France and the Holy Roman Empire, and 11.5 in the Spanish Netherlands. Sections of the Hungarian-Croatian border that were strategically more significant were even better fortified. In 1607, 60 garrisons protected the important border section between Murány and the Muraköz Region, the area between the Drava and Mura Rivers, now Medimurje in northern Croatia. This 400-kilometer-long section averaged 15 forts per 100 kilometers.[98] Such comparisons are somewhat misleading because they consider neither the types of armies, weaponry, and tactics that these forts faced, nor the differences in terrain and hydraulic systems. They still illustrate the significance of the Habsburg monarchy's Danubian frontier in the broader European context.

9

Military Transformations

Habsburg Military Transformation

The spectacular increase in military manpower in most European armies is one of the hallmarks of the transformation of European militaries in the seventeenth and eighteenth centuries. It has been explained alternatively by the rise of the "new monarchies" and their bureaucracies, by interstate rivalry, and by the emergence of the "artillery fortress."[1] In the case of the Habsburg monarchy, the Ottoman threat in Hungary and Croatia prompted a number of military and fiscal developments. Because of these efforts, by the late sixteenth century the Habsburgs were able to deploy better and larger armies against the Ottomans in Hungary than in the time of Süleyman. In Hungary, the Viennese government could rely on experience gained by the Spanish armies fighting in Flanders, troops that are considered by historians to have been on the cutting edge of the late sixteenth-century art of warfare. Some of the changes that the Viennese military leadership introduced in the field armies were, at least partly, prompted by Ottoman firepower superiority. Lazarus Freiherr von Schwendi—captain-general in Upper Hungary between 1565 and 1568 and one of the best experts on Ottoman military of his time—emphasized the importance of the arquebus as a counter to the janissaries. He advised the Habsburg emperor to enroll Spanish and Italian arquebusiers as well as horsemen equipped with this weapon.[2] Others seconded his views. At a Viennese military conference in 1577, which discussed the anti-Ottoman war and defense strategies, military experts and advisers underlined the need for more German horsemen armed with firearms, not only because the Turks outnumbered the Hungarian hussars along the frontier but also because the experts believed that "for the time being, hand firearms are the main advantage of Your Majesty's military over this enemy (i.e., the Ottomans)."[3] The Habsburg armies that fought against the Ottomans in the Long War of 1593–1606 in Hungary were on par with their western European contemporaries in terms of army structure, armaments, and tactics. In the German, Walloon, Lorrainese, and French infantry regiments deployed in Hungary, "gunners" (*Schützen*) greatly outnumbered the pikemen, their ratio ranging in the various companies from two to one to seven to one. The impressive firepower of these infantry regiments was due to the infantrymen's countermarch tactics and their matchlock muskets.[4] The deployment of mounted gunners—a mix of mounted arquebusiers, German "black cavalry" (named after the color of their breastplates), and cuirassiers—further enhanced Habsburg firepower. The arquebusiers, who had been fighting the Ottomans in Hungary since the 1560s, were armed with arquebuses as well as with pistols. The German black cavalry carried at least two (but occasionally as many as six) wheellock pistols and were especially effective owing to their caracole tactics. The cuirassiers, named after their heavy armor (cuirass), also carried two pistols but retained their heavy and long sword. The Habsburgs had used them against the Ottomans since 1595 as shock cavalry. The wheel-lock guns of the mounted gunners were shorter (97–98 cm) and lighter (2.8 kg) than the matchlock muskets and could be fired with one hand.[5]

The Hungarian army that Süleyman defeated at Mohács numbered about 26,000 men. In 1595, the Habsburg emperor deployed almost three times as many soldiers, some 80,000 men. The main army that recaptured Esztergom from the Ottomans in 1595 numbered 57,945 men.[6] Deployed troops were smaller than these paper numbers. Nevertheless, the imperial field armies fighting the Ottomans in Hungary constituted a formidable military force, significantly surpassing the armies that the Ottomans had faced earlier in the sixteenth century.

After the Thirty Years' War, the Habsburgs managed to keep some of their regiments together, establishing a standing field army in addition

TABLE 9-1. Effective and Paper (peacetime) Strength of the Habsburg Standing Army

Date	Effective	Paper/peacetime strength
1650	24,500	20,000
1655	13,732	
1656	41,400	
1661	53,000	
1668	29,633	
1673	59,700	
1675	60,187	
1677	77,621	
1679		36,160
1681	37,000	
Summer 1683	55,700	80,000
1684		80,000
1685		60,000
1687	63,800	
1697	77,736	88,795
1698		116,000
1699	86,388	59,626
1700/01	55,000	80,000
1701		108,670
1702		123,532
1703	76,000	125,000
1704	76,195	134,376
1705	113,000	135,075
1707		119,032
1711		130,622
1714		137,229
1715		141,843
1716		157,303
1717		160,722
1718		162,727
1721		121,537
1727		190,257
1732		141,713
1734		202,598
1735		205,643
1737		162,572
1739		159,519
1740		141,880

Source: Hochedlinger 2003: 104, 237; for 1698, see Zachar 2004: 161.

to their permanent garrisons in Hungary and Croatia. From the 1680s onward, the "provincial recruitment" system (*Landrekrutenstellung*) became the main method of raising troops in wartime, which still depended on the participation of the Estates. However, unlike in earlier times when the provinces could commute their obligations to a monetary payment, now they were required to provide recruits, making the system more efficient and less expensive. Estimates regarding the size of the Habsburg standing army vary, but table 9-1 will give the reader some sense as to the effective and paper strength of the Habsburg military.

In addition to the permanent garrison troops stationed in Hungary—numbering 14,000 to 15,000 in the mid-seventeenth century—the size of the effective Habsburg troops fluctuated between 14,000 and 53,000 men. In the 1680s and 1690s Vienna was able to deploy troops numbering between 64,000 and 86,000. In 1698, despite peace negotiations with the Ottomans, the Habsburgs still maintained 61,625 troops in Hungary, which was more than half of the monarchy's paper strength of 116,000 men.[7] In 1705 the effective forces numbered over 110,000 men, and during the Austro-Ottoman war of 1716–18 the total paper strength of the Habsburg army reached 160,000 men. The actual size of the army was much smaller. In 1706, for instance, the army was short 31,000 infantrymen and 13,000 horses; the next year the infantry was short 26,000 men. Heavy casualties further diminished troop strength. The twenty-five infantry regiments fighting against the Ottomans in Hungary in the 1716 campaign, for example, needed 17,500 new recruits for the following year's campaign.[8]

Habsburg War Finance and the Estates

Financing and administering the border defense proved to be an especially difficult task, and it led to the mutual interdependence of the Habsburg court and the Estates. Although the Court War Council served as the main office of Habsburg military administration, in the mid-sixteenth century the war paymaster (*Kriegszahlmeister*) could only authorize payments not exceeding 150 Rhine gulden. This limited financial authority of the Court War Council did not match the huge range of its military and organizational responsibilities, and undercut its abilities to recruit, arm, and supply troops and maintain military arsenals, warehouses, and border castles. Finances were further complicated by the fact that in the sixteenth century the Habsburg monarchy was transitioning from a "domain state" to a "tax-state." Revenues came from two main sources: *camerale* and *contributionale*. Designed to cover the expenditures of the court, the monarch's *camerale,* or ordinary revenues, came from his shrinking domain lands, mines, and customs duties. *Contributionale*, on the other hand, were considered extraordinary subsidies to meet emergency military expenses and required a vote by the Estates. While the Court War Council administered extraordinary taxes, the Court Chamber or Treasury (*Hofkammer*), set up by Ferdinand in 1527 in Vienna, collected ordinary cameral revenues.[9] The Viennese Court Chamber alone could not manage the revenues of the monarchy. Therefore, subordinate provincial treasuries (*Länderkammer*) were set up in Prague for Bohemia (1527), Breslau (Wrocław) for Silesia (1557), Pozsony for Hungary, and Kassa for Upper Hungary to administer *cameral* revenues.[10]

By the 1570s, three different treasuries administered revenues and paid the soldiers in Hungary. The Hungarian Chamber (*Camera Hungarica* or *Ungarische Kammer*) was established in 1528 in Buda but moved to Pozsony after the loss of its original home in 1529 to King John Szapolyai. Territories in Upper Hungary lay too far from the seat of the Hungarian Chamber in Pozsony. Therefore, in 1567 Vienna organized another treasury in Kassa, the Zipser Chamber (*Camera Scepusiensis* or *Zipserische Kammer*). According to its first instructions (1567 and 1571), the main function of the Zipser Chamber was to pay the garrison soldiers in Upper Hungary. In addition to these treasuries, the Lower Austrian Chamber (*Niederösterreichische Kammer*), established in 1527 in Vienna, also played a crucial role in managing the ordinary royal revenues from the Habsburgs' Hungarian Kingdom and in paying the soldiers in the castles along the Hungarian-Croatian border.[11]

Initially, the Habsburgs possessed a limited tax base in Hungary. In 1530 Ferdinand managed to collect revenues from only seven or eight counties of the seventy-two counties of pre-Mohács Hungary. By 1539, the number rose to twenty-eight. Ferdinand controlled the largest territory in 1551–55, when he temporarily ruled Transylvania, administering some sixty counties and parts of Transylvania. The number of counties controlled by Ferdinand shrank to thirty-two in 1557–58, a number that did not change substantially in the rest of his reign.[12] Consequently, the Hungarian Chamber collected negligible revenues (4,000 to 5,000 Hungarian florins) in the early 1540s, but those rose to 150,000 to 180,000 Hungarian florins in the early 1550s. Despite territorial losses, in the 1570s and 1580s revenues administered by the Hungarian Chamber rose to more than 190,000 Hungarian florins (about 240,000 Rhine gulden), owing to more efficient fiscal administration.[13] However, when the Estates rejected the extraordinary war tax known under the various names of *subsidium*, *contributio*, *dica*, and *Anschnitt*, as they did in 1586, 1589, and 1591, the Habsburgs suffered a serious loss of income—up to 40 percent in 1586.[14]

Despite difficulties, the Hungarian lands provided the Habsburgs with substantial revenue. Ferdinand managed to collect from his Hungarian Kingdom some 640,000 Hungarian florins in good years (and about 400,000 Hungarian florins in bad years). Of his successors, Maximilian I (as king of Hungary, r. 1564–76) collected 640,000 Hungarian florins (800,000 Rhine gulden), whereas Rudolf I (r. 1576–1608; as Emperor Rudolf II, r. 1576–1612) collected about 550,000 Hungarian florins. Since Ferdinand's and his successors' total revenues are estimated at 1,700,000 to 2,000,000 Hungarian florins (2,150,000 to 2,500,000 Rhine gulden), the revenues from Hungary amounted to 25 to 32 percent of the total.[15]

However significant these revenues may seem, it was not enough to cover the salaries of garrison soldiers stationed in the Hungarian-Croatian border forts, the cost of which reached approximately 800,000 Hungarian florins (1,000,000 Rhine gulden) by the last years of Ferdinand's reign. Even if all the Hungarian revenue went to cover soldiers' pay, only between 48 and 66 percent of the soldiers would have been fully compensated. However, only about 50 to 60 percent of the revenue from Hungary went to military expenses, with the rest allocated for administrative expenses and debt.[16] Soldiers' pay, though admittedly the most substantial, was but one of many defense-related expenses. Estimates place other defense-related costs—such as rebuilding and repairing forts, maintaining the Danubian flotillas in Komárom and Győr, military administration, intelligence gathering, and communication—at 400,000 to 500,000 Hungarian florins per year. Thus, the total annual cost of the Hungarian-Croatian military border amounted to 1,700,000 to 2,100,000 million Hungarian florins, which almost equaled Ferdinand's total annual revenues from his kingdoms and provinces.[17]

Border defense therefore required ongoing contribution from the Habsburgs' other kingdoms and from the Holy Roman Empire. The imperial aid, however, remained contingent on political factors. Unlike Bohemia, Hungary was not part of the Reich. The obligation of the imperial Estates to finance Hungary's defenses went into effect only if the Ottomans threatened the territory of the empire or Vienna, which after Ferdinand's election as emperor in 1558 assumed the position of imperial capital. Although the Hungarian frontier lay far from Speyer, Regensburg, and Augsburg, where the imperial diet held its meetings, the "Turkish Question" (*Türkenfrage*) and "Turkish Aid" (*Türkenhilfe*) recurred time and again as significant issues at the diet's meetings. Between 1576 and 1606 the income from the Turkish Aid amounted to 18.7 million Rhine gulden, averaging some 600,000 Rhine gulden per year—that is, about 25 percent of the monarchy's annual revenue. When the Court War Council in 1613 stated that "every province had to upkeep its respective confines in Hungary," it formulated a time-honored practice. The Estates of Carniola and Carinthia financed the Croatian section of the military border, while the Styrian Estates paid for the Slavonian section. The Estates of Inner Austria (Styria, Carinthia, and Carniola) spent more than 18 million Rhine gulden for the forts in neighboring Croatia and Slavonia in the sixteenth century. The Kanizsa border area drew funds from the Styrian, Hungarian, and imperial Estates; the Győr section drew money from the Estates of Lower Austria and the Reich; the mining town or Lower Hungarian border area was financed by the Bohemian and Moravian Estates; while the Hungarian, Silesian, and imperial Estates paid for the Upper Hungarian section of the border.[18]

Owing to their dependence on the emperor-king's other kingdoms, the Hungarian Estates lost control over military and financial affairs. However, administering and maintaining the border defense system depended on local knowledge and resources. Defense required the participation and cooperation of the Hungarian and Croatian nobility. Local aristocrats and nobles controlled the counties and their military forces and thus proved instrumental in maintaining smaller private forts in the second line of defense. The majority of the large estates also remained in the hands of the provincial landowning nobility. Revenues and food from such estates paid and supplied the border fortresses, an enterprise that would have been unthinkable without the cooperation of the provincial nobility. Moreover, the extraordinary war taxes had to be approved and voted for by the Estates at the Hungarian diet. Although in the 1570s and 1580s revenues from the war tax amounted to merely 10 percent of the total revenues that the Habsburgs collected from Hungary, it was nonetheless an important sum. Furthermore, the Hungarian nobility provided a much-needed workforce to strengthen the border forts. The Estates approved and administered the uncompensated peasant labor (*gratuitus labor*), a new extraordinary tax that Ferdinand introduced.

The interdependence of the Viennese government and the Estates resulted in the dual nature of the administration of the border defense system. Two types of captain generalcies emerged, controlled, respectively, by the Viennese Court War Council and the Hungarian Estates. The Border Fortress Captain Generalcies (*Grenzgeneralat*) fell under the purview of the captains-general of the borders (*Grenzobrist/Grenzoberst*) headquartered in key fortresses. The six generalcies were (1) the Croatian and Adriatic Captain Generalcy, commanded initially from Bihać and after 1579 from Karlstadt; (2) the Slavonian or Wendish Captain Generalcy, with Varasd as its center; (3) the Kanizsa Captain Generalcy (renamed after the Ottoman conquest of Kanizsa in 1600 as the Captain Generalcy facing Kanizsa); (4) the Győr Captain Generalcy; (5) the Mining Towns Captain Generalcy, with Léva and after 1589 Érsekújvár as its center; and (6) the Upper Hungarian or Kassa Captain Generalcy. Komárom, which defended Vienna, was the center of the monarchy's Danube flotilla and was under the direct control of the Viennese Court War Council. The division of the country into smaller border areas allowed these border captain-generals to control the main

fortresses that the central government built, modernized, and maintained. At the same time and in the same territories, so-called district
captain-generals (*Kreisobrist/Kreisoberst*) commanded smaller forts of
secondary importance with forces made up of noble, county, and town
troops and contingents of cavalry and infantry paid by the Habsburg
rulers. While the border captain-generals could be from the neighboring Habsburg lands or could be Hungarian lords acceptable to the
Court War Council, native Hungarians almost exclusively filled the
ranks of the less important district captain-generals.[19]

The establishment and manning of the military border led to increased
militarization of Hungarian society. By the 1570s, a quasi-permanent
military force made up of the Hungarian soldiers of the border forts had
emerged. Their number in the four captain generalcies in Hungary
proper was about 11,000 in the 1580s and about 14,000 to 15,000 in the
mid-seventeenth century. Although most of them were peasants, in return for their military service they gained privileges similar to those of
the nobility.[20] By the seventeenth century, all the captain-generals, save
those of the strategically most important, Győr, came from Hungary's
most influential landowning aristocrats. Thus, the Estates gained crucial
control over the Hungarian soldiery deployed in royal forts.

In addition to these garrison soldiers paid at least partly by Vienna,
the Hungarian landowning aristocrats also had their own private armies.
Estimates regarding the combined strength of the private armies of the
Hungarian landowning magnates vary between 10,000 and 20,000 men
in the seventeenth century. To this one should add at least 8,000 to
15,000 (or perhaps as many as 20,000 to 25,000) *hajdú* soldiers. Most of
these were regular soldiers serving in royal forts or imperial regiments,
while others were considered semiregular reserve forces, often employed by the magnates or the princes of Transylvania.[21]

The ultimate dependence of the soldiers of the border forts, the
hajdús, and the serving lesser nobility (*servitor*) on their aristocrat em-
ployers (*dominus*) provided the large landowners with an effective military force and military-administrative personnel that could be used
against the centralizing policy of the Habsburgs. The Hungarian soldiers
of the border forts along with the *hajdús* formed the bulk of the army of
Stephen Bocskai during his anti-Habsburg uprising of 1604–6. In 1605,

in return for their military service, Bocskai collectively ennobled some ten thousand *hajdú* soldiers, liberated them from their *corvée*, and settled them in his lands in eastern Hungary.[22]

The Estates' position was further strengthened by Ottoman-held Hungary and the Principality of Transylvania. Having strong personal, economic, and cultural ties with territories under Habsburg rule, these parts of the country offered refuge for the Hungarian rebels. They also effectively backed the Estates' political demands both on the battlefields and in international diplomacy. Unlike in Bohemia, where the anti-Habsburg rebellion of the Estates in 1618–20 was crushed ruthlessly (although the Estates did not disappear), Vienna had to be more cautious in Hungary to avoid losing further territories to its archenemy, the Ottomans. Harsh absolutism provoked anti-Habsburg rebellions with the military backing of the Hungarian soldiers of the border fortresses, Transylvania, and even the Ottoman-held territories, and led to repeated loss of territories, either to the Ottoman vassal princes of Transylvania or to the Ottomans. This is what happened when the Protestant princes of Transylvania, Gabriel (Gábor) Bethlen and George (György) I Rákóczi, led successful campaigns against the Habsburgs during the Thirty Years' War, often with the agreement and backing of the Ottomans. These princes could mobilize armies of eight thousand to twenty thousand, in which the overwhelming majority were *hajdús*.[23]

While Ottoman military pressure spurred military modernization and administrative-fiscal centralization in the Habsburg monarchy, it also strengthened the territorial Estates' position in managing taxation and army provisioning. Despite Habsburg centralization in the eighteenth century, the Estates—especially those of Lower Austria—continued to play a crucial role in Habsburg war finance. They financed the monarchy's debt by providing long-term loans at low-interest rates.[24]

Ottoman Army Growth

From the late sixteenth century on, the traditional Ottoman military, fiscal, and administrative systems went through major crises and adjustments. These were partly due to the changing nature of warfare and tactics in Europe, which the Ottomans faced for the first time during the Long Hungarian war of 1593–1606.[25] In a treatise composed shortly after the battle of Mezőkeresztes (1596), the single major field battle of the war, Hasan Kafi al-Akhisari (d. 1615) complained that the imperialists used modern arquebuses and cannons and showed a distinct advantage over the Ottomans.[26] The Ottoman chronicler Selaniki Mustafa contended that the Ottomans "could not withstand the musketeers from Transylvania." In 1602, the grand vizier reported that "in the field or during a siege we are in a distressed position, because the greater part of the enemy forces are infantry armed with muskets, while the majority of our forces are horsemen and we have very few specialists skilled in the musket."[27] The imperial forces fighting against the Ottomans in the war of 1593–1606 were in the forefront of contemporary military development in terms of the high proportion of gun-carrying infantry relative to pikemen. While the temporary tactical superiority of the Habsburg forces did not materialize in strategic advantages—the Treaty of Zsitvatorok (1606) left Eger and Kanizsa in Ottoman hands—the war had profound effects on the evolution of the Ottoman military. The Ottoman government attempted to counterbalance Habsburg firepower superiority in two ways: first, by setting up units of arms-bearing infantry troops hired from among the vagrant subject population, usually designated in the sources as *sekban* and *levend*, and second, by increasing the numbers of arms-bearing janissaries.

The Porte hoped to increase its military manpower by hiring *sekban* mercenaries, who knew how to use firearms and could be recruited for a campaign or two and then discharged at the close of the campaign season. However, the *sekban* mercenaries did not return to their villages but instead joined the Celali rebel bands in Asia Minor. Although the direct connection between the Hungarian wars and the Celali rebellions is problematic,[28] the employment of *sekban* and *sarıca* units in both wars is well documented.[29] The eyewitness Akhisari blamed the army's disorder and the flight of the Ottoman soldiers on the forced recruitment of peasants and artisans. He attributed the Christian success in the Long War of 1593–1606 to the lack of discipline, the cruelty, and the rebellion of the Ottoman soldiers, which coincided with the start of the Long War.[30]

TABLE 9-2. Paper Strength of the Ottoman Salaried Troops, 1568–1730

Date	Janissary	Artillery	Palace cavalry	Total
1568–69	11,535	2,460	5,395	**19,390**
1574	13,599	2,124	5,957	**21,680**
1582	16,905	3,736	8,346	**28,987**
1597	35,000	6,527	17,000	**58,527**
1609	37,627	7,966	20,896	**66,489**
1652–53	55,151	7,246	20,479	**82,876**
1654	51,047	6,905	19,844	**77,796**
1661–62	54,222	6,497	15,248	**75,967**
1666–67	47,233	6,193	13,267	**66,693**
1669–70	53,849	8,014	14,070	**75,933**
1687–88	62,826	17,995	19,800	**100,621**
1690–91	42,542	13,354	13,351	**69,247**
1691–92	35,839	8,309	10,807	**54,955**
1694–95	78,798	21,824	13,395	**114,017**
1696–97	69,620	14,726	15,212	**99,563**
1699	67,729	15,470	13,447	**96,646**
1700	50,102	11,934	12,992	**75,028**
1700–1701	42,119	11,485	13,043	**66,647**
1701–2	39,925	10,893	12,999	**63,817**
1702–3	40,139	10,010	12,976	**63,125**
1704–5	52,642	11,851	17,133	**81,626**
1709–10	16,609	3,265	14,101	**33,975**
1710–11	43,562	8,775	15,625	**67,962**
1712	36,383	—	21,208	**57,591**
1723–24	24,403	—	12,979	**37,382**
1727–28	24,733	—	18,178	**42,911**
1728–29	24,803	—	19,970	**44,773**
1729–30	98,726	—	16,809	**115,535**

Source: Özvar 2006: 237–38; Ágoston 2014: 113; 2018: 996–97. For 1690–91 (H. 1102), see BOA, KK.d. 2313 (here, the numbers for janissaries and artillery include those serving in the frontier castles).

The wars that the Ottomans waged against the Safavids, Habsburgs, and Venetians from the late sixteenth century onward profoundly affected the development of the Ottoman military, contributing to the growth of the salaried forces and their transformation.

Data presented in table 9-2 demonstrate the gradual expansion of the salaried troops from the late 1560s onward. The number of the Porte's salaried standing troops rose from 19,390 in 1569 to 28,987 in 1582, and to 58,527 in 1597. In the meantime, the number of janissaries rose from

TABLE 9-3. Paper Strength of the Janissaries, 1568–1699

1569	10,363
1573	13,565
1574	13,839
1574–75	14,355
1577	14,142
1578	14,955
1582	16,905
1589	19,708
1589–90	22,760
1591–92	23,372
1592	23,359
1593	24,250
1597	35,000
1609	37,627
1620	31,174
1624	37,809
1628	31,794
1632–33	43,000
1652	56,042
1654	51,047
1660–61	55,151
1661–62	54,222
1664	53,371
1666	49,556
1666–67	47,233
1669	53,849
1670	49,868
1687–88	62,825
1690–91	42,542
1691–92	35,839
1694–95	78,798
1696–97	69,620
1699	67,729
1700	50,102
1701–2	39,925
1702–3	40,139
1703–4	53,200
1704–5	52,642
1709–10	16,609
1710–11	43,562
1712	36,383

Source: Ágoston 2012a: 203; 2014: 96–97; 2018: 967–68; for 1569, 1573, and 1578, see BOA, KK.d. 1767, KK.d. 1769, and MAD.d. 2727, p. 794; for 1589 and 1589–90, see BOA, KK.d. 1773; for 1620, 1624, and 1628 see Murphey 1999: 47, For 1632–33, see Aziz Efendi 1985: 6; for 1664, see G. Yılmaz 2011; for 1690–91, see BOA, KK.d. 2313.

Note: The janissaries were paid quarterly and their numbers fluctuated from one quarter to the other in a given fiscal year. When more than one figure is available, I give the highest one.

10,363 in 1569 to 14,955 in late 1578 (the first year of the Ottoman-Safavid war), a 44 percent increase.[31] By the last months of the war (late 1589 and early 1590), 22,760 janissaries received salaries from the treasury. During the Ottoman-Safavid war, the size of the janissary corps increased by 52 percent (7,805 men).[32] The corps expanded even faster during the Long War of 1593–1606. In late 1593, in the first campaign season of the war, the Porte paid 24,250 janissaries, of whom 9,080 men were ordered to the Hungarian front).[33] The number rose to about 35,000 men in 1597, stabilizing for a while at about 37,000 men in 1609, three years after the war, only to increase further to about 43,000 men in 1632–33, during the last phase of the Ottoman-Safavid wars (1623–39) (Table 9-3).[34]

These figures reflect the general demand for, and availability of, military manpower during the Ottomans' Sixty Years' War (1578–1639), when Ottoman troops fought, often simultaneously, against the Safavids in the east (1578–90, 1603–12, 1615–18, 1623–39), the Habsburgs in the north (1593–1606), and the Celali rebels in eastern Asia Minor and Syria (c. 1595–1610). Other spikes in the numbers of the standing salaried army coincided with the wars against Venice over Crete (1645–69) and against the Holy League (1684–99).

The reasons behind the expansion of the Ottoman standing military are manifold. Successfully besieging modernized and Italian-bastioned fortresses in Hungary and Crete was a more difficult business than besieging outdated medieval Hungarian castles in the time of Süleyman. While the modernization of the Hungarian castles was only partially completed before the Long War of 1593–1606, owing to a lack of resources, these fortresses, with garrisons numbering several thousands of experienced mercenaries, required substantially more Ottoman troops, firepower, and time to invest. Moreover, the Habsburgs mobilized field armies in the range of 50,000 to 60,000 in the 1590s and 80,000 to 100,000 men a century later. To successfully fight these armies, the Ottomans needed to mobilize troops comparable in size to those of their rivals. The multiseason wars of the late sixteenth through the early eighteenth centuries also resulted in much higher rates of casualties and desertion than the wars of Süleyman, and thus required larger military potential and reserves.

Garrisoning the empire's border provinces demanded additional salaried troops as more and more janissaries and artillery gunners of the standing army were deployed in key fortresses. The number of janissaries of the Porte serving in the fortresses of Ottoman Hungary had risen from 2,282 in 1547 to 7,581 by 1596–97, amounting to 22 percent of the total number of janissaries paid by the imperial treasury in 1597.[35] Although these were war years and two of the castles with significant janissary garrisons were recently conquered, the figures reflected empire-wide trends. While the ratio of janissaries on garrison duty to their total number changed little from 1547, in absolute numbers the change was noticeable. In contrast to 1547, when 4,648 janissaries served in the empire's fortresses, in the seventeenth century between 14,000 and 36,000 janissaries were on garrison duty annually. Key border fortresses had janissary garrisons ranging from 1,500 to 6,000. Even in 1691–92, during the war against the Holy League, the proportion of janissaries in frontier garrisons was 42 percent.[36]

The increase in the number of salaried troops (and bureaucrats) was only partly driven by the exigencies of war. War created the need for more soldiers, which was seized upon by members of the military, who enrolled their sons and relatives into the salaried corps. Taxpaying subjects (*reaya*) found their way into the military, which gave them tax-exempt status and regular salaries, even if the latter were often in arrears. Soldiers of the Porte supplemented their salaries by working as tax farmers and tax collectors. Members of the standing cavalry forces accounted for 78 percent of the collectors of the *cizye*, the poll tax levied on non-Muslims, in 1570–71; by 1615–16 their share had risen to 90 percent.[37] In the first three years after the introduction of the life-tenure tax farm (*malikane*) in 1695, 682 out of 1,113 tax farms (61 percent) went to members of the military-bureaucratic-religious class. They paid 71 percent of the initial advance payment, amounting to 46.7 million *akçe*.[38] Ottoman governors, grand viziers, and commanders in chief used their positions to extract large sums from applicants for offices. At the end of the sixteenth century, for instance, Sinan Pasha accused his rival Ferhad Pasha of accumulating almost 135 million *akçe*, more than the treasury's annual revenues from Asia Minor and Rumeli, from appointment fees between 1586 and 1590 as commander in chief.[39]

The Metamorphosis of the Janissaries

The increased demand for military manpower could not be met by traditional recruiting techniques. New methods of recruitment had to be found, which opened the doors to the taxpaying subjects who wanted to enter the nontaxpaying *askeri* class. The two most consequential effects of the changed recruitment were the metamorphosis of the janissaries and the transformation of the provincial forces. The number of janissary cadets or novices (*acemi oğlan*) more than doubled between 1530 and 1574—from 3,640 men to 7,673 men—reaching 9,314 men in 1589. There was no similar sharp increase in later years, when the number of janissary cadets stayed at about 9,000–10,000 men until the early seventeenth century.[40] These data suggest that the Ottoman government filled the vacancies in the salaried corps principally with janissary novices, as opposed to the post-1590 period, when sons of janissaries and "outsiders" (*ecnebi*) (that is, commoners from the taxpaying subjects) were the main source of recruitment. The practice of the child levy also changed. A comparison of *devşirme* recruitment registers of the 1490s and 1603 demonstrated that the levied boys' average age had risen from 13.5 years to 16.6 years.[41] This indicates that in the early seventeenth century the Porte preferred older boys, who could immediately be turned into soldiers. This reflected not only the increased need for military manpower but also the changed nature of warfare. It took only a couple of months to train musketeers, whereas previously it took years to train a skilled janissary archer. However, bribed officials recruited lads who were not up to the job. In April 1590, the Habsburg resident envoy in Constantinople reported that in Silistra bribed officials collected poor Turkish lads instead of Christians, and that the agha of the janissaries earned 50,000 ducats from the corrupt business, for which he was dismissed.[42]

The number of janissary cadets was higher in the 1620s than in the 1590s (in 1624, for instance, 11,477).[43] Most of them were not recruited by the system of levy of boys, as the *acemi* corps too went through its own metamorphosis. In principle, the janissaries were not allowed to marry, but already in the fifteenth century they occasionally did so.[44]

The marriage restriction was lifted under Selim I, if not earlier, when the Porte granted permission to older members of the corps to marry.[45] By the second half of the mid-sixteenth century, the practice must have been quite ubiquitous, for the Porte paid stipends to hundreds of janissary orphans. Known in the sources under various names (*nanhoran, nanhoregan,* or *kuloğlu*), these orphans of deceased janissaries received a state stipend until they were old enough to enroll into the corps of janissary cadets. The number of janissary orphans more than doubled from 470 in 1543 to 1,000 in late 1589.[46] They amounted to about 10 percent of the janissary novices in the second half of the sixteenth century, which indicates that the share of sons of active janissaries among the novices must have been higher. The lifting of the janissary marriage prohibition resulted in the corps elite soldiers admitting their sons into their ranks in growing numbers.

In addition to the orphans and sons of janissaries, increasingly more novices were handpicked recruits in the personal service of the commander of the janissary corps (*ağa çırağı*) and sons of the salaried cavalry (*ferzend-i sipahi*). Complaining about these new opportunities of recruitment, Aziz Efendi noted in circa 1632 that these recruits were still required to work as janissary cadets and "were accepted into permanent regiments" of the janissaries only after they completed their training.[47] As these new sources of recruitment became available, the *devşirme* levy was gradually phased out over the course of the seventeenth century. Sir Paul Rycaut—who stayed in the Ottoman capital and the port city of Izmir for seventeen years in the 1660s and 1670s—claimed that by his time the levy of boys was disused.[48] Rycaut's observation reflected actual practice, even though there were sporadic attempts to levy boys in the early eighteenth century.

We saw that the "civilianization" of the janissaries in greater numbers started under Süleyman, partly as a consequence of the succession struggle between Princes Bayezid and Selim. Under Murad III (r. 1574–95) the government tried in vain to recall the *yasakçı* janissaries from the countryside. The failure also meant that the *timariot* cavalrymen lost not just their role of policing the countryside and maintaining public order, but also the transgression fees, which they had collected from commoners found guilty of criminal acts. These sums now enriched the janissaries, who desperately needed the extra revenue, as the real value of their salaries had substantially declined because of inflation and the repeated devaluation of the silver *akçe*, in which they were paid. Realizing the problem, the government provided the janissaries with an annual clothing allowance and set up a special fund to subsidize the janissaries' purchases of staple commodities such as bread and meat.[49] Such subsidies, along with revenues from transgression fees, artisanal activities, and trade, as well as the availability of credit from the corps fund, were important incentives for commoners aspiring to enter the corps. Janissary life in the provinces offered plenty of opportunities for amassing and investing substantial sums, which the janissaries used for various financial transactions.[50]

By the late seventeenth century, janissary service had been radically transformed. Many janissaries had become craftsmen, shop owners, merchants, and tax farmers, while ordinary tradesmen, merchants, and tax farmers bought their way into the corps using opportunities created by the exigencies of wartime economies. The life of the janissaries was a far cry from the rigid military discipline that characterized the corps in its early days. Janissaries married and settled in towns, established relationships with the civil population, and were more interested in providing for their families than fighting the enemy.[51]

Many of the janissaries were not mobilized for war either. Janissaries who were not fit for active military service were designated as pensioners (*mütekaid*) and guards (*korucu*). The *mütekaids* were retired janissaries, with no military obligations. From the time of Selim II (r. 1566–74) on, their pensions were paid from the imperial treasury, a practice that inflated the size of the corps. The *korucu* were charged with guarding the janissary barracks in the capital, or their fighting peers' tents, when the janissaries were mobilized for campaigns. In the first quarter of the century, the number of those who managed to get *korucu* and *mütekaid* status was more than 7,000, although fewer than 1,000 of them were in fact old and unfit for military service.[52] Ottoman treasury account books indicate that in 1654, out of the 33,463 janissaries stationed in the capital, 10,665 men (31 percent) were *kurucus* and *mütekaids*. The figures

in 1701 were 43,562 and 9,621 (22 percent).[53] Consequently, only a portion of the janissaries recorded in the treasury account books and janissary pay registers participated in campaigns: in 1597 about 26 percent,
and in the second half of the seventeenth century between 25 and
33 percent of the total.[54] The number of absentee janissaries who were
ordered to the campaign but were missing at periodic musters was also
high. During the failed Khotyn campaign of 1621, one inspection revealed that only half of the troops were present.[55] The ratios of mobilized to total troops are similar if one looks at the standing army as a
whole. In 1710, for instance, during the Russo-Ottoman war of 1710–11,
out of 52,337 total standing infantry (janissaries, gunners, gun carriage
drivers, armorers, and their pensioners), only 10,378 men (less than
20 percent) took part in the campaign.[56]

Provincial Forces and the Rise of the *Kapu Halkı*

The military demands and sociopolitical changes that shaped the evolution of the janissaries (and the standing *kapukulu* troops in general) also
profoundly affected the provincial *sipahi* cavalry. As with the janissaries,
the changes started under the reign of Süleyman, when the *timariot* cavalry's involvement in the succession struggles led to the government's
distrust of these forces. Not only did they gradually lose their privileges
of maintaining public order (and the associated revenues) to the *yasakçı*
janissaries, but many of the *timars* used to remunerate the provincial
sipahis were increasingly utilized by the government to pay garrison
forces and janissaries, especially in frontier regions.[57] Other *timar* prebends were turned into royal estates to pay the expanding standing army
and to hire state-funded peasant mercenaries (*miri levend*) for the army.
The policy aimed at easing the burden on the treasury, which faced recurring deficits from the early 1590s onward.[58]

As the real value of their assigned revenues gradually declined, ever
fewer *sipahis* were able to outfit themselves and their retinues.[59] Cash
loans made to the *timariot sipahis* from the central, inner, and provincial
treasuries during long-distance campaigns became more frequent from
the late 1560s onward.[60] Impoverished *sipahis* showed little desire to

report for military service. *Sipahis* mobilized from distant provinces often arrived late to the theaters of war. Some deserted the army, while others failed to report for military service.[61] Government responses to these actions varied. At times the Porte confiscated the *timar* prebends of those who failed to report for campaigns. At other times the *sipahis* were allowed to send a substitute to campaigns or pay a compensatory fee (*bedel*) in lieu of military service, which had become an accepted practice by the middle of the seventeenth century.[62] The Ottoman government also adjusted the minimum income after which ordinary *timariot sipahis* and holders of medium-size prebends (*zeamet*) were obliged to field an armed retainer (*cebelü*): in the case of the former the threshold was raised from 3,000 *akçe* to 6,000 *akçe*, in the latter from 4,000 *akçe* to 5,000 *akçe*. In other words, holders of smaller prebends were now exempted from military service. *Timar* holders possessing prebends worth 10,000 to 19,999 *akçe* annual revenue were required to maintain three retainers.[63]

Small prebend-holder *sipahis*, whose military ineffectiveness was laid bare by the wars against the Habsburgs, were less likely to be summoned for campaigns. Instead, the government either ordered them to keep the peace in their respective *sancaks* or assigned them temporarily to guard frontiers, whose more capable military forces were then ordered to join the imperial expeditionary armies elsewhere. This practice, like the other changes, started either under Süleyman or soon after his reign but became more common from the latter part of the sixteenth century onward. Consequently, at the end of the seventeenth century, only a small portion of the *timariot* army could actually be mobilized. The *sancak* and provincial governors' household armies, known as *kapu halkı*, or "troops of the gate," took their place. Provincial governors were now expected to maintain large household armies, and such a capability had become the condition for their appointments. Many of them enjoyed the revenues of whole *sancaks* as *arpalık* (literally "fodder money") to maintain their households and armies even when temporarily out of office, and had the title of *mutasarrıf*.[64]

Just as the Porte turned "extraordinary" war-time taxes (*avarız*) into regular taxes and increased their amount in order to pay for the enlarged salaried army, so did the governors increase the variety and amount of taxes they levied on their subjects to pay their households armies. While small *timariots* became poorer, provincial governors became richer. The annual revenue of the governor-general of Diyarbakır in 1670–71, for instance, was six times larger than that of his predecessors a century before, which is a significant increase even if accounting for inflation.[65] Ottoman governors, grand viziers, and army commanders used their positions to extract large sums from candidates applying for offices. For instance, Sinan Pasha accused his rival, Ferhad Pasha, of accumulating almost 135 million *akçe* (more than the treasury's annual revenues from Anatolia and Rumelia) from appointment fees between 1586 and 1590, when Ferhad served as army commander (*serdar*).[66]

The governors and pashas were expected to use their revenues to maintain their household armies and mobilize them for imperial campaigns. For the 1697 campaign, the grand vizier and the governor of Rumeli mobilized household troops numbering, respectively, 2,600 and 2,400 men. The governors in Asia Minor and the Arab lands had smaller armies. These armies numbered as many as 700 men in Anadolu; 600 men in Karaman, Diyarbakır, and Damascus; 500 men in Adana; 400 men in Sivas and Aleppo; and as few as 150 men in Maraş. The troops of some pashas, who administered rich *sancaks* as *arpalık,* could match or even exceed these numbers. However, ordinary *sancak* governors had much smaller armies, numbering as few as 25 men and as many as 150. The Porte also mobilized the hereditary Kurdish begs, who were supposed to bring between 35 and 150 soldiers.[67]

The manpower pool of these household armies was the same as that of the state-financed militiamen: landless peasants and vagabonds, created by the combination of the socioeconomic and environmental changes since the latter part of the sixteenth century. If not employed by provincial governors or the central government, these individuals usually turned to banditry, leading to an increase in rural disorder and violence. The number of such *levends* was already substantial by the mid-sixteenth century, when in 1555 a rebel ("Prince Mustafa") managed to gather some ten thousand *levends* and *timariot* cavalry under his banner.[68]

These changes affected the Ottoman provincial administration, too. As the importance of the household troops of *sancak* and provincial governors increased, so did the number of *sancaks* and provinces, from where the latter collected their revenues and soldiers. As noted, the empire was divided into 90 *sancaks* and some eight provinces in the early sixteenth century. The number of these military-administrative units had risen respectively to some 230 and 30 to 40 by the early seventeenth century, an increase that cannot be explained simply by the geographical expansion of the empire.[69]

Owing to these transformations, the Ottomans could still mobilize large expeditionary armies at the end of the seventeenth century. In fact, they deployed larger armies than in the empire's heyday under Sultan Süleyman I. In March 1697, for instance, an official register listed 104,514 troops, including 10,000 men of the Danube flotilla, mobilized for the Hungarian front. In addition, numerous smaller armies were mobilized to defend various strategically important fortresses and border areas against the Russians, Poles, Venetians, and Austrians. The largest contingents were sent against the Russians: 17,023 men were sent to defend Kerch and Taman and the Kerch Strait between the Black Sea and the Sea of Azov, and 16,608 soldiers were sent to guard Ochakiv and the border around it. Two smaller armies of 6,237 men and 4,812 men were sent to defend the Morea and the island of Negroponte against the Venetians. For Podolia, 5,451 soldiers were mobilized to defend Kamieniec Podolski. Belgrade and Temesvár on the Hungarian front were to receive 9,321 and 6,141 troops, respectively. Together with the main army, this amounts a total of more than 170,000 troops.[70]

The implications of military expansion and devolution for the composition of the Ottoman expeditionary armies and their military capabilities were also significant. Whereas the salaried troops of the court constituted only about 20–25 percent of Süleyman's armies, their share rose to 40–50 percent by 1697–98. Conversely, while in the early sixteenth century the *timariot* provincial cavalry accounted for 60–75 percent of the Ottoman combat forces, their proportion had dropped to 10–15 percent by the late 1690s. In 1526 Süleyman could mobilize some forty-five thousand *timariot* cavalrymen; in the 1697 campaign the provinces provided just eleven thousand *timariot sipahis*. By the late 1690s, the household armies of provincial governors and grandees gave 16–18 percent of the mobilized troops. Owing to the high proportion of infantry musketeers in the salaried central army and the household troops of governors, the infantry-to-cavalry ratio in the Ottoman army was 52:48 in 1697 and 57:43 the next year. If we add the soldiers serving on the Danube flotilla, the share of foot soldiers in the army rises to 56 percent in 1697 and 60 percent in 1698, mirroring the infantry-to-cavalry ratio of their Habsburg rivals.[71]

Ottoman War Finance

The growth of the salaried army generated fiscal pressure. Soldiers' pay almost tripled between 1582 and 1608 in nominal terms. Even if we account for the more than 50 percent devaluation of the silver *akçe* in 1585, salaries paid to the standing troops rose from 81.5 metric tons of silver in 1582 to 108 tons in 1608, and their share within the total expenditure of the central treasury increased from 48 percent to 64 percent. In general, soldiers' pay accounted for 60 to 85 percent of the imperial treasury's annual expenditure from the mid-seventeenth to the mid-eighteenth century. In addition to war-related expenditures, the accession bonuses or donatives paid to the salaried troops and state employees became an especially heavy burden. After the death of Sultan Ahmed I (r. 1603–17) in 1617, the rapid succession of Sultans Mustafa I (r. 1617–18, 1622–23), Osman II (r. 1618–22), and Murad IV (r. 1623–40) required the payment of four accession donatives in seven years, upsetting Ottoman state finances just before the long Ottoman-Safavid war of 1623–39. Between 1687 and 1695, an era that saw the most exhausting war thus far, three padishahs—Süleyman II (r. 1687–91), Ahmed II (r. 1691–95), and Mustafa II (r. 1695–1703)—succeeded each other. The total sum of accession bonuses often exceeded the annual salaries of the janissaries. Defterdar Sarı Mehmed Paşa claimed that in 1687, after the dethronement of Mehmed IV (r. 1648–87), Süleyman II had to pay 455,700,000 *akçe* for the accession donatives of the 70,394 janissaries, 12,653 armorers, 5,084 artillery gunners, 670 gun carriage drivers, and the cavalry regiments of the Porte. This amount exceeded by more than 88 million *akçe* the regular salaries of all the troops in the fiscal year of 1687–88, when the Ottoman Central Treasury paid 367,327,140 *akçe* to the active and retired soldiers. Desperate, the government paid part of the accession donatives from the padishah's private purse and other revenues destined to the private purse, and used melted gold and silver items from the imperial kitchen and armory to mint new coins.[72] Still, the soldiers—demoralized by their recent humiliating defeat at Nagyharsány—continued their mutiny. They sacked high-ranking officials and killed both the agha of the janissaries, Harpudlu Ali Agha, and Grand Vizier Siyavuş Pasha.[73]

To alleviate financial pressure, the Ottoman government used various tried-and-true methods. Confiscation of the assets of dismissed viziers and high officials,[74] minting copper coinage, and the debasement of the silver *akçe* were among the devices used by the government to come up with the necessary funds. Other policies with which the government experimented included the expansion of the tax-farming system (*iltizam*), under which the collection of revenues from crown lands (*hass*) and other revenue sources called *mukataa* were leased out to the highest bidder; the reorganization of the collection of the head tax payable by non-Muslims (*cizye*), and the widening of the tax base; the regularization of the extraordinary wartime taxes (*avarız*), and the introduction of new taxes.

As the military value of the *timariot* provincial cavalry declined from the late sixteenth century onward, vacant *timars* were not reassigned. Instead, they were attached to the padishah's *hass* lands and farmed out to tax farmers (*mültezim*) for collection, like other leased *mukataa*. If the tax farmer failed to collect the revenue for which he contracted, he had to pay the remaining amount from his own funds. When the Porte was in financial need, it could ask the tax farmer to pay the revenues in advance and recompense him later. In other words, the tax-farming system functioned as short-term borrowing.[75] The share of the mukataa incomes within the central treasury's total annual revenues amounted to 60 to 70 percent in the 1650s and 1660s, declining to about 45 to 50 percent by the last decade of the century, as other revenue sources increased.[76]

Of these other revenues, the most important was the *cizye,* or head tax, payable by non-Muslims. The amount of head tax was raised from 50 *akçe* in the mid-sixteenth century to 240 *akçe* in the mid-seventeenth century. With other supplementary taxes on sheep, wine, and wax, and fees for the collectors, the annual head tax payable per person rose to a total of 325 *akçe.*[77] Even if we account for inflation, these sums represented a considerably higher burden than in the sixteenth century. This was somewhat alleviated by the reform of the head tax, which was levied from 1691 onward according to the taxpayer's capacity. Tax reform also increased the efficiency of collection. As a result, the treasury's head tax revenues quadrupled in nominal terms between 1666 and 1698. More importantly, the share of the head tax within the treasury's annual revenues rose from 20 percent in the mid-1660s, to 30 percent in the mid-1690s, and to 48 percent in 1702. Thus, the empire's non-Muslim population shouldered more and more of the tax burden.[78]

The extraordinary taxes had become regular annual levies by the early seventeenth century and were demanded in cash, as opposed to the earlier practice, when these were collected in kind. Whereas their share within the treasury's annual revenues was less than 9 percent in 1652, it rose to 20 percent during the last year of the Cretan war in 1669. It fluctuated between 15 percent and 23 percent in the 1690s, dropping to 11 percent after the peace of Karlowitz.[79]

The expansion of taxation required the reorganization of the financial bureaucracy. In the mid-sixteenth century only four major bureaus managed the revenues of the central treasury under the leadership of the chief treasurer (*defterdar*) (responsible for revenue management in Rumeli), the second treasurer of Anadolu, and the treasurer of the Arab lands. Another treasurer and his colleagues managed the extensive *timar* revenues. These bureaus were assisted by specialized personnel heading sub-bureaus that dealt with various types of revenue sources. By the early seventeenth century many of these sub-bureaus had developed into independent bureaus. In the mid-seventeenth century, fourteen of these bureaus dealt with the collection of various leased revenue sources. In addition, seven bureaus oversaw the disbursement of payments from specific revenue sources, mainly to the central troops and garrison forces. However, these numbers are misleading because the largest bureau, the Office of the Chief Accounting, oversaw the collection and disbursement of more than 120 different sub-bureaus and revenue units. These sub-bureaus included the office of the commissioners of the Imperial Cannon Foundry, Armory, gunpowder works, the Imperial Naval Arsenal, Imperial Mint, various customs and *mukataas*, and provincial treasuries. In the sixteenth through eighteenth centuries, there were almost forty independent provincial treasuries that administered the collection and disbursement of revenues in their respective provinces, and submitted annual accounts to the Office of the Chief Accounting.

The Ottoman Empire first considered borrowing from foreign powers only in 1784, and started to borrow regularly only after the Crimean War. However, it had resorted to internal borrowing much earlier. The Ottoman tax-farm system can be considered as a form of short-term domestic borrowing, although its main function was tax collection. In addition, from the latter part of the sixteenth century there are several examples of short-term domestic borrowing from Jewish financiers, who also lent money to high-ranking Ottoman officials and members of the Ottoman dynasty, and in return gained access to lucrative tax farms.[80]

From the late sixteenth century onward, the central treasury began to resort to short-term borrowing from its high-ranking officials and bureaucrats. Sums borrowed in this way during the Long War of 1593–1606 ranged from hundreds of thousands of *akçe* to millions of *akçe*. By comparison, the annual salary paid to the janissaries in 1599 was almost 20 million, whereas that of the central troops and garrison soldiers in Hungary was 100 million *akçe*.[81] While the government was usually able to repay these loans, it paid no interest to the lenders.

Starting with the wars against Poland-Lithuania in the 1670s, transfers to the state or outer treasury from the padishah's privy purse or interior treasury (*hazine-i enderun, iç hazine*) in the 1670s and 1680s not only occurred annually, but their sum had increased from 36.5 million *akçe* in 1672 to more than 250 million *akçe* in 1683–84; the transfers reached their peak in 1685 with 401 million *akçe*, an amount that was sufficient to cover the salaries of the standing troops for almost two years.[82] Although the privy purse's main function was to meet the expenses of the padishah and his harem and to pay for gifts and alms, it also served as a reserve bank and transferred money to the outer or state treasury on the condition that the borrowed money would be repaid.

In 1695, the government extended the term of tax farms from three years to the lifetime of the tax farmer. The aim of the life-term tax farms (*malikane*) was to alleviate the treasury's cash shortages through the large purchase prices, which the successful bidders of the auctioned *malikane* tax farms paid to the treasury at the time of the auction. The lifelong tax farms made tax collection more predictable for a longer period of time because the treasury received steady—albeit more modest compared with the purchase price—annual payments from the *malikane* holders during the latter's lifetime. In short, by using state tax revenues as collateral, the life-term tax farms functioned as financial devices for long-term domestic borrowing, comparable to the sale of life annuities known in contemporary western Europe.[83] Unlike in western Europe, where borrowing rates for kings and princes could be as low as 3 to 5 percent, the cost of the *malikane* system was as high as 75 percent, as only twenty-four *guruş* out of the collected one hundred *guruş* reached the central treasury in the years after the introduction of *malikane*.[84] However, the picture is more complicated as many of the holders of life-term tax farms contributed armies and supplies to the Ottoman war efforts, in exchange for access to the revenue resources they managed. Changes in fiscal policy in the late seventeenth century stabilized Ottoman finances. In the first half of the eighteenth century, the government was able to pay its troops and the accession bonuses under Amhed III (r. 1703–30), Mahmud I (r. 1730–54), Osman III (r. 1754–57), and Mustafa III (r. 1757–74). The central treasury's incomes and expenditures remained balanced until the Russo-Ottoman war of 1768–74. However, fiscal and economic exhaustion caused by that war, along with the war indemnity payable to Russia—amounting to about half of the central treasury's annual income—upset the financial balance and led to further adjustments in the fiscal policy. These included the use of the Imperial Mint as a reserve bank and the reorganization of the *malikane* system in 1775. In the new system (*esham*), shares of the tax farm's annual revenues were sold to a large number of buyers. The aim was to further broaden domestic borrowing by reaching beyond the large financiers, who had dominated the *malikane* system, and to tap into the available financial resources of a larger number of lenders with more modest financial means.[85]

Despite continuous adjustments, Ottoman finances seemed inefficient especially when compared with the fiscal expansion of the Habsburg monarchy and Russia. Whereas in the early 1760s Saint Petersburg's and Constantinople's revenues were comparable in terms of tons of silver, by the end of the century Russian revenues were about ten times larger.[86] Yet one should be cautious to explain the Ottomans' declining military performance vis-à-vis their Austrian and Romanov rivals solely with the growing fiscal gap.[87] Dissimilar fiscal and military systems in the Habsburg, Romanov, and Ottoman Empires make it difficult to compare fiscal and military capabilities. Despite having revenues comparable to those of Constantinople in the early 1760s, the Russian government was able to maintain an army twice the size of the Ottoman army.

10

Lawfare and Diplomacy

ABOUT TEN YEARS AGO, I suggested that the reign of Süleyman I witnessed the formulation of an Ottoman grand strategy. In addition to the mobilization of human and economic resources and military power, Ottoman grand strategy involved the formulation of an imperial ideology and a universalist vision of empire.[1] Ottoman grand strategy also used what may be called soft power. By this I mean something different from the classical definition of modern soft power.[2] Unlike modern soft power, which is understood as a "power to attract" without the use of coercion, Ottoman soft power included a good deal of coercing. I see Ottoman soft power as a combination of lawfare, diplomacy, and intelligence gathering, by which the Sublime Porte and its agents managed their foreign policy and influenced other powers to act according to Ottoman interests. By Ottoman lawfare, I mean the Porte's manipulation of legal instruments—such as unilateral and bilateral commercial and political agreements, called *ahdname* by the Ottoman chancery—and the imposition of forms and ways of peacemaking on other states to realize the Porte's objectives. In addition to changing military capabilities, the Ottomans' success or failure in using lawfare, diplomacy, and intelligence gathering against the Porte's opponents also indicates the shifting balance of power in the Mediterranean and central Europe.

Competing Titles and Claims of Sovereignty

Titles by which monarchs addressed one another reflected perceptions of self and "other" and pretensions of monarchs. When appearing in mutually signed treaties, titles showed status and power relations.[3] The titles that the Ottoman chancery used for Christian monarchs were intended to demonstrate Ottoman superiority, especially when juxtaposed with the elaborate and lengthy titles of the Ottoman rulers.

Of these, the least prestigious was the Arabic title sultan, widely used by sovereign Muslim rulers. We have seen the claim that Sultan Bayezid I (r. 1389–1402) asked the shadow caliph in Mamluk Cairo for permission to use the title "sultan of Rum." However, he did not use it as a means of self-identification on his coins, and it was not widely accepted by his Muslim neighbors. For instance, while the Chinggisid ruler of the Golden Horde and the founder of the Khazan khanate, Ulugh Muhammad (1405–45), addressed Murad II as "the sultan of the land of Rum," he noted that his ancestor Tokatmış (d. 1406) regarded Bayezid I only as *beg* (that is, a divisional leader).[4]

The rulers of the House of Osman proudly used the Turco-Mongolian title of *khan*, and its Turkic variant, *khakan*, despite the fact that the Ottomans could not claim Chinggisid descent. These titles figure prominently both in official correspondence and in the rulers' official monogram (*tuğra*) used to authenticate documents issued in their name. The titles khan and khagan expressed the Ottoman rulers' claim over the vast steppe lands stretching from the Black Sea to Central Asia.[5]

After the conquest of Constantinople, Ottoman rulers added Byzantine titles to their Islamo-Turkish ones: Mehmed II went by caesar, *basileus* (supreme emperor), and padishah. In the 1502 treaty, concluded with Venice and written in Greek (as several previous treaties had been), Bayezid II titled himself "by the grace of God *basileus* and *autokrator* (unlimited ruler) of the two continents of Asia and Europe and other possessions."[6] In 1517, in the Latin *intitulatio* of the Italian version of the capitulation issued to Venice, Selim I titled himself "Sultan Selim Shah, Son of Sultan Bayezid Khan, Emperor of Emperors, by the Grace of God supreme Emperor of Asia, Europe, of the Persians, Syria, of the

Arabs and invincible ruler of Egypt."[7] Süleyman too titled himself supreme emperor, padishah, "Sultan of Sultans," and world conqueror. He listed no fewer than forty-two kingdoms and cities over which he claimed sovereignty, including Mecca, Medina, and Jerusalem, the three Holy Cities of Islam:

> Sultan of Sultans of East and West, world conqueror (*sahib-kıran*) of the domains of Rum, Persia and Arabia, Hero of the Cosmos, Neriman of the Earth and time, Padishah and Sultan of the Mediterranean and the Black Sea, the Kaaba the honored, Medina the illuminated, and Jerusalem the noble, of the throne of Egypt the promised of the age, and of the provinces of Yemen, Aden and San'a, of Baghdad the house of peace, of Basra, Lahsa and Ctesiphon, the lands of Algiers and Azerbaijan, the Qipchak Steppes, the land of the Tatars, Diyarbakır, Kurdistan and Luristan, all of Rumeli and Anadolu, Karaman, of the lands of Wallachia, Moldavia and Hungary, and of many highly esteemed kingdoms and lands besides, Sultan Süleyman Khan, son of Sultan Selim Khan.[8]

The Ottomans used the respective foreign titles for European monarchs and heads of states without listing the addressee's kingdoms and dominions: *doj* from the Italian *doge*, *kıral* from the Hungarian *király* (king), *çasar* from the Hungarian *császár* (caesar/emperor). Occasionally, the Ottoman title padishah, a term that the Ottoman emperors used for themselves, was also used for the doge of Venice and the king of France. However, the Venetian doge was also addressed as *beylerbeyi*, the title used for Ottoman provincial governors-general. Queen Elizabeth (r. 1558–1603) was addressed as queen (*kraliçe*).

In his letter in 1526, Süleyman addressed Francis I (r. 1515–47) of France—who asked the padishah for help after his capture at Pavia (1525) by Charles V's forces—as the "King of the province of France" (*França vilayetinin kıralı*). In another letter sent to the French king in September 1528, Francis was titled merely as "Beg of the kingdom of France" (*Françsa memleketinin beyi Françesko*).[9] However, Süleyman called Francis padishah in a letter sent to Ferdinand in 1541, and so did Grand Vizier Ibrahim Pasha in his letter to Charles V in 1533. The Ottomans also titled

Charles IX (r. 1560–74) of France as emperor in the French version of the treaty of 1569.[10] By elevating Francis I and Charles IX to the rank of emperor, Süleyman and his successors sent a clear message to the Habsburg brothers, whom the Porte titled as kings. The progression from beg to padishah also reflected the increased importance of the French monarchs for the Ottomans' anti-Habsburg policy in Europe.

In Ottoman-language correspondence, Charles V was king of Spain and king of the land of Spain (*İspanya vilayetinin kıralı*); Ferdinand was king of Vienna (*Beç kıralı*), King Ferdinand (*Ferenduş kıral*), king of Austria/Habsburg lands (*Nemçe kıralı*), and "king of the land of Austria and of territories belonging to it."[11] Letters in Latin mirrored these titles: Charles was "king of Spain" (*rex Hispaniarum, Hispaniae*) and Ferdinand "king of Germany" (*rex Alemanorum*) and "Ferdinand king" (*Ferdinandus rex*). By denying Charles V his imperial title, Süleyman also denied his rival's pretensions to universal kingship. At the same time, Süleyman's chancery made sure that when corresponding with the Habsburg brothers, King John Szapolyai—whom Charles and Ferdinand called *voivode* or count of Szepes (Slk. Spiš)—was titled as king (*kıral* or *rex*).[12] On other occasions, however, translators working for the Habsburg brothers made sure that the Latin translations of the sultan's letters addressed Charles and Ferdinand properly. For example, Süleyman's letter written to Ferdinand from the sultan's camp in Osijek on 17 July 1532 addressed Ferdinand as king of the Romans (*rex Romanorum*), using Ferdinand's most recent title.[13]

The Habsburg brothers, on their part, reciprocated the Ottoman approach. Not to be outdone by his Muslim nemesis, Charles V listed no fewer than sixty-nine of his titles in letters written to Süleyman in 1533. Some of his titles claimed sovereignty over territories and kingdoms that Süleyman had claimed for himself—such as Jerusalem, Hungary, Dalmatia, Croatia, and Slavonia. However, Charles and Ferdinand addressed the sultan as "Emperor of the Turks, Asia, and Greece."[14]

Unlike letters, treaties reflected mutually accepted titles, over which the parties often argued for weeks. As we have seen, historians have claimed that in the Peace of Zsitvatorok (1606) the padishah acknowledged Rudolf as his equal, although in the treaty Rudolf is called "emperor" (*imperador*) and caesar (*çasar*) instead of padishah. However, Süleyman already titled Ferdinand I as "Emperor (*imberador*) of the Germans, king and ruler of the Bohemian, Slavonian, Croatian and other lands" in the 1562 treaty (issued by the Ottomans as an *ahd-name*), thus reflecting some of Ferdinand's official titles. After the death of Ferdinand, the 1565 renewal of the 1562 treaty with Emperor Maximilian II (as king of Hungary, Maximilian I, r. 1564–76) also used these very same titles for the new emperor, as did the treaty of 1568, which Maximilian concluded with Süleyman's successor, Selim II (r. 1566–74). In letters, the titles remained less consistent.[15]

The Ottoman governors-general of Buda referred to Ferdinand I as emperor in the 1560s in their Hungarian-language correspondence with the Habsburgs. Again, they used the Hungarian term *császár*, retaining the term "padishah" for the Ottoman sovereign. But they considered the two terms as equal. For instance, İskender—governor-general of Buda in 1564–65—referred to the peace of 1562 between Ferdinand I and Süleyman as a pact concluded "between the two emperors," using the same term for both monarchs.[16] The Ottoman governors-general of Buda addressed Maximilian II and Rudolf II both as Roman emperors and kings of Hungary. Sokollu Mustafa Pasha (governor-general in 1566–78) almost always addressed Maximilian as Roman emperor (*romai cyazar*).[17] These letters were penned by the Hungarian secretaries of the pashas of Buda, working in their chanceries. Known in the sources as *tyato* (a corruption from the Turkish word *katib*, meaning "scribe"), these secretaries had been trained in Latin and Hungarian chancery language.[18] However, they must have used these titles and formulae—current in the Viennese chancery—with the knowledge of their superiors, the pashas of Buda. This is yet another example of the nuances of Ottoman diplomacy in the border provinces, where pragmatic compromise was required.

The evolving titles used by the Ottomans for the rulers of Muscovy and Russia also reflected changing geopolitical realities. Ivan IV, grand prince of Muscovy, was addressed as Moskof Beyi (1539)—that is, Süleyman's chancery used the same title for the grand prince as it did for the *sancak* governors of the Ottoman Empire. In the Peace Treaty of Karlowitz (1699), in which Russia and the Porte concluded a two-year truce, Peter is called "the Tsar of the country of Muscovy, the ruler/ sovereign of all Russian lands and the king/lord of the dependent realms and great cities, the Great/Almighty Tsar of Muscovy."[19] In the Treaty of Constantinople (1700), he was titled alternatively "Tsar of Muscovy and Russia" (*Moskov ve Rus Çarı*) and "Tsar of Muscovy" (*Moskov Çarı*) in the Turkish-language copy;[20] but in 1713 he was titled only "Tsar of Muscovy," perhaps reflecting Ottoman sentiments following Russian and Ottoman victories in the wars of 1686–1700 and 1711. By the treaty of 1720, Peter the Great was "Tsar of the whole of Russia," a title that his successors also inherited. Likewise, Empress Anna (r. 1730–40) is titled in the treaty of 1739 as "Empress of Muscovy" (*Moskof Çariçesi*).[21]

Instruments of Ottoman Lawfare: Truces and Peace Treaties

Since the beginning of their empire, Ottoman rulers used diplomacy to further their policy goals. In the early centuries of the House of Osman, diplomacy proved critical in forming alliances, ending wars, and neutralizing dangerous enemies. As Ottoman military power grew, threatened neighbors negotiated truces to halt Ottoman conquest. They also concluded commercial agreements with the Porte to gain privileges and benefit from the expanding Ottoman market. The Porte used peace treaties along with the capitulations as an effective tool of Ottoman lawfare. The capitulations extended commercial privileges to a handful of "favored nations" (Venice, France, Poland, England, and the Dutch Republic) and others, including Constantinople's archenemy, the Austrian Habsburgs. Through diplomacy and lawfare, the Porte divided and weakened its European rivals. The Franco-Polish-Ottoman alliance, for instance, aimed at weakening the Habsburgs. The capitulations served similar purposes.

European monarchs sent their diplomats to the Porte to negotiate, conclude, and renew truces and trade agreements with the Ottoman sultan. While the Ottomans reciprocated these missions, sending hundreds of envoys and emissaries to European monarchs, in the sixteenth century they negotiated most of their treaties in Constantinople, or the old capital Edirne, with European envoys and ambassadors. This, as discussed in chapter 7, changed with the Habsburg-Ottoman Peace of Zsitvatorok (1606). Concluded in the Habsburg negotiators' tent in Habsburg-controlled Hungary, this treaty symbolized the shift in power relations and demonstrated the weakening of Ottoman positions.

European states, threatened by the Ottomans' unmatched military capabilities and policy of expansion, tried to profit politically and economically from their relations with the Ottomans by maintaining resident ambassadors in the Ottoman capital. The institution of permanent or resident embassies originated in fifteenth-century Italy, where Venice became the first republic to employ a resident diplomatic representative, sending Zacharias Bembo as its envoy (*orator*) to Rome in 1435. Milan, Florence, Naples, and the papacy all had permanent representatives in the second half of the fifteenth century, first in Italy and later in other European capitals. Milan and Venice sent their first resident envoys to Paris in 1463 and 1479, and to London in 1490 and 1496. France and England sent their first resident envoys in 1509, and France had ten resident embassies by 1547.[22] As one of the leading centers of European diplomacy and intelligence gathering, Ottoman Constantinople played a pioneering role in the development of permanent diplomatic representation in Europe. The Porte allowed select European states to set up permanent embassies in Constantinople, beginning in 1454 with the Venetian *bailo*, the republic's resident ambassador-consul. Other European states followed suit: France established its permanent embassy in Constantinople in 1536, the Habsburg monarchy in 1547, England in 1583, and the Dutch Republic in 1612, whereas the Republic of Ragusa (Dubrovnik) appointed its first resident consul in the Ottoman capital in 1688. Conversely, the Ottomans did not station resident envoys in foreign courts until 1793.

There was a clear hierarchy among European diplomats in Constantinople. At the top stood the representatives of Venice, France, England, and the Netherlands, who had the title of ambassador (It. *ambasciatore*). They were followed by diplomats having the titles of resident (It. *residente*) and agent (It. *agente*), in declining order. The Habsburg permanent diplomats initially had the title of *agente*. After the long hiatus in Habsburg-Ottoman diplomatic relations during the war of 1593–1606, Michael Starzer started his work as an *agente* in 1610. His successor, Sebastian Lustrier von Liebenstein (resident from 1624 to 1629), held the rank of *residente*.[23]

By the mid-sixteenth century, Venice had become the model for other European states, which admired and imitated the republic's efficient diplomatic service and information-gathering network. In addition to Constantinople, Venice maintained its *baili* in Paris, the capitals of the Austrian and Spanish Habsburgs, and the Italian states. Vienna and Prague (the seat of Emperor Rudolf II's court) owed their central role in the Venetian diplomacy to the Serenissima's need to gather up-to-date information about Habsburg-Ottoman relations. Since the Ottomans threatened the republic's Adriatic and Mediterranean possessions, and since Venetian trade in the Ottoman domains was essential for the Venetian economy, Ottoman Constantinople figured prominently among the capitals where the Serenissima employed permanent diplomatic representatives. For the very same reasons, the position of the *bailo* in the Ottoman capital was a stepping-stone for future political carriers in the republic.[24]

Ottoman attitudes toward diplomacy and the Porte's reluctance to establish permanent embassies in European capitals—termed "diplomatic unilateralism"—have traditionally been explained by the Ottomans' sense of superiority, their contempt for Christian Europe, and their adherence to Islamic precepts. This resulted in an antagonistic relationship and permanent state of war between the Abode of Islam (*Dar al-Islam*) and the Abode of War (*Dar al-Harb*). Although such views—based on a superficial understanding of "orthodox Islam"—may occasionally resurface in popular works, studies about the diplomatic and commercial relations between the Islamic polities and their European contemporaries have long discredited them.[25]

The very notion of Ottoman diplomatic unilateralism is questionable. In the early modern era, there was hardly a year when there were no Ottoman envoys on their way to one or more of the European capitals. Besides, Ottoman *sancak* and provincial governors regularly communicated with their Venetian, Hungarian, Habsburg, and Safavid counterparts. The lack of resident Ottoman diplomats in European capitals (or anywhere for that matter) did not initially harm the Sublime Porte's interests. To the contrary, the lack of reciprocity allowed the Ottomans to put pressure on the European resident ambassadors at the Porte. In the long run, however, the lack of resident Ottoman diplomats in foreign capitals deprived the Porte of the most efficient institution of collecting information systematically and turning it into knowledge about the Porte's rivals and enemies.

To explain Ottoman diplomatic relations with Europe by merely referencing Islamic law and earlier Islamic practices would be a mistake. Ottoman foreign policy was pragmatic and reflected the continually shifting power dynamics between the Porte and its rivals. According to a widespread view, Islamic law required the Ottomans to conclude with their Christian opponents not genuine peace treaties but temporary truces, implying merely the suspension of war for one to three years. Indeed, in the fifteenth and sixteenth centuries, the expanding Ottoman Empire often concluded its treaties with its enemies for only one to three years. This practice put pressure on the Porte's neighbors, as they knew well that the Ottomans could attack them once the truce expired. However, as we will see from the examples below, when circumstances so dictated, the Ottomans were willing to conclude peace treaties for more extended periods—five, seven, and, occasionally, ten years. With friendly monarchs, such as the kings of France and Poland-Lithuania, the Ottomans made peace for indefinite time periods and even concluded "perpetual" peace lasting for the reign of the contracting monarchs. Because treaties were concluded not among governments but with monarchs, the death of the contracting monarch annulled the treaty, requiring its renewal. This, in turn, created opportunities for renegotiation.[26]

Another misconception is that the Ottomans granted peace to their rivals unilaterally. The confusion stems from the fact that the Ottoman sultans issued a document (*ahdname*) bearing the padishah's calligraphic monogram (*tuğra*) and containing the conditions of the treaty. However, the parties had accepted these conditions only after lengthy negotiations. In this process, the Ottomans created other documents (*temessük*) that contained the conditions of the peace/truce, which both parties had mutually agreed to.[27]

Most medieval treaties between the Ottomans and their European adversaries were negotiated for months and years according to elaborate diplomatic procedures, similar to those of European monarchs. The process started when one of the parties contacted the other party through his border governor, signaling his intentions for negotiations. He also requested a letter of safe conduct (Lat. *Salvus conductus*, Tr. *istimalet name*) for his envoy from the ruler or border governor of the opposite side. Emissaries crossed the border only in possession of such documents, which protected them from harm while traveling in enemy territory. However, the granting of safe conduct could be delayed—for example, the border official could not reach his monarch—or the monarch could deny the safe conduct, using it as leverage. Once the letter of safe conduct was obtained, the envoys traveled to meet the monarch of the opposite party. Upon arrival, the envoys were received at a festive audience by the ruler and handed their peace offer. The offer was discussed either on the spot, while the envoy was waiting, or in private. Once the decision was made, it was communicated to the envoy orally. Later it was put in writing and sent to the monarch with an embassy.

From Short-Term Truce to Perpetual Peace

The duration of treaties reflected legal traditions, Ottoman pragmatism, and the changing balance of power between the Ottomans and their rivals. The treaties with the medieval Hungarian monarchs, chief enemies of the Porte in the fifteenth century, were made for one to five years. The peace of 1444 was an anomaly. Initiated by the Ottomans and negotiated after John Hunyadi's victories and under the threat of both a new crusade and an attack from the rival Karaman emirate in Asia Minor, it was to last for ten years. According to some jurists, this was the maximum period a Muslim ruler could conclude a truce with an infidel. As we have seen, before Mohács, the Hungarians and Ottomans concluded and renewed existing truces in 1467–68, 1483, 1488, 1495, 1498, 1503, 1509, 1511, 1514, 1516, and 1519. These truces usually lasted for three years. The treaty negotiated in 1494–95 was planned for ten years, but in late 1495 King Wladislas II confirmed it for just three years. The treaty of 1503 was made for seven years and was renewed in 1511 for five years.[28] Earlier chapters discussed how the Ottomans tried to avoid war on multiple fronts by using these treaties to give the Porte respite along its Hungarian borders while dealing with enemies in other parts of the empire.

The treaty that the envoy of John Albert of Poland-Lithuania negotiated in Constantinople in 1501 was concluded for an indefinite period, partly because the Porte wanted to secure its northern borders as it was at war with the Venetians and faced rebellions in Anatolia by followers of Shah Ismail. But with the death of the Polish king that same year, the treaty was renewed for five years by Sultan Bayezid II in 1502 and ratified by the deceased king's brother and successor, Alexander, in early 1503. After the death of King Alexander in 1506, Bayezid II granted only a one-year truce in 1509 to the new king, Sigismund I "The Old" (r. 1506–48). This was renewed for another year in 1510, and five years in 1512. After the death of Bayezid II in 1512, Sultan Selim I renewed the truce in 1514 and 1519, in both instances for three years. As we have seen, the treaty of 1519, and the one that Süleyman issued as an *ahdname* in 1525 for three years, neutralized the Poles during Süleyman's campaigns against Hungary in 1521 and 1526.

Habsburg and Muscovite advances and the Moldavian voivode's attacks against Poland resulted in Ottoman-Polish rapprochement and the conclusion of the "perpetual" peace of 1533, which was limited for the lifetime of the contracting monarchs, Sigismund and Süleyman. The Polish envoys wanted to extend the treaty to the monarchs' successors, which Süleyman rejected. In 1533, Süleyman was preparing for a war against his Safavid neighbor and wanted to secure his empire's northwestern frontiers. By this time, Poland-Lithuania had emerged as a potential counterweight against the Habsburgs, which explains the fact that all other peace treaties between the parties in the sixteenth and seventeenth centuries were to last "in perpetuity."[29]

In the treaty with Venice in 1482, Sultan Bayezid II promised to have "good and permanent peace and friendship" with the doge and his successors.[30] This was hardly surprising as the sultan's brother, Prince Cem, had escaped to Rhodes and then to France in 1482. Bayezid feared that the Venetians and other European powers would use Cem for their planned crusade. The treaty with King Matthias of Hungary in 1483 hoped to achieve similar goals. The "good and secure peace and sincere concord"—which Jean de la Forêt, Francis I's envoy to Süleyman, negotiated in 1535–36 in Constantinople—was meant to be for "the lifetime" of each monarch.[31] While the validity of this treaty has been questioned,[32] the 1569 capitulations confirmed its conditions. France was considered a friendly nation, and its diplomats and merchants enjoyed privileges in the Ottoman Empire, as the Porte was well aware of the Habsburg-Valois rivalry and could use the French as a counterweight to Habsburg power. Encircled by the Habsburgs, France maintained friendly relations with the Ottomans for most of the sixteenth and seventeenth centuries; it even allowed the Ottoman navy under Grand Admiral Hayreddin Barbarossa to winter in the French harbor of Toulon in 1543–44 in order to launch a joint Franco-Ottoman attack against Spanish-controlled Sicily and Naples.[33] As noted, in 1573 the Venetians also concluded a "perpetual peace" with the Porte.[34]

The 1639 Safavid-Ottoman Treaty of Zuhab (also known as the Treaty of Kasr-i Şirin), signed on 17 May, was concluded as a perpetual agreement, which was to last "until the end of the centuries."[35] The 1692 Ottoman-Safavid peace treaty, concluded in the midst of the Ottomans' multifront war against the Holy League and shortly after their recent humiliating defeat at Slankamen, was also a perpetual peace that did not require renegotiation and reconfirmation upon the accession of a new ruler. Shah Sulayman assured Sultan Ahmed II of Iran's neutrality and friendship during the padishah's war in Europe. In return, the treaty promoted the shah's grade from two steps to one step below the Ottoman padishah and elevated the bilateral relations between the "two eternal states" to "perpetual peace in alliance." The treaty carried all the attributes of an eternal peace without the exact designation of eternal.[36]

Until the late eighteenth century, Ottoman padishahs concluded only limited truces with the Habsburgs, although it was not always the Sublime Porte that required such limitations. As noted earlier, in 1531 Ferdinand offered Süleyman a truce "for as long a time as possible," hoping to forestall another attack against Vienna, but the padishah rejected it.[37] In 1545–47, the Porte also rejected the Habsburg suggestion that the parties make an eternal treaty.[38] The treaties of 1547 and 1553 were both signed for five years. At the negotiations in 1559, Grand Vizier Rüstem Pasha (1555–61)—occupied as he was with the rivalry between Süleyman's sons—suggested that the truce be concluded for the reign of the padishah. This time, the Habsburgs wanted a truce for a limited period, concluding it for eight years. The remaining treaties in the sixteenth century (signed in 1562, 1565, 1568, 1574, 1577, 1583, and 1590) were all concluded for eight years, even when the Habsburgs wanted longer terms—for instance, suggesting ten years during the negotiations prior to the peace of 1568.[39] However, violations by the parties and the death of a party's reigning monarch, which required the renewal of all treaties by the new ruler, altered the duration of these treaties. Although the Habsburg resident diplomat, Bartholomäus Pezzen, hoped in January 1590 that the treaty would be confirmed in early 1592 and last until 1600, it was interrupted by hostilities in 1591 along the Bosnian-Croatian border, leading to the Long War of 1593–1606.[40]

Violations of truces did not necessarily lead to war. When the interest of the parties so dictated, it was possible to negotiate and renew the truce. This is what happened regarding the landmark Spanish-Ottoman truce of 1578, called capitulation (*vire*) and armistice (*treuga*) by the parties. The truce had to be renegotiated owing to "certain difficulties" that arose after its conclusion.[41] As noted, in the late 1570s the Spanish were busy with the Dutch Revolt while the Ottomans were fighting against the Safavids, and therefore both empires wanted to preserve the peace and were willing to solve their disagreements.

The death of the emperor and the padishah always led to great anxiety. The new monarch's situation was often precarious and emperors and padishahs could not be sure that the other party would not take advantage of their weakness at home. When Emperor Maximilian II died in October 1576, his successor, Rudolf II (r. 1576–1612), inherited an empty treasury, debts, and a shaky position in the Holy Roman Empire and Hungary. In the empire, the Protestant princes conspired with France against Rudolf and even sought Ottoman involvement. Receiving the

news of the death of Emperor Maximilian II, Archduke Ernst—
responsible for matters related to the anti-Ottoman border defense in
Hungary—hurriedly dispatched his envoy to the Sublime Porte with
the annual tribute. The move worked. By early January 1577, Rudolf II
had received the good news from the Habsburg resident envoy in Constantinople: Sultan Murad III, who was preparing for a war against the
Safavids of Persia, had renewed the peace for eight years.[42]

During the negotiations that resulted in the Peace of Zsitvatorok in
1606, the Ottomans wanted to limit the treaty to five or seven years, but
they eventually accepted the Habsburgs' demand for a longer term,
signing it for twenty years. Concluded with the mediation of Stephen
Bocskai, the treaty also included the successors of both emperors. Both
the mediation of a third party and the inclusion of the successors of the
monarchs—at the request of the Habsburgs (article 12)—were innovations that contradicted Ottoman diplomatic practice.[43] It was yet another sign of the Ottomans' weakening position. Interested in maintaining the status quo established in 1606, the parties renewed the
Treaty of Zsitvatorok repeatedly: in 1615–16 (Vienna), in 1618
(Komárom), in 1625 (Gyarmat), 1627 (Szőny), 1629 (Komárom), and
1642 (Szőny). This latter treaty had to be renewed after the deposition
of Sultan Ibrahim (r. 1640–48). With the war with Venice ongoing in
Crete and Dalmatia and trouble brewing in Asia Minor, in July 1649
Grand Vizier Kara (Black) Murad Pasha and the Habsburg internuncio
Johann Rudolf Schmid zum Schwarzenhorn (imperial resident in Constantinople between 1629 and 1643) renewed the treaty in Constantinople. It was to run for twenty-two and a half years.[44] These treaties
were mutually beneficial: the Habsburgs received a much-needed respite
on their eastern frontier during the Thirty Years' War, and the Ottomans—
engaged in wars against the Safavids (1603–39, with interruptions), the
Celali rebel pashas in Asia Minor, and Venice in Crete, Dalmatia, and
the Mediterranean (1645–69)—received peace of mind. However, war
broke out in 1663. Despite their defeat at Szentgotthárd/Mogersdorf on
the Rába River on 1 August 1664, the Ottomans succeeded in concluding a favorable peace at Vasvár (Eisenburg) on 10 August. Since Emperor Leopold I was preparing against France and Grand Vizier Fazıl

Ahmed Pasha wanted to complete the conquest of Crete, both parties were happy to conclude the peace for twenty years.[45] That all these treaties were concluded for longer periods on the request of the Habsburgs reflected changing power relations between the parties. So did the fact that the treaties (with the exception of the peace of 1649) were negotiated and signed not in Constantinople, as had been the custom in the sixteenth century, but in the Habsburg capital, Komárom, the center of the anti-Ottoman Habsburg military command, or in Habsburg-ruled Hungary.

By the eighteenth century, the Porte was no longer in a position to dictate the terms of treaties. The Treaty of Karlowitz (1699) with the Habsburgs, called in the Latin text as both armistice and peace, was to last for twenty-five years but ended when war broke out in 1716. The Treaty of Passarowitz (1718) with the Habsburgs, called both "peace" and "truce," was set for twenty-four lunar years. The Treaty of Belgrade (1739), which returned Belgrade to the Ottomans, was made for twenty-seven years. In 1747, the Habsburgs, engaged in the War of Austrian Succession (1740–48), managed to conclude peace for an unlimited period with the Porte, despite French machinations. This was followed by the first "perpetual and universal peace" between the parties in 1791 at Sistova, concluded on the basis of *status quo ante bellum*, although Austria was granted some border adjustments that improved Austrian defense capabilities.[46]

The Porte concluded the Treaty of Constantinople (1700) with Russia for thirty years. Although in the 1710–11 Russo-Ottoman war the Ottomans captured Peter the Great of Russia in the battle on the Pruth River, Grand Vizier Baltacı Mehmed Pasha signed a peace (12 July 1711), which was called "eternal peace" in all Russian text versions. Yet this "eternal peace" lasted for only a few months. Having been accused of concluding a premature treaty and accepting bribes from the Russians, Baltacı Mehmed Pasha was dismissed from his position. The Porte declared war on Russia three times between 1711 and 1713, accusing Peter of not fulfilling his obligations. But no fighting resumed. The conflict was resolved by talks between the Porte and the Russian ambassadors, who had been kept in the Ottoman capital as hostages. New treaties were signed in Constantinople (5 April 1712) and Edirne (13 June 1713).[47] In 1720, the Porte also made a "perpetual peace" (*sulh-i müebbedi*) with Russia,[48] which lasted until war broke out in 1736. This war ended in 1739 with another "perpetual peace" in Belgrade, which the monarchs and their heirs were to keep "forever" (*ilelebed*).[49] The Ottoman government also concluded a perpetual peace with Venice in 1733, which lasted until the end of the republic (1797). The transition from short-term truces to perpetual peace reflected the Ottomans' waning power as the Sublime Porte had to agree to terms increasingly dictated by its enemies.

Ad Hoc Embassies and Resident Ambassadors

At any given time there were numerous European envoys and ambassadors in Constantinople to negotiate and renew truces and commercial agreements with the Porte, to announce the accession of their monarchs, and to reciprocate Ottoman embassies that brought news of the accession of a new sultan or announced the padishah's most recent victory. Countries that owed yearly tribute to the padishah—such as Ragusa, Transylvania, Wallachia, Moldavia, and the Habsburgs after 1547—sent their envoys with the tribute annually to the Ottoman capital. The Ottomans, too, sent hundreds of messengers and envoys to European courts to negotiate truces and to witness the royal oath of European monarchs, a final act of Ottoman peacemaking. According to one count, the Porte sent more than 150 envoys to Venice between 1384 and the outbreak of the Cretan war (1645). Another list recorded almost 180 Ottoman missions to Venice between 1384 and 1762.[50]

Before departing, European and Ottoman envoys had to secure letters of safe conduct from the courts they were about to visit. In the case of Habsburg-Ottoman diplomatic relations, Habsburg envoys had to secure such letters from the pasha of Buda—"the viceroys/locumtenens of the Turkish emperor in Buda and Hungary" (*imperatoris Turcarum Budae et in tota Hungaria locum tenens*) in contemporary parlance.[51] After a farewell banquet in Vienna or Komárom, the Habsburg envoys and their suites—interpreters, secretaries, chaplains, musicians, cooks, and pages—boarded their ships and left for the Habsburg-Ottoman border. At the border, which was clearly marked by stakes and other physical markers, an Ottoman escort sent by the border *sancak* governor of Esztergom greeted the delegation. The *sancak* governors of Bosnia and Klis (after 1580, the *beylerbeyi* of Bosnia) performed similar duties for Venetian and Ragusan missions. After crossing the border, European envoys were under the protection of the Ottoman authorities, who were also responsible for provisioning them.[52] In Buda, the ambassador met with the governor-general, while members of the embassy, under strict surveillance, toured the city. After the audience, the embassy traveled on boats to Belgrade, where they loaded their baggage onto hundreds of carts. For Habsburg envoys, ceremonial receptions in Esztergom, Buda, and Belgrade were part of the protocol and a powerful tool of propaganda for both parties. Janissaries of the governor-general of Buda escorted the legation through Constantinople. Following the famous "Imperial Road" from Belgrade to Constantinople, they journeyed on land through Serbia and Bulgaria, stopping for overnight rest at caravanserais.[53] Janissaries from Buda stayed with them until they reached the Ottoman capital. The aim of the escort was not only to protect the foreign envoys and their suite along the route but also to provide surveillance. Members of European embassies often complained about how the constant Ottoman surveillance restricted their movement. Upon reaching the Ottoman capital, the delegation was greeted by the Habsburg resident diplomat. Accompanied by a janissary band, they entered the Ottoman capital in a procession, creating quite a spectacle for the locals, and providing both the mission and the Ottomans an opportunity to demonstrate the grandeur and power of their respective monarchs. In the Ottoman capital, they were escorted to the Envoys' Inn (*Elçi Hanı*), built between 1509 and 1512 as a caravanserai of Atik Ali Pasha's charitable building complex. Located opposite the Column of Constantine (Çemberlitaş in modern Istanbul) along the city's main route (modern Divanyolu Caddesi) leading to the Topkapı Palace, it was also known as the German/Habsburg Inn (*Nemçe Hanı*) because the Habsburg ambassadors stayed there.[54] The Ottomans routinely used the arrival of European embassies in Constantinople for propaganda purposes, often timing their reception to coincide with the distribution of payment to the army or the departure of the navy. As noted, in July 1572 the Habsburg embassy witnessed the departure of the navy, demonstrating the resurgence of Ottoman naval power after the disastrous battle of Lepanto the previous year.

The Ottomans made clear on several occasions that they knew that the European embassies were engaged in what can be called military intelligence gathering. The reports and memoirs of European legations contained a good deal of information about the architectural features and weaponry of Ottoman fortresses and the size and composition of their garrisons.[55] This is hardly surprising, as the Habsburgs routinely included military experts among the members of the delegation, like the captains of the Danube *naszád* flotilla of Komárom, future captains-general of the Habsburg defense system, and army engineers.[56] In 1618–20, Hans Mollart, the president of the Court War Council, traveled to Constantinople to congratulate Osman II on his accession and discuss disputed issues regarding Transylvania.[57]

Habsburg legations were able to observe Ottoman fortresses on their way to Constantinople because they traveled along the military corridor dotted with forts and fortresses. Despite diligent Ottoman surveillance, members of the Habsburg embassies managed to converse with the padishah's Christian subjects living along the route. Communicating with Hungarian, Croatian, Serbian, and Bulgarian subjects of the padishah was not difficult, as members of the delegations spoke Hungarian and Slavonic. Ferdinand I and Maximilian II (r. 1564–76) routinely charged their loyal noblemen from Dalmatia, Croatia, and Slavonia with diplomatic missions to Constantinople. For instance, they sent the Croatian nobleman and soldier-diplomat Nicholas (Nikola/Miklós) Jurišić/Jurisics in 1529 and 1530 and the Dalmatian humanist historian and diplomat Anthony (Antun) Vrančić (Hun. Antal Verancsics) in 1553–56 and 1567–68 to Constantinople because of these men's language skills and familiarity with Ottoman affairs.[58] Other members of the Habsburg legations knew Slavic. Some even knew Turkish and were knowledgeable about the Turks.

Anthony Vrančić (1504–73) was particularly knowledgeable about the Ottomans. Born in the Dalmatian town of Sebenico, then under Venetian rule (Šibenik in modern Croatia), he was educated in Dalmatia and Hungary under the strict guidance of his maternal uncle, John Statileo (Ivan Statilić), the future bishop of Transylvania. He briefly studied in Padua, Vienna, and Cracow. Besides his Croatian mother tongue, he was fluent in Hungarian, Latin, and Italian. In the 1530s, he served King John Szapolyai as ambassador to Venice, Popes Clement VII and Paul III, Francis I of France, the kings of Poland, and Ferdinand I. He also negotiated with the *sancak* governor of Bosnia. Although after Szapolyai's death he served the king's widow, Isabella, he could not get along with Friar George. In 1549 he entered the service of Ferdinand I, and in 1553 was appointed bishop of Pécs. That same year, Ferdinand sent him—in the company of Francis Zay—to Constantinople to negotiate a peace with Süleyman. In addition to his familiarity with the Ottoman border provinces, he also knew Ottoman history and the strengths of the enemy. In 1539 he translated from Italian to Latin Paolo Giovio's (1486–1552) *Commentary* on the origin and growth of Turkish power (*Commentario del le cose de' Turchi*), which Giovio dedicated to Charles V in January 1531 and published the next year (and reprinted in 1533, 1535, and 1538). Since the sultan was campaigning against the Safavids, Vrančić spent four years in Asia Minor and returned to Hungary only in 1557. After Süleyman's death at Szigetvár, Maximilian II again sent Vrančić to Constantinople—together with the Styrian Christoph von Teuffenbach—to negotiate a treaty with Sultan Selim II. Arriving in Constantinople in late August 1567, they successfully negotiated with Grand Vizier Sokollu Mehmed Pasha and Sultan Selim II, concluding the peace in Edirne in February 1568.[59]

Traveling for weeks from Austria or Poland to Constantinople was a hazardous task and occasionally cost the ambassador his life.[60] In addition to the hardships encountered on the long journey, diplomatic missions often meant a serious financial burden. Yet, the reward was substantial. Complaining about the small remuneration he had received, one Venetian ambassador to the French court remarked that the ambassadors of the Holy Roman emperor, France, Portugal, and England were generously rewarded. After their assignments, "their kings endow them with abbeys, dioceses, lifelong offices, of which the interest amounts to four thousand to ten thousand ducats."[61] Diplomatic missions to the Porte, which were especially delicate and dangerous, often meant a career leap for the diplomats. After his embassy to Süleyman in 1533, Cornelius Schepper (officially the envoy of the emperor's brother Ferdinand of Hungary and Bohemia) was promoted from secretary to councillor in the *Geheime Raad*. Emperor Charles V rewarded the services of Gerard Veltwyck with a similar promotion. Veltwyck was then made a member of the more prominent *Raad van State* and elected treasurer of the Order of the Golden Fleece, whose mission was to fight the Turks. Jean de Monluc (1508–79), whom Francis I sent to the Porte as his special envoy in 1545 to accompany Veltwyck, was made a member of the Conseil Privé after his return; in 1554 he received the episcopate of Valence and Dié, much to the indignation of Grand Vizier Rüstem Pasha, who thought that the Frenchman deserved to be impaled.[62] Although Vrančić was unsuccessful in his first mission, he was made bishop of Eger for his services. After his second embassy to Constantinople, which resulted in the Habsburg-Ottoman treaty of 1568, Maximilian appointed Vrančić archbishop of Esztergom.[63]

Once in the Ottoman capital, envoys and ambassadors tried to maintain communication with their monarchs, despite close Ottoman surveillance and the envoys' occasional confinement to their residence. In 1547, for instance, Gerard Veltwyck, who was under house arrest, managed to receive news and instructions from the emperor. When Veltwyck himself informed Grand Vizier Rüstem Pasha that he had received news about Charles V's victories over the Protestant princes (Mühlberg, 24 April), the grand vizier was furious and wanted to impale the guards charged with securing the ambassador's residence.[64]

Countries that stationed resident diplomats at the Porte had better access to the Ottoman government, but it was a double-edged sword. The Ottomans repeatedly arrested the European resident diplomats upon the outbreak of hostilities. In 1499, when war broke out between Venice and the Porte, the Ottomans arrested Andrea Gritti, the republic's unofficial representative. During the Cyprus war, Bailo Marc'Antonio Barbaro was put under house arrest from 1570 through 1573. Because he had a good relationship with Grand Vizier Sokollu Mehmed Pasha, he was allowed to visit the bath twice a week for his health. "I could not nor would I know how to desire a better disposition from the Magnificent Pasha, who on many occasions, with me and with others shows himself to be very humane and affable," reported Barbaro.[65] But not all the *baili* were as fortunate as Barbaro. At the outbreak of the Cretan war in June 1645, the Porte placed guards at the house of Bailo Giovanni Soranzo. In 1649, the *bailo* and his interpreters were paraded in chains through the streets of the Ottoman capital to the Seven Towers. In 1653, Giovanni Capello, the ambassador extraordinaire sent to negotiate peace, was imprisoned in Edirne. He remained in prison until his death at the age of seventy-eight in 1662.[66] Bailo Andrea Memo was also arrested when the Serenissima declared war on the Ottomans in December 1714. He was first sent to a special prison in the Tophane, and later transferred to one of the fortresses of the Dardanelles along with forty-two members of his staff or "family." The embassy's interpreter who resided in Galata was also detained on charges that he was spying for the *bailo*, informing him about the operations of the Ottoman army.[67]

We saw earlier that in 1514 Selim I kept Barnabas Bélay, the envoy of King Wladislas of Hungary, under house arrest for forty days and then took him along on his Iranian campaign. Bélay returned to Buda only in 1519. Selim also arrested the Safavid envoy who arrived at his court in Damascus in February 1518. As the Ottomans' archenemy in Europe, Habsburg diplomats often experienced harsh treatment in the Ottoman capital. In 1541, when Süleyman learned of Ferdinand's attack on Buda, his ambassador, Jerome Łaski, was imprisoned. As mentioned, Malvezzi, the first Habsburg resident diplomat in Constantinople, suffered the same fate in 1551, when Habsburg troops occupied Transylvania. Hostilities in Hungary led to another Habsburg ambassador, the Flemish Ogier Ghiselin Busbecq, being kept under house arrest most of his time in Constantinople between 1556 and 1562. The Habsburg resident diplomat Albert de Wijs (1562–69) was held captive between 1565 and 1567 at the time of hostilities.[68]

Occasionally, the Habsburgs also arrested the padishah's envoys. When war broke out between the Habsburgs and the Ottomans over Transylvania in 1565, the Habsburgs retained the Ottoman envoy,

Hidayet Çavuş, as a hostage, while sending their envoy to negotiate at the Porte. In response, the Ottomans retained the Habsburg envoy, Michael Černović. The Ottoman decision had to do with the appointment of the belligerent Sokollu Mehmed to the post of grand vizier—who assumed his post a day after Černović arrived in Constantinople (28 June 1565)—and with the panic at the Porte, which feared that the Habsburgs would conquer Transylvania, an Ottoman tributary state. When the governor of Temesvár informed the Porte about Ottoman victories in Hungary, Černović was allowed to return to Vienna.[69]

During the peace negotiations in 1568, the Habsburgs demanded that their envoys and resident diplomats be treated under the standards laid out by international law. Their request was granted. Article 19 of the treaty stated that the Habsburg representatives—be they *orator*, *agente*, or *procurator* or called by any other name—should enjoy the same liberty and privileges as other European resident diplomats whom the Porte's allies and friends stationed in Constantinople. Article 20 added that the representatives of the Habsburgs were free to hire as many interpreters as they deemed necessary and that Ottoman officials, the infamous *cavuşes* of the Porte, should not control them. Article 21 resolved that Habsburg residents were free to send messengers (*nuncios sive cursores*) with letters when they wished and via routes they chose. Emperor Maximilian II was also free to send his messengers and letter carriers (*nunciis vel tabellariis*), whom the Ottomans were not to obstruct but were to assist on their way to Constantinople. The Habsburgs justified their request by the need to be in regular contact with their resident diplomats at the Sublime Porte. This would ensure that Habsburg diplomats had up-to-date instructions and authorization to discuss matters concerning bilateral relations with the grand vizier and other viziers.[70]

Yet, the Ottoman practice of imprisoning and treating diplomats as hostages continued. Imperial resident Charles (Karel) Rijm van Estbeek (1570–74) was put under house arrest because the Habsburg annual tribute had not arrived in time. The fate of Friedrich von Kreckwitz, the last Habsburg resident envoy (*orator*, 1591–93) at the Porte before the outbreak of the Long War of 1593–1606, was especially tragic. Two members of the embassy—a young Bohemian nobleman, Wenceslas Wratislaw of Mitrowitz, and the embassy's apothecary, Friedrich Seidel—recorded the mission's tribulation.[71] Soon after assuming the office of grand vizier, Koca Sinan Pasha summoned Kreckwitz and demanded the annual tribute. However, Vienna did not send the tribute, claiming that the Porte violated the truce on account of the Bosnian governor-general's capture of Bihać. Sinan threatened the orator with prison and war. Later, the grand vizier's men surrounded Kreckwitz's house and arrested his interpreter, accusing him of intentionally mistranslating communications between the Porte and the Viennese court. When the Ottomans discovered that Kreckwitz was spying, Grand Vizier Sinan dragged him away to the Hungarian campaign in chains. Kreckwitz died in late November in the Ottoman military camp in Belgrade. Meanwhile, the rest of the embassy staff, including Wratislaw, were arrested. They were taken in chains to the gallows in Kumkapı. Although all rejected the Ottomans' call to convert to Islam, their lives were spared and they were put in the arsenal's prison. Thereafter, they were sent to the galleys to serve as rowers, then again imprisoned in the dreaded Black Tower of the Rumeli Hisarı fortress, so called because the tower had no windows. Having spent two years and five weeks in darkness, they were freed after Sinan Pasha's death in the spring of 1596, on Sultan Mehmed III's orders. The captives owed their freedom to the good offices of the old warden of the Black Tower, Mehmed Agha, and the new grand vizier, Damad Ibrahim Pasha. Both men hailed from Croatia and proved more merciful toward the prisoners.[72] Despite diplomatic relations that put them on equal footing in 1606, the Ottomans continued to treat the Habsburg diplomats as hostages. In 1663, for instance, the grand vizier dragged imperial resident Simon Reniger and his interpreters (*dragomans*) to the Hungarian campaign as hostages. Ali Pasha of Temesvár also treated the Habsburg ambassador, Johann Goes, as a hostage and took him to the grand vizier's camp.[73]

Russian ambassadors—representatives of the Porte's emerging rival—received similar harsh treatment. When Peter the Great of Russia attacked the Ottomans, the Porte declared war on Russia in November 1710 and imprisoned the Russian ambassador, P. A. Tolstoy, in the

Seven Towers. After the Ottoman-Russian peace treaty of 1711, which ended the Ottomans' Pruth campaign, P. P. Shafirov and M. B. Shereme-tev, the Russian ambassadors sent to Constantinople, were to remain in the Ottoman capital until Russia implemented its obligations. Ottoman documents called the ambassadors *emanet*, meaning "security," "deposit," and "hostage." Their stay lasted for years, as the Ottomans insisted that they remain in Constantinople until the parties demarcated the borders.[74]

Europeans vehemently protested against their diplomats' imprisonment and cruel treatment in Constantinople. During the (unsuccessful) Habsburg-Ottoman peace negotiations in 1603, the Habsburgs and Hungarians noted how at the beginning of the war the Ottomans arrested the Habsburg resident envoy, Kreckwitz, in Constantinople "against the law and justice," let him die in captivity, imprisoned members of his household, and sent some of them to the galleys.[75] Ottoman practices differed from European norms, where the notion of diplomatic immunity—based on the inheritance of Classical Greece and Rome—gradually became an accepted principle of continental relations.[76] However, occasional arrests of envoys were not unheard of in Europe either. In 1528, Charles V ordered the arrest of the ambassadors of France, England, Milan, Venice, and Florence—the remaining members of the League of Cognac. The diplomats remained in detention for four months.[77] When the Venetian vice *bailo* at the Porte, Pietro Zen, reported the arrest of the Venetian ambassadors in Spain to Ibrahim Pasha, the grand vizier was surprised, but perhaps happy to know that the Habsburgs also arrested diplomats.[78] In 1569, the English confined a Spanish envoy to his embassy, while in 1659 the French imprisoned the Dutch diplomat Abraham van Wicquefort for supplying secrets. Wicquefort's imprisonment prompted him to argue forcefully for the diplomats' legal privileges in his published works on diplomacy.[79] Emperor Maximilian II also arrested two envoys of the newly elected king of the Polish-Lithuanian Commonwealth, Stephen Báthory (r. 1576–86), bound for the imperial diet in Regensburg. Báthory had been the voivode and prince of Transylvania and Maximilian II's main rival to the Polish throne.[80] The envoys were released only after Maximillian's sudden death

(October 1576). His successor, Emperor Rudolf II, needed to normalize his relations with Báthory at a time when the emperor's suzerainty was threatened both in the Holy Roman Empire and in Hungary.[81]

Language and Diplomacy

Contemporary theoreticians of early modern diplomacy emphasized the importance of foreign languages. They recommended that the ambassador know Latin and the language spoken in the country of his residence. However, they argued that the ambassador should use his mother tongue when delivering his speech. Louis XII of France (r. 1498–1515), Emperor Maximilian I (r. 1493–1519), and Henry VII of England (r. 1485–1509) spoke Latin with ambassadors, though Henry VIII (r. 1509–47) was a better Latinist. Francis I of France (1515–47) rarely attempted to speak in Latin. Charles V preferred French with foreign monarchs and ambassadors and with his siblings.[82] But the Habsburg siblings were conversant in multiple languages: Charles also spoke Dutch and Castilian Spanish, and understood Latin, Italian, and some German. Ferdinand was born, raised, and educated in Spain and was fluent in Spanish. He also knew Latin, Italian, and German. Still, communicating with the elites of the multilingual Habsburg monarchy and the Holy Roman Empire was challenging. When Emperor Charles V's German secretary fell ill in 1541, Charles found "no one here to translate my instructions into German." He had to send his negotiator to the German princes and Estates with "a signed blank sheet." In 1542, Ferdinand complained that his emperor-brother had signed documents in which he granted toleration to Lutherans in lands of Catholic rulers. In his response, Charles admitted that he trusted that the documents "were as they should be, and because they were in German, I signed without reading them first."[83]

Italian was perhaps the most common language among European diplomats in the second half of the sixteenth century. Many diplomats had studied law at one of the flagship Italian universities, especially at Padua. After Spanish, Italian (rather than French) was preferred in Philip II's court, and it was used by the Austrian Habsburgs as well, in addition to Latin, German, and Spanish. Latin remained an essential medium in central Europe. In Hungary, it served as the language of education until 1792 and was the official language of legislation until 1844. Western European monarchs and diplomats, therefore, used Latin to correspond with the courts of central Europe. Ferdinand's chancery used both German and Latin to communicate with the Estates in the Holy Roman Empire, Bohemia, and Hungary-Croatia. German and Latin dominated Ferdinand's and his successors' correspondence with the Habsburg resident envoys in Constantinople. Most of the envoys were erudite scholars and fluent in Latin, like the humanist diplomats from the Low Countries: Ogier Ghiselin Busbecq, Albert de Wijs, and his successor Charles (Karel) Rijm van Estbeek. In the seventeenth century, the imperial residents in Constantinople wrote their dispatches to Vienna in Italian and German.[84] In April 1556, Ferdinand reprimanded his captain-general of Győr, Adam Gall zu Lossdorf, for sending his spy reports to Vienna in Hungarian, instructing him to translate these into either German or Latin.[85]

Transylvanian rulers spoke multiple languages. King John Szapolyai spoke south Slavic, Czech, Hungarian, and Latin. His wife, Queen Isabella, could converse in Italian, Latin, and German, in addition to her native Polish. Their son, John Sigismund, elected king of Hungary and prince of Transylvania, knew eight languages. According to his Italian guard, he spoke enough Latin to be able to express himself. He also spoke Italian, German, Polish, Hungarian, and Romanian quite well and knew a little Turkish and Greek. From his time spent in exile in the Ottoman Empire, Prince Gabriel Bethlen learned enough Turkish to carry on a conversation in that language. He also knew Romanian and a little German. His Spanish tutor in etiquette and dance, Don Diego de Estrada, noted that he conversed with foreign envoys in Latin, that he was eager to learn Spanish and Italian from him every day, and that he spoke those languages. In addition to their native Hungarian, the Rákóczi princes—George I (r. 1630–48) and George II (r. 1648–60)—also knew Latin, German, and French. Those who accompanied Bethlen to the Ottoman Empire also learned Turkish, and at least a dozen nobles around the prince were able to converse in Turkish. Many of them served Bethlen and George Rákóczi I as diplomats in the Ottoman Empire.[86]

However, knowledge of Turkish among the European princes and diplomats was a rarity.

Up to the middle of the fifteenth century, dynastic marriage alliances, which the Ottomans concluded with the Byzantine emperors and the monarchs of southeastern Europe, facilitated knowledge of Greek and Slavic in the Ottoman court. The overwhelming majority of the child-levy recruits were from the Slavic-speaking Orthodox Christians of the Balkan Peninsula and Muslims from Bosnia. Knowledge of Slavic was widespread among the janissaries and administrators of the Porte. As mentioned, in the fifteenth century the Ottoman chancery used Greek as a language of diplomacy with Venice. The republic reciprocated and sent diplomats who knew Greek, such as Alvise Sagudino, who knew both Greek and Turkish.[87] Greek, in addition to Turkish and Slavic, was also used in correspondence with the Republic of Ragusa (Dubrovnik).[88]

Serbian, written in Cyrillic, was an important medium between the Ottomans and the monarchs and peoples in southeastern, central, and eastern Europe. The chancery of Bayezid II wrote in Serbian to the king of Hungary and Bohemia, as did Selim I to the ruler of Muscovy. Ottoman governors in Rumeli and Bosnia used the same language in their correspondence with Ragusa, Venice, the Habsburg monarchs, and the bans of Dalmatia, Croatia, and Slavonia. One Ottoman governor-general in Buda sent letters to the Viennese court and its military commanders in Serbian. The Ottoman sultans and provincial governors retained Serbian clerks and translators, like the "grand chancellor Đurađ" in Murad II's chancery. They composed letters that exhibited mixed Serbian and Ottoman chancery formulae and practices.[89] The chanceries of both Mehmed II and Selim I used Slavic in their correspondence with the Moldavian voivodes.[90] In 1520, Ferdinand used Serbian as an intermediary language of diplomatic correspondence with the Ottomans.[91] Ferdinand's envoy to Süleyman in 1533, the Dalmatian Jerome of Zara, occasionally also wrote in Slavic.[92]

The Ottomans issued treaties in Serbian and Hungarian, while their Polish and Habsburg counterparts used Polish and Hungarian to craft their versions of the treaties. The articles of the 1595 treaty, concluded at Moldavian Țuțora with the Polish-Lithuanian Commonwealth, were drafted in Polish and Serbian. The latter version, written in Cyrillic, was issued and signed by the Ottoman-Tatar side.[93] Besides diplomatic correspondence, Ottoman judges in Rumeli accepted medieval charters written in the Serbian/Bulgarian language.[94]

Owing to their Serbian, Bosnian, and Croatian origins, numerous Ottoman grand viziers and pashas spoke Slavic, and this language remained an important medium in the Ottoman court in the sixteenth century. When in December 1568 the government of Ragusa sent the latest news from Europe to its ambassadors in Constantinople in Italian, it also enclosed a translation "in the Serbian language" for Grand Vizier Sokollu Mehmed Pasha.[95] In 1570, Anthony Vrančić—who spent years in the Ottoman Empire as Habsburg ambassador—insisted that the Habsburg envoys and their secretaries and spies, if they were to be efficient in Constantinople, had to know Bosnian and Croatian.[96] A hundred years later, the imperial resident in Constantinople maintained that European diplomatic interpreters should know Slavonic because many renegade dignitaries in the empire spoke that language.[97]

In the multilingual and multiethnic Ottoman Empire, both the Ottoman authorities and the European diplomats relied on a wide array of cross-cultural and cross-confessional intermediaries. Still, the lack of a common language in diplomatic relations between the Ottomans and the European powers hindered relations and was manipulated by both parties. Joseph Lamberg and Nicholas Jurišić, the heads of the diplomatic mission that Ferdinand sent to Süleyman in 1530, struggled to communicate with Grand Vizier Ibrahim Pasha. At their first audience, Lamberg spoke in German, which the Latin interpreter of the mission, Benedict Kuripešić, translated into Latin. However, Ibrahim's interpreter, who spoke Italian, claimed that he did not understand Latin. He did not even recognize the language, so he pretended, inquiring if this was the language used in learning sciences and writing scholarly books in Europe. In the end, Jurišić saved the day by switching to his native Croatian, which another interpreter of the Porte who knew Serbian translated for the grand vizier.[98]

Ibrahim himself spoke several languages, including Greek, Italian, and Slavic. He must have understood most of what Jurišić said in Croatian, but decided to manipulate the negotiations. However, when the grand vizier deemed it useful, he switched to Slavic. In January 1533, Ibrahim ordered his interpreter to leave the room so that he could converse privately in Slavic or Italian with Ferdinand's envoy, Jerome of Zara, who was fluent in both languages. On 24 June, during the final stages of the peace talks in Ibrahim's home, the grand vizier switched to Slavic/Croatian (*lingua sclavonica*) to reassure Jerome that Lodovico Gritti—who did not understand Slavic—could not act independently and had to follow his orders.[99] Gritti's fluency in Greek, Italian, Latin, and Turkish allowed him to play a significant role in Ottoman diplomacy. When Ibrahim left for the Safavid campaign in October 1533, second vizier Ayas Mehmed Pasha continued the negotiations with Ferdinand's representative, Vespasian of Zara, Jerome's son. At the meeting, Gritti translated for Ayas Mehmed.[100]

The Habsburgs remained aware of the importance of Slavic at the Porte, as can be seen from Schepper's mission to the Porte in 1534. As Charles V's envoy, Schepper was back in Constantinople by April 1534 to negotiate a peace "both in our (Charles V) name and in that of Christendom." Since Jerome of Zara was ill, Schepper took Jerome's secretary, Peter of Trau (Trogir), because he spoke Slavic and knew the Turks and their customs.[101]

By this time, the Viennese court employed several Turkish translators. However, they had difficulties in understanding the Ottoman chancery language, which was full of Arabic and Persian phrases. One interpreter remarked in 1535 on the back of the grand vizier's letter that he could not understand the lines written in Persian.[102] To minimize language difficulties, Vienna asked the Porte to send its letters in Italian or Latin. Occasionally, the Ottomans complied. Süleyman and Ibrahim Pasha wrote to Ferdinand in Italian.[103] Ferdinand sent his letters to Süleyman, Ibrahim, and the Ottoman frontier governors in Latin.[104]

Lack of language skills occasionally had grave consequences. As mentioned, John Habardanecz and Siegmund Weichselberger—Ferdinand I's envoys to Süleyman in 1528—could not communicate Süleyman's answer to their master as they were unable to read the padishah's Turkish-language letter and did not know its content. No qualified interpreter in

Vienna could translate the document. The content of the letter was revealed only when the Ottoman army was marching against Vienna in
1529.[105] Lacking qualified translators created security risks as well. Narrating his recruitment as the Turkish scribe or interpreter (Hun. *török
deák*) of Prince Michael Apafi of Transylvania, David Rozsnayi noted
that in 1663 there was no Turkish translator in Transylvania. "When there
arrived letters written in Turkish from the Turkish emperor, the Tatar
khan, the Grand Vizier and the vizier of Buda, or from other places, the
[Transylvanians] took these letters addressed to His Majesty [Michael
Apafi] to Moldavia, Wallachia, and [the Ottoman garrisons of] Lippa
and Várad, and therefore the secrets of His Majesty were learned by
others."[106]

Treaties were drawn up in more than one language, and the discrepancies between the versions often led to disputes between the parties.
The Treaty of Zsitvatorok (1606) illustrates the intricacies.[107] There is
no single extant copy of the treaty that has been signed by all three
parties—the delegates of the Habsburg emperor, Prince Bocskai of
Hungary and Transylvania, and the Ottoman padishah. The emperor's
and Bocskai's negotiators signed a Hungarian-language version (with
Latin *intitulatio* and *eschatocol*) of the peace agreement in Zsitvatorok
on 11 November. Three copies of this "version A" are extant, which were
given to the Habsburg and Transylvanian negotiators, and to the delegates of the Hungarian counties.[108] There is an extant Turkish translation made by the imperial translator Caesar Gallo. The Habsburg and
Transylvanian negotiators also signed this Turkish-language document,
believing that it was the faithful translation of the Hungarian-language
treaty (version A). However, this is a falsified translation, which corresponds to "version B." There are two extant copies of version B, which
only the Ottoman negotiators signed. One copy was written in Hungarian at Almás in the Ottoman camp. The other copy is its Turkish translation.[109] Latin, German, and French translations of version A were
printed in Prague, Nurenberg, and Paris in 1607. The Habsburgs used
the authorized and signed Hungarian version, whereas the Ottomans
relied on the Ottoman Turkish text and its authorized Hungarian translation, both signed by the two Ottoman commissioners, Ali Pasha and

Habil Efendi.[110] However, the Hungarians and Habsburgs soon discovered that the copies signed by the parties differed in some essential points. After lengthy negotiations in 1607–8, the parties managed to sort out the disputed issues. Their agreement in 1608 was prepared in Hungarian, as was the addendum of the document.[111]

The Treaty of Zsitvatorok in 1606 called for twenty years of peace. However, because of discrepancies in the various copies, violations of the peace, and the election of Matthias II as king of Hungary in 1608, Sultan Ahmed I and Matthias II deemed it necessary to confirm and renew the treaty multiple times (1610, 1612, 1614, and 1615). Three authentic copies of the 1615 treaty—concluded in Vienna "in His Majesty's castle" by the representatives of Ahmed I and Matthias II—were written in German, Turkish, and Hungarian. Both sides signed and sealed all three copies, unlike the Latin translation, made from the Hungarian version of the treaty, which had no signatures and seals.[112] The Treaty of Komárom (27 February 1618) settled further disputes, such as the status of villages beyond the Hungarian defense line being taxed by the Ottomans. Habsburg and Ottoman diplomats structured this treaty, written in Italian, as a renewal of the Peace of Zsitvatorok.[113]

In 1703–4, during the joint Ottoman-Russian enforcement of the new border regime, accepted in the Istanbul peace treaty (1700), communication problems plagued relations between the two sides. Although the parties used Russian and Ottoman Turkish, neither team had a suitable translator to render the letters to his mother tongue. The Ottomans had no Russian translator, and the Turkish translators in the Russian camp often could not understand the high Ottoman style owing to their ignorance of Arabic. They either mistranslated the documents or were slow in rendering them into Russian. Therefore, the Ottomans often wrote to the Russians in Italian and requested that the Russians use either Greek or French rather than Russian, since the head of the Ottoman delegation had readers of those two languages at hand.[114]

11

Embassies, Dragomans, and Intelligence

European Embassies as Centers of Espionage in Constantinople

The fifteenth and sixteenth centuries marked a turning point in the history of diplomacy and intelligence. Permanent diplomatic contacts emerged in Europe out of the need to improve information gathering and reporting on foreign states.[1] As in the field of diplomacy, Venice led the way in establishing what contemporaries rightly considered the world's leading intelligence or secret service, based in part on the republic's network of resident ambassadors. Headquartered in the Doge's Palace, the Venetian intelligence service operated under the direction of the Council of Ten—the government committee responsible for the republic's security—and three state inquisitors, chosen from among the members of the Council of Ten (these individuals should not be confused with Venice's infamous Inquisition [*Santo Ufficio*]). Unlike most European intelligence operations that relied on "idiosyncratic espionage networks of potentates," the Council of Ten created and administered one of the world's first centrally organized state intelligence organizations. A specialized annex of the state bureaucracy, Venice's intelligence apparatus operated a formidable and far-reaching intelligence network based on the republic's geographically dispersed state representatives—naval and military commanders, envoys, and consuls—and supported by its robust and well-trained

diplomatic corps. Just like the republic's strategy and international relations, its intelligence operations were driven by the republic's business
acumen, protecting and serving the commercial elite's economic
interests.[2]

Most European monarchs would have agreed with Spinola that "spying on the designs and secrets of princes is the very trade of ambassadors, and especially residents."[3] Of all European resident ambassadors
in Constantinople, the Venetian *baili* played the most prominent role in
intelligence gathering. The bailate in the Ottoman capital was regarded
as one of the most critical diplomatic offices of the Republic of Venice.
The *baili* came from a handful of influential families of the Venetian
patriarchate, such as the Contarini, Nani, Bernardo, and Capello. Most
had received a thorough education at the University of Padua and elsewhere, and excelled in philosophy, rhetoric, and Latin. Before their appointments to Constantinople, they held important political, legal, and
military positions in Venice and its maritime empire (*Stato da Mar*) or
served the Serenissima as ambassadors at the courts of Austria, the Holy
Roman Empire, Poland, Spain, France, and the Holy See. Although in
principle their tenure in Constantinople was two years, it often lasted
longer because of the lack of qualified candidates, the duties of the *bailo*-
elect, or wars, when the *baili* were put under house arrest.[4]

The Ottomans regarded the European resident diplomats in their
capital as spies. In 1563, Grand Vizier Semiz Ali Pasha told the Venetian
bailo that if the sultan wanted to remove all spies from his country, he
would also have to expel the *bailo* with the entire Venetian nation, as
well as all other envoys with their compatriots, since they were nothing
more than spies. As the Venetians reported on events in Christianity to
the sultan, they also told the Christian princes what they saw and experienced in Turkey. Although the sultan knew this, he cared little,
because, as the grand vizier put it, "a fly could not harm an elephant."[5]

Occasionally, the buzzing of a fly bothered the elephant. In 1492, the
Porte expelled Bailo Girolamo Marcello for sending secret letters to
Venice about Sultan Bayezid II's shipbuilding program. The Ottomans
told the Venetians not to replace Marcello.[6] However, the Venetians
continued to receive news from the *bailo's* unofficial successor, Andrea

Gritti (1455–1538). As mentioned, after the death of his wife in 1479, the young Gritti settled in Pera, beyond the walls of Galata, the Latin quarter of Constantinople across the Golden Horn. As a wealthy grain merchant, he soon became the leader of the Venetian colony, living a lavish life with his Greek mistress. She gave birth to their four illegitimate sons, including Lodovico, whom we met concerning Sultan Süleyman's Hungarian policy. Andrea Gritti's prominent role was due to his wealth and good relations with Hersekzade Ahmed Pasha and Sultan Bayezid II. Late in 1496, for instance, he persuaded the Ottoman government to lift the embargo on grain export, a decision from which Gritti profited handsomely. On other occasions, he aided the Venetian ambassador extraordinaire in the Ottoman capital, but he also informed the Porte about Venice's alliance with France, a prelude to the Ottoman-Venetian war of 1499–1503. Seeing the Ottoman war preparations, Gritti sent regular dispatches to Venice about Ottoman naval constructions, the numbers of ships, and the names of their commanders, urging the Signoria to strengthen the fleet. To avert the Ottoman authorities' suspicion, Gritti coded his letters in commercial jargon. In August 1499, at the outbreak of the war, the Ottomans intercepted his letters and arrested him on charges of spying. He remained in prison until 1501 and escaped execution on account of his friendship with Ahmed Pasha. Released from his confinement, Gritti negotiated a peace with the grand vizier, accompanying the Ottoman envoy to Venice and back to the Ottoman capital to finalize the treaty.[7] In it, the Porte limited the tenure of the Venetian *bailo* to one year (a decade later it was raised to three years).[8]

Despite close Ottoman surveillance, the *baili* established an elaborate intelligence-gathering operation in the Ottoman capital. They relied on a wide array of official and unofficial informants and paid spies, penetrating every level of the Ottoman administration and military establishment from the palace and the imperial council to the arsenal. They paid informants and planted moles in other embassies. The *baili* also traded information with the Ottoman grandees. Some of these men were Christian renegades from Italy and communicated with the *baili* in Italian, such as Cafer Pasha, the governor-general of Tunis and Cyprus. The *baili* enlisted their Jewish physicians (Solomon Ashkenazi, Abramo

Abensazio, David Valentino), who also served the Ottoman grandees. The Turkish language tutors (*hoca*) at the bailate, hired to train Venetian apprentice interpreters, relayed information they heard from the grand mufti of Constantinople or the padishah's tutor. The *baili* even managed to penetrate the sultan's chancery and palace. In 1566 a chancery scribe provided the *bailo* with a copy of a previous Habsburg-Ottoman treaty, and in 1588 the chief chancellor shared with the *bailo* copies of imperial orders sent to the Safavid frontier. Of the palace staff, the Venetian renegade Gazanfer Agha, chief eunuch of the imperial harem, met Bailo Marco Venier secretly. His sister, Fatma Hatun (alias Beatrice Michiel), provided the *bailo* with handwritten notes concerning Ottoman economic problems, military preparations, and factional rivalries. The *baili* also had informants in the Ottoman arsenal, including the steward of Grand Admiral Uluc Ali, a Calabrian renegade. The *baili* recruited informants from among the Ottoman capital's Christian and Jewish inhabitants, who offered their services for monetary rewards and privileges. The *baili* also used the republic's vast commercial network and merchant colonies along with the intelligence operations of the Venetian consuls in Aleppo, Alexandria, Izmir, Chios, Gallipoli, Rhodes, and other places.[9]

The *baili* succeeded in gathering and transmitting intelligence even during their imprisonment. Bailo Marc'Antonio Barbaro, whose house in Pera the Porte sealed off at the outbreak of the Ottoman-Venetian war in 1570, was still able to send letters to Venice. Barbaro's Jewish physician, Solomon Ashkenazi—who also served Grand Vizier Sokollu Mehmed Pasha—smuggled the *bailo's* letters out of his home in his shoes, sending them to Crete with his correspondence. When Sokollu Mehmed Pasha learned that Barbaro still managed to communicate with Venice, he had the windows of the embassy covered, confiscated all paper and ink, and placed spies around the building. But the grand vizier also used Solomon to negotiate a peace with Barbaro that would end the war.[10] The Porte's attempt to isolate the *bailo* during the Cretan war failed too. Although Ottoman officials placed guards at his house, Bailo Giovanni Soranzo was still able to regularly inform the Venetian Senate about Ottoman war preparations and politics in Constantinople via the Habsburg resident at the Porte. Count Hermann Czernin forwarded the *bailo's* letters in his diplomatic pouch to Vienna. Between June 1645 and February 1647, the doge and the Senate received some 260 dispatches from Soranzo.[11]

Occasionally, the *baili* shared sensitive information with foreign powers too. Girolamo Lippomano leaked state secrets to Spain. He was accused of treason, and the Council of Ten ordered his arrest. On 25 June 1591, the *bailo* was put on a Venetian ship but died before he reached Venice. He jumped (or was pushed) into the water and drowned, just as his ship came in sight of the Lido at Venice.[12]

The *bailli* were not immune to espionage either, as Bailo Daniele Barbarigo discovered in 1563. He had been suspicious of the embassy's chief interpreter, Michael Černović, for some time. He also resented the interpreter because in 1562 the Signoria (and the grand vizier) chose Černović over the *bailo* as the republic's special envoy to congratulate Prince Selim on the marriages of his three daughters. Barbarigo criticized the costs involved in the legation and began a secret investigation of Černović.

Michael Černović (Michele Cernovicchio de Macedonia) was a descendant of the medieval Serbian dynasty of Črnojevici.[13] When at the end of the fifteenth century the family had to leave Montenegro, some of its members immigrated to Italy. Michael probably came from the Venetian branch of the family, but he may have been brought up in Constantinople. Černović entered the service of Archduke Maximilian in 1556 in Vienna, on the recommendation of Zaccaria Delfino, bishop of Hvar. With the recent death of the secret agent in Constantinople, Vienna urgently needed a replacement. Černović accepted the job under the condition that the Habsburg resident in Constantinople would not be made aware of him. He was to use the regular Venetian courier service for his encrypted letters, addressed to a Viennese merchant, which Bishop Delfino's brother would forward from Venice to Vienna. Having received 200 Rhine gulden for his travel expenses and the promise of an annual salary, Černović left Vienna in April 1556. He stopped in Bosnia, where he had worked as a merchant and knew the *sancak* governor. He reported to Vienna about Ottoman war preparations, but continued his trip, arriving in the Ottoman capital in mid-July. He stayed in Constantinople until Süleyman and his court moved to Edirne for the winter. Back in Constantinople in May 1557, he again moved with the sultan back to Edirne for the winter. By mid-March 1558, he was back again with the court in the capital. He spent the rest of the year and most of 1559 in Constantinople, where the sultan decided to stay, on account of the rivalry among his sons.

European ambassadors coveted Černović for his connections to the Ottoman grandees and his exceptional language skills. He spoke Turkish, Arabic, some Persian, Italian, Slavic, and Albanian. Bailo Antonio Erizzo asked him to join the Venetian embassy as an interpreter in 1556, but Černović declined. He also declined an offer from the French ambassador Jean de la Vigne the next year, citing his close relations with the Venetians. Then, when Bailo Marino Cavalli approached Černović, he had little room for maneuvering. Černović accepted the offer in 1558, although only after the grand vizier threatened to expel him from Constantinople and forbid him to trade if he would not serve the *bailo*. The Venetians were pleased with his work. In 1562, Vice Bailo Andrea Dandolo praised Černović as a loyal servant who carried out his duties with respect and tact and was highly knowledgeable in all matters at the Porte. He added that Černović had freed eight ships and 415 Christian subjects captured by the Turks.

In January 1563, Barbarigo's investigation revealed that Černović had been a secret agent of the Habsburgs, communicating with Vienna via Venice. The Viennese archives preserved dozens of his reports (eleven letters from 1556, thirty-one from 1557, twenty-nine from 1559, and twenty-two from 1559), which he usually signed as "secret friend" or "secret spy" (*amicus secretus* or *explorator secretus*). The archives also preserved Süleyman's letters to Prince John Sigismund Szapolyai of Transylvania and Charles IX of France, whose Italian translations Černović attached to his reports in 1560 and 1562.[14] Černović's services were invaluable for the Habsburgs. As the *bailo's* diplomatic interpreter, he participated in the meetings of the imperial council with the Venetian diplomat or alone, representing the *bailo*. He also befriended Rüstem Pasha's treasurer, a eunuch from Naples, who had pro-Habsburg and anti-French feelings. The treasurer was frequently with the grand vizier when Rüstem had audiences with Christian diplomats, and had access to the wives of the grand vizier and the sultan. The eunuch spread the rumor that Černović was his relative, which enabled the Habsburg secret agent to visit him three times a week.

Following Bailo Barbarigo's discovery, the Venetian authorities seized all letters coming from Constantinople and found Černović's letters to the emperor from January and February. They also intercepted a package for Černović from Innsbruck, which included letters for the Habsburg resident in Constantinople, Albert de Wijs. Černović's activities were declared treason, and the *bailo* was instructed to arrest him with the help of the Ottoman authorities. The *bailo* had to inform Grand Vizier Semiz Ali Pasha that he had arrested Černović on behalf of the Signoria and that he wanted to take him to Venice for punishment with the grand vizier's permission. He could offer the grand vizier up to 2,000 ducats for his cooperation. The Signoria was not convinced of the success of these measures. Therefore, it ordered Barbarigo to do away with Černović either by poisoning him or by some other means, but making sure that the *bailo* was not implicated. Černović got wind of the Venetians' plans. At the beginning of February 1564, with the knowledge of the grand vizier, the emperor's secret agent disappeared from Constantinople, leaving his wife, Jovanka, and children in the Ottoman capital. He arrived in Vienna via Ragusa, Puglia, Naples, and Rome, escaping arrests and ambushes prepared by the Venetians. In Vienna, Emperor Maximilian II appointed him imperial councillor and special diplomatic agent. He returned to Constantinople as the emperor's envoy in 1564.[15]

Agents like Černović were indispensable for Vienna because the Ottoman authorities kept the Habsburg residents under close surveillance. Unlike the permanent representatives of Venice, France, and England, all of whom resided across the Golden Horn in Pera, the Habsburg resident envoys were forced to live in the old city, close to the Ottoman court. But closer surveillance in the old city did not stop the Habsburgs from establishing an information-gathering network in the Ottoman capital. An Ottoman search of the house of the imperial resident Kreckwitz in 1593 revealed that Habsburg intelligence gathering had reached the inner circles of the Ottoman court.[16] In the embassy's chancery, they found and confiscated the resident's dispatches written in cipher. Having deciphered and translated the letters into Turkish with the help of German renegades, Grand Vizier Sinan Pasha realized how much the Habsburg resident knew about the Ottoman war plans and preparations. Sinan was shocked to learn that Kreckwitz's sources of information included "many of the chief officials, and the Sultana [the queen mother] herself." Sinan, "like an old fox," did not wish "to fall into disfavor with the imperial ladies, for the emperor's mother and wife ruled everything, and did what they liked." Therefore, the grand vizier "kept this to himself, made little noise about it." He simply "informed the Sultan that secret writings had been found in the chancery of the Viennese ambassador . . . [and that] the ambassador betrayed to the Viennese king everything that took place in the city." After the incident, "the Sultan immediately placed my lord the ambassador, and all his people and servants, in the pasha's hands, to do with them what he pleased."[17] As mentioned in the previous chapter, Sinan took Kreckwitz with him to the Hungarian campaign. The chronicler, the eyewitness Wenceslas Wratislaw of Mitrowitz, and the members of the embassy staff were sent to prison.

The Habsburg diplomats also knew how to circumvent Ottoman surveillance and communicate secret information to Vienna. Suspicious of David von Ungnad, the Habsburg resident envoy in Constantinople between 1573 and 1578, the Porte instructed him "to submit the letters he wished to dispatch to the emperor for prior reading." All letters had to be shown to the renegade Ali Beg of Frankfurt and translated into Turkish. The Ottoman authorities summoned Ungnad to a hearing, where the letters were read to him in Turkish. Then the German originals were "stamped in front of his eyes" so that nothing could be added to them. Grand Vizier Sokollu Mehmed assigned a *sipahi* cavalryman to the Habsburg couriers and ordered the men to depart immediately. The grand vizier "also wrote to the Pasha of Buda, telling him to strip [the couriers] to their pants and vests, in case they had other letters with them."[18] However, Ungnad found a way to communicate news to Vienna. Letters meant for the eyes of Ottoman officials were written in such a way that "no fault could be found in them. Other letters, however, in which he [Ungnad] reports at length on all his activities and on events, he writes with lemon juice and presses them according to Turkish custom. Thus, not one single character can be seen on the paper. He adds all sort of silk [into the envelope], as if he were sending a greeting to a sweetheart. The emperor also wrote with lemon juice between the lines of his letter about things that he thought should not become known to the Pasha."[19]

Habsburg intelligence gathering in the Ottoman Empire remained haphazard in the sixteenth century and focused mainly on military intelligence concerning Ottoman-ruled Hungary and Bosnia. Vienna's primary source regarding the Ottomans was its resident diplomat in Constantinople. After Kreckwitz's death in November 1593, Vienna had no resident envoy at the Porte until 1610. It took some time for the Habsburg diplomats to establish themselves and their intelligence-gathering operations, which were handicapped by the lack of independent sources of information. In Europe, Vienna could count on the well-developed diplomatic and intelligence services of the dynasty's Spanish branch. But Spain had no permanent representative at the Porte. As a consequence, the Viennese government could not check from independent sources the intelligence that its resident envoy at the Porte sent to the Court War Council. This situation would soon change.

In 1623, Emperor Ferdinand II sent Johann Jacob Kurtz von Senftenau (1583–1645) to Constantinople to congratulate Sultan Murad IV on his accession to the throne. However, his mission was more ambitious. He was to organize a clandestine Habsburg intelligence network in the Ottoman Empire. According to his instruction, Kurtz was to set up a network of secret correspondents. They were to report on Ottoman affairs to the Viennese Court War Council—which was responsible for the Hofburg's Turkish policy and diplomacy—and to the Habsburg resident envoy in Constantinople. In his final report, Kurtz listed his successes, including the hiring of the Habsburgs' first secret correspondents in the padishah's domains: the physician Girolammeo Grassi in Sofia, and the merchants Giovanni Pellegrini in Buda and Matteo Sturanni in Belgrade. Their reports soon arrived in Vienna.[20]

The institution solidified during the long tenure of Johann Rudolf Schmid from 1629 through 1643. Schmid had been captured by the Turks as a young boy in Hungary and spent two decades in the Ottoman Empire. Kurtz met him in Constantinople as a privileged slave who had a good command of Turkish and occasionally worked as a translator between the Ottoman authorities and the Habsburg diplomats. Kurtz freed and took Schmid to Vienna, and with the help of the War Council's chief Turkish interpreter, he prepared him for future diplomatic service in the Ottoman Empire. Schmid's language skills, intercultural experience, and knowledge—a set of cognitive and behavioral skills that enable someone to interact in different cultural contexts effectively— along with his personal network in the Ottoman capital, made him a perfect imperial resident. Schmid moved his house to Constantinople's Phanar district, on the southern side of the Golden Horn. He preferred this location because it was farther from the eyes of the Ottoman authorities and because of its proximity to the water and Pera, where he could cross in case of fire.[21] In 1644, Alexander von Greiffenklau, Schmid's successor as Habsburg resident at the Sublime Porte in 1643– 48, would move into a new building in Pera, where the other European embassies had been for some time. The house would serve as the home of the imperial residents through the eighteenth century.[22]

Most secret correspondents were merchants or physicians. As such, they could maintain close contacts with Ottoman officials and subjects and gather information from them. The correspondents' duties and payment were outlined in a hiring contract, usually signed by an ad hoc Habsburg envoy or the imperial resident. In it, the correspondents undertook to maintain constant written communication with the Viennese Court War Council or the Habsburg resident in Constantinople, informing them about all important matters they learned. They were to send regular reports in encrypted letters, using the cipher keys provided by Vienna. Most of the correspondents used fake names. Others signed their letters simply as "a confidant" or "a friend," or avoided signing their reports. Some of them, such as Grassi, managed to infiltrate the higher echelons of the Ottoman administration. Born and educated in Ragusa, Grassi studied medicine at the University of Padua. He sent his reports from Sofia, Belgrade, and Buda, where he served the governor-general Nasuhzade Hüseyin (1635–37). When the latter was recalled to Constantinople, Grassi went with him. In the Ottoman capital, Grassi entered the service of Grand Vizier Bayram Pasha (1637–38), accompanying him to the Iranian campaign. He witnessed and reported on the Ottoman conquest of Baghdad. Upon the death of Bayram in August 1638, Grassi joined the circle of his successor, Grand Vizier Kemankeş Kara Mustafa Pasha (1638–44). He remained a Habsburg secret correspondent until he died in January 1642.[23]

Embassy Dragomans and Intelligence

Since most European ambassadors in Constantinople lacked knowledge of the Turkish language and the intricacies of Ottoman diplomacy, they relied on a wide array of cross-cultural and cross-confessional intermediaries. Of these, the sultan's Roman Catholic, Greek Orthodox, and Jewish subjects were the most influential. On account of their education, language skills, and commercial networks in the empire and Europe, they were the ideal trans-imperial subjects. European ambassadors often hired these men as translators and diplomatic interpreters, called *dragomans*, from the Arabic *tarjuman*, meaning "interpreter" or "translator."

The ambassadors resented their dependency on these linguistic and cultural brokers. In 1585, Bailo Lorenzo Bernardo lamented the situation with these remarks: "What else is a *bailo* to do but speak with the tongue of another, listen with the ear of another, and lastly, act with the help of the brain of another." A late eighteenth-century French ambassador in Constantinople echoed his sixteenth-century colleague's opinion by saying that "a consul cannot, nor will ever be something more than his dragoman's clerk."[24]

The Venetians drew on three primary sources of dragomans. Venetian citizens by birth constituted the first group. They were second-tier metropolitan elite, not eligible for holding offices. Therefore, becoming an apprentice interpreter to serve the Venetian *bailo* in the Ottoman capital offered a stepping-stone to more prestigious employment. A second group of possible recruits came from the republic's shrinking colonial elite, from the Dalmatian hinterland and Cyprus. The polyglot families of the Roman Catholic community of Pera (*Magnifica comunita di Pera*) constituted the third source. Employment as an apprentice interpreter and later as dragoman offered steady income, prestige, and protection. The *bailo*, on the other hand, gained access to this community's elite, as the dragomanal families served as leaders of the community and its Catholic churches.[25]

The community enjoyed protected status from the time that Mehmed II issued his charter of privilege to his Latin subjects in Galata/Pera after the conquest. By working for European embassies, these families acquired further protection, as the European powers gradually extended the privileges they and their fellow citizens enjoyed under the capitulary regime to members of their households. The Fornettis, Grillos, Navonis, Peronis, Tarsias, and Testas evolved into dragomanal dynasties, a network of families connected by marriages who served the European resident ambassadors.[26]

Initially, the Habsburg diplomats relied on the dragomans of the Porte and the Venetian and French embassies. However, these men could not be used for delicate jobs, as Giovanni Maria Malvezzi, the first Habsburg resident envoy in the Ottoman capital (1546–52) discovered. With the help of bribed Ottoman officials, Malvezzi regularly acquired copies of letters written by the French and Polish ambassadors and Friar George, the trusted statesman of King John I Szapolyai of Hungary. Malvezzi copied and sent these letters to Vienna. However, Friar George often outwitted the Habsburg resident. "The old fox"—complained Malvezzi—sent his letters to the Porte written in Turkish, which Malvezzi could not read and copy.[27] Malvezzi intended to solve the problem by having his own dragoman. He first thought to recruit the French embassy's interpreter, Jacobus Bondorius. However, nothing came of this, because it was feared that Bondorius would collude with the French. In the end, Malvezzi hired two interpreters: an Italian and a Greek from Pera, who spoke Turkish and Italian.[28] By employing Levantine dragomans, the imperial residents diminished the influence of the Porte's interpreters. The latter habitually manipulated letters and treaties by their faulty translations, omissions, and additions and were spying on the Habsburgs.

Since the Levantine dragomans were the sultan's subjects, their loyalty remained questionable, as the Porte could press them to leak or manipulate information. Moreover, they had to be cautious with the Ottoman authorities and could not effectively represent the *bailo's* interest. As early as 1518, Bailo Leonardo Bembo, who used the Ottoman grand dragoman Ali Beg in dealings with the Porte, suggested his government send a dragoman "who would be our subject and would have the spirit to speak up," which Ali Beg apparently did not dare to do.[29] In 1551, the Venetians began to train their own apprentice interpreters, called *giovani di lingua*. Other European monarchs followed suit. The French sent young boys to Constantinople to be trained as dragomans in 1559. However, it was not until 1669 that the systematic training of French apprentice dragomans (*enfants de langue*, later *jeunes de langue*) was fully established. In 1569, the Poles sent a young nobleman to Constantinople for the same purpose. He returned to Poland after six years to become the crown's official translator of Eastern languages and later trained his nephews, who succeeded him as dragomans.[30]

Albert de Wijs, imperial resident from 1562 to 1569, advised the emperor to send two or three young boys with each new envoy to Constantinople to be trained by a local tutor (*hoca*). De Wijs's successor, Charles (Karel) Rijm van Estbeek (1570–73), met a young Spanish boy whom de Wijs had trained. The boy would work as dragoman until 1608. Rijm himself added four slave boys to his suite and had them trained by an Ottoman tutor. Rijm also suggested to his superiors that the Habsburg government should train Turkish interpreters from among the emperor's subjects. In 1578, the imperial resident Joachim von Sinzendorf arrived in Constantinople with an orphan boy to be trained as an apprentice interpreter. The boy, Peter von Wolzogen, later made a career in Vienna as a Turkish diplomatic interpreter.[31]

In Vienna, the Habsburg government relied on diplomatic interpreters of Italian and Dalmatian origin, such as Cesare Gallo, the Genoese Andrea Negroni, and the Armenian Giovanni Pietro Damiani.[32] Owing to the influence of Italian translators, by the last third of the sixteenth century, Italian had become the dominant language in the Habsburg court concerning Ottoman diplomacy. It retained its status for the next hundred years.

However, the translators' Turkish-language skills often left much to be desired. Many could correspond in Turkish, but their translations of Ottoman chancery documents were often faulty. The Negroni affair demonstrated the problem. Negroni was tried on account of his faulty translation of the Peace of Zsitvatorok (1606). Although he died before his trial could be completed, the incident prompted the Viennese government to resume attempts to train professional diplomatic interpreters from among the emperor's subjects.[33]

Both the issue of reliable dragomans and the training of future interpreters improved considerably with the hiring of two talented and ambitious diplomatic interpreters: Michel d'Asquier and Josephus Barbatus. Born in Marseilles in 1598, d'Asquier had an extraordinary gift for foreign languages. When he entered the service of Emperor Maximilian in Vienna in 1617, he had a good command of Turkish. He was fluent in French, Italian, Spanish, and Latin but also learned Arabic, German, Hungarian, Czech, Persian, and Greek. In 1625 the Court War Council named d'Asquier chief interpreter of Oriental languages (*Hofdolmetscher für orientalische Sprachen*), meaning Eastern languages such as Arabic, Hebrew, Syriac, Turkish, and Persian. D'Asquier would remain the chief interpreter of Oriental languages for the next forty years, serving four emperors. He became an indispensable Turkish expert.[34]

In Constantinople, the Habsburgs' chief interpreter was d'Asquier's protégé, Josephus Barbatus (alias Yusuf ibn Abu Dhaqn). This Cairo-born Egyptian Copt Christian had spent years in Rome, Paris, Oxford, London, Antwerp, Louvain, and Munich as professor of Arabic and Hebrew, before entering the emperor's service in 1622. Besides Arabic and Hebrew, he also knew Syriac, Turkish, Latin, Italian, Spanish, and English. Barbatus's career took a turn after he met d'Asquier, who became his patron for the next twenty years.[35] The Viennese Court War Council hired Barbatus as an interpreter of Oriental languages and in 1623 sent him to Constantinople with Ambassador Kurtz. When Kurtz returned to Vienna, Barbatus stayed in Constantinople, now serving the imperial resident at the Porte, Sebastian Lustrier. The dragoman resented his work. Since he was born in Cairo, the Ottomans considered him the sultan's subject and continually insulted him. He also complained to his superior that Lustrier treated him as a lackey and did not pay him.[36] Facing chronic shortages of money and trying to maintain the status quo with the Ottomans during the Thirty Years' War in Europe, Lustrier was not a successful diplomat. His successor, Johann Rudolf Schmid, proved more able. During his long service as imperial resident (1629–43), Schmid strengthened the emperor's standing at the Porte and developed a network of secret agents. He also put the training of apprentice interpreters (*Sprachknaben*) on a more stable footing with the help of d'Asquier and Barbatus. In addition to his daily work as a translator, Barbatus was responsible for training the apprentice interpreters.

Schmid, d'Asquier, and Barbatus played a crucial role in Vienna's Turkish policy, directed by the Court War Council. There was no letter, report, or instruction of importance concerning the Ottomans that d'Asquier did not see. He worked closely with the imperial resident in Constantinople and read and summarized his dispatches for the Court War Council. He influenced Vienna's Turkish policy with his expert opinions and summaries (*estratto*) of the residents' reports. He was also in charge of the secret correspondents. He provided the correspondents with cipher keys and read and summarized their encrypted reports. He frequently traveled to Ottoman Buda and Constantinople and interpreted at the peace negotiations in Komárom (1618), Gyarmat–Szőny (1624–25), and Szőny (1641–42). In 1627, the imperial resident in Constantinople, Sebastian Lustrier, named d'Asquier as one of three men best suited to succeed him. But the chief interpreter stayed in Vienna. Despite his enmity with the Hungarian palatine Nicholas Eszterházy and accusations that he and Schmid had planned the poisoning of the Ragusan embassy's dragoman in 1633—the ambitious Vincenzo Bratutti (Vinko Bratutović)—d'Asquier kept his position. He eventually fell into disgrace and was dismissed during the reign of Leopold I, as he was held responsible for the outbreak of the Turkish wars in 1663.

The poisoning of Bratutti gives us a unique window through which to understand both Vienna's Turkish policy and the chief interpreter's power. Resident Schmid invited the young Ragusan to lunch on 7 February 1633. During lunch, Schmid offered the dragoman a glass of poisoned wine. The poison was effective. In pain and bleeding, Bratutti tried to escape, but the resident's servants blocked his way out. Luckily, the dragoman's servant heard the shouting and took Bratutti to the Ragusan embassy. There, the embassy physician and his colleague from the French embassy administered antidotes. Bratutti fought for his life for nine days and slowly recovered. Having investigated his poisoning for years, the Ragusan learned that d'Asquier and Schmid had tried to kill him already in 1632. After the unsuccessful poisoning, they continued plotting against him. In 1638, Bratutti presented his evidence to the Viennese Court War Council: written testimonies of those d'Asquier and Schmid had approached with their assassination schemes. He also informed Sebastian Lustrier, Schmid's predecessor and now Habsburg ambassador in France. Despite overwhelming evidence, the War Council concluded its investigation without punishing Schmid and d'Asquier. It did not want to risk disturbing the peace with the Sublime Porte, established in 1606. The War Council's long-serving leadership guaranteed the status quo. Under Heinrich Schlick's presidency (1632–49), Vice President Gerard Questenberg coordinated the work from 1624 until he died in 1646. He worked closely with d'Asquier, who did most of the day-to-day work in cooperation with Schmid in Constantinople. D'Asquier and Schmid feared that the young and ambitious Bratutti would threaten the status quo. They also realized that the Ragusan had an influential supporter, Lustrier, who, as ambassador to France, was not under the auspices of the War Council. The members of the War Council agreed. But they also realized that the Ragusan was ambitious and wanted to serve the emperor. Therefore, the War Council recruited him as an interpreter of Oriental languages, to work alongside d'Asquier. The Ragusan achieved his dream. But his relationship with d'Asquier, who called him "the poisoned" (*il Tossicato*), remained uneasy. Bratutti slowly built his career. He worked with the Hungarian palatine Nicholas Eszterházy, who often disagreed with Schmid and despised d'Asquier.

He also made a name for himself with his Italian translation of Hoca Saadeddin's (d. 1599) Ottoman chronicle. The Ragusan dedicated the first volume of his *Chronica dell'origini e progressi della Caso Ottomana* (Vienna 1649) to Emperor Ferdinand III. The second volume appeared in 1652 in Madrid, and the dragoman dedicated the work to his new master, Philip IV of Spain. Having escaped his enemies in Vienna, Bratutti achieved his goal. He died as a respected royal interpreter, author, and diplomat and outlived both Schmid and d'Asquier.[37]

In 1637, d'Asquier and Schmid proposed the establishment of an academy of Oriental languages in Vienna. They realized that some of the apprentice dragomans sent to Constantinople lacked the necessary skills and qualities. They suggested that future dragomans first be trained in Vienna. Once they had a good grasp of the Turkish language, they needed only minimal training in the Ottoman capital to perfect their chancery and everyday Turkish and familiarize themselves with Ottoman court protocol. The academy that d'Asquier and Schmid had envisaged was realized only in 1674, when Emperor Leopold I authorized Johann Baptist Podestà, the secretary of Oriental languages, to establish a College of Oriental Languages in Vienna.[38] By this time, there were new diplomatic interpreters in charge of the Habsburgs' Turkish policy and intelligence gathering both in Vienna and in Constantinople.

D'Asquier's successor in Vienna was François Mesgnien, better known by his Polish name as Meniski. Born in Lorraine in 1623, Mesgnien studied in Rome. In 1647 he moved to Poland, where he tutored the son of the Polish-Lithuanian aristocrat Alexander Radziwiłł. He traveled to Constantinople in 1654 in the company of ambassador Mikołaj Bieganowski and the future Polish king Jan Sobieski. He stayed in the Ottoman capital for two years, where he perfected his Turkish with the help of Ali Ufki Efendi (alias Wojciech Bobowski), one of the Porte's chief dragomans. Upon his return to Poland, he worked as the crown's chief Turkish translator. He was dispatched two more times to the Ottoman capital on diplomatic missions. In 1661 he went to Vienna, and early the next year was appointed Turkish dragoman, succeeding d'Asquier as the chief interpreter of Oriental languages after the latter's dismissal in 1664. Commissioned by Schmid, he played an important role in organizing Walter von Leslie's embassy to Constantinople in 1665. In 1669 he traveled to Jerusalem and Syria, returning to Vienna only in 1671. In 1680, he published the first three volumes of his dictionary, *Thesaurus Linguarum Orientalium Turcicae, Arabicae, Persicae*, which he dedicated to Emperor Leopold I. He was appointed as councillor of the War Council in 1686 and—despite his health problems in the 1690s—maintained his office and influence on Vienna's Turkish policy until his death in the spring of 1698.[39]

In Constantinople, the imperial resident, Alexander von Greiffenklau, dismissed Barbatus, who by now was unable to fulfill his duties because of his old age. In 1645, Greiffenklau hired a thirty-year-old Arab interpreter from Aleppo, Gian Battista Corel, and a young Orthodox Greek interpreter, Panagiotes Nikousios. Corel spoke Arabic, Turkish, and Italian and had worked under Barbatus at the embassy, and later in Vienna and Graz. He returned to Constantinople in 1649 with the embassy of Schmid. A former imperial resident and one of the top Ottoman experts in the Viennese government with a good command of Turkish, Schmid soon realized Corel's insufficient language and personal skills. The Ottomans also complained about Corel's Turkish, which was heavily influenced by his Arabic. But it was his questionable loyalty toward the emperor and his shady dealings in Constantinople that resulted in his dismissal.[40] Panagiotes, on the other hand, proved to be a capable interpreter. He studied in Constantinople with theologians of the Orthodox Greek Patriarchate, and he later studied medicine at the University of Padua. He had an exceptional talent for languages. In addition to his native Greek, he knew Turkish, Arabic, Persian, Italian, and Latin. He came from a wealthy Phanariot family, was familiar with Ottoman customs, and had a broad personal network.[41] He was well regarded by his colleagues and European ambassadors at the Porte, who competed for him. After the death of the resident ambassador Greiffenklau in a horse accident in June 1648, Panagiotes managed the embassy staff until the new resident ambassador, Simon Reniger, arrived in the spring of 1649.[42]

Meanwhile, the training of apprentice dragomans continued. In 1644 the Habsburg ambassador extraordinaire, Hermann Czernin von

Chudenitz, took four boys to Constantinople. For the next four to five years, they were to be trained in the Turkish language by the embassy dragoman and a Turkish tutor in the house of the imperial resident, Alexander von Greiffenklau. However, one of the boys died and another converted to Islam. The two remaining boys continued their training with the help of Barbatus. Once they attained proficiency, they were assigned to serve in Vienna or key frontier fortresses, under the supervision of the War Council's chief interpreter of Oriental languages.[43]

By the mid-seventeenth century, Vienna not only had qualified interpreters, but several of these men proved to be expert scholars of Oriental languages and that of the Ottoman Empire. The best of them, the chief dragomans of Vienna, also supervised the emperor's clandestine intelligence operations of secret correspondents in the Ottoman Empire, which complemented the spy network operated by the Habsburg residents in Constantinople.

The Porte's Dragomans and Intelligence

In the sixteenth century, most of the Porte's dragomans were men of Greek, German, Austrian, Hungarian, or Polish lineage who had arrived at the empire as captives. Yunus Beg, the chief dragoman under Süleyman, was originally a Venetian subject of Greek descent from the Greek town of Methoni (Venetian Modon), which the Venetians lost to the Ottomans in 1500. Yunus's sister and his nephew lived on the Ionian island of Zakynthos (Venetian-controlled Zante), while his brother, Mustafa Agha (d. 1565), served as chief gatekeeper in Süleyman's court. Throughout his career, Yunus maintained personal and business ties with his relatives and acquaintances across political and religious borders and lobbied for his relatives in Venice. Owing to his knowledge of Greek, Italian, Latin, and Turkish, he positioned himself well to undertake diplomatic missions in Europe, especially to Venice, where the Porte sent him more than six times between 1519 and 1542. In 1519, he came to Venice to demand the release of some Turks captured by Venetian subjects in Dalmatia. In 1522, in addition to dealing with Ottoman taxpaying subjects who had fled to Venetian territory, Yunus was to seek

justice for Defterdar Mehmed Beg, whose jewels had been stolen by a
Venetian subject. In 1529 and 1533, he brought Ottoman victory procla-
mations to the doge. In 1537, he was to settle outstanding debts of Venetian merchants. But he also had a secret mission: to arrange an alliance
among Venice, France, and the Porte.[44]

Yunus's successor as the chief dragoman of the Porte was Ibrahim
Beg. He was a scion of a Polish noble family, baptized as Joachim Strasz.
Captured by Tatar raiders and sold to the Ottomans as a young boy, he
was converted to Islam. He succeeded Yunus in 1551 as the padishah's
chief dragoman and held his office until his death in June 1571.[45] Ibrahim
had close relations with the Polish and Hungarian elite, including Andreas Dudith, bishop of Pécs and Emperor Maximilian II's diplomat.[46]
At the Sublime Porte, Ibrahim was an expert in Polish, Hungarian, and
Habsburg affairs. He became famous in Europe when as Süleyman's
"orator" he delivered a speech at the coronation ceremony of Maximilian in Frankfurt in 1562. The Hungarian chronicler Nicholas (Miklós)
Istvánffy reported that Ibrahim's performance in Frankfurt was one of
the most memorable events of the celebration. In his capacity as chief
dragoman, Ibrahim accompanied his sovereign on the 1566 Hungarian
campaign. He interpreted at the audience during which John Sigismund
of Hungary and Transylvania paid homage to Süleyman in the Ottoman
military camp. Ibrahim also played an instrumental role in restoring
Transylvania to Queen Isabella and John Sigismund, under whose rule
the Principality of Transylvania as an Ottoman tributary state was born.
Habsburg diplomats had a rather negative view of Ibrahim. They regarded the chief dragoman as "the most dangerous, most cunning and
most deceitful enemy of Christendom." He was also very revengeful and
had a German ambassador sent into exile to Caffa in the Crimea because
the latter dubbed him a billygoat in one of his letters.[47]

Mahmud Tercüman (alias Sebold) was the son of a Viennese merchant, Jacob von Pibrach. The Ottomans captured Sebold either during
the battle of Mohács or in Süleyman's 1529 Vienna campaign. Having
converted to Islam, he rose to become one of the leading interpreters of
the Sublime Porte, owing to his language skills in Latin, German, and
Hungarian. From 1541 on, Mahmud was considered to be an individual

of considerable influence at the Porte. He represented the padishah on diplomatic missions to Transylvania, Poland, France, Venice, and Vienna. Mahmud played an important role in the Habsburg-Ottoman peace negotiations that led to the treaty of 1547, whose German translation he prepared. In 1551 Mahmud lost his office, a dismissal perhaps linked to the death of Yunus Beg and the nomination of Ibrahim Beg as chief dragoman.[48] He soon returned to the office and was sent on diplomatic missions. Nevertheless, in 1558 he was removed once more, and historians thought that Mahmud was unable to regain his former significance at the Ottoman court. However, in 1567–68, he was still working as a dragoman, furnishing the Habsburg embassy with information. He also continued to perform diplomatic duties, and his prestige and influence grew. Prince John Sigismund of Transylvania commissioned Mahmud as his ambassador to propose (unsuccessfully) marriage to Margaret of Valois, daughter of Henry II of France. Mahmud's last diplomatic mission occurred in 1574 when he delivered the final version of the Ottoman-Habsburg peace treaty to Emperor Maximilian II in Prague. Philibert of Brussels—brother-in-law of Charles Rijm, the Habsburg resident ambassador at the Sublime Porte (1570–74) who brought the yearly tribute in 1574 to the sultan and whom Mahmud dragoman accompanied on his way home—noted in February 1575 that Mahmud "offered a toast to the emperor's health with a jug of beer, 'because he does not drink any wine.'"[49]

Two interpreters of Hungarian origin, Murad and Ferhad, were also key figures at the Porte, especially with regard to Hungarian and Habsburg affairs. Murad dragoman, alias Valentine (Balázs) Somlyai, came from Nagybánya/Szatmárbánya (today Baia Mare in Romania). The Ottomans captured him either in 1526 or in 1529. He played an important role in Habsburg-Ottoman peace negotiations at the Porte in the 1550s and the 1570s. The Hungarian Murad and the Viennese Mahmud worked closely together on a number of diplomatic and cultural projects, which suggests cooperation among dragomans hailing from the same geographical region.[50]

Ibrahim dragoman may have been hostile to the Habsburgs, but he had more cordial relations with the Polish court. He corresponded regularly in Polish with the king and his chancellor and received 100 gold pieces for his services. He also lobbied for his fellow Poles and Christians in Ottoman service, asking for the chancellor's help in obtaining letters of recommendation from the king to the padishah for his acquaintances. The Porte considered Ibrahim an expert in Polish and central European affairs and sent him on diplomatic missions just as it did Ibrahim's older countryman, Said Beg.[51]

Said Beg (alias Jan Kierdej) was born in 1490 as the son of Zygmunt Kierdej, the governor (*starosta*) of Krasnystaw and Trembowla. He was captured as a child in 1498 during a Turkish raid against his father's castle at Pomorzany in Ruthenia. He was brought up as a page in the Ottoman court, and his language skills were noted by Grand Vizier Ibrahim Pasha, who charged him with diplomatic missions to Poland, starting in 1531. During his mission to Cracow, he met his mother and tried in vain to regain his family's Pomorzany estate from the Sieniawski family. Between 1531 and 1543, he visited his country of birth eight times. Most of his missions concerned Ottoman merchants trading in Poland-Lithuania. On his last mission, however, he tried, albeit unsuccessfully, to spoil the marriage between the future Sigismund II Augustus Jagiellon (r. 1548–72) (son of the reigning Polish king, Sigismund I) and Elisabeth of Austria (1526–45), eldest daughter of Ferdinand I.[52]

These examples demonstrate the scope of work that the Porte's dragomans performed. In addition to their service as translators of incoming and outgoing documents and interpreters for Ottoman officials and European diplomats, they also acted as the Porte's envoys and experts on European politics. Like their European colleagues, Ottoman dragomans played an important role in the production of knowledge about the Ottomans and Islam for European audiences. They also authored treatises about their countries of birth for their Muslim patrons. Just like the works of their European colleagues, which reflected Europe's view of the Ottoman other, the writings by Ottoman dragomans also functioned as propaganda tools that promoted the superiority of Islam and the Ottomans and justified Ottoman conquests.[53]

Of these works, the best known is the treatise on the Ottoman government that Yunus Beg authored in collaboration with Lodovico Gritti in the Venetian dialect.[54] Murad dragoman was the author of numerous religious, literary, and historical works. In 1557 he wrote his self-narrative conversion, *Guide for One's Turning toward Truth*, which he translated into Latin a decade later. Around 1559 he presented the Venetian *bailo*, Marino de Cavalli, an Ottoman Turkish text, inspired by Cicero's *De Senectute*. Equally significant is his historical work, a translation of an anonymous Ottoman chronicle into Latin—one of the basic texts of the famous fifteenth-century Ottoman chronicler Neşri (d. 1520)—which Murad prepared for Philip Haniwald, the secretary of the Habsburg ambassador. The work, known as *Codex Haniwaldanus*, was an important source of the Westphalian humanist Hans Löwenklau's Ottoman history. Dismissed from imperial service because of his "immoderate enjoyment of wine," the elderly Murad continued to produce religious hymns in Turkish about the unity of God, providing his audience with their Hungarian and Latin translations.[55]

Mahmud dragoman's Turkish-language *Chronicle of Hungary* (*Tarih-i Ungurus*) narrates the history of Hungary from the conquest of the region by Alexander the Great to the death of Louis II at the battle of Mohács in 1526. Mahmud wrote his chronicle between 1543 and 1566 for Süleyman the Magnificent, to acquaint the padishah with the history of his newest conquest. But the *Tarih-i Ungurus* also served as a propaganda tool. The anecdotes from the life of Alexander the Great and his conquest of the region were used to justify the conquest of Hungary (and future conquests beyond Hungary) by Süleyman, the rightful successor of Alexander. Mahmud's chronicle therefore should be read as part of a corpus of propaganda literature that intended to justify and broadcast Süleyman's policy of world dominion, his claim to inherit the universal sovereignty of the Roman emperors.[56] Mahmud may have prepared his work with the help of collaborators who had a better grasp of Ottoman Turkish and Arabic than the author. One such collaborator was his Hungarian fellow dragoman, Murad. The Viennese manuscript of the *Illustrated Chronicle* of Mark of Kalt, one of Mahmud's sources, contains short notes in Hungarian and Latin in Arabic script, reminding the reader to pay special attention to certain events in the chronicle—notes that Murad dragoman could have made during his collaboration with Mahmud on the *Tarih-i Ungurus.*[57]

By the latter part of the seventeenth century, Phanariot Greeks had assumed the positions of dragoman of the Porte. The name Phanariot alludes to Constantinople's Phanar quarter (from the Greek *phanarion*, meaning "lantern" and Turkish *fener*, meaning "lighthouse"), the home of the Orthodox Patriarchate since 1586. The Phanariots retained their commercial and personal connections to the Italian states especially through the Genoese and Venetian colonies in Galata, and educated their sons at the universities of Padua, Rome, Milan, Genoa, and Paris. On their return from Europe, many of these young men came into close contact with the Ottoman political elite. Ottoman viziers and the Imperial Court were all keen to employ these young men to benefit from their knowledge of European languages, politics, and sciences. Many Phanariots were employed as family or court physicians, political advisers, and interpreters. Owing to their medical knowledge, European contacts, and superior language skills, the Phanariot Greeks quickly replaced the Sephardi Jews who had filled such positions of trust in earlier periods. Moreover, the Phanariots succeeded where the Sephardim had earlier failed. They institutionalized their political influence by monopolizing the office of the chief dragoman of the Sublime Porte and the Ottoman navy until the Greek Revolution of 1821.[58]

Panagiotes Nikousios laid the basis for the unmatched influence of the Phanariot Greek community at the Sublime Porte. After serving the Habsburg residents in Constantinople for more than ten years, he entered the service of the Porte around 1659. Köprülüzade Fazıl Ahmed Pasha recognized Panagiotes's abilities and appointed him chief interpreter of the Porte, a position that Panagiotes held until his death in October 1673.[59]

Recognizing the importance of the dragomans of the Porte, European legations paid them regular salaries, hoping to gain their goodwill and cooperation. Dragoman Yunus received 500 ducats per year from the Habsburg court, but the French regularly sent him gifts too. Services that the dragomans rendered to European embassies paid off. Yunus's wealth at his death amounted to 200,000 ducats and precious stones, a hefty sum for someone whose official annual revenue was a little more than 400 ducats, less than what he received from the Habsburgs.[60] Yunus's successor, the Polish renegade Ibrahim, received 300 ducats annually from the Habsburg emperor. In 1563 he left no stone unturned in his effort to obtain from the Habsburg emperor an annual stipend equivalent to that of his predecessor.[61] His junior interpreter colleagues, Ferhad and Murad, also received gifts from the Habsburgs, and from the prince of Transylvania, as did Mehmed dragoman, Ferhad's son.[62]

Agents of Many Masters

Copying and trading letters at the Ottoman court and the European embassies in Constantinople seems to have been a customary practice and a lucrative business for the dragomans. While some of the Porte's dragomans leaked and traded information to influence European diplomacy and decision making, there were those whose acts undoubtedly harmed Ottoman interests. Such was the case with one of Süleyman's dragomans, Peter Esztéri, a former Hungarian Christian. Ottoman marauders kidnapped him shortly after the battle of Mohács in 1526, while his friend and schoolmate Peter Pécsi Kis managed to escape. In captivity, Esztéri converted to Islam. He returned to Hungary in 1541 as an interpreter with the padishah's army. His former schoolmate Pécsi Kis was now the secretary of Paul Várday, archbishop of Esztergom. In 1541 he was serving as secretary and interpreter of the Habsburg envoys whom Ferdinand sent to Süleyman, following the Ottoman capture of Buda. Thus, fifteen years after their traumatic separation, the two childhood friends met once again in the Ottoman military camp near Buda as interpreters of two opposing empires. Pécsi Kis recounted their encounter in his treatise about the Ottoman military (*Exegeticon*), which he dedicated to Emperor Maximilian II in 1564. The work is based on his observations in the Ottoman camp and his Ottoman dragoman friend's explanations.[63]

Every day, in the greatest and most carefully guarded secrecy, I had friendly and gentle conversations with the Turkish dragoman, my old schoolmate. From him, I received a thorough knowledge regarding the appearance, manner, and form of the Turkish Emperor's camp, how it was preparing for war and the decisive battle. He even showed me all the new military equipment for land and water in the Turkish camp. He explained all this to me accurately and in good faith. What I was able to understand . . . I wrote down according to my best abilities.[64]

That the two men were often seen together aroused no suspicion because they were both interpreters and their jobs required that they work together. The information about the Ottoman military was passed to the best possible person to receive it: Pécsi Kis had been in military service for almost a decade, and his knowledge of the Ottoman army must have been considerable. On two occasions in 1540, Archbishop Paul Várday sent Pécsi Kis, disguised as a poor peasant, on reconnaissance missions to the Ottoman army camp near Buda. His task was to gather information about the Ottoman troops helping the followers of the recently deceased King John I Szapolyai, whom Ferdinand's forces were besieging. In 1564 Pécsi Kis recorded his experiences in his *Exegeticon*, which contains descriptions of the Ottoman military camp.

As noted, Mahmud dragoman also furnished the Habsburg embassy with information during their stay in Constantinople in 1567–68. Anthony Vrančić, a member of the delegation, later noted to Archduke Charles that Mahmud "was so faithful to us that he copied all the letters of both the French and the Venetians by his own hand. He also diligently informed us about what he had learned from the Transylvanian envoys and regarding issues that the pashas had discussed in the sultan's *divan*."[65] Panagiotes also emphasized his goodwill towards European diplomats and monarchs. He stated on several occasions that he was a good Christian who wanted to support the prince of Transylvania and his men at the Porte—in return for a small gift. During the Érsekújvár campaign in 1663, Panagiotes had asked his Transylvanian colleague David Rozsnyai to invite the prince of Transylvania to the Turkish camp to "assure him of my Christian faith, and that no harm shall befall him."[66]

Of course, not only the dragomans of the Porte could serve the Europeans. The converse was also true. One of the Venetian embassy's apprentice dragomans, a man called Colombia, defected to the Ottomans and converted to Islam. Known henceforth as Mehmed, he was recruited to work at the sultan's chancery as a translator. He helped decipher the letters of the Venetian *bailo*, rendering an invaluable service to his new master, as the Ottomans lacked such experts and themselves seldom used ciphers. As someone intimately familiar with Venetian politics, Mehmed was designated to the Serenissima as envoy in 1578 by the Porte, against which the Venetian authorities vehemently protested.[67]

Communication presented a problem in the European frontier provinces as well. Few people in Vienna knew Turkish, and even fewer in the office of the pasha of Buda knew German or Latin. However, it was relatively easy to find educated Hungarians with good knowledge of Turkish. As a consequence, Hungarian quickly became the favored language of communication between the Ottoman governors-general of Buda and the Habsburg authorities in Vienna. Alas, the loyalty of the pashas' "Turkish scribes" (Hun. *török deák*), as these interpreters were known, was questionable. In 1551, Ferdinand had three spies in Ottoman Hungary. One was the scribe of the governor-general of Buda by the name of Adrian, who shared the pasha's letters with Ferdinand.[68] Another scribe, Yahya Yazıcı (alias János deák), served as the secretary of the *sancak* governor of Székesfehérvár and Arslan Pasha of Buda. Yahya approached John Pethő of Gerse, commander-general in the Habsburg fortress of Komárom in 1565, with the following:

I want to let your Esteemed Lordship know that I am a Christian boy. When I was captured, along with my father, I was just a child. My father was ransomed, but I was turned Turk [converted to Islam]. I am the captive of Mahmud Beg, *sancakbeyi* of Székesfehérvár. After my capture, I was sent to a Turkish school and learned Turkish. I also serve Arslan Pasha now. When letters arrive from His Majesty, the King, I translate them to Turkish for the pasha. Therefore, my Lord, I know the business of the Turks well and am knowledgeable about their perfidious matters, be they matters of the emperor, viziers, or begs. There cannot arrive any secret news here that I would not know about quickly. I want the best for the poor Christian people as I want it for myself. I do not dare to write more about this, for I fear that your Lordship would give me away. But I sent word with Matthias Bélay, the content of which your Lordship can trust and answer me in secret. May God keep your Lordship. Yahya Yazıcı, in Hungarian János, your Lordship's trusted servant.

At the end of his letter he added: "Whether I am here [in Buda] with the pasha or in Fehérvár, your Lordship should find a trusted man by whom I can send you fresh news, so much do I want to serve His Majesty, our king."[69] That these were not empty promises, János deák proved soon. In his letter on 1 April 1566, he alerted Pethő about Süleyman's campaign and the padishah's departure from Constantinople. He informed Pethő that one of the pasha's men had just returned from Constantinople with details about the attack. The scribe assured the addressee that he would not send news "which he heard at the market" but only solid news that the sultan wrote to the pasha. He heard that Süleyman's targets were Szigetvár and then Komárom, the seat of Pethő.[70] As we know, Süleyman marched against Szigetvár and died there during the siege.

Ottoman Intelligence Gathering

While Ottoman information gathering never quite reached the level of sophistication of the Venetian or Spanish secret service, it served Ottoman policy-makers well. Contemporaries were often surprised how well informed the Ottomans were about both major political and military events in Europe and about less important day-to-day policy decisions. The fire in the Venetian arsenal in September 1569 and the defeat of the Spanish Armada in 1588 are just two of the most revealing examples. The Ottomans quickly learned about the 1569 arsenal fire, purportedly from Joseph Nassí. Nassí was a member of the influential Jewish Mendes family, with numerous agents and vast commercial networks in Europe, who had relocated to the Ottoman capital and become a confidant of several grand viziers. The Venetians were convinced that the Ottoman-

Venetian war of 1570–73 had been "launched against them by the Turks on account of espionage and the evil machinations of Jews." Some even suspected that the agents of Nassí were responsible for the arsenal fire's destruction of the Venetian navy.[71] No wonder Süleyman called Nassí "a true mirror, in which he saw all the developments in Christendom and from which he obtained information about all countries."[72] The information regarding the 1569 fire in the Venetian arsenal and the war party's manipulation of the news in the Ottoman court proved crucial in launching the war against the Republic of St. Mark. By exaggerating the fire's destruction of the Venetian Armada, pro-war politicians in the Ottoman court succeeded in winning over their opponents.

Another example is equally telling. In 1588 the English ambassador was eager to share with the grand vizier the news of the great English victory over Spain's "invincible Armada." To his surprise, the Ottoman government had already been informed about the outcome of the battle. The source of the information was Don Alvaro Mendes, alias Salamon Abenaes (Ibn Yaish), brother-in-law to Queen Elizabeth's physician, who had resided in Constantinople since 1585. He had assumed Joseph Nassí's influential position in the Ottoman court. The information about the destruction of the Spanish Armada was all the more important because the Ragusan representative in Constantinople claimed that the naval engagement ended with Spanish victory, causing apparent anxiety in the Ottoman capital.[73]

The unilateral nature of European-Ottoman diplomacy and the lack of Ottoman permanent embassies in European capitals was a disadvantage for the Ottomans and a major advantage for the Europeans. European resident ambassadors' regular dispatches from the Ottoman capital to their home countries furnished European courts and governments with valuable information about Ottoman politics and rivalries within the highest echelons of the Ottoman government and among the European diplomatic corps of the Ottoman capital. Owing to the lack of comparative Ottoman source material, recent works on Ottoman espionage and Ottoman-European diplomatic relations have also been based on European diplomatic dispatches even when the researchers had access to the Ottoman archives.

At least four levels of Ottoman information gathering may be discerned: (1) central intelligence in Constantinople; (2) information gathering by local Ottoman authorities, especially along the empire's frontier provinces; (3) information services provided by Ottoman vassals; and (4) espionage and counterespionage carried out by the Porte's spies and saboteurs in foreign countries.[74]

We have seen that the European resident ambassadors were busy gathering information in Constantinople. They acquired and copied incoming and outgoing letters by paying and bribing the Porte's dragomans. But the Ottomans also used these embassies to collect information. The resident ambassadors of the competing European governments willingly shared information concerning their rivals to manipulate the Porte. As mentioned earlier, in 1527 the Venetian *bailo* in Constantinople not only regularly informed Grand Vizier Ibrahim Pasha about the power struggle between the two newly elected Hungarian kings, John Szapolyai and Ferdinand of Habsburg, but also urged Ibrahim Pasha to help King John. Through its *bailo*, the Venetian government reminded the Ottoman viziers that Emperor Charles V's power would grow excessively if his younger brother, Ferdinand, archduke of Austria and already king of Bohemia, acquired the Hungarian crown.[75]

One of the primary sources of Ottoman information gathering was the Porte's dragomans, who were in daily contact with European diplomats residing in Constantinople. Equally important was their role in assessing incoming intelligence regarding the empire's European rivals. These men were able to provide background information on the history and the present state of these countries. Their sojourns as the Porte's envoys offered them ample opportunity to gather information in the lands of the padishah's foes and allies. In 1519 severe winter conditions and heavy snow forced Yunus dragoman to extend his stay in Venice. Accompanied by Secretary Alvise Sabbadino, Yunus toured the city, spending most of his time in the arsenal and "learning a lot of things." His city tours stretched the Venetian protocol that imposed strict restrictions on the movement of foreign diplomats. His stay and tours in Venice endowed Yunus with valuable experience and contacts that would serve him well in his future career. During his second visit to

Venice in 1522, Yunus's host, Valerio Marcello, presented the dragoman with a map of Dalmatia and Istria. Due to the map's apparent military value, Marcello was investigated by the Council of Ten. In the end, he escaped punishment.[76] Other dragomans also had interest in European maps. In 1573, for instance, Mahmud dragoman ordered from Vienna two copies of Abraham Ortelius's *Theatrum Orbis Terrarum* (Theater of the world), the first true modern atlas, which contained uniform map sheets and supporting text bound together in book format, summarizing the cartographical knowledge of the sixteenth century. Mahmud was surprisingly up to date, as Ortelius first published his work in 1570.[77] Still, the number of these maps in Ottoman possession must have been limited, especially considering their ready availability in European courts.

Intelligence on the Frontiers

In addition to intelligence gathered in Constantinople, Ottoman officials in the frontier provinces also collected valuable information regarding the empire's neighbors. Ottoman *sancak* governors in the Balkans regularly watched Venetian Dalmatia and Habsburg Croatia. During the Venetian-Ottoman war of 1499–1503, the *sancak* governors of Trikala (Tırhala), Morea (Mora), Herzegovina (Hersek), Shkodër (Iskenderiye), and Valona (Avlonya) informed the Porte about Venetian naval and troop movements and plans. The information was based on intercepted Venetian communication and reports of Ottoman spies returning from Venetian lands.[78] The Porte ordered countermeasures, including the strengthening of Ottoman fortresses (Anavarin, Modon, Koron) and increasing their garrisons.[79]

Ottoman *sancak* and provincial governors in Hungary sent information to Constantinople about Vienna's policy regarding Transylvania, Poland-Lithuania, and Ottoman-held Hungary. These reports concerned Habsburg-Safavid diplomatic relations, Habsburg troop concentrations, strengths, and mobilizations, military campaigns, and campaign plans, to name just a few topics.[80] Ottoman governors and officials in Hungary collected valuable intelligence from captured soldiers serving in Habsburg fortresses. In 1547, for instance, the governor of Buda learned important details regarding Habsburg military preparations, Ferdinand I's whereabouts, and his consultations with his brother, Charles V, from a captured soldier who served in Komárom, the main Habsburg garrison in northwestern Hungary and the base of the Habsburg Danube flotilla. The "tongue" (*dil*), as the Ottomans called these captured men, also gave a realistic assessment of the strength of Komárom's garrison: "There is a Beg called Ugnod [Johannes Ungnad] and there are 1,000 gunmen. The . . . castle has thirty-two *şayka* boats on the Danube and there are thirty men in each *şayka*, which comes to nine hundred and sixty people altogether." The information soon arrived at the Porte.[81]

Apart from captured enemy soldiers and agents, Ottoman governors employed their own spies. While governors in eastern Asia Minor and Iraq used Turks, Kurds, and Arabs, those in Hungary relied mainly on Hungarians and Slavs. Ottoman spies regularly traveled between Ottoman-held Hungary and the Habsburg domains. One such spy, called *pribék* in Ottoman and Hungarian documents, confirmed in early 1548 the news extracted from the above-mentioned captured soldier from Komárom.[82] This indicates that the Ottoman authorities tried to authenticate foreign intelligence through multiple sources. Spies in the service of Ottoman *sancak* governors in Hungary were often Hungarians. They shared information with their coreligionists or conationals. In 1584, leaked information of a planned Ottoman attack against a Hungarian fortress ended in an Ottoman defeat because the Ottoman spies informed the warden of the targeted fortress, who thus was able to surprise the attackers.[83]

Still, Ottoman frontier commanders apparently felt comfortable with their knowledge of the enemy. In 1561, when the Habsburgs threatened to send a large army against the *sancak* governor of Székesfehérvár, Hamza Beg, he reminded King Ferdinand I that the Habsburg monarch could not possibly have enough soldiers at his disposal for the undertaking. Had Ferdinand had enough troops, Hamza would have been informed,

> because I have had a spy living in Vienna for six years, whose wife and child are there, a man who can say mass if he wants, or be a scribe, or

a German, a Hungarian, or a good improviser, a soldier, a man with a limp, or someone who walks as steady as you do; a man with a good knowledge of every language.[84]

From their spies and informants, Ottoman authorities along the Ottoman-Habsburg frontier received up-to-date information about the state of the Hungarian garrisons. Shortly after the Habsburg military authorities modernized the Hungarian fortresses around Kanizsa in Transdanubia, Üveys Pasha of Buda (1578–80) prepared a detailed and surprisingly accurate map of the region with all the fortresses and the major river crossings. The pasha sent the map to Constantinople. There, Joachim von Sinzendorf, Habsburg resident ambassador in the Ottoman capital between 1578 and 1581, succeeded in preparing an Italian copy of the map and sent it to Vienna, demonstrating the efficacy of the residents' intelligence gathering.[85]

The Porte's tributary states were also expected to provide the Ottoman government with information about neighboring territories. Ottoman intelligence could rely mainly on the Republic of Ragusa (Dubrovnik), Transylvania, and the Romanian Principalities. Ragusa provided the Porte with information about Venice and the Spanish and Austrian Habsburgs. The Ragusan authorities obtained such information from the republic's elaborate network of agents and informants, several of whom turned out to be double and triple agents. Spanish, Venetian, and French agents residing in or passing through Ragusa were another source.[86] The Transylvanian princes sent news about Vienna's policies regarding the principality and Hungary, planned and actual Habsburg troop movements, and the conditions of Hungarian and Habsburg garrisons.[87] These tributary states, especially Ragusa, also spied on the Ottomans and informed the Habsburgs and Venetians. Between 1551 and 1556 Transylvania was in Habsburg hands. Ferdinand charged his voivodes with gathering intelligence, allocating them an annual sum of 1,000 florins to employ spies.[88]

In addition to spies sent to neighboring countries by Ottoman provincial governors, the central government in Constantinople employed its own agents and spies in Europe. Bayezid II's agents traveled to France and Italy to spy on the sultan's brother, Cem, who had challenged Bayezid's claim to the sultanate and escaped to Europe.[89] The Ottoman government masterfully exploited its renegade dragomans' language skills and knowledge of their original homelands. Yunus Beg, whose Christian relatives were Venetian subjects, visited Venice six times between 1519 and 1542. He visited Venice twice (1519, 1522) before he became chief dragoman in 1525, and at least four times afterward (1529, 1532–33, 1537, 1542). He also traveled to Vienna (1533) and Hungary (1534). His successor in the office of the chief dragoman, the Polish renegade Ibrahim Beg, carried out various diplomatic tasks in Venice (1553, 1566), Poland (1564), Vienna, and France (1568). We have seen that the Porte sent Said Beg (alias Jan Kierdej) to Poland at least eight times between 1531 and 1543. The Ottomans dispatched the Viennese-born Mahmud dragoman to Vienna in 1549, with a report describing the Ottoman victory against the Safavids. Arriving in Vienna on 10 March 1550, Mahmud visited his mother and family, who lived in the city. He also traveled on official business to Transylvania (1550, 1554), Poland-Lithuania (1543, 1554), Venice (1570), Paris (1569), and Prague (1575). When in Vienna in 1550, he gathered important intelligence regarding the negotiations between Ferdinand and Friar George.[90] Mahmud's junior colleague (and perhaps former fellow student in Vienna), the Hungarian renegade Murad, was charged with handling Transylvanian affairs during his legation to Hungary in 1551. He was captured by Gianbattista Castaldo, ransomed by Grand Vizier Rüstem Pasha (after thirty months in captivity), and made an interpreter. In 1554 and 1566 the Porte sent the other Hungarian renegade interpreter, Ferhad, to John Sigismund of Transylvania.[91]

The Porte valued the expertise and contacts of these renegade dragomans and trusted them in missions to their former homelands. Several of the renegades offered information to their former countrymen, but accusations of treason rarely occurred. This happened to Hidayet Agha (alias Markus Scherer), a Hungarian/Saxon renegade from Szeben (Hermannstadt/Sibiu), in Transylvania. He served as a Hungarian and Latin interpreter and secretary under several Ottoman governors of Buda, and dragoman of the Porte. The government sent him to Vienna in 1565 to conclude a peace treaty. However, in the meantime the war party regained control in Constantinople. Upon his return to the Ottoman capital, Hidayet Agha was executed for working for peace between the Habsburgs and the Ottomans.[92]

Apart from official envoys, the Ottoman government also employed agents and spies in foreign countries. Ottoman spies were especially active in Spain, Venice, and the Austrian Habsburg lands. The activities of these agents are revealed by reports of the Venetian *baili* in Constantinople or by the Habsburg resident ambassadors stationed in the Ottoman capital and Venice. During the Ottoman-Venetian war of 1570–73, for instance, the Venetian *bailo* exposed several Ottoman spies operating in Venice. In May 1581, Joachim von Sinzendorf, Habsburg resident ambassador in Constantinople, uncovered an Ottoman spy pretending to be a Swiss merchant.[93] Although some of these spies were double agents, others remained loyal to the Ottomans even at the expense of their lives. Habsburg counterintelligence led to the capture of "a spy of the Turk . . . who called himself Friar Ludovico of Martinengo." Although "he began to confess . . . fearing for his life, he took a dagger from one of the guards and struck himself four times, slitting his throat. Which, by the way, is a great inconvenience since from him we could have learned many things," lamented the Habsburg agent.[94]

News and information from the provinces to the Ottoman capital, whether concerned with domestic or foreign affairs, as well as orders from the center to the provinces, were transmitted by an elaborate courier and communications network, the so-called *ulak* or *menzilhane* system. The Ottoman *ulak* (state courier) and *menzilhane* (posting/ relay station) system was built on a sophisticated road network inherited from Roman and Byzantine times. The Ottoman road network had three main routes (left, center, and right arm/wing), both in Europe and in Asia Minor. Each of the six main routes had several smaller branches radiating from the capital toward Thessaloniki–Athens, Edirne–Sofia–Belgrade–Buda, and the Crimea in Europe, and toward Erzurum–Van–the Caucasus, Diyarbakır–Mosul–Baghdad–Basra, and Aleppo–Damascus–Cairo or Mecca in Asia Minor and the Arab provinces, respectively. Posts established along the road network at intervals

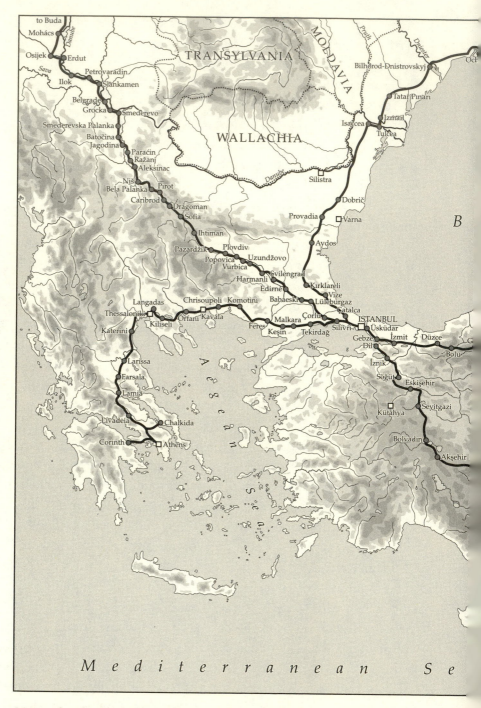

Main roads and postal or halting stations in the Ottoman Empire. (Drawn by Béla Nagy.)

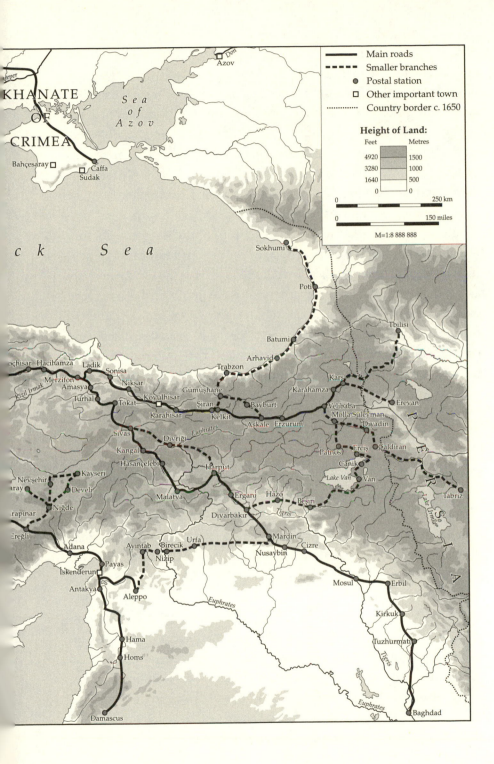

Main roads
Smaller branches
● Postal station
□ Other important town
Country border c. 1650

Height of Land:

Feet	Metres
4920	1500
3280	1000
1640	500
0	0

0 — 250 km
0 — 150 miles

M=1:8 888 888

KHANATE
OF
CRIMEA

Bahçesaray □
Caffa ●
Sudak □

Sea
of
Azov

Dɐn
Azov

ck Sea

Sokhumi ●

Poti ●

Tbilisi ●

Batumi ●
Arhavid ●
Trabzon ●

Kars ●
Karahamza ●
Erevan ●

…oçhisar Hacihamza ● Ladik
Merzifon Sonisa ●
Amasya ● Niksar ●
Turhal ● Tokat Koyulhisar □ Gümüşhane Şiran ● Bayburt ● Velibaba
Kızıl Irmak Karahisar Kelkit Molla Süleyman Diyadin ●
Sivas ● Divriği Aşkale Erzurum ● Patnos Erciş Çaldıran
Kangal ● Euphrates Çanik Van
Hasançelebi ● Harput ● Lake Van
Nevşehir ● Kayseri ●
…aray ● Develi Malatya ● Ergani ● Hazo Beşiri ● Tabrız
…rapinar Niğde ● Diyarbakır Tigris Lake Urmia
Ereğli Urfa Mardin ●
Adana Ayıntab Birecik ● Cizre
İskenderun Nizip Nusaybin ●
Payas □ Mosul ● Erbil ●
Antakya ● Aleppo Kirkuk ●
Hama ● Euphrates Tuzhurmatı ●
Homs ●
Tigris
Euphrates
Damascus ● Baghdad ●

P
E
R
S
I
A

of six to twelve hours' ride (or at distances of between twenty and seventy kilometers), depending on the terrain, provided the couriers with post horses and made sure that reports and orders were transported swiftly and efficiently. While abuses of the system occurred even in the time of Süleyman the Magnificent, the Ottoman communications network played a crucial role in transmitting intelligence, news, and reports of all kinds, as well as imperial orders. The network is rightly regarded as one of the main instruments that held the empire together.[95]

As a result of its information-gathering system and its road and communications network, the Ottoman Empire of the sixteenth century remained an integral part of European politics and information flow. Juan de Vega, the viceroy of Sicily, stated in 1557 that the Ottomans were as quick as the Spanish government in receiving information about events in the Spanish and Italian Mediterranean.[96] A look at Ottoman foreign policy vis-à-vis the Habsburgs under Süleyman the Magnificent corroborates this assumption and suggests that the masters of the imperial council possessed sufficient information on which to base their policies.

However, Ottoman intelligence gathering never reached the efficiency and sophistication of its Venetian, Spanish, or Austrian counterparts. It was too decentralized, relying on the intelligence networks of grand viziers, provincial governors, and grandees. These, in turn, employed agents of questionable expertise and loyalties. Reliance on renegade and Phanariot dragomans of questionable loyalties compounded the deficiencies of Ottoman intelligence gathering. In the long run, the absence of permanent Ottoman embassies and a professional, well-trained diplomatic corps proved to be a significant handicap. Many of the Habsburg residents and the Venetian *baili* in Constantinople were experts in Turkish affairs. Some even learned the language, studied the Ottoman Empire's history, and understood its military strengths and weaknesses. Johann Christoph von Kindsberg, the imperial resident between 1672 and 1678, had a library of more than one hundred books, including histories of the Ottomans, Venice, Spain, France, Transylvania, and the Ottoman-Habsburg wars.[97] The Habsburgs also had an ever-growing professional staff of experts—dragomans, clerks, and spies.

In contrast, the Ottomans never established a central bureau that could have acted as an intelligence headquarters, gathering and analyzing incoming intelligence. This explains why there are no large files of intelligence reports in the Ottoman archives similar to those found in the Venetian, Spanish, and Austrian archives. The fractured and haphazard nature of Ottoman intelligence gathering made it impossible for the Sublime Porte to turn information into systematized knowledge about their enemies' strengths and weaknesses.

PART IV

Frontiers and Wars of Exhaustion

12

Borders and Border Provinces

Survey Books and Sovereignty

Ottoman expansion slowed by the mid-sixteenth century. Power relations on all fronts became balanced, and the Ottoman armies operated at the limits of their radius of action. In this era, the vastness of Ottoman lands forced the government to adopt a defensive policy and to mobilize abundant economic and human resources to defend the empire's borders. Ottoman security strategy called for strengthening the defense capabilities of border provinces and launching imperial campaigns either to restore the status quo or to capture new fortresses and territories, considered vital for securing the empire's borders. Apart from the long and exhausting wars that drained the empire's resources, limited border warfare typified confrontation along the empire's borders. This type of war, known to contemporaries in the Hungarian frontiers as "small war" (Hun. *apró csata*, Ger. *Kleinkrieg*), was characterized by limited operations of local forces, mainly involving cavalry engagements, raids, and smaller sieges. These long and small wars—along with the construction, reinforcement, and maintenance of fortresses, and the remuneration and supply of ever-larger garrisons along an increasingly stretched frontier in Bosnia, Hungary, the northern Black Sea, the Caucasus, and Iraq—affected the very basics of the Ottoman economy, finance, and administration. This chapter, therefore, examines evolving Ottoman boundary conceptions and frontier defense strategies by focusing on the most heavily fortified Ottoman-Habsburg frontier in

Hungary, Croatia, and Bosnia; it also makes comparative observations regarding the empire's other frontier provinces.

The Ottomans had long used border fortresses or limit towns to mark the boundaries of the empire.[1] Ottoman, Latin, Hungarian, and German sources from the sixteenth to the eighteenth centuries all distinguished between the broader military frontier and the border fortresses or limit towns, which demarcated political boundaries. The Ottoman Turkish *kale* or *palanka*, the German *Grenzfestung*, the Latin *castrum* or *castellum*, and the Hungarian *végvár* and *végház* all referred to the various types of fortifications proper. By contrast, the Ottoman Turkish *serhad*, the German *Grenzgebiet* or *Kreis*, the Latin *confinia* or *partes*, and the Hungarian *végvidék* were terms used to describe the broader territory between and beyond the fortresses. Similarly, the Ottoman expression *serhad kaleleri*, "fortresses of the frontier," clarifies the contemporaries' use of the term *serhad*.

The Ottomans considered the lands of their Christian neighbors the "domain of war" (*darü'l-harb*) and the "land of the infidel" (*memleket-i küffar*), where the "enemy of the faith" (*düşman-i din*) lived. Ottoman chroniclers and official documents referred to their polity as the "lands of Islam" (*memalik-i İslamiyye*) or the "well-guarded lands of Islam" (*memalik-i mahrusa-yi İslamiyye*) and its borders as "the borders of Islam" (*hudud-i İslamiyye, sugur-ı İslamiyye*). The troops who defended these borders against enemy attacks were the "soldiers of Islam" (*asker/asakir-i İslam*), "holy warriors/ghazis of Islam" (*guzat-i İslam*), or "ghazis of the frontier" (*serhad gazileri*).[2] The empire's frontiers were called the "victorious frontier" (*serhadd-i mansure*), and Ottoman subjects close to enemy lands perceived themselves as being on the "frontier of Islam" (*serhadd-i İslamiyye*). Strategically important border provinces or fortresses such as Buda, Eger, Belgrade, Zvornik, Bender, and Azak, which guarded the empire against the Habsburgs and Muscovites/Russians, were known as the "strong rampart/bulwark of Islam" (*sedd-i sedid-i İslam, sedd-i sedid-i İslamiyye*) or the "strong/firm rampart of the frontiers of Islam" (*sugur-ı İslamiyyenin sedd-i sedidi*).[3] The Ottomans also designated Belgrade the "house of the holy war" (*darü'l-cihad*), similar to Tripoli in North Africa. In the last quarter of the seventeenth century,

Ottoman Kamaniçe (the former Polish fortress of Kamieniec Podolski) joined these fortresses as "house of the holy war," along with Temesvár and Banjaluka in the early eighteenth century. Temesvár was also called the "rampart of the frontiers of Islam" (*sedd-i sugur-ı İslamiyye*). Ochakiv (Özü) was known as "the strong rampart of the victorious frontier" (*sedd-i serhadd-i mansure*). After 1718, following the loss of Belgrade, acknowledged in the Treaty of Passarowitz, Vidin had become the new "house of the holy war and holy warriors" (*darü'l-cihad ve'l mücahidin*).[4] Fortresses and provinces along the empire's eastern and southern frontiers assumed similar significance. The fortress of Van on the frontier with Shiite Safavid Persia was known from the time of Süleyman the Magnificent as the "strong rampart of the [Sunni Islamic] faith" (*sedd-i iman*). Erzurum was referred to as "the limit of the frontier of Persia" (*intiha-yi serhadd-i Acem*), whereas the province of Yemen was called "firm rampart of Mecca" (*sedd-i sedid-i Mekke-i Mükerreme*).[5]

Despite attempts to demarcate sections of the empire's borders, Ottoman border areas were often vaguely defined, and intentionally so, for their expansion and fluidity remained essential features, as did cross-border raids and ransom slavery. Military raids proved an effective strategy to extend Ottoman taxation into enemy territory, and thus enlarge the realms of the House of Osman. In the sixteenth and seventeenth centuries, Ottoman soldiers habitually forced villages that were legally under Habsburg rule to pay at least a nominal lump sum to the Ottomans. The Ottomans also recorded such villages in their revenue surveys, indicating that they considered them part of the padishah's domains. This idea, which privileged jurisdiction and sovereignty over subjects rather than over a territory delineated by physical border markers, was also familiar to early modern Europeans, and created a confusing and overlapping jurisdictional geography.[6]

In the sixteenth century, the Ottomans regarded the first revenue surveys of the newly conquered Hungarian lands, prepared by Çandarlızade Halil Beg, as a primary document regarding border disputes.[7] Appointed in 1545 to survey the revenues of the *sancaks* of Mohács and Székesfehérvár, Halil Beg in the following years prepared the revenue registers of numerous *sancaks* in the province of Buda.[8] The aim of these surveys was to provide the government with realistic estimates regarding the possible revenues of every single locality of the surveyed lands. The government then used these registers to determine which of the surveyed villages and towns were to be distributed as *timars* to soldiers and their commanders or be kept as crown lands—that is, *hass* estates of the padishah.

Soon after their completion, Halil Beg's survey books became essential documents because the Ottomans regarded every settlement listed in them as theirs and demanded taxes from them. The pasha of Buda was already using these surveys in 1548 to extort taxes from villages that had not previously paid taxes to the Ottomans. In 1550, the Habsburg resident in Constantinople, Giovanni Maria Malvezzi, reported that the grand vizier supported the Ottomans' claim to Szolnok and Vál by showing him "a book of incomes that was compiled before the truce" of 1547, an apparent reference to Halil Beg's survey registers.[9] Ottoman soldiers and officeholders, too, used Halil's survey books to claim villages and towns for themselves.[10]

Halil Beg's defter played an important role during peace negotiations leading to the treaties of 1562 and 1568. According to Stephan Gerlach—chaplain-adviser and member of the Habsburg delegation that negotiated the peace of 1568—during the talks in Constantinople, the Ottomans showed the Habsburg envoys a book. In the book,

> the Turks inscribed several villages, market towns, and castles that lay some miles in His Majesty's territories, which the Turks had never conquered. Still, [the Turks] wanted that all those towns, market towns, and villages that had been recorded in that book pay taxes to them so that their soldiers can be paid from these revenues. . . . If they [the Habsburgs] did not accept what was in that book, the peace would be void. . . . Therefore, the cursed author of this book—the book is known as Halil Beg's register—conquered more territory with his pen than [the Ottoman soldiers] with their sword. The Turks would in no way deviate from this book. All the villages and towns inscribed in the book had to pay taxes.[11]

During these negotiations, the Ottomans suggested that Halil Beg's defter be used to settle the status of those subjects who lived between the

Ottoman and Habsburg fortresses, paying taxes to both sides. Using border markers, they wanted to demarcate the border as precisely as possible and distribute the subjects between the parties. The envoys of Emperor Maximilian II rejected the offer, citing their ignorance of Halil's registers, and suggested instead that a bilateral border commission establish the precise border, following the promulgation of the treaty.[12]

In the eyes of the Ottomans, *tahrir* registers in general remained the basis for settling border disputes. Precisely on these grounds, Üveys Pasha of Buda demanded in 1579 from Archduke Ernst that sixty-seven villages listed in the Ottoman tax registers as belonging to the *sancak* of Szolnok pay their taxes to the Ottoman side. In his letter to the archduke, Üveys complained that the villages in question (which had 1,161 taxpaying households) stopped paying their taxes after the Habsburgs erected the castle of Kálló, although in the past they had duly paid their taxes to their *sipahi* and the padishah. The pasha, who attached the list of the villages in question to his letter, asked the archduke to order the fortress commander of Kálló, who obstructed the payment of taxes, to let the said villages pay their taxes to the Ottoman side.[13] Unable to challenge the policy on the ground, Habsburg and Hungarian authorities eventually accepted the *tahrir* registers as basic documents reflecting the spatial claims of Ottoman taxation and sovereignty.[14] The Transylvanian princes also used Halil Beg's survey books as a basis to protect their domains from Ottoman taxation. In 1591, for instance, Prince Sigismund Rákóczi complained to Sultan Murad III that the new surveyor of the province of Temesvár was adding villages to his survey book that had from ancient times belonged to Transylvania and had not been listed in Halil Beg's defter. Rákóczi therefore requested the sultan to order the governors-general in Buda and Temesvár to respect Halil Beg's defter, which Murad III did.[15] Ottoman taxation was financially essential in maintaining Ottoman rule in the conquered lands. The livelihood of the Ottoman provincial cavalrymen—and from the latter part of the sixteenth century, increasingly that of garrison soldiers paid via collective *timars*—depended on these sources of revenue. As Sinan Pasha of Buda wrote to Archduke Ernst in 1591, these were villages "from where the *sipahis* got their horse, weapon, cloth, and food."[16] This is why the pashas of Buda argued so vehemently for all villagers who were re-corded in the Ottoman survey and tax registers to duly pay their taxes.[17]

Border Demarcations

While the Ottomans lacked the cartographic mapping of the padishah's domains, imperial orders sent to provincial governors give a good sense of what members of the Ottoman political elite considered the empire's border provinces to be at any given moment. In documents from the mid-sixteenth century, the provinces of Buda, Temesvár, and after 1580 Bosnia (Bosna) in Europe consistently appear as provinces on the frontier, as do Erzurum, Diyarbakır, Kars, Van in Asia Minor, Damascus in Syria, Shahrizor, Baghdad, and Basra in Iraq, and Lahsa in present-day Kuwait. Despite ambiguities regarding Ottoman borders, the widespread view that the Ottomans did not accept border demarcations before the Treaty of Karlowitz is in need of revision.[18] In fact, the Ottomans negotiated linear borders with Venice and Moldavia in the late fifteenth century, and with the Austrian Habsburgs, Poland-Lithuania, and the Safavids in the sixteenth and seventeenth centuries.[19] The technical terms for defining boundaries and demarcating borders were known in Ottoman documents as *kat-i sınır* and *tayin-i sınır*—that is, to appoint, to mark out, or to define a boundary. The Ottomans also widely used the term *hududname* or *sınırname*, meaning "documents containing the descriptions of boundaries." Domestically, such documents demarcated the boundaries of villages belonging to religious endowments, to prevent members of the provincial cavalry corps remunerated via *timar* prebends in the vicinity from interfering with them. Internationally, these documents marked the boundaries between the domains of the Ottoman padishah and those of his neighbors.[20]

An early Ottoman border demarcation document was prepared between Venice and the Ottoman Empire after the Venetian-Ottoman treaty of 1479, which concluded the war of 1463–79. For centuries, the Republic of Venice and the Ottoman Empire shared a long frontier along the Dalmatian and Albanian coasts, the Adriatic and Ionian Seas, the Peloponnese, the Sea of Create, the Aegean Sea, and the eastern

Mediterranean. Along this vast frontier, the two states strove to negotiate reciprocal raids and conquests, mark and administer their respective lands and peoples, foster trade, and control the movements of peoples and disease. All these tasks required the demarcation of lines or areas lying between the two states, an activity usually initiated by the republic but accepted by the Ottomans. To delineate the boundaries after the war of 1463–79, Sultan Mehmed II sent his emissary, Halil Beg, to Albania and the Morea. The sultan's instructions to his emissary—which were communicated to the Venetians in the form of a royal document (*name-i hümayun*) written in Greek—were precise: lands conquered by the sultan's armies must remain in Ottoman hands, even if this meant disregarding natural borders such as the Bojana River near Shkodër. This document is one of the first known examples in which the principle of *uti possidetis* was used to demarcate borders. It meant that each party kept whatever territory it possessed at the conclusion of hostilities. This principle continued to guide the parties in the centuries to come. While the borderline satisfied the Venetians in Albania, the borders in the Morea remained contested. Therefore, the parties commissioned two official representatives, an Ottoman and a Venetian, to jointly establish the border in the Morea upon physical inspection. Negotiations continued in the Ottoman capital between the sultan and the Venetian *bailo*, after which Mehmed II unilaterally issued a *sınırname* describing the established border.[21] The Venetian ambassador in Constantinople and the orator received the document in 1481. In the *ahdname* of 1482, Mehmed II's successor, Sultan Bayezid II, also accepted the borders as described in his father's *sınırname*.[22] Bayezid II later adjusted the borders, as did Süleyman the Magnificent in the district of Klis.

The Ottomans justified the declaration of war against the Republic of Venice in February 1570 with the assertion that the Venetians built castles and villages beyond the borderlines established during the reign of Sultans Mehmed II, Bayezid II, and Süleyman I.[23] The Ottoman conquests in the Cyprus war resulted in another demarcation of the border between Venice and the Ottoman Empire in Dalmatia. The Venetian-Ottoman treaty of 1573 in principle restored the boundaries of both Ottoman and Venetian possessions in Albania and Dalmatia as they were before the war, and obliged the Ottomans to give back all conquered territories to Venice. However, the Bosnian *sancak* governor Sokollu Ferhad demarcated the border unilaterally, leaving only a thin coastal strip in Dalmatia in Venetian hands, including the towns of Novigrad, Nin, Zadar, Šibenik, Trogir, Split, and Kotor. Several fortresses remained in Ottoman hands. The border between the Venetian possessions and the Ottoman *sancaks* of Bosnia and Klis was revised in 1576, though without significant changes. This time, the Ottoman border commission consisted of Ferhad and the *sancak* governor of Klis, Mustafa, the jurisconsult and judge of Sarajevo, and the judge of Skradin. Ambassador Francesco Soranzo represented the Venetians. This border established by the commission remained relatively stable until the end of the seventeenth century, although the parties disputed the border from time to time. Such disagreements occasionally led to border revisions, like that in 1626, conducted by the Venetian dragoman. One of the complaints was that the border of 1576 left the Venetian coastal communities with little territory to produce food, forcing them to import food from the Ottoman domains.[24]

As mentioned, after the Ottoman-Moldavian treaty in April 1486, the parties demarcated the border between the two states in a separate "boundary document" (*sınırname*).[25] Similarly, the Ottoman-Hungarian treaties of 1503 and 1519 listed more than fifty and seventy fortresses and forts, respectively, which the Ottomans and Hungarians possessed, thus defining the boundaries and the respective domains of the contracting monarchs.[26] In the mid-sixteenth century (1538–44), attempts were made to demarcate the border between Poland-Lithuania and the Ottoman Empire. But these attempts failed, because the appointed commissioners never met. The parties demarcated the borders only in 1633. Despite the lack of delimited borders before 1633, the Poles and Ottomans enjoyed relatively peaceful relations, except for the short Polish-Ottoman war of 1620–21. Both parties tacitly accepted that the border ran along the Dniester, Jahorlyk, and Kodyma Rivers, the latter of which defined the southern border of the Commonwealth.[27] The borders changed with the Ottoman conquest of Kamieniec Podolski in 1672. However, with the outbreak of a new Polish-Ottoman war that lasted until 1676, Polish and Ottoman commissioners demarcated the border only in 1680.[28]

Ferdinand I also tried to establish defined borders between his and Süleyman's domains in Hungary. He asked for fixed borders thirteen times before 1546, but the Ottomans rejected this request each time. Yet the Ottomans did not oppose fixed borders as a principle. During the negotiations that led to the treaty of 1562, Grand Vizier Semiz Ali Pasha wanted to settle the issue of common villages that paid taxes to both sides in Hungary by dividing them between the parties and establishing a fixed boundary.[29] As mentioned, after the conquest of Szigetvár and Gyula in 1566—the largest extent of Ottoman rule in Hungary up to that point, encompassing some one hundred thousand square kilometers—the Ottomans proposed to their Habsburg counterparts that the parties establish a fixed border between their respective possessions using boundary stones. The border had to be based on previous Ottoman revenue surveys. Grand Vizier Sokollu Mehmed Pasha rejected the idea that the padishah's subjects pay taxes to the Habsburgs and the Hungarians, suggesting that the parties demarcate the borders. Mehmed Pasha also wanted to destroy Tata and Veszprém and burn the lands between the Ottoman and Habsburg fortresses, thus creating a no-man's-land. However, this time the Habsburg authorities in Vienna rejected the idea of demarcated borders.[30]

By establishing delimited borders, the Ottomans intended to end Hungarian taxation in Ottoman-ruled areas. In 1567, the Porte sent numerous orders to its *sancak* and provincial governors, charging them with stopping Hungarian taxation.[31] Habsburg rejection of fixed borders indicated that by this time the Viennese government had realized both the legal and financial advantages of extending Habsburg and Hungarian taxation and jurisdiction into territories beyond the Ottoman border forts, a policy that demarcated borders would have made impossible. This also explains why the Viennese government refused the scorched-earth tactics—that is, destroying villages between the Ottoman and Habsburg fortresses. Lazarus Freiherr von Schwendi, captain-general in Upper Hungary, and some Hungarian fortress captains argued for such tactics in the 1560s. They proposed that the Habsburgs burn the environs of Ottoman fortresses to hinder Ottoman military operations. Schwendi repeated his suggestion a decade later at the military conference in Vienna in 1577, and Hans Rueber von Püchsendorf— Schwendi's disciple and successor as captain-general of Upper Hungary from 1568 to 1584—seconded his opinion. However, the Viennese government rejected their proposal.[32]

Ottoman-Habsburg truce agreements and peace treaties, in general, did not specify the borders but tried to resolve the problem of sovereignty over the taxpaying population. The issue first appeared during the negotiations that led to the treaty of 1547. In it, the parties acknowledged each other's right to the territories in their de facto possession at the time of the treaty. However, the Ottomans insisted that Hungary belonged to Süleyman, for he had conquered it by his sword. Grand Vizier Ibrahim Pasha had made this clear in 1528 to King Ferdinand I's envoys by saying that "wherever the hoof of the Sultan's horse has trod, there the land belongs to him."[33] Indeed, Ferdinand had to pay the annual tribute of 30,000 Hungarian ducats or florins to Süleyman in exchange for the territories (and their taxes) under his rule in Hungary.[34]

As in the case of Venetian-Ottoman relations, standard practice in Ottoman-Habsburg peace negotiations dictated that the demarcation of the border be left to border commissions, which were to draw the border in the months after the signing of the treaty. Military commanders and border governors habitually headed such commissions, and this practice of border negotiation is yet another example of how the padishah and his grand vizier delegated authority to border governors. The latter carried out the job either personally or via their proxies, with the help of "knowledgeable" local people. This is how the Habsburg-Ottoman treaties of 1562 and 1564 under Süleyman dealt with the issue of borders.[35] In a letter sent to Emperor Maximilian in 1565, Süleyman ordered that for the establishment of the border (*tayin-i sınır*) both parties appoint "useful and reliable people."[36] This practice continued with subsequent peace treaties, such as those of Edirne (1568), Zsitvatorok (1606), and Gyarmat (1625). The latter two treaties ruled that the issue of disputed villages situated in southwestern Hungary and Croatia, in the vicinity of the newly conquered fortress of Kanizsa, fell under the jurisdiction of such commissions.[37] Ottoman provincial and *sancak* governors knew well where the borders of their respective provinces and subprovinces were. Therefore, they continually protested against Hungarian and Transylvanian interference and taxation beyond these borders. In 1671, for instance, the governor of Temesvár protested to the Ottoman-vassal prince of Transylvania, Michael Apafi (r. 1661–90) that the Transylvanians did not respect the borders of the district of Karánsebes, which followed the Marga River (the left tributary of the Bistra River in the Banat).[38]

The parties knew well how difficult it was to maintain peace "in a country so vast and divided." Therefore, to settle anticipated border disputes, the parties decided to establish a permanent joint border commission after the conclusion of the treaty in 1568. The commission included an equal number of delegates from both parties. The members had to be "honest, diligent, peace- and truth-loving people, who knew the situation on the frontier well." If this joint commission failed to settle the disputes, they had to refer the issue to the governor-general of Buda and the Habsburg captain-general. If, however, even they could not solve the matter, it was turned over to the Ottoman and Habsburg emperors (paragraph 18 of the Treaty of Edirne, 1568). Indeed, such mechanisms settled most border disputes and maintained peace for the next quarter century, until the outbreak of the Long War of 1593–1606.

Demarcation of the border also existed along the empire's eastern frontiers. However, the loyalty of the Kurdish and Turkmen tribes mattered more than demarcated borders, for with the shift of their loyalties whole areas changed sides, as we saw concerning the province of Shahrizor. The parties first demarcated the border after the Peace of Amasya in 1555, which served as a reference for later treaties and border demarcations such as those in 1611–12 and 1639. On the other hand, the Treaty of Constantinople in 1590, which concluded the Safavid-Ottoman war of 1578–90, allowed the Ottomans to keep their recent conquests, including most of the southern Caucasus and the former Safavid capital Tabriz. The five-member Safavid delegation accepted the territorial claims. The Ottoman *ahdname* listed the territories by name. However, to more precisely delineate the new border, the Ottoman governor of Erevan and his associates, along with the Safavid emissaries, traveled to the border from the Ottoman capital. Border demarcation lasted into the fall of 1592. Starting with the province of Tabriz, the joint border commission demarcated the borders without any apparent problems, consulting elderly locals and using border markers. The parties also agreed in principle on the Shahrizor-Baghdad border, listing the respective territories in a joint protocol, although numerous place-names were erroneously registered in the document. But demarcating the borders around Nahavand proved more difficult and led to protracted correspondence between the parties. During the demarcation, the commission not only marked the border on the ground, using border markers, but also compiled a detailed register listing all the important place-names. The register then had to be authenticated by both parties using their respective seals and sent to the Ottoman capital.[39] The border was demarcated again in 1639, leaving Kars, Ahıska, Shahrizor, Baghdad, and Basra in Ottoman hands. This demarcation served as a reference for later border delimitations.[40]

Attempts to demarcate sovereignty existed even at sea. In principle, most Europeans accepted the Roman law that no polity controlled the open seas. Mehmed II's famous chief jurisconsult, Molla Hüsrev, seconded this opinion by noting that the sea belonged neither to the "domain of war" nor to the "domain of Islam," for lines in the sea could not be drawn. However, many powers ignored these notions in practice. Venice, for instance, considered the Adriatic its own gulf, and the Ottomans adopted the phrase *Venedik Körfezi*, that is, "the Gulf of Venice," although they used it more narrowly than the Venetians. In an agreement with the Knights of Saint John of Rhodes, Sultan Bayezid II accepted the delimitation of the sea, and both the Christian privateers and the Muslim sea corsairs (*levend*) respected the agreement. After the Ottoman conquest of Crete, the Venetian-Ottoman agreement included the issue of jurisdiction over coastal waters. Several small islands along the waters within cannon-shot range remained in Venetian possession. The idea of territorial waters, which recognized jurisdiction over a portion of sea waters adjacent to coastal states and limited it to the distance of cannon-shot range from the coast, reflected an emerging practice in

Europe, which went back to the dispute sparked by the publication of Hugo Grotius's *Mare Liberum* (*The Free Seas*) in 1609.[41] However, the notion of coastal waters existed in the Ottoman Empire much earlier. An imperial decree from 1560 made the captain of the Ottoman fortress of Preveza responsible for an attack by the Muslim sea corsairs against Ragusan merchants, who were carrying wheat from the empire to the republic, because the attack occurred within cannon-shot range of the castle.[42] Later, during the Seven Years' War, the French insisted that "the shores of [the lands of] Islam should in all ways be secure and spared from any dispute or conflict" (that is, Ottoman territorial waters should remain neutral). This position reflected French rather than Ottoman interests, as the French wanted to protect themselves against English privateering in Ottoman territorial waters.[43]

Another attempt to demarcate sovereignty at sea emerged during the first Portuguese-Ottoman peace negotiations in the early 1540s. Despite recurring Portuguese incursions into the Red Sea, by the 1540s the Porte considered the Red Sea an Ottoman sea and tried to keep the Portuguese out of it. During the peace negotiations in 1540–44, the Portuguese insisted that they be able to freely trade in the Red Sea port of Jeddah. They also demanded that the Ottomans not build a fleet with which they could sail to the Indian Ocean. Sultan Süleyman rejected these demands. In his counteroffer in January 1541, the padishah proposed that the parties demarcate their respective spheres of influence along the line drawn from Shihr through Aden to Zayla, and that neither empire's war fleets cross this line of demarcation. The padishah repeated his demands in May 1542, stating that one of the conditions of the peace was that no Portuguese ship visit Shihr and Aden on the southern Yemeni coast, Zabid, Jeddah, and Suakin in the Red Sea, or any other port belonging to the Ottoman province of Habeş.[44]

The Ottomans readily ceded territories to their Venetian, Hungarian, and Habsburg neighbors or exchanged villages with them when circumstances dictated such expediencies. They did this despite the widespread belief that the Ottomans could not give up any land on which the sultan's horse stepped, an idea frequently voiced by Ottoman officials during peace negotiations. The Ottomans ceded territories to the

Venetians in 1531, 1558, and 1559.[45] Articles 6 and 7 of the Habsburg-Ottoman Treaty of Edirne (1568) discussed the issue of territories between "the ancient borders of Transylvania," which the Ottomans acknowledged, and the Tisza River, which had been disputed by John Sigismund of Transylvania (an Ottoman vassal) and Emperor Maximilian II. The treaty left both parties in the possession of their respective castles and towns, but allowed for future swaps of territories to minimize the possibility of territorial disputes and violations of the treaty.[46] Perennial disputes and raids ensued since both parties retained castles, towns, villages, and subjects in territories of the other party. John Sigismund and Emperor Maximilian II finally settled the issues in 1570 in the Treaty of Speyer.[47] The Ottomans closely followed these disputes and knew well where the borders between their vassal Transylvania and Habsburg-ruled Hungary were.[48]

The Ottomans, Venetians, and Habsburgs produced one of the most detailed demarcations of political borders after the Treaty of Karlowitz in 1699. In November 1698, with winter arriving with snow and icy wind, the plenipotentiaries agreed that after they determined the general outlines of the new frontier, the details should be left to commissioners. As the Ottoman chief dragoman, Mavracordato, put it: "The best and obvious solution is to refer the details of the proposed 'artificial' boundaries to mature, expert and sensible men who—proceeding quite differently from people here at the condference—can erect landmarks on the spot, and make the boundary clear and unmistakable. This is the old expedient of our predecessors, and we should pay attention to the precedent."[49] Commissioners, cartographers, and military engineers demarcated these borders in the months and years after the conclusion of the treaty.[50] While it was the most detailed border demarcation made along the Triplex Confinium, it did not represent "the first of its kind in early modern European history."[51] Empires and states, both in Europe and in Asia, have long been familiar with such demarcations. In addition to the examples examined above, one can point to the border established between Russia and China at the Treaty of Nerchinsk (1689) along the Argun River. The border was demarcated by stone markers, and the text of the treaty was inscribed on a stele in Russian, Chinese, Manchu,

Mongol, and Latin.[52] From an Ottoman perspective, the Treaty of Karlowitz should be considered only one stage, admittedly important, rather than a major turning point in the evolving Ottoman boundary conceptions and policies from frontiers to delimited borders. The importance of Karlowitz lay not in the delimitation of the border but in the fact that the Ottomans accepted, albeit reluctantly, European concepts of sovereignty and the territorial integrity of their neighbors.

Geography and Border Defense

As in other parts of the world, border defense systems along the Ottoman-Hungarian/Habsburg frontier often followed major rivers, utilizing river systems, marshlands, mountains, and other natural defensive features offered by the land's geography. The Danube played a crucial role as a natural border of empires since Roman times. As we have seen, the medieval Hungarian kingdom (1000–1526) built its anti-Ottoman defense system along the Danube and Sava Rivers. This defense line successfully halted Ottoman advance for 150 years, until it collapsed in the 1520s, when Süleyman's forces captured Belgrade (1521), Zemun (1521), Orşova, (1522), and Severin (1524).

Ottoman authorities studied the defense lines of the countries they planned to conquer. During their 1541 Hungarian campaign, which ended with the capture of Buda, the capital of the medieval Kingdom of Hungary, the Ottomans prepared a "plan of conquest" that listed strategically important Hungarian castles whose capture seemed especially warranted. The document listed the forts according to their owners, the most prominent aristocrats and politicians of Hungary. It also gave the locations of the castles, accompanied by short comments regarding their immediate past. An unknown author summarized the importance of the castles of Friar George, the most influential politician in eastern Hungary, as follows:

In Transylvania [there is] the castle called Várad, which was the seat of several kings and brave barons. As long as this castle is not in hand, Transylvania cannot be occupied. The fortress called Kassa is towards

Poland. It belongs to Buda and has several castles, villages and towns galore, and many gold and silver mines. When it is occupied, the region stretching as far as Poland, as well as the dominions of Peter Perényi (d. 1548) and the bans Bebek [the Bebek brothers, Emeric and Francis (d. 1558)] and Gáspár Serédy (d. 1553) will be occupied.[53]

The security of Ottoman territories also concerned military strategists. Listing the garrisons at the hand of Peter Petrović, the document made the following comment: "Until the fortresses called Lippa, Temesvár, Becskerek and Becse have been taken, the province of Srem will not be free from evildoers. It has several fortresses, towns and villages. It is a genuine Serbian province, a refuge for trouble-makers escaping from Smederevo and the Srem, [who] pillage our other provinces."[54] Ten years later, the Ottomans captured all these garrisons save for Kassa.

By the 1550s, the Ottomans controlled the Danube as far as Esztergom. Most of the former Hungarian castles between the Danube and Lake Balaton, the forts in the Nógrád Mountains north of Ottoman Buda, and all the major castles along the Tisza River and its tributaries in the eastern parts of the country were in Ottoman hands. The Ottoman authorities repaired, strengthened, and rebuilt the captured castles when they thought them suitable for defense, and demolished those they considered useless.

The majority of Ottoman castles and forts in Hungary were captured from the Hungarians. The Ottomans did build new forts and altered the inherited ones when their defense strategy so required. Moreover, their conquests and the organization of new provinces and subprovinces show that they took environmental and strategic issues into consideration. The establishment of a defensive ring of forts around Buda, the administrative and logistical center of the first Ottoman province in Hungary by the same name, illustrates this strategic thinking. Esztergom stood as the most important fortress guarding Buda from Hungarian and Habsburg attacks from the west. Since it also controlled both river and overland communication routes, Esztergom received special attention from the Ottoman authorities. They reinforced Esztergom proper by building several new bastions both in the fortress and in the

"Lower Castle" and a gunpowder work, and erected two new forts, mainly palisades (known as *parkan* in Ottoman Turkish and *parkány* in Hungarian): Szent Tamás-hegy (Turkish: Tepedelen), right next to Esztergom, and Párkány (Turkish: Ciğirdelen), on the other side of the Danube.[55] In the Danube bend, Visegrád and Vác guarded Buda from the north/northwest, whereas Érd and Korkmaz, at the southern tip of Csepel Island near Adony, secured the city from the south. From Vác, the protective ring defending Buda from the north followed the line of the Nógrád Mountains, where most of the Hungarian castles, such as Drégely, Szécsény, Hollókő, and Buják, were captured in 1552. South of Buják, the Ottomans built a new fort at Hatvan (1544) and made it the center of a newly established *sancak.* The fort controlled both the Zagyva River, a tributary of the Tisza, and the royal route (*via regia*) coming from Buda. The capture of Siklós, Pécs, and Fehérvár in Transdanubia in 1543 helped connect Buda with Ottoman-held Srem. All these forts were reinforced and became *sancak* centers. The conquest of Ozora, Tamási, and Simontornya in 1545 secured Ottoman communication and transport along the right bank of the Danube.[56]

The 1551–52 campaigns are significant because several of the forts occupied during these campaigns secured important river routes and crossings. As we have seen, the Ottomans conquered Becse on the Tisza, Becskerek on the Béga River, Csanád, Lippa, and Arad on the Maros River, and Temesvár, the region's most important fortress, on the Temes River. They also captured Szolnok, at the confluence of the Tisza and Zagyva Rivers. The conquests of 1551–52 reflected the Ottomans' understanding of the region's geography. The strategic significance of these forts—already noted in the "conquest plan" of 1541—is illustrated by the fact that in 1522 Temesvár became the center of the second Ottoman province in Hungary. Becse-Becskerek, Csanád, Arad, and Lippa all became *sancak* centers in the new province. The Ottomans also organized a new *sancak* around Szolnok and attached it to the province of Buda. In 1554, Ottoman officials promptly completed the first revenue surveys of the *sancaks* of the Temesvár province, mapping all collectable revenues.[57]

The Ottomans used their forts in Hungary for both defensive and offensive purposes. During the long Habsburg-Ottoman war at the turn of the century (1593–1606), the Ottomans again endeavored to capture Vienna. By occupying Veszprém, Palota, Tata, Győr, Szentmárton (Pannonhalma), Pápa, and Tihany they came very close to reaching their goal. However, in the second phase of the war, the Ottomans lost all their recent conquests, except for Palota, in the counterattacks of the Habsburg and Hungarian forces. Still, by occupying Eger (1596) and Kanizsa (1600), they further expanded the padishah's domains in Hungary. Additional significant border changes took place only in the middle of the seventeenth century. The conquest of Várad (1660), the center of Hungarian Partium, ceded control of the Sebes-Körös River, and thus of Transylvania. The occupation of Érsekújvár (1663) eliminated the key fortress and the center of Habsburg defense in Lower Hungary, and brought Ottoman rule dangerously close to the monarchy's and empire's capital city, Vienna. As the unsuccessful Habsburg siege of Buda in 1684 proved, Ottoman Uyvar also significantly increased the protection of Ottoman Buda; to conquer Ottoman Buda in 1686, the Habsburgs first had to capture Ottoman Uyvar the previous year.

Both the Hungarians and the Ottomans utilized the waterways of their common frontier to strengthen their defense capabilities by creating protective marshes around their fortifications. On plain lands, protection was secured by building castles in river estuaries and river bends or by routing water via canals from nearby rivers, streams, or marshes into ditches dug around the castles. Such waters protected the riverside and "swamp forts" of Győr, Tokaj, Szolnok, Gyula, Temesvár, Szigetvár, Kaposvár, Ecsed, and Tata. To contemporaries, many of these forts appeared as strong structures on islands, surrounded by lakes and marshes.

The Ottoman geographer Behram Dimişki (d. 1690/91) commented on these features: "Temesvár had deep moats, and therefore looked like an island. Its surroundings were inaccessible reed and marshes. Behind its inner castle there was a lake, formed out of the waters of the Temes River." He had similar comments on Becskerek, "which could be seen from Belgrade, and after crossing the Danube could be reached in a day. It stood in the Temes River on an island," surrounded by vast bogs. Szolnok, at the confluence of the Tisza and Zagyva Rivers, and "about an hour from the Belgrade-Eger route, had a strong castle, built on 3,600 pillars."

It was surrounded by the Zagyva, "which became a large lake to the south of the castle." Kanizsa was "enclosed by the Zákány River, which branches into two. The area around the castle is impassable marshland on every side for a *mil* [about three kilometers]." Szigetvár "is a strong castle, whose surroundings are vast waters and marshes. This castle is a double fortress in the middle of a large lake. Traffic between its two parts is restricted to a single bridge. . . . It is an imposing fortress, which forms a triangle with Buda and Esztergom."[58] Contemporary Ottoman and European topographical illustrations of Szigetvár and other "swamp forts" were in accord with these descriptions, and the maps prepared by Luigi Ferdinando Marsigli at the end of the seventeenth and the beginning of the eighteenth centuries provide vivid illustrations of the marshlands of Hungary and the Habsburg-Ottoman frontier.

Border Provinces and Administrative Strategies

In general texts, apart from the vassal or client states not integrated into the empire, differences between the provinces get only cursory attention, and only in the context of the so-called *timarlı* and *salyaneli* provinces. In the *timarlı* provinces, agricultural revenues in the form of *timars* were assigned to cavalrymen (*sipahi*), the backbone of the Ottoman provincial army. Ottoman provinces in Europe and Asia Minor and some Arab territories are said to have belonged to this first category. In more remote regions in the Maghrib and the Middle East— which lay outside the main direction of Ottoman advance—political, military, and economic factors tended to favor a different type of revenue management. Tax revenues in these regions were not distributed as *timars* but were instead collected with the help of tax farmers (*mültezim*). Provincial governors then used the collected revenue to pay themselves, the *sancak* governors, and troops under their command. If his province produced a surplus, the governor submitted the money— known as *hazine* (treasury) or *irsaliye* ("that was sent/transmitted")— to the imperial treasury in the capital. Such provinces were known as *salyaneli* after the governor-general's annual salary (*salyane*). The geographical distribution of the *salyaneli* provinces—Egypt, Yemen, Habeş

(Abyssinia), Basra (southern Iraq), Lahsa (al-Hasa, present-day Kuwait), Baghdad (northern Iraq), Trablus-i Garb (northern parts of present-day Libya), Tunis, and Cezayir-i Garb (the coastal strip of Algeria)—illustrates the political and economic pressure that led to their formation.[59] While it is useful to differentiate between the provinces on the basis of revenue management, such a model fails to show the differences between the empire's core areas and frontier provinces.

At first glance, the Ottomans seem to have introduced the same provincial administrative system in their Danubian frontier that they used in the empire's core provinces. If one looks at the imperial decrees sent from Constantinople to the provinces during the mid-sixteenth century, the impression gained is one of an Ottoman central government whose will prevailed even in the most remote frontier areas. Provincial revenue surveys also suggest uniform and efficient administrative and taxation systems. However, Ottoman administrative strategies differed significantly in the core and frontier provinces. The minutes of local judicial courts, complaints of provincial authorities, and the communication between the central and local authorities present a different picture and demonstrate the limits of Ottoman centralization in the frontier provinces. In these sources, local and central governments appear to have enjoyed a far more complex and less one-sided relationship than those put forward by historians in the past.[60]

Ottoman Hungary consisted of six long-standing provinces: Buda (1541–1686), Temesvár (1552–1716), Eger (1596–1687), Kanizsa (1600–1690), Várad (1660–92), and Újvár (1663–85).[61] Initially, the province of Buda possessed little hinterland. Consequently, the *sancaks* of Smederevo, Kruševac, Vulčitrn, Zvornik, and Požega—all of which lay to the south of the Drava River and at a great distance from Buda—came under the authority of the pasha of Buda. With the growth of Hungarian territory under Ottoman rule, Buda annexed more *sancaks*. The province had ten *sancaks* in 1545, fifteen in 1555, and twenty in 1568.[62] Only four of them lay south of the Drava River. To create new provinces in Hungary after conquests, *sancaks* originally belonging to the province of Buda were attached to these new administrative units. Thus, the *sancaks* of Smederevo and Kruševac were attached to the province of

Temesvár in 1552, the *sancaks* of Szolnok, Hatvan, Szeged, and Fülek to the province of Eger in 1596, and the *sancaks* of Szigetvár, Požega, and Pécs to the province of Kanizsa in 1600.[63]

Compared with the much larger Balkan Peninsula, which until the creation of the province of Bosnia in 1580 fell under the authority of a single governor (that of Rumeli), the number of provinces and *sancaks* established in Hungary seems rather high. This density of administrative subdivisions can be explained in part by the geostrategic location of Ottoman Hungary. As the empire's key military frontier in central Europe, standing face-to-face with the Habsburg archenemy, this region required a large concentration of forts and garrisons, and thus of provincial and *sancak* governors to command these troops.

These Ottoman administrative strategies, however, were not unique to Hungary. Similar patterns can be observed along the empire's eastern frontiers during its gradual expansion. The province of Diyarbakır split into at least twenty-six *sancaks* in 1568–74, the province of Baghdad had between twenty-one and twenty-nine *sancaks*, the considerably smaller province of Basra comprised sixteen *sancaks*, and the easternmost province of Shahrizor had twenty-four *sancaks*.[64] Attaching *sancaks* to recently established provinces was an administrative strategy practiced in the empire's eastern frontiers as well. The province of Damascus was originally established with eighteen *sancaks*, but already in the early 1520s five *sancaks* were attached to the newly created province of Dulkadır. As a consequence, the number of *sancaks* in the province of Damascus had dropped to thirteen by 1523. In 1549, the province of Aleppo was established with nine *sancaks*, most of which were detached from Damascus. By 1549, the province of Damascus had only eight *sancaks*.[65]

The province of Erzurum, formed roughly at the same time as the province of Buda, originally emerged with seven *sancaks*, but this number increased to nine during the term of the first governor. The province consisted of seventeen *sancaks* in 1550, twenty-six in 1556, and thirty-one by 1585. This is eleven *sancaks* more than what the pasha of Buda commanded in 1568. Following the establishment of the provinces of Çıldır, Kars, and Batum in 1579–80, several *sancaks* belonging to Erzurum were

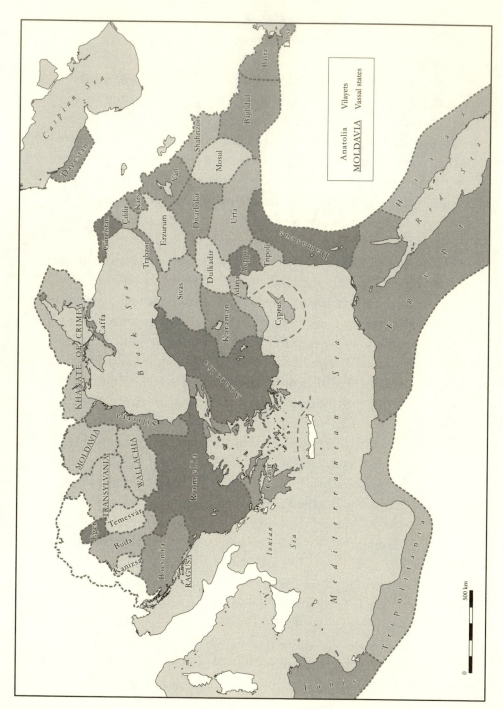

Ottoman provinces in 1609. (Drawn by Béla Nagy, based on Pitcher 1972, map xxiv.)

Anatolia   Vilayets
MOLDAVIA   Vassal states

Caspian Sea

Dagestan

KHANATE OF CRIMEA

Caffa

Black Sea

Gürcistan

Çıldır

Kars

Trabzon

Erzurum

Van

Diyarbakır

Urfa

Mosul

Shahrizor

Baghdad

Basra

Lahsa

Sivas

Dulkadir

Adana

Aleppo

Tripoli

Damascus

Karaman

Anatolia

Cyprus

Egypt

Hijaz

Red Sea

Silistre

MOLDAVIA

TRANSYLVANIA

WALLACHIA

Temesvár

Eger

Buda

Kanizsa

Bosnia

RAGUSA

Rumelia

Cezâyir

Ionian Sea

Mediterranean Sea

Tripolitania

Tunis

500 km

0

attached to these new provinces. Thus, in 1609, the governor of Erzurum could command the military force of only twelve *sancaks*.[66]

The process of increasing the number of provinces and *sancaks* was an empire-wide phenomenon under Süleyman, aimed partly at consolidating Ottoman rule in newly conquered territories. In the 1520s, in the empire as a whole, there were 8 provinces consisting of some 90 *sancaks*. By the 1570s, these numbers had grown to 24 and 250, respectively. The empire's territorial expansion can only in part explain the growing number of *sancaks* and provinces. The principal reason was the transformation of the Ottoman provincial military. As discussed in chapter 9, in the latter part of the sixteenth century ordinary *timariot* provincial *sipahis* found it difficult to earn a living and outfit themselves and their retinues. Therefore, the Porte increasingly relied on the cavalry troops brought into battle by *sancakbeyis* and *beylerbeyis*, which in turn necessitated the establishment of more and more *sancaks* and provinces.[67]

The geographical distribution of *sancaks* not only reflected strategic considerations but was also shaped by existing geographical conditions. In Hungary, both the Ottomans and the Habsburgs built their forts along major rivers and in the hills of Transdanubia and northern Hungary. The Ottomans established nine *sancaks* in the territories to the west of the Danube and six along their northern border. Both were regions that faced Habsburg Hungary, heavily dotted with forts and garrisons. On the other hand, only two *sancaks* existed in the much larger but better protected region between the Danube and Tisza Rivers. Five *sancaks* were formed in the trans-Tisza region and around the forts of the Temes and Maros Rivers, which monitored the Ottoman tributary Transylvania. The Porte established only two *sancaks* in the Hungarian Great Plain, a large area with few forts.[68] Of the six provinces, Buda, Kanizsa, and Újvár stood as the main bases for further Ottoman expansion against the Habsburgs and faced the strongest Hungarian/Habsburg garrisons on the other side of the military border. Their strategic significance affected the size and composition of their garrisons, their weaponry and equipment, and the everyday lives of the soldiers and their families.

13

Contested Bulwark of Islam

Fortifications and Garrisons

To defend the borders of such a vast empire required major military and financial commitments, as well as organizational and logistical prowess. Of the 125,000-strong military potential available for Süleyman in 1527, only some 15,000 soldiers served in the empire's capital. The rest were stationed in the provinces as *timar*-holding cavalry and garrison soldiers. In 1527, almost 42,000 troops served in the empire's 292 fortresses and provincial centers. About 77 percent of these soldiers received salaries in cash; the rest were compensated with *timars*. The strategic importance of the Balkan Peninsula, the Adriatic, and the Mediterranean is demonstrated by the fact that 58 percent of the soldiers served in the Balkan Peninsula, and 16 percent served in Cairo and a handful of coastal forts of Egypt (Alexandria, Rosetta/Rashid, and Damietta). Of the 292 castles, 200 were in the Balkan Peninsula. The provinces of Asia Minor housed a mere 24 percent of the garrison troops in 92 castles. The remaining 2 percent of the soldiers were stationed in Syria.[1]

For the rest of the sixteenth century we lack similar sources. In the sixteenth and seventeenth centuries, the garrison forces consisted of two main groups: local (*yerli* or *yerlü*) troops and contingents of the standing salaried army, who served in border fortresses on a rotational basis for a limited term, usually three years (at least in principle). In many frontier provinces, the bulk of the garrison forces were local troops. Pay for local troops came from, if at all possible, the provincial treasuries. However, most frontier provinces could not finance their garrisons and remained dependent on subsidies from the central imperial treasury and from neighboring interior provinces. The imperial treasury paid the central salaried troops serving in the fortresses. This decentralized financial and accounting practice makes it very difficult to arrive at any reliable estimates regarding the size of the empire's garrison forces.

The majority of Ottoman garrison soldiers were concentrated in a few strategically essential fortresses. Each Ottoman province counted the protection of one or two major forts with thousands of soldiers in each, several smaller second-tier ones with garrisons numbering a couple of hundred soldiers, and smaller third-tier castles, usually palisades (Ottoman *parkan* and *palanka*), in which typically fewer than 100 troops served. In 1530, for instance, 9,325 garrison soldiers served in the twenty forts of the *sancak* of Smederevo. Two-thirds of these garrison troops were deployed in the *sancak's* three main fortresses.[2] The situation was similar in the *sancak* of Caffa in 1520. More than half of the *sancak's* 1,003 soldiers served in Azak (31 percent) and Caffa (23 percent). The number of soldiers in the *sancaks* of Smederevo and Caffa also demonstrates the strategic importance of the Danube frontier as opposed to the Black Sea frontier in the early decades of the sixteenth century.

In Europe, the Ottoman government stationed the largest concentration of its garrison troops in the province of Buda. The number of forts in Ottoman Hungary grew steadily from 29 in 1545, to 61 in 1569, and to about 130 by the mid-seventeenth century. The Hungarians and Habsburgs originally built most of these castles, with the Ottomans making relatively minor architectural updates. The few new castles that the Ottomans built in Hungary consisted of smaller palisades.[3] The number of Ottoman castles in Bosnia, another frontier province that faced both the Venetians and the Habsburgs, also grew steadily in the sixteenth and seventeenth centuries. In 1530 the Ottomans surveyed 56 castles in the *sancak* of Bosna. Elevated to the rank of province in 1580, Bosnia had 108 castles, palisades, and smaller watchtowers in 1616. By 1643, the number of castles and other smaller fortified structures in the province had risen to 126.[4]

In Ottoman-held Hungary, the key fortresses had between 1,000 and 4,000 soldiers, and second-tier ones had between 200 and 500 troops. Just as in the *sancaks* of Caffa and Smederevo, the strategically significant fortresses housed the majority of garrison forces in Hungary too. About two-thirds of the 15,000 troops serving in the province of Buda in 1545 defended the four key fortresses of Buda, Pest, Esztergom, and Székesfehérvár. After further conquests and the consolidation of Ottoman rule in the 1550s, the Ottomans redeployed their troops into their newly conquered forts. This reduced the troop strength of the four key fortresses by 50 percent, although the overall strength of Ottoman garrison troops in Hungary increased.[5] Ottoman Hungary contained an unusually high number of fortifications. Other provinces housed fewer castles, and the concentration of garrison soldiers in a couple of strategically important fortifications remained higher.

In 1545, the Ottomans paid 12,975 garrison soldiers in their twenty-nine forts in Hungary. Including janissaries of the Porte (2,282 men in 1547), the occupying military force of the province of Buda numbered between 15,000 and 16,000 men.[6] After further Ottoman conquests in 1551 and 1552, and the creation of the province of Temesvár, the number of garrison soldiers in the province of Buda somewhat decreased. Some of the men serving in the province of Temesvár had been redeployed from the forts of the province of Buda. Accordingly, the provincial treasury in Buda paid only 10,300–10,400 soldiers in the fifty-one forts of the province in 1556–59, a decrease of 2,500 men compared with 1545. However, by 1569 the Buda treasury again paid 12,485 soldiers, deployed in sixty-one forts of the province. If one adds 945 janissaries of the Porte, and 1,350–1,500 soldiers remunerated by collective *timar* revenues instead of cash, the overall strength of the provinces' garrison force approaches 15,000 men. During the consolidation of the 1570s, the number of garrison soldiers paid through collective *timars* in the province of Buda doubled to about 3,200 men. Correspondingly, the number of garrison soldiers paid in cash by the provincial treasury decreased to below 11,000 men. This was in response to repeated orders from the Porte, which attempted to lessen the burden of soldiers' pay on the Buda treasury, whose deficit in the 1550s and 1560s had to be balanced by subsidies from Constantinople.[7] In 1591, before the Long War of 1593–1606, the number of garrison troops in the two provinces of Ottoman-held Hungary—Buda and Temesvár—is estimated between 19,000 and 20,000. Buda had some 15,000 men, and Temesvár 4,000–4,500 men.[8]

The aggregate military power of frontier provinces also included auxiliary troops, peasant militias, and other semiprofessional soldiers. The number of such troops is difficult to gauge, but the following example is eye opening. According to Ottoman salary registers and treasury account books, in the 1570s about 16,000 salaried garrison troops served in the province of Buda, in addition to some 5,000 *timariot* cavalry—a combined military force of about 21,000 men. At the same time, a Habsburg spy report, prepared for a military conference in Vienna in 1577, put the Ottoman military strength in the province of Buda at 35,043 men, and in Ottoman-occupied Hungary at 47,049 men. While spy reports often exaggerated the military strength of the enemy, and the Habsburg report certainly could have done so to pressure the Viennese authorities to commit more troops and resources against the Ottomans in Hungary, the discrepancy between the two figures is too high and requires some reflection. It is likely that the Habsburg report counted all available Ottoman soldiers, including regular forces paid in cash and prebends, military escorts and private armies of the provincial and *sancak* governors, and unpaid volunteers.[9]

When estimating the military potential of a province, one should take into consideration redeployments and reorganizations after conquests and military defeats, which resulted in gaining and losing fortresses and territories. For instance, after the conquest of central Hungary in 1541, thousands of soldiers had to be redeployed from Rumeli to Hungary. As mentioned, to defend the newly acquired territories in Hungary, Süleyman deployed 2,653 and 914 soldiers to the castles of Buda and Pest, respectively, in 1541. To reinforce the defenses, 4,196 additional soldiers were transferred from Golubac, Haram, Smederevo, Belgrade, Slankamen, Titel, Petrovaradin, Ilok, Vukovar, Osijek, Požega, and other Ottoman castles south of the newly conquered province.[10]

The eastern frontier witnessed similar readjustments after Ottoman conquests and defeats. For instance, the frontier fortress of Van,

Ottoman, Habsburg, and Transylvanian fortresses in 1568. (Drawn by Béla Nagy.)

KINGDOM OF POLAND

ssa
NGARY Munkács
Várda Tisza
Ecsed Szatmár Szamos
SZATMÁR
ebrecen Szentjobb
Várad
arkad Belényes
ota Jenő
Solymos
Tótvárad Illye
ippa Facset
svár Déva
Lugos
Karánsebes
ršac Mehadia
m Orsova Severin
olubac Vidin

Huszt
Nagybánya
Kővár
Szamosújvár
Kolozsvár Maros
T r a n s y l v a n i a
Gyulafehérvár Segesvár
Szeben Olt
Brassó

Kamieniec
Dniester
Hotin
Prut

M o l d a v i a
Suceava
Iaşi Prut
Seret

Galaţi
Brăila

W a l a c h i a
Târgovişte
Bucharest
Giurgiu Ruse Silistra
Danube
Danube
Nikopol

Captain-generalcy of
Ottoman fortress
Ottoman Empire
Ottoman vassal states

Transylvanian fortress
Contry border
Provincial border

100 miles/
160,9 km
0 20 40 60 80
Scale 1: 4,300,000

conquered from the Safavids in 1548, had about 300 to 500 local troops after the Ottoman-Safavid peace of 1555. At the outbreak of the war with the Safavids in 1578, however, the number of local salaried troops doubled and remained at about 800 to 1,000 men. When in 1585 the Ottomans temporarily conquered Tabriz, they transferred part of the Van garrison there. After Shah Abbas retook Tabriz in 1603, Van again became a frontier fortress, threatened by renewed Safavid attacks. Consequently, its garrison bolstered its strength and the number of local troops fluctuated between 1,750 and 2,300 in the years 1609–11. The number of local troops further increased to 3,000 in 1636. It remained at this size after the Peace of Zuhab, which again made Van a frontier province.[11]

As we have seen, the Ottomans ended the Long War of 1593–1606 against the Habsburgs with modest territorial gains in Hungary: they occupied Eger in 1596 and Kanizsa in 1600. After the conquest of these key castles, which served the Hungarian-Habsburg defense for decades before their Ottoman capture, the Ottomans created two new provinces around them with dozens of castles.[12] Yet, the number of Ottoman garrison troops guarding the empire's Danubian frontier did not significantly increase, for the newly conquered forts were partly manned by soldiers from the neighboring province of Buda. In the second decade of the seventeenth century, the number of Ottoman garrison troops (including some 1,000 janissaries of the Porte) came to about 21,000 men in the now four Ottoman provinces of Buda, Temesvár, Eger, and Kanizsa.[13] To this we should add the garrison forces in the fortresses of the province of Bosnia, which numbered between 10,000 and 11,800 men.[14] These numbers give us a total of about 32,000 to 33,000 Ottoman garrison soldiers in Bosnia and Hungary in the first quarter of the seventeenth century.

Another pay list from about 1613 recorded 28,024 garrison soldiers in the same provinces. This number amounted to about 73 percent of the 38,196 garrison soldiers documented as serving in the empire's castles, which would demonstrate the importance of the Hungarian and Bosnian frontier.[15] However, the numbers of garrison soldiers listed in the document as serving in the empire's eastern frontier are so low that they distort the picture. The document contains only the number of soldiers paid in cash. Inclusion of the *timar*-holding cavalry significantly changes the picture of Ottoman military commitments. In 1631, the total number of *timar*-holding *sipahis* is estimated at 106,600 men. Only 8,050 of them (7.5 percent) were stationed in Hungary. Even if we add an additional 5,082 *timar*-holding provincial cavalry of Bosnia, the result is that only 12 percent of the empire's provincial cavalry troops were stationed in Bosnia and Hungary.[16] These data also demonstrate that *timariot* provincial cavalry troops were more useful in Asia Minor and in the eastern frontier provinces, where they fought against the Safavids, who also retained a high number of horsemen.

In the second half of the seventeenth century, two major events affected the number and distribution of Ottoman forts and garrison soldiers in Hungary: the conquest of Várad (1660) and Érsekújvár (1663), and the creation of two new provinces named after these two fortresses. In 1662–63, 18,043 soldiers received pay in the castles of the provinces of Várad, Buda, and Érsekújvár, almost as many as in all of the Ottoman fortresses and forts in Hungary in the first half of the century.[17] We have no data regarding the soldiers serving in the provinces of Temesvár, Eger, and Kanizsa, whose garrisons numbered 10,877 men in the 1610s. While some of these soldiers were certainly transferred to the newly conquered castles in the provinces of Várad and Érsekújvár, sizable garrisons must have remained in at least the major forts of the above three older provinces. Estimating the number of soldiers at 5,000 men and adding to them some 6,500 janissaries of the Porte serving in Hungary, one would arrive at an aggregate number of about 30,000 garrison soldiers serving in the six Ottoman provinces in Hungary. This represents a considerable increase compared with the first half of the century.[18] As for the *timar*-holding cavalry, the earlier pattern did not change. While in 1653 the number of *timar*-holding cavalry is estimated at 201,000 in the empire, in the twenty-four *sancaks* of the provinces of Buda, Eger, Kanizsa, and Temesvár there served only 14,000 *timar*-holding cavalry and retainers—less than 7 percent of the potential strength of the empire's provincial cavalry.[19] With them, the garrison soldiers and the *timariot* cavalry in Hungary can be estimated at 44,000 men.

A similar increase is visible in the province of Bosnia, where the number of garrison soldiers rose from 11,473 in 1635 to more than 14,000 men in 1645, the year of the outbreak of the Cretan War with Venice. As in Hungary, key fortresses boasted the largest garrisons. About one-third of the soldiers served in the *sancak* of Bosna, which had several key fortresses along the Sava River. To these should be added some 8,000 *timar*-holding cavalrymen, who served in the province's seven *sancaks* in 1653. Thus, the military potential of the province of Bosnia in the mid-seventeenth century can be estimated at 22,000 men.[20]

In short, in Hungary and Bosnia the Ottomans boasted a powerful military force of about 65,000 men in the mid-seventeenth century. Since the number of garrison forces defending the Hungarian kingdom under Habsburg rule is estimated at 14,000 men in the 1660s,[21] the above figures regarding Ottoman military commitments in Hungary and Bosnia suggest that the Ottomans managed to significantly outnumber their Habsburg opponents in terms of deployed soldiers along their mutual frontier zone. This is all the more remarkable because the Ottomans also committed large numbers of troops in the empire's eastern frontiers and in the Cretan War against Venice.

To maintain adequate troop strength along the empire's most vulnerable border regions, the Ottomans habitually redeployed soldiers to key border fortresses from castles that did not face imminent threat. After the capture of Érsekújvár, the garrison of this new provincial capital augmented its strength with janissaries from Buda and Eger. These transferred janissaries served in Érsekújvár for six months on a rotational basis and left the fortress only when new contingents arrived.[22] The Porte also strengthened the frontier garrisons during the campaign season—defined in the sources as the period from Ruz-i Hızır (23 April) through Ruz-i Kasım (26 October)—when enemy attacks most commonly occurred. For instance, in the spring of 1665 the deputy *sancak* governors of Požega and Pécs were ordered to serve in Kanizsa and Szigetvár.[23] Such seasonal troop redeployments involved soldiers from more distant *sancaks* as well. The *timariot* cavalry from the province of Jenő, for instance, received orders to serve in 1665 in Érsekújvár, a fortress that lay more than four hundred kilometers to the northwest. In 1680, the *timariot* cavalrymen from the *sancak* of Požega were also redeployed to Érsekújvár, which lay some four hundred kilometers north of Požega.[24]

Numbers regarding the size of garrisons in various frontier provinces should be handled with caution. In addition to frequent troop redeployments, one should also take into consideration the discrepancies between paper figures and actual numbers. Garrisons lost their men because of death, enemy capture, and desertion. Fortress commanders in principle had to fill such vacancies promptly. However, they often delayed these tasks and pocketed the wages of dead and missing soldiers. During wartime, the central government tried to force its border governors and fortress commanders to fill vacancies as promptly as possible. Some of the governors initiated the procedure themselves.[25] Still, in war years, many border garrisons were severely undermanned. The musters in 1631 and 1634 found 93 and 98 percent, respectively, of the local soldiers present in the fortress of Temesvár.[26] However, in 1691 only 79 percent of the required 1,406 soldiers were present.[27] When in 1696 the commander of Babadağ inspected Kamieniec, he found 257 men (13 percent) missing of the alleged strength of 1,911 local troops. Another inspection a year later found 187 additional vacant positions, chiefly due to death, but also to desertion. The number of local troops dropped to 1,410 men, a mere 74 percent of the expected number.[28]

The aggregate data presented earlier regarding Ottoman garrisons along the empire's northern frontiers mask an important development. In the seventeenth century, more and more janissaries of the Porte served in fortifications. As mentioned, in the mid-sixteenth century about 4,700 janissaries performed garrison duty. According to Marsigli, in the 1680s the Porte garrisoned 28,426 janissaries in the empire's fortresses.[29] The number of janissaries on garrison duty fluctuated between 14,000 and 36,000 in the 1660s through the 1680s. On average, about 45 percent of the janissaries served in the empire's border fortresses in these years.[30]

Local circumstances and the exigencies of warfare determined the size of janissary contingents in border fortresses. In some cases, the initially high numbers decreased considerably over time as provincial governors managed to fill their garrisons with local troops. In Kanizsa, conquered in 1600, the number of janissaries of the Porte dropped from 1,838 in 1603 to just 170 in 1629. By the latter date, local troops numbered

1,650 men.[31] Várad, in the eastern parts of Ottoman-held Hungary, had 1,577 janissaries in the spring of 1661 (less than a year after its conquest) but only 602 in the spring and summer of 1669.[32] Similar trends apply to Érsekújvár. Its garrison had 1,781 janissaries of the Porte just months after its conquest in 1663, but this number dropped to 955 by the fall of 1669.[33] However, after the failed Ottoman siege of Vienna (1683), the Ottomans strengthened the garrison, expecting a Habsburg siege. In 1685, before the Habsburg siege, 2,462 janissaries of the Porte served in Érsekújvár.[34] After its conquest, Candia housed 5,925 janissaries of the Porte in the spring of 1670, but this number dropped to 2,689 men by 1686, and to 1,485 men by 1691.[35] In the empire's northernmost province of Kamieniec (T. Kamaniçe), janissaries and other central salaried troops of the Porte remained substantial, although their number too declined, dropping from 3,724 men in 1676 to 2,016 men by the end of Ottoman rule. A parallel process occurred with regard to local troops, whose number dropped from 3,429 men in 1672 to 1,609 men in 1699.[36] One of the largest janissary contingents guarded Baghdad, where in the 1660s between 4,400 and 5,500 janissaries served. Their number too dropped to 3,353 men in 1677, and to 2,530 men in 1688. However, this number increased sharply to 7,123 men in 1699–1700 as the Ottomans concluded their war in Europe and soldiers became available to reconquer Basra under the command of the governor of Baghdad. The number of janissaries in Baghdad rose again from 2,981 in 1723 to 8,300 in 1736, just before the outbreak of the war against Iran (1724–46).[37]

Guardians of the Frontier

As part of a larger Ottoman strategy of burden sharing, the government expected the frontier authorities to meet most of the costs relating to the maintenance of their respective border regions from local revenue sources. Thus, the Ottoman government designated part of the agricultural revenues as prebends (*timar*, *zeamet*, and *hass*) to be assigned to cavalrymen and to their military commanders, the *sancak* governors. *Timar* revenues assigned to ordinary *sipahi* usually yielded an annual sum of up to 20,000 *akçe*; *zeamets* yielded an annual sum between

20,000 and 99,999 *akçe*, although the upper limit occasionally grew considerably higher, in rare cases reaching 300,000 *akçe*.[38] High-ranking officials, such as *sancak* and provincial governors, drew their income from *hass* prebends, which in principle yielded over 100,000 *akçe* revenue annually. In the sixteenth century, the starting salary for *sancak* governors in the European part of the empire was 200,000 *akçe*.

The best-paid *sancak* governors along the Danubian frontier often received *hass* grants yielding 400,000 *akçe* annually, but some managed to obtain prebends worth as much as 600,000 *akçe*. In 1530, as *sancak* governor of Bosnia, Hüsrev Beg expected to collect 643,979 *akçe* from his *hass* estates.[39] The *sancak* governors of Szigetvár in the 1570s and 1580s drew compensation with *hass* prebends worth 590,000 to 640,000 *akçe*. However, these figures reflected the nominal or estimated value of the *hasses* to which these *sancak* governors were entitled. The collectable income often fell far below these estimated totals. One governor, for instance, managed to lay claim to less than half of his nominal revenue.[40] These figures illustrate the everyday realities along the frontier. Following the slowing down of conquests in the latter part of the sixteenth century, offices and revenues became more difficult to come by than in midcentury, and officers and officials contented themselves with less revenue than they were entitled to. In addition to his military service as commander of the provincial cavalry forces in his *sancak*, the *sancakbeyi* maintained law and order with the help of the *timariot* cavalry under his command. He and the judge of the *sancak* collected taxes, managed revenues, and assisted the officials appointed by the government to carry out revenue surveys.

After the conquest of Buda in 1541, the Ottomans had only limited financial resources at their disposal in their newly conquered territory and relied on revenues from distant territories. The *hass* revenues assigned to the first two governors of the province of Buda lay more than 200 kilometers south of their seat and were scattered in the *sancaks* of Požega, Smederevo, Vidin, Zvornik, and Kruševac. Furthermore, the high income of 1,000,391 *akçe* of the second governor came from more than 450 poor settlements. Later, as the Ottomans consolidated their administration and revenue management in Hungary, the *hasses* granted to the governor of Buda lay closer to Buda, and by the 1580s all were located north of the Sava River. By the 1560s, the pashas of Buda collected some 50 to 60 percent of their annual income of 800,000 to 1,000,000 *akçe* from the *sancak* of Buda.[41]

During 145 years of Ottoman rule, seventy-six governors served in Buda. Since several of them held the post more than once, the total number of appointments is about one hundred. The longest-serving governor was Sokollu Mustafa Pasha, who held his post for twelve years (1566–78) thanks largely to the protection of his uncle, Grand Vizier Sokollu Mehmed Pasha (1565–79). Before his appointment as *beylerbeyi* of Buda, Mustafa Pasha served as *sancak* governor of Fülek, Klis, Szeged, Hercegovina, and Bosnia. He was also the first governor of Buda to be granted the rank of vizier, in 1574. Among his successors, only a few had attained this title before the 1620s. After that, almost all the governors of Buda doubled as viziers, owing to the depreciation of titles. With his new title, Mustafa Pasha's yearly revenues increased to 1,200,000 *akçe*, the largest known *hass* revenue given to a Buda governor in the sixteenth century. It represented a twentyfold increase in Sokollu Mustafa's annual salary since the start of his career on the Hungarian frontier two decades earlier. He converted most of his wealth into charitable endowments, which paid for the upkeep of four congregational and six smaller mosques, two secondary schools (*medrese*), twelve hostels for travelers, and sixteen bathhouses whose construction the pasha had commissioned.[42] Two more Sokollus, Gazi Ferhad (1588–90) and Mehmedzade Vizier Hasan (1593–94), served much shorter periods in Buda, although both men had distinguished carriers. Ferhad, cousin of Grand Vizier Mehmed, served as *sancak* governor of Klis (1566–74) and Bosnia (1574–80). When Bosnia was elevated to the rank of province in 1580, he became its first provincial governor-general, a post he held until the summer of 1588. After more than twenty years of distinguished service on the Dalmatian and Bosnian frontier, he was appointed to Buda in late November 1588. However, he was killed during a rebellion of the Buda garrison in September 1590.[43] Hasan, son of Sokollu Mehmed, was four times governor of Damascus, three times of Rumeli, and twice of Bosnia. He also served as *beylerbeyi* of Diyarbakır, Erzerum, Anadolu, and Temesvár. He was appointed governor of Buda in January 1593 with the rank of vizier. He was also commander in chief of the remaining army in Hungary after the 1596 campaign and of the troops fighting against the Celali rebel leader Kara Yazıcı ("Black scribe") Abdülhalim (1601).[44]

Many of the Ottoman governors coveted appointments on the Hungarian frontier and were willing to pay large sums to secure them. In 1590, Osman, the former *sancak* governor of Esztergom, reportedly secured the *sancak* governorship in Szolnok only after paying 10,000 thalers for the salaries of the garrison soldiers of Buda.[45] Kadızade ("son of the judge") Ali Pasha served as governor of Buda several times between 1602 and 1616, with brief interruptions. His father, Habil Efendi, served as judge, or *kadı*—hence Ali's name—in Buda from 1597 to 1608 and thereafter as jurisconsult in Belgrade until his death in 1621. Habil and Ali proved instrumental in concluding the Peace of Zsitvatorok in 1606. Ali must have enjoyed his position in Hungary. After his reassignment to the eastern frontier to fight against the Safavids, he pleaded with the Habsburg monarch to intervene on his behalf in the Ottoman court regarding his reappointment to Buda. He also contacted the interpreter Andrea Negroni, with whom he had worked closely during the peace negotiations. Ali reminded Negroni of his promise that the latter would intercede with the king of Hungary. Since recent raids and skirmishes threatened the peace, Ali lobbied for his reappointment to Buda. In 1614, Ali was quick to inform his Viennese and Hungarian counterparts—Johann von Molart, president of the Viennese War Council (1610–19), and Francis II Batthyány, captain-general of the Transdanubian District—about his return. He also promised that "I will do my best to uphold the provisions of our covenant so that sacred peace will be maintained fully and without any flow."[46] His final two years before his death in December 1616 were devoted to preserving the peace. In one of his letters to Molart, Ali informed his Viennese colleague that upon his recommendation the Sublime Porte dismissed the pasha of Kanizsa from his post "for disturbing the peace." However, that the new governor of Kanizsa previously served as

Ali's deputy suggests that he may have had other motives in arranging the sacking of the former governor of Kanizsa beyond the noble goal of "striving for increased friendship and amity between us."[47]

As Ali Pasha's career illustrates, social capital and networks were instrumental in attaining offices and accumulating wealth along the frontier. The relations of the Sokollu pashas, who spent most of their lives in Ottoman Bosnia and Hungary, show a similar pattern. Sokollu Mustafa had friendly relations with the Transylvanian princes from his time in Temesvár. John Sigismund and Christopher Báthory donated four villages to him, which Mustafa then converted into private property and later made part of his pious endowments in support of his *medrese* in Pest. Two other Sokollus, Sarhoş (Drunk) İbrahim and his son Yakovalı Hasan Pasha, also enjoyed cordial relations with the Transylvanian princes. The family was known in Bosnia as Memibegović, named after Hasan's grandfather Memi Beg. Originally from Albania, Memi had served as *sancak* governor of Krka (Lika), Srem, Požega, Pakrac, Zvornik, and Esztergom. He was killed in the battle of Sisak in 1593. Sarhoş Ibrahim was Memi's son from Sokollu Mehmed's sister. Ibrahim served as *sancak* governor of Silistra and Szeged and as *beylerbeyi* of Kanizsa, Eger, Temesvár, and Bosnia. He belonged to the Ottoman faction that supported Prince Gabriel Bethlen of Transylvania against Vienna. Ibrahim's politics temporarily cost him his position, for Kadızade Ali Pasha of Buda, who headed the anti-Bethlen Ottoman faction, had him dismissed from Eger. Having later returned to Eger, in 1623 Ibrahim led the Ottoman troops in support of Bethlen against the Habsburgs. As an old man, Ibrahim participated in the 1663 Hungarian campaign, during which his son Hasan was appointed to Kanizsa. Hasan knew the Hungarian frontier well, as he hailed from this region. In the 1630s he had served in Kanizsa for almost ten years, due (at least partly) to the lobbying of the Transylvanian princes and their envoys in Constantinople. Following the rise of the Köprülüs, Hasan supported Grand Vizier Köprülü Mehmed during Abaza Hasan's revolt. Since the family was related to the Sokollu or Sokolović Bosnian dynasty of Ottoman statesmen, Hasan signed some of his letters as Şahin (Falcon/Hawk) Hasan, *şahın* being the Persian/Ottoman Turkish translation of the Slavic word for "falcon," *sokol*.[48]

The Sokollu/Sokolović family is notable because—in addition to their Muslim members who held high administrative offices in the Ottoman Empire—its Orthodox Christian members played an important role in the administration of the Serbian Orthodox Church in the second half of the sixteenth century. As mentioned, after the Ottoman conquest of Serbia in 1459, the autocephalous Serbian church gradually lost its independence and came under the influence of the Ohrid archbishopric. However, in 1557 Sokollu Mehmed restored the Serbian Orthodox Patriarchate of Peć (in Kosovo), appointing his close relative Makarije Sokolović as its first patriarch. Variably reported as being Mehmed Pasha's brother, nephew, or cousin, and titled as "Archbishop of Peć and Patriarch of Serbs, Bulgarians, and the maritime and northern parts," Makarije headed the Peć Patriarchate until 1571. When illness made him unable to fulfill his duties, his nephew Anthony (Antonije) Sokolović succeeded him. After Anthony, four more members of the Sokolović clan headed the Serbian Patriarchate until 1592. Since its patriarchs were appointed by the sultan's decree, the Peć Patriarchate played an important role in controlling the padishah's Serbian subjects. However, as church services under its jurisdiction were held in Serbian rather than Greek, the Peć Patriarchate was instrumental in maintaining Serbian culture in a vast territory from the Dalmatian coast to Bosnia, Serbia, Hungary, parts of Bulgaria, and parts of Habsburg Croatia.[49]

In addition to the Sokollus, many other governors-general in Hungary hailed from Serbia, Croatia, Bosnia, and Albania. A few were of Hungarian origin. In the seventeenth century pashas of Abkhazian, Circassian, and Georgian origin joined them. Similarly, most members of the Ottoman religious establishment serving in the administration as judges, jurists, and jurisconsults or in mosques, schools, and dervish lodges in Hungary also came from the Balkan Peninsula.[50] The Balkan Peninsula, especially Bosnia and Serbia, provided the main source of Ottoman garrison soldiers in Hungary. After its Ottoman conquest in 1543, 89 percent of the 812 fortress soldiers serving in Székesfehérvár came from the Balkan Peninsula, and less than 1 percent consisted of recruits from Hungary. In 1558, more than 90 percent of the newly recruited 814 garrison soldiers of Buda originated from the Balkan Peninsula. The majority (63 percent) of these recruits were Muslims, but new converts and Christians were also well represented (22 percent and 15 percent, respectively).[51] Archeological finds and the architectural characteristics of Ottoman buildings in Hungary also show heavy Balkan influences. Members of the Ottoman provincial administration and garrison soldiers engaged in trade and moneylending. When a Ragusan trading company in Buda declared bankruptcy in 1591, the authorities recorded Ottoman janissaries, *sipahis*, *çavuşes*, and a jurisconsult among its creditors. The bankrupted company owed them hundreds of thalers, the largest sums (1,200 and 1,400 thalers) to the jurisconsult and a *çavuş*. Both sums were several times greater than their regular annual salaries.[52]

Financial and administrative services offered lucrative opportunities for talented and ambitious soldiers. The career of Osman Agha is a case in point. In 1564, Osman, the agha of a cavalry unit of Fülek, gained the right to collect taxes from three neighboring villages as a tax farmer. Later he managed the imperial *hass* estates of Fülek. In 1568, he and his business partner obtained the right to manage the tax farm (*mukataa*) of Vác, one of the most lucrative revenue sources in Ottoman Hungary due to its customs. Osman agreed to collect 15,800,000 *akçe* during his three-year term—a sum almost 1 million *akçe* more than his predecessors had promised—but he failed to deliver. Although he temporarily lost his position to a five-member consortium in the 1570s, he later resurfaced as the tax farmer of the same *mukataa*. In return for his services, his former salary was converted into a *zeamet* prebend, yielding almost 13,000 *akçe* annually. By 1581 he had become the fiscal inspector of the Vác *mukataa,* with the tax farmers under his supervision offering to collect 20,700,000 *akçe* in three years. In 1586 the Porte rewarded his financial and military services by appointing him *sancakbeyi* of Szécsény. In 1588, he became *sancak* governor of Hatvan and in 1590 that of the militarily more prestigious Szolnok, with an annual *hass* revenue of 385,000 *akçe*. This former cavalry soldier had become one of the most powerful men in Ottoman Hungary.[53]

The Cost of Defense

Maintaining the border forts and paying the soldiers cost a considerable sum. By the mid-sixteenth century most border provinces were unable to finance their garrisons from local resources and became dependent on subsidies from the central treasury and neighboring provinces. The central and local administration employed various techniques to ease the financial burden and make frontier provinces self-sufficient when possible. The reallocation of available resources emerged as a favorite technique. A significant portion of revenue resources from the provinces of Aleppo, Diyarbakır, and Erzurum funded the garrisons of the neighboring Iranian border zone. Similarly, revenues from the Balkan *sancaks* in the seventeenth century were transferred to the border provinces in Hungary to pay the garrison soldiers. The financial situation may have changed several times, and generalizations based on random data are misleading. In any examination, one should differentiate between the initial period of Ottoman rule when the administration and taxation had not yet been consolidated and the period of consolidated Ottoman rule. Long wars that characterized the late sixteenth and seventeenth centuries brought about devastation and economic ruin. The books of the most affected war-torn frontier provinces, however, could be balanced only with the help of the interior regions. However, after wars, the economic and financial situation improved.

After the conquest of Buda in 1541, the provincial treasury faced considerable deficits. As early as 1542, the Habsburg ambassador to Constantinople reported that Süleyman's treasury was empty and that the Ottomans had not been able to pay their soldiers for two years because the defense of Buda had consumed all available money.[54] According to the account books of the Buda treasury, in fiscal years 1558–59 and 1559–60 the annual payment made to the 10,328 soldiers stationed in the castles of the province was 23 and 23.5 million *akçe* (307,500 and 313,300 gold florins), respectively. At the same time, the Buda treasury collected just 6.4 and 8.8 million *akçe* (58,794 and 117,784 gold florins) in revenue from local sources. In other words, local revenues of the province covered only 28 percent and 38 percent of the expenses.[55] These figures reflect the dire financial situation of a new frontier province, whose hinterland had not yet been established, and where revenue collection remained haphazard and unsteady.

As the Ottomans consolidated their rule during the governorship of Sokollu Mustafa Pasha (1566–78) and Üveys Pasha (1578–80), local revenues of the Buda treasury increased. By the early 1570s, the financial situation of the province had improved considerably. Local revenues grew to cover about 90 percent of the soldiers' wages.[56] The first significant change took place in 1575. For the first time, no annual subvention from the imperial treasury was needed.[57] No subvention arrived to Buda from the imperial treasury until 1581. The treasury account book of Buda contains a proud reference:

> Previously 350,000–400,000 gold pieces had been provided by the imperial treasury annually to cover the wages of the garrison troops in the province of Buda. It has been nine years since Mustafa pasha became governor of the province of Buda. In this time, he has brought order to the province and the Padishah's revenues so that the revenues now cover the expenses. The imperial treasury no longer sends gold pieces [to Buda]: only 4 million *akçe* are received from the treasury of Temesvár.[58]

Better protected from Habsburg and Hungarian attacks, the province of Temesvár emerged as self-sufficient by 1574 and its local provincial treasury subsidized Buda.[59]

The increase in local revenue in the province of Buda can be explained by two main factors: territorial expansion following Süleyman's successful campaign in 1566 and the consolidation of Ottoman administration and taxation. As a result of the 1566 campaign, large territories fell under Ottoman rule. By 1566 the territory of Ottoman Hungary formed a huge triangle in the middle of the country, extending over an area of one hundred thousand square kilometers.[60] The increase in tax revenues after the peace of 1568 resulted from administrative measures and more efficient tax collection. Following former Hungarian custom regarding the taxpaying liability of subjects, at the beginning of their rule in Hungary the Ottoman authorities collected the poll tax (*cizye*) from only those heads of families who had 300 *akçe* (6 Hungarian florins) worth of movable property.[61] Determining tax liability in this way allowed the Ottomans to follow the Hungarian custom, formulated in 1547 by the Hungarian diet. Following local customs in taxation was a tried-and-true Ottoman practice in accordance with pragmatic Ottoman administration. However, it also meant that about 30 percent of all potential taxpayers in Hungary were exempt from the *cizye* tax in the early years of Ottoman rule.[62] Shrinking finances and increased defense costs forced the government to abolish the 300 *akçe* threshold and collect the *cizye* from all potential taxpayers regardless of financial circumstances. The Ottomans introduced the new system in the *sancak* of Buda in 1562, and over the 1570s extended it to other regions.[63] Consequently, the number of *cizye* payers increased considerably, as did revenues. While in 1558–59 only 1.5 million *akçe* came from the *cizye* tax in the province of Buda, twenty years later this sum increased by 3.5 million to a total of 5.3 million *akçe*.[64]

Incomes from the padishah's *hass* estates, which constituted another important part of provincial revenues, also increased. Üveys Pasha took new measures to utilize this revenue source. He prevented the *sipahis* from laying their hands on the padishah's *hasses*, which may have diminished treasury revenues. He also suggested that abandoned estates not be distributed among the *sipahis,* as had been the practice, but instead be attached to the padishah's *hass* estates.[65] Üveys Pasha's actions brought about the desired results. While in 1559 *hass* estates yielded only 2.3 million *akçe* to the Buda treasury, in 1580 their income was more than 9 million *akçe*.[66] This rise of nearly 300 percent is considerable even though the value of the *akçe* had somewhat diminished (the great devaluation of 1585 had not yet occurred). Income from tax farms (*mukataa*) increased even more. These were revenues from customs duties, fair tolls, market fees, and monopolies and formed 50 to 70 percent of the province's total revenue. The treasury's income from tax farms rose from 3.4 million *akçe* in 1558 to 18.5 million *akçe* in 1580.[67] By the late 1570s, the Ottoman administration accomplished its goal. Local revenues covered most of the expenses. Parallel to the consolidation of Ottoman taxation, Hungarian taxation in territories under Ottoman rule also expanded in the relatively peaceful years following the Habsburg-Ottoman treaty of 1568. Agricultural productivity on the Great Hungarian Plain was revived, and the Hungarian peasants living under Ottoman rule managed to pay their taxes and dues to both the Ottoman and Hungarian landlords. But this economic consolidation was short-lived.

The long wars in the Caucasus and Hungary against the Safavids and Habsburgs, respectively, upset the finances of the frontiers. Annual remittances (*irsaliye*) that the eastern provinces of Aleppo, Damascus, Karaman, Erzurum, and Baghdad sent to the imperial treasury decreased substantially just years after the outbreak of the Ottoman-Safavid war of 1578–90. The burden on these treasuries did not ease after the conquest either. To maintain about 10,000 garrison troops defending the eastern borders cost about 400,000 to 500,000 gold pieces annually, which the local provincial treasuries could only partially cover.[68] To finance the garrisons in the newly established Georgian and Azerbaijan frontiers, the resources of the neighboring interior provinces of Diyarbakır, Erzurum, and Aleppo had to be redirected. The treasury of Diyarbakır paid the soldiers in the forts of Erevan (1585), Tbilisi (1594), Tabriz (1594–95), and Ganja (1593). The provincial treasury of Aleppo paid the garrisons in Van (1585) and Kars (1589–90), whereas the soldiers serving in the Georgian forts of Gori (1593–94), Akhaltsikhe, and Azgur (1596) received their pay from the treasury of Erzurum. The Porte surveyed the lands and tried to redistribute the resources in the conquered lands. It reorganized the provincial administration on multiple occasions, hoping to improve its finances. Nonetheless, garrison soldiers were not paid for months. Even when the imperial treasury authorized the transfer of funds from the neighboring provincial treasuries to cover the wages of the soldiers defending the eastern frontier, it took months to deliver the money. When the Porte realized that it took eight to nine months to send the wages from Diyarbakır and Aleppo to the soldiers of the castle of Erevan, it ordered that the funds henceforth be transferred from the treasury of Van, which lay closer to Erevan. This transaction still took three months.[69] Seeing the disastrous financial consequences of the Ottoman conquest of Georgia, Grand Vizier Sinan Pasha commented: "Since the fortresses were built, have we taken possession of a single village having two houses? Has a single *akçe* of revenue been obtained? It is beyond my comprehension what sort of a conquest this is."[70]

In the Hungarian borderlands, the Long War of 1593–1606 also resulted in the collapse of Ottoman finances. In 1600, the revenues of the provincial treasury of Buda covered only 21 percent of the expenditures and about 23 percent of the wages of soldiers serving in the province's castles. The devastating effects of the war are reflected in the fact that about half of the province's much-reduced revenue came from the soldiers themselves (in payments for food and provisions). This indicates the decimation and flight of much of the taxpaying population—those who remained were unable to pay their taxes and dues. In subsequent years of the war, the financial situation deteriorated further. From 1601 through 1603, the province's local revenues covered just 15 to 18 percent of expenditures. The situation was similar in the province of Kanizsa, established in 1600. Almost all of the expenditures (90 percent) had to be covered from the imperial treasury in Constantinople.[71]

A budget draft for 1613, which contains only *cizye* and *mukatta* revenues of the now four provinces in Ottoman Hungary (Buda, Temesvár, Eger, and Kanizsa), indicates that the effects of the war were devastating and that these provinces had to be heavily subsidized from the Balkan Peninsula for years after the war. In regions that lay in western Hungary and thus were most affected by the war, the bulk of the projected revenue—83 percent in the province of Buda and 80 percent in the province of Kanizsa—came from the Balkans. The treasuries of Temesvár and Eger—in southeast and northeast Hungary—were able to collect 63 and 54 percent of their revenue from their own provinces. However, they too had to collect the missing revenues from the Balkans. In general, the 1613 budget draft calculated almost 47 million *akçe* in revenue—that is, somewhat more than 313,000 Venetian ducats. However, less than 30 percent of this amount would be collected in the provinces themselves. Taxpayers living hundreds of kilometers to the south, in villages from Bosnia to Vidin, were expected to pay more than 70 percent of the amount needed to cover the wages of soldiers of the four frontier provinces in Hungary.[72]

The taxpayers in the two most affected provinces of Kanizsa and Buda recovered very slowly. In 1619, almost 70 percent of the money (12.6 million *akçe*) needed to pay soldiers' wages in the province of Kanizsa still came from the Balkans. The finances of the province of Buda were equally miserable. In 1631, less than 28 percent of the province's *cizye* and *mukataa* revenues (almost 29.5 million *akçe*) were collected locally. Taxpayers in the Balkans provided the remaining 72 percent. The finances of the province of Buda had not improved much a generation later. In 1662–63, a little more than one-third of the province's revenues originated from the province. The rest was collected from the Balkans. The situation in the newly established province of Érsekújvár was even direr. Érsekújvár lay in Vienna's approaches, only about 130 kilometers (as the crow flies) from the Habsburg capital, and its military force was substantial (2,800 local troops and 1,430 central janissaries in 1667). Almost all of their wages were covered by the central imperial treasury and revenues from the Balkans. The situation was much better in the small province of Várad in the east. The province had only about 1,200 soldiers in Várad and four minor forts. Since the region's densely populated areas were relatively undamaged by the recent war, it seems that the provincial treasury was capable of paying most of the soldiers from local revenues. In short, available budgets indicate a substantial deficit in all three western frontier provinces of Ottoman Hungary (Buda, Kanizsa, and Érsekújvár), all of which were ransacked by the wars of 1593–1606 and 1663–64. In these provinces, the wages of the local garrison troops had to be paid by taxpayers in the Balkan Peninsula and from the imperial treasury. The situation was better in the two eastern provinces of Temesvár and Várad. Even Eger in the northeast managed to recover from the devastations of the Long War of 1593–1606.[73] The relatively small province of Érsekújvár, which had a disproportionately large military garrison but meager financial resources, was not a unique case. In Kamaniçe, the empire's northernmost province that existed between 1672 and 1699, local revenues covered only 3 percent of the province's expenditure, most of which was spent on the salaries of the local garrison soldiers. The missing funds had to be transferred from the imperial treasury and from provinces as remote as Aleppo and Saida.[74]

Condominium and the Geography of Sovereignty

Although the Hungarian provinces were part of the regular Ottoman administrative system with *timars* and cadastral surveys, actual administrative and taxation practices were different from those of the core zones. The military balance of power and the armed strength of the Hungarian border fortress soldiers resulted in joint sovereignty, or *condominium*, and double Hungarian-Ottoman taxation. Villagers had both an Ottoman *sipahi* and a Hungarian landlord and paid taxes to both. This situation seemed natural for contemporaries. The Ottoman warden (*dizdar*) of the castle of Koppány wrote to the commander of the Hungarian forces in southern Transdanubia that "Your Lordship's village, Nagyegrös, is in my possession in Turkey, I mean, it is in Your Lordship's possession in Hungary."[75] Throughout the Ottoman era, the Hungarian Estates considered their subjugation to the Ottomans to be temporary, and the Ottoman-ruled areas as inalienable parts of the Hungarian crown, wherein the rights of both the Hungarian king and nobility remained in effect. Consequently, the Hungarian nobles and authorities insisted on their rights to collect taxes and dues from their subjects living under Ottoman rule. In 1573, the Lutheran chaplain Stephan Gerlach praised the Hungarian citizens of the market town Tolna, south of Buda, for their loyalty. "Tolna's inhabitants, like those living in the villages and market towns south of Buda, are loyal to our emperor. Although they have to serve the Turks, they pay their taxes to His Majesty, the emperor. They remained loyal to him and wished to stay faithful until they die."[76] However, the good Lutheran minister was mistaken. Heartfelt allegiance to their king, church, and native landlords did not persuade the Hungarian peasants to continue paying taxes to the Hungarian side over and above the poll tax (*cizye*) and tithe (*öşr*) they owed to the padishah and his *sipahis*. The emperor-king's subjects happily forgot to pay their taxes and dues to their Habsburg and Hungarian masters. Only the soldiers and tax collectors living in the Hungarian border fortresses reminded them of their duties, collecting their share of the taxes, if necessary, at the point of a gun.

The condominium existed because the Hungarian political elite and their institutions in Royal Hungary survived. The Hungarian Estates found refuge on the far side of the military border. From their base in Habsburg-ruled Hungary, the Estates defended their interests vis-à-vis the Ottoman central government and its local representatives with the assistance of the Hungarian garrisons and the Habsburg diplomacy. Apart from the Serbian-populated Srem in southern Hungary, no major region in the country avoided paying some kind of tax to the Hungarian side. Taxes to landlords were collected regularly. State and church taxes could be collected only from two-thirds of the Ottoman-held territories in the sixteenth century and only from half of it in the seventeenth century. The Hungarian taxation in Ottoman-ruled areas was surprisingly efficient just years after the Ottoman conquest. For instance, in the region between the Danube and Tisza Rivers, more than 77 percent of the families who paid the poll tax (*cizye*) to the Ottomans in 1546 also paid the Hungarian state tax (*dica*) in 1550. The Hungarian garrisons of Szigetvár, Eger, and Gyula played a key role in establishing Hungarian taxation under the Ottoman-ruled areas. As early as 1549, the Porte received complaints that the garrison soldiers of Eger demanded taxes from villagers living around Sremski Karlovci and Petrovaradin.[77] Both had been in Ottoman hands for more than twenty years and lay some four hundred kilometers south of Eger. The Ottomans repeatedly demanded the surrender of both castles and attempted to take Eger in 1552 and Szigetvár in 1556. Although they finally conquered both fortresses in 1596 and 1566, respectively, the Hungarian nobles took over the task of taxation, which continued. Most nobles had fled their former estates (now under Ottoman rule) and settled in Royal Hungary. Many assumed the captainships of the border castles. Using the soldiers under their command, they collected manorial, state, and church taxes. The soldiers in the border fortresses, whose wages were in arrears, happily assisted their lords, as these taxes became a significant revenue source for them as well.[78] Initially, the Ottoman authorities vehemently rejected the idea that the subjects of the padishah—subjugated by his mighty sword—pay taxes to their former Hungarian lords, churches, and the Habsburg kings.[79] However, the local Ottoman soldiery was unable to seal the borders and prevent soldiers in the Hungarian border forts from extracting these taxes. Conversely, the Hungarian authorities never succeeded in completely halting Ottoman tax collection in territories that were, according to treaties and border demarcations, under the control of the Hungarian crown. While double taxation also existed in other frontier provinces of the Ottoman Empire for shorter or longer periods, it became neither as prevalent nor as systematized as in Hungary.

In addition to taxation, the Hungarian nobles also administered their estates as if the Ottomans were not present. They mortgaged their estates, sold them, and included them in their wills, according to Hungarian common law. The weakest of all the former Hungarian institutions that continued to exert some influence in Ottoman-ruled territories were the noble counties. Most fell apart shortly after conquest. The work of the few remaining "refugee counties" operating from Royal Hungary was confined to the legal transactions among the Hungarian nobles. Although these "refugee counties" passed regulatory decrees and statutes regarding issues not governed (or insufficiently governed) by the kingdom's laws, they did not replace the Ottoman authorities. The Ottomans often debated the same affairs. At the beginning of the seventeenth century, the Hungarian authorities at the county level strengthened their positions vis-à-vis the local Ottomans, owing in part to the withdrawal of the Ottoman administration from the countryside to Ottoman fortresses during the long Habsburg-Ottoman war of 1593–1606.[80]

Market towns in the padishah's Hungarian domains were more successful than the noble counties in their attempt to administer justice independently of the Ottomans. Ottoman judges worked in only a handful of garrison towns. In the more numerous Hungarian market towns with no Ottoman garrison, Muslim judges were rarely present, and all of them had left by the 1620s. As a consequence, the task of maintaining law and order, crime prevention, inquiry, and judgment remained the prerogative of the local Hungarian authorities.[81] In the border zone, raiding and pillaging were part of everyday life. Robbers, criminals, marauding Hungarian and Ottoman soldiers, and German, Spanish, and Italian mercenaries in Habsburg service posed a constant threat to the people living in towns unprotected by walls and soldiers. The Long War of 1593–1606 saw the collapse of public safety and the creation of local self-defense mechanisms. Municipal records show that many towns in Ottoman Hungary had already obtained the right to pursue and arrest looting soldiers and criminals, pass justice, and issue death sentences in the decades after the Ottoman conquest. Towns that lay closer to Royal Hungary or Transylvania acquired these rights immediately. Debrecen—one of the largest market towns in Hungary, with some 12,000 inhabitants in the second half of the seventeenth century—accepted Ottoman suzerainty and paid an annual tribute of 50,000 *akçe* in 1555. The Ottoman authorities classified the town as crown land or imperial *hass*, and its revenue was allocated for the payment of the garrisons of Buda, Eger, Szolnok, and—after its conquest in 1660—Várad.[82] In 1564, the town acquired from Zal Mahmud Pasha of Buda (1563–64) the right to punish troublemakers and malefactors "according to their futile laws." The privilege included capital punishment.[83] Municipal records demonstrate that the town repeatedly exercised these rights in the sixteenth and seventeenth centuries. For settlements that lay in territories that the Ottomans could better control, the process that led to complete judicial autonomy lasted longer. These towns first acquired the right to pursue, capture, and try in their court malefactors who harmed their citizens or caused damage to their property. At this early stage, however, many towns needed permission from their respective Ottoman *sancak* governors and judges to exercise these juridical rights. At a later stage, the towns obtained the right to hang convicted criminals, mostly robbers and looting soldiers, according to their laws. In such cases, the Ottoman officials had no right to demand blood money. At a still later stage—for example, in the case of the Jász towns to the north of Szolnok only in the 1640s and 1650s—several market towns obtained permission to exercise these juridical rights over their citizens and not just over foreign criminals and looting soldiers. In addition, these municipal authorities administered disputes concerning guilds, artisans, and matters of probate and imposed and collected fines.[84] The captain-general of the Mining Towns Generalcy reminded his soldiers in 1555 that although "the Turks have occupied parts of our country . . . they have been unable to introduce their institutions or laws. They must tolerate that those [occupied] parts continue to use their own institutions and laws."[85]

Similar condominiums developed in areas where the Ottomans could not fully occupy and integrate into their core territories, and where the former elites retained their positions and the strength of their armed forces. Examples include the Balkan Peninsula, eastern Asia Minor, Georgia in the Caucasus, and the Arab provinces. While exhibiting significant differences over time and according to place, this sharing of authority for a shorter or longer period extended to areas such as taxation, public administration, and justice. In the hereditary *sancaks* of the provinces of Diyarbakır, Van, Shahrizor, Aleppo, Baghdad, and Mosul— generally headed by the leaders of Turkmen, Kurdish, and Arab tribes— the Ottoman government neither introduced the *timar* system nor carried out any revenue surveys. The revenue of the territory went to the local power holders, and the central Ottoman government received no income from these areas. The situation differed in the so-called *ocaklık* (family estate) *sancaks* of the eastern provinces, where part of the revenue may have been remitted to the sultan's treasury. Arab tribal leaders could also keep their former territories in return for cooperation with the Ottoman authorities. The annual income of an Arab tribal leader often reached 200,000–300,000 *akçe*, which roughly corresponded to the income of a junior *sancak* governor in the empire's core provinces. In some cases, the sum was several times more. The nominal income of the *sancak* governor of Karadağ in the province of Baghdad from his hereditary district (*hükümet*) exceeded 800,000 *akçe* annually. This sum was on par with the income of an Ottoman provincial governor-general.[86]

In many places, the Ottoman authorities preserved pre-Ottoman legal customs concerning land ownership and taxation. The first law books (*kanunname*) of the *sancaks* in eastern Asia Minor often copied the Akkoyunlu, Dulkadır, and Mamluk regulations and laws. The laws of Alaüddevle of Dulkadır, for instance, served as a model for the legal code of the *sancak* of Bozok. The *kanunname* of the *sancak* of Diyarbakır read the same as the legal code of Uzun Hasan of Akkoyunlu. The first *kanunnames* of many other eastern *sancaks* and smaller administrative units (Ergani, Urfa, Mardin, Çimrik, Siverek, Erzincan, Kemah, and Bayburt) were based in part on the laws of Hasan Padishah (that is, Uzun Hasan). All of these legal codes, as well as the special regulations that applied to the nomadic Turkmen tribes, preserved the pre-Ottoman tribal customs of the Turkmens, which often contradicted the Ottoman *kanuns*, and retained the former rules regarding property relations. The abrogation of some of the pre-Ottoman regulations and the introduction of Ottoman provincial tax regulations took place only decades later. The reduction of the tax burden on subjects motivated these administrative changes. Still, in many places double taxation survived for many generations.[87]

After the conquest of the Caucasus, the Porte left members of the former Georgian ruling families at the head of the newly established Georgian *sancaks*. In some cases, families whose members were still Christians received these territories as family estates. Only later did they convert to Islam to keep their lands and pass them to their sons. In 1578 the Ottomans established the new province of Çıldır (Akhaltsikhe) and appointed the region's former Georgian prince as its first *beylerbeyi*. Together with his brother, who had been given the *sancak* of Oltu (near Erzurum), they were awarded an Ottoman *hass* with an annual revenue of 900,000 *akçe*. With some exceptions, the Georgian princes of Samtskhe administered the new province as hereditary governors until the mid-eighteenth century. In the mountainous areas of Guria, Imeretia, Mingrelia Svaneti, and Abkhazia that were more difficult to conquer, the Ottomans wisely permitted the rule of vassal Georgian princes, who recognized the authority of the padishah by paying symbolic (and often irregular) tributes.[88]

When neither the Ottoman authorities nor the local indigenous elites could maintain law and order and provide security and safety for villagers from bandits and marauding soldiers, villagers formed their own militias and self-defense organizations. These militia groups or gatherings of peasants were known in Hungary as "peasant county" (*paraszt vármegye*) and *zapis* in territories inhabited by Slavic peoples. These armed insurrections of peasants led by their captains provided for the villagers' defense.[89] In Asia Minor, such self-defense organizations were known as *il-erleri*, "militiamen of the province." Members of such groups were young men from the villages who elected their leaders. Their task was to ensure public order and security in the villages and surrounding areas. When the regular provincial forces led by the *sancak* and provincial governors proved incapable of protecting the countryside from raids, brigandage, and banditry, the authorities turned to these peasant militia organizations. The government tried to keep these organizations under its control by insisting that, after being elected by village chiefs, the leader's name be submitted to the Porte by local judges and then confirmed by the government via a certificate of appointment.[90] In the sixteenth century, such peasant militias operated both in the core territories and in the frontier regions: in the provinces of Anadolu, Karaman, Sivas, and Rumeli and the villages of the Aegean and Black Sea coasts that were vulnerable to enemy attack. The authorities used the militias against robbers, brigands, rebels, insurgents, and *levends* who were ravaging the countryside, storming villages and markets, devastating the gardens and vineyards, and laying waste to the stables and flocks.[91] The village militias often operated under the command of *sancak* governors, and the Porte authorized them to kill the rebels, assuring them that they would not be punished and no blood money would be collected from them.[92] The pragmatism of the Ottomans allowed for as much flexibility as was needed for the maintenance of occupation.

14

Wars of Exhaustion

War with Venice: Dalmatia and Crete

After the Ottoman-Venetian war of 1570–73, Venice and the Ottoman Empire enjoyed the longest peace in their history until the outbreak of the Cretan war in 1645. Although there had been smaller incidents in the Adriatic, the Porte was willing to overlook them as it was fighting against the Celalis in Asia Minor and the Safavids in Iraq. Interested in maintaining their commerce operations in the Ottoman domains, the Venetians also tried their best to maintain peace with the Porte. However, it was impossible to prevent incidents along the 2,400-kilometer-long (1,500 mile) border.

In late September 1644, six Maltese galleys of the Knights Hospitaller, who had been plundering in the Greek Archipelago for a decade, attacked a small Ottoman fleet heading to Mecca. The main Ottoman galleon was carrying the newly appointed judge of Mecca, Bursevi Mehmed Efendi, the recently dismissed Chief Black Eunuch of the Imperial Harem, Sünbül Agha—with all his riches, concubines, and horses—and hundreds of Muslim pilgrims heading to the annual pilgrimage. The Maltese pirates stopped in Venetian Crete, whose southern shores the Venetians were unable to control. The Venetian government had done its best to deter the Maltese pirates preying on Ottoman shipping. Venice worried that the Ottomans might use such an incident as an excuse to declare war on the republic and attack Crete, the last major Venetian island in the Mediterranean. The Ottoman Empire still looked formidable. The Venetians knew that despite constant intrigues and factional strife at the Ottoman court of Sultan Ibrahim (r. 1640–48), the Porte was capable of mobilizing a great armada.

The time was opportune for war. The Porte had just concluded its last major war against the Safavids, and it had been at peace with the Habsburgs in Hungary since 1606. Nobody could predict that the war with the Venetians would drag on for twenty-five years and deplete the resources of both parties. After the incident, the Venetian *bailo* diligently kept the Signoria informed about the extensive construction work at the Ottoman naval arsenal in Constantinople and about the mobilization of troops and resources throughout the empire. However, Ottoman propaganda duped the Venetians into believing that the padishah's armada would strike at the Knights of Malta.[1]

The war party at the Porte, led by the young padishah's influential tutor Cinci ("Demon-Chaser") Hüseyin Hoca, decided to seize Crete from the Venetians. According to Venetian sources, Grand Admiral Silahdar Yusuf Pasha allied with the war party. Born as Josef Masković, Yusuf was a convert to Islam from Dalmatia and the favorite companion of the padishah. The padishah gave his daughter, Fatma Sultan, in marriage to Yusuf, making him an imperial son-in-law. In 1643 Yusuf was promoted to the padishah's arms bearer. The next year the padishah appointed him grand admiral of the imperial navy with the rank of vizier. After the decision to go to war against Venice, he was made commander in chief of the expedition.[2]

The Ottoman fleet left Constantinople on 30 April 1645. The Porte had already sent 90 smaller transport ships and galleons to Thessaloniki and 60 vessels to the harbor of Çeşme to get soldiers and supplies. The Ottomans also chartered about 200 merchant ships, which carried 840 metric tons (15,000 kantars) of gunpowder, 50,000 cannonballs, and 50 heavy basilisks. Yusuf's fleet of two galleasses, a great galleon, ten chartered vessels from the Dutch and English, and about 250 transport ships reportedly carried some 50,000 men. After it was stocked with water and supplies at the Venetian island of Tinos in the Cyclades Archipelago, the fleet rounded the Morea and stopped at Navarino on the western coast as though it was indeed heading against Malta. Having joined with the galleys from Tripoli and Tunis, the armada raised anchor two weeks later. Yusuf now read the imperial order to the ship captains, revealing the campaign's actual target, Crete. By 23 June, the fleet arrived in the Bay of Chania and started to land troops, including 7,000 janissaries, 14,000 *sipahis* of the Porte, 3,000 sappers, and tens of thousands of *timariot sipahis*. After fifty-four days of siege, the defenders of Chania signaled their intention to surrender. Four days later (22 August) Yusuf took possession of the fortress. Having repaired the fortress, he appointed the governor-general of Rumeli to Chania, left a garrison of some 12,000 troops (including 4,000 janissaries and 4,000 *sipahis*), and ordered the survey of the conquered lands. However, upon his return to Constantinople, the rivalry between Yusuf and Grand Vizier Semin Pasha resulted in the latter's removal from office and Yusuf's execution (22 January 1646).[3] In the first two years of the war, Ottoman troops also conquered Rethymnon. In May 1648, they laid siege to Candia, the island's strongest fortress and the capital of Venetian Crete. Nobody could predict that Candia, a cannon-fortress built by the Venetians to withstand modern firepower, would resist Ottoman sieges for the next twenty-one years.

In the first eleven years of the Cretan war, the Ottoman leadership launched thirteen naval campaigns to bring reinforcements and supplies to the army and garrisons on the island. Three times (in 1648, 1650, and 1652) the navy was unable to leave Constantinople, as the Venetians blockaded the Dardanelles Straits. Three other times (in 1649, 1654, and 1655) the Ottomans broke the Venetian blockade and sailed to the Aegean. But only in 1654—at the first battle of the Dardanelles (16 May)—were the Ottomans superior to the Venetians. Although in the remaining campaigns the Straits were not under Venetian blockade, the Ottomans still suffered defeat in naval battles.[4]

Realizing the inferiority of their oar-rigged galleys against the Venetian sailing galleons, the Ottomans started to increase the number of their galleons, which they had used regularly as transport ships. The English ambassador, Sir Thomas Bendish, reported in the spring of 1651 that the Ottomans had built some fifteen to twenty galleons the previous year "framed after the Dutch fashion carrying 35, 40 and 50 great brass guns apiece." Bendish predicted that if the Turks would be able to use them effectively, "they would doubtless in a few years become at sea very formidable."[5] Nevertheless, the Ottoman experiment with galleons proved unsuccessful. In May 1651, a newly built large galleon sunk as soon as it was launched into the Golden Horn. The Ottoman shipbuilders were able to construct smaller galleons. Of the navy's 150 vessels in 1651, 30 were galleons. But this navy suffered a severe defeat in June, near Naxos in the Cyclades, because the janissaries who were aboard refused to fight and forced the ship captains to ground their vessels. After the defeat, the Ottomans suspended the construction of galleons.[6]

The Venetians soundly defeated the Ottomans in 1655 and 1656, at the second and third battles of the Dardanelles. Of the two battles, the second was more consequential. As soldiers serving on galleys close to the shore deserted (26 June 1656), the Ottomans suffered their gravest defeat since Lepanto. The Venetians captured eight Ottoman galleys and destroyed the rest of the navy, save for the admiral's vessel and twenty other ships. More dangerously for the Ottomans, the Venetians captured Tenedos (Tr. Bozcaada) in July and Lemnos (Tr. Limni) in August, effectively controlling the entrance of the Dardanelles Straits and blocking the Ottomans from sending reinforcements and supplies to their troops besieging Candia.[7] The loss of the two islands sent shock waves through the empire. In Constantinople many feared an imminent Venetian attack. At this critical moment, Hadice Turhan Sultan, the mother of Sultan Mehmed IV (r. 1648–87), who acted as regent for the fourteen-year-old padishah, suggested the appointment of the aged Köprülü Mehmed Pasha as grand vizier.

Mehmed Pasha had been recruited from Albania via the *devşirme*. While he considered Albania his "original home," he was named Köprülü after his adopted hometown of Köprü in north-central Asia Minor.[8] He had a long and distinguished record of government service and had been suggested to the grand vizierate in 1651. Later he was sidelined by the then grand vizier Gürcü (Georgian) Mehmed. His appointment in 1656 surprised many of the political elite because he had not held significant positions and had been absent from the capital for some years. The fact that he had not been part of the court factions' intrigues of the preceding years helped his chances of appointment.

Arriving in the capital in early July 1656 in the company of Grand Vizier Boynu Yaralı Mehmed Pasha, Köprülü Mehmed shared his ideas with his influential friends in the capital as to how to handle the grave situation the government faced. These friends then persuaded the queen mother and the sultan to appoint him to the highest office of the empire. In mid-September, Boynu Yaralı Mehmed was dismissed, and Köprülü Mehmed was appointed as grand vizier. Mehmed Pasha accepted the grand vizier's seal only after the queen mother had promised to honor his conditions: nobody would interfere with his governing, and his policies would not be opposed; they would accept his appointments so that the ablest men would get offices; and both the young padishah and his mother would back him up if he faced opposition.[9] Such conditions were not unheard of but previously had brought little stability.[10] Factionalism, court intrigues, rivalries, fights between the infantry janissaries and the standing cavalry, and uprisings of soldiers and merchants in the capital, and of provincial governors in Asia Minor and Syria defeated eighteen grand viziers in the past ten years. Factionalism and uprisings also cost the lives of Sultan Ibrahim in 1648 and the old queen mother Kösem in 1651. Few in the empire and abroad thought that Köprülü Mehmed's tenure would be any different.

The new grand vizier was determined to break the Venetian blockade and retake the lost islands. The fourth battle of the Dardanelles (17–19 July 1657) ended with an Ottoman victory after an Ottoman cannonball ignited the gunpowder and bombs on the Venetian flagship. Later that year, the Ottomans recovered Tenedos (31 August) and Lemnos (12 November). Köprülü Mehmed also had plans to attack Venetian Dalmatia and Friuli using the Ottomans' traditional strength in land warfare and thus forcing the Venetians to give up Candia.

Dalmatia had been a subordinate front in the Cretan war since the beginning of the conflict. In 1647 and 1648, the Venetians secured Novigrad and Skradin and conquered the important fortresses of Knin and Klis (It. Clissa).[11] The losses had severe repercussions. The janissaries who orchestrated the dethronement of Sultan Ibrahim in 1648 cited among their grievances the loss of Klis together with the inability of the Ottoman navy to break the Venetian blockade of the Dardanelles.[12] Venetian successes encouraged rebellion among the Ottomans' Christian subjects, driving semiautonomous regions to seek Venetian protection, while forcing others, including the seminomadic Morlacchi of Ottoman Dalmatia and Lika, to migrate to Venetian-controlled lands. By 1649 the Venetian operations had reached their limits. The Serenissima's attempt in 1649 to instigate rebellion among the Albanian Christians failed.

In 1657, Köprülü decided to conquer the strategically important Venetian fort of Kotor (It. Cattaro) at the Bay of Kotor, near Herzeg-Novi, the center of the *sancak* of Herzegovina. However, Köprülü was unsuccessful in his attempt. The failure of the expedition illustrates how factionalism and rivalry among the local elite could sabotage and derail the Porte's plans. The grand vizier assigned the task to his man, the newly appointed *sancak* governor of Shkodër, Hisim Mehmed Pasha, known in Venetian sources as Mehmed Pasha Varlac. But the former *sancak* governor of Shkodër, Yusufbegović, and his kinsman Çengizade Ali sabotaged Hisim Mehmed. Ali, the *sancak* governor of Herzegovina, was a member of the powerful Çengi clan of southern Bosnia and Herzegovina. Throughout the expedition, Çengizade Ali cooperated with Antonio Bernardo, the Venetian governor-general in Dalmatia and Albania, who personally directed the defense of the fort. Ali arrived for the siege with only a thousand troops, half of them Christians. During the siege, he kept Bernardo informed about the Ottoman siege plans and arranged for the Ottoman siege cannons not to damage the walls. Çengizade Ali also claimed credit for the many "accidents" that befell the Ottoman besiegers, such as exploding cannons and the mysterious fire that consumed fifteen sacks of gunpowder. Ali also convinced the governor-general of Bosnia, Seydi Ahmed Pasha, that the siege held no prospect of success. The Circassian Seydi Ahmed required little convincing, as he was the rival of the Albanian grand vizier. Apart from tensions between Ottoman statesmen of Caucasian (Abkhazian, Circassian, and Georgian) and Balkan (Bosnian and Albanian) origin,[13] Seydi Ahmed resented Köprülü Mehmed for personal reasons as well. Upon assuming the grand vizierate, Köprülü Mehmed dismissed Ahmed from his post as grand admiral of the navy and appointed him governor of Bosnia, which Ahmed considered tantamount to exile.[14] Therefore, it came as no surprise that in 1657 Seydi Ahmed too sabotaged the siege of Kotor, arriving only in late September. Days later in early October, after more than two months of halfhearted fighting, the grand vizier's man and the campaign's commander in chief, Hisim Mehmed, lifted the siege of Kotor, without the Ottomans attempting to storm the walls of the fort even once.[15]

In the winter of 1657 and the spring of 1658, the Venetian Senate continued receiving alarming reports about Ottoman war preparations and the grand vizier's plans to lead the Ottoman army into Dalmatia. The Ottomans even approached the Habsburgs, asking them to let the Ottoman army march through Habsburg territory to strike the Venetian mainland. By this time, the grand vizier and the young sultan Mehmed IV had arrived in Edirne to oversee the preparations for the planned campaign against Venice. But events that unfolded in Poland-Lithuania and Transylvania derailed the grand vizier's war plan.[16] The ensuing wars in Transylvania and Hungary tied up Ottoman troops and resources for the next seven years; thus, the grand vizier could not concentrate on Dalmatia and Crete.

Transylvania and Its Rebel Princes

During the Thirty Years' War in Europe, the Ottomans were engaged in their own thirty years' war (1603–12, 1615–18, 1623–39) against the Safavids. The official policy in Vienna and Constantinople was to maintain the peace. As we have seen, the parties repeatedly renewed the Treaty of Zsitvatorok (1606). However, this does not mean that the Porte was neutral during the Thirty Years' War. The Ottoman government and its factions in Constantinople and the Hungarian frontier followed the events in Europe carefully. They participated in the conflict by supporting or sabotaging the Transylvanian princes' attacks against the Habsburgs. Occasionally, the Porte also accepted the Transylvanian princes' requests for military help and ordered its governors in Hungary and Bosnia to help the Transylvanians. However, to maintain peace with

Vienna, the Porte officially condemned these campaigns and denied its involvement.

Having consulted and received permission from the Porte, Prince Gabriel (Gábor) Bethlen of Transylvania launched a campaign against Emperor Ferdinand II in late August 1619. The Porte initially supported Bethlen because he promised an Ottoman-vassal Hungarian Kingdom. His troops conquered Kassa, the center of the Habsburg military command in Upper Hungary, and Pozsony, the capital of the Kingdom of Hungary. By late November he joined the Protestant armies besieging Vienna. However, after pro-Habsburg Hungarian and Polish forces defeated his general in Upper Hungary, Bethlen lifted Vienna's siege and withdrew. He hoped in vain that the Porte would support his ambitions for the Hungarian and Czech thrones. Having received Sultan Osman II's approval to elect their king, the pro-Bethlen nobles assembled at the Diet of Besztercebánya (Slov. Banská Bystrica). They dethroned Ferdinand II and elected Bethlen king of Hungary (25 August 1620). However, Bethlen was never crowned. Earlier historiography maintained that the Porte did not allow Bethlen—or anyone else—to rule the vassal Principality of Transylvania and Hungary (or any other kingdom in the region) at the same time. However, this premise does not seem to be a general Ottoman policy. In Bethlen's case, it was the anti-Bethlen frontier faction, supported by the grand mufti Esad Efendi in Constantinople, that did not allow Bethlen to be crowned as king of Hungary and keep Transylvania at the same time.[17] In light of imperial success and the lack of any tangible Ottoman support, Bethlen made peace with Ferdinand II. At the Treaty of Nikolsburg (Mikulov in the Czech Republic, 31 December 1621–6 January 1622) he conceded his claim to St. Stephen's crown to Ferdinand, while Ferdinand ceded seven counties in Upper Hungary to Bethlen and guaranteed to continue financing their garrisons.

Meanwhile, Sultan Osman II declared war on the Poles in 1621 and personally commanded the Ottoman army in the failed Khotyn (Pol. Chocim) war. Before that campaign, viziers and members of the ulama argued that recent Polish interference in Moldavia and Cossack attacks against the Ottoman Black Sea coast did not warrant a campaign commanded by the padishah. They believed that provincial governors or an army led by a military commander in chief could have dealt with the problem, as they had done for years. However, Sultan Osman II hoped that a successful campaign would enhance his legitimacy and empower him to overhaule the military and governance, just as his ancestors Mehmed II and Süleyman I did after their conquests of Constantinople (1453), Belgrade (1521), and Rhodes (1522). As it turned out, the sultan's plan backfired. The campaign ended in failure, and Osman II was deposed and murdered. It was the first regicide in Ottoman history.[18]

As a client of the padishah, Bethlen regularly informed the Sublime Porte about his anti-Habsburg policies and plans. He also sought Ottoman military assistance for his campaigns from the beginning of the conflict. During the Khotyn campaign, there was little chance that the Ottoman sultan would be involved in Bethlen's anti-Habsburg wars. But he tried to influence the Porte's Habsburg and central European policies by actively lobbying in Constantinople. In the spring of 1623, Bethlen asked the grand vizier to appoint Sufi Mehmed Pasha of Buda as commander in chief of an Ottoman army that would support his campaign against Emperor Ferdinand II. Bethlen asked for thirty thousand troops for Mehmed and an additional twelve thousand men under the command of the governor-general of Bosnia. He promised that he would lead his army of twenty-four thousand men. In the end, the Porte appointed the governor-general of Bosnia, Sarhoş Ibrahim, to aid Bethlen's campaign with some ten thousand men, and ordered the governor of Silistra with the troops under his command to help Ibrahim.[19] However, Ottoman military assistance had little impact as neither Behlen nor his Ottoman allies wanted to attack Ferdinand II. Bethlen, therefore, renewed the peace with the emperor in Vienna (8 May 1624). A year later, Sultan Murad IV and Ferdinand II restored the peace in Gyarmat (28 May 1625). But neither treaty lasted long. In 1626, Bethlen launched his third campaign against the Habsburgs with military support from the Porte. Ottoman troops under the command of Murteza Pasha of Buda did not alter the conflict. Bethlen concluded another treaty with Ferdinand (20 December 1626, Pozsony) based on the 1620 pact. The emperor and the sultan shortly followed suit, renewing the Ottoman-

Habsburg peace (13 September 1627, Szőny) that had been disturbed by Bethlen's campaign. The ever-changing power relations and factional struggle between the Ottoman frontier and the metropolitan elite shaped Ottoman policy regarding Bethlen's anti-Habsburg wars. It was also influenced by the Habsburg and Transylvanian diplomats in Constantinople. During Vienna's and Constantinople's respective Thirty Years' Wars, the parties managed to maintain the peace. A generation later, the Transylvanian prince's attempt to secure the Polish-Lithuanian Commonwealth's throne triggered a retaliatory Ottoman campaign. Ottoman attacks in Transylvania and Hungary quickly erupted in an Ottoman-Habsburg war.

Hetman Bohdan Khmelnytsky of the Zaporozhian Cossacks rebelled against the Poles in 1648, allying himself with the Crimean khan, the Porte's vassal. In 1652 Khmelnytsky entered into an alliance with the Porte, but having received little tangible assistance from Constantinople, he turned to Moscow. Following protracted negotiations, Khmelnytsky swore allegiance to Tsar Alexis (r. 1645–76) in early 1654 in Pereiaslav. This not only led to a joint Muscovite-Cossack attack on the Polish-Lithuanian Commonwealth, but also engineered a long-standing Polish–Crimean Tatar alliance (1654–66) against Muscovy and the Hetmanate. By the time the Sejm (the lower chamber of the Commonwealth's parliament) voted to raise eighteen thousand Lithuanian and thirty-five thousand Polish troops, a seventy-thousand-strong Muscovite army and some twenty thousand Cossacks were marching against the Commonwealth. In early October the tsar's forces took the strategically important Smolensk. A year later, on 9 August 1655, Tsar Alexis made a triumphal entry to the Lithuanian capital Wilno (Vilnius), occupying most of the Grand Duchy of Lithuania.[20] Attacked by its eastern rival, John II Casimir (Jan Kazimierz) Vasa of Poland-Lithuania (r. 1648–68) sought help in Constantinople but received no military assistance. Meanwhile, fearing that Russia would overrun the Commonwealth, Charles X Gustav of Sweden (r. 1654–60) attacked Poland in July 1655. In doing so, he claimed the crown from his cousin John Casimir and started what would later be called the Second Northern War (1655–60), and in Polish historiography "the Deluge." As most of the

regular army was still fighting Khmelnytsky's Cossacks and their Muscovite allies in Ukraine, the Poles could not defend themselves. In July,
the Greater Poland (Wielkopolska) noble levy surrendered to the
Swedes. A month later the Protestant grand hetman of Lithuania, Janusz
Radziwiłł, accepted Swedish protection. Another treaty in October recognized Charles X Gustav as the grand duke of Lithuania, annulled the
1569 union with Poland, and proclaimed the union with Sweden.
Charles X Gustav entered Warsaw on 8 September. With John Casimir
leaving for exile in Habsburg Silesia, Poland's ancient capital Cracow
capitulated on 19 October 1655. However, the atrocities and the invaders' looting of churches and monasteries energized the Poles and Lithuanians. Nobles and peasants mounted a spirited defense, especially after
protecting the Pauline monastery of Jasna Góra in Czestochowa, which
became the symbol of resistance to the "heretic" invaders. By early 1656,
John Casimir was back in Poland, and the Polish and Lithuanian magnates returned to his fold. However, the Commonwealth's forces and its
Crimean Tatar allies suffered defeat at Warsaw (28–30 July 1656) at the
hands of the joint army of Charles X Gustav and the Calvinist Frederick
William, elector of Brandenburg. The latter had broken his vassal allegiance to John Casimir; at the treaties of Marienburg (25 June 1656) and
Labiau (20 November 1656), Frederick William allied with Charles X
Gustav in return for hereditary sovereignty over Greater Poland. But the
Swedes could not capitalize on their victory. Having placed his forces
in Greater Poland, Frederick William refused further military action. In
November Tsar Alexis signed an alliance with the Commonwealth in
return for the promise of the Polish throne. The tsar also annulled his
peace with Charles X Gustav, attacking Swedish Livonia, where the
Swedish king had to redeploy part of his troops.[21]

Looking for a new ally, Charles X Gustav turned to George (György) II
Rákóczi (r. 1648–60) of Transylvania, an Ottoman vassal. The Transylvanian prince had been in communication with the Swedes for years.
Some five years earlier, Rákóczi had told the Swedish envoy that he
could get either the Hungarian or the Polish crown. During the conversation, the parties raised the idea of the Commonwealth's partition. The
Lithuanian and Polish nobles—including Janusz Radziwiłł, Stanisław

Potocki, and Jerzy Sebastian Lubomirski, a distant relative of Rákóczi's—had in the early 1650s also encouraged the Transylvanian prince to come to their defense. The Polish emissaries offered Spisz (Hun. Szepes, Slov. Spiš)—pawned to Poland by Sigismund of Luxemburg—and the remote possibility of the Polish crown, provided that Rákóczi raise his son as Catholic and arrange his marriage to one of Casimir's cousins. However, in return for military assistance, Charles X Gustav had a more tempting offer for Rákóczi: Lesser Poland (Pol. Małopolska), including Cracow. On 6 December 1656 in Radnót in Transylvania (today, Iernut in Romania), Rákóczi signed an anti-Polish alliance with the Swedish emissaries.[22] Rákóczi had signed similar treaties on 7 September at his court in Gyulafehérvár with Khmelnytsky's envoy and the Wallachian and Moldavian voivodes. In late January 1657, fourteen thousand Transylvanian and six thousand Wallachian and Moldavian troops attacked the Commonwealth. On 18 February, twenty thousand Cossacks joined Rákóczi.[23]

The Porte knew about Rákóczi's campaign from the outset, and it could not let his vassals jeopardize the balance of power in the region. As Zülfikar Agha—the Hungarian renegade chief interpreter and "expert" in Hungarian, Transylvanian, and eastern European affairs at the Porte—had noted in September 1656 to Jacob (Jakab) Harsányi, Rákóczi's resident diplomat at the Porte, Grand Vizier Köprülü Mehmed Pasha could have accepted Rákóczi on the Polish throne only if the Poles requested this from the padishah, and if Rákóczi ruled the Commonwealth as an Ottoman vassal (akin to Stephen Báthory, whom the Poles had elected their king in 1576). However, in 1657 the situation was rather different. Rákóczi was not elected to the Commonwealth throne, and he launched his campaign disregarding the Porte's orders. In January 1657, via the Transylvanian resident in Constantinople, Köprülü Mehmed ordered Rákóczi to abort his campaign. The grand vizier repeated his warnings through the Ottoman governors in Buda, Temesvár, and Eger and multiple envoys. In his apology, Rákóczi stated that he had answered the Poles' request and that the campaign served the Porte's interest. But in early May 1657, Sultan Mehmed IV rejected his vassal's excuses.[24]

By this time Rákóczi had taken possession of Cracow. Some two weeks later he joined the Swedish monarch. In May, the coalition army took Brest on the Bug River, near the border between Poland and Lithuania. On 17 June, Warsaw surrendered to Rákóczi, who was supported by Swedish troops. However, the campaign quickly lost momentum. The Polish and Lithuanian magnates withdrew their support from the Transylvanian prince. The Polish armies escaped open battles, constantly harassing the enemy in guerilla-type attacks.[25] The Swedish troops had to be withdrawn after the battle of Warsaw, as Denmark's Frederick III declared war on Sweden in June, signing an alliance with the Commonwealth in July. Disobeying their generals, most Cossacks also left Rákóczi after Brest, as they wanted to return to the Ukraine with their loot. Rákóczi now was caught between the Poles and the Crimean Tatars, who had been helping the Poles since 1654. The Transylvanian prince sued for peace on 22 July 1657. According to the humiliating terms of the treaty, Rákóczi had to end his alliance with Sweden and the Cossacks, return the occupied territories and captives, and pay a war indemnity of 1,200,000 gold pieces to the Commonwealth. Having left his troops under the command of John (János) Kemény, Rákóczi left for Transylvania with three hundred men. His army, however, did not reach Transylvania. The Lithuanian grand hetman Paweł Sapieha led the Transylvanian army into the arms of the Crimean Tatars near Trembowla (Terebovlia in western Ukraine). While Kemény was taken to meet the khan, the Tatars attacked the Transylvanian camp. They massacred many of the four thousand to five thousand troops, taking the survivors to the Crimea as slaves. Kemény would return to Transylvania from his Crimean captivity only in August 1659.[26]

Disciplining Vassals and Stabilizing the Northern Frontier

Rákóczi's Polish campaign alarmed the Ottoman leadership. The Porte could not tolerate the rebel vassal, who threatened to build an independent power base, jeopardizing the empire's Pontic defense ring against

Cossacks, Muscovites, and Poles. In addition to launching his Polish campaign against the Porte's orders, Rákóczi also brought the neighboring voivodes of Wallachia and Moldavia to his side. The Porte could not allow this. The Porte had a long-standing policy against one prince ruling two neighboring countries, a policy that Köprülü Mehmed Pasha reiterated in September 1659 in his letter to the Crimean khan.[27]

Historians often lump the Principality of Transylvania and the two Romanian voivodeships together as Ottoman vassals. However, the relationship among these three polities vis-à-vis the Porte differed considerably and changed over time, as did their relationship with each other. In general, Transylvania had more freedom of action, and its ties to the Porte were not as close as those of Wallachia and Moldavia. The Porte usually accepted and confirmed the Estates' election of the Transylvanian princes and did not station Ottoman troops in the principality's castles. Moreover, ever since the Treaty of Speyer (1570), the princes of Transylvania had acknowledged the suzerainty of the Habsburg kings of Hungary. This created a dual dependency for the Transylvanian princes.[28] Also, the voivodes of Wallachia and Moldavia from time to time pledged loyalty to the Transylvanian princes, who maintained their Hungarian secretaries at the voivodes' chanceries. These men duly informed the prince about the voivodes' policies. Occasionally, the Transylvanian princes also kept (with the Porte's consent) several hundred soldiers in Moldavia and Wallachia.[29]

Occupied as he was with war preparations against Venice, Köprülü Mehmed sought to resolve the Transylvanian problem by forcing the Transylvanians to get rid of Rákóczi and putting an obedient prince on the principality's throne.[30] The Venetians hoped that the Transylvanian problem might force Köprülü to make peace with the republic and leave Candia in Venetian hands, but the grand vizier quickly disappointed them. The Porte continued its war preparations against Friuli, and Köprülü told the Venetians that the padishah had enough resources to deal with the Transylvanians, Wallachians, and the Venetians at the same time.[31] In August 1657, on the Porte's orders, the Crimean Tatars ravaged Transylvania. In early November the Transylvanian diet deposed Rákóczi and elected as prince the old Francis (Ferenc) Rhédey—Rákóczi's proxy in Transylvania during the Polish campaign. In early 1658, the Porte ousted the pro-Rákóczi voivodes of Wallachia and Moldavia and replaced them with seemingly loyal ones: Mihnea III Radu and Gheorghe Ghika. Mihnea had lived in the household of Koca Kenan Pasha in the Ottoman capital until he was about forty years old. Since 1653, Ghika too had been living in Constantinople, where he befriended Köprülü Mehmed Pasha.[32]

Things did not turn out the way the grand vizier hoped. Rákóczi did not accept the Porte's decision. He controlled the principality's armed forces and key fortresses and thus wielded real power in the principality. He discredited Rhédey by citing the latter's willingness to surrender the key fortress of Jenő (R. Ineu) to the Ottomans. In late January 1658 the Transylvanian diet forced Rhédey to abdicate and reinstated Rákóczi as prince of Transylvania. Rákóczi now tried to help Constantin Şerban (the Wallachian voivode whom the Ottomans had ousted) regain his throne and that of Moldavia. Rákóczi also sought help from the Habsburgs. The Hungarians had elected Leopold king of Hungary in 1657 with the promise that he would liberate their country from the Turks. However, Habsburg armies were still fighting in Poland-Lithuania, and the Viennese government wanted to preserve the status quo with the Porte, established at the Peace of Zsitvatorok (1606). The German princes, for their part, were preoccupied with the election of a new emperor. As a consequence, Rákóczi's envoys got no tangible help at the imperial diet in Frankfurt.[33] By the time the diet elected Leopold Holy Roman emperor (18 July 1658), Grand Vizier Köprülü Mehmed Pasha was on his way to Transylvania to depose and eliminate Rákóczi.

The grand vizier decided to resolve the Transylvanian problem himself. In March 1658 he informed Leopold that the elimination of the rebel Rákóczi was necessary and beneficial for both parties, as Rákóczi's actions disturbed the peace between the two empires. Leopold assured the Porte via his resident there that he did not want to upset the status quo either.[34] Rákóczi and the Transylvanian nobles tried to negotiate with the Porte, offering gifts and more taxes, but to no avail. The grand vizier wanted to not only teach his disobedient vassal a lesson but also settle an old score with Rákóczi[35] The Porte demanded that the Transylvanians either kill or expel Rákóczi. The Venetians heard that Köprülü wanted to eliminate the Transylvanians' right to elect their prince, and instead appoint a voivode as in Wallachia and Moldavia. The grand vizier also entertained the possibility of putting a Cossack on the Transylvanian throne, an idea that the queen mother, Hadice Turhan, supported on account of her Cossack/Ukrainian origin.[36] Köprülü ordered the Crimean khan to attack Transylvania again, and Gürci ("the Georgian") Kenan Pasha of Buda to march against Rákóczi.[37] However, on 6 July, Kenan's army of about nine thousand men from the provinces of Buda, Eger, and Temesvár suffered a defeat near Pálülés (Pauliş in Romania). Kenan lost two thousand to three thousand of his men, including the provincial governor of Eger and the *sancak* governor of Esztergom.[38]

Köprülü Mehmed Pasha left Edirne on 23 June and arrived in Belgrade in late July 1658 with thirty thousand troops.[39] By late August, the Ottoman army had reached the strategically important Jenő—which Ottoman chroniclers called "the key to the infidel kingdoms."[40] Seeing the overwhelming strength of the Turks and receiving no help from Rákóczi, the defenders surrendered the castle on 2 September, without the besiegers firing a single gunshot.[41] Meanwhile, the Tatars ravaged Transylvania. They destroyed the principality's capital city Gyulafehérvár (Alba Julia) and took hundreds of people captive. To save their country, the Transylvanian Estates dispatched a delegation to the grand vizier, headed by Ákos Barcsay, a loyal statesman and experienced diplomat of the Rákóczis. On 6 September, at their first meeting in the Ottoman camp near Jenő, Vizier Kenan Pasha of Buda informed the delegation about the harsh conditions that the grand vizier had put forward for not turning Transylvania into an Ottoman province. These conditions included surrendering to the Turks the Hajdúság (the special-status towns in eastern Hungary where Stephen Bocskai had settled his *hajdú* mercenaries and granted them collective nobility), making Barcsay prince of Transylvania, raising the principality's annual tribute, and paying special tribute for Lugos and Karánsebes. Barcsay told Kenan Pasha that he could not accept the princely title as the princes had to be elected at the Transylvanian diet. In later meetings, the grand vizier increased his demands: now he also wanted the *Partium* with the key fortress of Várad and the castles of Lugos and Karánsebes. He also made clear that he would turn Transylvania into an Ottoman province if Barcsay did not accede to his conditions. In the end, Barcsay was declared prince of Transylvania. He agreed to hand over Lugos and Karánsebes and to raise Transylvania's annual tribute from 15,000 to 40,000 gold pieces.[42]

Köprülü stabilized the Porte's hold over Transylvania for the time being, but he failed to eliminate Rákóczi, who escaped to Habsburg territory and was organizing his return. The grand vizier could not deal with him, as his position at the Porte had become precarious. His opponents at the Porte accused him of squandering time and resources with his campaign against Rákóczi and neglecting the war against Venice.[43] More dangerous for the grand vizier was the rebellion of his old nemesis, Abaza ("the Abkhazian") Hasan Pasha.

Abaza Hasan, governor of Aleppo, had been ordered to join the Transylvanian campaign. Instead, he gathered a rebel army of thirty thousand men in Konya, mainly consisting of the provincial and private troops of some fifteen acting and former provincial governors. The rebels besieged the old capital Bursa to lend legitimacy to their cause, but to no avail. Then they marched against Constantinople, demanding the execution of Köprülü Mehmed. However, the young padishah stood firm on the side of his old grand vizier, who hastily returned to Edirne from Transylvania in mid-October. The government then returned to Constantinople and ordered an inspection of the central troops, disguised as a distribution of outstanding salaries. Some seven thousand cavalry of the Porte, who had failed to join the Transylvanian campaign, were dismissed from the corps. Those whom the grand vizier's agents could capture were executed. The harsh measures provoked disobedience among the janissaries, who now thought of siding with Abaza Hasan. However, winter came, and Abaza Hasan withdrew to Anatolia. Having seen his support eroded, he made a deal with Murteza Pasha, whom the government had sent against the rebels. The rebel commanders stayed in Aleppo in Murteza Pasha's mansion, awaiting news from Constantinople regarding their petition for pardon. On 24 February 1659 Murteza Pasha murdered the rebel leaders, sending their heads, stuffed with straw, to Constantinople and hanging their bodies on the city gate.[44] Although Ottoman chroniclers branded Abaza Hasan's insurrection as yet another Celali revolt, it was more dangerous. Unlike previous rebel leaders who had sought provincial governorship or other high government positions, Abaza Hasan wanted his state: "From now on, consider us as implacable a foe as the Shah of Iran; you [the padishah] shall have Rumeli and we Anatolia."[45]

In Transylvania, Rákóczi persisted. He concluded an alliance with the Wallachian voivode, Mihnea III Radu, and together they put Constantin Şerban (Rákóczi's vassal) in charge of the Moldavian voivodeship, ousting the pro-Ottoman Gheorghe Ghika. The Porte would not tolerate Rákóczi's rebellion that threatened Ottoman rule in the vassal principalities. In the fall of 1659, Seydi Ahmed Pasha (governor-general of Buda since March 1659) defeated Rákóczi, while the pasha of Silistra destroyed Mihnea's Wallachian-Transylvanian troops. In the meantime, the Porte acknowledged that Leopold had succeeded his deceased father as Holy Roman emperor and that Leopold had requested that peace be maintained between the two empires. The padishah ordered his viziers and frontier governors to keep the peace as long as the Habsburgs kept it. However, Köprülü made clear that the "traitor" Rákóczi should be punished and that the "soldiers of Islam" would pursue him until they caught him.[46]

In January 1660, Rákóczi besieged Barcsay in Szeben but had to lift the siege in mid-May to confront Ahmed Pasha's army, which again invaded the principality. On 22 May, Rákóczi suffered a defeat against Ahmed Pasha's superior army in the battle of Szászfenes (Floreşti in Romania), in which the prince was wounded. Two weeks later (7 June 1660) Rákóczi died of his wounds in Várad. Ahmed ordered Barcsay to his camp, demanding the payment of Transylvania's still outstanding indemnity of 500,000 thalers from 1658.[47] In the meantime, after a siege of forty-five days, on 27 August Köse (Varvar/Vardar) Ali Pasha, commander in chief of the Transylvanian campaign, took Várad, the center of the "Parts" (*Partium*) on the Sebes Körös River.[48]

The Ottomans organized their new conquests into the province of Várad. The province's first governor, Vizier Sinan Pasha of Adana, was a loyal statesman of Köprülüs, who had accompanied Mehmed Pasha to the 1658 Transylvanian campaign. Sinan solidified Ottoman control over the province by building a new palisade (Belényes) and conquering Szentjobb (21 February 1661). To secure the province's defenses and its communication with the Ottoman provinces to the south, the governor of Temesvár, Sarı Hüseyin, erected yet another palanka (Feketebátor) that guarded the crossing point on the Fekete-Körös River. After Sinan's death in mid-September 1661, Sarı Hüseyin was appointed governor of Várad and tasked with organizing the first land survey of the province. For the defense of the province, the Ottomans placed some twelve hundred to twenty-five hundred soldiers into its castles and palisades.[49]

With Várad in their hands, the Ottomans controlled most of the *Partium* that had in the past protected Transylvania from the Ottoman troops in Hungary.[50] In both Transylvania and Vienna it was feared that the Porte would turn Transylvania into an Ottoman province. To avoid such a scenario, the Transylvanian Estates elected John Kemény (Rákóczi's trusted man and commander in chief during the Polish campaign) as their prince and declared the principality's independence from the Porte. Kemény promptly imprisoned Barcsay, the Ottomans' handpicked vassal prince, whom his men murdered in July. Through Palatine Francis (Ferenc) Wesselényi, Kemény sought military help in Vienna. He also signaled his willingness to let Habsburg troops into key Transylvanian castles and to accept Habsburg sovereignty if Transylvania was allowed to elect its princes.

Anti-Ottoman policies gained currency at both the Viennese court and the Holy Roman Empire. Johann Philipp von Schönborn, the archbishop of Mainz and the leader of the Rhenish Alliance (*Rheinbund*), offered the emperor his services against the Turks. It was a notable offer, as the Rhenish Alliance of some fifty German princes and cities (Catholics and Protestants alike) had been created in 1658 to counter Habsburg influence in the empire. In January 1661, Johann Ferdinand Portia—Emperor Leopold's chief minister and the leader of "the Spanish party" at the Viennese court that had previously avoided war with the Ottomans—accepted the leading Hungarian politicians' plan against the Ottomans. Submitted to a conference convened by Portia, the plan envisioned a multifront coalition war against the Ottomans, hoping to end their rule in Hungary. The Croatian ban, Nicholas Zrínyi, would attack Kanizsa in southwestern Ottoman-ruled Hungary; the imperial forces were to march along the Danube against Ottoman Esztergom and Buda; and the Habsburg garrisons in Upper Hungary were to assist Kemény against an expected Ottoman expedition in Transylvania. Although the operation in the spring of 1661 started according to plan, the Viennese War Council kept changing the orders to Field Marshal Raimondo Montecuccoli, whom Emperor Leopold had sent to Upper Hungary and Transylvania. This was due to the Viennese court's policy, which, fearing war with France, hoped to settle the Transylvanian issue by diplomatic means. Grand Vizier Köprülü Mehmed Pasha, who wanted to concentrate on Crete, had signaled to the Habsburg court his willingness to halt Ottoman operations in Transylvania and accept the election of a new prince. His offer, however, was dependent on these conditions: the emperor was to acknowledge the Ottoman conquest of Várad, withdraw his support from Kemény, and dismantle the fortress of Zrínyi-Újvár. Zrínyi had started to build the castle in mid-June 1661 on the right banks of the Mura (Mur) River on Ottoman-ruled territory, across from Kanizsa. The castle endangered Ottoman Kanizsa and frustrated the Porte's plans to attack Venetian Friuli through the Croatian passes.[51]

In the meantime, Montecuccoli and Kemény joined forces, and by mid-September had reached Kolozsvár. However, Montecuccoli's orders did not allow the general to attack the Ottomans. He also had to withdraw the imperial forces if the Porte honored the agreement, which it did. On the order of Ali Pasha of Silistra, commander in chief of the Ottoman expedition against Transylvania, the Transylvanian diet "freely" elected Michael (Mihály) I. Apafi as Transylvania's new prince (14 September 1661). Upon learning about the election, Montecuccoli promptly left Transylvania, though he placed imperial troops in the country's castles and towns. Insufficiently provisioned, his army plundered and pillaged, causing anti-Habsburg peasant revolts in the Trans-Tisza region. By late December Ali Pasha also had left Transylvania. Kemény was unable to reassert his sovereignty. He was defeated and was killed in a battle against the joint forces of Prince Apafi and Küçük

Mehmed Pasha of Jenő/Temesvár, fought on 23 January 1662 at Nagyszőlős (Transylvania).[52]

Habsburg-Ottoman Wars

Days before his death, Köprülü Mehmed Pasha told the Habsburg resident in Constantinople that the Porte would not accept Habsburg meddling in Transylvania. His son, Köprülüzade Fazıl Ahmed Pasha, was present at the audience and succeeded his father as grand vizier after Mehmed's death (30 October 1661), the first such example in Ottoman history. At only twenty-six years of age, Ahmed Pasha decided to settle the Transylvanian problem once and for all. He also hoped to strengthen his position at the Porte with a successful campaign against the Habsburgs.

To prepare for the war, Fazıl Ahmed placed his loyal men in key governorships in Bosnia and Hungary. When he left Edirne for Hungary two years later, pro-Köprülü pashas governed all the principal provinces in Hungary and Bosnia. Moreover, they were familiar with Ottoman-ruled Hungary, as they had grown up there or had been serving in the northern frontier for years. Sarı Hüseyin Pasha of Buda had served in Hungary since 1658 as governor-general of Eger, Temesvár, and Várad. Although of Abkhazian origin—who usually opposed the Albanian Köprülüs—Sarı Hüseyin was loyal to both Mehmed and Ahmed Pasha because he owed his positions to them. Köse Ali Pasha, a trusted man of the late Köprülü Mehmed, had been governing Bosnia for the past three years. Küçük Mehmed had been the governor-general of Temesvár/Jenő since September 1661. Sarı Hüseyin and Küçük Mehmed had been instrumental in consolidating Ottoman rule in Transylvania. Mehmed stayed in Transylvania from late 1661 through the summer of 1663 to strengthen the position of the pro-Ottoman prince Michael Apafi. Since May 1663, another Köprülü loyalist, Gürci ("the Georgian") Kenan, governed Várad. Kenan was a veteran of the Hungarian frontier and Buda's former governor-general. In June 1663, the grand vizier appointed Yakovalı ("from Đakovo") Hasan Pasha to govern the province of Kanizsa, in southwestern Hungary. A veteran of the Hungarian-Bosnian frontier, Hasan represented the third generation of the frontier dynasty of the Memibegoğlu (Memibegović), named after Hasan's grandfather. All these men played essential roles in Fazıl Ahmed's 1663 campaign, either by supporting the grand vizier's main army or by leading military operations in secondary theaters of the war.[53]

The Habsburg court hoped to renew the peace with the Porte and was willing to sacrifice Zrínyi-Újvár. When Zrínyi refused to demolish his castle, the Viennese court told the Porte that they would not protest if the Turks destroyed it. It was too late. Fazıl Ahmed had already decided to lead the Ottoman army to Hungary. He left Edirne on 14 April 1663. The Habsburg representatives—who had started the negotiations back in the Ottoman capital and had met with the grand vizier on numerous occasions during the campaign—had standing orders for the renewal of the truce. However, the grand vizier rejected Vienna's offer. He was so sure of his success that he demanded the reinstatement of the tribute that the Habsburg emperors had paid to the padishah before the Treaty of Zsitvatorok (1606). The Habsburg envoys could not accept such humiliating conditions.

The main Ottoman army crossed the border river Drava at Osijek on 5–6 July. Following the old military road along the Danube, the army arrived at Buda on 17 July. At a council meeting, the grand vizier changed his original plan. He accepted the local pashas's advice and decided to conquer Érsekújvár instead of Győr or Komárom, the campaign's other possible targets. "If we conquer Győr," declared the grand vizier at the end of the meeting, "we get a castle but do not get a province." If, however, "Újvár, the chief castle of Middle Hungary, trusting in God, would be besieged," we "will conquer a province and a country"; Újvár was known as "a merry, rich, and vast province" that had "some thirty castles and palisades, countless villages and towns, and silver and gold mines."[54] Fazıl Ahmed reached Érsekújvár on 16 August. After five weeks of siege, on 25 September the headquarters of the Habsburg border defense system in Lower Hungary surrendered to Fazıl Ahmed. The Ottomans quickly conquered the neighboring castles, expanding their control up to the Vág River.[55]

The Ottomans turned Érsekújvár into the key fortress on their northwestern frontier. It lay only about 130 kilometers (as the crow flies) from

Grand Vizier Köprülüzade Fazıl Ahmed Pasha conquered Érsekújvár (Ger. Neuhäusel, Slov. Nové Zámky) in 1663. Notice the modern Italian-bastioned fortress and the distribution of the Ottoman besiegers indicated by the names of their commanders. This contemporary German broadsheet also shows the remaining two thousand German and four hundred Hungarian defenders leaving the fortress on 26 September toward Komárom. (Courtesy of the Hungarian National Museum, Budapest, TKCs, T 5442.)

the Habsburg capital of Vienna, and about 50 kilometers from Pozsony, capital of the Kingdom of Hungary. With their conquest, the Ottomans separated the remaining parts of Lower Hungary from Upper Hungary and Transylvania. The Ottomans placed in Érsekújvár 1,781 janissaries of the Porte, in addition to local provincial troops. In the first decade, janissaries, armorers, and gunners of the central army made up about two-thirds of the garrison of 2,800 soldiers. The size of its garrison and weaponry (109 cannons) underlined Érsekújvár's great strategic significance.[56] After Érsekújvár's conquest, the grand vizier decided to winter his troops in northern Bosnia and Hungary. Having tasked Gürci Mehmed Pasha of Aleppo with the defense of Osijek, Fazıl Ahmed settled in Belgrade with the high command. This suggested that he wanted to start next year's campaign early in the season. Ottoman chroniclers claimed that in 1664 Fazıl Ahmed Pasha wanted to deepen his conquest in northwestern Hungary by attacking Győr. But Zrínyi's winter campaign forced the grand vizier to alter his plans.

Older historiography presented the winter campaign as a splendid page from the Hungarians' heroic struggle against the Turks, but new research has shown that it was part of a major coalition war. The Rhenish Alliance sent imperial troops to Hungary. Louis XIV of France, who liked the idea that his Habsburg rival would be occupied with a bloody war against the Turks, promised six thousand troops. The imperial diet at Regensburg discussed various war plans. Pro-war politicians in Hungary and the empire put pressure on the decision makers and used contemporary media and propaganda to prepare the public for a major war against the Turks. Newspapers and pamphlets detailed the siege and fall of Érsekújvár, and the number of broadsheets published in Germany about the Turkish wars in Hungary tripled in 1663. They detailed the atrocities of the Turks and Tatars in Moravia, stunning Europe with images of naked dead bodies left on the roadside by the Turks.[57] As the sharp-eyed Venetian *bailo* in Vienna noted, "The Habsburgs now wanted to show something to the world but they did not want to provoke a war with the Turks."[58] Zrínyi's planned winter campaign along the Drava River seemed like the right solution for the dilemma. Sending the ten-thousand-strong imperial army of the Rhenish Alliance to Zrínyi's expedition from their winter quarters in the Austrian hereditary provinces would also relieve those provinces' burden.

The campaign started on 21 January 1664 from Zrínyi-Újvár. The local Ottoman forces were unable to oppose the twenty-thousand-strong Christian army, consisting of the league's army, noble armies, and soldiers of the border districts from Transdanubia and the Wendish and Croatian borderlands. The surprised Ottoman guards of smaller forts in Transdanubia quickly surrendered, while the fleeing guards of Barcs, an important crossing point on the Drava River, set their fort on fire. The coalition army surprised and captured the town of Pécs—the center of Ottoman Transdanubia where the Ottomans accumulated large amounts of food and supplies for their planned 1664 campaign. Since the Ottoman soldiers in the castle put up a stubborn defense, the Rhenish

Alliance's army continued the siege of the fortress. Meanwhile, Zrínyi and his horsemen raced to Osijek and burned down its fortified bridge over the marshes of the Drava's floodplain, the Ottoman imperial armies' main crossing point to Hungary.

The twenty-six-day winter campaign penetrated more than two hundred kilometers deep into the Ottoman domains. It was a significant feat militarily and had considerable propaganda value. The publicity, generated in part by Zrínyi, put further pressure on the decision makers in Vienna and Regensburg. Upon his return, Zrínyi decided to abandon the siege of Pécs. It would have been difficult to defend the fort and town against the gathering Ottoman relief army. Zrínyi set Pécs on fire and, using a scorched-earth strategy, devastated the countryside, making the provisioning of the expected Ottoman campaign more difficult. His main aim was Kanizsa, which the winter campaign isolated. The Viennese decision makers decided to support Zrínyi's plan to capture Kanizsa, despite the opposition of Montecuccoli, who worried that the siege would derail the primary campaign along the Danube. Owing to slow decision making, mobilization, and supply, the attack commenced only in late April 1664 with an army of eighteen thousand to twenty thousand men, which, however, lacked sufficient siege artillery. In the meantime, Habsburg forces commanded by Louis de Souches besieged and captured Nyitra (15 April–3 May) and closed on Érsekújvár. Although Fazıl Ahmed had been informed about the planned siege of Kanizsa in mid-April, it was not until mid-May, at a council meeting in Osijek, that the Ottoman command discussed the campaign's targets. This delay was due to slow mobilization and the rebuilding of the Osijek bridge. Érsekújvár had plenty of soldiers, weaponry, and supply and was defended by the experienced governor of Buda. To strengthen the defense of Érsekújvár and the northwestern frontier, the grand vizier sent the provincial forces of Eger, Temesvár, and Várad and the Tatars to Érsekújvár.

Now Fazıl Ahmed could relieve the isolated Kanizsa. The loss of that key fortress would have endangered the principal military corridor along the Danube and Ottoman positions in Transdanubia. The grand vizier arrived at Kanizsa via Szigetvár on 3 June. A day before his arrival,

This engraving by an anonymous Italian artist shows the map of Nicholas Zrínyi's winter campaign in 1664 and his equestrian portrait. (Courtesy of the Hungarian National Museum, Budapest, TKCs, 4640.)

the Christians retreated to Zrínyi-Újvár and beyond the Mura River. A few days earlier they had emptied and set fire to the recently reconquered smaller forts (Babócsa, Berzence, and Segesd). Fazıl Ahmed Pasha relieved Kanizsa, but the Christian army retreated without a loss. Moreover, its strength was growing as Montecuccoli was ordered to join them with his troops, thus making the southern army the main imperial force operating in Hungary. The grand vizier could not leave this army intact and march to the north as originally planned. Destroying this Christian army at an open battle, however, could have forced Vienna to conclude peace on the Porte's terms, pacify the Hungarian frontier after six years of fighting, and free the main Ottoman forces to return to Candia.[59]

The grand vizier marched to Zrínyi-Újvár to force the Christians into a battle. However, by the time he captured and destroyed the castle and managed to cross the river, the Christian forces had withdrawn to the north of the Rába River, whose defense against the Turks was essential for both Graz and Vienna. The famous battle and Christian victory of Szentgotthárd (Mogersdorf, 1 August 1664) evolved from the Ottomans' attempt to cross the river. Although the psychological and propaganda value of the victory was considerable, one should not overrate its military significance. After all, the Christians defeated only part of the Ottoman army, which managed to cross the river. The rest of the grand vizier's army still stood intact on the other side of the river. This situation, together with Vienna's fear of a possible war with France, explains why the Habsburgs were eager to conclude the Peace of Vasvár (10 August 1664) with the Porte, allowing the Ottomans to keep their recent conquests in Hungary.[60]

The Last Conquests: Candia and Kamieniec

The Peace of Vasvár with the Habsburgs enabled Fazıl Ahmed Pasha to complete the conquest of Crete. The final phase of the war started on 28 May 1667. Most of the siege consisted of slowly sapping and advancing the approach trenches toward the walls of the fortress and laying down gunpowder mines and exploding countermines. Commanded by Ahmed Pasha, the Ottoman troops in 1667 were engaged in a war of mines that lasted seven months. The besiegers and defenders together used about 600 mines and countermines. The Venetians kept the Ottomans under constant bombardment. However, already in the spring of 1667, there was a need for Venetian bombardiers in Candia, as the remaining 163 men were insufficient to handle the 500 cannons within the fortress.[61] Venetian mines and bombardment caused heavy casualties for the Ottomans, killing 2 governors-general of Rumeli and 8,000 miners, sappers, *sipahis*, and janissaries. The toll on miners was so heavy that in late August Fazıl Ahmed ordered 600 oarsmen from the Ottoman galleys waiting in the harbor to the trenches as sappers. For the 1668 campaign season, an additional 2,500 trench diggers, miners, and sappers were mobilized, arriving on the island in April and July.[62] In 1668 the Ottomans launched 18 assaults and triggered 69 mines, while the Venetians carried out 47 sorties and triggered 292 countermines. The casualties were brutal: the Venetians lost 6,971 men, whereas Ottoman losses amounted to 36,839 dead and 6,667 wounded, according to Venetian sources.[63] Before the end of the year, the Venetians sent their peace offer to the padishah. Fazıl Ahmed pleaded with his sovereign not to accept the peace offers as he thought victory was near. The siege continued for almost another year, until Francesco Morosini surrendered the city on 6 September 1669. The last months of the siege witnessed unprecedented violence. An Ottoman account of war casualties claimed almost 260,000 dead or wounded, certainly an exaggeration. The Venetians recorded for 1668–69 more than 12,700 losses on their side, and more than 37,700 dead and 7,900 wounded on the Ottoman side. After the surrender, it took another year and a half to draw the borders in Dalmatia, which signaled the official end of the most exhausting conflict in both Venetian and Ottoman history.[64]

After the death of Sultan Süleyman during the Szigetvár campaign in 1566, it was rare for Ottoman padishahs to personally lead their armies. Sultan Mehmed III commanded the Ottoman troops in 1596 into Hungary and captured the fortress of Eger. So did Murad IV in 1639 when the Ottomans recaptured Baghdad from the Safavids. The last time an Ottoman monarch marched against the Poles was in 1621, during Sultan Osman II's failed Khotyn campaign. In 1672, Sultan Mehmed IV (r. 1648–87) personally led his armies to western Ukraine on the right (west) bank of the Dnieper River to support the Cossack hetman Petro Doroshenko (r. 1666–76) against his former Polish-Lithuanian suzerain. Commanded by Fazil Ahmed Pasha rather than the padishah, the Ottoman army reached Kamieniec Podolski, the center of the historic region of Podolia, after almost three months of arduous march, often in heavy rain. Kamieniec was one of Christianity's bulwarks against Islam. For the Ottomans, however, it was "the key to northern Europe." The Ottoman army of 100,000 men was an assemblage of janissaries (about 25 percent of the combatants), mercenaries, and household troops of Ottoman pashas, *timariot* cavalry relegated to auxiliary services, Tatars,

Cossacks, Moldavians, Wallachians, Kurds, Arabs, and a few French renegades. The 1,500 defenders of Kamieniec were no match for such a large army. They capitulated after just a week's siege (19–27 August) and surrendered the well-fortified fortress on 29 August. The Ottomans glorified the conquest of Kamieniec in campaign books and chronicles, full of technical details and poetic symbolism.[65] In the Treaty of Buchach (17 October), King Michael (Michał) Korybut Wiśniowiecki ceded Podolia to Sultan Mehmed IV and recognized the independence of Right Bank Ukraine under Doroshenko. After the treaty, the Ottomans attempted to organize their conquest into a province. But their efforts were frustrated by the outbreak of a new Polish-Ottoman war. John (Jan) Sobieski and other commanders persuaded the Sejm to reject the Buchach truce and resume the fight. By 1673, some 60,000 troops (31,000 and 12,000 soldiers from Poland and Lithuania, respectively, plus militiamen and private troops) were available for a campaign. Sobieski's three-pronged attack resulted in his victory near Khotyn, where the Turks reportedly lost 20,000 men. Although the triumph at Khotyn helped Sobieski succeed the deceased King Michael on the Commonwealth's throne, political factionalism and lack of troops and resources did not allow him to recapture Kamieniec. With Crimean mediation, the parties signed the Truce of Žuravno (1676). Only after the Sejm accepted Podolia's loss and a Polish embassy in Constantinople in 1677–78 confirmed the agreement were Polish and Ottoman commissioners able to demarcate the border in 1680. The next year, Ottoman officials prepared the first land survey of the province, which remained in Ottoman hands until the Treaty of Karlowitz in 1699.[66] With the conquests of Candia and Kamieniec, the empire reached its largest territorial extent of approximately 3.8 million square kilometers (1,482,000 square miles), if one includes loosely held lands and unproductive deserts.

Less impressive was the Ottomans' performance in their first war against Muscovy. In 1676 Hetman Doroshenko handed his capital Chyhyryn to the tsar. The Porte appointed Bohdan Khmelnytsky's son Iurii, a prisoner of the Ottomans since 1672, as the new hetman (February 1677) and decided to take Chyhyryn. The government charged Vizier Ibrahim Pasha, the castellan of Ochakiv and commander of the campaign, and Selim Giray of the Crimean Tatars with recapturing Chyhyryn and investing Iurii in the Right Bank Ukraine. The fall of Chyhyryn to the Ottomans would have enabled the Porte and its Tatar allies to use the fortress as a staging ground for attacks against Kyiv. The Muscovite government refortified the fortress, which now had about 12,500 defenders. It also sent Grigorii Romodanovskii with 32,000 men from the Belgorod and Sevsk armies and Hetman Ivan Samoilovich of the Left Bank Ukraine with his 20,000 Cossacks against Ibrahim Pasha's approaching army of 45,000 men. The Ottomans reached Chyhyryn by early August but could not take it before the Russian-Ukrainian relief force arrived. Romodanovskii and Samoilovich attacked the Ottomans in late August. According to prisoner testimonies, they inflicted heavy casualties (the Ottomans and Tatars lost 20,000 men), forcing Ibrahim Pasha to lift the siege of Chyhyryn. In 1678, the Ottomans launched another campaign. The padishah went with the army as far as Dobrič in Bulgaria (Hacıoğlu Pazarı). There, he appointed Grand Vizier Merzifonlu Kara Mustafa Pasha (1676–83), Köprülü Mehmed's successor and son-in-law, the commander in chief of the army of 70,000 men to take Chyhyryn. This time Muscovy was less prepared for the assault. Prince Romodanovskii's request for additional troops from the nearby reserves (commanded by his rival) was denied. Romodanovskii, therefore, did not risk engagement. He ordered the evacuation and destruction of Chyhyryn, which cost him his command. The next year the Russians again assembled a large army, but the Ottomans did not return. However, the Ottomans were unable to keep Chyhyryn. On 13 January 1681, Muscovy, the Porte, and the Crimean khanate signed a twenty-year truce in the khanate's capital Bakhchisaray. The parties accepted the Dnieper River as the border between the Ottoman and Muscovite domains. The Porte recognized Muscovy's suzerainty over Left Bank Ukraine (east of the Dnieper River) and Kyiv. Muscovy, on the other hand, gave up its claims to Right Bank Ukraine and Chyhyryn. The 1677–81 Russo-Ottoman war took the Ottomans to the northernmost point of their conquest in eastern Europe, some 250 kilometers southeast of Kyiv, the capital of modern Ukraine. A consequence of Ottoman-Muscovite rivalry over the Cossack hetmanate, the campaign also marked the beginning of direct Russo-Ottoman military conflicts.[67]

The Ottoman Siege of Vienna

In 1683, about a century and a half after the first unsuccessful siege of Vienna in 1529, the Ottomans were again in front of the walls of the Habsburg capital. Increased Ottoman military activity and capability in the second half of the seventeenth century were linked to the reforms introduced by the Köprülü grand viziers. These reforms strengthened the Ottoman central government's authority and improved its administrative and financial capabilities. The recent revival of Ottoman military fortunes and Vienna's conciliatory policy toward the Ottomans—exemplified by the Treaty of Vasvár (1664), which acknowledged the latest Ottoman conquests in Hungary despite the Habsburg victory at Szentgotthárd—were interpreted in the Ottoman capital as signs of Habsburg weakness. Emperor Leopold's (r. 1658–1705) ineptness against the Hungarian insurgents in the 1670s and Imre Thököly's successful insurrection reinforced the Ottomans' perceptions of Habsburg vulnerability. Thököly received his *ahdname* from Ibrahim Pasha of Buda (16 September 1682) for his "Middle Hungarian Principality" (1682–85). His Ottoman vassal principality lay in Upper Hungary between the Habsburg-controlled Royal Hungary and the Ottoman-vassal Principality of Transylvania. It covered about a hundred thousand square kilometers and was guarded by 17,662 *kuruc* soldiers.[68] The renewed Franco-Habsburg rivalry, caused by Louis XIV's (r. 1643–1715) policy of "reunions," and perceived Habsburg military weakness convinced Kara Mustafa Pasha that the time had come to attack Vienna. As it turned out, his assessment of international politics and of Ottoman and Habsburg military capabilities proved incorrect.

Rumors of a possible Ottoman attack against the Habsburg capital circulated from the 1670s onward. Emperor Leopold I tried in vain to renew the 1664 peace. In February 1682 he sent Alberto Caprara (1630?–85) as ambassador extraordinaire to the Porte. However, by the fall of 1682 the Viennese court had realized that the war was unavoidable and started defensive preparations. By that time, Kara Mustafa had secured the support of Sultan Mehmed IV for his planned campaign.[69]

The padishah declared war on the Habsburgs on 20 February 1683 and left Edirne at the head of his army on 1 April 1683. They reached Belgrade in early May, where the janissaries, cannoneers, and the bulk of the provincial cavalry from Asia Minor and the Arab provinces joined the army. Sultan Mehmed IV decided to stay in Belgrade, appointing Kara Mustafa commander in chief. According to Ottoman chronicles, the decision to lay siege to the Habsburg capital—instead of Komárom and Győr, which had been the proclaimed targets of the campaign—was made at a military council first in Székesfehérvár and then in Győr. At the meeting in Győr, Uzun (Tall) Ibrahim Pasha of Buda, who was experienced in matters of the frontier, opposed the siege of Vienna. Instead, he suggested taking Győr and spending the winter in Buda and then moving against Vienna. However, Kara Mustafa Pasha decided to take Vienna. He went with the army to Vienna on 7 July, leaving Ibrahim with twenty-five thousand Ottoman and ten thousand Tatar soldiers to besiege Győr.[70]

Emperor Leopold I and his court left Vienna on 7 July 1683 for Linz and Passau. The defenders of Vienna under Count Ernst Rüdiger von Starhemberg numbered sixteen thousand men (ten thousand infantry and six thousand cuirassiers). Some eight thousand citizens and seven hundred university students fit for military service also helped the defenders. The city's fortifications had been modernized in the 1670s and reinforced before the siege. Owing to the indefatigable diplomacy of Pope Innocent XI (1676–89), effective military assistance was also on the way.

The grand vizier reached Vienna on 14 July with an army of ninety thousand men. Of the Ottoman vassals, only the Crimean Tatars took part in the actual fighting. After a failed preventive siege against Érsekújvár, the Habsburg forces, commanded by the talented Duke Charles of Lorraine (1643–90), Emperor Leopold's brother-in-law, tried to secure the left bank of the Danube while waiting for the Polish allied troops. The latter were to join the relief army according to an "everlasting offensive and defensive alliance" signed on 31 March in Cracow by the representatives of the emperor and Jan III Sobieski, king of Poland-Lithuania (r. 1674–96). Leopold and Sobieski concluded their alliance despite the intensive lobbying of the French ambassador in Poland-Lithuania against such an alliance.[71] Habsburg and papal diplomacy also secured the participation of some ten thousand Bavarian troops and a similar number of Saxon soldiers, led by the electors of Bavaria and Saxony, Maximilian II Emanuel and Johann Georg III, respectively.

By 15 July, Vienna had been encircled and cut off. The siege began in earnest that very same day, with heavy bombardment that lasted for the next two months. Throughout the siege, the Ottomans concentrated their attacks against the walls between the Burg Bastion and the Löbl Bastion. However, as in 1529, the Ottomans lacked heavy siege artillery and their 130 field guns and 19 medium-caliber cannons were inferior in number to the defenders' 260 cannons and mortars. The defenders lacked sufficient ammunition, however, which explains why they fired only one or two shots per weapon daily. Ottoman trench and mine attacks, in which the Ottoman soldiers were experts, proved more effective than bombardment. But the defenders stood firm, made frequent sorties, repaired the walls, and stopped the besiegers with hastily erected fortifications behind the breaches. It was not until 2 September that the Ottomans could take the Burg Ravelin. On 6 September, another mine exploded under the Burg Bastion. By this time, the defenders, who had lost about half of their strength and were weakened by dysentery and food shortages, were expecting a decisive final assault. Instead, Kara Mustafa paraded his army in front of the walls to force the city to surrender. But had the grand vizier launched a final assault, he may have been able to take the city before the arrival of the relief army.

The relief army of 75,000 to 80,000 men and 160 cannons was gathering northwest of Vienna. The troops from Bavaria, Saxony, Franconia, and Swabia numbered about 35,000 to 40,000 men and joined the imperial forces of 20,000 men under Lorraine. Arriving last, King Sobieski's Polish troops could have numbered some 20,000 men. The decisive battle took place on 12 September near Kahlenberg, at the edge of the

Vienna Woods. Underestimating the strength of the relief army, Kara Mustafa left most of his janissaries in the trenches and planned to destroy the allied Christian army in a decisive cavalry charge. Although Ottoman chroniclers put the number of the Ottoman forces at Kahlenberg at 28,400 men, with Tatar and other auxiliaries the Ottoman army must have reached some 50,000 men. It was an insufficient force that had only 60 field guns. Owing to bad intelligence, Kara Mustafa expected the Christian attack on 11 September and ordered his soldiers to stay awake all night. However, the battle started a day later, at dawn on 12 September, between the Ottoman advance forces under Kara Mehmed Pasha and the Christian left wing under Charles of Lorraine near Nussberg. Lorraine's forces, strengthened by the Saxons, soon reached the Ottoman right wing. The Bavarians and Franconians descended from the slopes farther inland and also joined the fight against the Ottoman right wing and the middle. Sobieski's Poles on the Christian right wing advanced slowly because of the difficult terrain. They were led by the famed winged hussars. Modeled after the Hungarian hussars and reorganized by King Stephen Báthory, the Polish winged hussars were an elite heavy cavalry. They were protected by helmet, metal-plated body armor and armed with a long lance (*kopia*) of about 5 meters, as their primary offensive weapon. They also carried a saber (*szabla*) with a curved blade, a long thin sword (*koncerz*) about 1.3 to 1.6 meters in length that was used as a lance to pierce ring-mail or thrust between the armor plates, and/or a shorter broadsword (*palasz*, from the Hungarian *pallos*). Slow to adopt firearms at first, by the mid-seventeenth century most hussars sported a pair of pistols in the saddle holster. They also carried bows, though few knew how to use them effectively. Less effective against the volley fire of disciplined Western armies, the heavy-winged hussars proved a deadly shock force against the Ottoman light cavalry and janissaries. Around 1 p.m., the Polish vanguard reached Dornbach, about a mile to the west of the Ottoman encampment. Although the Ottomans fought bravely, an overall Christian attack that started in the fiercest heat after 3 p.m. decided the fate of the battle. The Ottoman left wing and the Tatars were unable to withstand the charge of the Polish cavalry and dragoons, who were the first to

fol. 275.

Den grooten Vizier verwurgd. in't Iaar. 1683.

This Dutch engraving from 1689 is one of many European depictions of Grand Vizier Kara Mustafa Pasha's execution in Belgrade, following his failed siege of Vienna in 1683. He suffered death by strangulation by a silk cord, the usual capital punishment of high-ranking Ottoman officials. (Courtesy of the Rijksmuseum, Amsterdam, RP-P-1896-A-19368-751.)

reach the Ottoman encampment. By 6 p.m., the Ottomans were defeated. Those who had not been slaughtered fled the battlefield, leaving ample booty—the whole Ottoman camp—for the Christians.[72]

Vienna was saved by a coalition of central European countries, whose army proved to be tactically superior and, for the first time in the history of Ottoman-European confrontations, matched the Ottomans in terms of deployed manpower and weaponry, as well as in logistical support. Polish and Habsburg forces pursued the fleeing Kara Mustafa, defeating him at Párkány (9 October) and taking Esztergom (27 October). The grand vizier's defeat led to his downfall and execution in Belgrade on Christmas Day 1683.[73]

Wars against the Holy League

Kara Mustafa's siege of Vienna provoked the creation of an effective anti-Ottoman coalition of Christian states, called the Holy League (*Liga Sacra*). Formed on 5 March 1684 on the initiative and under the patronage of Pope Innocent XI, the Holy League included King John Sobieski of Poland, Emperor Leopold I, and Doge Marc' Antonio Giustinian of Venice. Muscovy joined the alliance two years later, when it signed the "eternal peace" with the Polish-Lithuanian Commonwealth (16 May 1686), confirming the Treaty of Andrusovo (13 January 1667) and the division of Ukraine. The league's members launched their respective campaigns in coordination on three different fronts: the Habsburgs in Hungary, the Poles in Podolia, and the Venetians in the Adriatic and the Morea. They also agreed not to conclude a separate truce with the Porte.

The victorious campaigns of the allied forces from 1683 through 1699 have been labeled alternatively in contemporary sources and later Austrian, Hungarian, and Venetian historiography as the Great Turkish War (*Große Türkenkrieg*) and the Age of Heroes (*Heldenzeitalter*), the Liberation of Hungary (*Hungaria Eliberata*), and the Morean War (*Guerra di Morea*) and the Turkish-Venetian War.

In the pursuit of the defeated enemy, the allied forces compelled the surrender of Esztergom on 27 October 1683. However, in 1684 they failed to take Buda, the center of Ottoman rule in Hungary. Realizing that a successful siege of Buda required the capture of Érsekújvár, the allied forces focused on this task the next year, forcing the castle's Ottoman defenders to give up the center of their northernmost province in Hungary (15 August 1685). The goal of the following year's expedition was again Buda. Buda fell to the imperial forces led by Charles of Lorraine and Maximilian II Emanuel on 2 September 1686. The conquest of Buda, the seat of the most important Ottoman provincial governor in central Europe since 1541, was a major loss for the Ottomans. For the Hungarians and Habsburgs, it was both a symbolic and strategic victory.

Expecting a Turkish counterattack the following spring, the Habsburg government took measures to rebuild Buda, which was destroyed in the siege. Pope Innocent offered large sums for rebuilding Buda and turning

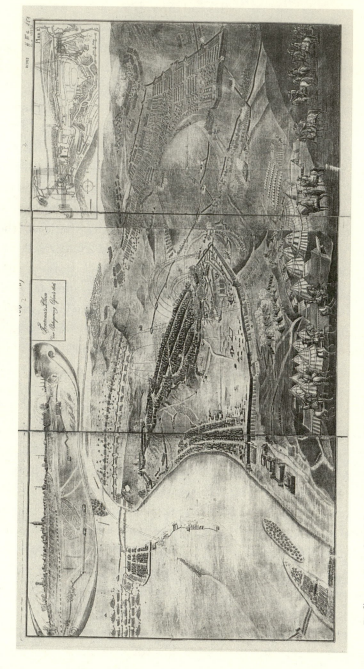

Bird's-eye view of Buda's reconquest on 2 September 1686, showing the military camps, troop movements, and prominent Ottoman landmarks inside and outside the city walls. (Courtesy of the Military History Museum, Budapest, HIII c 151.)

it into a "strong bulwark of Christendom." In the fall of 1686, the imperial armies captured several castles and the seats of the Ottoman *sancak* governors of Simontornya (23 September), Pécs (22 October), and Szeged (21 October). Vienna also rejected the Porte's offer for a truce, as protracted talks would have enabled the Ottomans to reorganize their armies.[74]

The next three years brought swift victories for the Christian alliance.[75] On 12 August 1687, the Christian army—commanded by Charles of Lorraine and Maximilian II Emanuel—soundly defeated Grand Vizier Sarı Süleyman Pasha's sixty-thousand-strong army at Nagyharsány, near Mohács. The victors estimated that the Turks lost sixteen thousand men in the battle and that ten thousand more died in the marshes while fleeing. The battle is also called the second Mohács and had been celebrated as a victorious revenge for the catastrophic defeat in 1526. The Christians captured the entire Ottoman camp with artillery, ammunition, and provisions worth 5,000,000 imperial thalers.[76]

Receiving approval from the Viennese War Council just days after Nagyharsány, Lorraine marched to Transylvania to secure the principality for the emperor and winter the exhausted imperial troops of some forty thousand men in the principality. After lengthy negotiations, Prince Michael I Apafi's representatives and the duke of Lorraine reached an agreement at Balázsfalva (27 October 1687). The agreement confirmed the principality's independence, the Estates' privileges, and the four Christian denominations' religious freedom. Transylvania was to pay 700,000 guldens and provision the Habsburg troops during the winter. Leaving his troops and Antonio Caraffa in Transylvania, the duke of Lorraine returned to Vienna to plan the next year's campaign. The next spring, the Transylvanians renewed their allegiance to Emperor Leopold and his heir, Joseph I, broke all ties with the Porte, offered to fight against the Turks ("the hereditary enemy"), and opened further towns in front of the Habsburg troops.[77] When Michael Apafi I died in mid-April 1690, Leopold did not recognize Michael Apafi II's election. Instead, in his edict of 4 December 1691, known as the *Diploma Leopoldinum*, he tied Transylvania to the monarchy, preserving its autonomy in domestic affairs.

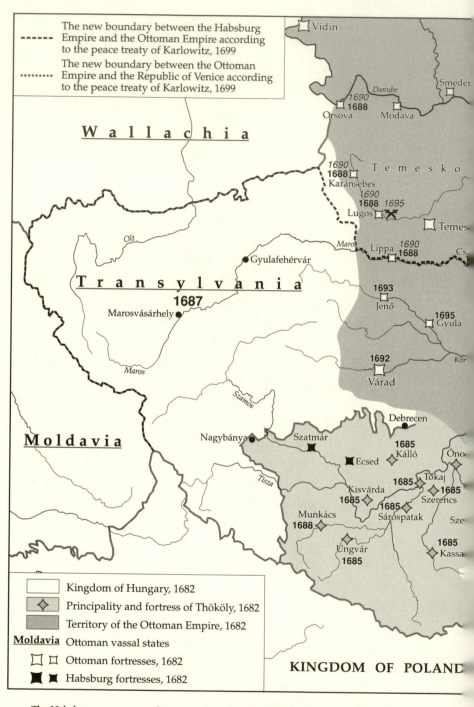

Vidin

Danube Smeder

1690
1688
Orsova Modava

W a l l a c h i a

1690 T e m e s k ö
1688
Karánsebes
1690 *1695*
1688
Lugos ✕ Temes

Maros Lippa *1690*
1688 Cs

Olt

● Gyulafehérvár

T r a n s y l v a n i a
1687 **1693**
Marosvásárhely ● Jenő

1695
Gyula

Maros

1692
Várad

Szamos

Debrecen

Nagybánya ● Szatmár **1685**
Kálló Óno
M o l d a v i a ■ Ecsed
1685 Tokaj
Kisvárda **1685**
1685 Szerencs
Tisza **1685**
Munkács Sárospatak Sze
1688
1685
Ungvár Kassa
1685

KINGDOM OF POLAND

The Habsburg reconquest of Hungary from the Ottomans as seen from Vienna.
(Drawn by Béla Nagy.)

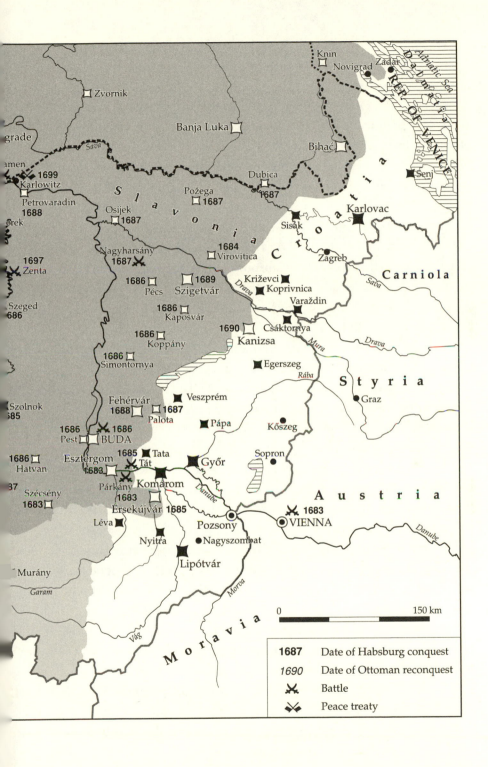

Knin

Novigrad Zadar

Adriatic Sea

Dalmatia

REP. OF VENICE

Zvornik

grade

amen

Sava

Banja Luka

Bihać

Senj

1699
Karlowitz

Petrovaradin
1688

rek

Dubica
1687

Požega
1687

Slavonia

Osijek
1687

Sisak

Karlovac

Croatia

1697
Zenta

Nagyharsány
1687

Virovitica
1684

Zagreb

Carniola

Szeged
686

1686
Pécs

1689
Szigetvár

Drava

Križevci
Koprivnica

Sava

Varaždin

1686
Kaposvár

1686
Koppány

1690
Kanizsa

Csáktornya

Mura

Drava

Szolnok
685

1686
Simontornya

Egerszeg

Rába

Styria

Fehérvár
1688

1687
Palota

Veszprém

Pápa

Kőszeg

Graz

1686
Pest

1686
BUDA

Esztergom
1683

1685 Tata
Tát

Győr

Sopron

Austria

1686
Hatvan

Párkány
1683

Komárom

Danube

37 Szécsény

1683

Érsekújvár 1685

Léva

Pozsony

Nagyszombat

VIENNA

1683

Danube

Murány

Nyitra

Lipótvár

Garam

Morva

0   150 km

Vág

Moravia

1687	Date of Habsburg conquest
1690	Date of Ottoman reconquest
✗	Battle
⚔	Peace treaty

In the meantime, in pursuit of the fleeing grand vizier, Sarı Süleyman Pasha, the Christian armies crossed into Slavonia and Srem. In September and October 1687, they captured Osijek, Valpó, and Požega. Eger, the center of the Ottomans' third province in Hungary since 1596, had been isolated since 1685. In the second half of July 1687, allied forces blockaded the fortress, denying the garrison reinforcements and food. Eger's 3,500 defenders entered into negotiation in late November and surrendered on 18 December. While most of the garrison left for the closest Ottoman fortress, Várad, some 300 Turks decided to remain and convert to Catholicism.[78] At their diet at Pozsony (18 October 1687), the Hungarian Estates, grateful for the reconquest of their capital and country, accepted the House of Habsburg's hereditary right to the Hungarian crown and gave up their right to resist and contradict their monarch (*ius resistendi et contradicendi*), which they had enjoyed since King Andrew's Golden Bull of 1222.

Demoralized by their recent humiliating defeat at Nagyharsány, the unpaid Ottoman troops mutinied. The grand vizier fled to Belgrade and then to Constantinople. Sultan Mehmed IV sacked and executed him. However, the rebellious troops deposed Mehmed IV and put his half brother, Süleyman II (r. 1687–91), on the throne (8 October). The rebellion lasted for months. It was not until April 1688 that Sultan Süleyman II and his frequently changing statesmen managed to quell the troops. Süleyman dismissed several of his incapable viziers and advisers and melted down the gold and silver plates of the Topkapı Palace to pay his soldiers. The sultan also co-opted one of the rebellion's ringleaders, Yeğen Osman Pasha, by appointing him as commander of the Hungarian front. However, he too proved unable to halt the Holy League's advance and lost Belgrade (6 September 1688), the key to Hungary and the most critical Ottoman logistical center on the Danube River.

The fall of Belgrade opened the way to the Ottoman Balkans for the Christians. When the Holy League troops captured Vidin (14 October 1689), it became apparent that the empire's dire situation required an experienced and capable statesman. The sultan appointed Köprülüzade Fazil Mustafa Pasha as his grand vizier. Like his predecessors from this distinguished family of grand viziers before him, Mustafa brought order to the administration and the military by purging corrupt officials and incapable officers. He instituted strict roll calls to eliminate the widespread practice by which soldiers collected their deceased comrades' salaries. He also proclaimed a general mobilization of the empire's Muslim subjects and the conscription of Turkmen and Kurdish nomads. The latter had to send thousands of soldiers to the Balkan front. Other measures were aimed at winning over the population of the hinterland. The grand vizier reinstituted the custom by which the poll tax, paid by the empire's non-Muslim subjects, was assessed on individual adults. In earlier years, the government had switched to collective assessment. However, this practice hurt communities whose population had dwindled, as the same taxes had to be paid by fewer people. It was especially unjust in regions ravaged by war. The government also encouraged repopulation by tax incentives. Permits to fix or rebuild Christian churches were also issued more easily.[79]

The 1690 campaign brought much-needed military success. The Ottomans recaptured Niš in September, along with several strong forts along the Danube River, such as Vidin, Smederevo, and Golubac. By the beginning of October 1690, Fazil Mustafa Pasha besieged Belgrade with his forty thousand infantry and twenty thousand cavalry. On 8 October, after an explosion destroyed the armory, Belgrade's Habsburg commander capitulated. Although Mustafa had about three weeks before the campaign season's traditional end, heavy rain prevented him from continuing the fight. The grand vizier's success was partly due to Vienna's renewed war with France, known as the War of the League of Augsburg or the Nine Years' War, which required the Habsburgs to redeploy their best forces from Hungary to the Rhine front. However, not even a Köprülü could produce a miracle. In the 1691 campaign, the Ottomans suffered a crushing defeat at Slankamen (19 August), north of Belgrade, at the hands of Ludwig Wilhelm of Baden, the Habsburg commander in chief in Hungary (fittingly nicknamed "Türkenlouis" [Louis the Turk] for his splendid victories against the Ottomans). In the battle, recognized by contemporaries as "the bloodiest battle of the century," the Ottomans lost some twenty thousand men, including the grand vizier. Under Fazıl Mustafa Pasha's successors, the Ottomans suffered further defeats. In June 1692, the Habsburgs conquered Várad, the seat of an Ottoman governor since 1660. Although the best Habsburg forces were fighting the French, the Ottomans were unable to regain their possessions in Hungary. In 1694 they tried to recapture Várad but to no avail. In January 1695, they gave up the fortress of Gyula, the center of an Ottoman *sancak* since 1566. With the fall of Gyula, the only territory still in Ottoman hands in Hungary was to the south of the Maros River, with its center at Temesvár.[80]

After his accession, Sultan Mustafa II proclaimed a holy war against the empire's enemies. Despite opposition from the imperial council, the padishah decided to confront the enemy at the head of his army in the hope that he would recover Hungary. His first campaign in 1695 was a success. Ottoman troops led by the padishah recaptured Lippa (7 September). At the battle fought near Lugos (21 September), Ottoman troops inflicted a disastrous defeat on Federico Ambrosio Veterani, the commander of the Habsburg troops in Transylvania, who himself died in the fight. Mustafa II then proceeded to capture Karánsebes before leaving the front for wintering. The padishah entered Constantinople with the spoils of his successful campaign, including some three hundred Christian captives, a rare occurrence in recent Ottoman history.[81]

The 1696 campaign was less successful. On 7 August 1696 Muscovy captured Azak, "Islam's strong bulwark." The Ottomans suffered yet another disastrous defeat in 1697 at Zenta in northern Serbia on the Tisza River. The defeat was not for lack of troops, as the Ottomans could still mobilize more than ninety thousand soldiers.[82] Despite the advice of the warden of Belgrade, Amcazade Hüseyin Pasha, who proposed to attack Habsburg-held Petrovaradin northwest of Belgrade on the Danube River, the padishah sided with Grand Vizier Elmas Mehmed Pasha and decided to consolidate Ottoman positions around Temesvár. The Habsburg command had no idea about the Ottomans' intended target, because the Ottomans were engaged in diversionary operations. Until the Ottomans crossed the Danube at Pančevo on 19 August, the Habsburg command had to consider several options: Ottoman attacks against Petrovaradin (regarded as the most likely target), Slavonia, Transylvania, or Upper Hungary. After the Ottomans crossed the Danube, the Habsburgs still considered the latter two targets, but also an Ottoman attack against Titel. Indeed, the Ottoman army marched against Titel, while their flotilla split at Slankamen. Part of it sailed northward on the Tisza River toward Titel, while the larger ships moved on the Danube, indicating a possible attack against Petrovaradin. However, after the Ottomans captured Titel and continued on the right bank of the Tisza to the north, Eugene of Savoy, commander in chief of the Habsburg forces in Hungary, realized that he had to stop them before they crossed the Tisza and attacked Transylvania. By 10 September, Eugene was at Becse, where he learned that the Ottomans had started to cross the left bank of the Tisza at Titel. According to Eugene's report, by 11 September the padishah and most of the cavalry had crossed the river on the pontoon bridge, which the Turks built from sixty vessels with the expert help of French engineers. The infantry, under the command of the grand vizier, was still in the process of crossing the river when Eugene attacked with his fifty thousand men. After intense bombardment, Eugene destroyed the Ottoman wagon lager and the entrenchment protecting the bridgehead, slaughtering half of the Ottoman army. Some twenty-five thousand Ottomans, including the grand vizier, were reported to have been killed.[83] A crowning victory for the Habsburgs, Zenta was a major disaster for the Ottomans. Through English and Dutch mediation, the Porte sped up the peace negotiations that had started in 1688.[84] To increase his leverage during the peace talks, the new grand vizier Amcazade Hüseyin was heading toward Belgrade with his army in 1698 when he met the Habsburg envoys in Sofia. Negotiations started in earnest, and the peace was signed on 26 January 1699 at Karlowitz.

At the Peace of Karlowitz, the Ottomans surrendered much of Hungary, the Ottoman vassal the Principality of Transylvania, Croatia, and Slavonia to the Austrian Habsburgs, but kept Temesvár and the Ottoman province around it, south of the Maros River. Podolia, with the dismantled fortress of Kamieniec, was restored to the Polish-Lithuanian Commonwealth, but the Ottomans kept Moldavia. Parts of Dalmatia and the Morea remained Venetian. With Muscovy, whose envoys signed a two-year truce at Karlowitz, negotiations continued. A peace for thirty years was reached on 3 July 1700 at Constantinople. In the treaty, the Porte ceded Azak to Russia and freed the tsar from his tribute obligations to the Crimean khan. Russia was allowed to send a resident ambassador (*kapu kethüdası*) with his dragomans to Constantinople, who during peacetime could freely communicate with the Russian court. Russia's pilgrims were free to go to the Holy Land, and in return, Russia dropped its claim to the Straits of Kerch.[85]

After the Treaty of Karlowitz, Sultan Mustafa retired to Edirne, the old Ottoman capital. Karlowitz was perceived by many as a humiliation. The implementation of the treaty—including delineation of the new borders by the border commissions and curbing raids into enemy territory (traditionally a lucrative activity for the border garrisons)— adversely affected many in the Ottoman elite. After the resignation of Grand Vizier Amcazade Hüseyin Pasha in 1702, Mustafa II's tutor and adviser, Feyzullah Efendi, was able to significantly increase his influence on the affairs of the state. He had also managed to secure many of the highest government posts for his sons and relatives. A new generation of statesmen began to plot against Feyzullah's nepotism and for regime change. When some two hundred soldiers rebelled in Constantinople, demanding the salaries the treasury owed them, the uprising spread swiftly and the rebels, now demanding the deposition of Mustafa, marched toward Edirne. The opposing forces met halfway between Constantinople and Edirne on 19 August. Mustafa's troops deserted, and the sultan fled to Edirne, where he abdicated in favor of his brother Ahmed III (r. 1703–30). Five months later, Mustafa II died in Edirne.

In November 1710, the Porte declared war on Russia, hoping to avenge the loss of Azak, "Islam's strong bulwark." Both Charles XII of Sweden and the khan of the Crimea lobbied in Constantinople for the war. After Peter the Great of Russia defeated him at Poltava (1709), Charles found refuge at the Ottoman fortress of Ochakiv at the mouth of the Dnieper River and later near Tighina on the Dniester. The Crimean khans feared Russian aggression and manipulated politics at the Porte. The Ottomans spent the winter preparing for war and recruiting soldiers for the janissary corps, whose number dropped to its lowest before the war. On 22 July 1711, the Ottomans defeated the Russians at the Pruth River, a tributary of the Danube. Captured by the Ottomans, Peter proposed negotiations. Grand Vizier Baltacı Mehmed Pasha accepted the offer. Azak was restored to the Ottomans, who regained all the territories lost to Russia in 1700. Peter was denied a representative in Constantinople and access to the Black Sea. Charles XII was free to return to Sweden. The Ottomans also eliminated the Wallachian and Moldavian rebel leaders, and henceforth the Porte appointed Phanariots Greeks from Constantinople to govern the two Romanian principalities. Contemporaries and later historians have long speculated whether the destruction of the captured Russian army and the continuation of the war could have altered the power balance between the two empires and changed the course of history. Some suggested that Peter bribed the grand vizier. Others claimed that the truce and the treaty in 1713 reflected Sultan Ahmed III's magnanimity.[86]

Rebellion in Montenegro, incited and supported by the Russians and Venetians, and Venetian corsair attacks in the Adriatic and the Mediterranean led to war with Venice in the Morea. The rebels found refuge in Venetian Dalmatia and Venice refused to turn the rebel leader over to the Ottomans. Venetian corsair attacks endangered the vital communication between Egypt and Constantinople. Since the Karlowitz Treaty prohibited aiding rebels and corsairs, the Porte accused Venice of breaching the peace and declared war in December 1714. The Ottoman leadership considered the reconquest of the Morea imperative for religious and strategic reasons. The Porte was also aware of the Venetians' military weakness and the Orthodox Moreotes' hatred of their Catholic Venetian overlords.[87] The republic's *bailo* duly noted the Ottoman military buildup. The Ottoman court chronicler claimed that the Porte increased the number of janissaries to 100,000. While the Porte was able to raise the number of the corps from 16,600 to 43,000 before the Prut campaign, it is unlikely that it could have tripled that number before the Morea war. The Ottomans faced difficulties in mobilizing their troops. Official documents showed that 14,800 *timariot sipahis* failed to report for military service (especially from eastern Asia Minor and Syria). Before the army reached the Morea some 57,000 provincial troops attempted to escape.[88] Sultan Ahmed III accompanied his favorite son-in-law, Grand

Vizier Damad Ali Pasha, and the troops to northern Greece. Despite difficulties, the Ottoman army, commanded by the grand vizier, crossed the Isthmus of Corinth into the Morea. It quickly captured all strategic fortresses (Corinth, Nauplia, Navarino, Koroni, and Modon), a testament to the Ottoman soldiers' skills in siege warfare. The Ottoman fleet also proved victorious and by late November expelled the Venetians from the islands of the archipelago.[89]

By 1716, Emperor Charles VI (Charles II as king of Bohemia and Charles III as king of Hungary) had become alarmed by the Ottomans' recent conquests in the Morea and their attacks in Dalmatia. He also felt that his Rhenish frontiers were secure as a consequence of the conclusion of the War of Spanish Succession and the death of his archrival Louis XIV. He now had enough troops and military capital to attack the Ottomans. In the spring of 1715 the emperor ordered the strengthening of the Hungarian fortresses. A year later, on 13 April 1716, he concluded an offensive and defensive treaty with Venice. June 1716 marked the start of the mobilization of the imperial forces. Led by Eugene of Savoy, they were to gather at Futog, on the left bank of the Danube River.

The imperial army, seventy thousand strong and commanded by Eugene, met the Ottoman army under Grand Vizier Damad Ali Pasha, the victor of the Morea campaign, near Petrovaradin. Located at almost the same distance from both Osijek and Belgrade and built on a rock at the curve of the Danube on its right bank, Petrovaradin occupied a strategic location for the defense of Slavonia, Syrmia, and Hungary. It had been strengthened and made into a major Habsburg military base after its reappropriation from the Ottomans in 1692.

According to an eyewitness, the grand vizier set up his camp on 2 August, some five kilometers southeast of Petrovaradin at a defendable elevation, and strengthened it with wagons. Without Tatar and Wallachian auxiliaries, the regular Ottoman forces' paper strength was about 70,000 men: 40,000 janissaries and 30,000 provincial troops. Eugene crossed the Danube on 2 August. Two days later, the Ottoman artillery opened fire on the imperialist infantry defended by trenches. To recover the initiative, a known quality of his leadership, Eugene decided to attack. The imperialists started the battle on 5 August on the left wing.

They managed to dislodge the janissaries from their trenches. However, the janissaries, noticing the confusion on the Habsburg right wing, started a successful counterattack. The counterattack, in turn, was stopped by the cavalry forces commanded by John (János) Pálffy. The relieved Habsburg infantry pushed back the janissaries some five kilometers. Seizing the initiative, Eugene led his troops against the enemy, whose cavalry fled. The janissaries fought bravely but were overwhelmed. The estimate of 30,000 casualties seems disproportionately high, compared with that of the imperialists' 4,500 wounded and dead. More realistic estimates put Ottoman casualties at 6,000, including Grand Vizier Damad Ali Pasha. Prince Eugene wrote his report about his victory from the grand vizier's tent, claiming to have captured 172 cannons, 156 banners, and 5 horsetails.[90] Despite severe imperial losses, Eugene decided to besiege Temesvár, the capital of the Banat and the center of an Ottoman province since 1552. Temesvár was a strong Ottoman fortress, guarded by some 8,000 men.[91] Its defenders resisted the siege for forty-three days but eventually surrendered the fortress, despite abundant supplies. On 16 October 1716, the Ottomans left Temesvár for Belgrade, having negotiated favorable terms of surrender.

During the winter, Eugene made preparations for the following year's campaign, whose goal was to recapture Belgrade, the only remaining Ottoman fortress along the Danube. On 15 June 1717, using modern pontoon bridges, the imperial army crossed the Danube at Pančevo, east of Belgrade. By 18 June, Belgrade was surrounded, and the imperialists were busy building their defensive entrenchments against the fortress and the approaching relief army. Eugene's army had a paper strength of one hundred thousand men with more than one hundred field guns and a healthy siege artillery train. Contemporaries estimated Belgrade's artillery at six hundred cannons and its garrison at thirty thousand men. This figure seems high. However, if one considers that thousands of soldiers from the battle of Petrovaradin must have stayed in the fort in anticipation of a Habsburg siege, it is not entirely implausible. By the time the Ottoman relief army from Niš arrived on 27 July, Belgrade had been heavily damaged by the five-week Habsburg bombardment.

The paper strength of the Ottoman forces under Grand Vizier Hacı Halil Pasha, Belgrade's former commander, was well above one hundred thousand men. However, contemporaries noted that the army comprised only few regular troops. Most of it consisted of undisciplined and untrained recruits with no chance of making a stand against the Habsburgs' better-trained regular forces. Knowing his forces' weakness, the grand vizier chose not to engage Eugene's army in open battle. Instead, he kept up deadly artillery fire on the imperialists from his elevated position to the east of the city. The imperialists were caught between two artillery fires from the fortress and from the Ottoman field army. Eugene had to act quickly if he was to save his army, which was suffering not only from enemy fire but also from dysentery. Hoping that the besieged enemy would not be able to fight for some days after the massive explosion in the city on 14 August, Eugene decided to attack the Ottoman army on 16 August. While leaving ten thousand men in the trenches, Eugene unleashed his remaining forces on the Ottomans in the early-morning hours when the thick fog that had concealed the imperialists' movements cleared away. Thanks to the Bavarians' bravery, the imperialists destroyed the Ottoman army. Eugene captured all 150 pieces of Ottoman artillery and the grand vizier's camp. The Ottomans, who lost perhaps as many as ten thousand men, retreated toward Niš. A day after the battle, the defenders of Belgrade surrendered—they had remained passive during the battle because the weather conditions prevented them from seeing anything. On 22 August 1717, Eugene and his men moved into Belgrade.[92] In the Treaty of Passarowitz (Požarevac in Serbia, 21 July 1718), the Ottomans surrendered the Banat of Temesvár, parts of northern Serbia, and western Wallachia (Oltenia) to Austria. However, the Ottomans kept the Morea, and Venice ceded its last outposts in Crete to the padishah.[93]

In 1716–17, the Habsburgs matched the Ottomans' military capabilities both numerically and logistically. Moreover, thanks to Eugene of Savoy's military leadership and reforms under his three-decade-long tenure as president of the Court War Council (1703–36), Habsburg armies were also better trained and possessed superior leadership. Yet, the Viennese government still considered the Ottomans a threat and

distrusted the Hungarians—an attitude that was a legacy of the Ottoman era. In 1718, 46 percent of the monarchy's estimated 160,000 troops
(paper strength), amounting to 76,000 men, were stationed in Hungary
and its new annexes. This was the highest concentration of Habsburg
forces in the monarchy, with the second highest concentration being
the 60,000 troops deployed in Italy, which was a theater of war at that
time.[94] Ordinary soldiers in the Habsburg army continued to fear their
Ottoman peers, especially the janissaries and the Turkish cavalry. The
cavalry's shock attacks often proved fatal for the Austrians in the 1737–39
war. Field Marshal Sachse-Hildburghausen blamed the Austrian officers
and generals for planting the belief among the Austrian rank and file
that Ottoman attacks could not be stopped. He added that fables about
the Turks' superhuman courage and their invincibility played a vital role
in the flight of some Austrian troops in that war.[95] The Treaty of Belgrade (18 September 1739) ended Austria's Turkish War of 1737–39,
fought in coalition with Russia. In the treaty, Austria ceded Habsburg
Serbia, including Belgrade, and northern Bosnia to the padishah. However, Ottoman hopes to regain Hungary never materialized.

Epilogue

THE EARLY OTTOMANS and their sultans proved to be capable warriors and commanders. They used varied strategies of conquest, which went beyond the application of sheer military force and prowess. They claimed to be holy warriors, and used these claims to attract soldiers and followers to their camp, as well as to legitimize both their wars and their rule. Other strategies of conquest and rule included dynastic marriages, forced resettlement, and the co-optation of the conquered people into the Ottoman military and bureaucracy. In this regard, the Ottomans were similar to other dynastic empires of their time.

The Ottoman conquest of Byzantine Constantinople in 1453 reshaped power relations in the Mediterranean, southeastern Europe, and beyond. It eliminated the Byzantine Empire, which had separated the Ottomans' European and Asian lands and organized crusades against the Ottomans. The conquest also offered the Ottomans a commanding position over the trade routes between Europe and Asia and a perfect capital city with thousand-year-old imperial traditions. Straddling the shores of the Bosporus Straits and linking Europe with Asia, Ottoman Constantinople was the city that Napoleon I Bonaparte called the capital of the world because of its strategic location. Owing to Constantinople's location, its natural harbor (the Golden Horn), and the empire's resources and organizational skills, the Ottoman Empire soon emerged as a Mediterranean naval power.

The conquest enabled Sultan Mehmed II to transform the frontier principality of the House of Osman into a patrimonial empire, and the young sultan to aspire for universal rulership as heir of past empires of the Turco-Mongol, Islamic, and Roman/Byzantine traditions. In its heyday in the sixteenth century, Ottoman Constantinople was the cosmopolitan hub of a mighty empire. In an age in which European capitals followed the religion of the ruling dynasty, Ottoman Constantinople was a multi-confessional and multi-ethnic city of boundless opportunities, attracting talent from all corners of the empire and beyond. The Ottoman brain gain afforded the sultans an expanding pool of talented men of all creeds, ethnicities, and professions seeking political, military, economic, and cultural advancement. This diverse pool of statesmen, scholars, military men, and artisans was chiefly responsible for developing and continuously fine-tuning the institutions and policies that lay behind the Ottoman success story for the next two hundred years or so.

The Ottomans played a crucial role in the emergence of modern diplomacy and the gathering of information. By the sixteenth century, Ottoman Constantinople had become one of Europe's most important centers of diplomacy and espionage, and the Ottomans successfully exploited this position; they remained well-informed about European politics and rivalries. The Porte used truces, peace treaties, and trade agreements to neutralize possible adversaries and to sow division among the leading European powers. Before the Porte launched campaigns, it routinely concluded treaties with other powers to secure its borders and avoid military conflict on other fronts at the same time. However, in the long run, the lack of permanent embassies, a professional diplomatic corps, and centralized intelligence gathering proved to be a major disadvantage for the Ottomans. It denied the Ottomans the opportunity to gather information about their rivals and to turn such data into systematized knowledge. By contrast, European resident ambassadors and their translator-interpreters accumulated a great amount of information about the Ottomans and their culture. Many diplomats and dragomans became avid students of Ottoman culture and Islam. Programs to train translator-interpreters in Oriental languages for their embassies and governments led to the establishment of Oriental Academies in European capitals and the emergence of Oriental studies as a field of scholarly endeavor.

The Ottoman conquest impacted a vast region, from the Mediterranean to Egypt and Greater Syria, and from central and eastern Europe to Iraq and Iran. We have seen how the Ottoman-Safavid rivalry and wars over Iraq strengthened Shiism in Persia and solidified the split between Sunni and Shiite Islam. To halt Ottoman conquest, the countries of central Europe united their resources under the same ruler or dynasty, resulting in personal unions of the kingdoms of Hungary, Bohemia, and Poland under the Jagiellons and Habsburgs. The Ottoman victory over the Hungarians in 1526 and the death of Louis II Jagiellon cleared the way for the Habsburgs to acquire the crowns of Hungary and Bohemia when the Estates elected the Austrian archduke, Ferdinand, their king. However, along with Hungary's crown, Ferdinand also inherited the obligation to halt the Ottoman advance in Hungary, which also threatened Austria. Ferdinand's brother, Holy Roman Emperor Charles V, and Süleyman engaged in an epic and exhausting, yet ultimately futile, rivalry for supremacy in Europe. The Habsburg-Ottoman rivalry was closely connected to the Habsburg-Valois struggle for European supremacy as Francis I of France, "the most Catholic king," was Charles V's archenemy and the sultan's reluctant ally. These rivalries also affected the spread of the Protestant Reformation as the Habsburgs' fight against the Ottomans in the Mediterranean and Hungary tied down precious resources and military forces. The Protestant Estates also demanded and acquired more religious freedom in return for their contribution to the Habsburg war effort against the Ottomans.

The Ottoman threat also spurred military and fiscal-bureaucratic reforms, the establishment of new types of armies, and the reorganization of border defense in central and eastern Europe from the late fourteenth century through the early eighteenth century. Whether real or perceived, the Ottoman threat had a dual impact on the development of the Habsburg monarchy. On the one hand, it spurred military modernization and administrative centralization, which laid the groundwork for more comprehensive centralization projects in the second half of the eighteenth century. Mapping and demarcation of border areas facilitated the development of military cartography in the Habsburg monarchy. On the other hand, the Viennese government remained dependent on the

Estates of the Hereditary Lands, Bohemia, and Hungary for financing, manning, and supplying its anti-Ottoman defenses. This dependence perpetuated a system of military devolution and administrative decentralization, which in turn maintained the distinct political, constitutional, and cultural institutions of the Habsburg kingdoms and domains.

The Habsburg takeover of Hungary and Transylvania after the reconquest of Hungary from the Ottomans fundamentally altered Vienna's relations to the Hungarian Estates. The Estates lost the military and diplomatic support that they had previously enjoyed during their anti-Habsburg insurrections. As noted, in late 1687, the Hungarian Estates gave up their centuries-old right to resist their sovereign along with their right to elect their kings, thus accepting the Habsburgs as their hereditary sovereigns. While on the surface the insurrection and anti-Habsburg war of Francis (Ferenc) Rákóczi (1703–11) seemed yet another anti-Habsburg insurrection of the type of Bocskai and Bethlen, it in fact took place in radically changed circumstances and with higher stakes. By 1703, both the Principality of Transylvania and Ottoman-held Hungary, where the insurgents had received military support and found refuge in the seventeenth century, were in Habsburg hands. What was at stake in the 1703–11 insurrection was the new administration of the country and the Estates' role in it. The defeat of the 1703–11 insurrection and the ensuing compromise further strengthened the Habsburg sovereign's power vis-à-vis the Hungarian Estates and his hold over the newly acquired kingdom and its resources.

The post-Ottoman era favored bureaucratic consolidation, centralization, and military modernization. Yet we should not overstate these processes, for the monarchy remained less centralized, and its military and finances less effective, than most of its Western rivals. As noted, the Estates remained crucial partners of the monarchy in financing Austria's wars. They provided low-interest loans to finance the monarchy's wars and debt. Cooperation with the Estates and increased control of the Viennese governmental bodies over the means of organized violence gave substantially more oversight to the emperor with regard to war making than the Ottoman sultans and their viziers ever enjoyed in the eighteenth century.

The Ottomans followed a reverse path. In the sixteenth century, the Ottoman sultans had substantially more control over their resources and armed forces than did their Habsburg rivals. This is true even if we recognize that the Ottoman central administration had to compromise and negotiate with its provincial elites, and that Ottoman authority was never as omnipotent as former historiography has led us to believe. We have seen that the Ottomans governed their empire with great pragmatism. The provinces experienced varying degrees of government control: the closer the province was to the capital, the more control the government had over it. Thus one can speak of core zones, more remote frontier provinces, and loosely attached vassal or client states. In their core provinces in southeastern Europe and Asia Minor, the Ottomans distributed most of their revenues as military fiefs. The beneficiaries served the state as soldiers and administrators. In the distant provinces such as Egypt or Yemen, the Ottomans did not introduce the *timar* land-tenure system and collected taxes with the help of tax farmers.

From the fifteenth through the seventeenth centuries, the Ottomans were successful in adjusting their militaries, weapons, and strategies to match those of their European and Muslim rivals. Owing to the *timar* service land grants and the large *timariot* provincial cavalry, along with the sultans' stipendiary standing corps, the Ottomans routinely outnumbered their opponents on the battlefield. However, the defense of the empire's overextended borders and the long and exhausting wars against the Safavids and Habsburgs from 1578 through 1639—what might be called the Ottomans' sixty years' war—required yet more soldiers. The wars against the Habsburgs also exposed the Ottoman armies' weaknesses. The Porte relied on provincial governors and grandees to mobilize and provision soldiers and raise the necessary funds. By the early eighteenth century provincial elites appropriated a good share of the empire's resources, which they used to establish and maintain their household armies. Owing to the deterioration of the *timar* system and the provincial administration, the sultans became increasingly dependent on local elites in administering the empire, maintaining law and order in the provinces, and raising and provisioning armies.

European diplomats, army commanders, and military engineers studied the strengths and weaknesses of the Ottoman Empire and its military. Works by Lazarus Freiherr von Schwendi (Emperor Maximilian II's captain-general in Hungary in 1565–68), Giorgio Basta (Emperor Rudolf II's commander in Hungary and Transylvania in 1596–1606), Raimondo Montecuccoli (field marshal and commander in chief of the Habsburg armies in 1664–80), and Nicholas Zrínyi (the Hungarian-Croatian statesman and military commander, 1620–64) contain some of the best observations regarding the strengths and weaknesses of the Ottoman military. They gave the Europeans useful advice on how to defeat the Ottomans. Luigi Ferdinando Marsigli, a Bolognese military engineer and polymath who fought against the Ottomans in Habsburg service in the 1680s and 1690s, compiled the best concise description of the contemporary Ottoman army (*Stato militare dell'Imperio ottomano*, 1732). Most of this knowledge was systematized and taught to the ever-growing number of military engineers and officers in newly established military academies.

Military treatises such as those that Schwendi, Montecuccoli, and Marsigli wrote about the Ottoman army were wanting in the Ottoman Empire. The Ottomans lacked works that would systematically describe the available resources, strengths, and weaknesses of their opponents. Even more important was the lack of Ottoman war and naval academies and ministries. By the mid-seventeenth century the French ministry of war and marine had emerged as central bureaucratic organizations responsible for the planning and conduct of war. Other European states followed suit. The Austrian Habsburgs opened their Engineering Academy in Vienna in 1718, and the Military Academy in Wiener Neustadt was opened in 1752. Staffed by administrators, clerks, soldiers, engineers, and mapmakers, European war ministries were responsible for a wide array of tasks—from weapons improvement to clothing, and from training to the supplies of weapons, food, and fodder. Improvements in weapons technology, organization, and logistics owed a lot to the experiments of such ministries. They were instrumental in improving the effectiveness of European resource mobilization, recruitment practices, and weapons and munitions industries. The new types of knowledge accumulated, taught, and systematized in the new European bureau-cratic centers of war making could not be transmitted quickly. These academies also trained the new cadres of officers familiar with the latest improvements in military-related sciences and skills that Ottoman of-ficers usually lacked. Moreover, as contemporary Ottoman observers recognized, the number of officers (including noncommissioned offi-cers) and the ratio of officers to the rank and file was substantially higher in the Habsburg armies than in their Ottoman counterparts.

As a result, Habsburg commanders were better able to control their armies, organized into smaller and more agile units than those of the Ottoman army. Equally important, by the end of the seventeenth century, the Ottomans seemed less capable of adjusting their military personnel and tactics to the changing nature of warfare, which in east-central Europe was dominated by open battles rather than sieges. This failure to adjust was partly due to Ottoman military culture, but also partly to Ottoman successes in siege warfare—the dominant type of warfare throughout the 150-year-long period of Ottoman confrontation with the Habsburgs in Hungary. The Habsburg military, fiscal, and bu-reaucratic reforms of the sixteenth and seventeenth centuries, including the establishment of a standing army with related bureaucratic and fiscal institutions responsible for manning and supplying it, as well as experi-ence in pitched battles, ultimately shifted the balance of military power toward the Habsburgs.

The strength of the European armies and the weaknesses of the Ot-toman military were also noticed by Ottoman observers. Ibrahim Müt-eferrika (1674–1754), the Hungarian renegade and founder of the Arabic letter printing in the Ottoman Empire, revealed as early as 1732 those characteristics that, in his opinion, ensured the strength of the European armies, and argued that it was precisely the absence of these elements that weakened Ottoman military capabilities. He praised the structure of the Christian armies, the balanced proportions of infantry, cavalry, and dragoons, and the excellent cooperation among these groups. Other lauded qualities included superior methods of training and drilling soldiers, discipline, the high proportion of officers (at least 25 percent), the competency of the high command, the order and defense of the camps, military intelligence and counterintelligence, "geometric" troop formations, "la manière de combattre," and the volley technique to maintain continuous fire.[1]

Many of the deficiencies of the Ottoman troops, so accurately analyzed by Ibrahim Müteferrika, were on display in the wars agains the Habsburgs in 1684–99 and during the Ottoman-Venetian and Ottoman-Habsburg wars in 1715–17. Ottoman victories in the Morea can be explained by Ottoman strength in numbers, good logistics and skills in siege warfare, the dominant form of confrontation in that war, and a traditionally strong feature of the Ottoman art of war. However, the weaknesses of the Ottoman military in the Morea war—the uneven quality of the troops and lack of discipline—were also visible. Such deficiencies proved fatal to the Ottomans against the Habsburgs. The Habsburgs were a different type of enemy. They not only matched the Ottomans in terms of mobilized forces, but owing to Eugene's military brilliance, the expertise of his officer corps, and the discipline of his forces, the Habsburgs managed to overcome the often poorly led and undisciplined Ottoman army. But Habsburg superiority was also misleading and should not be overstated. After Eugene's death in 1736, Vienna lacked comparably expert and efficient military leadership, and incompetent command would lead to defeat, including in the Austro-Ottoman war of 1737–39, during which the Porte regained Belgrade.

Even so, the divergent paths that the Habsburgs and Ottomans took fundamentally changed the military balance between the Ottomans and their enemies. They also changed the outlooks of the two rival empires. By the end of the eighteenth century, the Habsburg monarchy had evolved into a military-fiscal state. As a result of their military devolution and fiscal decentralization, the Ottoman Empire became a limited monarchy.

ACKNOWLEDGMENTS

UNDERSTANDING THE OTTOMAN conquest and its impact in Europe has occupied my mind ever since I was a student in the Departments of History and Turkish Studies at the University of Budapest (ELTE) in the early 1980s. I am indebted to my professors Gyula Káldy-Nagy and Géza Dávid, who introduced me to Ottoman studies, and Ágnes R. Várkonyi and Matyás Unger, who taught me Hungarian and Transylvanian history. If I became fluent in Modern Turkish, I owe that to Cemil Öztürk, who went beyond his duties as a language instructor, spending long hours with us outside the classroom, in both Budapest and Istanbul.

From the mid-1980s on, I was fortunate to have the opportunity to discuss my thoughts about Ottoman, European, and Hungarian history with colleagues. Gábor Barta wisely suggested that I choose a topic other than János Szapolyai, whom he had been studying for years. Pál Engel read and commented on my first scholarly article, which examined the 1444 Ottoman embassy to Hungary, and shared his views about medieval Hungary. I learned a great deal from Erik Függedi about late medieval Hungary and from Géza Perjés about military history. Ferenc Szakály taught me about sixteenth- and seventeenth-century Hungarian history and offered his friendship. Klára Hegyi shared her knowledge of Ottoman rule in Hungary. I learned a great deal about the Turkic peoples and their cultures from István Mándoky-Kongur and his wife, Ayşe. They regularly welcomed me into their home in my college years and beyond, until István's untimely death in 1992.

I had the good fortune to teach courses on Ottoman and Hungarian history at the Universities of Budapest (ELTE) and Pécs (JPTE) to small groups of exceptionally dedicated students, many of whom went on to become historians. Zsuzsa Barbarics-Hermanik, István Kenyeres,

Dóra Kerekes, Mónika Molnár, Géza Pálffy, Balázs Sudár, and Éva Sz. Simon kept in touch and sent their works to me after I left Hungary for Georgetown in 1998. Among my Hungarian friends, Teréz Oborni, who also taught and mentored many of the same students, has remained my strongest connection to my colleagues in Hungary. Árpád Rácz of the historical journal *Rubicon* commissioned and published my first book and numerous articles about the Ottomans for his journal and helped me stay connected with fellow *Rubicon* authors.

Looking over my old syllabuses and the present monograph, I see many common topics, reminding me of my colleagues' nagging that I should have written this book a long time ago. However, I would like to think that teaching courses on the Middle East, the Ottoman Empire, the Black Sea, and Ottoman-Habsburg and Ottoman-Russian relations at Georgetown over the past two decades has broadened my horizons. I am fortunate to be part of such a collegial department. I especially cherish the friendship of Jim Collins, Catherine Evtuhov, Andrzej Kamiński, and Jim Shedel. Before her move to Columbia University in 2016, Catherine and I co-taught several undergraduate and graduate courses on the Black Sea and the Ottoman and Russian Empires and co-mentored some exceptionally talented graduate students, as I also did with Andrzej Kamiński, Jim Collins, and John McNeill. Over the years I have kept in touch with many of my graduate students and have profited from their works. I would acknowledge here Fatih Çalışır, Selim Güngörürler, Emrah Safa Gürkan, Faisal Husain, Said Salih Kaymakçı, Andrew Robarts, Felicia Roşu, and Kahraman Şakul, many of whom sent their works to me and drew my attention to new publications. Kahraman and Emrah offered their friendship and hospitality in Istanbul, as did Tuba Çavdar, Heath Lowry, Cemil Öztürk, and Fikret Yılmaz, as well as Antony Greenwood and Gülden Güneri of the American Research Institute. I also thank my undergraduate students in my seminars, especially those in "Pirates, Soldiers and Diplomats" and "Islam and War," who have challenged my views with their questions.

I have fond memories of my spring 2003 semester, which I spent at the University of Vienna. I learned a great deal from my Habsburg historian colleagues, Thomas Winkelbauer and Martin Scheutz, who honored me with their participation in my seminar on Ottoman-Habsburg relations. In Vienna, I discussed Ottoman history with Markus Köhbach and Claudia Römer. I have admired Claudia's language and paleographical skills since 1983, when we first met at an Ottoman paleography workshop in Visegrád, Hungary. Two semesters of teaching in Georgetown's overseas programs in Alanya (Turkey) in 2008 and 2009 took me to Syria and Cyprus and helped me appreciate the Mediterranean dimensions of the Ottoman Empire. I thank Kathryn Ebel and Scott Redford for inviting me to Alanya. In my year of teaching at the Georgetown University–Qatar campus in Doha, Qatar, in 2018, I developed a better understanding of the empire's connections to the Persian Gulf and the Indian Ocean. I thank James Reardon-Anderson and Amira Sonbol for inviting me to Doha, and Dean Ahmad Dallal and GU-Q's faculty, students, librarians, and staff for the welcoming and intellectually vibrant environment I found there.

I could not have written this book without the help of my colleagues. My indebtedness to other scholars is evident from the source notes. I especially paid attention to works written in Turkish and in languages less accessible to English speakers. I use these publications to acknowledge the contribution that historians writing in those languages have made to scholarship. I thank my fellow Ottoman historians who shared their thoughts with me at workshops and in the Istanbul archives. Others invited me to their institutions to give talks. I especially acknowledge Virginia Aksan, Günhan Börekçi, İdris Bostan, Palmira Brummett, Linda Darling, Géza Dávid, Feridun Emecen, Mehmet Yaşar Ertaş, Suraiya Faroqhi, Caroline Finkel, Kate Fleet, Pál Fodor, Alexandar Fotić, Mehmet Genç, Rossitsa Gradeva, Molly Greene, Klára Hegyi, Colin Heywood, Doug Howard, Ekmeleddin İhsanoğlu, Özlem Kumrular, Heath Lowry, Rhoads Murphey, Victor Ostapchuk, Hüseyin Özdeğer, Erol Özvar, Ali Yaycıoğlu, and Fikret Yılmaz. I thank Kate Fleet for inviting me to serve on the editorial board of the *Turkish Historical Review*. I also thank my fellow editors—Antonis Anastasopoulos, Ebru Boyar, Amina Elbendary, Ben Fortna, and Svetla Ianeva—and Brill's editor and Ottoman historian Maurits van den Boogert for sharing their knowledge about Ottoman studies.

I thank my colleagues who over the past two decades commissioned articles and book chapters for their projects. I am grateful to Virginia Aksan, Jeremy Black, Pál Fodor, Michael-David Fox, Daniel Goffman, David Graff, Charles Ingrao, Selim Kuru, David Parrott, Andrew Peacock, Matt Romaniello, Martin Scheutz, Hamish Scott, Karin Sperl, Frank Tallett, David Trim, and Christine Woodhead. They forced me to synthesize, often for the general reader, what I know about the Ottoman Empire. For those projects, I occasionally tapped into my book manuscript and I use some of the material here.

I am indebted to the staff of the Ottoman archives in Istanbul (BOA). I thank Ayten Ardel for her assistance with digital copies of documents and decades of friendship that started in 1985 in Konya, well before her employment in the archives. I also acknowledge Georgetown University's Lauinger Library, especially the Interlibrary Loan staff, for handling my constant requests for obscure works expeditiously.

I am grateful to Andrzej Kamiński and Eulalia Łazarska, who invited me to Warsaw in June 2017 to discuss my book manuscript as part of their project Recovering Forgotten History. I benefited from the detailed comments of Andrzej Kamiński, Jim Collins, Dariusz Kołodziejczyk (University of Warsaw), Rigels Halili (University of Warsaw), and Endre Sashalmi (University of Pécs).

I thank my editors at Princeton University Press. The book owes its existence to Brigitta van Rheinberg, who commissioned the book and patiently waited for it well beyond the deadline our contract stipulated. Eric Crahan managed the manuscript through the initial editorial process and suggested changes regarding the book's title and emphases. I am grateful to the two anonymous readers for their careful reading and thoughtful comments. Priya Nelson and Thalia Leaf at Princeton University Press and Angela Piliouras at Westchester Publishing Services oversaw the production in a difficult time with expertise. Copyeditor Liz Schueler did a meticulous job and Alex Trotter provided a thorough index. I thank Béla Nagy of the Institute of History of the Hungarian Academy of Sciences for preparing the maps and putting up with my unending requests for changes. I also thank László Szende and Mátyás Gödölle of the Hungarian National Museum and Katalin Mária Kincses and Kristóf Csákvári of the Institute and Museum of Military History (Budapest), and the Rijksmuseum (Amsterdam) for the illustrations.

An ACLS Fellowship in 2013 helped me launch this project in earnest. Georgetown University supported my research and writing with a sabbatical leave, a senior research grant, and numerous summer research grants. The latter, along with Georgetown University–Qatar's summer research grant, enabled me to work in the libraries in Turkey and Hungary, and return to the Ottoman archives in Istanbul regularly over the past ten years.

I am most grateful to my family. My parents had supported my career with love, even when my research and work took me ever farther from them. My sister, Ildikó, has offered constant help in Hungary. The hospitality she and my brother-in-law, Zsolt, offered during our summer vacations enabled our sons, Márk and Zoltán, to roam Hungary's most famous Ottoman-era castle, Eger. The support and love of my sons and wife, Kay, helped me find the balance between research, teaching, and family.

CHRONOLOGY

1071	Seljuk Turks defeat the Byzantines at the battle of Manzikert; Seljuks established in Asia Minor.
1204–61	Latin Empire of Constantinople founded by crusaders after the sack of the Byzantine capital, Constantinople.
1243	Mongols rout the Seljuks at the battle of Kösedağ; Seljuk power in Asia Minor wanes.
1250–1517	Mamluk sultanate of Syria and Egypt.
1271–91	The Mamluks expel the crusaders from Krak des Chevaliers (1271), Marqab (1285), and Acre (1291). The Knights of St. John (Hospitallers) transfer their headquarters to Cyprus.
1309	The Knights of St. John conquer Rhodes and move their headquarters there.
?–1324	Osman I (Ghazi), eponymous founder of the Ottoman dynasty.
c. 1324–62	Orhan I (Ghazi).
1326	Ottomans capture Byzantine Prusa (Bursa) from the Byzantines, which becomes the Ottoman capital.
1326–27	Earliest known Ottoman coin.
1331	Ottomans capture Byzantine Nicaea (İznik).
1331–55	Stephen Dušan in Serbia, largest territorial expanse.
1331–71	John Alexander (Dušan's brother-in-law) in Bulgaria; the country is divided into the two kingdoms of Trnovo and Vidin, and Dobrudja.
1337	Ottomans capture Byzantine Nicomedia (İzmit).
1345–46	Ottomans are allies of the Byzantine claimant John VI Kantakouzenos; Kantakouzenos gives his daughter, Theodora, in marriage to Orhan.
c. 1345–46	Ottomans annex Karasi Emirate.
1352	Ottomans cross over into Europe (Thrace), establish their first bridgehead in Tzympe on the Gallipoli peninsula.
1354	Byzantine Gallipoli destroyed by an earthquake, captured by Orhan's eldest son, Süleyman; beginning of Ottoman advance into Thrace.

1355	Stephen Dušan of Serbia dies; his kingdom is divided among his successors.
1361?–69?	Ottomans capture Byzantine Adrianople (Edirne) at the confluence of the Marica and Tundža Rivers; Edirne becomes Ottoman capital.
1362–89	Murad I.
1371	Ottoman victory over Serbs at Černomen (Çirmen) on the Marica River; conquest of Macedonia and neighboring areas.
1373	Byzantine Empire and the Balkan rulers become tributaries of the Ottomans.
1385	Ottomans capture Sofia from the Bulgarians.
1386	Ottomans capture Niš from the Serbians.
1389	First battle of Kosovo; Ottomans defeat a Balkan coalition led by the Serbian prince Lazar; Lazar and Murad I both killed; Serbia becomes Ottoman tributary.
1389–1402	Bayezid I.
1390	Ottomans capture Philadelphia, last Byzantine city in Asia Minor.
1390s	Ottomans annex west Anatolian emirates.
1393	Ottomans capture Trnovo, capital of Bulgarian ruler Šišman.
1394–1402	Unsuccessful siege and blockade of Byzantine Constantinople.
1396	Battle of Nikopol; Bayezid I defeats a crusader army led by Sigismund, king of Hungary.
1397–99	Conquest of large part of Asia Minor.
1402	Battle of Ankara; Bayezid I defeated and taken prisoner by Timur (Tamerlane); Anatolian Turkish emirates regain independence; Byzantine Empire ceases being tributary and recovers substantial territory.
1402–13	Bayezid's sons struggle for throne; Mehmed I triumphs, supported by Byzantine emperor Manuel II (r. 1391–1421) and by Serb princes.
1413–21	Mehmed I.
1415	Ottoman expansion in western Anatolia; conflict with Venice; Mehmed's brother, "False" Mustafa, challenges the sultan in Anatolia.
1416	Venetians destroy the Ottoman fleet at Gallipoli (29 May); Sheikh Bedreddin revolts in Rumelia but is defeated and executed (summer); Mustafa in Rumelia; both aided by King Sigismund of Hungary and Mircea of Wallachia.
1417	Mehmed's punitive campaign in Wallachia; Mircea becomes Ottoman vassal.
1421–22	Revolt of "False" Mustafa (Murad's uncle), aided by the Byzantines.
1421–44	Murad II (first reign).
1422	"False" Mustafa is executed (January); punitive Ottoman siege of Constantinople (June–September) fails; rebellion of "Little" Mustafa, Murad II's brother, in Anatolia.

1423	Murad defeats Mustafa.
1423–30	Thessaloniki under Venetian control; Ottoman-Venetian war.
1424	Ottoman-Byzantine treaty; Byzantines again become Ottoman tributary.
1426	Treaty of Tata between King Sigismund of Hungary and Despot Stephen Lazarević of Serbia regarding the childless despot's succession.
1427	Lazarević dies; according to the Treaty of Tata, the despot's nephew, George Branković, becomes ruler of Serbia; Hungarians enter Belgrade.
1430	Ottoman capture of Thessaloniki.
1438	Byzantine emperor John VIII Palaiologos leads the Byzantine delegation to the Council of Ferrara to discuss the union of the Western and Eastern churches.
1439	Ottomans annex Serbia; Decree of Union of the Western and Eastern Churches is signed in Florence.
1439–53	Çandarlı Halil Pasha grand vizier.
1440	Unsuccessful Ottoman attempt to take Belgrade from Hungarians.
1441–42	John Hunyadi repels Ottoman raids in Transylvania, defeats the governor of Smederevo.
1442	John Hunyadi defeats and kills the marcher lord of Nikopol and routs the governor-general of Rumeli.
1443	Hungarian campaign into the Balkans leads to Ottoman retreat from Serbia; insurrection of Skanderbeg (George Kastrioti) in northern Albania.
1444	Ottomans defeat the crusaders led by King Wladislas of Hungary and Poland and Hunyadi at Varna; debasement of Ottoman silver coinage.
1444–46	Mehmed II (first reign).
1446	Venetian-Ottoman treaty.
1446–51	Murad II (second reign).
1448	Second battle of Kosovo; Ottomans defeat Hungarian army led by Hunyadi.
1451–81	Mehmed II (second reign).
1452	Pope Nicholas V crowns Emperor Frederick III as Holy Roman emperor in Rome (last coronation in Rome); with a short exception (1742–45), all emperors would come from the House of Habsburgs until the empire's dissolution in 1806 by Napoleon I.
1453	Ottoman conquest of Constantinople ends Byzantine Empire; execution of Çandarlı Halil Pasha.
1453–56	Zağanos Pasha, first *devşirme* grand vizier.
1454	Venetian-Ottoman treaty, first *bailo* in Ottoman Constantinople.
1455	Moldavia becomes Ottoman tributary.

1455–61	Construction of the Grand Bazaar in Constantinople/Istanbul.
1456	Ottoman attempt to capture Belgrade defeated by Hunyadi.
1456–68	Mahmud Pasha Angelović, first grand vizierate.
1457–58	Construction of the Seven Towers (Yedikule) fortress and the Old Palace in Ottoman Constantinople.
1459	Annexation of Serbia; construction of Topkapı Palace begins.
1460	Conquest of Duchy of Athens; conquest of Byzantine Despotate of Mistra.
1461	Ottoman capture of Trebizond (Trabzon) ends last Byzantine state.
1463	Ottoman conquest of most of Bosnia and Herzegovina.
1463–79	Ottoman-Venetian war.
1468	Ottomans annex Karaman Emirate.
1469–74	Pacification of Karamanids.
1470	Ottomans capture Negroponte in Euboea from Venice.
1472	Ottoman raids in Venetian Friuli.
1472–74	Mahmud Pasha Angelović, second grand vizierate.
1473	Ottoman victory over Uzun Hasan of the Akkoyunlu Turkmen confederation; consolidation of Ottoman rule in Anatolia.
1475	Ottomans capture Genoese colonies in the Crimea.
1478	Crimean Tatars become Ottoman vassals.
1479	Ottoman-Venetian peace ends war of 1463–79.
1480	Ottomans regain control of most of Albania, capture Otranto, Italy; Ottoman siege of Rhodes fails.
1481–1512	Bayezid II.
1481	Ottomans surrender Otranto to the Neapolitan troops of Ferrante (Ferdinand) I of Naples; the Ottoman pretender Cem flees to Mamluk Egypt.
1482	Cem takes refuge first in Rhodes, then in France.
1483	Ottoman conquest of Herzegovina.
1484	Ottoman conquests of Kilia and Akkerman deprive Moldavia of access to Black Sea.
1485–91	Ottoman-Mamluk war.
1489	Cem is taken to Rome; Cyprus becomes Venetian.
1492	Jews are expelled from Spain, offered new home in the Ottoman Empire.
1493–1519	Emperor Maximilian I.
1494	Treaty of Tordesillas; Portugal and Castile partition newly discovered lands; French invasion of Italy.

1495	Ottoman pretender Cem dies.
1497–1516	Hersekzade Ahmed Pasha, five times grand vizier with interruptions.
1499–1503	Ottoman-Venetian war; Ottomans capture Venetian strongholds in Greece and Albania, including Lepanto and Modon (1500).
1501	Shah Ismail I establishes Shiite Safavid state in Iran.
1508	League of Cambrai.
1509–17	War of the League of Cambrai, fought between Venice and its allied foes: France, the empire, Spain, the papacy, Ferrara, and Mantua.
1509–47	Henry VIII, king of England.
1510–12	Succession struggle among sons of Sultan Bayezid II.
1511	Shiite partisans of Shah Ismail rebel in southwestern Anatolia.
1512	Selim forces his father, Bayezid II, to abdicate.
1512–20	Selim I.
1513–21	Pope Leo X (Giovanni de' Medici).
1514	Battle of Chaldiran; Ottoman victory over Shah Ismail; eastern Anatolia incorporated into empire.
1515–47	Francis I of France.
1516	Ottoman victory over the Mamluks at the battle of Marj Dabik; conquest of Syria; Archduke Charles of Habsburg becomes king of Castile.
1516–26	Louis II Jagiellon, king of Hungary and Bohemia.
1517	Ottoman victory over the Mamluks at the battle of Raydaniyya; conquest of Egypt; fall of the Mamluk sultanate; the sharif of Mecca submits to Selim I.
1519	Charles I of Spain elected Holy Roman emperor; Pope Leo X condemns Luther.
1520s	Ottoman-Portuguese rivalry in the Indian Ocean.
1520–66	Süleyman I.
1521	Ottomans capture Belgrade from Hungary; Pope Leo X excommunicates Luther.
1521–22	Archduke Ferdinand assumes governance of Austria; double marriage of Ferdinand and Anna Jagiellon (1521) and Louis II Jagiellon and Mary of Habsburg (1522).
1522	Ottoman conquest of Rhodes; end of the rule of Knights of St. John in Dodecanese (they would eventually move to Malta [1530]).
1523–36	Ibrahim Pasha, Süleyman's childhood friend and confidant, grand vizier.
1523–38	Andrea Gritti doge of Venice.
1525	Charles's forces capture Francis I of France at the battle of Pavia.

1526	Battle of Mohács, collapse of the medieval Kingdom of Hungary; John Szapolyai elected and crowned king of Hungary; Archduke Ferdinand elected king of Bohemia, Hungary, and Croatia; Ottoman-Habsburg rivalry in Hungary.
1529	Failed Ottoman siege of Habsburg Vienna.
1530s	Ottoman-Habsburg rivalry in North Africa.
1533	Hayreddin Barbarossa, governor of Algiers, appointed to command Ottoman navy.
1534	Ottoman conquest of Tabriz and Baghdad.
1537–40	Ottoman-Venetian war.
1538	Ottoman campaign in Moldavia; Ottomans annex northwestern Black Sea coast; Ottoman naval victory at Preveza over the allied fleet of the papacy, Venice, and the Habsburgs.
1539–41	Lutfi Pasha (of Albanian origin) becomes grand vizier; married Süleyman's sister, Shah.
1541	Ottomans annex central Hungary (Buda province); Transylvania becomes a tributary principality.
1544–61	Rüstem Pasha (of Croatian origin) becomes grand vizier (with interruption in 1553); married to Süleyman's daughter, Mihrimah.
1548	Süleyman's campaign against Safavids of Iran.
1553–55	War with Safavid Iran.
1554	Süleyman's campaign in Iran; Ottoman conquest of Nakhichevan and Erivan; Muscovy conquers Astrakhan.
1555	Ottoman-Safavid peace at Amasya stabilizes the eastern frontier and Ottoman-Safavid border.
1565	Ottoman siege of Malta defeated by Knights of St. John.
1565–79	Sokollu Mehmed Pasha (of Serbian origin) grand vizier.
1566	Süleyman dies during his last campaign at the siege of Szigetvár (Hungary).
1566–74	Selim II.
1569	Failed Ottoman attempt to dig a canal between the Don and Volga Rivers.
1570–73	Ottoman-Venetian war triggered by the Ottoman attack on Cyprus.
1571	The Holy League (papacy, Spain, Venice) defeats the Ottomans at the battle of Lepanto.
1573	Peace with Venice; Cyprus (conquered in 1570–71) remains in Ottoman hands.
1574–95	Murad III.
1578–90	War with Iran; Ottoman conquest of Azerbaijan; financial crisis and inflation.

1580–81	Ottoman-Habsburg truce in the Mediterranean.
1590s	Start of Celali revolts in Anatolia.
1593–1606	Long War against the Habsburgs in Hungary.
1595	Rebellion of Romanian principalities.
1595–1603	Mehmed III.
1603–12	Renewed war with Safavid Iran ends in first major loss, that of conquests made in war of 1578–90.
1603–17	Ahmed I.
1606	Peace of Zsitvatorok with Austrian Habsburgs; the parties rule over their respective territories in Hungary.
1609	End of first phase of Celali revolts.
1613–35	Rebellion of Fahreddin Ma'noğlu.
1614–18	War with Safavid Iran.
1617–18	Mustafa I (first reign).
1618–22	Osman II.
1618–48	Thirty Years' War.
1620	Battle of White Mountain; Habsburg victory over Bohemian Estates.
1621–22	War with Poland-Lithuania.
1622–23	Mustafa I (second reign).
1622–28	Revolt of Abaza Mehmed Pasha.
1623–39	War with Iran.
1623–40	Murad IV.
1639	Treaty of Zuhab with Safavids restores frontiers of 1555 and 1612.
1640–48	Ibrahim I.
1645–69	War with Venice over Crete.
1648	Treaty of Westphalia ends Thirty Years' War.
1648–87	Mehmed IV.
1656–61	Köprülü Mehmed Pasha grand vizier with full powers.
1657–58	Ottoman campaign against Transylvania to subdue Prince George (György) II Rákóczi.
1660	Ottomans capture Várad; province of Várad created.
1661–76	Köprülüzade Fazıl Ahmed Pasha grand vizier.
1663–64	War with Austrian Habsburgs and Hungarians.
1669	Ottomans conquer Crete.

1672–76	War with Poland-Lithuania ends in annexation of Podolia; maximum Ottoman expansion in Europe.
1676–83	Kara Mustafa Pasha grand vizier.
1677–81	War with Muscovy.
1683	Second Ottoman siege of Vienna; Austrian-Polish army defeats Ottomans.
1684	Holy League (Austria, Poland-Lithuania, Venice, papacy) against Ottomans.
1684–99	Habsburgs conquer Ottoman-held Hungary; Venice captures the Morea (first war of Morea); Poland reconquers Podolia.
1686	Fall of Buda; Muscovy joins the Holy League.
1687	Holy League defeats Ottomans at Nagyharsány ("Second Mohács"); Mehmed IV forced to abdicate.
1687–91	Süleyman II.
1688	Austrian Habsburgs capture Belgrade, occupy parts of Serbia; Serbs revolt in support of Habsburgs.
1690	Ottoman reconquest of Serbia and Belgrade; first great Serbian migration from Kosovo and southern Serbia to Slavonia and Hungary.
1691	Habsburgs defeat Ottomans at Slankamen.
1691–95	Ahmed II.
1695	Introduction of lifelong tax farms.
1695–1703	Mustafa II.
1697	The Holy League defeats Ottomans at Zenta.
1699	Treaty of Karlowitz (in modern Serbia): Slavonia, Croatia, and Transylvania ceded to Habsburgs; Morea and lesser Dalmatian territories ceded to Venice; Podolia ceded to Poland; Ottomans retain Serbia and Moldavia.
1700	Treaty of Istanbul: Azak ceded to Muscovy.
1703	Revolt of the army (Edirne Incident); Mustafa II deposed.
1703–30	Ahmed III.
1710–11	War with Russia.
1711	Ottoman victory over Peter I (the Great) of Russia.
1713	Peace with Russia; Azak recovered.
1715–18	War with Venice (second war of Morea); Ottomans recover Morea.
1716–18	War with Austria.
1718	Treaty of Passarowitz (Serbia) with Austria and Venice: Morea recovered; Banat, northern Serbia, and western Wallachia ceded to Habsburgs.

GLOSSARY OF TERMS

agent (It. *agente*): A lower-level permanent envoy; in rank, he was below a resident and an ambassador.

agha (Tr. ağa): Title used for senior officers of the military and of the Ottoman imperial household, such as the *agha* (commander) of the janissaries.

ahdname: Letter of contract; treaty; capitulations; from the Arabic *ahd* (contract, agreement, oath) and the Persian *name* (letter, document).

akçe: Small Ottoman silver coin that was the basic currency in the Ottoman Empire and also served as a unit of account; between 1532 and the end of the century, 60 *akçe* = 1 sultani of gold, about 1 Venetian ducat.

***bailo* (It. plural: *baili*):** Representative of the Republic of Venice and the head of a Venetian community abroad; the Venetian ambassador-consul at the sultan's court in Constantinople.

Balkans / Balkan Peninsula: Meaning mountainous region and peninsula, the Balkans is the name of southeastern Europe that includes present-day Romania, Bulgaria, Greece, European Turkey, Albania, and the countries of the former Yugoslavia.

ban (from the Latin *banus*): Royal governor in medieval and early modern Hungary, usually of frontier regions or countries.

banate (from the Latin *banatus*): Frontier province or dependency governed by a *ban* in the name of the king of Hungary.

beg (Tr. bey): Military commander; lord; prince; ruler of an emirate/principality; governor of a *sancak* (subprovince).

***beylerbeyi* (literally "bey of the beys" or "lord of the lords"):** Provincial governor-general; commander of the *sancakbeyis*.

capitulation (from the Latin *capitula*, meaning the articles of a treaty): Commercial agreement by which the Ottoman sultans granted extraterritorial immunity from local laws and taxes to subjects of European countries.

çavuş: An officer in the palace and the imperial council who is responsible for escorting envoys and carrying imperial decrees; messenger; an army officer who conveys messages from the commanders to the army.

Celali (Jelali): Rebels against the Ottoman government in Anatolia and Syria in the sixteenth and seventeenth centuries, named after Sheikh Celal, who had rebelled in 1519.

Çelebi: "Gentleman," "Young Master," prince; name given to the sons of early Ottoman rulers; later, honorific given to learned men, such as Evliya Çelebi.

chief mufti: The mufti or jurisconsult of Constantinople/Istanbul, also known as *Şeyhülislam*; the highest-ranking legal and religious officer in the Ottoman Empire.

cizye (**Ar.** *jizya*): Islamic head tax imposed on non-Muslim adult males and households.

defter: A register or record book, such as tax/revenue surveys (sing. *tahrir defteri*), registers of the poll tax (sing. *cizye defteri*), or soldiers' pay lists (sing. *mevacib defteri*).

defterdar: The keeper of the defter; treasurer or chief accountant in the Ottoman government; head of provincial treasuries and finances.

despot: "Lord"; a Byzantine title also used in the successor states of the Byzantine Empire established after the Latin conquest of Constantinople in 1204 and in Bulgaria and Serbia.

devşirme: "Collection"; child levy; the system by which the Ottoman authorities recruited non-Muslim lads in their empire for the army and administration.

diet (**Lat.** *dieta*): Assembly of the Estates; parliament, Estates General.

doge: Elected leader of the Venetian state.

dragoman (**Ar.** *tarjuman*, **Tr.** *tercüman*): Translator; diplomatic interpreter; especially those translating from and to Turkish in the Ottoman capital and the provinces.

ducat: Money of account; Venetian gold and silver coins.

emirate: A polity ruled by a semi-independent ruler (*emir*); a principality.

Estates (**of the realm**): The nobles, clergy, and burghers (in some European countries, the peasants); those who are represented at the assembly of the Estates or diet.

florin (**Tr.** *filori*): Gold coin, named after the European golden coinage *fiorino*; also used in the Ottoman Empire with the value of 50–66 *akçe* in the sixteenth century.

fusta: Small galley with twelve to fifteen rowing benches.

galiot: Small galley with sixteen to twenty-three rowing benches.

galleass: Heavily armed galley that could fire broadside, created by the Venetians.

galley: The principal fighting ship in the Mediterranean and adjacent waters, powered by oars and sails, with twenty-five rowing benches on each sides and three oarsmen to a bench. It could fire cannons from the prow.

ghaza: Raid; warfare in the name of Islam; "holy war."

ghazi: A man who participates in a *ghaza*.

ghulam: A boy, lad, or male slave; in the Safavid Empire, the shah's slave soldiers of Circassian, Armenian, or Georgian origin.

grand vizier (**Tr.** *vezir-i azam, sadr-i azam, sadrazam*): Chief vizier, the highest-ranking administrative officer in the Ottoman Empire, and the head of the government and the absolute deputy of the sultan.

harem: "forbidden"; "sacred"; the private quarter of the house and its female inhabitants in Islamic lands, forbidden for males who are not family members.

hass: (1) Sultanic or crown lands/revenues; (2) lands/revenues of *provincial* governors and *sancak* governors, usually (but not always) yielding an annual revenue of more than 100,000 *akçe* in the sixteenth century.

hoca: Muslim teacher or tutor; Ottoman title used for religious functionaries.

khutba (**Tr.** *hutbe*): The Friday sermon in Islam in which the ruler's name is mentioned.

janissary: The sultan's elite infantry corps; derived from the Turkish term *yeni çeri* (new army).

jihad: Struggle to defend and extend Islam; war to achieve these goals.

kanun: Customs, codes, regulations; customary law; customary and sultanic law promulgated in the name of the reigning sultan, which supplemented the Islamic sacred law (*sharia*).

kanunname: A collection of customary and sultanic laws; shorter law code of a *sancak* dealing with issues of criminal law and taxation.

kapudan pasha: The admiral of the Ottoman navy.

kapukulu (kapıkulu): "Slave of the Porte"; slave of the sultan's household who served in the military, the administration, and the palace.

kul: Slave, servant (mainly of the sultan).

levend: Privateer, often with the imperial navy; irregular soldier; militia.

Lower Hungary (Ger. *Niederungarn,* Lat. *Cisdanubia*): Ten or eleven counties in the northwestern territory of the Kingdom of Hungary, as viewed from Vienna and Pozsony, where during the Ottoman era most government offices resided.

Moldavia: Historical region in modern Romania; Ottoman vassal or tributary principality disputed by Poland-Lithuania.

Morea: A large peninsula in southern Greece; also known as the Peloponnese.

mufti (Tr. *müfti*): Jurist or jurisconsult who issued legal opinion.

mukataa: Revenues from parceled fiscal units administered as tax farms.

Muscovy: Russian principality centered around Moscow that by the eighteenth century expanded to become the Russian Empire.

orator (Lat.): Public speaker; envoy who speaks for his monarch; same as *legatus*.

padishah: Sovereign; great king; Ottoman term used for Ottoman rulers, sultans.

palatine (Lat. *Palatinus regni*): The highest office in the Kingdom of Hungary; leader of the nobility.

Partium (Lat.): The Latin phrases *Partium Regni Hungariae* (parts of the Hungarian Kingdom) and *Partes adnexae* (the annexed parts) refer to the eastern and northern parts of the Hungarian Kingdom in the sixteenth century and thereafter.

pasha (Tr. *paşa*): Title given to viziers and governors-general.

Phanariots: Greek elite living in Constantinople's Phanar (Tr. Fener) district, where the Orthodox patriarchate was situated.

Qizilbash ("Red-head"): Followers of Shah Ismail of the Safavid Empire, so named after their twelve tasseled red hats, a symbol of their belief that Ismail was the promised twelfth imam of Shiite Islam.

reaya: Flock; originally all taxpaying subjects of the sultan, regardless of their religion, as opposed to the *askeri* ruling elite.

Reis: Ottoman title of naval commanders.

resident (It. *residente*): A permanent diplomat, envoy; in the hierarchy of permanent diplomats, the resident was below the permanent ambassador (It. *ambasciatore*) but above the agent (It. *agente*).

Rum: A geographical term in Arabic, Persian, and Turkish that refers to Anatolia (Asia Minor), the land of Rome, or the Eastern Roman Empire.

Rumeli (Rumelia): "Land of the Romans [Byzantines]"; Ottoman possessions in southeastern Europe south of the Danube; the Balkans.

sancak (Ar. *liva*): Banner; a subdivision of a province; subprovince or district.

sancakbeyi (*mirliva*): The governor of a *sancak*.

Serenissima (It.): The Republic of Venice; short for the Most Serene Republic of Venice (*Serenissima Repubblica di Venezia*)

şeyhülislam: Head of the Ottoman religious establishment (*ulema*); the chief *mufti* of Constantinople and the empire.

sharia: Islamic sacred law.

Signoria (It.): Venice's governing body.

sipahi: Light cavalryman remunerated through military fiefs or *timars*; *sipahi* of the Porte, member of one of the six *kapıkulu* cavalry divisions of the Porte's standing army.

sultan: Ruler of the Ottoman Empire; princes and senior female members of the Ottoman dynasty also used the title.

tahrir: Land and revenue survey.

timar: Military or administrative "fief" or prebend that was given to soldiers and officials in return for their service.

Transylvania: Historical region in the eastern part of medieval Hungary; the Principality of Transylvania was a tributary of the Ottoman Empire.

ulama: The Ottoman religious establishment.

Upper Hungary (Ger. *Oberungarn*): The territory of thirteen counties in the northeastern part of the Kingdom of Hungary.

vilayet: A province headed by a governor-general or *beylerbeyi*.

vizier (Tr. *vezir*): The sultan's minister with military and administrative power who was a member of the imperial council; title given to high-ranking officials like the commander of the janissaries, the admiral of the navy, and important provincial governors-general (Egypt, Baghdad, Buda, etc.).

voivode: Royal governor of Transylvania in medieval Hungary; ruler of the Ottoman vassal states of Wallachia and Moldavia.

GLOSSARY OF PLACE-NAMES

Bos. = Bosnian, Bul. = Bulgarian, Cz. = Czech, Ger. = German; Gr. = Greek; Hun. = Hungarian; It. = Italian, Lat. = Latin; Pol. = Polish, Serb. = Serbian; Slov. = Slovak; Rom. = Romanian; Russ. = Russian; Tr. = Turkish, Ukr. = Ukrainian

The Balkan Peninsula, Black Sea Littoral, Poland-Lithuania, Muscovy

Name in the book	Current name	Other name forms
Akkerman (Tr.)	Bilhorod-Dnistrovskyi (Ukr.)	Cetatea Albă (Rom.), Dnyeszterfehérvár (Hun.), Walachisch Weissenburg (Ger.)
Aleksinac (Serb.)	Aleksinac (Serb.)	Alekşice (Tr.)
Azak (Tr.)	Azov (Rus.)	Tana (It.)
Bela Palanka (Serb.)	Bela Palanka (Serb.)	Palanka-i Musapaşa (Tr.)
Caffa	Feodosiya (Rus. Ukr.)	Kefe (Tr.)
Chalcis (Gr.)	Chalcis (Gr.)	Negroponte (It.), Ağriboz, Eğriboz (Tr.)
Chrysoupolis (Gr.)	Chrysoupolis (Gr.)	Sarı Şaban (Tr.)
Chyhyryn (Ukr.)	Chyhyryn (Ukr.)	Chigirin (Rus.), Czehryn (Pol.), Çehrin (Tr.)
Corinth (Gr.)	Corinth (Gr.)	Gördüs (Tr.)
Eleftheroupoli (Gr.)	Eleftheroupoli (Gr.)	Praviște (Tr.)
Grocka (Serb.)	Grocka (Serb.)	Hisarcık (Tr.)
Isaccea (Rom.)	Isaccea (Rom.)	İsakçı (Tr.)
Izmail (Ukr.)	Izmail (Ukr.)	İsmail (Rom.), İsmail Geçidi (Tr.)
Jagodina (Serb.)	Jagodina (Serb.)	Yagodina (Tr.)
Jajce (Bos.)	Jajce (Bos.)	Jajca (Hun.), Yayçe (Tr.)
Kamieniec (Pol.)	Kamianets-Podilskyi (Ukr.)	Kamaniçe (Tr.)
Karlowitz (Ger.)	Sremski Karlovci (Serb.)	Karlóca (Hun.)
Khotyn (Ukr.)	Khotyn (Ukr.)	Chocim (Pol.), Hotin (Rom. and Tr.)
Kilia	Kiliya (Ukr.)	Kili (Tr.)
Komotiní (Gr.)	Komotiní (Gr.)	Gümülcine (Tr.)

(Continued)

The Balkan Peninsula, Black Sea Littoral, Poland-Lithuania, Muscovy (continued)

Name in the book	Current name	Other name forms
Koron (It. Venetian)	Koroni (Gr.)	Koron (Tr.)
Kruševac (Serb.)	Kruševac (Serb.)	Alacahisar (Tr.)
Lamía (Gr.)	Lamía (Gr.)	İzdin (Tr.)
Langadas (Gr.)	Langadas (Gr.)	Langaza (Tr.)
Larissa (Gr.)	Larissa (Gr.)	Yenişehir (Tr.)
Livadeia (Gr.)	Livadeia (Gr.)	Livadiye (Tr.)
Modon (It. Venetian)	Methoni (Gr.)	Moton (Tr.)
Negroponte (It.)	the island of Euboia (Gr.)	Ağriboz, Eğriboz (Tr.)
Nikopol (Bul.)	Nikopol (Bul.)	Nicopolis (Lat.) Niğbolu (Tr.)
Ochakiv (Ukr.)	Ochakiv (Ukr.)	Cankerman, Özü, Özi (Tr.)
Orfani (Gr.)	Orfani (Gr.)	Orfan (Tr.)
Pazardžik (Bul.)	Pazardžik (Bul.)	Tatarpazarı (Tr.)
Petrovaradin (Serb.)	Petrovaradin (Serb.)	Pétervárad (Hun.), Varadin (Tr.), Peterwardein (Ger.)
Pirot (Serb.)	Pirot (Serb.)	Şehirköy (Tr.)
Plovdiv (Bul.)	Plovdiv (Bul.)	Filibe (Tr.)
Popovica (Bul.)	Popovica (Bul.)	Papaslı (Tr.)
Požega (Cro.)	Požega (Cro.)	Pojega (Tr.)
Ragusa (Lat./It.)	Dubrovnik (Cro.)	
Šabac (Serb.)	Šabac (Serb.)	Szabács (Hun.), Böğürdelen (Tr.)
Skopje (Macedonian)	Skopje (Macedonian)	Üsküb (Tr.)
Skradin (Cro.)	Skradin (Cro.)	Scardona (Lat., It.)
Slankamen (Serb.)	Slankamen (Serb.)	Szalánkemén (Hun.)
Smederevo (Serb.)	Smederevo (Serb.)	Szendrő (Hun.), Semendire (Tr.)
Srebrenik (Bos.)	Srebrenik (Bos.)	
Srem (Serb.)	Srem/Srijem (Serb./Cro.)	Syrmium (Lat.), Szerémség (Hun.), Sirem (Tr.)
Svilengrad (Bul.)	Svilengrad (Bul.)	Cisr-i Mustafapaşa (Tr.)
Thessaloniki (Gr.)	Thessaloniki (Gr.)	Thessalonika, Thessalonica, Salonica (Gr.), Selanik (Tr.)
Tulçea (Rom.)	Tulçea (Rom.)	Tulça (Tr.)
Uzundžovo (Bul.)	Uzundžovo (Bul.)	Uzuncaabad-I Hasköy (Tr.)
Vulčitrn (Serb.)	Vulčitrn/Vushtrri (in Kosovo)	Vulçitrin (Tr.)
Zvornik (Bos.)	Zvornik (Bos.)	İzvornik (Tr.)

Habsburg and Ottoman Hungary, Transylvania

Name in the book	Current name	Other name forms
Arad (Hun.)	Arad (Rom.)	Arad (Tr.)
Becse (Hun.)	Novi Bečej (Serb.)	Beçey (Tr.)
Becskerek (Hun.)	Zrenjanin (Serb.)	Beçkerek (Tr.)
Besztercebánya (Hun.)	Banská Bystrica (Slov.)	Neusohl (Ger.)
Buda (Hun.)	Budapest (Hun.)	Budin, Budun (Tr.), Ofen (Ger.)
Csanád (Hun.)	Cenad (Serb.)	Çanad (Tr.)
Eger (Hun.)	Eger (Hun.)	Erlau (Ger.) Eğri (Tr.)
Érsekújvár (Hun.)	Nové Zámky (Slov.)	Neuhäusel (Ger.), Uyvar (Tr.)
Esztergom (Hun.)	Esztergom (Hun.)	Gran (Ger.), Strigonium (Lat.), Estergon, Ostorgon (Tr.)
Fülek (Hun.)	Filakovo (Slov.)	Filek (Tr.)
Győr (Hun.)	Győr (Hun.)	Raab (Ger.), Yanık (Tr.)
Gyulafehérvár (Hun.)	Alba Iulia (Rom.)	Weissenburg/Karlsburg (Ger.)
Kanizsa (Hun.)	Nagykanizsa (Hun.)	Kanischa (Ger.), Kanije (Tr.)
Karánsebes (Hun.)	Căvăran (Rom.)	Karansebesch (Ger.)
Kassa (Hun.)	Košice (Slov.)	Kaschau (Ger.)
Kolozsvár (Hun.)	Cluj-Napoca (Rom.)	Klasenburg (Ger.)
Komárom (Hun.)	Komárno (Slov.)	Komorn (Ger.)
Kőszeg (Hun.)	Kőszeg (Hun.)	Güns (Ger.)
Lippa (Hun.)	Lipova (Rom.)	Lipova (Tr.)
Lugos (Hun.)	Lugoj (Rom.)	Lugoş (Tr.)
Mohács (Hun.)	Mohács (Hun.)	Mohaç (Tr.)
Nagyszombat (Hun.)	Trnava (Slov.)	Tyrnau (Ger.)
Osijek (Cro.)	Osijek (Cro.)	Eszék (Hun.), Ösek (Tr.)
Pécs (Hun.)	Pécs (Hun.)	Fünfkirchen (Ger.), Peçuy (Tr.)
Pozsony (Hun.)	Bratislava (Slov.)	Pressburg (Ger.), Posonium (Lat.)
Szatmár (Hun.)	Satu Mare (Rom.)	Sacmar (Ger.)
Szeben (Hun.)	Sibiu (Rom.)	Hermannstadt (Ger.)
Szigetvár (Hun.)	Szigetvár (Hun.)	Sigetvar (Tr.)
Temesvár (Hun.)	Timişoara (Rom.)	Temeschwar (Ger.), Temeşvar (Tr.)
Turnu Severin (Rom.)	Drobeta-Turnu Severin (Rom.)	Szörény (Hun)
Várad/Nagyvárad (Hun.)	Oradea (Rom.)	Wardein/Grosswardein (Ger.), Varad (Tr.)
Vasvár (Hun.)	Vasvár (Hun.)	Eisenburg (Ger.)

NOTES

Abbreviations of Archival and Published Sources
Used in the Notes

AE.SMST.II = Ali Emiri Mustafa II

AT = Džaja, Srećko M., et al. *Austro-Turcica 1541–1552.*

BOA = Başbakanlık Osmanlı Arşivi (Prime Ministry's Ottoman Archives, Istanbul)

CSP. Spain = *Calendar of Letters, Despatches and State Papers relating to the Negotiations between England and Spain, preserved in the Archives at Simancas and Elsewhere.* London 1862–1954. Also available via Medieval and Early Modern Sources Online (MESO)

D. BKL.d. = Büyük Kale Kalemi Defterleri

D.BŞM. BDH.d. = Bab-ı Defteri Başmuhasebe Budin Hazinesi Defterleri

D.BŞM. BNH.d. = Bab-ı Defteri Başmuhasebe Bosna Hazinesi Defterleri

D.BŞM. UYH.d. = Bab-ı Defteri Başmuhasebe Uyvar Hazinesi Defterleri

D.PYM.d.=Bab-ı Defteri Piyade Mukabelesi Kalemi Defterleri

D.YNÇ.d. = Bab-ı Defteri Yeniçeri Kalemi Defterleri

EOE I = Erdélyi országgyűlési emlékek. Vol. 1. (1540–1556). Edited by Sándor Szilágyi. Budapest. 1876.

HHStA = Haus, Hof- und Staatsarchiv of the Österreichisches Staatsarchiv (Vienna)

KK.d. = Kamil Kepeci Defeterleri

MAD.d. = Maliyeden Müdevver Defterleri

MNL OL DL = Magyar Nemzeti Levéltár Országos Levéltára, Diplomatikai Levéltár

MÜD = Mühimme Defterleri

ÖStA = Österreichisches Staatsarchiv (Vienna)

TSMA = Topkapı Sarayı Müzesi Arşivi (Archives of the Topkapı Palace Museum)

TT = Történelmi Tár

TT.d. = Tapu Tahrir Defterleri

Prologue

1. See, for example, Mack 2002; Brotton 2002; ; Dursteler 2006; Isom-Verhaaren 2013.

2. See, for instance, Howard 1994, 2007; Kafadar 1997–98; Darling 1996; Khoury 1997; Salzman 2004; Murphey 1999; Ágoston 2005a; Aksan 2007.

3. Tezcan 2010.

Chapter 1: The Early Ottomans

1. Korobeinikov 2010: 218–23; 2014: chapter 4.

2. Korobeinikov 2014: 295–96; Ostrogorsky 1969: 478–98, Bartusis 1992.

3. Ostrogorsky 1969: 492.

4. Wittek 1938, 2012. On Wittek and the reception of his ideas, see Kafadar 1995: 35–59; Heywood 1999: 231–40.

5. Jennings 1986; Kafadar 1995; Lowry 2003; Oikonomides 1993.

6. In 1267, the Genoese acquired the right to settle in Galata/Pera, owing to their alliance with the Byzantine emperor, Michael Palaiologos, against Venice. Though the treaty contained humiliating terms (the emperor considered the Genoese vassals), the Genoese attained the status of resident aliens with their place of residence and commercial quarter in Pera. Their Venetian rivals, on the other hand, had to rent houses in Constantinople. See Nicol 1988: 190–91.

7. İnalcık 1979: 79–80; Luttrel 1993; Fleet 1999; Kyriakidis 2011: 28–31.

8. Emecen 1993; Zachariadou 1993b.

9. Lowry and Erünsal 2010; Lowry 2012: 3–15; Kiprovska 2016.

10. Levend 1956: 181–84; Sabev 2002; Kiprovska 2008, 2013.

11. Lowry 2012; Lowry and Erünsal 2010. The fourth such dynasty, the Turahanoğulları ("Sons of Turahan"), is of uncertain origin.

12. Quoted in Lowry 2003: 46.

13. Lowry 2003: 58–66; Kastritsis 2007a.

14. Lowry 2003: 141–42.

15. Kafadar 1995: 79–80.

16. Darling 2011: 15–16.

17. In March 1302, floods temporarily diverted the course of the Sakarya River into its ancient riverbed. Byzantine forts had been built along the river's more recent course, on the left (Byzantine) bank of the river. But after the flood altered the course of the river, these forts became ineffective. This change made it easier for Osman and his small band to cross the river and defeat the Byzantines. See Lindner 2007: 102–16.

18. Schamiloğlu 2004. However, the claim that the Ottomans "would have suddenly gained in relative size and strength" vis-à-vis the other Turkish principalities, which "suffered from depopulation and instability" (271), cannot explain Ottoman victory over the latter. After all, the Ottomans managed to defeat the emirs of Menteşe and Aydın around 1390, decades after the plague, and even then just temporarily.

19. İnalcık 1989: 228–35; Oikonomides 1994; Chrysostomides 2009: 33–36; Laiou 2008; Zachariadou 1999: 7–11.

20. N. Necipoğlu 2009: 120–23. Venetian sources claimed that Andronikos also offered his sister to Murad in marriage, but, as one of the sources added, God prevented this "abominable sin" by taking her life.

21. Tekin 1989: 156; Zachariadou 1993b: 229.

22. Aşıkpaşazade (A.H.1332) 1916: 125–28, quoted in Levend 1956: 185. After the conquest of Smederevo, Aşıkpaşazade sold five slaves in Skopje for 900 *akçe*. After the conquest of the Morea, the *akıncıs* sold a female slave for 100 *akçe*.

23. Lowry 2003: 48–49 (I slightly modified his translation). In the mid-fifteenth century the *akıncıs* opposed the conquest of Belgrade because they thought it would mean the end of their profitable raids. See Aşıkpaşazade (1332) 1916: 147, quoted in Levend 1956: 185.

24. Arnakis 1951: 106–7.

25. Lowry 2010: 65–106.

26. Lowry 2003: 36–37 (I slightly altered his translation). Heywood 2004 offered alternative readings for sections of the inscription. He (1999: 238; 2004) also noted that in his translation, Wittek conveniently omitted titles that did not fit into his *ghazi* thesis. See also Howard 2017: 30.

27. Emecen (1995) 2003: 83–84; Imber 2000: 168–69; Lowry 2003.

28. Lindner 1983: 24.

29. Leube 2015b, 2015c, both accessed on 19 April 2016.

30. Kyriakidis 2011: 38–40.

31. Fine 1994: 345–48. Alexander declared John Šišman (his son from his second marriage) his heir, granting Vidin and the northwestern part of his realm to his disinherited son from his first marriage, John Stracimir, as compensation.

32. In 1353, the Hungarian king married Elizabeth Kotromanić (d. 1387), the daughter of King Stephen II Kotromanić of Bosnia (r. c. 1314–53). He demanded that the king's teenage nephew and heir Stephen Tvrtko I surrender western Hum as Elizabeth's dowry. In 1363, after a Hungarian invasion, Tvrtko I surrendered the fortress of Ključ to the Hungarian king. When his Bosnian rivals ousted him in 1366, Tvrtko I fled to Hungary. Having accepted Hungarian suzerainty, he recovered his lands in 1367 with Hungarian help.

33. Dorothy had been living in the Hungarian capital Buda as a hostage ever since Louis I conquered Vidin in 1365 and established a Hungarian frontier province, or *banate*, under a Hungarian royal governor (*ban*) in Vidin. The Banate of Vidin existed until 1369, when Louis restored Stracimir into his possessions as a Hungarian vassal. Engel 2001: 164–66.

34. Quoted in Housley 1984: 202.

35. Several dates (1361, 1362, 1367, 1369, 1371) have been suggested for the Ottoman conquest of Adrianople. See Zachariadou 1970. İnalcık (1989: 241) claimed that Bursa remained the Ottoman capital until 1402. Bursa retained its significance thereafter as the burial place of the dynasty.

36. İnalcık 1989: 243; Fine 1994: 379–82.

37. Housley 1984: 192, 204–6.

38. Sigismund claimed the Hungarian throne after the death of King Louis I—the last male descendant of the Hungarian branch of the House of Anjou—on account of his betrothal (1379) and marriage (1385) to King Louis's older daughter Mary, who succeeded her father on the Hungarian throne in 1382 under the regency of her mother, Elizabeth of Bosnia. King Charles III

of Naples, the last male representative of the House of Anjou, who had been brought up in Hungary, also laid claim to the Hungarian throne. Charles III was crowned king of Hungary (1385) but was soon assassinated (1386), after which the Neapolitan party declared his son Ladislaus heir to the Hungarian throne. The anti-Sigismund factions remained active for years in Croatia, Slavonia, Dalmatia, and Bosnia. Although Sigismund was crowned king of Hungary in 1387, he managed to suppress the Angevin party only in 1394, restoring royal authority by 1403. In the meantime, Louis's younger daughter, Hedwig (Jadwiga), was crowned king (*rex*) of Poland in Cracow in 1384, though other sources mention her as queen (*regina*). In 1385 she married Władysław of Jagiellon, the grand duke of Lithuania and the founder of the Jagiellonian dynasty. Władysław ruled Poland as comonarch until Hedwig's death (1399), and then as sole king. While Sigismund and Władysław laid claims to each other's crowns, the main threat to Sigismund's rule came from the Angevin party. See Engel 2001.

39. See Mályusz 1984: 12; Árvai 2013. Lazar arranged the marriages of his three other daughters to two Serbian rival lords (Vuk Branković, the lord of Kosovo and its surroundings, and George [Djuradj] Balšić, the lord of Upper Zeta/Montenegro and prince of Albania), and the son of the Bulgarian tsar.

40. This reconstruction of events, based on Serbian and Byzantine sources, questions Lazar's acceptance of Ottoman suzerainty at this point, claimed by the Ottoman chronicler Neşri and the older historiography. See Reinert 1993: 174–79. I thank Alexander Fotić for drawing my attention to this article. For the older views, see İnalcık 1989: 246–48.

41. Reinert 1993: 191–94.

42. Reinert 1993: 205.

43. After the death of Vuk Branković—Stephen's rival and brother-in-law—in late 1397, Sultan Bayezid gave Stephen most of Vuk's lands. See Spremić 2014.

44. Engel 1998.

45. This reconstruction of the sultan's Wallachian campaign (fall 1394) and of the battle of Rovine (10 October 1394, instead of 17 May 1395 as suggested by earlier studies) follows Diaconescu 1998: 250–51.

46. Gradeva 2004: 26.

47. Engel 2001: 203; Diaconescu 1998: 258–59, 274.

48. Mályusz 1984: 105.

49. Schnerb 1998; Veszprémy 2001: 226–27; Pálosfalvi 2018: 57–59. On Mircea's contingent, which previous historiography estimated at eight thousand to ten thousand men, see Diaconescu 1998: 260.

50. A generation after Nikopol, the Burgundian traveler Bertrandon de la Brocquière noted that while the Hungarian archers used "bows like those of the Turks, they are not as good or as strong. Nor are the people as good shots. The Hungarians shoot with three fingers and the Turks with the thumb and the ring finger." Quoted by Nicolle 2005: 22.

51. Veszprémy 2001.

52. Nicolle 2005.

53. Mályusz 1984: 104–7; Diaconescu 1998: 262.

54. Panaite 2000: 102–3.

55. Gradeva 2004: 27.

Chapter 2: Defeat and Recovery

1. İnalcık 1993c: 44–45; Murphey 2008: 78. Following the Mongol destruction of the Abbasid Caliphate and the killing of the last caliph in 1258, the Mamluk sultan Baybars revived the caliphate in Cairo in 1261–62 by installing two scions of the Abbasid dynasty, who had excaped to the Mamluk Sultanate. See Amitai-Preiss 1995: 56–63.

2. G. Necipoğlu 2019: 126.

3. Alexandrescu-Dersca 1977: 112–15.

4. Dincel 2002.

5. Ibn 'Arabshāh 1936: 178–79.

6. Alexandrescu-Dersca 1977: 68–79; Matschke 1981.

7. The "Law Code of Mehmed II" is quoted in Turkish in Uzunçarşılı (1945) 1984: 45–46.

8. Colin Imber has suggested that Mehmed II's Law Code is a later compilation and that the "law of fratricide" intended to justify the last and most horrendous fratricide, the execution of Mehmed III's nineteen infant brothers after Mehmed's accession to the throne in 1595, which caused public outrage. See Imber 2009: 96; 2013: 208–9.

9. Regarding the Ottoman dynastic succession and fratricide, see Uzunçarşılı (1945) 1984: 45–49; İnalcık 1959, 1993a; Peirce 1993: 25; Akman 1997: 47–58.

10. İnalcık 1993a: 57–58; Kastritsis 2007a: 203–5.

11. Finkel 2006a: 33–34.

12. Finkel 2006a: 34–36; Imber 1990: 82–87.

13. Gemil 2009: 36.

14. For the above, see Imber 1990; Finkel 2006a.

15. İnalcık 1954; Kunt 1983; Fodor 2009: 198.

16. Kunt 1978: 15–20; Emecen 1996: 89–90; T. Gökbilgin 1965: 53–54; İpşirli 1994; Göyünç 1999; İ Şahin 1999.

17. The *müsellem* and *yaya* soldiers were organized into units called *ocaks*. An *ocak* consisted of three to five men who were settled on a plot of land. Only one of these men went to war (*eşkinci*), while the rest were designated as helpers (*yamak*). The latter paid 50 *akçe* to cover the expenses of their fighting peer. The *müsellem* and *yaya* soldiers were paid by the ruler during campaigns. They returned to their villages after campaigns and were exempted from certain taxes in return for their military service. See Káldy-Nagy 1977b: 171–72; Fodor 2009: 213.

18. Káldy-Nagy 1977b: 163.

19. Imber 2011.

20. İnalcık and Oğuz. 1978; Georgius de Hungaria 1977: 74; Jefferson 2012: 458.

21. Wittek 1955.

22. Demetriades 1993.

23. Imber 2011.

24. Anonymous (1706) 1987: 9b–10b. (I am following Petrosian's page numbers on the facsimile.) Anonymous (1795–96) 1990: 138–43. See also Imber 2009: 123–24.

25. Anonymous (1706) 1987: 11b

26. Rycaut 1686: 149.

27. The above section on the *devşirme* is based on Anonymous (1706) 1987: 7a–8a, 16b–18b; Uzunçarşılı (1943) 1984, vol. 1: 13–30; Imber 2009: 123–27; G. Yılmaz 2009.

28. Bryer 1975, Appendix II and notes.

29. Leading members of two powerful Qizilbash tribes, the Ustajlu and Shamlu, married sisters of Shah Ismail, as did a prominent member of the Qaramanlu tribe. Ismail twice married into the powerful Mawsillu tribe, and the mother of his oldest son and successor, Shah Tahmasb (r. 1524–76), was a Mawsillu. Ismail arranged the marriage of one of his daughters to Sultan Khalil Shirvanshah. Later Shah Ismail himself married the sister of Sultan Khalil. See Newman 2009: 15, 22, 29.

30. Peirce 1993: 28–32, 34–35; N. Necipoğlu 2009: 121.

31. On these dynastic marriages, see Imber 2009: 81–83; Fine 1994: 407, 530; Popović 2009, 2012.

32. Peirce 1993.

33. İnalcık 1954; Papademetriou 2015.

34. İnalcık 1954; Šabanović 1982: 39, 116; Imber 2009: 171; Kiprovska 2016: 82.

35. Ágoston 2003.

36. Including the thirty-four soldiers serving as fortress guards (*kale eri*), of whom only three were Christians, would lower the proportion of Christian *timariots* to about 50 percent.

37. İnalcık 1953: 215–22; Miljković-Bojanić 2004: 73–74. Darling 2014: 219 shows that in 1454 in Tırhala the proportion of Christian *timar* holders was 25 percent (seventy-one men), which later declined to 2 percent (twelve men). In Serbia in 1454 their share was 29 percent (seventy-four men), whereas in Bosnia in 1485 it was 12 percent (thirty-six men).

38. İnalcık 1953: 225, 227–28; Fine 1994: 522, 556–58. See also Schmitt 2009.

39. İnalcık 1953: 223; 1954: 112–17; Zirojević 1974: 162–69; Ercan 1986; Kiprovska 2016.

40. Lowry 2002: 173; 2003.

41. Barkan 1949–54; İnalcık 1954: 122–29; 1993b; (1994) 1997: 31–41.

42. Rázsó 1973; Mályusz 1984; Engel 1994a.

43. Terbe 1936: 304.

44. Mályusz 1984: 60; Popović 2010.

45. Spremić 2014: 145–48; Kastritsis 2007a: 190–91; 2007b.

46. Engel 1994a: 279.

47. For the text of the treaty, which exists only in later copies, see Szalay 1861: 119–22. For the Hungarian translation, see Thallóczy and Áldásy 1907: xxiv–xviii. See also Prlender 1991.

48. Fine 1994: 524–27.

49. Veszprémy 2008. A raiding party had already crossed into Hungary at Golubac in 1411. The siege of Golubac in 1428 was relatively short, lasting from 27 April through 3 June.

50. Brocquière 1807: 283.

51. Fine 1994: 30; Popović 2009: 358–59; 2012: 60; Beydilli 2017: 387, 390–91; Nicol 1968: doc. 96; 1994b: 110–19.

52. Nicol 1968: doc. 96; 1994b: 110–19.

53. See Sigismund's letter from 1399, quoted in Rázsó 1973: 424.

54. Kastritsis 2007a: 51, 130–33, and chapter 4.

55. Diaconescu 1998.

56. Veszprémy 2008: 287.

57. Engel 2001: 236–37.

58. Filipović 2012: 138.

59. Szakály 1979: 77–78; Fine 1994: 464–65, 472–73; Engel 1997; 2001: 236; Árvai 2013: 114.

60. Rázsó 1973: 431; Engel, Kristó, and Kubinyi 1998: 147.

61. Pósán 1998: 109–10.

62. Other estimates were much higher. In 1429, Nicholaus von Redewitz estimated the annual costs of maintaining the border fortresses entrusted to the Teutonic Order at 314,822 gold florins. See Mályusz 1984: 117.

63. Because Pope Boniface IX supported Ladislaus of Naples over Sigismund in their struggle for the Hungarian throne, Sigismund decreed in 1404 that papal bulls were valid in Hungary only with the king's approval (*placetum regium*). Sigismund also claimed full patronage over ecclesiastical offices and church property, which thus could be filled and granted only with the monarch's consent. At the death of Sigismund in 1437, the archbishopric of Kalocsa, along with the bishopric of Csanád (Cenad in Romania) and Zagreb, and the priority of Vrana had been vacant for years and governed by the Talovac brothers. See Engel 1993; Engel, Kristó, and Kubinyi 1998: 138–40, 146.

64. Borosy 1982; 1971: 15–63.

65. Engel, Kristó, and Kubinyi 1998: 146.

66. Rázsó 2002.

67. Doukas 1975: 176; Teleki 1852a: 225–30; Szabó 2010.

68. Fraknói 1921: 63–68.

69. Fraknói 1921: 69–70; Kottannerin 1971.

70. Quoted in Fraknói 1921: 70; Engel 2001: 281, 393.

71. Engel 2001: 281.

72. Quoted in Fraknói 1921: 70; Fügedi 1980: 179–80; Engel 2001: 281.

73. On the institution in English, see Rady 1992.

74. Teleki 1852a: 225–29, 240–47, 257–58; Engel 2001: 280–85.

75. Székely 1919–21; Elekes 1952; İnalcık 1989; Jefferson 2012; Pálosfalvi 2018: 97–120.

76. Engel 1982, 1984, 1994b; Ágoston 1986; Kołodziejczyk 2000: 100–109.

77. Halecki 1943; Engel 1994b.

78. Engel 1982, 1984, 1994b; Imber 2006.

79. İnalcık and Oğuz 1978; İnalcık (1954) 1987; Elekes 1952. For the sources and events in English, see Imber 2006 and Jefferson 2012.

80. Georgius de Hungaria 1976: 42; 1977: 74.

81. Özveri 2006: 82–83; 2014.

82. Chase 2003; Andrade 2016: 4.

83. This is a point made by Hale 1985: 50.

84. Ágoston 2005a: 28–29. The standard work on the sultan's standing household army remains Uzunçarşılı (1943) 1984.

85. BOA, MAD 15334, pp. 42, 44, 46, 49–50, 54–58, 44m–45m, 63, 71; KK 4725, p. 24b. See Ágoston 2014: 94, table 2.

86. Ágoston 2005a: 16–21; 2014: 88–90.

87. Ágoston 1995: 12–13; 2014: 91–92; Antoche 2004.

Chapter 3: Constantinople

1. Nicol 1994a: 16–17.

2. Doukas 1975: 210. On the controversy of this statement and interpretations, see Setton 1976–84, vol. 2: 105.

3. DeVries 1997; Smith and DeVries 2001: 50; Ágoston 2005a: 64–67; 2013: 130; Philippides and Hanak 2011: 413–25.

4. Philippides and Hanak 2011: 377–87.

5. The date given in the *fethname,* or imperial letter, announcing victory is 26 Rebiülevvel 857, Friday. See Ateş 1953: 24–25; Emecen 2012: 232. This corresponds to 6 April, which, according to the Julian calendar, was indeed Friday. There is a discrepancy (usually one day) regarding the dating of events in Western and Ottoman sources.

6. Doukas claimed that this was suggested to the Ottoman gunners by a Hungarian envoy. Doukas 1975: 216. Few historians gave much credit to Doukas's tale, suggesting that the Ottomans knew this firing technique. See Philippides and Hanak 2011: 370–1.

7. Kritovoulos 1954: 51.

8. Ágoston 2005a: 68.

9. DeVries 1997: 360.

10. Emecen 2012: 265–72.

11. I am using Nicol's translation of Doukas: Nicol 1994a: 65. See also Doukas 1975: 218.

12. On the volcanic eruption's effects on the siege, see the news release of the Jet Propulsion Laboratory, California Institute of Technology, December 6, 1993: https://www.jpl.nasa.gov /news/releases/93/release_1993_1543.html. For an alternative view, see Erik Klemetti, "Kuwae Euption of the 1450s: Missing or Mythical Caldera?" published on wired.com 05.24.2012: https://www.wired.com/2012/05/kuwae-eruption-of-the-1450s-missing-or-mythical-caldera/.

13. Ágoston 2013.

14. Mihailović 2011: 47. Mihailović may have been present at the siege as part of a contingent of miners from Mihailović's hometown, Novo Brdo, whom Mehmed ordered to the siege. See Soucek's note in Mihailović 2011: 120. On the legends regarding Emperor Constantine's death, see Nicol 1994a: 74–108.

15. Some modern scholars claim that the sultan terminated the sack after one day, but eyewitnesses insisted that the plunder went beyond the first day. See Philippides and Hanak 2011: 93.

16. O. Turan 1955: 89; Fodor 2000.

17. Muslu 2014: 112.

18. Muslu 2014: 110–14.

19. I thank Dariusz Kołodziejczyk for this information.

20. Apostolopoulos 2007; Nicol 1993: 72; Lowry 2003: 119; Kołodziejczyk 2012b.

21. Population estimates vary; see İnalcık (1994) 1997, 2012. Regarding problems of earlier calculations, see Dávid 2016.

22. Babinger 1978: 208.

23. G. Necipoğlu 1991: 10.

24. G. Necipoğlu 1992; Kafesçioğlu 2009; Faroqhi 2010: 242.

25. Genç 2000: 318–22.

26. Pryor 1992; Brummett 1994; Bostan 2007a.

27. Ágoston 2005a: 128–35, 178–89; 2011b; Pedani 2014.

28. On Çandarlı Halil, see Uzunçarşılı 1974: 56–84. His start date as grand vizier is disputed. Uzunçarşılı 1974: 56 gave 1428/29; Danişmend (1947–61) 1971–72, vol. 1:195 and vol. 5: 10 gave 1438/1439; while Ménage (art. "Djandarli") suggested that he became grand vizier by 1443.

29. Arslan 2013: 12. On Çandarlı İbrahim, see Uzunçarşılı 1974: 100–2.

30. Lowry 2003: 115–30; Imber 2009: 149–53.

31. Stavrides 2001: 87–88, 90; Finkel 2006a: 62; Bostan 2006: 48, 58.

32. Fine 1994: 578.

33. Lowry 2011; Reindl 1983: 129–46; Reindl-Kiel 2013. On Ahmed Pasha's offices, see Lowry 2011: 14–15.

34. Mahmud may have had another wife: the daughter of Mehmed I and first cousin of Mehmed II. See Stavrides 2001: 101–3.

35. Peirce 1993: 65–69; Finkel 2006a: 78.

36. Uzunçarşılı (1943) 1984, vol. 1: 162–64, 167–68. Writing in the early sixteenth century in Italy, Theodore Spandounes, a descendant of the Byzantine Kantakouzenos (Cantacuzene) family, claimed that the number of janissaries rose to 8,000 "in the time of the second Murad ('Amurat')." See Spandounes 1997: 22. The standing army numbered 12,147 men in 1484, including 7,841 janissaries but excluding the armorers, gunners, and gun carriage drivers. See BOA, MAD 23; Ágoston 2012a: 177–78, and table 8.1 in the present book.

37. Following Ottoman chroniclers, scholars claimed that under the reign of Sultan Bayezid II (r. 1481–1512), the number of janissaries reached 13,000 men as the sultan established new companies under the corps commanders. See Veinstein 2013: 118–19. However, in the last year of Bayezid II's reign, the treasury paid merely 8,164 janissaries, suggesting only a modest increase under him. See BOA, MAD 23; Ágoston 2012a: 177; and chapter 8 in the present book.

38. Lowry 2003: 51–54. For more on this, see Kiprovska 2004, where the register is examined, and Kiprovska 2016: 101.

39. Antov 2013: 229–30.

40. Levend 1956: 187–95; Zirojević 1971; Miljković-Bojanić 2004: 53; Kiprovska 2004: 31–33. Following his victory in 1460 over the famous Hungarian commander and statesman Michael Szilágyi, Ali Beg was appointed sancak governor of Vidin, and served there until 1462, and again in 1464–67 and 1473–75. He served as sancakbeyi of Smederevo in 1463–64, 1467–72, 1475–79, 1481–88, 1492–94, and 1498–99.

41. Gradeva 2004: 26. The rest of the conquered lands was attached to the Paşa sancak.

42. G. Necipoğlu 1991: 3–13, 160.

43. On the divan, see Uzunçarşılı (1945) 1984: 1–248; İnalcık (1973) 1994: 89–100; Imber 2009: 141–63; 2019: 124–42. On the transformation of the bureaucracy, see A. Atçıl 2017.

44. Repp 1986; A. Atçıl 2017.

45. Aydın and Günalan 2007.

46. Ünal, Türe, and Kaynar 2017: 19, 22–27.

47. Quoted in Imber 2019: 127.

48. Philippides and Hanak 2011: 12.

49. Although the Byzantines recaptured Constantinople "by a concatenation of coincidences" before any Genoese ship arrived, the emperor granted the privileges in 1267 and the Genoese established their quarter in Pera. Nicol 1988: 176–78, 190–91.

50. Shortly after 6 July 1454, the doge confirmed the treaty with his oath in front of the Ottoman envoys. See Theunissen 1998: 125.

51. Pedani 1994: 99–100; 2002: 13, doc. 45; Coco and Manzonetto 1985: 24.

52. Goffman 2007; Ágoston 2005c; Gürkan 2017.

53. De Groot 2003; Boogert 2005; Eldem 2006.

54. One such Genoese, Angelo Zaccaria, informed the Ottomans of the defenders' plan to burn the boats that the Ottomans had transported over dry land into the Golden Horn. See Philippides and Hanak 2011: 13.

55. Lybyer 1915; İnalcık 1979; Fleet 1999.

56. Preto 1975, 1993; Brummett 1994, chapters 2 and 5; Goffman 2002: 137–64; Pedani 1994, 1996, 2005.

57. De Groot 2003; Boogert 2005; Eldem 2006.

58. İnalcık 1944: 198; 1979: 74; Ürekli 1989: 14; Y. Öztürk 2000: 21.

59. Geanakoplos 1989; Wilson 1992; Harris 1995.

60. G. Necipoğlu 1991: 10; Kafesçioğlu 2009.

61. I thank Fikret Yılmaz for this observation.

62. Zirojević 1987. After the conquest of Hungary in 1541, the road's other end point was Buda, the former Hungarian capital and now the seat of an Ottoman governor-general. See Zirojević 1976.

63. Reinsch 2003: 304–6.

64. Raby 1983; Blanchet 2008. Similar considerations may explain the execution of Lucas Notaras. Notaras was a former Byzantine grand duke whom the sultan had considered for a leadership position in the post-conquest city but later changed his mind as Notaras had strong ties to the Genoese and the Western powers in general. The fact that Notaras had good relations with Grand Vizier Çandarlı Halil Pasha—who opposed the siege and was executed after the conquest—did not help. See Papademetriou 2015: 26–28.

65. Lowry 2003; Imber 2009: 149–50.

66. Delilbaşı 1993. The last Ottoman victory proclamation (*fethname*) written in Greek and extant in the Venetian archives is dated from 1529. See Pedani 1998; 2010: xv.

67. See, for instance, Fotić 2005.

68. See, for example, Kafesçioğlu 2009; Mack 2002; Brotton 2002.

69. See, for example, two influential captive narratives by the "Transylvanian captive" George of Hungary (Georgius de Hungaria, d. 1502) and the Croatian Bartolomej Đurđević (d. 1566), published in 1480 and 1544, respectively. I have used the Hungarian translations in Fügedi 1976. The literature on the "image of the Turk" is vast. See, for instance, Göllner 1961–68, 1978; Bisaha 2004; Fichtner 2008; Malcolm 2019.

Chapter 4: Conquests

1. Teleki 1852b: 321–29.

2. Teleki 1852b: 330–45; Elekes 1952: 430–31; Szakály 1979: 91–92.

3. Babinger 1978: 126–27.

4. Tursun Beg 1978: 38; 1977: 78.

5. Mihailović 2011.

6. Tursun Beg 1978: 38; 1977: 79.

7. For the campaign and text of the bull, see Visy 2000.

8. Bölcskey 1924, vol. 2: 297.

9. Teleki 1852b: 412.

10. Ágoston 2014: 92.

11. Ágoston 2013: 133.

12. Teleki 1852b: 422; Bölcskey 1924, vol. 2: 296–301; Elekes 1952: 460–65.

13. Bölcskey 1924, vol. 2: 313.

14. Bölcskey 1924, vol. 2: 314–28; Ágoston 2000b; 2013: 133–34; Pálosfalvi 2018: 179–86.

15. Tursun Beg 1977: 93; 1978: 40.

16. Babinger 1978: 165–66; Imber 1990: 169–73.

17. Popović 2009: 360.

18. Teleki 1853: 77; İnalcık 1960: 420–21; Babinger 1978: 163–65; Stavrides 2001: 128–29.

19. Szakály 1979: 94; Pálosfalvi 2018: 201–2. The Venetian *bailo* reported his execution on 5 February 1461; see Fraknói 1890: 109. Levend (1956: 190) mistakenly dated the event 1466.

20. Filipović 2012.

21. The subdivisions in question are the lands of "the king" and the lands of the lords of Pavlović and Kovačević (*Vilayet-i Kral, Vilayet-i Pavel/Pavli-ili*, and *Vilayet-i Kovaç*). See the 1485–86 summary survey (BOA, TT.d 18) and the 1488–89 detailed *tahrir* survey (TT.d 24). The new survey of 1530–31 (TT.d 157), however, did not contain these names. For these sources, see Hersek, Bosna ve İzvornik (1520–33) 2005: 14, 18.

22. Šabanović 1982: 39, 116.

23. Nicol 1993: 403–8; Stavrides 2016: 60–61.

24. İnalcık 1944; A. Fisher 1987: 8–11; Y. Öztürk 2000: 22–30. Kâtib Çelebi (2008: 71) gave the number of ships as 300, but other sources reported 380. The Crimean civil war was part and parcel of the regional rivalry among King Casimir IV of Poland-Lithuania (r. 1440/47–92), Ivan III of Muscovy (r. 1462–1505), the Crimean khanate, and the Great Horde. See Kołodziejczyk 2011: 16–21.

25. Tursun Beg 1977: 205; see Bilge 2012: 65–69, who also quoted Tursun Beg (65).

26. Gemil 1983: 235–38; 2009: 211.

27. Quoted in Ostapchuk 2001: 28.

28. Ostapchuk 2001; Kołodziejczyk 2007; Ostapchuk and Bilyayeva 2009.

29. A. Fisher (1980) 1999: 115.

30. Kołodziejczyk 2006: 151–52; C. Davis 2003: 23. The population loss was actually much higher, as the Tatars captured and killed tens of thousands during their raids. The *wojewoda* of Chernigov who permitted the Poles' Tatar allies in 1655 to "feed" off the villages in the Bratslav palatinate noted that the Tatars, reportedly some one hundred thousand men, took more than two hundred thousand captives and strangled some ten thousand children, dumping their bodies along the roadsides. See Davies 2007: 120.

31. Teleki 1853: 58–59.

32. Fraknói 1890; Rázsó 1982; 2002: 64–65.

33. Fraknói 1921: 95–102; Kubinyi 2008: 65–66.

34. R. Horváth 2013.

35. Mihailović 2011.

36. E. Kovács 2005, based on three eyewitness reports from the besieged castle.

37. Szakály 1979.

38. Fraknói 1890: 236; Fenyvesi 1990: 84; Tardy 1983: 35–43; 1986: 248–51.

39. Fraknói 1890: 235–40; Kubinyi 2008: 109–10; Veszprémy 2009; Pálosfalvi 2018: 243–53.

40. Szakály 1982; Pálffy 2000a.

41. Fügedi 1982; Kubinyi 1990: 104–16; Kenyeres 2008: 360–61.

42. E. Kovács 1995: 39.

43. Kubinyi 1991: 32; E. Kovács 1995: 40–46; Engel 2001: 345–47; Neumann 2010; 2011: 300–301.

44. Woods (1976) 1999: 89, 106.

45. Woods (1976) 1999: 106; Leube 2015a.

46. Vatin 1997; Isom-Verhaaren 2013: 82–113.

47. Posch 2013. Kafadar 1995: 76 used the term and approach for Anatolia.

48. Newman 2006: 13–14.

49. For an extensive treatment of the events, the struggle for power, and the issue of the possible poisoning of Bayezid, see Emecen 2010a: 29, 37, 45–70. In English, see Finkel 2006a: 96–102; Çipa 2017: 56–60, which, however, should be read along with Fikret Yılmaz's book-length review article (F. Yılmaz 2018).

50. Setton 1976–84, vol. 3: 123, 127–28, and relevant footnotes.

51. For Shaybani's conquests, see Haidar 2002: 89–122. In 1501 Babur had to surrender Samarkand to Muhammad Shaybani and give his beloved sister, Khanzada Beghum—a descendant of both Chinggis Khan and Amir Timur on her maternal and paternal sides, respectively—to the Shaybanid ruler in marriage. The various sources depict the event differently. Babur, in his memoirs, wrote that his sister fell captive to Muhammad Shaybani after Babur had to abandon Samarkand following a four-month siege. The *Shaybani Nama*, on the other hand, claims that Babur offered his sister as part of a peace agreement, a view supported by the *Humayun Nama*, written by Khanzada Beghum's niece, Gulbadan Beghum. See Haidar 2002: 99–100.

52. Haidar 2002: 106, 119.

53. Eberhard 1970; Tekindağ 1970; Dressler 2005; Çipa 2017.

54. Dávid and Fodor 1994b: 29, 43–45.

55. Dávid and Fodor 1994b.

56. Ágoston 2012a: 177–78.

57. Khvānd Mīr 1994: 546–605; Thackston 2012: 596 [546] (the latter number refers to the page number of the original work). We have seen that there were only ten thousand janissaries, and only about half of them carried firearms.

58. Thackston 2012: 596 [547].

59. The above reconstruction draws on Ágoston 2013: 134–37.

60. Thackston 2012: 596 [548].

61. The report (TSMA E. 6320) was published in Bacqué-Grammont 1987: 158–61.

62. Floor 2001: 178–79, 189. The Venetian *bailo* in Constantinople reported on 6 March 1516 that the shah had seventy cannons and two thousand matchlockmen. See Bacqué-Grammont 1987: 171, footnote 662.

63. Babur 1922; 1993: 347rv, 354rv (page numbers refer to the manuscript folios used by both Beveridge and Thackston and indicated in the various English translations). See also Dickson 1958: 128, 130–34.

64. Setton 1976–84, vol. 3: 143, 146–49, 150–51.

65. Tansel 1969: 101–7, 112; Finkel 2006a: 106.

66. Eberhard 1970; Tekindağ 1970; Uğur 1985; Imber 1995: 147.

67. Kosáry 1978: 108–10.

68. Irwin 2004: 136; Lellouch 2006: 1–8.

69. Yavuz 1984: 180. According to other sources, this happened in February 1517 in Cairo, after Selim's final victory over the Mamluks.

70. Tansel 1969: 164–88; Emecen 2010a: 258–61, 283–96; Lellouch 2006: 13.

71. For details, see 370 Numaralı 2001–2 and 401 Numaralı 2011: 13–14.

72. Yavuz 1984: 181; Emecen 2010a: 303–4; Stripling 1942: 88; Lellouch and Michel 2013.

73. H. Yılmaz 2018.

74. Genç and Özvar 2006, vol. 2: 23; Sahillioğlu 1985: 434; Özvar 2006: 204; Barkan 1953–54: 286, 291. Counting *timar* revenues, the total revenue of the Ottoman treasury amounted to 477.4 million *akçe* (8.7 million ducats), of which about a quarter came from Egypt, where the *timar* system was not introduced. See Özbaran 2009: 74.

75. Genç and Özvar 2006, vol. 2: 31, 38; Çakır 2006: 173.

76. The treasury of Egypt sent 299,591 gold coins in December 1526; 509,683 gold coins in December 1527; 600,000 gold coins in March 1529; and an additional 200,000 gold coins in early May of that same year. See Mahmud 1990: 119.

77. Soucek 2013: 87; Bostan 2014: 32.

78. Dames 1921: 8–11; Ross 1921: 547–51; Mughul 1987: 35–44; Mathew 1986: 30–31; Brummett 1994: 35, 114–15; Soucek 2012: 326.

79. Dames 1921: 8–11. A contemporary Arab chronicler of the western Yemeni town Zabid, Abd al-Rahman Ibn Ali Ibn ad-Dayba (1461–1537), claimed that Amir Husain was accompanied by another experienced naval captain in Ottoman service, Selman Reis, mistakenly suggesting that Selman had been sent by the Ottoman sultan Selim I, who, however, ruled from 1512 through 1520. See Ross 1921: 549. This is an interesting piece of information, because historians have generally thought that Selman Reis arrived in Mamluk Alexandria in November 1511 with yet another shipment of Ottoman military aid, and that he entered Mamluk service only after this date. The exceptions are Ross (1922: 2) and Brummett (1994: 115), who claimed that the Mamluk fleet of 1507–8 was jointly commanded by Husain al-Kurdi and Selman Reis. Is it possible that Ad-Dayba and Fihrishta conflated the 1508 Chaul campaign with the 1515–16 Mamluk expedition, which was indeed jointly commanded by Husain al-Kurdi and Selman Reis? The fact that the Arab chronicler claimed that Selman had been sent by Sultan Selim I, who ascended the throne in 1512, seems to indicate this latter possibility.

80. Quoted in Turkish in Mughul 1987: 59–60, and in English in Soucek 2012: 326; see also Mughul 1965: 39.

81. Mughul 1987: 52–59. See also Albuquerque to King Manuel, 20 October 1514, in Danvers 1894: 304–5 (English) and Mughul 1987: 60–62 (Turkish).

82. Ross 1922: 2–3; Mughul 1965: 40; 1987: 66–77; Yavuz 1984: 40; Brummett 1994: 118–19; Fuess 2001: 60–63.

83. TSMA E. 8337. Selman Reis's letter, dated 25 Ra 923/17 April 1517, published in Mughul 1965: 42–47 and in Bacqué-Grammont and Kroell 1988: 32–34.

84. This reconstruction follows Guilmartin 2003: 26–29. See also Orhonlu (1974) 1996: 7; Mughul 1987: 80–83; Bacqué-Grammont and Kroell 1988.

85. Soucek 2012: 327, but see Mughul (1987: 85), who disputes Selman's arrest and adds that we know nothing about his life in Istanbul until 1520, when he returned to Egypt.

86. The news of his death arrived in Mamluk Cairo in February 1511. See Soucek 2013: 87.

87. Soucek 1996: 50; Pinto 2012.

88. Soucek 2012: 329.

89. This is suggested by Casale 2010: 25, without evidence. He refers to Adnan Adıvar, who first raised the idea that Selim kept the map's eastern portion for himself. See Adıvar 1982: 76.

90. Soucek 2012: 335.

91. Tansel 1969: 242–43; Finkel 2006a: 112–13; Emecen 2010a: 309, 311, 318–20.

92. Setton 1976–84, vol. 3: 174, 185.

93. Fleischer 1992: 163.

94. Setton 1976–84, vol. 3: 174–75.

95. Setton 1976–84, vol. 3: 193.

96. Tansel 1969: 242–44; Emecen 2010a: 338–43.

97. Setton 1976–84, vol. 3: 176–79.

98. Bohnstedt 1968: 35–36.

99. Celalzade Mustafa (d. 1567), a member of the imperial council in 1516, claimed that the Ottoman navy was preparing against the "infidels"; see Kerslake 1978: 43. For similar opinions by Hoca Sadeddin (d. 1599) and Gelibolulu Mustafa Ali (d. 1600), see Tansel 1969: 242.

100. Kâtib Çelebi 2008: 78; Soucek 1971; Vatin 2011.

101. Soucek 2013: 82 (al-sultān al-mujāhid fī sabīl rabb al-'ālamīn).

102. Kâtib Çelebi 2008: 82; Tansel 1969: 191; Soucek 2013: 82–83.

103. Kâtib Çelebi 2008: 82; see also Soucek (2013: 83), who quoted the relevant passage in English.

104. Gürkan 2010: 128–33.

105. Setton 1976–84, vol. 3: 184.

106. Whaley 2012, vol. 1: 143.

107. Quoted in Hillerbrand 2007: 172.

108. Quoted in Abbott 1859: 102.

109. Citations from Luther in Francisco 2007: 69–70.

110. Citations are from Tardy 1983: 74–78, who quotes the Hungarian diplomats and chroniclers Francis (Ferenc) Zay (1498–1570) and Nicholas (Miklós) Istvánffy (1538–1615). See also Dávid and Fodor 1994b: 37.

111. Papp 2004: 61, for the reconstruction of the negotiations in 1488.

112. For a Turkish-language (draft?) version of the 1488 treaty, see Istanbul, TSMA E 5861, published in Hazai 1955: 294–95.

113. The Latin ratification copy of the treaty (MNL OL DL 30498) was published in Thallóczy and Horváth 1915, 167–70, doc. CVI. Sultan Bayezid II confirmed the 1503 treaty on 5 November. For the Turkish-language version, see TSMA E 7675, published in T. Gökbilgin 1958. Both are incomplete. For a complete version, see Hammer 1827–35, vol. 2: 616–20. On the Hungarian side, the treaty mentioned (from west to east) only Jajce (attacked by the Ottomans the previous year); Srebrenik, "at the edge of the king's domains" (in the Turkish text); Šabac, "the glorious castle" of Belgrade (in the Latin text); and Severin. By contrast, it listed almost fifty fortresses and towns of the sultan.

114. For the Latin-language copy of the 1519 treaty, ratified by King Louis II, see MNL OL DL 24393. Published in Thallóczy and Horváth 1912: 279–86, doc. CLXVII. Modern Hungarian and Turkish translations are in Yekeler 2016: 13–18. See also Kosáry 1978: 81–82, 146–47; Papp 2004: 62–65; 2018: 91.

115. Istvánffy 2001–9: 122; Margalits 1900–1902, vol. 1: 195–203; Szakály 1979: 101–2; Pálosfalvi 2018: 335, 343.

116. Istvánffy 2001–9: 153–56. According to Istvánffy, the Turks, Serbs, and Dalmatians knew the castle as Cavalla (Havale), whereas the Hungarians called it Zsarnó. Istvánffy adds that Bali Beg was known among his contemporaries as Küçük (small) because he was short. On Szapolyai's battle, see also Barta 1983: 47; Pálosfalvi 2018: 351–53.

117. Çakır 2016.

118. C. Tóth 2016.

119. For more data and their sources, see table 4.1. For earlier comparisons, see Ágoston 2000b; Pálffy 2009: 25.

120. Kubinyi 2000: 74–77. The cost to pay the border garrisons amounted to 116,000 florins.

121. In 1521, the *sancak* governor of Bosnia commanded some 7,000 footmen and 3,000 horsemen (see chapter 5.). In 1530, 9,325 garrison soldiers served the twenty fortresses of the *sancak* of Smederevo, which included Smederevo and Belgrade, but the *sancak* governor could also mobilize the provincial cavalry remunerated by *timar* prebends (see chapter 13).

122. Quoted in Whaley 2012, vol. 1: 159.

Chapter 5: Süleyman in Hungary

1. The imperial treasury loaned almost 9,000,000 *akçe* (about 160,000 Venetian ducats) to the troops. Amounting to more than 10 percent of the treasury's annual revenue, the loan was repaid to the treasury when the army returned to Damascus. See Emecen 2010a: 313–14.

2. Bacqué-Grammont 1987: 172; Fodor 2015: 63.

3. Fodor 1991: 292. Bali sent this undated letter as *sancakbeyi* of Bosnia, a position he held until mid-September 1521, when he was appointed *sancak* governor of Smederevo. Fodor thought that Bali served as *sancakbeyi* of Bosnia in 1524–25, and thus dated the letter "around 1524–25." However, from 1524 to 1527, Bali Beg was *sancakbeyi* of Smederevo; therefore, the letter must have been written in 1521, in connection with the sultan's 1521 campaign, as I noted in my Szigetvár talk in September 2016. Since this section was omitted from the published version of my paper, see the original article (Ágoston 2017). In a recent article (Fodor 2019b), Fodor also placed Bali's report in the context of the 1521 campaign.

4. Reindl 1983: 336–45.

5. He served as *sancak* governor of Valona (Albania, 1506–9?), Silistra (1509–11), Nikopol (1511–13), Smederevo (1513–15, 1517–18, mid-September 1521–late 1523, and 1524–27), Shkodër (1519?–21), Bosnia (1521), and Vidin (1524). See Bojanić 1985; Fotić 2001: 439; Zirojević 1974: 261–64; Fodor 2019b.

6. Quoted in Fodor 1991: 335 (I slightly altered his translation). Situated between Hram and Golubac, Požažin was the Ottomans' usual crossing point on the Danube from Serbia to Hungary.

7. Feridun Bey 1867, vol. 1: 518; Hungarian translation in Thúry 1893–96, vol. 1: 373–76; see also Yurdaydın 1961: 15.

8. He sought help from Shah Ismail, Venice, and the Knights of Rhodes and asked Ramazanoğlu Piri Beg and Şehsüvaroğlu Ali Beg to side with him against the Ottomans. See Stripling 1942: 65; Yurdaydın 1961: 8–12; Hathaway 2008: 52–53; Masters 2013: 28.

9. Quoted in Artner 1926: 70; Kosáry 1978: 70.

10. Károlyi 1880: 273; Kosáry 1978: 70.

11. Óváry 1890–1901, vol. 1: 260, doc. 1132.

12. For the 1521 campaign, see Yurdaydın 1961; Káldy-Nagy 1974b; Szakály 1994. For the numbers, see BOA, MAD 23 and Ágoston 2012a: 178 (standing troops); Káldy-Nagy 1977b: 170 (*akıncı*).

13. Feridun Bey 1867, vol. 1: 508; Thúry 1893–96, vol. 1: 289; Káldy-Nagy 1974a: 46; Káldy-Nagy 1974b: 166.

14. Quoted in Szakály 1994: 57.

15. Szakály 1994.

16. Bojanić 1985; Miljković-Bojanić 2004: 50, 128. Despite the relocation of the *sancak's* seat to Belgrade, the *sancak* kept the name Smederevo (Tr. Semendire). However, in Hungarian sources its governor was alternatively known as the beg of Smederevo and Belgrade, leading to occasional confusion.

17. BOA, MAD 23.

18. Zirojević 1974: 114; BOA, MAD 506: 16; see 506 Numaralı 2009: 13 (facsimile: 16).

19. Quoted in Szakály 1994: 71.

20. Zay 1980: 82.

21. Tracy 2016: 99–102. Klis was under attack almost every year: in 1515, 1520, 1521, 1522, 1523, 1526, 1528, 1531, 1532, 1534, 1535, 1536, and 1537. On the role of the Danube in Ottoman strategy, see Ágoston 2009.

22. Óváry 1890–1901, vol. 1: 261, doc. 1136; 264, docs. 1152, 1155; 265, doc. 1160; and 266, docs. 1162–63. Süleyman notified Ragusa of his conquest of Belgrade on 10 September 1521. Venice's representative in Buda reported the news four days later. The Venetian historian Marino Sanuto recorded the fall of Belgrade a month later. The Latin translation of Süleyman's Persian-language letter is published in Sanuto 1878: 248–49. Óváry 1890–1901, vol. 1: 264, doc. 1150 (Venetian report from Buda, 14 September 1521).

23. Quoted in Setton 1976–84, vol. 3: 199, note 6.

24. Setton 1976–84, vol. 3: 199, 201. After the fall of Belgrade to Süleyman, the Signoria instructed its *bailo* in Constantinople in early December to deny any financial assistance to the Hungarians.

25. Setton 1976–84, vol. 3: 205–13.

26. Setton 1976–84, vol. 3: 205–13; Soucek 2004: 223–24. Süleyman was less generous toward Murad, the son of his great-uncle Cem, and his family, who lived on the island as converted Christians. Murad and his two sons were executed for apostasy, while Murad's wife and daughters were enslaved and sent to Constantinople. See Spandounes 1997: 67–68; Setton 1976–84, vol. 3: 213; Vatin 1994: 500–502; Vatin 1997: 175, 301.

27. Ahmed initially managed to escape but was caught when troops loyal to the Porte surrounded the bathhouse as he was shaving. For his story, see Mahmud 1990: 77–81; Ross 1922: 6–7; Stripling 1942: 68–70; Winter 1992: 14–15; Hathaway 2008: 55–56. For Ibrahim's activities in Egypt, see the account of the eyewitness Celalzade Mustafa as summarized in K. Şahin 2013: 54–59. See also Mahmud 1990: 84–90; Winter 1992: 15–17.

28. See the letters of Louis II to Pope Clement VII between 4 February 1524 and 13 April 1526, in Artner 2004: 166–79, docs. 131–37. On 21 June 1526, the king informed the pope that the sultan was three or four days from Belgrade and that his bridges over the Sava River were completed. A month later, he reported about the siege of Petrovaradin. Artner 2004: 183–85, docs. 140–41.

29. Kołodziejczyk 2000: 116.

30. Ortvay 1910: 6.

31. Parker 2019: 158–62; quotation, 168. Charles was also busy enjoying his marriage to his cousin, Isabella of Portugal, who conceived their first son and heir, the future Philip II.

32. Schaendlinger 1978: 57, 66; Káldy-Nagy 1974b; Perjés 1989; B. Szabó 2015.

33. Kalous 2007; B. Szabó 2015. Contemporary sources are available in Hungarian translation in Katona 1987 and B. Szabó 2006.

34. Shortly before Palm Sunday, Szapolyai still believed that Süleyman would invade Transylvania. See Louis II's letter to Ferdinand of Habsburg, dated Palm Sunday 1526. Quoted in Setton 1976–84, vol. 3: 248.

35. After Szapolyai's election and coronation as king of Hungary (10 and 11 November 1526), Ferdinand and his propagandists claimed that Szapolyai had stayed away from the battle because he was in league with the sultan so that he could get the Hungarian crown, a fabrication that has long been discredited. See, for instance, Pataki 1976; Barta 1983. At the time of the battle, the Transylvanian army stood near Szeged.

36. Kemal Paşa-zâde 1893: 217, 248; Celalzade 1896: 163.

37. Murphey 1999: 38 (for the higher numbers), but see Káldy-Nagy 1977b; Ágoston 2013: 140; and Ágoston 2016 (for the lower estimates).

38. According to a list of *sancak* governors ordered to join the padishah in 1526 (see Emecen 2010b: 209–12), the Porte mobilized almost all the provincial cavalry of Rumeli, numbering about twenty-six thousand men. From Asia Minor, only the *sipahis* of ten western *sancaks* were mobilized, a total of about nineteen thousand men. Missing from the 1526 campaign were the *sipahis* of the provinces of Karaman, Rum, Diyarbakır, and Damascus, about twenty-four thousand cavalry from forty-four *sancaks*. See Ágoston 2013: 141. Káldy-Nagy, who did not use the above lists, also estimated the strength of Süleyman's *timariot* cavalry at forty-five thousand.

39. For the sources and my calculations, see Ágoston 2013: 140–42; Ágoston 2016. For Tomori's estimate, see Katona 1987: 22.

40. An inventory of weapons listed 5,200 bows and 1,400,000 arrows. See Emecen 2010b: 213–16.

41. Celâlzade 1981: fols. 146b–47a.

42. Ágoston 2005a: 24; Börekçi 2006: 431.

43. This draws on Ágoston 2013. See also Perjés 1989; B. Szabó 2015; Pálosfalvi 2018: 437–43.

44. Thúry 1893–96, vol. 1: 315–16; Schaendlinger 1978: 83, facsimile: 50/10.

45. Jászay 1846: 14–15.

46. Ortvay 1914: 190–92. A partial list, compiled in 1528, of the treasures taken by the queen in 1526 from Buda is published in TT 1890: 367–69.

47. Szerémi 1857: 122–25; 1979: 124–26. See also Bostan Çelebi in Thúry 1893–96, vol. 2: 71. This chronicle, attributed to Ferdi until 1955, was written by Bostan Çelebi. See Yurdaydın 1950, 1955.

48. Büchler 1901: 75; Káldy-Nagy 1988: 257. See also Veinstein 2014: 135, citing A. Galante, İ. H. Uzunçarşılı, Alexandrescu-Dresca, M. A. Epstein, and E. Radushev, who all repeat the story.

49. In addition to the sources reviewed by Veinstein (2014: 136–37), see the account of eyewitness George Szerémi (1857: 125), which references an unnamed merchant (*mercator*) in Buda.

50. An imperial order issued to the *kaymakam* and *kadı* of Istanbul in 1693 (MÜD 104, doc. 932) and published by Gilles Veinstein in facsimile and French translation (2014: 132–35) claims that the original deed of exemption (*muafname*) was given by Süleyman to a German (Ashkenazi) Jew by the name of Israil son of Yasef, who had surrendered the keys of Buda to Süleyman and received tax exemptions in return for his services. The 1693 document is a confirmation given to a certain Yasef, the grandson of Israil. For a later confirmation of the exemptions from 1800, see BOA, C. ML 3161.

51. Thúry 1893–96, vol. 2: 71.

52. First published in 1554 and revised twice and updated to 1575, Joseph ha-Kohen's chronicle is a work of a careful historian. Some of the details regarding Hungary are surprisingly accurate and go back to other historical sources, such as Paolo Giovio. See Kohn 1881: 93; see also Büchler 1901: 75. On the author and his work, see Jacobs 2004.

53. Káldy-Nagy 1988; Veinstein 2014: 137–40.

54. Habardanecz (1528–29) 1996: 176.

55. Thúry 1893–96, vol. 1: 256 (campaign journal), 318 (Kemal Paşa-zade).

56. Figani is quoted in Peçevi (1864–66) 1980, vol. 1: 99–100 (Turkish); Fekete 1944: 7 (Hungarian); G. Necipoğlu 1989: 419 (English). See also J. Balogh 1966: 141–42; Mikó 2000: 42–46; G. Necipoğlu 2019: 117–21.

57. Labib 1979.

58. Perjés 1979, 1989.

59. Szakály 1975, 1994; Fodor 1991, 2015.

60. These authors utilized Halil İnalcık's study (İnalcık 1954) about the method of Ottoman conquest. İnalcık found that the Ottomans conquered the Balkan Peninsula in two distinct stages: first, they "sought to establish some sort of suzerainty over the neighboring states," and then, in the second stage, introduced direct control "by the elimination of the native dynasties." İnalcık 1954: 103.

61. Łaski (1527–28) 1996: 136.

62. The treasury's annual revenue was 141.3 million *akçe* in 1525. See Sahillioğlu 1985. The 56,000 gold ducats were about 3 million *akçe*.

63. Schaedlinger 1978: 57, and facsimile 25/5; Katona 1987: 168.

64. Katona 1987. On Celalzade, see K. Şahin 2013.

65. Ortvay 1914: 190–206.

66. John Szapolyai's date of birth is given in the sources variably as 1487, 1490, 1491, and 1492. The most likely date is 1490. See, Neumann 2020: 30–31. On Duchess Hedwig of Cieszyn, her marriage to Stephen Szapolyai, and her marriage policies, see Sroka 2005; Kucharská 2014.

67. Kubinyi 2004; Botlik 2004; Neumann 2014, 2020.

68. Fraknói 1921: 158–66.

69. Jászay 1846: 270–79, 321.

70. Jászay 1846: 275.

71. Charles V to Ferdinand, Granada, 29 November 1526, in Gévay 1838–42, vol. 1: 23–26, doc. 15; P. Török 1930: 6–7.

72. Fraknói 1921: 167–74.

73. Fraknói 1921: 174–76. See Ferdinand's election diploma in Šišić 1912: 50–53; Jászay 1846: 386–90. For Ferdinand's charter containing his promises, see Jászay 1846: 390–92.

74. The election was the basis for the Croatian Estates' decision to acknowledge the right of the female Habsburg line to become hereditary queen of Croatia (see Article 7 of the Croatian diet of 1712, the so-called Pragmatic Sanction of 1712), against the Hungarian diet's position. Following Ferdo Šišić's works in the early twentieth century, Croatian historians interpreted the election as the end of the Croatian-Hungarian personal union (established in 1102) and the "reunification of the Croatian Kingdom," Croatia and Slavonia, under Ferdinand I of Habsburg. On these, see Margetić 1990; Sz. Varga 2008.

75. Krsto Frankopan, who defected to King John and was appointed ban of Dalmatia, Croatia, and Slavonia, played an important role in the election.

76. Sz. Varga 2013.

77. Jovan initially served Szapolyai, who charged him with organizing a mercenary army of Serbian refugees from the sultan's domains to fight the Ottoman enemy. However, Jovan declared himself tsar and attempted to establish an independent principality in southern Hungary, south of Szeged. In the spring of 1527, Ferdinand succeeded in luring Jovan to his side. Emeric Czibak, King John's trusted captain of Temes and bishop of Várad, defeated Jovan in late June 1527. See Szerémi 1979: 126–29, 150–66; Szakály 1978.

78. King John's diplomat was the Dalmatian John Statileo, bishop of Transylvania. Francis's negotiator was his chancellor, Cardinal Antoine Duprat, bishop of Sens. The treaty and the related letters of authorization are published in Charrière 1848–60, vol. 1: 162–67. See also Szalay 1859: 89–91. King John ratified the treaty in his camp near Buda a year later, on 1 September 1529, when Süleyman was marching against Vienna. See also Bárdossy 1943: 75–77; Setton 1976–84, vol. 3: 322; Barta 1983: 133–49; Botlik 2013: 840–41.

79. Charles V to Ferdinand, 6 March and 26 April, in Gévay 1838–42, vol. 1: 48–49, doc. 31, and 67–68, doc. 47; P. Török 1930: 9–10.

80. Both quoted in Setton 1976–84, vol. 3: 213.

81. Iványi 1941: 35.

82. Podmaniczky pledged loyalty to Ferdinand in July 1527.

83. Barta 1979: 25–28; 2001: 595–96.

84. Barta 1995.

85. P. Török 1930: 9, with reference to Salinas's letter to Ferdinand (Valladolid, 19 February 1527). See also the instruction to and reports of the Venetian vice *bailo* in Constantinople from May through September 1527. Óváry 1890–1901, vol. 2: 10–14, docs. 31, 33, 36, 43–45.

86. Kretschmayr 1901; Szakály 1995. Lodovico was also known as Alvise—the Venetian variant of Aloisio, which goes back to the Italian Luigi (Aligi, Aloisio) and Latin Ludovico/Lodovico. Hence the various name forms (Alvise, Luigi, Ludovico/Lodovico) used for him in the literature. According to Kretschmayr (1901: 8), he signed his letters mostly as Lodovico.

87. Quoted in Szakály 1995: 45.

88. Papp 2004: 70.

89. Łaski (1527–28) 1996: 160.

90. Szakály 1995: 47; Barta 1971.

91. Papp 2004: 71–83; Papp 2013: 31.

92. Barta 1986: 296.

93. Iványi 1941: 37–38.

94. CSP, Spain, vol. 3, part 2: 613; P. Török 1930: 23.

95. Instructions to Pietro Zen and Tommaso Contarini, respectively, on 22 April 1528 in Óváry 1890–1901, vol. 2: 21–22, docs. 85–86.

96. See the dispatch of Pietro Zen, 29 April 1528, in Óváry 1890–1901, vol. 2: 22, doc. 88.

97. Ottoman troops from Bosnia maintained pressure on Croatia. The *sancak* governor of Smederevo attacked the Temes region in southeastern Hungary, where Ferdinand's captain had recently established himself. Returning from Constantinople with the Ottoman-Hungarian treaty of alliance, Łaski arrived in Smederevo around the same time, carrying Süleyman's orders to the *sancak* governors to assist King John. See Barta 1995.

98. Gévay 1838–42, vol. 1: 36–37, 43–45, docs. 22 and 27; Süleyman and Ibrahim Pasha to Ferdinand, 15 April 1527, in Gévay 1838–42, vol. 1: docs. 40–42. See also Szalay 1859: 127; Matuz 1971: 32, doc. 52; Petritsch 1991: 22–23, docs. 3–4; Barta 1996: 25 (Barta's introduction). Ferdinand's man, Nicholo, was a messenger (*nuncio*), who had no right to negotiate. For the letter to Mehmed Beg, see Gévay 1838–42, vol. 1: 70–71, docs. 50–51. Yahyapaşazade Mehmed would play a crucial role along the frontier as *sancak* governor of Smederevo (1527–34, 1536–43, 1548–50) and governor-general of Buda (1543–48).

99. Óváry 1890–1901, vol. 2: 10–11, docs. 31–32. The Signoria promptly forwarded the letter to its *bailo* in France so that the latter could inform the French monarch about Ferdinand's recent overtures at the Porte.

100. P. Török 1930: 8. They also reminded their allies that Ferdinand had previously used rebels such as the Serbian Jovan Črni against King John.

101. Gévay 1838–42, vol. 1: docs. 70–71; Szalay 1859: 128.

102. Óváry 1890–1901, vol. 2: 23–27, docs. 94, 100–101, 107–8, 112.

103. Habardanecz (1528–29) 1996: 189.

104. Habardanecz (1528–29) 1996: 192.

105. Habardanecz (1528–29) 1996: 197.

106. Habardanecz (1528–29) 1996: 193–203; P. Török 1930: 16–19. They attributed their delay to the intrigues of the Venetian *bailo* and the envoy of Sigismund I of Poland.

107. See Süleyman's campaign diary in Thúry 1893–96, vol. 1: 324.

108. Thúry 1893–96, vol. 1: 385–86.

109. Ferdinand authorized all his envoys sent to Süleyman between 1529 and 1541 to offer an annual tribute up to 100,000 gold coins in return for Hungary. See Petritsch 1993: 50.

110. The campaign diary and Ottoman chroniclers claimed that King John kissed Süleyman's hand, a sign of his subjugated status. News of the "hand kissing" quickly spread in Europe, but Hungarian sources remained silent about it. See Szerémi 1979: 230–35; Feridun Bey 1867, vol. 1: 569; Celalzade 1981: 186a–b; Papp 2004: 74.

111. Szerémi 1979: 236–38; Feridun Bey 1867, vol. 1: 571; Thúry 1893–96, vol. 1: 335; Celalzade 1896: 179–80. Before the Ottoman siege, Ferdinand's castellan, Thomas Nádasdy, offered to surrender Buda to King John. The latter, however, rejected the offer, not wanting to offend Süleyman and also distrusting Nádasdy, who had betrayed him twice before.

112. See the account of eyewitness Szerémi 1979: 238–39; quoted in English in Szakály 1995: 52. The Ottoman campaign diary mentions the "enthronement" only in passing.

113. Named for the town in the Netherlands where it was proclaimed, the treaty is known as the Ladies' Peace, because Margaret of Austria (Charles's aunt and the regent of the Netherlands) and Louise of Savoy (the French queen mother) negotiated it. In the treaty, Francis I renounced his claims to Milan, Naples, and Flanders, whereas Charles gave up his claims to Burgundy. Francis also promised to pay more than 1 million crowns for the return of his sons, who were being held hostage, and to marry Charles's sister Eleanor.

114. Celalzade 1896: 182–86; 1981: 191b–92a; Feridun Bey 1867, vol. 1: 574; Thúry 1893–96, vol. 1: 341–42; Turetschek 1968.

115. Celalzade 1896: 180, 1981: 187a.

116. G. Necipoğlu 1989: 416, 419. According to the miniature's Persian inscription, Süleyman handed King Louis's crown to King John.

117. Papp 2004: 74–77; 2013: 103. The phrase is included among his titles in the Ottoman-Polish treaty of 1525. See Kołodziejczyk 2000: 223.

Chapter 6: Imperial Rivalries

1. Parker 2019: 190–93.

2. Charles had 12,000 *Landsknechts*, 10,000 Spanish and 10,000 Italian infantrymen, 4,000 heavy and 2,000 light cavalrymen, 3,000 to 4,000 "pioneers" for digging trenches, and 40 cannons. Ferdinand had 4,300 carriages with 17,200 horses and 8,600 people, 30 guns with 120 persons and 500 horses, and 300 wagons with 600 people and 1,200 horses. His camp numbered 97,120 people and 30,000 horses. For these figures, see Ferdinand to Maria, Vienna, 2 October 1532, in Gévay 1838–42, vol. 2, part 2: 51, quoted in P. Török 1930: 68. See also Bárdossy 1943: 344; Turetschek 1968: 311–12; Tracy 2002: 139. In April 1532, Charles ordered his wife to send 400,000 ducats from Spain to Italy, "with all possible secrecy and dissimulation." See Parker 2019: 229. For Giovio's calculation, see Zimmermann 1995: 124.

3. Bárdossy 1943: 108–9, citing Ferdinand's instruction to his envoys.

4. Published in Gévay 1838–42, vol. 1, part 5: 88 (Latin); Bariska 1982: 170 (Hungarian). I follow Parker's English translation (Parker 2019: 227), with the addition of the last sentence.

5. G. Necipoğlu 1989; 2019: 130–31. European observers mistakenly identified the headpiece as Süleyman's crown. But Ottoman sultans did not wear crowns. During the processions, Süleyman was wearing a large turban and a gold brocade caftan embroidered with jewels.

6. Charles to Ferdinand, Brussels, 25 November 1531, in Gévay 1838–42, vol. 1, part. 5: 64–66, quoted in Bárdossy 1943: 106.

7. Jerome received his instructions on 3 October 1532. He was accompanied by Cornelius Duplicius de Schepper, Charles V's diplomat, counselor, and inquisitor in the Low Countries. Schepper, however, was not authorized to negotiate in the name of the emperor. The well-informed Venetians knew about the embassy by early November, and the Signoria alerted its *bailo* in Constantinople on 10 November. See Óváry 1890–1901, vol. 2: 55, doc. 264.

8. Gévay 1838–42, vol. 2: 63, quoted in P. Török 1930: 69 and Bárdossy 1943: 113 (Hungarian) and 345 (Italian original). On 31 December 1532, the Venetian *bailo* reported that the arrival of the Habsburg envoys was imminent. On 15 January 1533, the *bailo* relayed that Ibrahim Pasha received Ferdinand's envoys on 12 January. See Óváry 1890–1901, vol. 2: 55–56, docs. 266, 269.

9. Petritsch 1991: 26–27, docs. 14–16; Gévay 1838–42, vol. 2: docs. LXIV–LXVII and Gritti's letter, dated 15 July, ibid., doc. LXVIII. See also P. Török 1930: 67; Setton 1976–84, vol. 3: 383.

10. By killing Gritti, they were avenging the murder of Emeric Czibak, bishop of Várad (1526–34), by Gritti's men. See Szakály 1995.

11. Kâtib Çelebi 2008; Bostan 2009b: 144–46.

12. On these circumstances, and for the quotation (originally from Peçevi 1864–66, vol. 1: 493), see Soucek 2013: 95.

13. Burke 1999: 433–34; Kohler 1999: 106–8; Seipel 2000; Tracy 2002: 145–46.

14. The tactical and strategic mistakes of the Christian leadership—as well as the shifting winds, which when fell calm rendered the round ships unable to move—also played a role. Guilmartin 2003: 42–69.

15. Glete 2000: 99; Charrière 1848–60, vol. 1: 523.

16. Bostan 2009c: 180; 2014.

17. Sz. Varga 2016: 116.

18. Sz. Varga 2016: 129–35; Tracy 2016: 121–22.

19. George was the son of the Croatian Gregory Utješenović and Anna Martinušević, related to the patrician Venetian family of Martinuzzi. Since 1534 he was bishop of Várad and King John's treasurer and councillor. See Barta 1988; Oborni 2017.

20. The relevant sources are published in Gooss 1911: 49–113. See also Károlyi 1879; Lukinich 1918: 1–4; Bárdossy 1943: 187–232; Oborni 2017: 57–58.

21. See the eyewitness Celalzade 1981: 291a–398b and Guboğlu 1986, who follows Celalzade, Süleyman's campaign diary, and other Ottoman and Western sources. See also Gemil 2009: 257–58.

22. Faroqhi 1994.

23. Quotation is from Imber 1992: 179. The fifteenth-century Ottoman chronicler Tursun Beg called both Edirne and Constantinople "the house of the Caliphate." See Tursun Beg 1977: 110,

145, 149, 193, 203. The chronicler and Şeyhülislam Kemal Paşa-zade (1468–1534) had noted that in 1520 Süleyman acceded "to the throne of the caliphate." See Kemal Paşa-zade 1996: 21. The draft of the Venetian Capitulation of 1540 (28 July) was issued in the "well-guarded Constantinople." However, the final copy of the same document (2 October) was written in the "House of the Exalted Caliphate . . . the protected city of Constantinople." See Theunissen 1998: 447, 469.

24. The following draws on Ágoston 2005b: 213–17; 2007: 94–98. See also chapter 10.

25. See, for instance, Süleyman's letters to Charles V, Ferdinand I, and Maximilian II in Schaendlinger and Römer 1983, docs. 1, 6, 7, 19, 23, 25, and 32.

26. See, for instance, Charles V to Süleyman, Alexandria, 26 March 1533, in Gévay 1838–42, vol. 2: 106–7, doc. 43.

27. Burke 1999: 411–18, 426–33.

28. Quoted in Parker 2019: 151–52; see also plate 12 for a picture of his suit of armor.

29. Fleischer 1992.

30. Headley 1982: 22.

31. Finlay 1998: 22.

32. Łaski 1996: 105.

33. Quoted in Setton 1976–84, vol. 3: 338.

34. Tracy 1996: 195.

35. Quoted in Fraknói 1899: 323 (Latin); Barta 1979: 68 (Hungarian); and Barta 2001: 610 (English).

36. Süleyman to Maylád, 13–22 September 1540, in Schaendlinger and Römer 1986: 3–4, doc. 1; see also Petritsch 1991: 39, doc. 56.

37. The garrison consisted of a thousand Bohemian infantrymen, a thousand hussars, and two battalions of *Landsknechts*. See Iványi 1941: 54–60.

38. Ferdinand obtained a Latin translation of the letter, dated 23 December. See Iványi 1941: 62–63.

39. Oborni 2020: 210–16, based on eyewitness and other contemporary accounts. The sultan's message to Isabella is quoted ibid., 215.

40. Thúry 1893–96, vol. 1: 395.

41. Barta 1979, 2001; Oborni 2004, 2013b, 2015a, 2020: 216–25. See also Queen Isabella to John (Jan) Tarnowsky, castellan of Cracow, 18 October 1541, in Óváry 1890–1901, vol. 2: 81, doc. 390.

42. Oborni 2013a, 2013b, 2013c, 2015a.

43. For a summary of the intricate discussions, see Károlyi 1880: 445–56.

44. Fekete 1944: 26–28; Károlyi 1880.

45. On the disease known to contemporaries as *febris Hungarica, ungarisches Fieber, morbus Hungaricus,* and *Ungarische neue Krankheit,* see Győry 1900.

46. Quoted in Parker 2019: 287.

47. Quoted in Knecht 1982: 225.

48. Charrière 1848–60, vol. 1: 567–80; Ursu 1908: 141–47; Rouillard 1941: 119–21; Deny and Laroche 1969; Setton 1976–84, vol. 3: 470–73; Veinstein 1990: 318–20; Isom-Verhaaren 2013: 121–38.

49. For the campaign, see Káldy-Nagy 1974b: 194–95; Szántó 1985: 20–28; İpçioğlu 1990. See also Várday to Pope Paul III, Pozsony, 20 August 1543, in Óváry 1890–1901, vol. 2: 87–88, doc. 418.

50. Káldy-Nagy 1974b: 194, who also notes an entry in the *kadı* register of Manisa that named Vienna as the target of the campaign. The *kadı* may have learned this from Süleyman's son Prince Mehmed, who had arrived at Manisa as prince-governor.

51. Fekete 1926b.

52. The friar may have surmised this from the padishah's messenger. Károlyi 1881: 115, doc. LXXX/b.

53. The campaign account book recorded about 62 million *akçe* (more than a million ducats) expenditure in cash (İpçioğlu 1990). The annual cash revenue of Süleyman's treasury in 1547 was almost 199 million *akçe* and about 242 million *akçe* the previous year (Barkan 1957–58: 900).

54. The *sancaks* of Szeged (1543), Székesfehérvár (1543), Esztergom (1545–46), Hatvan (1545–46), Nógrád (1545–46), and Simontornya (1545–46). See Káldy-Nagy 1977a: 9.

55. Hegyi 2007, vol. 1: 157.

56. It was recorded in the campaign's account book of revenues and expenditures: BOA, KK 1765, 8v; İpçioğlu 1990: 144.

57. *Partium Regni Hungariae*—that is, the [eastern] parts of the Hungarian Kingdom. See Lukinich 1918: 52.

58. Parker 2019: 300–306, quotation 306.

59. Veltwyck to Charles V, Nagyszombat, 2 February 1545, in Hatvani (Horváth) 1857–59, vol. 2: 119–26, doc. 187, quotation from 119–20.

60. Setton 1976–84, vol. 3: 480. His envoys were Girolamo (Hieronimo) Adorno and Niccolo Sicco. Sicco was to offer an additional 3,000 ducats to Grand Vizier Rüstem Pasha and 1,000 ducats to each of the three other viziers.

61. Petritsch 1991: 50–52, docs. 93–95; Veltwyck's letter from Büyükçekmece, 22 June 1547, in AT: 160–62, doc. 47; P. Török 1930: 101–11; Petritsch 1985: 55–66; Severi 2001: 240–41; Rodríguez-Salgado 2015.

62. Petritsch 1985: 66–80; 1991: 50–51, doc. 93, with all translations and ratifications. Severi 2001: 242–44; Schaendlinger and Römer 1983, docs. 6–7, which are not the Turkish originals (see Römer and Vatin 2019: 344). Hungarian translation of the Turkish version in Thúry 1893–96, vol. 2: 396–400. The Latin version that Ferdinand issued is published in Hatvani (Horváth) 1857–59, vol. 2: 142–48.

63. Petritsch 1993.

64. See, for example, Ferhad to Archduke Ernst, 1 December 1578, in Takáts, Eckhart, and Szekfű 1915: 162, doc. 153.

65. Ferdinand's letter, Augsburg, 5 December 1547, in Hatvani (Horváth) 1857–59, vol. 2: 142–48.

66. Allouche 1983; Matthee 2003.

67. T. Gökbilgin 1957.

68. Kennedy 2006.

69. Sahillioğlu 1990; Özbaran 2004b; Khoury 1997.

70. 401 Numaralı 2001, vol. 1: 4–5.

71. Ş. Turan 1997; Akman 1997: 84–92; Z. Atçıl 2016.

72. Posch 2013; Murphey 1993: 231–33; Matthee 2003: 165.

73. Kırzıoğlu (1993) 1998: 241–49; R. Kılıç 2001: 71–78.

74. For 1611–12, see Naima 2007, vol. 2: 383–84, 387, 390–91. For border negotiations before 1639, see ibid., 905 and 927–28; Feridun 1867, vol. 1: 620–25.

75. Ş. Turan 1997: 148–57; Kappert 1976: 140–49; Finkel 2006a: 211.

76. Unless otherwise indicated, the following is based on Ágoston 1992: 52–61; Barta 2001: 619–38; Fodor 2015: 103–28; Sz. Varga 2016: 224–38; Oborni 2017, 2020.

77. Gooss 1911: 110–14; Oborni 2017: 177–78, 2020: 227–28.

78. Dávid and Fodor 2003: 126–28.

79. The letter is published in EOE I: 307–11; see also ibid., 258–61. ; Lukinich 1918: 58–59; Barta 1979: 100; Ágoston 1992: 54; Oborni 2017. In early February 1550, there were three *cavuşes* at the Transylvanian diet in Kolozsvár to investigate the situation.

80. Lukinich 1918: 61. The treaty—signed on 19 July 1551 at Gyulafehérvár and ratified on 18 October—is published in Gooss 1911: 119–36. John Sigismund continued to use the title of elected king until 1570. See Oborni 2013b, 2020: 231.

81. Oborni 2020: 230–32.

82. The Ottoman campaigns of 1551–52 have been the subjects of numerous studies. The following is based on Szántó 1985; Sinkovics 1985: 261–67; Sugár 1991.

83. Kropf 1896; Oborni 2020: 228–29.

84. Szántó 1985: 65.

85. Szántó 1985: 58–69.

86. Quoted in Setton 1976–84, vol. 4: 576. The assassination and Friar George's deeds are detailed in the (often distorted and tendentious) testimonies of the papal investigation of 1552–54, after which Pope Julius III exonerated Ferdinand and the friar's assassins on 14 February 1555. See Barta 1988; Oborni 2017: 239–46; Setton 1976–84, vol. 4: 576–81.

87. Sokollu Mehmed Pasha to Friar George, 1 December 1551, in Károlyi 1881, quoted in English by Setton 1976–84, vol. 4: 574.

88. Szondi's heroism is immortalized by one of Hungary's greatest poets, János Arany (1817–82), in his *Two Pages of Szondi* (1856). The Hungarian original, an English translation by Adam Makkai, and recitation by Zoltán Latinovits (1931–76) are found at https://www.visegradliterature .net/works/hu/Arany_J%C3%A1nos-1817/Szondi_k%C3%A9t_apr%C3%B3dja/en/1972-The _two_pages_of_Szondi.

89. Szántó 1985: 107–36; Sinkovics 1985: 264–65.

90. Szántó 1985: 153–255; Sugár 1991.

91. The heroic defense is commemorated in Géza Gárdonyi's 1899 novel, *Egri csillagok* (The stars of Eger). Published in English as the *Eclipse of the Crescent Moon*, the novel is one of Hungary's most popular books and is part of the literature curriculum in middle and high schools.

92. Kropf 1896; Oborni 2002, 2003, 2015a.

93. Barta 1979: 115–21; 2001; Quotations are from Barta 1979: 118–19; 2001: 630–31.

94. Benda 1966: 34–38, 46–49; Sz. Varga 2016: 183–84, 198–99, 214–23. For sources regarding the 1556 siege, including Horváth Stančić's report to Ferdinand, see Fodor 2016.

95. On these theories, see T. Gökbilgin 1966; Sz. Varga 2016: 226–32; Tracy 2013, 2019.

96. T. Gökbilgin 1966: 53; G. Necipoğlu 2005: 54. Nureddinzade joined the campaign as "army sheikh." One of Nureddinzade's pupils, the Bosnian Ali Dede, later served as sheikh of Süleyman's tombs at Szigetvár (Hungary), which was built around 1576 on the site where the

sultan's inner organs were buried after his death on 7 September 1566. See Ágoston 1991: 198–99.

97. In 1561 and 1562, Süleyman arranged the marriages of three of his granddaughters (daughters of his son and heir Selim with Nur Banu) to influential Ottoman statesmen. Şah Sultan, Gevherhan/Cevher-i Müluk Sultan, and İsmihan/Esmehan Sultan married, respectively, Janissary Agha Hasan, Grand Admiral Piyale Pasha, and Second Vizier Sokollu Mehmed Pasha. See Peirce 1993: 68.

98. For the reconstruction of the campaign and the sieges of Gyula and Szigetvár, see Bende 1966; Sz. Varga 2016: 239–48; Kelenik 2019.

99. The tomb and the adjacent mosque were protected by a small fort (*palanka*), guarded by some fifty soldiers. See BOA, MÜD 27: 354; Ágoston 1991: 197–98. The site of the tomb, which was destroyed in 1688 during the Habsburg-Ottoman wars, was only recently discovered and excavated.

Chapter 7: Overreach

1. Ross 1922: 7–9; Mughul 1974: 90–91; Yavuz 1984: 42–44. All follow the contemporary Meccan ulama and chronicler Qutb al-Din al-Nahrawali al-Makki's (1511–82) history about the Ottoman conquest of Yemen, which Ottoman chroniclers also used. See Yavuz 1984: 216–18.

2. TSMA E. 6455. Published in Kurdoğlu 1934 (Turkish); Lesure 1976 (French translation); Özbaran 1978; 1994: 99–110 (English translation). The English translation is reproduced in Özbaran 2009: 330–35 and is quoted here. See also Özbaran (2011) 2013, which gives an improved Turkish transliteration of the report (52–58). The report is anonymous. Orhonlu ([1974] 1996: 13) noted that the only evidence for Selman Reis being its author is his presence in Yemen and Cairo at that time and his extensive knowledge of the Red Sea and the Indian Ocean.

3. Quotations are from Özbaran 2009: 331–34. The report has been widely used and examined. See, for instance, Orhonlu (1974) 1996: 13–14; Mughul 1974: 92–99; İnalcık (1994) 1997: 323–25; Özbaran 2009: 70–72; Casale 2010: 42–43.

4. Ross 1922: 9–10; Mughul 1974: 99–101; Yavuz 1984: 43. Contemporary sources used by Ross, Mughul, and Yavuz give the date of Selman's death variously as late 1527, September 1528, and 1528–29. The lack of Ottoman central planning is noted in Özbaran 2009: 73, and Özbaran 2013b: 178. For an alternative view, see Casale 2010: 44–45. This work convinced few experts that the Indian Ocean was at the heart of Ottoman strategy, owing to the author's questionable methodology, which presents random acts of local agents as part of the Sublime Porte's strategy. One scholar called the book "not only useless but also dangerously misleading" (Fodor 2015: 12). For a detailed rebuttal of the book, see Soucek 2010.

5. Soucek 2013: 91–94.

6. See Ross 1922: 10–11 and Mughul 1973–74: 247–54; 1974: 102–10, who devotes two short chapters to these events and includes separate sections on the Gujarati diplomatic mission to the Ottoman Porte in 1536–37 and the relations between Bahadur Shah and the Portuguese. To present Mustafa Bayram's activities as an official Ottoman imperial policy (Casale 2010: 47–50, 55–56) is baseless and misleading.

7. Hadim Süleyman Pasha was removed from his post and left Egypt on 26 February 1535. See Orhonlu (1974) 1996: 15; Mughul 1974: 132–33; Yavuz 1984: 44.

8. Işıksal 1969: 55. In July 1540, the Portuguese envoy returning from the Porte via Cairo reported that there were forty-six vessels in Suez, but some of them were unsuitable for oceanic navigation. See Özbaran 2009: 86. For Gallipoli, see Bostan (2001) 2006: 38–40.

9. There is no evidence that this raiding expedition was part of a larger Ottoman plan against the Portuguese or that it was synchronized with the campaign against Basra in the Persian Gulf, launched from Baghdad by that province's governor-general. Casale (2010: 77) tried to present it as such, but furnished no evidence.

10. The Ottomans mobilized some 400 ships (including 100 galleys and 150 light galleys) in 1470 against the island of Negroponte. See Imber 1990: 201. We have seen that they had 300 to 380 ships in their naval expedition against Caffa in 1475. For Preveza, see Bostan 2009c: 176.

11. The order is quoted in Turkish in Mughul 1974: 130–31, and in English in Ross 1922: 14 and Özbaran 2009: 82. Casale (2010: 82, 224) gives a somewhat different translation and transliteration. The order is preserved in Abd al-Samad al-Diyarbakri's (d. after 1538–39) chronicle (British Library Ms. Add. 7846). Casale cites a different manuscript (MS. Add. 1846) but gives the same folio number as Mughul. Diyarbakri's work contains translations from the chronicles of Hasan b. Husayn b. Ahmed b Tulun (b. 1528) and Ibn Iyas, with substantial additions, reflecting the Ottoman point of view. Arriving in Egypt with Sultan Selim, Diyarbakri stayed in Egypt and served as a judge. See Winter 1992: 76. It is possible that Diyarbakri saw the actual order, as these were routinely sent to the governors and judges and copied into the latter's record books.

12. The fleet included six great galleys (baştarda), seventeen galleys of standard size (kadırga), and twenty-seven small galleys (fuste).

13. For the campaign, see Mughul 1974; Önalp 2008; Özbaran 2009: 80–84; (2012) 2013, 2013b: 179; Vlašić 2015. Estimates regarding the size of the crew are varied in the literature. Casale's alternative history that presented these events as "Hadim Süleyman Pasha's world war" against the Portuguese is not convincing.

14. Özbaran 2009: 107–11.

15. Orhonlu 1970b; 1970c: 240–48; Özbaran 2009: 112–14. Seydi Ali recounts his travels and observations in The Mirror of Countries (Mirat al-Mamalik).

16. Göksoy 2004; Casale 2010: 127–32; Reid 2014; Römer and Vatin 2015; Couto 2015.

17. Istanbul, BOA, MÜD 7: 258, doc. 721. This decree has long been known and is often quoted; see, for example, Uzunçarşılı (1951) 1983: 32–33.

18. Özbaran 2009, 2013a, 2013b; Brummett 1994; Soucek 2009.

19. Reid 2014. On the transmission of firearms technology, see İnalcık 1975; Özbaran (1986) 1994; Ágoston 2019b.

20. Davies 2007: 29–32; Boeck 2009.

21. The Muscovite government mobilized 30,991 troops in 1563, 32,325 men in 1577, and 36,625 men in 1578. See Smith 1993: 38–39.

22. A. Fisher 1973; Y. Öztürk 2000: 276–79.

23. Kurat 1961: 11; 1966: 57–65; Khodarkovsky 2002: 108–15.

24. The number of garrison soldiers rose from 1,003 in 1520 to 1,102 in 1574–75 in the ten/eleven forts of the sancak of Caffa. See Y. Öztürk 2000: 178. One hundred janissaries also served in the fort of Caffa in 1547. See Barkan 1957–58: 270. In 1560, eight sancak governors in the vast region from Lepanto to Akkerman were ordered to help the sancakbeyi of Silistra.

25. Bostan 1992: 26; Y. Öztürk 2000: 174. They also increased Azak's garrison from 307 men in 1520 to 428 men in 1574. See Y. Öztürk 2000: 178.

26. İnalcık 1948: 366–68; Kurat 1966: 93–98; 1972: 277–80; Ö. Gökbilgin 1973: 43–46. In the spring of 1565, Devlet Giray Khan sought Ottoman aid against Muscovy, but the Porte had already mobilized its troops and navy for the Malta campaign.

27. İnalcık 1948: 373, doc. 4; Kurat 1961: 14; 1966: 103–4.

28. Kurat 1961: 16–23; 1966: 107–48. In addition to Ottoman sources, Kurat also used eyewitness accounts, such as those of the Polish nobleman and envoy Andrzej Taranowski, whom the Ottomans invited to join the campaign as a liaison, and the Muscovite envoy to the Nogays, Mal'tsev, who was present during the campaign as a captured prisoner. See also Vásáry and Tardy 1974; Ö Gökbilgin 1973: 48–50, 71–72, doc. 13, with somewhat different chronology.

29. The raided settlements included Sarıyer, Tarabya, İstinye, Büyükdere, and Yeniköy—all parts of Istanbul today. The devastation was especially severe in Yeniköy, home of the rich Greek merchants, who regularly brought wheat, flour, and other provisions from the Crimean ports to the capital.

30. Ostapchuk 2001; Ostapchuk and Bilyayeva 2009; İnalcık 2008.

31. Neither Ottoman chroniclers nor a well-informed local historian of Cyprus mentions Nassí's involvement. Nassí's role was popularized by Joseph von Hammer-Purgstall (1774–1856), the influential Austrian historian of the Ottoman Empire. Hammer-Purgstall spread the oft-repeated story that Sultan Selim II, a supposedly avid consumer of wines from Cyprus, decided to conquer the island to ensure a steady supply of its wine. See Strauss 1992: 328–29.

32. Bostan 2006: 91; Setton 1976–84, vol. 4: 971. Data regarding the number of galleys and troops vary a good deal in the sources.

33. Setton 1976–84, vol. 4: 1027–44; Bicheno 2003: 180–224; Capponi 2006: 231–35.

34. Setton 1976–84, vol. 4: 1015.

35. For the estimated forces and battle order, see Guilmartin 2003: 254–57; Konstam 2003: 23–25; Bicheno 2003: 300–318.

36. On the battle, see Kâtib Çelebi 2008: 113–14; Guilmartin 2003: 258–62; Konstam 2003: 49–87; Bicheno 2003: 249–78; Capponi 2006: 253–86.

37. Kâtib Çelebi 2008: 115. In the Topkapı manuscript (77b), Kılıç Ali Pasha talks about "tools (alat), sails and other equipment" instead of "cordage (halat), sails and other equipment." However, most other manuscripts and editions have riggings (halat), and in his reply, the grand vizier too talks about anchors, riggings, and sails. Quoted in English in Setton 1976–84, vol. 4: 1075.

38. François de Noailles to Charles IX, 8 May 1572, quoted in Setton 1976–84, vol. 4: 1075.

39. The imperial resident David von Ungnad arrived in the Ottoman capital when the "Turkish armada" left the city for the campaign season of 1572. On 12 July, the resident's chaplain counted 120 galleys, including 5 bigger ones. The next day other galleys arrived, and the total number reached 180 galleys. See Ömich (1582) 1986: 51. Kâtib Çelebi (2008: 115) mentions 234 galleys and 8 mavnas.

40. Setton 1976–84, vol. 4: 1091 (quoting de Noailles). See also Hess 1972.

41. Capponi 2006: 308.

42. Setton 1976–84, vol. 4: 1089; Capponi 2006: 310–12; Theunissen 1998: 490–95 (the transliteration of the Turkish text of the ahdname, dated 14 Zilkade 980 / 18 March 1573). See also Işıksel 2016: 169–74.

43. Setton 1976–84, vol. 4: 1095.

44. Skilliter 1971; Hess 1978: 97–99.

45. De Groot 1994: 169–70.

46. Since among the Ottoman chroniclers only Peçevi ([1864–66] 1980, vol. 2: 33–37) reported Sokollu's opposition, it should be treated with caution. See B. Kütükoğlu 1993: 29.

47. B. Kütükoğlu 1993: 197–206, 223–36; Matthee 2014.

48. Feridun 1867, vol. 2: 96–100 (Turkish text); Verancsics (1567–68) 1860: 220–21 (Latin text); Sinkovics 1968: 143 (Hungarian translation).

49. Oborni 2011: 85–99. For the treaty, see Gooss 1911: 182–204; Sinkovics 1968: 156–68.

50. Dávid and Fodor 2007.

51. Sinan to Archduke Matthias, Buda, 12 May 1591, in Bayerle 1972: 86–89, doc. 41. See also S. Tóth 2000: 73. The Hungarian terms used in the letter are: "apró csata" for smaller skirmishes, and "derék csata" for major battles.

52. Sinan to Archduke Ernst, Buda, 23 June 1591, in Bayerle 1972: 90–91, doc. 43.

53. Câfer Îyânî 2001: 5–27.

54. Selâniki 1999, vol. 1: 285–86.

55. Wratislaw 1862: 100–101.

56. Akhisarî 1909: 12; 1979–80: 253.

57. Peçevi (1864–66) 1980, vol. 2: 129. See also S. Tóth 2000, the most detailed modern history of the war, especially 7–81. In English, see Tracy 2016: 260–62, 284–90. There is confusion in the sources and literature regarding the names and titles of the deceased sancak governors. Selâniki (1999, vol. 1: 321) names Sultanzade Mehmed the sancak governor of Klis. Ruprecht von Eggenberg's report to Archduke Ernst, Sisak, 24 June 1593 (in Hugyec 1894: 264), calls him the "son of the sister of the Turkish Emperor." Mehmed and Mustafa were the sons of Ayşe Sultan, from her marriage to the late grand vizier Semiz ("the fat") Ahmed Pasha (d. 1580). Ayşe Sultan was the daughter of Mihrimah (Süleyman's daughter) and Rüstem Pasha.

58. Selâniki 1999, vol. 1: 320–22. For the Ottoman chroniclers' views regarding the outbreak of the war, see S. Tóth 2000: 72–81 and Emecen 2007. During Ferhad Pasha's governorship in Buda (1588–90), the chronicler Ibrahim Peçevi himself was present when two years' worth of tribute arrived in Buda. See Peçevi (1864–66) 1980, vol. 2: 134.

59. Âlî 2000, vol. 3: 570–79; see also Fleischer 1986: 297–98.

60. One should remember that Peçevi was biased against Sinan Pasha, who had quarreled with Hasan Pasha (the brother of Peçevi's mother). Sinan was the rival of the chronicler's patron, Lala Mehmed Pasha, in whose retinue Peçevi served from 1591 through 1606.

61. Peçevi (1864–66) 1980, vol. 2: 131–33.

62. Selâniki 1999, vol. 1: 322–23. The Hungarian statesman and chronicler Nicholas Istvánffy (1538–1615) believed it was the former, whereas the Venetian bailo and another Hungarian chronicler, John (János) Baranyai Decsi, believed it was the latter. See S. Tóth 2000: 81.

63. Wratislaw 1862: 104. See also the dispatch of the imperial resident in Constantinople, Kreckwitz, on 17 July 1593, quoted in S. Tóth 2000: 82. Both mistakenly thought that the mother of the fallen Mehmed and Mustafa was the sister of the sultan.

64. S.Tóth 2000: 130–32.

65. S. Tóth 2000: 133. The aristocrats whom Sinan and the governor of Temesvár approached (Francis Nádasdy, Stephen Báthory of Ecsed, and his brother-in-law, Francis Dobó) rejected

the offer. Later, the Porte offered Kassa, Munkács, and Huszt to Poland to neutralize the Poles, a familiar Ottoman tactic. See Kołodziejczyk 2000: 127.

66. S. Tóth 2000: 135–44.

67. The Ottomans perceived it as a betrayal. Hasan Kafi suggested that the padishah should not appoint Christians to Christian provinces close to Edirne and Constantinople. He advocated for turning these tributary states into Ottoman vilayets, an idea that had been entertained before and would resurface after George II Rákóczi's Polish campaign in 1657. See Akhisari 1909: 22; 1979–80: 271.

68. Paolo Mirandola, Pietro Ferabosco, and Carlo Theti prepared the plans. Ottavio Baldigara directed the works of modernization between 1569 and 1582. See Domokos 2000.

69. S. Tóth 2000: 129–262; Sugár 1991: 112–30.

70. S. Tóth 2000: 203–62. Contemporary sources greatly exaggerated the numbers of combatants on both sides. Hungarian, Habsburg, and other European sources estimated the size of the Ottoman army between 150,000 and 600,000 men. The Ottoman chroniclers and the sultan's victory proclamation put the number of the Christian troops at 100,000 to 300,000 men.

71. S. Tóth 2000: 281–98, 309–23.

72. Peçevi (1864–66) 1980, vol. 2: 301; Papp 2013: 109–13.

73. Teszelszky 2014: 156–61.

74. Teszelszky 2009: 140–58.

75. Akdağ 1995; Griswold 1983; Barkey 1994; White 2011; Özel 2016.

76. Illésházy's report about the negotiations is quoted in Salamon 1884: X–XI.

77. This temporary treaty was concluded by crown grand hetman Jan Zamoyski and the Ottoman commander Ahmed Pasha. Two years later, it was confirmed by a formal *ahdname* given to the Polish envoy in Constantinople. See Kołodziejczyk 2000: 52.

78. Bayerle 1980: 5–6; Nehring 1986: 10.

79. Köhbach 1992.

80. For instance, while the copies that the Habsburg delegates signed contained the phrase that the gift of honor of 200,000 florins should be paid only "once and for all," this phrase was missing from the copies signed by the Ottoman delegates. See Nehring 1986: 14, and the section "Language and Diplomacy."

81. Peçevi (1864–66) 1980, vol. 2: 187–88. Hungarian translation in Peçevi 1916: 126–27. Quoted in English in Imber 2005: 10–11. Koca/Kuyucu Murad Pasha was governor-general of Diyarbakır at the time. Peçevi claimed to have replied to Pálffy that it was not Pálffy's ancestors who were mistaken but Pálffy, as "you opened only the upper layer of the box, but you have not yet opened its lid. Once you open its lid, you will see the destruction of those stingy animals."

82. Newman 2009: 73–74; Matthee 2014; Küpeli 2014.

83. Rota 2015: 239 (on the *ghulams*); Tezcan 2010, chapter 6 (on the janissaries).

84. Monshi 1978, vol. 2: 809–10, 812. See also Floor 2001: 181.

85. Newman 2009: 71–72.

86. Kunt 1971: 67–69. For a detailed narrative and evaluation of Ottoman-Safavid relations, see Güngörürler 2016: 134–83.

87. Güngörürler 2016: 181–88; Newman 2009: 87.

Chapter 8: Resources and Military Power

1. Modelski and Thompson 1988: 44. But see Brummett 2001.

2. Valensi 1993: 24–29.

3. Parker 1998: 59–65.

4. Arbel 2002: 23.

5. Karamustafa 1992.

6. See, for example, Sahillioğlu 1965.

7. Kurşun 2012.

8. Dankoff and Tezcan 2011; Dankoff, Tezcan, and Sheridan 2018.

9. J. Rogers 1992: 231; Soucek 1996.

10. Uzunçarşılı 1940; Finkel and Barka 1997.

11. Ebel 2008. The two chronicles are *Beyan-i Menazil-i Sefer-i Irakeyn-i Sultan Süleyman Han* (The description of the stages of his imperial majesty Sultan Süleyman's campaign in the Two Iraqs)—better known by its shorter title *Mecmua-i Menazil* (Compendium of stages)—and *Tarih-i Feth-i Şikloş, Üstürgon ve İstolni Belgrad* (History of the conquest of Siklós, Esztergom, and Székesfehérvár).

12. The number of revenue survey books extant in the principal Ottoman archives in Istanbul (BOA) is close to two thousand, the great majority of which concern the sixteenth and seventeenth centuries. In addition, the archives in Ankara house more than twenty-three hundred survey books regarding *timars* and their beneficiaries, as well as of endowment deeds of charitable trusts.

13. Motyl 2001: 4.

14. Parker 1998.

15. Evans 1979: 447, and Winkelbauer 2003, vol. 1: 25, respectively. Winkelbauer also called the Habsburg monarchy "a monarchical union composed of monarchical unions of states with Estates."

16. Pitcher 1972: 134–35; Issawi 1993; Ágoston and Oborni 2000: 10; Pálffy 2010: 65.

17. J. McNeill 2000: 376–77.

18. Ágoston 2005a: 96–104, 164–78.

19. For earlier comparisons, see Issawi 1993: 145–47; Ágoston and Oborni 2000: 11; Winkelbauer 2003, vol. 1: 13–14, 23; Pálffy 2010: 65.

20. Tracy 2004: 73; Winkelbauer 2003, vol. 1: 488; Rauscher 2004: 188–248; Kenyeres 2010: 41–42; 2013: 549. For the difficulties in estimating the Habsburg monarchy's revenues, see Rauscher 2019.

21. For such an attempt, see Karaman and Pamuk 2010.

22. Barkan 1953–54: 303.

23. Kunt 1983, 2012; Dávid 1992a. There were exceptions. Semiz Ali Pasha was transferred from the governorship of Rumeli to Egypt in 1549 with *hass* revenues of 2,300,000 akçe, whereas Ayas Pasha was appointed from Baghdad to Diyarbakır with 2,000,000 akçe. See Emecen and Şahin 1998.

24. Barkan 1953–54. The geographical distribution of *sipahis* was as follows: Rumeli: 10,688 men; Anadolu: 7,536 men; Karaman, Rum, and Dulkadır: 6,318 men (Barkan's transliteration mistakenly gives 6,518); Diyarbakır: 1,071 men; Damascus and Aleppo: 2,275 men.

25. Barkan 1953–54: 281, 300; İnalcık (1994) 1997: 89, with different distribution.

26. See, for instance, İnalcık 1980.

27. After its conquest in 1521, Belgrade got 485 janissaries from the 8,349 janissaries mobilized for the campaign (BOA, MAD.d. 23). During the 1543 campaign Süleyman left 1,500 janissaries in Buda and the newly conquered Esztergom (BOA KK.d. 1765 fol. 29v).

28. Barkan 1957–58; Hegyi 2007, vol. 1: 157. In Buda, 1,556 janissaries served in 1563–64, but their number dropped to 945 men in 1569. BOA, KK.d. 1866, p. 48. Data for the period 1569–81 are available in Ágoston 2000a: 206, and data for some of the years between 1578 and 1591 in Hegyi 2007, vol. 1: 144; 2018: 146.

29. For instance, 1,385 to 1,440 janissaries served in Baghdad in 1549. BOA, MAD.d. 12872: 161, 333, 361 (jpg. 83, 167, 179 [there are two different sets of page numbers]).

30. Ş. Turan 1997: 81–84, 93–95, 103–4, 145–49; Akdağ 1995: 108–9.

31. İnalcık 1975: 196–97; İlgüler 1979.

32. Ş. Turan 1997: 150–52; Akdağ 1947; İnalcık 1975; 1980: 286; Kafadar 2007.

33. Sugar 1978, but see Goffman 2002: 1–4, and Faroqhi 2004: 8.

34. In 1552, Süleyman ordered the governors-general of Erzurum and Diyarbakır to gather twenty thousand to thirty thousand *azabs* and "put them under arms and have them fully equipped with their hatchets, shovels and spades," an indication that they were to be used as auxiliaries. Quoted in Káldy-Nagy 1977b: 163.

35. Káldy-Nagy 1977b: 170; Levend 1956: 186–87.

36. Ivanics 1994: 177.

37. In Anatolia, the authorities conscripted 7,668 *yaya* and 2,584 *müsellem* units (*ocak*) in 1521. In Rumeli, they registered 1,377 *yürük* and 810 *müsellem* units (*ocak*) in 1552. Only one man from each *ocak* went to war at a time. See Káldy-Nagy 1976; 1977b: 172.

38. Mobilized troops in 1543: 2,624 palace cavalry, 8,166 janissaries, 1,609 artillery gunners, 1,773 armorers, and 721 gun carriage drivers. See İpçioğlu 1990. In 1549: 7,894 janissaries out of the total of 12,822. See BOA, MAD 12872: 161. As noted, 4,648 janissaries were on garrison duty in 1547.

39. Fleet 2001.

40. On Ottoman naval power, see Bostan 2005, 2006, 2007a; Imber 2009: 295–323; Panzac 2009.

41. Kâtib Çelebi 2008: 73–74; Esin 1985; Bilge 2012: 79–87.

42. Soucek 1993, 1994, 1996.

43. Soucek 1971; Brummett 1994: 89–121; Özbaran 2009.

44. This section uses material from Ágoston 2011c.

45. Ágoston 2000b: 239.

46. Imber 1990: 248–50.

47. Tansel 1966: 172; Bostan 2009a: 116.

48. Among the bigger ones were three galleasses, two carracks, and two *barza* of about 350 and 500 tons. The Ottomans also had fifty *fuste* and fifty brigs (*grippi*, Ottoman *iğribar*, smaller vessel than the *fuste*). S. Fisher 1948: 51–52; Pryor 1992: 180.

49. Pryor 1992: 180. Near-contemporary Ottoman chroniclers claimed that the Porte mobilized three hundred, five hundred, and six hundred ships for the 1499 campaign. See Tansel 1966:

186; Bostan 2009a: 117. For the types of Ottoman ships, see Soucek 1975; Kahane, Kahane, and Tietze 1988.

50. Imber 2009: 312–15.

51. Bostan 2006: 94.

52. Ultimately from the Arabic *dar as-sina'a*, which had become a pan-Mediterranean designation for the arsenal. See Kahane, Kahane, and Tietze 1988: 428–30.

53. Bostan 1992: 6.

54. Imber 1980: 235–47; Bostan 1992: 14–29.

55. Imber 1996; 2009: 295–323.

56. Imber 1980: 255–56; 2009: 308; Bostan 1994.

57. As mentioned, in 1433 there were one hundred light galleys in Golubac, each with sixteen or eighteen oars on a side. See Brocquière 1807: 283.

58. Imber 1980: 275–77; Gülderen 1983; Hegyi 2007, vol. 1, 101–4; 2018: 105–9; Szántó 1980: 54.

59. Parker 1999. W. McNeill (1982) also raised the importance of "the gunpowder revolution" in "the rise of Atlantic Europe."

60. C. Rogers 1995; Black 1991, 2011.

61. Parrott 2012: 2.

62. Ágoston 1994, 1999, 2005a, 2014; Chase 2003; Lorge 2008; Andrade 2016.

63. Guilmartin 1995: 304, 306; DeVries 1997.

64. Hodgson 1974; W. McNeill 1989.

65. Guilmartin 1995: 307–8; Kelenik 2000.

66. The list of authors who share these views is long and includes Kenneth M. Setton, Paul Kennedy, Eric L. Jones, Carlo Maria Cipolla, Victor David Hanson, Arthur Goldschmidt, and Bernard Lewis. See Ágoston 2005a: 7–8. Despite evidence to the contrary, such views have been enduring. See, for example, Pagden 2009: 354: "Why had they failed to maintain their advantage? The simplest, most compelling answer was and would remain: religion."

67. Ágoston 2005a: 61–88, 184–87; Mattio 2013: 46. The *bailo's* positive opinion is cited in Pedani 2014: 463. The discrepancy between the calibers of Ottoman and Venetian cannons must have been another reason for recycling and recasting Ottoman cannons in Venice.

68. Ágoston 2013.

69. Ágoston 2005a: 88–93.

70. Ágoston 2005a: 178–89; Şakul 2011.

71. Ágoston 2005a: 128–63. However, by the Russo-Ottoman war of 1768–74 production had fallen, and the Ottoman government had to import substantial quantities of powder. This prompted the establishment of the modern Azadlu gunpowder works, which started production in 1796. See Şakul 2020.

72. Ágoston 2011b.

73. Hall 1997: 104, 148, 156.

74. Hall 1969: 18–22.

75. Wolf 1969: 33.

76. Finkel 1988; Murphey 1999: 65–103; Aksan 2007: 67–75, 147–51.

77. Ágoston 2005a: 48–56. In the seventeenth-century campaigns against Poland, the Cossacks, and Muscovy, cannons were shipped closer to the theater of war. In the Chyhyryn

campaign in 1678, for instance, they were shipped to Kilia. See Defterdâr Sarı Mehmed Paşa 1995: 91.

78. Imber 1980: 276.

79. BOA, MÜD 5: 201, doc. 496 (Smederevo), 530, doc. 1449 (Vidin), and 394, doc. 1042. See also Zirojević 1974: 232–33 (Smederevo and Zvornik); Káldy-Nagy 1977b: 175 (Smederevo); and Imber 1980: 276 (Smederevo and Vidin).

80. On the Shatt al-Arab in 1698–99, there were sixty frigates with seventy *levend* soldiers aboard each ship, which meant a fighting force of forty-two hundred troops. See BOA, MAD 975: 15, 17. See also Husain 2018, chapter 2.

81. Matthee 1996.

82. Ágoston 2005a: 154.

83. González de León 2004: 28, 30–32.

84. Pálffy 2000a: 18–22.

85. Bohnstedt 1968: 39.

86. Tracy 2004: 69–70.

87. Glete 2000: 99; Charrière 1848–60, vol. 1: 523; Károlyi 1880: 375.

88. Pálffy 2011b.

89. Ágoston 1998: 130.

90. Pálffy 2011b: 180.

91. Regele 1949; Ember 1946: 48–74, 119–47; Hochedlinger 2003: 89.

92. Pálffy 2009: 98; 2010: 176–81.

93. Z. Török 2004, 2015; Pálffy 2000b, 2011.

94. Pálffy 2011.

95. Kenyeres 2008: 89–95; 2011.

96. Ágoston 1998: 131–33; Domokos 2000: 20–29.

97. Pálffy 2009: 99; 2010: 150; Zachar 2004: 156. In 1609, of the intended 20,097 troops, only 12,124 men were present in the garrisons.

98. Czigány 2004: 67–68.

Chapter 9: Military Transformations

1. Parker 1995: 344.

2. Parry 1975: 225.

3. Geőcze 1894: 658; Kelenik 2000.

4. Kelenik 2000. His figures should be used with caution, as they are based on *Bestallungen*, or recruitment contracts, which reflect desired rather than actual troop composition.

5. Kelenik 2000; Bagi 2011: 105–15. The pistols weighed about 1.6–2.0 kilograms and were 14 millimeters in caliber.

6. Bagi 2011: 47–49, 371–74.

7. Zachar 2004: 161.

8. Hochedlinger 2003: 236.

9. Schulze 1995. On the types of "domain state," see Bonney 1995b: 447–63; regarding the Austrian Habsburgs, see Winkelbauer 2006: 184–87.

10. Ember 1946; Hochedlinger 2003: 32–33; Fazekas 2019: 185; Rauscher 2019: 197–202.

11. Kenyeres 2003: 95–97; 2013: 545–46.

12. Kenyeres 2005.

13. Kenyeres 2013: 548.

14. Kenyeres 2003: 97–101; 2013: 548.

15. Kenyeres 2005: 145–46; 2013: 549. While the two Hungarian chambers together marshaled some 60–68 percent of the kingdom's revenues, the Lower Austrian Chamber administered the most lucrative and stable revenue sources: mines and mints and, above all, customs duties (*tricesima* or *Dreissiger*), levied on the profitable cattle trade.

16. Kenyeres 2003: 116. Calculating somewhat different revenues, Pálffy (2003a: 127) estimated that in 1556 revenues covered 40 percent of soldiers' pay; this shrank to 31.5 percent in 1572 and fluctuated between 22 and 28 percent from the mid-1570s through 1593.

17. Pálffy 2003b: 32–33; 2009: 99, 129–34; Winkelbauer 2003, vol. 1: 440, 479, 482, 488; Rauscher 2004: 188–248; Kenyeres 2007: 86–87.

18. Pálffy 2003b: 34–39, 43; Czigány 2004: 63.

19. Pálffy 2000a: 39–49.

20. Czigány 2004: 102–3.

21. László Nagy 1985: 81–96.

22. Rácz 1969; László Nagy 1986.

23. Bethlen could have commanded eight thousand troops in 1619–20, ten thousand in 1623, and perhaps twenty thousand in 1626, whereas Rákóczi's army is estimated at fifteen thousand men in 1644–45. See László Nagy 1985: 91, though he gives larger figures.

24. On the continued significance of the Estates in the monarchy and their cooperation with the central Viennese authorities regarding war finance, see Rauscher 2010; Godsey 2018. Although Godsey's focus is on Lower Austria, he makes frequent references to other parts of the monarchy, including the lands of St. Wenceslaus: the kingdom of Bohemia proper, the margraviate of Moravia, and the duchy of Silesia. On the latter, see, Maťa 2006.

25. İnalcık 1980.

26. Akhisarî 1909: 20; 1979–80: 268, quoted from the German translation of Akhisarî 1909 by Parry 1975: 228.

27. Orhonlu 1970a: 70–71, quoted in English by İnalcık 1975: 199.

28. The connection was suggested by İnalcık (1980) but questioned by Finkel (1988: 39–46), who pointed out that most *sekbans* deployed in Hungary were hired not from Asia Minor but from Bosnia and Albania and therefore had no major effect on the Anatolian Celali rebellions.

29. For the conscription and deployment of infantry *sekbans/segbans* armed with firearms (*tüfengendaz segban*), see Abdülkadir 2003, vol. 1: 205, 242, 310, 312, 322, 387; on the *sarıca* units, see Abdülkadir 2003, vol. 2: 1172. Data suggesting that some provincial governors in Syria started to employ *sekbans* in their retinue in the late 1580s independently of the demands of the Safavid and Hungarian wars do not deny the significance of these wars as important catalysts for the Ottoman government's hiring of *sekban* mercenaries. Such data were presented in Tezcan 2010: 142. However, Tezcan himself refers to the contemporary Ottoman chronicler Mustafa Ali, who claimed that the first use of *sekbans* as mercenaries occurred during the Safavid war, when Hadim Cafer Pasha, commander of the Ottoman troops in 1585–90, recruited *sekbans* in large numbers.

30. Akhisarî 1909: 12, 23; 1979–80: 253, 274–75.

31. 1569: BOA, KK.d. 1767, p. 55 (covering the period of Recec 977, that is, from 13 September through 9 December 1569); 1578: BOA, MAD.d. 7227, p. 794. Of these, 5,017 janissaries were ordered to the Persian front. In 1582, the fifth year of the war, the Porte paid between 16,456 and 16,905 janissaries. BOA, KK.d. 1771 gives 16,594, 16,456, and 16,738 for Masar, Recec, and Reşen 990, corresponding to the period from 26 January to 28 October 1582. The Venetian *bailo* in Constantinople put the number of janissaries in 1585 at about 16,000 (J. Davis 1970: 131), a rather good estimate.

32. BOA, KK.d. 1773, p. 243, which covers the period from 10 November 1589 to 6 February 1590. The parties concluded their war with a treaty on 21 March 1590.

33. BOA, KK.d. 1775, p. 235.

34. Murphey 1999: 45–47.

35. Finkel 1988: 77. The 22 percent represented a slight increase from 19 percent in 1547.

36. See chapter 13. This increase in the number of janissaries on garrison duty happened despite the fact that the bulk of the garrison forces continued to be local troops, including local janissaries.

37. Darling 1996: 169–70; Tezcan 2010: 187.

38. Özvar 2003: 60–61.

39. Tezcan 2010: 181, 184–90.

40. Ágoston 2012a: 177–79; 2014: 113, table 7.

41. G. Yılmaz 2011: 75–77.

42. Pezzen to Archduke Ernst, 13 April 1590, HHStA, Turcica. Türkei I. Karton 72. Konv 3. 1590. III–IV, 171–80. See Fazekas, Kenyeres, and Sarusi Kiss 2011.

43. Uzunçarşılı 1984a [1943], vol. 1: 80.

44. Lowry 2002; 2003: 103–4.

45. Uzunçarşılı (1943) 1984, vol. 1: 306.

46. BOA, KK.d. 1765 fol. 10v; KK.d. 1773 p. 243.

47. Aziz Efendi 1985: 6, 10. See also Murphey's note, ibid., 55; G. Yılmaz 2011: 79.

48. Rycaut 1686: 360.

49. Murphey 1999: 85.

50. Tezcan 2010: 25, for the importance of credit.

51. Aksan 1998; Kafadar 2007; Tezcan 2010: 175–90.

52. Uzunçarşılı (1943) 1984a, vol. 1: 378–81.

53. Genç and Özvar 2006, vol. 2: 112, 287.

54. Ágoston 2010: 128–29.

55. Abdülkadir (Kadrî) Efendi 2003, vol. 2: 727. See also Rhoads Murphey's note in Aziz Efendi 1985: 47, endnote 17. The absentees were either ahead of or behind the army.

56. Genç and Özvar 2006, vol. 2: 289.

57. In the province of Buda, for instance, about 10 percent of the fifteen thousand garrison soldiers were already being paid by collective *timars* in 1568. Hegyi 2007, vol. 1: 162–63; on janissaries obtaining *timars,* see ibid.,148.

58. For Ottoman "budgets" and deficits, see Pamuk 2000; Genç and Özvar 2006.

59. İnalcık 1980.

60. Tekgul 2016.

61. Finkel 1988: 51, regarding the war of 1593–1606. In the 1715 Morea campaign against Venice, 14,800 *sipahis* failed to report for military service. Ertaş 2007: 231.

62. Röhrborn 1973: 83; Kunt 1983: 88; Finkel 1988: 256–57; Ertaş 2007: 224–32; Fodor 2006: 157–61, 305; 2018: 184–88.

63. Dávid and Fodor 2005.

64. Kunt 1983: 87–93. *Mutasarrıf* means "the one who possesses something," usufruct holder; here, it refers to governors who enjoyed the revenues of a *sancak*. Administrators and representatives of absentee governors also had this title.

65. Kunt 1983: 87–93.

66. Tezcan 2010: 181, 184–90.

67. BOA, MAD.d. 7483.

68. Akdağ 1995: 71.

69. Dávid and Fodor 2005.

70. BOA, MAD 7483, pp. 8, 16–22; Ágoston 2014: 193; 2018: 977–78.

71. For 1697, see BOA, MAD.d. 7483: 2–5; for 1698, see Dávid and Fodor 2005: 177–78, 188.

72. Defterdâr Sarı Mehmed Paşa 1995: 271. The sum of the donatives listed in the sources as given to the various troops should be 462,900,000 *akçe*. The imperial treasury paid 367,327,140 *akçe* to the troops in 1687–88. See Özvar 2006: 232.

73. Defterdâr Sarı Mehmed Paşa 1995: 275–77; Finkel 2006a: 298–99.

74. Fodor 2006: 125; 2018: 125.

75. Darling 2006: 120.

76. Çakır 2006: 184.

77. Darling 2006: 119.

78. Çakır 2006: 184–87. See also Darling 1996; and Finkel 2006a: 325–26, 329–33, for fiscal policy and the political turmoil caused by fiscal crises.

79. Çakır 2006: 184.

80. Pamuk 2000: 85.

81. Finkel 2006b: 258.

82. Özvar 2006: 232; Tabakoğlu 2006.

83. Genç 1975; 2000: 99–149; Özvar 2003; Salzmann 2004.

84. Genc 2000; Çizakça 2013: 255.

85. Genç 2000: 186–95; Pamuk 2004.

86. Ágoston 2011a: 310.

87. Karaman and Pamuk 2010.

Chapter 10: Lawfare and Diplomacy

1. Ágoston 2007.

2. For soft power, see Nye 2004.

3. I briefly address the importance of titles in the context of Habsburg-Ottoman imperial rivalry in Ágoston 2007. For a thorough discussion of titles as a reflection of self-reference and claims to sovereignty, see Murphey 2008: 77–98.

4. Murphey 2008: 77–78.

5. İnalcık 2010; Kołodziejczyk 2012b; Çolak 2015.

6. Ziegler 2004: 341.

7. Theunissen 1998: 407.

8. Süleyman to Ferdinand, Constantinople, 2 August 1562, in Schaendlinger and Römer 1983, doc. 25.

9. Charrière 1848–60, vol. 1: 118, 131. The title beg/bey is misprinted in the Turkish text.

10. Schaendlinger and Römer 1983, doc. 2; Köhbach 1992, footnote 5; Bacque-Grammont 1963: 90, footnote 3.

11. Fekete 1926a, docs. 2, 5–6; Schaendlinger and Römer 1983: xxii, 68.

12. Süleyman and Ibrahim Pasha to Charles and Ferdinand, 4 July 1533, in Gévay 1838–42, vol. 2: 135–39, docs. 64–66. The use of titles was political among European monarchs as well. In the early 1530s, for instance, King Sigismund I of Poland, in his letters to Charles and Ferdinand, avoided calling Szapolyai "king," referring to him as "the adversary of the Most Serene King of the Romans" (*adversarium Serenissimi Regis Romanorum*). See Óváry 1890–1901, vol. 2: 50, doc. 236.

13. Gévay 1838–42, vol. 1, part 5: 87–89, docs. 25–26. However, Charles is referred to as the "king of Spain."

14. See the numerous letters by Charles and Ferdinand to Süleyman in Gévay 1838–42.

15. Schaendlinger and Römer 1983: xxii, docs. 25, 32. For the versions and editions of the treaty of 1568, see Petritsch 1991: 187–88, doc. 551. In letters written in 1565, Süleyman addressed Maximilian as "emperor of Vienna" (*Beç imperadori*) and "king of Austria/the Habsburg lands and Germany" (*Nemçe ve Alaman kıralı*), but referred to the deceased Ferdinand as "your father, Emperor Ferdinand" (*babanız imparador Ferenduş*). See Fekete 1926a, doc. 13; Schaendlinger and Römer 1983, docs. 33–35.

16. İskender to Archduke Charles, 26 May 1565, in Takáts, Eckhart, and Szekfű 1915: 12–14, doc. 14.

17. Takáts, Eckhart, and Szekfű 1915, docs. 18, 24, 34, 36, 39, 43, 45, 47–49, 51, 53, 62–64, 66–72, 164, etc.

18. Takáts 1915a.

19. Ahmed Cavid 2004: 163: *"Moskov vilayetinin çarı ve cümle Rus memleketinin hükümdârı ve anlara tâbi diyâr ve emsârın mâliki ulu Moskov Çarı."*

20. Defterdâr Sarı Mehmed Paşa 1995: 693.

21. For the titles, see M. Kütükoğlu 1994: 106, 150–51, 224; Ahmed Cavid 2004: 239.

22. Black 2010: 44–45, 53. The classic study on Renaissance diplomacy remains Mattingly 1955.

23. Hiller 1998: 205; 2016: 264.

24. Coco and Manzonetto 1985; Pedani 2009, 2002, 2013; Dursteler 2001.

25. For the criticism of the older literature, see Yurdusev 2004; Goffman 2007.

26. Kołodziejczyk 2000: 70–71; Ziegler 2004.

27. M. Kütükoğlu 1994.

28. Kosáry 1978: 81–82; Dávid and Fodor 1994b; Papp 2004: 62–65.

29. Kołodziejczyk 2000: 70–71, 112–18, 232–33; Czamanska 2004: 92–93, 101.

30. Ziegler (2004: 341) uses the Greek text of the 1482 treaty. For the Turkish text, see Theunissen 1998: 372.

31. Charrière 1848–60, vol. 1: 283–94; Setton 1976–84, vol. 3: 400.

32. Veinstein 2008, and the literature quoted.

33. Rouillard 1941: 119–22; Isom-Verhaaren 2013: 134–38.

34. Setton 1976–84, vol. 4: 1089.

35. See the Ottoman version of the treaty sent to the Safavids. BOA, Name-i Hümayun Defteri #7, vol. 1: 4–6. For the territorial demarcation, see Naima 2007, vol. 2: 927–28.

36. Güngörürler 2018: 183; 2019, 167.

37. Setton 1976–84, vol. 3: 363.

38. Török 1930: 102.

39. See Schaendlinger and Römer 1983, docs. 23, 25, and 32 for the treaties of 1559, 1562, and 1568. See also Salamon 1884: VIII; Petritsch 1993: 56.

40. Pezzen to Archduke Ernst, Constantinople, 13 January 1590, HHStA, Turcica. Türkei I. Karton 72. Konv 1. 1590. I. 68–88, 104–117. See Fazekas, Kenyeres, and Sarusi Kiss 2011.

41. Skilliter 1971: 492 (Turkish text), 493 (Italian text).

42. The report of the Habsburg resident in Constantinople is dated 8 December 1576. It arrived in Rudolf II's court in Prague on 4 January 1577. See Kárpáthy-Kravjánszky 1933: 14.

43. Salamon 1884: IX. See the diary of János Rimay, who recorded daily developments of the peace conference, in Salamon 1884: X–XI. See also Bayerle 1980: 12–17, 28–37.

44. Setton 1991: 157.

45. Sperl, Scheutz, and Strohmeyer 2016; Tóth and Zágorhidi 2017.

46. Ingrao, Samardžić, and Pešalj 2011; Roider 1972: 155–72; Ziegler 2004.

47. Bazarova 2015: 122.

48. Ahmed Cavid 2004: 187–89.

49. See article 1 of the treaty, as preserved in Ahmed Cavid 2004: 239. This treaty lasted until the outbreak of the Russo-Ottoman war of 1768–74.

50. Pedani 1994: 195–202; 1996: 187.

51. See, for example, Zal Mahmud Pasha's letter to Michael Černović, Ákos Csaby, and George Albani, 19 June 1564, in Takáts, Eckhart, and Szekfű 1915: 12. doc. 13.

52. The Ottoman archives have preserved the receipts and financial reports regarding the provisioning of foreign envoys. These documents give precious details about the missions.

53. On the road, see Zirojević 1976, 1987.

54. Ömich (1582) 1986. Based on contemporary ambassadorial reports and journals, the journey is reconstructed in Teply 1968. See also Brummett 2015: 249–53. On the Elçi Hanı, see Eyice 1970, 1995.

55. This kind of information was used when creating European maps and engravings of the empire. See Brummett 2015.

56. Captains, vice captains, and voivodes of the flotilla who traveled to Constantinople as members of Habsburg embassies included Sigismund Pozsgai (1545, 1549); Vid Ugrinović, who traveled as Weltwyck's secretary; Francis Zay, who accompanied Antun Vrančić in 1553–57 and in 1560–65 served as captain-general of Upper Hungary; Paul Palinay (1563); Ákos Csaby (1563, 1564–65, 1565–66); and Peter Briznik (1565–66). Other military experts included Christoph von

Teuffenbach, the future captain-general of Upper Hungary, and the military engineer Marcantonio Pigafetta (1567–68). See Fenyvesi 1986.

57. Spuler 1935: 332.

58. Szakály 1983; Petritsch 2005.

59. For Vrančić's succinct biography and works, see Bartoniek 1975: 35–44. For his second mission to the Ottoman Porte (1567–68), see Szalay 1860. On Giovio, see Zimmermann (1995), who gives 1486 (instead of the usually accepted 1483) as his year of birth. Giovio's *Commentary* was published in 1532. Italian printings in 1533, 1535, 1538, 1540, 1541, and 1560 indicate its popularity, as did the editions of another Latin translation in 1537, 1538, and 1539. The German translation in 1537 appeared with Melanchton's preface. See Zimmermann 1995: 121.

60. The Polish envoy in 1590 fell off his horse during his journey. When he entered Constantinople with his entourage on 26 January 1590, he was rather ill and died two weeks later (7 February). Pezzen to Archduke Ernst, Constantinople, 10 February 1590, HHStA, Turcica. Türkei I. Karton 72. Konv 1. 1590. II. 99–110, 113–24, 125–34. See Fazekas, Kenyeres, and Sarusi Kiss 2011.

61. Severi 2001: 246.

62. P. Török 1930: 103; Severi 2001: 246–47.

63. Bartoniek 1975: 35–44.

64. P. Török 1930: 105.

65. Quoted in Dursteler 2006: 177.

66. Dursteler 2001: 18.

67. Râşid Mehmed Efendi 2013, vol. 2: 944; Doğan 2017: 28–29. On 7 August 1715, he informed the doge of his release "from the terrible prison in which I was shut up for four months." See Setton 1991: 427.

68. Severi 2015.

69. T. Gökbilgin 1966: 54; Žontar 1971: 217.

70. Szalay 1860: 229–30 (Latin version); Sinkovics 1968: 149–50 (Hungarian translation).

71. Wratislaw 1862; Seidel 1711, 2010.

72. The search of the embassy building and the imprisonment of the ambassador are narrated in detail in Wratislaw 1862: 109–16. See also S. Tóth 2000: 68–71.

73. Kerekes 2004b.

74. Bazarova 2015: 122.

75. Istvánffy 2001–9, vol. 1, part 3: 421.

76. Black 2010: 20, 62.

77. Parker 2019: 177.

78. Report of Zen, 29 April 1528, in Óváry 1890–1901, vol. 2: 22, doc. 88.

79. Black 2010: 62, 83.

80. On Báthory, see Roşu 2017.

81. Kárpáthy-Kravjánszky 1933: 10–12.

82. Mattingly 1955: 236.

83. Parker 2019: 506.

84. Severi 2015; Hiller 2016: 263.

85. Later in June, he praised Gall for sending his spy reports to Vienna in the Czech language. See HL, TGy 1556/9 (Ferdinand I to Adam Gall, 4 April 1556) and 1556/56 (Ferdinand I to Adam Gall, Vienna, 29 June 1556), summaries in Farkas 2000.

86. Horn 2009.

87. S. Fisher 1948: 51.

88. In 1430, Murad II's chancery issued a charter in Greek, Serbian, and Turkish to Ragusan authorities granting their merchants freedom of commerce in his lands. See Ivanović 2017: 54.

89. Boškov 1980: 219–20, 229. For instance, two translators, Kasim Beg and Skender Beg, composed the Cyrillic letters in Mehmed II's and Bayezid II's chanceries. The *sancak* governor of Bosnia, İshak Beg, used the Serbian clerks (*dijak*) Branislav and Mihailo. For these and other examples, see Boškov 1980: 229–31.

90. Guboglu 1968.

91. Hazai 1977; Bojović 1998; Römer 2008: 216.

92. Jerome of Zara's letters to Ferdinand and his chancellor and generals were usually in Italian, and occasionally in German, Latin, and Slavic. He chose Slavic (in Cyrillic) when writing to Francis Batthyán (ban of Dalmatia, Croatia, and Slavonia) and Louis Pekry (*Landeshauptmann* in Slavonia) about his negotiations. See his letter from Constantinople, 11 February 1533, in Gévay 1838–42, vol. 2: 74–75, doc. 21.

93. Kołodziejczyk 2000: 52.

94. Fotić 2005.

95. Malcolm 2015: 95.

96. Pálffy 1999b:44.

97. Cziráki 2016: 42.

98. Gévay 1838–42, vol. 1, part 4: 75, doc. vi; P. Török 1930: 35. Petritsch (2005: 256) claims that Ibrahim and Jurišić conversed in Croatian; Kuripešić, who also spoke Croatian, does not mention the incident.

99. P. Török 1930: 71, 76; Setton 1976–84, vol. 3: 383.

100. P. Török 1930: 78.

101. Setton 1976–84, vol. 3: 385.

102. Although he showed the letter to another translator, this man was equally unable to understand the Persian lines in question. The remark, written in Latin, is quoted in Holub 1923: 83.

103. See Süleyman's and Ibrahim's letters to Ferdinand from 1527, written by the Porte's interpreter, Yunus Beg, who hailed from Venetian Modon. Gévay 1838–42, vol. 2/1: 62–63, 64, docs. 40 and 42; Petritsch 1991: 23, docs. 3–4.

104. Ferdinand to Hüsrev Pasha, *sancakbeyi* of Bosnia, and to Grand Vizier Ibrahim Pasha, Vienna, July 1527. Gévay 1838–42, vol. 2/1: 90–91, docs. 70, 71.

105. Turetschek 1968: 18.

106. Szalay 1861: 17. This also indicates that interpreters who were working for the Ottoman governors of Lippa and Várad in the 1660s could translate from Turkish to Hungarian or Latin. In fact, George Branković, the younger brother of the Orthodox bishop of Gyulafehérvár (modern Alba Julia in Romania), Sava, had learned some Turkish while living in Lippa. He was thus hired together with Rozsnyai as the Transylvanian prince's Turkish *deák* and sent to Constantinople in 1663.

107. The following is based on Bayerle 1980 and Nehring 1986, which corrects some of Bayerle's mistakes.

108. Published in Salamon 1884: 257–61.

109. Published in Fekete 1932: 207–313; Bayerle 1980: 42–44. As mentioned, Almás was the site of the Ottoman delegation's camp on the right bank of the Danube, opposite the imperial camp.

110. Bayerle 1980: 6–8.

111. The Hungarian original is published in Salamon 1884: 262–64. The document was signed and sealed by Ahmed, the deputy of the governor of Buda, Kadızadeli Ali Pasha; Hüseyin, the *sancak* governor of Simontornya; and Mustafa, the treasurer (*timar defterdarı*) of Buda. The addendum was signed and sealed by Kadızadeli Ali Pasha himself and Habil Efendi, chief mufti and kadı of Buda, on 19 June 1608.

112. The Hungarian version is published in Salamon 1884: 265–71. See also Papp 2018: 95–96.

113. Salamon 1884: 274–78.

114. Boeck 2009: 150.

Chapter 11: Embassies, Dragomans, and Intelligence

1. Black 2010: 28.

2. Iordanou 2019, especially 1–15, and chapter 3.

3. Quoted in Dursteller 2001: 3.

4. Dursteller 2001.

5. Žontar 1971: 210.

6. S. Fisher 1948: 46; J. Davis 1974: 100; Iordanou 2019: 36. Later in her book (173), Iordanou confuses the expulsion of Girolamo Marcello with the case of Bailo Girolamo Lippomano, who is discussed below.

7. S. Fisher 1948: 52; J. Davis 1974; Benzoni 2002.

8. Theunissen 1998: 391, 397.

9. Gürkan 2018: 74–77. For the consulates, see Dursteler 2001: 5.

10. Arbel 1995: 79–80; Gürkan 2017: 242–45; 2018: 70.

11. Setton 1991: 124–25.

12. For his tragic story, see Tormene 1903–4; Coco and Manzonetto 1985: 51–55; Dursteler 2006: 28; Malcolm 2015: 374.

13. The following is based on Žontar 1971; 1973: 121–62. "Macedonia" was a vague geographical name adapted from antiquity, referring to a vast area from Bosnia to Bulgaria, including Albania.

14. Petritsch 1991, docs. 371–73, 380, 398–99.

15. Žontar 1971, 198–212; 1973: 152–54.

16. In April, the Ottomans searched the embassy with the help of the renegade Ali Beg, alias Ladislaus Mörth, the steward of the imperial resident Kreckwitz, who had recently escaped from the embassy and converted to Islam. Wratislaw 1862: 100–112. On Mörth, see Graf 2017: 90ff.

17. Wratislaw 1862: 109–16 (quotation from 116).

18. Gerlach 1986: 174.

19. Gerlach 1986: 173–74.

20. Hiller 1998: 208–11.

21. Meienberger 1973: 101–6; Hiller 1998; Hamilton 1994: 143.; Duregger 2015. For the definition of intercultural knowledge, see Bennett 2008.

22. Petritch 1982: 218.

23. Meienberger 1975: 83–86; Hiller 1998; Hiller (2016: 262) claims that he was the sultan's physician.

24. Quoted in English in Miović 2013: 195 and Gürkan 2015: 115; see also De Groot 1997: 241.

25. Rothman 2009: 776–78.

26. De Groot 1997: 240–45.

27. P. Török 1930: 89.

28. P. Török 1929: 423, 426; AT 243–50, doc. 83.

29. Rothman 2012: 168.

30. Hitzel 1997; Severi 2015; Kołodziejczyk 2000: 178–79.

31. Severi 2015; Kerekes 2014–15: 65.

32. Another interpreter, John (János) Illésy, was a Székely from Transylvania. Negroni and Illésy translated for the Habsburg delegation in 1603 during the unsuccessful Habsburg-Ottoman peace negotiations, while Balázs Szőcs, a Hungarian living in Ottoman Buda, was translating for the Ottoman envoys. Illésy interpreted during the negotiations that led to the Treaty of Zsitvatorok in 1606, and translated Turkish documents concerning its renewal in 1610. See Istvánffy 2001–9, vol. 1, part 3: 420; Papp 2013: 228; 2018: 96.

33. Kerekes 2014–15: 65.

34. On d'Asquier, see Meienberger 1975: 80–81; Hamilton 1994: 139–40; 2009; Hiller 1992: 72–75; 1998: 208; Kerekes 2004a: 1199.

35. Hamilton 1994: 123–38.

36. Hamilton 1994: 140–41.

37. Hiller 1993.

38. Kerekes 2010.

39. Kerekes 2010: 94–95. The fourth volume was published in 1687.

40. Cziráki 2016: 33–35.

41. Hering 1994; Janos 2005–6. The place (Chios, Constantinople, or Nicosia) and date (1613 or 1621) of his birth are disputed.

42. Cziráki 2016: 40.

43. Hamilton 1994: 139–42; Meienberger 1975; Hiller 1998: 206–8; Kerekes 2010: 100; 2014–15: 65.

44. Pedani 1994: 141–53; Bacqué-Grammont 1997; Warner 2001. Pedani narrates six of Yunus's missions between 1519 and 1542, whereas Setton (1976–84, vol. 3: 384) mentions six of his missions to Venice between May 1522 and January 1533. Earlier historiography (Matuz 1975; Szakály and Tardy 1989) maintained that Yunus was the chief interpreter of the Porte between 1525 and 1541. However, it is clear that he continued to work until his death in 1551. See AT 610, doc. 237.

45. MÜD 12: 477, doc. 916. He died on 9 June 1571. An imperial decree ordered Deputy Vizier Pertev Mehmed Pasha, who was on the Cyprus campaign, to immediately send a certain *sipahi* of his, used as an interpreter, to Constantinople so that he could perform his services at the Porte. The death of Ibrahim dragoman had resulted in a shortage of qualified translators.

46. Ibrahim was the uncle of Regina Straszówna, the first wife of Dudith. As the daughter of an impoverished noble family, Regina, along with her mother, was living on the annuity that the Polish ruler had given Ibrahim. When Dudith lost his bishopric and income after his marriage, the couple continued to rely on this annuity, in addition to revenues that Dudith received from Maximilian, as the emperor's secret agent. See Ács 2006. Malvezzi's secretary, Angelo Rachani, mentions Ibrahim's appointment in a letter dated 5 July 1551. See AT: 612, doc. 238; see also Matuz 1975: 45–46.

47. Selâniki 1999: 21–22; Bánffy 1993: 130; Ács 2006: 61.

48. References to his possible Jewish origin have been questioned; in 1550 he called himself a true Christian. Rachani reported on 5 July 1551 Mahmud's removal from office along with the death of Yunus Beg and the nomination of Ibrahim Beg as chief dragoman. AT: 612.

49. Petritsch 1985: 60–62; Ács 2000; 2006: 60; Papp 2016; Severi 2015: 6 (Philibert of Brussels's remark).

50. For a similar ethnic-regional solidarity and rivalry in the Ottoman political elite, see Kunt 1974.

51. Wawrzyniak 2003: 81–82.

52. Reychman and Zajączkowski 1968: 182. See Said Beg's short biography by Hubert Wajs in Yekeler 2014: 27. The marriage between Sigismund and Elisabeth had long been planned, and took place in Cracow on 6 May 1543.

53. Rothman 2009; Krstić 2011a, 2011b.

54. Published in Lybyer 1913, Appendix II.

55. Babinger 1927; Matuz 1975; Ács 2000; Krstić 2011a: 103–6. Löwenklau's *Muselmanische Histori Türckischer Nation* appeared in 1590, followed by the Latin version, *Historiae Musulmanae Turcorum, de monumentis ipsorum exscriptae*, the next year.

56. Borzsák 1988: 37; Krstić 2011b; Sudár 2017a.

57. Borzsák 1988; Mahmud 1996, 2019.

58. Runciman 1988: 363–64; Philliou 2009; Lewis 1984: 130–31.

59. Janos 2005–6.

60. Gürkan 2015: 114. Yunus's daily wage was just 43 *akçe* (0.7 ducat) and a medium-size military prebend (*ziamet*) with a minimum value of 10,000 *akçe* (166 ducats) per annum.

61. Lesure 1983: 140, footnote 51.

62. Szalay 1862: 57–59; Ács 2000.

63. Szakály and Tardy 1989, 1992; József Bessenyei's introductory essay in Pécsi Kis (1564) 1993.

64. Pécsi Kis (1564) 1993: 54.

65. Verancsics to Archduke Charles, 28 September 1570, quoted in Pálffy 2000b: 49.

66. Rozsnyai 1867: 329, 349, 350, 514.

67. Pedani 1994: 39; Gürkan 2017: 145.

68. Ferdinand to Castaldo, Vienna, 14 May 1551, in Óváry 1890–1901, vol. 2: 108, doc. 514.

69. János deák to János Pethő, 27 October 1565, in Takáts, Eckhart, and Szekfű 1915: 17–18, doc. 19; Takáts 1915a: 59–60.

70. Takáts, Eckhart, and Szekfű 1915, doc. 23; Takáts 1915a: 60. The scribe gave precious details regarding the size and weaponry of the approaching army: 42,000 *sipahis* just from Rumeli, 62 cannons, and 12,000 cannonballs sent via the Black Sea and the Danube River.

71. Pullan 1997: 179; Arbel: 1995: 55–63.

72. Baron 1983: 91.

73. Galanti 1995: 138.

74. This section draws on Ágoston 1999, 2005c. See also Gürkan 2017.

75. Bárdossy 1943: 62–63.

76. Pedani 1994: 82.

77. ÖStA, HHStA, Turcica karton 30, Konv. 1. Fol. 29. (22 January 1574). I am indebted to the archivist István Fazekas, my colleague and friend, for this information. See also Takáts 1915a.

78. Şahin and Emecen 1994: xxv–xxvi, and docs. 334, 342.

79. Şahin and Emecen 1994, docs. 112, 136, 137.

80. MÜD, 9: 107; 10: 338, doc. 550; 64: 121. Sahillioğlu 2002: 173–74, doc. 215; 310, doc. 428.

81. Dávid and Fodor 2003: 124.

82. Dávid and Fodor 2003: 126–28.

83. Morosini's report regarding the Hungarian frontier, Constantinople, 23 April 1584, in Óváry 1890–1901, vol. 2: 207, doc. 1009.

84. Takáts 1916: 170.

85. Pálffy 2000b, facsimile III.

86. Biegman 1963, 1968.

87. See, for instance, MÜD 7: 230, doc. 637; 12: 339, doc. 689; 67: 150; 69: 107; 71: 97. On the Romanian principalities, see MÜD 3: 391, 490, docs. 1165, 1457.

88. See King Ferdinand's instruction to his voivodes, István Dobó and Ferenc Kendy, 18 May 1553, in Oborni 2002: 169.

89. Ménage 1965; Vatin 1997.

90. Schaendlinger and Römer 1983: 27; Petritsch 1985: 62–63.

91. Matuz 1975: 55; Schaedlinger and Römer 1983: 27 (on Mahmud); MÜD 5: 443, doc. 1185 (on Murad and Ferhad).

92. Takáts 1915a.

93. Ágoston 1999: 139.

94. "He was a very wise man and a friend of Juan Mida, who has also visited Your Majesty and is a relative of Angulema, and whom I am certain is a spy who pretends to want to serve Your Majesty." Quoted in Bunes Ibarra 2002: 169.

95. Heywood 1976–77, 1996; Halaçoğlu 2002.

96. Rodríguez-Salgado 1988: 263.

97. See his probate inventory, prepared by his secretary shortly after Kindsberg's death on 14 December 1678 and published in Kerekes 2003. Among the works concerning the Ottomans, he possessed a 1664 German-language edition of Ogier Ghiselin Busbecq's *Turkish Letters* and Bratutti's *Chronica dell'origini e progressi della Caso Ottomana*.

Chapter 12: Borders and Border Provinces

1. See, for example, the fifteenth-century chronicle of Tursun Beg 1977: 108, regarding Koylu-Hisar as being on the "boundary of the [Ottoman] realms" (*serhadd-i memleket*) in 1461. Koylu-Hisar is situated in the Kelkit valley, northeast of Tokat. In the summer of 1461, when Mehmed II

captured it, the castle was under the control of Sultan Uzun Hasan of Akkoyunlu. See Imber 1990: 177.

2. See, for instance, Defterdâr Sarı Mehmed Paşa 1995: 192 (*hudud-i İslamiyye*, 1684), 199 (*guzat-i İslam*). In 1663, the Ottomans declared war against the Habsburg monarchy (*Nemçe*) because, in the words of one chronicler, they attacked the "borders of Islam." See Râşid 2013, vol. 1: 23, who here follows a chronicle contemporaneous with the events. There are countless references in Evliya Çelebi's *Seyahatneme* regarding the "*ghazis* of the frontier"; see especially vols. 5 and 6.

3. Defterdâr Sarı Mehmed Paşa 1995: 40 (Azak), 327 (Zvornik), 431, 453, 465, 678, 701, 726 (Belgrade), 588, 595, 726 (Temesvár). For Buda as "strong bulwark of Islam," see Fekete 1944: 41. For Belgrade, see Fekete 1926b: 155 (1601). Kanizsa, conquered in 1600, is called in a *fethname* the "key and iron gate of Hungary" (ibid.). By the 1690s, Belgrade had become the "strong bulwark of Hungary" (*sedd-i şedid-i Engürüs*) both in imperial documents and in local parlance (İnalcık 1943: 7). For Eger, see BOA, KK. d. 4898: 2, and Gezer 2016: 138. According to an Ottoman manuscript from circa 1740, Bender (Bendery) on the Dnister River was known as both a "strong bulwark of Islam" and the "boundary/frontier of the Ottoman domains" (*serhadd-ı Al-i Osman*); see Kornrumpf 1989: 243.

4. For Belgrade as "domain of the holy war" (*darü'l-cihad*), see Râşid 2013, vol. 1: 23 (1663); Defterdâr Sarı Mehmed Paşa 1995: 453; BOA, MÜD 145: 472 (1739), D.BKL 32718 (1217/1802–3); for Tripoli, see MÜD 6, doc. 950; for Kamieniec, see Kołodziejczyk 1994; for Temesvár and Banjaluka, see Gezer 2016: 12; for Vidin, see M. Aydın 2018: 115 (citing the Vidin *kadı* court records); for Ochakiv, see Defterdâr Sarı Mehmed Paşa 1995: 734.

5. O. Kılıç 2012: 94; Bayır 2014: 42.

6. Sahlins 1989; Benton 2010.

7. Ágoston 2009: 63.

8. He prepared the revenue surveys (sing. *tahrir defteri*) of the *sancaks* of Buda, Esztergom, Nógrád, Hatvan, Szeged, Simontornya, Szolnok, and Temesvár. See Káldy-Nagy 1968: 183–84; 1977a: 11. The early survey of Szolnok is not extant; it is referred to in a later one. See Ágoston 1989: 236.

9. AT: 505, doc. 190, also quoted by Tracy 2015. I thank James Tracy for sharing his unpublished paper with me. See also Tracy 2016: 218.

10. See, for instance, Tomkó 2004: 37–38, doc. 1.

11. Gerlach 1986: 137–38, also quoted in Sz. Simon 2014: 40.

12. Salamon 1886: 337; Sinkovics 1985: 278.

13. Üveys Pasha to Archduke Ernst, Buda, July 27 and August 12, 1579, in Takáts, Eckhart, and Szekfű 1915: 174, 176–78, docs. 162, 164.

14. See, for instance, Sinan Pasha to Archduke Matthias, Buda, 12 May 1591, in Bayerle 1972: 86–89, doc. 41. In the letter, Sinan Pasha assured his counterpart that, as requested by the archduke, the Ottomans would demand taxes only from those villages that had been recorded in the Ottoman survey registers at the time of the conquest of Szigetvár (1566).

15. Murad III to Sigismund Rákóczi, 6 December 1591, in Karácson 1914: 172, doc. 229.

16. Sinan Pasha to Archduke Ernst, Buda, 18 June 1591, in Bayerle 1972: 89–90, doc. 42.

17. The issue was a recurring theme in their correspondence; see Takáts, Eckhart, and Szekfű 1915; Bayerle 1972, 1991; Fekete 1932.

18. For this older view, see Abou-el-Haj 1969.

19. Gemil 1983: 235–38; Kołodziejczyk 2000: 57–67; Pedani 2002: 40.

20. Kreiser 1976. Such domestic *sınırnames* had been recorded in the *tahrirs*. See, for example, Ágoston 1989; Káldy-Nagy 2000.

21. Pedani 2002: 40–41.

22. Theunissen 1998: 376.

23. Pedani 2005: 23.

24. Traljić 1973: 447–53; Panciera, 2006, 2013; Mayhew 2008: 27–28. I thank Josip Faričić of the University of Zadar and his colleagues for providing me with copies of the relevant Croatian-language studies concerning the borders in Dalmatia.

25. Gemil 1983: 235–38; 2009: 211.

26. Both treaties listed more Ottoman castles than Hungarian ones. In 1519, for instance, the treaty listed seventeen border castles on the Hungarian side, whereas fifty-nine castles and towns were listed in the possession of Sultan Selim I. Many of these castles and towns lay well beyond the border but were listed in the treaty to ensure that the Hungarian side would not attack or harm them.

27. Veinstein 1986; Kołodziejczyk 2000: 59; 2012a: 209; 2014: 30–31.

28. Kołodziejczyk 1994, 2004.

29. Tracy 2015.

30. Verancsics to Ferdinand, Constantinople, 7 October 1567, in Szalay 1860: 115–37, doc. 35; see also Salamon 1886: 334–35; and Tracy 2015, who refers to other sources.

31. Szakály 1981: 99.

32. Geőcze 1894: 515, 533; Pálffy 2008: 181–83.

33. Habardanecz 1996: 177; see also Jenkins 1911: 73.

34. Szakály 1981.

35. Salamon 1886: 343.

36. Süleyman to Maximilian, 16 February 1565. See MÜD 6: 436, doc. 796, also quoted in Emecen 2009: 205.

37. See paragraph 15 of the Treaty of Zsitvatorok, and paragraph 4 of that of Gyarmat. See also Petritsch 2014.

38. Szakály 1981: 404.

39. B. Kütükoğlu 1993: 197–206, 223–36.

40. For details, see Küpeli 2014: 276–77.

41. Pedani 2005: 29–30. By 1625, Grotius, initially a defender of the idea of the free sea, had accepted the view of his opponent (the Scottish jurist William Welwood) that territorial waters could be possessed. See his *De Iure Belli ac Pacis*, II. 3. 13–15, and David Armitage's "Introduction" in Grotius (1609) 2004: 10.

42. MÜD 3, doc. 1120, written to the *kadı* of Yanya on 14 May 1560 and given to the envoys of the Republic of Ragusa (Dubrovnik) on 25 May. See also Bostan 2007b: 36.

43. Eldem 2013: 47.

44. The first Portuguese-Ottoman negotiations are detailed in Özbaran 1977: 105–11; on the conditions, including the border demarcation, see ibid., 106–7, and in English, Özbaran 2009: 86–88.

45. Pedani 2002.

46. Turkish text: Feridun 1867, vol. 2: 96–100; Latin text: Szalay 1860: 220–21; Hungarian translation: Sinkovics 1968: 143.

47. The treaty and the related sources were published in Gooss 1911: 182–204; Hungarian translation: Sinkovics 1968: 156–68. See also Oborni 2011: 85–99.

48. "The Turkish emperor knows the borders between Transylvania and Hungary as well as we do," wrote Prince Gabriel Bethlen of Transylvania in 1613. Quoted in Sudár 2011b: 975.

49. Quoted in Stoye 1994: 175.

50. There is a burgeoning literature on the post-Karlowitz border demarcation. See, for instance, Marsili 1986; Stoye 1994; Deák 1993, 1994, 1996; F. Molnár 2006, 2013; Doğan 2017: 141–217. For versions of the Ottoman-Turkish text, see BOA, MAD.d. 4157, AE.SMST.II. 956.

51. Abou-el-Haj 1969: 467.

52. Perdue 2005: 169. Because of the influence of the two Jesuits representing the Qing, Latin was the language of the negotiations.

53. Published in Fodor 1991: 320.

54. Published in Fodor 1991: 321.

55. I. Horváth 2003.

56. Hegyi 2007, vol. 1: 94–100; 2018: 100–105.

57. Káldy-Nagy 2000: 7.

58. Quoted in Fekete 1930: 15–16, 141–42.

59. İnalcık (1973) 1994: 104–7; Kunt 1983; Pitcher 1973: 126–28; İpşirli 1994; İ. Şahin 1999; Göyünç 1999, 2000. Many of these provinces were governed for shorter or longer periods according to the classical system, whereas at other times only certain *sancaks* of the province were administered as *salyaneli*.

60. This section builds on and uses material from Ágoston 2003.

61. During the turbulent years of the war of 1593–1606, the Ottomans established the short-lived provinces of Győr (Yanık, 1594–98), Pápa (1594–97), and Szigetvár (1594–97?).

62. The *sancaks* of Buda, Smederevo, Zvornik, Vulčitrn, Požega, Pécs, Fehérvár, Esztergom, Szeged, Srem, Hatvan, Simontornya, Koppány, Fülek, Szekszárd, Szigetvár, Szécsény, Nógrád, Szolnok, and Szekcső.

63. Káldy-Nagy 1977a: 9–10; Kunt 1978: 134–35; Fodor 1996.

64. Kunt 1978: 142–48, 167–69.

65. 370 Numaralı 2001–2; 401 Numaralı 2011: 13–14.

66. D. Aydın 1998; Ágoston 2003.

67. Dávid and Fodor 2005.

68. Hegyi 1995: 118–30; Ágoston 2009.

Chapter 13: Contested Bulwark of Islam

1. Barkan 1953–54: 282, 284–85, 294–96.

2. Smederevo (1,490 men), Belgrade (1,479 men), and Osijek (3,203 men). See Semendire 1530: 13, 16.

3. Hegyi 2007. In English, see Hegyi 1994, 2000, 2018.

4. Hersek, Bosna ve İzvornik (1520–33) 2005: 4–5, for the list of castles in 1530. The number of fortresses proper in Bosnia was seventy-eight and eighty-three in 1616 and 1643, respectively (Hanciç 1985: 264–65).

5. Hegyi 1995: 91.

6. Hegyi 2007, vol. 1: 157.

7. Fekete and Káldy-Nagy 1962a, 1962b; Ágoston 2000a: 206; Hegyi 2007, vol. 1: 161–65.

8. Hegyi 2007, vol. 1: 166; 2018: 168–69.

9. Szántó 1980: 24; Hegyi 2007, vol. 1: 170; 2018: 172–73.

10. Káldy-Nagy 1977a: 7.

11. O. Kılıç 1997: 316–21.

12. The fortresses of Eger, Heves, Szarvaskő, Sirok, Cserépvár, Szolnok, Szentmiklós, and Csongrád became part of the province of Eger. The province of Kanizsa comprised the castles of Kanizsa, Szeged, Berzence, Babócsa, Szigetvár, Barcs, Pécs, Kaposvár, Baranyanádasd, and Szászvár and the garrison guarding the famous bridge at Osijek.

13. Hegyi 2018: 171.

14. 11,000 men in 1613 (BOA, D.BŞM. BNH.d. 16768 ek 10/1a), 10,107 men in 1616 (Hanciç 1985: 268), and 11,773 men in 1635 (S. Öztürk 1999).

15. Hegyi 1995: 116.

16. Murphey 1999: 40; Ágoston and Oborni 2000: 107–12.

17. BOA, MAD.d. 106, fols. 2r-22v; D.BŞM. UYH.d. 17082; D.BŞM. BDH.d. 16728, 16729.

18. Hegyi (2007, vol. 1: 169–72; 2018: 171–72) estimated the aggregate troop numbers at twenty-four thousand.

19. İ. Şahin 1979: 908, 912–13.

20. BOA, D. BKL.d. 32182; İ Şahin 1979: 912. Hanciç (1985: 268) estimated that the number of garrison soldiers in Bosnia could have reached 16,000 men in 1643.

21. Czigány 2004: 73–79.

22. Fekete 1929: 92–93, docs. 261–62. The Porte ordered the governors-general of Buda and Eger in May 1665 to send, respectively, five hundred and two hundred janissaries to Érsekújvár.

23. Fekete 1929: 90–91, docs. 254–55.

24. Fekete 1929: 98, doc. 284; 103, doc. 297.

25. The governor of Eger petitioned the Porte in the spring of 1664 to fill vacancies in the ranks of the janissaries as they occurred and not at the end of the year as custom dictated. The Porte approved the petition. See Fekete 1929: 68, doc. 177.

26. Hegyi 2007, vol. 3: 1357, 1364.

27. BOA, D.BKL.d. 32235.

28. BOA, D.BKL.d 32260 and 32263. The actual number present should have been 1,467 men, and one related source (Ek 15-1-b of 32263) has this correct number.

29. Marsigli 2007: 62.

30. See Ágoston 2010: 129. The list of 14,376 janissaries in 1669 contains only those who served in the fortresses of Hungary and the eastern frontier. Their actual number must have been closer to 20,000 in the 1670s, and above 30,000 in the late 1680s.

31. Hegyi 2007, vol. 3: 1537, 1543, 1547.

32. BOA, MAD.d. 6616, p. 159; MAD.d. 1951, pp. 137–38.

33. BOA, KK.d. 6599 (see G. Yılmaz 2011: 114); MAD.d. 1951, p. 138.

34. BOA, D.YNÇ.d. 33980, p. 34.

35. BOA, MAD.d. 1951, p. 144; MAD.d. 1975, p. 12; D.PYM.d. 35148, p. 1; D.YNÇ.d. 34217, p. 2.

36. Kołodziejczyk 1994: 163–65.

37. BOA, MAD.d. 6616, p. 160; MAD.d. 1951, p. 140; MAD.d. 4042, p. 156; D.YNÇ.d. 33993, p. 7.

38. Dávid 1992–93.

39. Hersek, Bosna ve İzvornik (1520–33) 2005: 7.

40. Dávid 1992b: 96; 1992–93: 156.

41. Dávid 1992a.

42. Gévay 1841: no. 15; Káldy-Nagy 1990.

43. Gévay 1841: no. 21; Biščević 2006: no. 66. There is a discrepancy between the data given in these two works.

44. Gévay 1841: no. 24; Biščević 2006: no. 58.

45. Pezzen to Archduke Ernst, October 1590. HHStA, Turcica. Türkei I. Karton 74. Konv 1. 1590. X-XII, 66–69. See Fazekas, Kenyeres, and Sarusi Kiss 2011.

46. Bayerle 1991: X.

47. Bayerle 1991: X, 186–88, docs. 146–47, and 255–57, docs. 203–5.

48. Sudár 2009; Zahirović 2012.

49. Hadrovics 1991: 30–31; Fotić 2009.

50. Ágoston 1991.

51. Hegyi 2007, vol. 1: 239–43.

52. A. Molnár 2009: 328–30.

53. Fodor 2010.

54. P. Török 1932: 77. The report is published in AT: 21–30.

55. Fekete and Káldy-Nagy 1962a: 770–71. The deficit was 225,506 and 196,828 gold florins, respectively. The account book calculated the exchange rate at 75 akçe = 1 gold florin.

56. BOA, MAD.d. 1561, and MAD.d. 498, as examined in Ágoston 2000a.

57. In 1574, the imperial treasury transferred an unusually large sum that was three times the amount transferred in previous years to Buda.

58. BOA, MAD.d. 1561, p. 156, and Finkel 1988: 292, where the comment is quoted in Turkish.

59. Fodor 1996: 33. The provincial treasury of Temesvár annually sent 4 to 5 million akçe to Buda and an additional sum of 50,000 guruş to the imperial treasury.

60. Szakály 1981: 38.

61. The value of the house, land, and vineyard were excluded from movable property assets.

62. Káldy-Nagy 1968: 194–95. The diet of 1547 declared that the state tax (subsidium) "should be levied upon all those who possess six florins worth in moveable property."

63. Káldy-Nagy 1960; 1970: 89–93.

64. Fekete and Káldy-Nagy 1962a: 770, and BOA, MAD.d. 498, pp. 2, 44.

65. T. Gökbilgin 1950–51: 25.

66. Hegyi 1995: 43.

67. BOA, MAD.d. 498, as examined in Ágoston 2000a: 216–22.

68. Fodor 2006: 43–44; 2018: 45; Murphey 1999: 54.

69. B. Kütükoğlu 1993: 228–31.

70. Quoted in Fodor 2006: 44 (Hungarian); 2018: 45 (English).

71. Finkel 1988: 290, Appendix 13–6; Hegyi 2018: 187–89.

72. Hegyi 2018: 191–97. Temesvár's financial situation in 1613 must have been better, because the source recorded only the province's *mukataa* revenues but not those from the *cizye* tax.

73. Hegyi 2018: 198–207.

74. Kołodziejczyk 1994: 208–16.

75. Quoted in I. Tóth 1992: 18.

76. Gerlach (1674) 1986: 119; Szakály 1981: 470.

77. Szakály 1981: 52, 56.

78. Szakály 1981: 99–139.

79. See the numerous protests by the Ottoman governors-general to the Habsburg authorities in Takáts, Eckhart, and Szekfű 1915.

80. Szakály 1997: 315–29, 376.

81. Hegyi 1995: 131–45.

82. Fekete 1925: 43–44, 46, doc. 1.

83. Fekete 1925: 45–47, docs. 4 and 7, where the Turkish text used the Hungarian word *törvín* for law. See also Hegyi 1995: 132.

84. Several such cases are documented by the correspondence between these towns and the local Ottoman authorities. See, for instance, the Turkish letters of Jászberény. Hegyi 1988: 16–17, 64–69, 71–72, 79, 108, 126, 144–45, docs. 38–43, 47–48, 56, 90, 113, 128, 130.

85. Quoted in Szakály 1997: 7.

86. Sahillioğlu 1990: 1249.

87. Barkan 1943: 119–71.

88. Kırzıoğlu (1993) 1998; B. Kütükoğlu 1993.

89. Szakály 1969.

90. Akdağ 1995: 210–11.

91. For example, BOA, MÜD 3: 76, doc. 192: against the brigands ravaging gardens and vineyards in the vicinity of Malkara in 1559; MÜD 5: 78, doc. 180: against a bandit in the *sancak* of Hüdavendigar; MÜD 3: 185, doc. 511: against robbers in the vicinity of Alacahisar in 1559; MÜD 3: 353, doc. 1044: in the *kaza* of Tekirdağ against thirty or forty robbers; MÜD 3: 166, doc. 452: in the vicinity of Çorum and Amasya against the brigands and *levends*; MÜD 5: 473, doc. 1274: chasing Albanian robbers who escaped from the prison of Bursa; MÜD 5: 322, doc. 843: in the *sancak* of Menteşe against brigands; MÜD 5: 154, doc. 365, and 189, doc. 463: against outlaws and nomads who plundered the horses, camels, and sheep of the Muslims from the meadows (1565).

92. BOA, MÜD 3: 153, doc. 411, and 166, doc. 452.

Chapter 14: Wars of Exhaustion

1. Setton 1991: 110–20; Gülsoy 2004: 26, Finkel 2006a: 225–26.

2. Bostan 2014: 107–9.

3. Setton 1991: 125–27; Gülsoy 2004: 27–45; Panzac 2009: 141–45. There is a discrepancy between the Ottoman and Western sources regarding the dates and number of troops.

4. Gülsoy 2004: 123; Setton 1991: 182–85.

5. Quoted in Kunt 1971: 18.

6. Kunt 1971: 18–19; Setton 1991: 163–64.

7. Abdurrahman Abdi Paşa 2008: 90, 93–95; Naima 2007, vol. 4: 1674–77; Kâtib Çelebi 2008: 135. There are discrepancies between the Ottoman and European sources regarding the dates of these events and the size of the opposing navies. See Setton 1991: 182–84; Gülsoy 2004: 109–10.

8. Mehmed Pasha called the village of Ruznik in Albania his "original home" (*vatan-ı asli*) in his endowment deed for his mosque and school that he had built. See Kunt 1974: 235.

9. Naima 2007, vol. 4: 1700–1701; Abdurrahman Abdi Paşa 2008: 98; Silahdar 2012: 99. See also Kunt 1973: 58.

10. In 1650, Melek Ahmed Pasha accepted the grand vizier's seal only after he was assured that the janissaries would not meddle in state affairs. However, his tenure ended abruptly a year later when he mishandled a violent uprising of the tradesmen of the capital, who rebelled because of the grand vizier's devaluation of the Ottoman silver coin. Melek Ahmed Pasha's short-lived tenure was typical of the turbulent years that followed the outbreak of the Cretan war in 1645. See Naima 2007, vol. 3: 1266; Finkel 2006a: 339.

11. Setton 1991: 148–49.

12. Kunt 1971: 17.

13. On which, see Kunt 1974.

14. Köprülü Mehmed was suspicious of Seydi Ahmed, who had allied with Abaza Hasan and İpşir Mustafa, two Abkhazian statesmen who had rebelled against the Porte. Abaza Hasan Pasha first rebelled in 1651, after his dismissal from the lucrative position of *voyvoda* of the Yeni Il Turkmens in eastern Asia Minor. The Porte sent the governor of Sivas, the Abkhazian İpşir Mustafa, against Hasan; however, İpşir Mustafa sided with his kinsman. Hasan was eventually restored to office, and İpşir Mustafa was appointed the governor of Aleppo and later, in October 1654, grand vizier. He was dismissed and executed in May 1655, and the Albanian Kara Murad succeeded him. See Abdurrahman Abdi Paşa 2008: 82–84; Aktepe 1970; Sudár 2011a: 893.

15. See Madunić 2013. On Çengizade Ali and Seydi Ahmed, see also Sudár 2011a: 893–95, 896–97.

16. Grand Vizier Köprülü Mehmed to Mehmed Giray Khan, Safer 1068/Nov. 1657, in Karácson 1914: 227–28, doc. 262. See also Naima 2007, vol. 4: 1777; Kunt 1971: 86.

17. Papp 2011; Sudár 2011b.

18. Tezcan 2009; 2010: 136–40.

19. See Bethlen's instruction to his envoy, 15 June 1623, in Szilády and Szilágyi 1868–73, vol. 1: 383–93, doc. 161. Bethlen asked for twelve thousand cavalry, ten thousand Tatars, and eight thousand infantry musketeers for Mehmed Pasha of Buda, and five thousand cavalry, five thousand Tatars, and two thousand infantry for the governor-general of Bosnia.

20. Davies 2007: 103–22.

21. Frost 2000: 164–69; Gebei 2007: 149, 158, 163, 165; Kołodziejczyk 2011: 163–74.

22. For the treaty, see Szilágyi 1890–91, vol. 2: 190–96.

23. This section builds on Ágoston and Oborni 2000: 187–91. See also Gebei 2007: 185–93. For the sources, see Szilágyi (1890–91, vol. 2: 232), who gives eighteen thousand horsemen and five thousand infantry from Transylvania, twenty thousand Cossacks, and six thousand Wallachian and Moldavian soldiers. Gheorghe Ştefan often concluded his letters as Rákóczi's willing servant (*servitor paratissimus*). See Jakó 2016: 292.

24. Szilágyi 1890–91, vol. 2: 212–27, 357–62. Mehmed IV to Rákóczi, Edirne, Şaban 1067/ May 1657, in Karácson 1914: 225–26, doc. 261. See also Gebei 2004: 156–58.

25. Already in early spring, Lubomirski told the Transylvanian envoys that he considered Rákóczi an invader. In retaliation for the looting of his Lancut estates, he pillaged Rákóczi's estates in the counties of Bereg, Szatmár, and Ugocsa.

26. Szilágyi 1866, vol. 2: 262–65; Frost 2000: 178–79; Markowicz 2011; Kołodziejczyk 2011: 166–67; Gebei 2007: 202–19; Ivanics 2007: 204–6. The Tatar attack is described in Kemény's short pamphlet, *Ruina exercitus Transylvanici*, published in Kemény 2000.

27. Karácson 1914: 230, doc. 264.

28. Oborni 2011: 85–99; 2013b; Papp 2003, 2013; Panaite 2013.

29. Jakó 2009, 2016.

30. Dispatch of Giovanni Battista Ballarino, secretary of the Venetian embassy (acting as de facto *bailo* during Giovanni Soranzo's house arrest), Pera, 18 August 1657, in Óváry 1890–1901, vol. 3: 141, doc. 928.

31. Ballarino's dispatch, Pera, 1 March 1658, in Óváry 1890–1901, vol. 3: 143, doc. 942; see also Naima 2007, vol. 4: 1777.

32. Naima 2007, vol. 4: 1756–59, 1770–71; Szalárdi 1980: 511.

33. R. Várkonyi 1978; Péter 2002: 147–49.

34. Köprülü Mehmed to Leopold, Receb 1068/March 1658, in Karácson 1914: 228–29, doc. 263. See R. Várkonyi 1978: 165.

35. Rákóczi believed that Köprülü wanted to get even with him because, as governor of Eger province in 1646–47, Köprülü had felt humiliated by Rákóczi's father, Prince George I Rákóczi. See Hadnagy 2010.

36. Ballarino from Pera, 14 March 1658, in Óváry 1890–1901, vol. 3: 144, doc. 943. Hadice Turhan was captured at the age of twelve by Crimean Tatars in what is today Ukraine and was brought to the harem to serve Queen Mother Kösem, mother of Sultan Ibrahim. Later, Hadice Turhan bore a son to Ibrahim, the future sultan Mehmed IV. Upon the dethronement and execution of Sultan Ibrahim in 1648 and the accession of her son Mehmed IV to the throne, Hadice Turhan became the queen mother. See Thys-Şenocak 2006.

37. Ballarino's dispatches, 28 April, 29 May, and 15 July 1658, in Óváry 1890–1901, vol. 3: 146–47, docs. 957, 964, 965; Kunt 1971: 92.

38. Szalárdi 1980: 411–13.

39. Mehmed Halife 2000: 60; Ballarino from Edirne, 20 August 1658, in Óváry 1890–1901, vol. 3: 148, doc. 973.

40. Naima 2007, vol. 4: 1792.

41. Szalárdi 1980: 428–31.

42. See Barcsay's letter to Palatine Francis Vesselény, Dés (Dej in Romania), 16 January 1659, in Szilágyi 1890–91, vol. 2: 525–30. The negotiations and conditions are detailed in an anony-

mous Hungarian eyewitness account, published in Németh 1996. For the Turkish, Latin, and Hungarian versions of the agreement, see Uzunçarşılı 1952. See also Ballarino from Edirne, 1 November 1658, in Óváry 1890–1901, vol. 3: 149–50, doc. 979. The Ottoman chronicles also detail the events; see, for instance, Abdurrahman Abdi Paşa 2008: 125–28; Naima 2007, vol. 4: 1793–97. See also Kolçak 2017.

43. Ballarino from Edirne, 8 August 1658, in Óváry 1890–1901, vol. 3: 148, doc. 972.

44. Abdurrahman Abdi Paşa 2008: 122–24, 130–32; Naima 2007, vol. 4: 1787; Finkel 2006b: 257–62.

45. Mehmed Halife 2000: 62; Naima 2007, vol. 4: 1789 (who follows Mehmed Halife, d. 1697). Quoted in English in Finkel 2006b: 259.

46. Mehmed IV and Köprülü Mehmed to Emperor Leopold, n.d. (second half of 1659), in Karácson 1914: 231–34, docs. 265–66.

47. Mehmed Halife 2000: 71–75. Estimates vary from six thousand to eight thousand men for Rákóczi's army and from fifteen thousand to thirty thousand men for Ahmed's army. Despite Ahmed's services in reestablishing Ottoman control in Transylvania, Köprülü Mehmed ultimately got rid of his rival, using Habsburg protests that Ahmed crossed the border and defeated Rákóczi's fleeing troops on Habsburg territory. He was dismissed from the governorship in Buda and executed in Temesvár a year later (17 July 1661). See Gévay 1841: 44.

48. The siege is described in detail in the contemporary Hungarian chronicle of János Szalárdi (1980). See also Sultan Mehmed IV's letter to Gazi Mehmed Giray Khan, early September 1660, in which the padishah ordered the khan to celebrate the conquest of Várad. Karácson 1914: 236–37, doc. 268.

49. Sudár 2015. This *tahrir* survey was physically carried out by yet another frontier man, Piri Pasha, the former governor of Kanizsa, as land surveyor (*muharrir*). The earliest known pay list from November–December 1660 showed 2,019 soldiers in Várad and 469 soldiers in the province's four other forts. However, it seems that these were not actual but planned numbers. One of the forts listed (Szentjobb) was not even in Ottoman hands. In the next summer and fall, a roll call found only 1,200 men. See BOA, D-PYM 35139; data published in Ágoston 2000a: 204; Hegyi 2007, vol. 3: 1603–4; 2018: 570–73.

50. At that time, it comprised the counties of Máramaros, Bihar, Kraszna, Közép-Szolnok, Zaránd, and Szörény.

51. On Zrínyi-Újvár, see Hausner and Padányi 2012.

52. R. Várkonyi 2002: 236–43; 2016: 92–95. After the reconquest of Jenő in 1658, the governors-general of the province of Temesvár (to which Jenő had belonged between 1566 and 1595 and again between 1658 and 1693) resided in either Jenő or Temesvár, and therefore they titled themselves (and were referred to by contemporaries) alternatively as pashas of Jenő or Temesvár. See Fodor 1996.

53. Gévay 1841: 41–45; Sudár 2011a, 2015; Zahirović 2012.

54. Silahdar 2012: 281, and a summary quotation in English in Çalışır 2016: 208.

55. Şimşirgil 2012: 73–92; Çalışır 2016: 208–9; for the castles and the captaincy of Lower Hungary, see Pálffy 1999a, 2000a.

56. BOA, KK.d. 6599, quoted by G. Yılmaz 2011: 114; Hegyi 2007, vol 3: 1621–31; 2018: 574–76. The number of janissaries of the Porte dropped to 955 by the fall of 1669. See MAD.d. 1951, p. 138.

57. G. Etényi 2016: 302–3; R. Várkonyi 2016.

58. Quoted in Jászay 1990: 293–94, and Kelenik 2016: 145. (English).

59. Kelenik 2016: 152–64; Sudár 2017b.

60. Sudár 2017b, 2017c. See also Sperl, Scheutz, and Strohmeyer 2016; Tóth and Zágorhidi 2017.

61. Setton 1991: 194.

62. Gülsoy 2004: 133–40.

63. Mugnai 2018: 216.

64. Mugnai 2018: 217–24.

65. İnbaşı 2004; Doğru 2006; Şakul 2019; Davies 2007: 155–56.

66. Kołodziejczyk 1994, 2004; Davies 2007: 157.

67. Defterdâr Sarı Mehmed Paşa 1995: 80–81, 91–103; Finkel 2006b: 282; Heywood 2006; Davies 2007: 159–62; Stevens 2007: 189–93.

68. Czigány 2004: 149; J. Varga 2007: 33, 35.

69. J. Varga 2007: 67–68.

70. Silahdar 2012: 819; Defterdâr Sarı Mehmed Paşa 1995: 143, 146–48.

71. Leitsch 1988: 69.

72. For the winged hussars, *see* Brzezinski and Vuksic 2006. For the siege and battle, see Stoye 1965; Barker 1967; Wheatcroft 2009.

73. Finkel 2006b: 286–87.

74. Lajos Nagy 1987: 18.

75. These are discussed in detail in Szakály 1986: 73–91; Setton 1991: 271–300.

76. Lajos Nagy 1987. The booty included sixty-eight cannons, ten mortars, eight thousand cannonballs, eleven thousand hand grenades, ammunition, abundant provisions, seven thousand oxen, six thousand horses, and fifteen hundred camels; treasury, archives, and the grand vizier's tent.

77. The event is known as the Declaration of Fogaras (9 May 1688). See Szita 1987b: 55–59; R. Várkonyi 2002: 367–72.

78. Sugár 1979, 1991.

79. Finkel 2006a: 310–11.

80. Szakály 1986: 92–108.

81. Szakály 1986: 108–11.

82. As mentioned in chapter 9, in March 1697 an official register listed 104,514 troops (including 10,000 men of the Danube flotilla), mobilized for the war in Hungary. Carlo Ruzzini, Venice's resident in Vienna between 1683 and 1699 and the Signoria's chief negotiator with the Ottomans at Karlowitz, reported that the Ottomans prepared similar lists and battle orders with inflated numbers to deceive the enemy, claiming that the Porte never had that many soldiers. However, Ottoman pay lists and treasury accounts give similar numbers, reflecting paper numbers, if not numbers of troops actually deployed. For a list found in the Ottoman camp and commented on by Ruzzini, see Szita and Seewann 1997: 269–75, doc. 55. Silahdar Fındıklı Mehmed Agha also accused Grand Vizier Elmas Mehmed Pasha (in office, 1695–97) of exaggerating the size of the army. The chronicler claimed that the Grand Vizier supposedly showed registers that listed 104,000 soldiers (a number similar to that of Ruzzini's figure), when there

were not even 50,000 men in the army. See Silahdar 2001: 297; Finkel 2006a: 317. However, the above register looks like a genuine draft document, reflecting the number of mobilized troops thus far, as well as missing and expected contingents.

83. Szita 1997; Finkel 2006a: 317–18.

84. On these negotiations, see Heywood 1984.

85. Davies 2007: 187; Defterdâr Sarı Mehmed Paşa 1995: 692–98.

86. Finkel 2006a: 333–36; Aksan 2007: 90–98.

87. Setton 1991: 426–27; Ertaş 2007: 18–23.

88. Ertaş 2007: 231.

89. Creasy 1961: 339; Setton 1991: 427–32; Aksan 2007.

90. J. Varga 1994.

91. Dávid 2005.

92. Setton 1991: 436–40; Creasy (1858) 1968: 344–45, who followed Hammer 1827–35, vol. 7: 217–21, who in turn followed Raşid's chronicle.

93. Ingrao, Samardžić, and Pešalj 2011.

94. Hochedlinger 2003: 220.

95. Balisch 1983: 48.

Epilogue

1. Müteferrika 1995.

BIBLIOGRAPHY

Abbreviations Used in the Bibliography

AHASH = Acta Historica Academiae Scienciarum Hungaricae

AO = Archivum Ottomanicum

AOH = Acta Orientalia Academiae Scientiarum Hungaricae

BSOAS = Bulletin of the School of Oriental and African Studies

BTTD = Belgelerle Türk Tarih Dergisi

CH = Cartographica Hungarica

DİA = Türkiye Diyanet Vakfı İslam Ansiklopedisi 44 vols. (Istanbul, 1988–2016)

DTCFD = Ankara Üniversitesi Dil ve Tarih-Coğrafya Fakültesi Dergisi

EI2 = Encyclopedia of Islam, 2nd ed. Leiden and London, 1960–2007.

HK = Hadtörténelmi Közlemények

İA = İslam Ansiklopedisi, 13 vols. Istanbul, 1965–88.

İFM = İstanbul Üniversitesi İktisat Fakültesi Mecmuası

IJTS = International Journal of Turkish Studies

JEMH = Journal of Early Modern History

JRAS = Journal of the Royal Asiatic Society of Great Britain and Ireland

JTS = Journal of Turkish Studies

LK = Levéltári Közlemények

MHR = Mediterranean Historical Review

MÖStA = Mitteilungen des Österreichischen Staatsarchivs

OA = Osmanlı Araştırmaları

OTAM = Osmanlı Tarihi Araştırma ve Uygulama Merkezi Dergisi (Ankara Üniversitesi)

SoF = Südost-Forschungen

TAD = Tarih Araştırmaları Dergisi (Ankara Üniversitesi Dil ve Tarih-Coğrafya Fakültesi, Tarih Bölümü)

TD = İstanbul Üniversitesi Edebiyat Fakültesi Tarih Dergisi

TED = İstanbul Üniversitesi Edebiyat Fakültesi Tarih Enstitüsü Dergisi

THR = Turkish Historical Review

TİD = Tarih İncelemeleri Dergisi

TSz = Történelmi Szemle

Turcica = Turcica. Revue d'études turques

TV = Tarih Vesikaları

WZKM = Wiener Zeitschrift für die Kunde des Morgenlandes

370 Numaralı. 2001–2. 370 Numaralı Muhâsebe-i Vilâyet-i Rûm-ili Defteri (937/1530): Dizin ve Tıpkıbasım. 2 vols. Ankara.

401 Numaralı. 2011. 401 Numaralı Şam Livâsı Mufassal Tahrîr Defteri (942/1535). 2 vols. Ankara.

506 Numaralı. 2009. MAD 506 Numaralı Semendire Livâsı İcmâl Tahrîr Defteri (937/1530). Ankara.

Abbott, John Stevens Cabot. 1859. *The Empire of Austria: Its Rise and Present Power*. New York.

Abdurrahman Abdi Paşa. 2008. *Vekâyi'-nâme. Osmanlı Târihi (1648–1682)*. Edited by Fahri Ç. Derin. Istanbul.

Abdülkadir (Kadrî) Efendi. 2003. *Topçular Kâtibi Abdülkâdir (Kadrî) Efendi Tarihi*. Edited by Ziya Yılmazer. 2 vols. Ankara.

Abou-el-Haj, Rifa'at A. 1969. "The Formal Closure of the Ottoman Frontier in Europe: 1699–1703." *Journal of the American Oriental Society* 89, 467–75.

Ács, Pál. 2000. "Tarjumans Mahmud and Murad: Austrian and Hungarian Renegades as Sultan's Interpreters." In Wilhelm Kühlmann and Bodo Güthmüller, eds., *Europa und die Türken in der Renaissance*. Tübingen, 307–16.

———. 2006. "Andrea's Dudith Turkish Brother-in-Law." *Camoenae Hungaricae* 3, 59–64.

Adıvar, A. Adnan. 1982. *Osmanlı Türklerinde İlim*. 4th ed. Istanbul.

Ágoston, Gábor. 1986. "Az 1444. évi török követjárás." *TSz* 29, 2, 261–76.

———. 1989. "A szolnoki szandzsák 1591–92 évi összeírása. II rész." *Zounuk* 4, 191–287.

———. 1991. "Muslim Cultural Enclaves in Hungary." *AOH* 45, 181–204.

———. 1992. *A hódolt Magyarország*. Budapest.

———. 1994. "Ottoman Artillery and European Military Technology in the Fifteenth to Seventeenth Centuries." *AOH* 47, 15–48.

———. 1995. "15. Yüzyılda Batı Barut Teknolojisi ve Osmanlılar." *Toplumsal Tarih* 18 (Haziran 1995), 10–15.

———. 1998. "Habsburgs and Ottomans: Defense, Military Change and Shifts in Power." *Turkish Studies Association Bulletin* 22, 126–41.

———. 1999. "Információszerzés és kémkedés az Oszmán Birodalomban a 15–17. században." In Petercsák and Berecz 1999, 129–54.

———. 2000a. "The Costs of the Ottoman Fortress-System in Hungary in the Sixteenth and Seventeenth Centuries." In Dávid and Fodor 2000, 195–228.

———. 2000b. "La strada che conduceva a Nándorfehérvár (Belgrade): L'Ungheria, l'espansione ottomana nei Balcani e la vittoria di Nándorfehérvár." In Visy 2000, 203–50.

———. 2003. "A Flexible Empire: Authority and Its Limits on the Ottoman Frontiers." *IJTS* 9, 15–31.

———. 2005a. *Guns for the Sultan: Military Power and the Weapons Industry in the Ottoman Empire.* Cambridge.

———. 2005b. "Ideologie, Propaganda und politischer Pragmatismus: Die Auseinandersetzung der osmanischen und habsburgischen Großmächte und die mitteleuropäische Konfrontation." In Fuchs, Oborni, and Újvári 2005, 207–33.

———. 2005c. "Birodalom és információ: Konstantinápoly, mint a koraújkori Európa információs központja." In Hausner and Veszprémi 2005, 31–60.

———. 2007. "Information, Ideology, and Limits of Imperial Policy: Ottoman Grand Strategy in the Context of Ottoman-Habsburg Rivalry." In Aksan and Goffman 2007, 75–103.

———. 2009. "Where Environmental and Frontier Studies Meet: Rivers, Forests and Fortifications along the Ottoman–Habsburg Frontier in Hungary." In Peacock 2009, 57–79.

———. 2010. "Empires and Warfare in East-Central Europe, 1550–1750: The Ottoman–Habsburg Rivalry and Military Transformation." In Frank Tallett and David J. B. Trim, eds., *European Warfare, 1350–1750.* Cambridge, 110–34.

———. 2011a. "Military Transformation in the Ottoman Empire and Russia, 1500–1800." *Kritika* 12, 2, 281–319.

———. 2011b. "The Ottoman Empire and the Technological Dialogue between Europe and Asia: The Case of Military Technology and Know-How in the Gunpowder Age." In Günergun and Raina 2011, 27–40.

———. 2011c. "Ottoman Military Organization (up to 1800)." In Gordon Martel ed., *The Encyclopedia of War.* 5 vols. Online edition. https://doi.org/10.1002/9781444338232 .wbeow465.

———. 2012a. *Osmanlı'da Strateji ve Askeri Güç.* Translated by M. Fatih Çalışır. Istanbul.

———. 2012b. "Defending and Administering the Frontier: The Case of Ottoman Hungary." In Woodhead 2012, 220–36.

———. 2013. "War-Winning Weapons? On the Decisiveness of Ottoman Firearms from the Siege of Constantinople (1453) to the Battle of Mohács (1526)." *JTS* 39, 129–43.

———. 2014. "Firearms and Military Adaptation: The Ottomans and the European Military Revolution, 1450–1800." *Journal of World History* 25, 1, 85–124.

———. 2016. "Mohács és Szulejmán szultán magyarországi hadjáratai." In Horn et al. 2016, 59–73.

———. 2017. "Ottoman and Habsburg Military Affairs in the Age of Süleyman the Magnificent." https://www.academia.edu/38682935/Ottoman_and_Habsburg_Military_Affairs_in_the _age_of_S%C3%BCleyman_the_Magnificent.

———. 2018. "Oszmán hadügyi változások a 16–18. században." *Századok* 152, 5, 961–80.

———. 2019a. "Ottoman and Habsburg Military Affairs in the Age of Süleyman the Magnificent." In Fodor 2019a, 287–307.

———. 2019b. "Firangi, Zarbzan, and Rum Dasturi: The Ottomans and the Diffusion of Firearms in Asia." In Fodor, Kovács, and Péri 2019, 89–104.

Ágoston, Gábor, and Bruce Masters, eds. 2009. *Encyclopedia of the Ottoman Empire*. New York.

Ágoston, Gábor, and Teréz Oborni. 2000. *A tizenhetedik század története*. Budapest.

Ahmed Cavid. 2004. *Osmanlı-Rus İlişkileri Tarihi (Ahmed Câvid Bey'in Müntehabâtı)*. Edited by Adnan Baycar. İstanbul.

Akdağ, Mustafa. 1947. "Yeniçeri Ocak Nizamının Bozoluşu." *DTCFD* 5, 3, 291–309.

———. 1995. *Türk Halkının Dirlik ve Düzenlik Kavgası: "Celalî İsyanları."* Istanbul.

Akhisarî, Hasan Kâfî. 1909. *Az egri török emlékirat a kornmányzás módjáról—Eger vár elfoglalása alkalmával az 1596 évben irja Molla Haszan Elkjáfi*. Translated by Imre Karácson. Budapest.

———. 1979–80. Usûlü'l-Hikem fî Nizâmi'l-Âlem." Edited and transliterated by Mehmet İpşirli. In "Hasan Kâfî el- Akhisarî ve Devlet Düzenine Ait Eseri: Usûlü'l-Hikem fî Nizâmi'l-Âlem," *TED* 10–11, 239–79.

Akman, Mehmet. 1997. *Osmanlı Devletinde Kardeş Katli*. Istanbul.

Aksan, Virginia. 1998. "Whatever Happened to the Janissaries? Mobilization for the 1768–1774 Russo-Ottoman War." *War in History* 5, 23–36.

———. 2007. *Ottoman Wars, 1700–1870: An Empire Besieged*. Harlow.

Aksan, Virginia, and Daniel Goffman, eds. 2007. *The Early Modern Ottomans: Remapping the Empire*. Cambridge.

Aktepe, M. Münir. 1970. "İpşir Mustafa Paşa ve Kendisile İlgili Bazı Belgeler." *TD* 24, 45–58.

Alexandrescu-Dersca, M. M. 1977. *La campagne de Timur en Anatolie (1402)*. London.

Âlî, Mustafa bin Ahmet. 2000. *Gelibolulu Mustafa Âlî ve Künhü'l-ahbar'ında II. Selim, III. Murat ve III. Mehmet Devirleri*. Edited by Faris Çerçi. Kayseri.

Allouche, Adel. 1983. *The Origins and Development of the Ottoman-Ṣafavid Conflict (906–962/1500–1555)*. Berlin.

Amitai-Preiss, Reuven. 1995. *Mongols and Mamluks. The Mamluk–Ilkhanid War, 1260–1281*. Cambridge.

Andrade, Tonio. 2016. *The Gunpowder Age: China, Military Innovation, and the Rise of the West in World History*. Princeton, NJ.

Anonymous. (1706) 1987. *Mebde-i Kanun-ı Yeniçeri Ocağı Tarihi*. Facsimile and Russian translation by I. E. Petrosian. Moscow.

Anonymous. (1795–96) 1990. *Kavanin-i Yeniçeriyan*. In Ahmed Akgündüz, *Osmanlı Kanunnameleri ve Hukuki Tahlilleri*. Istanbul, vol. 9/1, 127–268 (transcription), 269–367 (facsimile).

Antoche, Constantin Emanuel. 2004. "Du Tábor de Jan Žižka et de Jean Hunyadi au *Tabur Çengi* des armées ottomanes." *Turcica* 36, 91–124.

Antov, Nikolay. 2013. "The Ottoman State and the Semi-Nomadic Groups along the Ottoman Danubian Serhad (Frontier Zone) in the Late 15th and the First Half of the 16th Centuries: Challenges and Policies." *Hungarian Studies* 27, 219–35.

Apostolopoulos, Dimitris G. 2007. "Du sultan au basileus? dilemmes politiques du conquérant." In Paolo Odorico, ed., *Le patriarcat œcuménique de Constantinople aux XIVe-XVIe siècles: rupture et continuité; Actes du colloque international, Rome, 5-6-7 décembre 2005*. Paris, 241–51.

Arbel, Benjamin. 1995. *Trading Nations: Jews and Venetians in the Early Modern Eastern Mediterranean*. Leiden and New York.

————. 2002. "Maps of the World for Ottoman Princes? Further Evidence and Questions concerning the 'Mappamondo of Hajji Ahmed.'" *Imago Mundi* 54, 1, 19–29.

Arnakis, Georgiades G. 1951. "Gregory Palamas among the Turks and Documents of His Captivity as Historical Sources." *Speculum* 26, 1, 104–18.

Arslan, Mehmet, ed. 2013. *Hadikatü'l-Vüzera ve Zeylleri: Osmanlı Sadrazamları.* Istanbul.

Artner, Edgár. 1926. "Magyarország és az apostoli szentszék viszonya a mohácsi vészt megelőző években, 1521–1526." In Imre Lukinich, ed., *Mohácsi Emlékkönyv.* Budapest, 63–124.

————. 2004. *Hungary as Propugnaculum of Western Christianity: Documents from the Vatican Secret Archives (ca. 1214–1606).* Edited by Kornél Szovák, József Török, and Péter Tusor. Rome and Budapest.

Árvai, Tünde. 2013. "A házasságok szerepe a Garaiak hatalmi törekvéseiben." In Tamás Fedeles, Márta Font, and Gergely Kiss, eds., *Kor-szak-határ: A Kárpát-medence és a szomszédos birodalmak (900–1800).* Pécs, 103–18.

Aşıkpaşazade. (A.H. 1332)1916. *Tevârih-i Âl-i Osman: Âşıkpaşazâde Tarihi.* Edited by Ali. Istanbul.

Atçıl, Abdurrahman. 2017. *Scholars and Sultans in the Early Modern Ottoman Empire.* Cambridge.

Atçıl, Zahit. 2016. "Why Did Süleyman the Magnificent Execute His Son Şehzade Mustafa in 1553?" *OA* 48, 67–103.

Ateş, Ahmet. 1953. "İstanbul'un Fethine Dair Fatih Sultan Mehmed Tarafından Gönderilen Mektuplar ve Bunlara Gelen Cevaplar." *TD* 4, 7, 11–50.

Aydın, Bilgin, and Rıfat Günalan. 2007. "XVI. Yüzyılda Osmanlı Eyalet Defterdarlıklarının Ortaya Çıkışı ve Gelişimi." *OA* 30, 57–73.

Aydın, Dündar. 1998. *Erzurum Beylerbeyiliği ve Teşkilatı.* Ankara.

Aydın, Mahir. 2018. "The Belgrade Fortress before the Treaty of Passarowitz (1697–1717)." In Srđan Rudić, Selim Aslantaş, and Dragana Amedoski, eds. *Belgrade 1521–1867.* Belgrade, 101–27.

Aziz Efendi. 1985. *Kanûn-nâme-i Sultânî Li Azîz Efendi (Aziz Efendi's Book of Sultanic Laws and Regulations; An Agenda for Reform by a Seventeenth-Century Ottoman Statesman).* Edited by Rhoads Murphey. Cambridge, MA.

B. Szabó, János, ed. 2006. *Mohács.* Budapest.

————. 2015. *Mohács. Régi kérdések, új válaszok. A Magyar Királyság hadserege az 1526. évi mohácsi csatában.* Budapest.

Babinger, Franz. 1927. "Der Pfortendolmetsch Murad und seine Schriften." In Franz Babinger et al., ed., *Literaturdenkmäler aus Ungarns Türkenzeit.* Berlin, 33–53.

————. 1978. *Mehmed the Conqueror and His Time.* Translated by Ralph Manheim. Edited by William C. Hickman. Princeton, NJ.

Babur, Zahiruddin Muhammed. 1922. *Babur-Nama (Memoirs of Babur).* Translated from the original Turki Text by Annette Susannah Beveridge. 2 vols. New Delhi.

————. 1993. *Bâburnâme.* Part Three. Chaghatay Turkish Text with Abdul-Rahim Khankhanan's Persian Translation. Turkish Transcription, Persian Edition, and English Translation by W. M. Thackston. Cambridge, MA.

Bacqué-Grammont, Jean Louis. 1963. "Kanunî Sultan Süleyman'ın I. François'ya İki Mektubu." *TAD* 8, 14, 89–98.

————.1987. *Les Ottomans, les Safavides et leurs voisins: contribution à l'histoire des relations internationales dans l'Orient islamique de 1514 à 1524*. Istanbul.

————. 1997. "À propos de Yûnus Beg, *Baş Tercüman* de Soliman le Magnifique." In Hitzel 1997, 23–39.

Bacqué-Grammont, Jean Louis, and Anne Kroell. 1988. *Mamlouks, Ottomans et Portugais en mer rouge. L'affaire de Djedda en 1517*. Cairo.

Bagi, Zoltán Péter. 2011. *A császári-királyi mezei hadsereg a tizenöt éves háborúban: Hadszervezet, érdekérvényesítés, reformkísérletek*. Budapest.

Bak, János, and Béla K. Király, eds. 1982. *From Hunyadi to Rákóczi: War and Society in Late Medieval and Early Modern Hungary*. New York.

Balisch, Alexander. 1983. "Infantry Battlefield Tactics in the Seventeenth and Eighteenth Centuries on the European and Turkish Theaters of War: The Austrian Response to Different Conditions. *Studies in History and Politics* 3, 43–60.

Balogh, István. 1929. *Velencei diplomaták Magyarországról (1500–1526)*. Szeged.

Balogh, Jolán. 1966. *A művészet Mátyás király udvarában*. 2 vols. Budapest.

Bánffy, György. 1993. *Második János, Magyarország választott királyának Második Szulejmán török császárhoz menetele rendje és módja*. Edited by József Bessenyei. Budapest.

Bang, Peter F., and Dariusz Kołodziejczyk, eds. 2012. *Universal Empire: A Comparative Approach to Imperial Culture and Representation in Eurasian History*. Cambridge.

Bárdossy, László. 1943. *Magyar politika a mohácsi vész után*. Budapest.

Bariska, István, ed. 1982. *Kőszeg ostromának emlékezete*. Budapest.

Barkan, Ömer Lütfi. 1943. *XV ve XVIıncı Asırlarda Osmanlı İmparatorluğunda Zirai Ekonomisinin Hukuki ve Mali Esasları. Kanunlar*. Istanbul.

————. 1949–54. "Osmanlı İmparatorluğunda bir İskan ve Kolonizasyon Metodu Olarak Sürgünler." *İFM* 11 (1949–50), 524–70; 13 (1951–52), 56–78; 15 (1953–54), 209–37.

————. 1953–54. "H. 933–934 (M. 1527–1528) Malî Yılına ait Bir Bütçe Örneği." *İFM* 15, 251–329.

————. 1957–58. "954–955 (M. 1547–1548) Malî Yılına ait Bir Osmanlı Bütçesi." *İFM* 19, 219–76.

Barker, Thomas Mack. 1967. *Double Eagle and Crescent: Vienna's Second Turkish Siege and Its Historical Setting*. Albany, NY.

Barkey, Karen. 1994. *Bandits and Bureaucrats: The Ottoman Route to State Centralization*. Ithaca, NY.

Baron, Salo Wittmayer. 1983. *A Social and Religious History of the Jews*. Vol. 18. *The Ottoman Empire, Persia, Ethiopia, India and China*. New York.

Barta, Gábor. 1971. "Ludovicus Gritti magyar kormányzósága (1531–1534)." *TSz* 14, 3–4, 289–319.

————. 1979. *Az erdélyi fejedelemség születése*. Budapest.

————. 1983. *A Sztambulba vezető út (1526–1528)*. Budapest.

————. 1986. "Egy magyar politikus a középkori Magyarország széthullása éveiben (Werbőczy István kancellár, 1526–1541)." In Rúzsás and Szakály 1986, 275–322.

————. 1988. *Vajon kié az ország?* Budapest.

————. 1995. "Az elfelejtett hadszíntér 1526–1528. (Megjegyzések a török-magyar szövetség előtörténetéhez.) *TSz* 37, 1, 1–34.

———, ed. 1996. *Két tárgyalás Sztambulban*. Budapest.

———. 2001. "The First Period of the Principality of Transylvania (1526–1606)." In László Makkai and András Mócsy, eds., *History of Transylvania*. Vol. 1, *From the Beginnings to 1606*. Highland Lakes, NJ.

Bartoniek, Emma. 1975. *Fejezetek a XVI–XVII. századi magyarországi történetírás történetéből*. Budapest.

Bartusis, Mark C. 1992. *The Late Byzantine Army: Arms and Society, 1204–1453*. Philadelphia, PA.

Bayerle, Gustav. 1972. *Ottoman Diplomacy in Hungary: Letters from the Pashas of Buda 1590–1593*. Bloomington, IN.

———. 1980. "The Compromise at Zsitvatorok." *AO* 6, 5–53.

———. 1991. *The Hungarian Letters of Ali Pasha of Buda: 1604–1616*. Budapest.

Bayır, Önder. 2014. *Sultan Dördüncü Murad'ın Hatt-ı Hümayunları*. Istanbul.

Bazarova, Tatiana. 2015. "The Process of Establishing the Border between Russia and the Ottoman Empire in the Peace Treaty of Adrianople (1713)." In Maria Baramova, Grigor Boykov, and Ivan Parvev, eds., *Bordering Early Modern Europe*. Wiesbaden, 121–32.

Benda, Kálmán. 1966. "Zrínyi Miklós, a szigetvári hős." In Ruzsás 1966, 15–51.

Bende, Lajos. 1966. "Sziget ostroma 1566-ban." In Ruzsás 1966, 61–104.

Bennett, Milton, J. 1998. "Intercultural Communication: A Current Perspective." In Milton J. Bennett ed., *Basic Concepts of Intercultural Communication: Selected Readings*. Yarmouth, ME.

Benton, Lauren. 2010. *A Search for Sovereignty: Law and Geography in European Empires, 1400–1900*. New York.

Benzoni, Gino. 2002. "Gritti, Andrea." *Dizionario Biografico degli Italiani*. Vol. 59. Rome. http://www.treccani.it/enciclopedia/andrea-gritti_%28Dizionario-Biografico%29/ (retrieved 7 March 2019).

Bethencourt, Francisco, and Florike Egmond, eds. 2007. *Cultural Exchange in Early Modern Empire, II. Correspondence and Cultural Exchange in Europe, 1400–1700*. Cambridge.

Beydilli, Kemal. 2017. "II. Murad'in Eşi Sırp Prensesi Mara Branković." *OA* 49, 383–412.

Bicheno, Hugh. 2003. *Crescent and Cross: The Battle of Lepanto 1571*. London.

Biegman, Nicolaas H. 1963. "Ragusan Spying for the Ottoman Empire: Some XVIth-Century Documents from the State Archives of Dubrovnik." *Belleten* 26, 106, 237–55.

———. 1968. *The Turco-Ragusan Relationship: According to the Firmāns of Murād III (1575–1595) Extant in the State Archives of Dubrovnik*. The Hague.

Bilge, Reha. 2012. *II. Bayezid: Deniz Savaşları ve Büyük Strateji*. Istanbul.

Bisaha, Nancy. 2004. *Creating East and West: Renaissance Humanists and the Ottoman Turks*. Philadelphia, PA.

Biščević, Vedad. 2006. *Bosanski namjesnici Osmanskog doba (1463–1878)*. Sarajevo.

Black, Jeremy. 1991. *A Military Revolution? Military Change and European Society, 1550–1800*. London.

———. 2010. *A History of Diplomacy*. London.

———. 2011. *Beyond the Military Revolution: War in the Seventeenth-Century World*. Houndmills, UK.

Blanchet, Marie–Hélène. 2008. *Georges-Gennadios Scholarios (vers 1400– vers 1472). Un intellectuel orthodoxe face à la disparition de l'empire byzantin*. Paris.

Boeck, Brian J. 2009. *Imperial Borderlands: Cossack Communities and Empire-Building in the Age of Peter the Great.* Cambridge.

Bohnstedt, John W. 1968. "The Infidel Scourge of God: The Turkish Menace as Seen by German Pamphleteers of the Reformation Era." *Transactions of the American Philosophical Society* 58, 1–58.

Bojanić, Dušanka. 1985. "Požarevac u XVI veku i Bali-beg Jahjapašić." *Istorijski časopis* 32, 49–77.

Bojović, Boško I. 1998. *Raguse (Dubrovnik) et l'Empire ottoman (1430–1520), les actes impériaux ottomans en vieux-serbe de Murad II à Sélim Ier.* Paris.

Bölcskey, Ödön. 1924. *Capistranói Szent János élete és kora.* 3 vols. Székesfehérvár.

Bonney, Richard, ed. 1995a. *Economic Systems and State Finance.* Oxford.

———. 1995b. "Revenue." In Bonney 1995a, 423–505.

Boogert, Maurits H. van den. 2005. *The Capitulations and the Ottoman Legal System: Qadis, Consuls, and Beraths in the 18th Century.* Leiden and New York.

Börekçi, Günhan. 2006. "A Contribution to the Military Revolution Debate: The Janissaries Use of Volley Fire during the Long Ottoman-Habsburg War of 1593–1606 and the Problem of Origins." *AOH* 59, 407–38.

Borosy, András. 1971. *A telekkatonaság és a parasztság szerepe a feudális magyar hadszervezetben.* Budapest.

———. 1982. "The *militia portalis* in Hungary before Mohács." In Bak and Király 1982, 63–80.

Borzsák, István. 1988. "A 'Hungarian History' through Turkish Eyes and the Alexander the Great Tradition." In Róbert Dán, ed., *Occident and Orient: A Tribute to the Memory of Alexander Scheiber.* Leiden and New York, 31–38.

Boškov, Vančo. 1980. "Odnos Srpske i turske diplomatike." *Jugoslovenski istorijski časopis* 19, 3–4, 219–36.

Bostan, İdris. 1992. *Osmanlı Bahriye Teşkilâtı: XVII. Yüzyılda Tersâne-i Âmire.* Ankara.

———. 1994. "Derya Beyi." *DIA* 9, 200–201.

———. (2001) 2006. "Osmanlıların Denizlere Açılma Sürecinde Gelibolu." In *Avrupa'ya İlk Adım. Uluslararası Sempozyum.* Istanbul, 2001, 47–61. Reprinted and cited here from Bostan 2006, 33–46.

———. 2005. *Kürekli ve Yelkenli Osmanlı Gemileri.* Üsküdar, Istanbul.

———. 2006. *Beylikten İmparatorluğa Osmanlı Denizciliği.* Istanbul.

———. 2007a. *Osmanlılar ve Deniz: Deniz Organizasyonu, Teşkilat, Gemiler.* Istanbul.

———. 2007b. "Osmanlılarda Deniz Sınırı ve Karasullar Meselesi." In Özlem Kumrular, *Türkler ve Deniz.* Istanbul, 2007, 29–46.

———. 2009a. "II. Bayezid Döneminde Osmanlı Denizciliği." In Bostan and Özbaran 2009, vol. 1, 111–19.

———. 2009b. "Barbaros Hayreddin Paşa. İlk Deniz Beylerbeyi." In Bostan and Özbaran 2009, vol. 1, 143–53.

———. 2009c. "Preveze Deniz Zaferi ve Sonrasında Akdeniz Dünyası." In Bostan and Özbaran 2009, vol. 1, 173–83.

———. 2014. *İstanbul'un 100 Denizcisi.* Istanbul.

Bostan, İdris, and Salih Özbaran, eds. 2009. *Türk Denizcilik Tarihi.* 2 vols. Istanbul.

Botlik, Richárd. 2004. "A Szapolyai család lengyel kapcsolata." *Kút* 3, 2, 18–31.

———. 2013. "Statileo János diplomáciai küldetései János király (1526–1540) uralkodásának idejéből." *Századok*, 147, 813–54.

Brzezinski, Richard, and Velimir Vuksic. 2006. *Polish Winged Hussar, 1500–1775*. Oxford.

Brocquière, Bertrandon de la. 1807. *The Travels of B. de la Brocquière to Palestine, and His Return from Jerusalem Overland to France during the Years 1432 and 1433*. Translated by T. Johnes, Etc. L.P. J. Henderson. n.p.

Brotton, Jerry. 2002. *The Renaissance Bazaar: From the Silk Road to Michelangelo*. Oxford.

Brummett, Palmira Johnson. 1994. *Ottoman Seapower and Levantine Diplomacy in the Age of Discovery*. Albany, NY.

———. 2001. "The Ottomans as a World Power: What We Don't Know about Ottoman Sea-Power." *Oriente Moderno* 81, 1, 1–21.

———. 2015. *Mapping the Ottomans: Sovereignty, Territory, and Identity in the Early Modern Mediterranean*. Cambridge.

Bryer, Anthony. 1975. "Greeks and Turkmens: The Pontic Exception." *Dumbarton Oaks Papers* 29, 113–48.

Büchler, Sándor. 1901. *A zsidók története Budapesten a legrégibb időktől 1867-ig*. Budapest.

Bunes Ibarra, Miguel Ángel de. 2002. "Charles V and the Ottoman War from the Spanish Point of View." *Eurasian Studies*, 1, 2, 161–82.

Burke, Peter. 1999. "Presenting and Re-presenting Charles V." In Wim Blockmans and Hugo Soly, eds., *Charles V and His Time: 1500–1558*. Antwerp, 411–33.

C. Tóth, Norbert. 2016. "A Magyar Királyság 1522. évi költségvetése." In Boglárka Weisz, ed., *Péz, posztó, piac: Gazdaságtörténeti tanulmányok a magyar középkorból*. Budapest, 117–127.

Çakır, Baki. 2006. "Geleneksel Dönem (Tanzimat Öncesi) Osmalı Bütçe Gelirleri." In Genç and Özvar 2006, vol. 1, 167–95.

———. 2016. "Osmanlı Devletinin Bilinen En Eski (1495–1496) Bütçesi ve 1479–1495 Yılı İcmali." *OA* 47, 113–45.

Çalışır, Muhammed Fatih. 2016. "The Grand Vizier Köprülüzade Fazıl Ahmed Pasha (1635–1676) and the Battle of Mogersdorf/Saint Gotthard (1664)." In Sperl, Scheutz, and Strohmeyer 2016, 207–14.

Capponi, Niccolò. 2006. *Victory of the West: The Story of the Battle of Lepanto*. London.

Casale, Giancarlo. 2010. *The Ottoman Age of Exploration*. Oxford.

Celalzade, Mustafa. 1896. Az országok osztályai és az utak felsorolása. In Thúry 1893–96, vol. 2, 112–278.

———. 1981. *Geschichte Sultan Süleymān Ḳānūnīs von 1520 bis 1557, oder, Ṭabaḳāt ül-Memālik ve Derecāt ül-Mesālik*. Edited by Petra Kappert. Wiesbaden.

Cezar, Mustafa. 1965. *Osmanlı Tarihinde Levendler*. Istanbul.

Cezar, Yavuz. 1986. *Osmanlı Maliyesinde Bunalım ve Değişim Dönemi*. Istanbul.

Charrière, Ernest. 1848–60. *Négociations de la France dans le Levant . . .* 4 vols. Paris.

Chase, Kenneth Warren. 2003. *Firearms: A Global History to 1700*. Cambridge.

Chrysostomides, Julian. 2009. "The Byzantine Empire from the Eleventh to the Fifteenth Century." In Fleet 2009, 6–50.

Çipa, Hakki Erdem. 2017. *The Making of Selim: Succession, Legitimacy, and Memory in the Early Modern Ottoman World*. Bloomington. IN

Çizakça, Murat. 2013. "The Ottoman Government and Economic Life: Taxation, Public Finance and Trade Controls." In Faroqhi and Fleet 2013, 241–75.

Coco, Carla, and Flora Manzonetto. 1985. *Baili veneziani alla sublime porta: Storia e caratteristiche dell'Ambasciata veneta a Costantinopoli*. Venice.

Çolak, Hasan. 2015. "Tekfur, fasiliyus and kayser: Disdain, Negligence and Appropriation of Byzantine Imperial Titulature in the Ottoman World." In Marios Hadjianastasis, ed., *Frontiers of the Ottoman Imagination: Studies in Honour of Rhoads Murphey*. Leiden and New York, 5–28.

Couto, Dejanirah. 2015. "Entre confrontations et alliances: Aceh, Malacca et les Ottomans (1520–1568)." *Turcica* 46, 13–61.

Creasy, Edward Shepherd. (1858) 1968. *History of the Ottoman Turks*. Beirut.

Czamanska, Ilona. 2004. "Poland and Turkey in the First Half of the 16th Century–Turning Points." In Zombori 2004, 91–101.

Czigány, István. 2004. *Reform vagy kudarc? Kísérletek a magyarországi katonaság beillesztésére a Habsburg Birodalom haderejébe 1660–1700*. Budapest.

Cziráki, Zsuzsanna. 2016. "Language Students and Interpreters at the Mid-seventeenth-century Habsburg Embassy in Constantinople." *Theatrum Historiae* 19, 27–44.

Dames, Longworth. 1921. "The Portuguese and Turks in the Indian Ocean in the 16th Century." *JRAS* 53, 1, 1–28.

Danişmend, İsmail H. (1947–61) 1971–72. *İzahlı Osmanlı Tarihi Kronolojisi*. 5 vols. Istanbul.

Dankoff, Robert, and Nuran Tezcan. 2011. *Evliyâ Çelebi'nin Nil Haritası "Dürr-i bî misîl în ahbâr-i Nîl."* Istanbul.

Dankoff, Robert, Nuran Tezcan, and Michael D. Sheridan. 2018. *Ottoman Explorations of the Nile: Evliya Çelebi's Map of the Nile and the Nile Journeys in the Book of Travels (Seyahatname)*. Ginko.

Danvers, Frederick Charles. 1894. *The Portuguese in India: Being a History of the Rise and Decline of Their Eastern Empire*. Vol. 1. London.

Darling, Linda T. 1996. *Revenue-Raising and Legitimacy: Tax Collection and Finance Administration in the Ottoman Empire, 1560–1660*. Leiden and New York.

———. 2006. "Public Finances: The Role of the Ottoman Centre." In Faroqhi 2006, 118–31.

———. 2011. "Reformulating the Gazi Narrative: When Was the Ottoman State a Gazi State?" *Turcica* 43, 13–53.

———. 2014. "Nasihatnameler, İcmal Defterleri, and the Timar-Holding Ottoman Elite in the Late Sixteenth Century." *OA* 43, 193–226.

Dávid, Géza. 1992a. "Incomes and Possessions of the *Beglerbegis* of Buda in the Sixteenth Century." In Veinstein 1992, 385–98.

———. 1992b. "Die Bege von Szigetvár im 16. Jahrhundert." *WZKM* 82, 67–96.

———. 1992–93. "The Sancakbegis of Arad and Gyula." *AOH* 46, 2–3, 143–62.

———. 2005. "Adalékok a temesvári ejálet 18. századi történetéhez." In Géza Dávid, *Pasák és bégek uralma alatt*. Budapest, 203–14.

———. 2016. "Maximilian Brandstetter törökországi utazása és Isztambul 16–17. századi népessége." In Horn et al. 2016, 75–90.

Dávid, Géza, and Pál Fodor, eds. 1994a. *Hungarian-Ottoman Military and Diplomatic Relations in the Age of Süleyman the Magnificent*. Budapest.

———. 1994b. "Hungarian-Ottoman Peace Negotiations in 1512–1514." In Dávid and Fodor 1994a, 9–45.

———, eds. 2000. *Ottomans, Hungarians and Habsburgs in Central Europe: The Military Confines in the Era of Ottoman Conquest*. Leiden and New York.

———. 2003. "Ottoman Spy Reports from Hungary." In Ugo Marazzi, ed., *Turcica et Islamica. Studi in memoria di Aldo Gallotta*. Naples, 121–31.

———. 2005. "Changes in the Structure and Strength of the Timariot Army from the Early Sixteenth to the End of the Seventeenth Century." *Eurasian Studies Yearbook* 4, 2, 157–88.

———eds., 2007. *Ransom Slavery along the Ottoman Borders, Early Fifteenth-Early Eighteenth Centuries*. Leiden and New York.

Davies, Brian L. 2007. *Warfare, State and Society on the Black Sea Steppe: 1500–1700*. London.

Davis, James C. 1970. *Pursuit of Power: Venetian Ambassadors' Reports on Spain, Turkey, and France in the Age of Philip II, 1560–1600*. New York.

———. 1974. "Shipping and Spying in the Early Career of a Venetian Doge, 1496–1502." *Studi veneziani* 16, 97–108.

Davis, Robert C. 2003. *Christian Slaves and Muslim Masters: White Slavery in the Mediterranean, the Barbary Coast, and Italy, 1500–1800*. Houndmills, Basingstoke.

Deák, Antal András. 1993. "Ki rajzolta Luigi Ferdinando Marsigli Duna-térképeit?" *Cartographica Hungarica* 3, 30–31.

———. 1994. "Johann Christoph Müller határmenti térképei." *Cartographica Hungarica* 4, 42–45.

———. 1996. "Luigi Ferdinando Marsigli Duna és Magyarország-térképeinek nürnbergi készítői." *Cartographia Hungarica* 5, 18–21.

Defterdâr Sarı Mehmed Paşa. 1995. *Zübde-i Vekayiât: Tahlil ve Metin (1066–1116/1656–1704)*. Edited by Abdülkadir Özcan. Ankara.

De Groot, Alexander. 1994. "The Ottoman Mediterranean since Lepanto (October 7th, 1571): Naval Warfare during the Seventeenth and Eighteenth Centuries." *Anatolica* 20, 269–93.

———. 1997. "Protection and Nationality: The Decline of the Dragomans." In Hitzel 1997, 235–55.

———. 2003. "The Historical Development of the Capitulatory Regime in the Ottoman Middle East from the Fifteenth to the Nineteenth Centuries." *Oriente Moderno, Nuova serie* 22, 83, 575–604.

Delilbaşı, Melek. 1993. "Greek as a Diplomatic Language in the Turkish Chancery." In N.G. Moschonas, ed., *Hē epikoinōnia sto Vyzantio: Praktika tou 2. Diethnous Symposiou, 4–6 Oktōvriou 1990*. Athens, 145–53.

Demetriades, Vassilis. 1993. "Some Thoughts on the Origins of the Devşirme." In Zachariadou 1993a, 23–31.

Deny, Jean, and Jane Laroche. 1969. "L'expédition en Provence de l'armée de mer du Sultan Suleyman sous le commandement de l'amiral Hayreddin pacha, dit Barberousse (1543–1544). (d'après des documents inédits)." *Turcica* 1, 161–211.

DeVries, Kelly. 1997. "Gunpowder Weapons at the Siege of Constantinople, 1453." In Yaacov Lev, ed., *War and Society in the Eastern Mediterranean, 7th-15th Centuries*. Leiden and New York, 343–62.

Diaconescu, Marius. 1998. "The Relations of Vassalage between Sigismund of Luxemburg, King of Hungary, and Mircea the Old, Voivode of Wallachia." *Mediaevalia Transilvanica* 2, 2, 245–82.

Dickson, M. B. 1958. *Shah Tahmasb and the Uzbeks: The Duel for Khurasan with 'Ubayd Khan: 930–946/1524–1540.* PhD Dissertation, Princeton University.

Dincel, Turgut. 2002. "Did the Diversion of a Small Water Course Change the Course of the History?" *EOS. Transactions, American Geophysical Union* 83, 31, 333 and 348. http://onlinelibrary.wiley.com/doi/10.1029/2002EO000246/pdf.

Doğan, Güner. 2017. *"Venediklü ile Dahi Sulh Oluna." 17. ve 18. Yüzyıllarda Osmanlı Venedik İlişkileri.* Istanbul.

Doğru, Halime. 2006. *Lehistan'da bir Osmanlı Sultanı: IV. Mehmed'in Kamaniçe-Hotin Seferleri ve Bir Masraf Defteri.* İstanbul.

Domokos, György. 2000. *Ottavio Baldigara: Egy itáliai várfundáló mester Magyarországon.* Budapest.

Doukas. 1975. *Decline and Fall of Byzantium to the Ottoman Turks.* Edited by Harry J. Magoulias. Detroit.

Dressler, Markus. 2005. "Inventing Orthodoxy: Competing Claims for Authority and Legitimacy in the Ottoman-Safavid Conflict." In Hakan Karateke and Maurus Reinkowski, eds., *Legitimizing the Order: The Ottoman Rhetoric of State Power.* Leiden and New York, 151–73.

Duregger, Sarah. 2015. *Diplomatische Kommunikation zwischen Kaiserhof und Hoher Pforte. Die Berichte der kaiserlichen Residenten Johann Rudolf Schmid zum Schwarzenhorn und Alexander Greiffenklau von Vollrats.* Saarbrücken.

Dursteler, Eric R. 2001. "The Bailo in Constantinople: Crisis and Career in Venice's Early Modern Diplomatic Corps." *MHR* 16, 1–30.

———. 2006. *Venetians in Constantinople: Nation, Identity, and Coexistence in the Early Modern Mediterranean.* Baltimore.

Džaja, Srećko M., Günter Weiß, Mathias Bernath, and Karl Nehring, eds. 1995. *Austro-Turcica 1541–1552: Diplomatische Akten des habsburgischen Gesandtschaftsverkehrs mit der Hohen Pforte im Zeitalter Süleymans des Prächtigen.* Munich.

E. Kovács, Péter. 1995. "Miksa magyarországi hadjárata." *TSz* 37, 35–49.

———. 2005. "Jajca 1464. évi ostroma." In Hausner and Veszprémi 2005, 403–18.

Ebel, Kathryn A. 2008. "Representations of the Frontier in Ottoman Town Views of the Sixteenth Century." *Imago Mundi* 60, 1, 1–22.

Eberhard, Elke. 1970. *Osmanische Polemik gegen die Safawiden im 16. Jahrhundert.* Freiburg im Breisgau.

Edelmayer, Friedrich, Maximilian Lanzinner, and Peter Rauscher, eds. 2003. *Finanzen und Herrschaft: Materielle Grundlagen fürstlicher Politik in den habsburgischen Ländern und im Heiligen Römischen Reich im 16. Jahrhundert.* Wien.

Eldem, Edhem. 2006. "Capitulations and Western Trade." In Faroqhi 2006, 283–335.

———. 2013. "'Strangers in Their Own Seas?' The Ottomans in the Eastern Mediterranean Basin in the Second Half of the Eighteenth Century." In Piero Sanna, ed., *Il Mediterraneo nel Settecento: Identità e scambi.* Naples, 25–58.

Elekes, Lajos. 1952. *Hunyadi.* Budapest.

Ember, Győző. 1946. *Az újkori magyar közigazgatás története Mohácstól a török kiűzéséig.* Budapest.

Emecen, Feridun M. 1993. "Ottoman Policy of Conquest of the Turcoman Principalities of Western Anatolia with Special Reference to Sarukhan Beyliği." In Zachariadou 1993a, 35–40.

―――. (1995) 2003. "Gazaya Dair: XIV. Yüzyıl Kaynakları Arasında Bir Gezinti." In *Prof. Dr. Hakkı Dursun Yıldız Armağanı.* Ankara, 191–97. Cited here from Emecen, *İlk Osmanlılar ve Batı Anadolu Beylikler Dünyası.* 2nd ed. Istanbul, 2003, 75–85.

―――. 1996. "Beylikten Sancağa: Batı Anadolu'da İlk Osmanlı Sancaklarının Kuruluşuna Dair Mülahazalar." *Belleten* 60, 227, 81–91.

―――. 2007. "Çağdaş Osmanlı Kaynaklarında Uzun Savaşlar ve Zıtvatorok Antlaşması ile İlgili Algılama ve Yorum Problemleri." *OA* 29, 87–97.

―――. 2009. "Osmanlı Sınırları Nerede Başlar, Nerede Biter." In *Osmanlı Klâsik Çağında Siyaset.* Istanbul, 195–217.

―――. 2010a. *Zamanın İskenderi, Şarkın Fatihi: Yavuz Sultan Selim.* Istanbul.

―――. 2010b. "Mohaç (1526): Osmanlılara Orta Avrupa'nın Kapılarını Açan Savaş." In *Osmanlı Klâsik Çağında Savaş.* Istanbul, 159–216.

―――. 2012. *Fetih ve Kıyamet, 1453: İstanbul'un Fethi ve Kıyamet Senaryoları.* Istanbul.

Emecen, Feridun M., and İlhan Şahin. 1998. "Osmanlı Taşra Teşkilatının Kaynaklarından 957–958 (1550–1551) Tarihli Sancak Tevcih Defteri I." *Belgeler* 19 (23), 53–98 (and appendix).

Engel, Pál. 1982. "János Hunyadi: The Decisive Years of His Career, 1440–1444." In Bak and Király 1982, 103–23.

―――. 1984. "A szegedi eskü és a váradi béke. Adalék az 1444. év eseménytörténetéhez." In Éva H. Bálázs, Erik Fügedi, and Ferenc Maksay, eds., *Mályusz Elemér Emlékkönyv.* Budapest, 77–96.

―――. 1993. "A magyar királyság jövedelmei Zsigmond korában." In Ferenc Glatz, ed., *A tudomány szolgálatában. Emlékkönyv Benda Kálmán 80. születésnapjára.* Budapest, 27–31.

―――. 1994a. "Magyarország és a török veszély Zsigmond korában (1387–1437)." *Századok* 128, 273–87.

―――. 1994b. "János Hunyadi and the Peace 'of Szeged' (1444)." *AOH* 47, 241–57.

―――. 1997. "Zur Frage der bosnischen-ungarischen Beziehungen im 14.-15. Jahrhundert." *SoF* 56, 27–42.

―――. 1998. "A török-magyar háborúk első évei, 1389–1392." *HK* 111, 3, 12–28.

―――. 2001. *The Realm of St Stephen: A History of Medieval Hungary, 895–1526.* Translated and edited by Tamás Pálosfalvi and Andrew Ayton. London and New York.

Engel, Pál, Gyula Kristó, and András Kubinyi. 1998. *Magyarország története 1301–1526.* Budapest.

Ercan, Yavuz. 1986. *Osmanlı İmparatorluğu'nda Bulgarlar ve Voynuklar.* Ankara.

Ertaş, Mehmet Yaşar. 2007. *Sultanın Ordusu (Mora Fethi Örneği).* Istanbul.

Esin, Emel. 1985. "İkinci Bayezid'in H. 904–906/1498–1500 Yıllarında Adalar Denizine Seferi." *Erdem* 1, 3, 789–94.

Evans, R. J. W. (1979) 2002. *The Making of the Habsburg Monarchy, 1550–1700: An Interpretation.* Oxford.

Eyice, Semavi. 1970. "Elçihanı." *TD* 24, 93–130.

———. 1995. "Elçi Hanı." *DİA* vol. 11, 15–18.

F. Molnár, Mónika. 2006. "Tárgyalási technikák és hatalmi játszmák: A Habsburg és az Oszmán Birodalom közötti határ meghúzása a karlócai békét követően." *Századok* 140, 1475–502.

———. 2013. "Der Friede von Karlowitz und das Osmanische Reich." In Spannenberg and Strohmeyer 2013, 197–220.

Farkas, Gyöngyi. 2000. *A török kor, a kuruc kor, a nemesi felkelés, a királyi magyar nemesi testőrség irataimak levéltári segédlete.* Budapest.

Faroqhi, Suraiya. 1994. *Pilgrims and Sultans: The Hajj under the Ottomans, 1517–1683.* London.

———. 2004. *The Ottoman Empire and the World Around It.* London.

———, ed. 2006. *Cambridge History of Turkey.* Vol. 3, *The Later Ottoman Empire, 1603–1839.* Cambridge.

———. 2010. "The Ottoman Ruling Group and the Religions of Its Subjects in the Early Modern Age, a Survey of Current Research." *JEMH* 14, 239–66.

Faroqhi, Suraiya, and Kate Fleet. 2013. *The Cambridge History of Turkey.* Vol. 2, *The Ottoman Empire as a World Power, 1453–1603.* Cambridge.

Fazekas, István. 2019. "The Central European Habsburg Monarchy in the Middle of the Sixteenth Century—Elements of Cohesion and Division." In Fodor 2019a, 179–92.

Fazekas, István, István Kenyeres, and Béla Sarusi Kiss, eds. 2011. *Segédletek az Osztrák Állami Levéltár [Haus-, Hof- und Staatsarchiv, Finanz- und Hofkammerarchiv] magyar vonatkozású irataihoz.* [PC CD-Rom] Budapest.

Fekete, Lajos. 1925. "Debrecen város levéltárának török oklevelei." *LK* 3, 42–67.

———. 1926a. *Einführung in die osmanisch-türkische Diplomatik der türkischen Botmässigkeit in Ungarn.* Budapest.

———. 1926b. "A velencei állami levéltár magyar vonatkozású fethnáméi." *LK* 4, 139–57.

———. 1929. "A berlini és drezdai gyűjtemények török levéltári anyaga. Második, befejező közlemény." *LK* 7, 55–106.

———. 1930. "A hódoltságkori törökség Magyarországra vonatkozó földrajzi ismeretei." *HK*, 31, 1–17, 134–54.

———. 1932. *Türkische Schriften aus dem Archive des Palatins Nikolaus Esterházy, 1606–1645.* Budapest.

———. 1944. *Budapest a törökkorban.* Budapest.

Fekete, Lajos, and Gyula Káldy-Nagy. 1962a. *Rechnungsbücher türkischer Finanzstellen in Buda (Ofen) 1550–1580. Türkischer Text.* Budapest.

———. 1962b. *Budai török számadáskönyvek 1550–1580.* Budapest.

Fenyvesi, László. 1986. " A (Habsburg)-magyar diplomáciai kapcsolatok krónikája." In J. Kovács 1986, 332–54.

———. 1990. "Magyar-török diplomáciai kapcsolatok Mátyás király haláláig." *HK* 103 (1), 74–99.

Feridun Bey. 1867. *Mecmua münşeat üs-selatin.* [Istanbul]. 2 vols.

Fichtner, Paula Sutter. 1982. *Ferdinand I of Austria: The Politics of Dynasticism in the Age of the Reformation.* Boulder, CO.

———. 2008. *Terror and Toleration: The Habsburg Empire Confronts Islam, 1526–1850.* London.

Filipović, Emir O. 2012. "Ardet ante oculos opulentissimum regnum . . . Venetian Reports about the Ottoman Conquest of the Bosnian Kingdom, A.D. 1463." In Iulian Mihai Damian et al., eds., *Italy and Europe's Eastern Border: (1204–1669)*. Frankfurt, 135–55.

Fine, John V. A. 1994. *The Late Medieval Balkans: A Critical Survey from the Late Twelfth Century to the Ottoman Conquest*. Ann Arbor, MI.

Finkel, Caroline. 1988. *The Administration of Warfare: The Ottoman Military Campaigns in Hungary, 1593–1606*. Vienna.

———. 2006a. *Osman's Dream: The Story of the Ottoman Empire, 1300–1923*. New York.

———. 2006b. "Macaristandaki 1593–1606 Osmanlı-Habsburg Savaşının Maliyeti." In Genç and Özvar 2006, 237–91.

Finkel, Caroline, and Aykut Barka. 1997. "The Sakarya River—Lake Sapanca—İzmit Bay Canal Project: A Reapprisal of the Historical Record in the Light of New Morphological Evidence." *Istanbuler Mitteilungen* 47, 429–42.

Finlay, Robert. 1998. "Prophecy and Politics in Istanbul: Charles V, Sultan Süleyman, and the Habsburg Embassy of 1533–1534." *JEMH* 2, 1–31.

Fisher, Alan W. 1973. "Azov in the Sixteenth and Seventeenth Centuries." *Jahrbücher für Geschichte Osteoropas* 21, 2, 161–74. Reprinted in Fisher 1999, 59–75.

———. (1980) 1999. "Chattel Slavery in the Ottoman Empire." *Slavery & Abolition* 1, 1, 25–45. Cited here from Fisher 1999, 105–27.

———. 1987. *The Crimean Tatars*. Stanford, CA.

———. 1999. *A Precarious Balance: Conflict, Trade, and Diplomacy on the Russian-Ottoman Frontier*. Istanbul.

Fisher, Sydney Nettleton. 1948. *The Foreign Relations of Turkey, 1481–1512*. Urbana, IL.

Fleet, Kate. 1999. *European and Islamic Trade in the Early Ottoman State: The Merchants of Genoa and Turkey*. Cambridge.

———. 2001. "Early Turkish Naval Activities." In Kate Fleet, ed., *The Ottomans and the Sea*, special issue of *Oriente Moderno* 20, 1, 129–38.

———, ed. 2009. *Cambridge History of Turkey*. Vol. 1, *Byzantium to Turkey, 1071–1453*. Cambridge.

Fleischer, Cornell. 1986. *Bureaucrat and Intellectual in the Ottoman Empire: The Historian Mustafa Ali (1541–1600)*. Princeton, NJ.

———. 1992. "The Lawgiver as Messiah: The Making of the Imperial Image in the Reign of Süleyman." In Veinstein 1992, 159–77.

Floor, Willem. 2001. *Safavid Government Institutions*. Costa Mesa, CA.

Fodor, Pál. 1991. "Ottoman Policy towards Hungary, 1520–1541." *AOH* 45, 2–3, 271–345.

———. 1996. "Das Wilajet von Temeschwar zur Zeit der osmanischen Eroberung." *SoF* 55, 25–44.

———. 2000. "The View of the Turk in Hungary: The Apocalyptic Tradition and the Red Apple in Ottoman-Hungarian Context." In Pál Fodor, *In Quest of the Golden Apple: Imperial Ideology, Politics, and Military Administration in the Ottoman Empire*. Istanbul, 71–103.

———. 2006. *Válallkozásra kényszerítve. Az oszmán pénzügyigazgatás és hatalmi elit változásai a 16–17. század fordulóján*. Budapest.

———. 2009. "Ottoman Warfare, 1300–1453." In Fleet 2009, 192–226.

————. 2010. "A váci harmincad és egy hódoltsági főember a 16. századból: Oszmán aga, cselebi és bég." *TSz* 52, 329–40.

————. 2015. *The Unbearable Weight of Empire: The Ottomans in Central Europe–a Failed Attempt at Universal Monarchy (1390–1566)*. Budapest.

————, ed. 2016. *Egy elfeledett ostrom emlékezete: Szigetvár, 1556—Remembering a Forgotten Siege: Szigetvár 1556*. Budapest.

————. 2018. *The Business of State: Ottoman Finance Administration and Ruling Elites in Transition (1580s–1615)*. Berlin. [English translation of Fodor 2006]

————, ed. 2019a. *The Battle for Central Europe*. Leiden and New York.

————. 2019b. "Wolf on the Border: Yahyapaşaoğlu Bali Bey (?–1527)." In Fodor, Kovács, and Péri 2019, 57–87.

Fodor, Pál, Nándor E. Kovács, and Benedek Péri, eds. 2019. *Şerefe: Studies in Honour of Prof. Géza Dávid on His Seventieth Birthday*. Budapest.

Fodor, Pál, and Szabolcs Varga eds. 2020. *Egy elfeledett magyar királyi dinasztia: A Szapolyaiak*. Budapest

Fotić, Aleksandar. 2001. "Yahyapaşa-oglu Mehmed Pasha's Evkaf in Belgrade." *AOH* 54, 437–52.

————. 2005. "Non-Ottoman Documents in the Kadi's Courts (Moloviya, Medieval Charters): Examples from the Archive of the Hilandar Monastery (15th–18th C.)." In Imber, Kiyotaki, and Murphey 2005, vol. 2, 63–73.

————. 2009. "Serbian Orthodox Church." In Ágoston and Masters 2009, 519–20.

Fraknói, Vilmos. 1890. *Hunyadi Mátyás király, 1440–1490*. Budapest.

————. 1899. *Werbőczi István életrajza*. Budapest.

————. 1921. *A magyar királyválasztások története*. Budapest.

Francisco, Adam S. 2007. *Martin Luther and Islam: A Study in Sixteenth-Century Polemics and Apologetics*. Leiden and Boston.

Frost, Robert. 2000. *The Northern Wars: War, State, and Society in Northeastern Europe, 1558–1721*. Harlow, England.

Fuchs, Martina, and Alfred Kohler, eds. 2003. *Kaiser Ferdinand I: Aspekte eines Herrscherlebens*. Münster.

Fuchs, Martina, Teréz Oborni, and Gábor Újváry, eds. 2005. *Kaiser Ferdinand I: Ein mitteleuropäischer Herrscher*. Münster.

Fuess, Albrecht. 2001. *Verbranntes Ufer: Auswirkungen mamlukischer Seepolitik auf Beirut und die syro-palästinensische Küste (1250–1517)*. Leiden and New York.

Fügedi, Erik. 1976. *Kimondhatatlan nyomorúság. Két emlékirat a 15–16. századi oszmán fogságról*. Budapest.

————. 1980. "Coronation in Medieval Hungary." *Studies in Medieval and Renaissance History* 3, 157–89.

————. 1982. "Mátyás király jövedelme 1475-ben." *Századok* 116, 484–506.

G. Etényi, Nóra. 2016. "Miklós Zrínyi through the Public Eye in the Holy Roman Empire." In Hausner 2016, 282–337.

Galanti, Avram. 1995. *Türkler ve Yahudiler*. Istanbul.

Geanakoplos, Deno John. 1989. *Constantinople and the West: Essays on the Late Byzantine (Palaeologan) and Italian Renaissances and the Byzantine and Roman Churches*. Madison, WI.

Gebei, Sándor. 2004. *II. Rákóczi György külpolitikája*. Budapest.

———. 2007. *Az erdélyi fejedelmek és a lengyel királyválasztások*. Szeged.

Gemil, Tasin. 1983. "Quelques observations concernant la conclusion de la paix entre la Molda-vie et l'Empire Ottoman (1486) et la delimitation de leur frontière." *Revue roumaine d'histoire* 3, 225–38.

———. 2009. *Romanians and Ottomans in the XIVth–XVIth Centuries*. Translated by Remus Bejan and Paul Sanders. Bucharest.

Genç, Mehmet. 1975. "Osmanlı Maliyesinde Malikane Sistemi." In Osman Okyar, ed., *Türkiye İktisat Tarihi Semineri*. Ankara, 231–96. Reprinted in Genç 2000, 99–149.

———. 2000. *Osmanlı İmparatorluğunda Devlet ve Ekonomi*. Istanbul.

Genç, Mehmet, and Erol Özvar, eds. 2006. *Osmanlı Maliyesi. Kurumlar ve Bütçeler*. 2 vols. Istanbul.

Geőcze, István. 1894. "Hadi tanácskozások az 1577-ik évben." *HK* 7, 502–37, 647–73.

Georgius de Hungaria. 1976. *Magyarországi György barát értekezése a törökök szokásairól, viszonyairól és gonoszságáról*. In Fügedi 1976, 5–148.

———. 1977. *Értekezése a törökök szokásairól, viszonyairól és gonoszságáról*. Translated by Győző Kenéz. In Tardy 1977, 49–153.

Gerlach, Stephan. (1674) 1986. *Stephan Gerlach naplója*. In Kovács 1986, 89–258.

Gévay, Antal. 1838–42. *Urkunden und Actenstücke zur Geschichte der Verhältnisse zwischen Öster-reich, Ungern und der Pforte im XVI. und XVII. Jahrhunderte. Aus Archiven und Bibliotheken*. 3 vols. Vienna.

———. 1841. *A budai pasák*. Vienna.

Gezer, Ömer. 2016. *Kale ve Nefer. Habsburg Sınırında Osmanlı Askeri Gücünün Yeniden Örgütlen-mesi (1699–1715)*. PhD thesis, Hacettepe Üniversitesi Sosyal Bilimler Enstitüsü Tarih Anabilim Dali, Ankara.

Glete, Jan. 2000. *Warfare at Sea, 1500–1650*. London.

Godsey, William D. 2018. *The Sinews of Habsburg Power: Lower Austria in a Fiscal-Military State 1650–1820*. Oxford.

Goffman, Daniel. 2002. *The Ottoman Empire and Early Modern Europe*. Cambridge.

———. 2007. "Negotiating with the Renaissance State: The Ottoman Empire and the New Diplomacy." In Aksan and Goffman 2007, 61–74.

Gökbilgin, Özalp. 1973. *1532–1577 Yılları Arasında Kırım Hanlığı'nın Siyasi Durumu*. Ankara.

Gökbilgin, Tayyib M. 1952. "Kara Üveys Paşanın Budin Beylerbeyliği (1578–1580)." *TD* 2, 3–4, 17–34.

———. 1957. "Arz ve Raporlara Göre İbrahim Paşanın İrakeyn Seferindeki İlk Tedbirleri ve Fütuhatı." *Belleten* 21, 83, 449–87.

———. 1958. "Korvin Mathias (Mátyás)'ın Bayezid II'e Mektupları, Tercümeleri ve 1503 (909) Osmanlı–Macar Muahedesinin Türkçe Metni." *Belleten*. 22, 87, 369–81.

———. 1965. "15. ve 16. Asırlarda Eyalet-i Rum." *VD* 6, 51–61.

———. 1966. "Kanuni Süleyman'ın 1566 Szigetvar Seferi Sebepleri ve Hazırlıkları." *TD* 16, 21, 1–14.

Göksoy, İsmail Hakkı. 2004. *Güneydoğu Asya'da Osmanlı-Türk Tesirleri*. Isparta.

Göllner, Carl. 1961–68. *Turcica. Die Europäische Türkendrücke des XV Jahrhunderts*. 2 vols. Bu-charest and Berlin.

———. 1978. *Turcica. Die Türkenfrage in der öffentlichen Meinung Europas im 16. Jahrhundert*. Bucharest and Baden-Baden.

González de León, Fernando. 2004. "Spanish Military Power and the Military Revolution." In Geoff Mortimer, ed., *Early Modern Military History, 1450–1815*. Basingstoke, 25–42.

Gooss, Roderich, ed. 1911. *Österreichische Staatsverträge: Fürstentum Siebanbürgen, 1526–1690*. Vienna.

Göyünç, Nejat. 1999. "Osmanlı Devletinde Taşra Teşkilatı." In Güler Eren, ed., *Osmanlı*. Vol. 6, *Teşkilat*. Ankara, 77–88.

———. 2000. "Provincial Organization of the Ottoman Empire in Pre-Tanzimat Period." In Kemal Çicek, ed., *The Great Ottoman-Turkish Civilisation*. Vol. 3. Ankara, 519–32.

Gradeva, Rossitsa. 2004. "Administrative System and Provincial Government in the Central Balkan Territories of the Ottoman Empire, 15th Century." In Rossitsa Gradeva, *Rumeli under the Ottomans: Institutions and Communities*. Istanbul, 23–51.

Graf, Tobias. 2017. *The Sultan's Renegades: Christian-European Converts to Islam and the Making of the Ottoman Elite, 1575–1610*. Oxford.

Greene, Molly. 2000. *A Shared World: Christians and Muslims in the Early Modern Mediterranean*. Princeton, NJ.

Griswold, William J. 1983. *The Great Anatolian Rebellion, 1000–1020/1591–1611*. Berlin.

Grotius, Hugo. (1609) 2004. *The Free Sea*. Indianapolis, IN. E-book

Guboglu, Mihail. 1968. "Fatih Sultan Mehmed ve Yavuz Sultan Selim'in Boğdan Voyvodalarına Yazdıkları Slavca Mektuplar." In *BTTD* 19, 31–36.

Guilmartin, John Francis. 1995. "The Military Revolution: Origins and First Tests Abroad." In C. Rogers 1995, 299–333.

———. 2003. *Gunpowder & Galleys: Changing Technology and Mediterranean Warfare at Sea in the 16th Century*. Revised ed. Annapolis, MD.

Gülderen, Jusuf. 1983. "Turska brodogradilišta na Dunavu i njegovim pritokama u drugoj polovini XVI veka." In Vasa Čubrilović, ed., *Plovidba na Dunavu i njegovim pritokama kroz vekove*. Belgrade, 1983, 179–91.

Gülsoy, Ersin. 2004. *Girit'in Fethi ve Osmanlı İdaresinin Kurulması (1645–1670)*. Istanbul.

Günergun Feza, and Dhruv Raina, eds. 2011. *Science between Europe and Asia: Historical Studies on the Transmission, Adoption and Adaptation of Knowledge*. New York.

Güngörürler, Selim. 2016. *Diplomacy and Political Relations between the Ottoman Empire and Safavid Iran, 1639–1722*. PhD dissertation, Georgetown University.

———. 2018. "Fundamentals of Ottoman-Safavid Peacetime Relations, 1639–1722." *THR* 9, 151–97.

———. 2019. "Fraternity, Perpetual Peace, and Alliance in Ottoman-Safavid Relations, 1688–98: A Diplomatic Revolution in the Middle East." *Turcica* 50, 145–207.

Gürkan, Emrah Safa. 2010. "The Centre and the Frontier: Ottoman Cooperation with the North African Corsairs in the Sixteenth Century." *THR* 1, 125–63.

———. 2015. "Mediating Boundaries: Mediterranean Go-Betweens and Cross-Confessional Diplomacy in Constantinople, 1560–1600." *JEMH* 19, 107–28.

———. 2017. *Sultanın Casusları*. Istanbul.

———. 2018. "Laying Hands on Arcana Imperii: Venetian Baili as Spymasters in Sixteenth-Century Istanbul." In Paul Maddrell et al., ed., *Spy Chiefs*. Vol. 2, *Intelligence Leaders in Europe, the Middle East, and Asia*. Washington, DC, 67–96.

Győry, Tibor. 1900. *Morbus Hungaricus: Orvostörténelmi tanulmány*. Budapest.

Habardanecz, János. (1528–29) 1996. *"Habardanecz, János jelentése 1528. nyári sztambuli tárgyalásairól."* In Barta 1996, 173–203.

Hadnagy, Szabolcs. 2010. "Köprülü Mehmed egri kormányzósága–egy oszmán államférfi életrajzának kérdőjelei." *Keletkutatás* 2010 tavasz, 107–13.

Hadrovics, László. 1991. *Vallás, egyház, nemzettudat. (A szerb egyház nemzeti szerepe a török uralom alatt)*. Budapest.

Haidar, Mansura. 2002. *Central Asia in the Sixteenth Century*. New Delhi.

Halaçoğlu, Yusuf. 2002. *Osmanlılarda Ulaşım ve Haberleşme (Menziller)*. Ankara.

Hale, J. R. 1985. *War and Society in Renaissance Europe, 1450–1620*. London.

Halecki, Oskar. 1943. *The Crusade of Varna: A Discussion of Controversial Problems*. New York.

Hall, A. Rupert. 1969. "Science, Technology, and Warfare, 1400–1700." In Wright and Paszek 1969, 3–24.

Hall, Bert. 1997. *Weapons and Warfare in Renaissance Europe: Gunpowder, Technology, and Tactics*. Baltimore, MD.

Hamilton, Alastair. 1994. "An Egyptian Traveller in the Republic of Letters: Josephus Barbatus or Abudacnus the Copt." *Journal of the Warburg and Courtlauld Institutes* 57, 123–50.

———. 2009. "Michel d'Asquier, Imperial Interpreter and Bibliophile." *Journal of the Warburg and Courtlauld Institutes* 72, 237–41.

Hammer, Joseph von. 1827–35. *Geschichte des osmanischen Reiches . . .* 10 vols. Pest.

Hanciç, Adem. 1985. "XVII. Yüzyılda Bosna Eyaletinde Sınır Karakollarının Teşkilatı Hakkında." In *Beşinci Milletler Arası Türkoloji Kongresi. Tebliğler. III. Türk Tarihi*. Istanbul, 263–70.

Harley, J. B., and David Woodward, eds. 1992. *The History of Carthography*. Vol. 2, book 1, *Cartography in the Traditional Islamic and South Asian Societies*. Chicago and London.

Harris, Jonathan. 1995. *Greek Emigres in the West 1400–1520*. Camberley.

Hathaway, Jane. 2008. With contributions by Karl Barbir. *The Arab Lands under Ottoman Rule, 1516–1800*. London and New York.

Hatvani (Horváth), Mihály. 1857–59. *Magyar történelmi okmánytár: A Brüsseli országos levéltárból és a Burgundi könyvtárból*. 4 vols. Pest.

Hausner, Gábor, ed. 2016. *Zrínyi Album*. Budapest.

Hausner, Gábor, and József Padányi, eds. 2012. *Zrínyi-Újvár emlékezete*. Budapest.

Hausner, Gábor, and László Veszprémi, eds. 2005. *Perjés Géza Emlékkönyv*. Budapest.

Hazai, György. 1955. "A Topkapu Szeráj Múzeumának magyar vonatkozású iratai." *LK 26*, 286–95.

———. 1977. "Zur Rolle des Serbischen im Verkehr des Osmanischen Reiches mit Osteuropa im 15–16 Jahrundert." In Gyula Decsy et al., eds., *Eurasia Nostratica: Festschrift für Karl Heinrich Menges*. Wiesbaden, 82–88.

Headley, John M. 1982. "Germany, the Empire and *Monarchia* in the Thought and Policy of Gattinara." In Heinrich Lutz, ed., *Das römisch-deutsche Reich im politischen System Karls V*. Munich, 15–47.

Hegyi, Klára. 1988. *Jászberény török levelei*. Szolnok.

———. 1994. "The Ottoman Military Force in Hungary." In Dávid and Fodor 1994a, 131–48.

———. 1995. *Török berendezkedés Magyarországon*. Budapest.

———. 2000. "The Ottoman Network of Fortresses in Hungary." In Dávid and Fodor 2000, 163–93.

———. 2007. *A török hódoltság várai és várkatonái*. 3 vols. Budapest.

———. 2018. *The Ottoman Military Organization in Hungary: Fortresses, Fortress Garrisons and Finances*. Berlin. [Condensed English translation of Hegyi 2007]

Hering, Gunnar. 1994. "Panagiotis Nikousios als Dragoman der kaiserlichen Gesandtschaft in Konstantinopel." *Jahrbuch der österreichischen Byzantinistik* 44, 143–78.

Hersek, Bosna ve İzvornik. (1520–33) 2005. Yusuf Sarınay et al., eds. *91,164, MAD 540 ve 173 Numaralı Hersek, Bosna ve İzvornik Livaları İcmal Tahrir Defterleri (926–939/ 1520–1533)*. Ankara.

Hess, Andrew C. 1972. "The Battle of Lepanto and Its Place in Mediterranean History." *Past and Present*, 57, 53–73.

———. 1978. *The Forgotten Frontier: A History of the Sixteenth-Century Ibero-African Frontier*. Chicago.

Heywood, Colin. 1976–77. "Some Turkish Archival Sources for the History of the Menzilhane Network in Rumeli during the Eighteenth Century (Notes and Documents on the Ottoman Ulak, I)." *Boğaziçi Üniversitesi Dergisi* 4–5, 39–54.

———. 1984. "English Diplomatic Relations with Turkey, 1689–1698." In William Hale and Ali Ihsan Bağış, eds., *Four Centuries of Turco-British Relations*. Walkington, 1984, 26–39.

———. 1996. "The Via Egnatia in the Ottoman Period: The *Menzilhane*s of the *Sol Kol* in the Late 17th/Early 18th Century." In Zachariadou 1996, 129–44.

———. 1999. "The Frontier in Ottoman History: Old Ideas and New Myths." In Daniel Power and Naomi Standen, eds., *Frontiers in Question: Eurasian Borderlands, 700–1700*. New York, 228–50.

———. 2004. "The 1337 Bursa Inscription and Its Interpreters." *Turcica* 36, 215–31.

———. 2006. "The Shifting Chronology of the Chyhyryn (Çehrin) Campaign (1089/1678) According to the Ottoman Literary Sources, and the Problem of the Ottoman Calendar." In Kermeli and Özel, 2006, 283–95.

Heywood, Colin, and Colin Imber. 1994. *Studies in Ottoman History in Honour of Professor V. L. Ménage*. Istanbul.

Hiller, István. 1992. *Palatin Nikolaus Esterházy: Die ungarische Rolle in der Habsburgerdiplomatie, 1625–1645*. Vienna.

———. 1993. "A tolmácsper." In Ildikó Horn, ed., *Perlekedő évszázadok. Tanulmányok Für Lajos történész 60. Születésnapjára*. Budapest, 147–86.

———. 1998. "A titkos levelezők intézménye." In Péter Tusor et al., eds., *R. Várkonyi Ágnes emlékkönyv születésének 70. évfordulója ünnepére*. Budapest, 204–15.

———. 2016. "A Habsburg diplomáciában játszott magyar szerep kérdései (1606–1648)." In Horn et al. 2016, 255–70.

Hillerbrand, Hans Joachim. 2007. *The Division of Christendom: Christianity in the Sixteenth Century*. Louisville, KY.

Hitzel, Frédéric, ed. 1997. *Istanbul et les langues orientales*. Paris and Montreal.

Hochedlinger, M. 2003. *Austria's Wars of Emergence: War, State and Society in the Habsburg Monarchy, 1683–1797*. Harlow.

Hodgson, Marshall G. S. 1974. *The Venture of Islam: Conscience and History in a World Civilization*. Vol. 3. *The Gunpowder Empires and Modern Times*. Chicago. IL

Holub, József. 1923. "Kutatások a párisi levéltárakban." *LK* 1, 69–97.

Horn, Ildikó. 2009. "Nyelvtanulás—nyelvtudás az Erdélyi Fejedelemségben." *TSz* 51, 1, 45–58.

Horn, Ildikó, et al., eds. 2016. *Művészet és mesterség: Tisztelgő kötet R. Várkonyi Ágnes emlékére.* Budapest.

Horváth, István. 2003. "Ottoman Military Construction in Esztergom." In Ibolya Gerelyes and Gyöngyi Kovács, eds., *Archeology of the Ottoman Period in Hungary.* Budapest, 75–87.

Horváth, Richárd. 2013. "The Castle of Jajce in the Organization of the Hungarian Border Defence System under Matthias Corvinus." In Ante Birin, ed., *Stjepan Tomašević (1461.–1463.)—slom srednjovjekovnoga Bosanskog Kraljevstva.* Sarajevo, 89–98.

Housley, Norman. 1984. "King Louis the Great of Hungary and the Crusades, 1342–82." *Slavonic and East European Review* 62, 192–208.

Howard, Douglas A. 1994. "With Gibbon in the Garden: Decline, Death and the Sick Man of Europe." *Fides et Historia* 26, 22–34.

———. 2007. "Genre and Myth in the Ottoman Advice for Kings Literature." In Aksan and Goffman 2007, 137–66.

———. 2017. *A History of the Ottoman Empire.* Cambridge.

Hugyecz, Antal. 1894. "Eggenberg Rupert jelentése Ernő főherceghez a sziszeki csatáról, 1593. Június 24." *HK* 7, 264–66.

Husain, Faisal. 2018. "The Tigris-Euphrates Basin Under Early Modern Ottoman Rule, c. 1534–1830." PhD. Dissertation, Georgetown University.

Ibn ʿArabshāh, Aḥmad ibn Muḥammad. 1936. *Tamerlane, or, Timur, the Great Amir.* Translated by J. H. Sanders. London.

İhsanoğlu, Ekmeleddin, ed. 1994. *Osmanlı Devleti ve Medeniyeti Tarihi.* Istanbul.

İlgüler, Mücteba 1979. "Osmanlı İmparatorluğu'nda Ateşli Silahların Yayılışı," *TD* 32, 301–18.

Imber, Colin. 1980. "The Navy of Süleyman the Magnificent." *AO* 6, 211–82.

———. 1990. *The Ottoman Empire, 1300–1481.* Istanbul.

———. 1992. "Süleyman as Caliph of the Muslims: Ebu's-Su'ud's Formulation of Ottoman Dynastic Ideology." In Veinstein 1992, 179–84.

———. 1995. "Ideals and Legitimation in Early Ottoman History." In Kunt and Woodhead 1995, 138–53.

———. 1996. "The Reconstruction of the Ottoman Fleet after the Battle of Lepanto, 1571–1572." In Colin Imber, *Studies in Ottoman History and Law.* Istanbul, 85–101.

———. 2000. "What Does Ghazi Actually Mean?" In Çiğdem Balım-Harding and Colin Imber, eds., *The Balance of Truth: Essays in Honour of Professor Geoffrey Lewis.* Istanbul, 165–78.

———. 2005. "Ibrahim Peçevi on War: A Note on the European Military Revolution." In Imber, Kiyotaki, and Murphey 2005, vol. 2, 7–22.

———, ed. 2006. *The Crusade of Varna, 1443–45.* Aldershot, England.

———. 2009. *The Ottoman Empire, 1300–1650: The Structure of Power.* 2nd ed. Houndmills, UK.

———. 2011. "The Origin of the Janissaries." In Colin Imber, *Warfare, Law and Pseudo-history.* Istanbul, 165–71.

———. 2013. "Government, Administration, and Law." In Faroqhi and Fleet 2013, 205–40.

———. 2019. *The Ottoman Empire, 1300–1650: The Structure of Power.* 3rd ed. Houndmills, UK.

Imber, Colin, Keiko Kiyotaki, and Rhoads Murphey, eds. 2005. *Frontiers of Ottoman Studies.* 2 vols. London.

İnalcık, Halil. 1943. "Saray Bosna Şer'iyye Sicillerine Göre Viyana Bozgunundan Sonraki Harp Yıllarında Bosna." *Tarih Vesikaları* 2, 11, 1–13.

———. 1944. "Yeni Vesikalara Göre Kırım Hanlığının Osmanlı Tabiliğine Girmesi ve Ahidname Meselesi." *Belleten* 8, 31, 185–229.

———. 1947. "The Origins of the Ottoman-Russian Rivalry and the Don-Volga Canal." *Annales de l'Université d'Ankara* 1, 47–110.

———. 1948. "Osmanlı–Rus Rekabetinin Menşei ve Don–Volga Kanalı Teşebbüsü (1569)." *Belleten* 12, 46, 349–402.

———. 1953. "Stefan Duşan'dan Osmanlı İmparatorluğuna: XV. Asırda Rumeli'de Hıristiyan Sipahiler ve Menşeleri." *60. Doğum Yılı Münasebetiyle Fuad Köprülü Armağanı.* Istanbul.

———. (1954) 1987. *Fatih Devri Üzerinde Tetkikler ve Vesikalar.* Ankara.

———. 1954. "Ottoman Methods of Conquest." *Studia Islamica* 2, 103–29.

———. 1959. "Osmanlılarda Saltanat Veraseti Usulü ve Türk Hakimiyet Telakkisiyle İlgisi." *Ankara Üniversitesi Siyasal Bilgiler Fakültesi Dergisi* 14, 1, 69–94.

———. 1960. "Mehmed the Conqueror (1432–1481) and His Time." *Speculum* 35, 3, 408–27.

———. (1973) 1994. *The Ottoman Empire: The Classical Age, 1300–1600.* London.

———. 1975. "The Socio-political Effects of the Diffusion of Fire-Arms in the Middle East." In Parry and Yapp 1975, 195–217.

———. 1979. "The Question of the Closing of the Black Sea under the Ottomans." *Arxeion Pontou* 33, 74–110.

———. 1980. "Military and Fiscal Transformation in the Ottoman Empire." *AO* 6, 283–337.

———. 1989. "The Ottoman Turks and the Crusades, 1329–1451." In Kenneth M. Setton, ed., *A History of the Crusades.* Vol. 6: *Impact of the Crusades on Europe,* eds. Harry W. Hazard and Norman P. Zacour. Madison, WI, 222–75.

———. 1993a. *The Middle East and the Balkans under the Ottoman Empire: Essays on Economy and Society.* Bloomington, IN, 37–69.

———. 1993b. *Osmanlı İmparatorluğu: Toplum ve Ekonomi Üzerinde Arşiv Çalışmaları, İncelemeler.* Istanbul.

———. 1993c. "The Ottoman Succession and Its Relations to the Turkish Concept of Sovereignty." In İnalcık 1993a, 37–69. [English translation of İnalcık 1959]

———. (1994) 1997. *An Economic and Social History of the Ottoman Empire: 1300–1600.* Cambridge. [First published as "The Ottoman State: Economy and Society, 1300–1600." In İnalcık and Quataert 1994, 9–409]

———. 1995. *Sources and Studies on the Ottoman Black Sea.* Vol. 1, *The Customs Register of Caffa, 1487–1490.* Cambridge, MA.

———. 2008. "Karadenizde Kazaklar ve Rusya: İstanbul Boğazı Tehlikede." In Mustafa Demir, ed., *Çanakkale Savaş Tarihi.* Vol. 1. Istanbul, 59–64.

———. 2010. "Osmanlı Sultanlarının Unvanları (Titulatur) ve Egemenlik Kavramı." In *Doğu Batı, Makaleler* II. Ankara.

———. 2012. *The Survey of Istanbul 1455: The Text, English Translation, Analysis of the Text, Documents.* Istanbul.

İnalcık, Halil, and Cemal Kafadar, eds. 1993. *Süleyman the Second and His Time.* Istanbul.

İnalcık, Halil, and Mevlûd Oğuz. 1978. *Gazavât-ı Sultân Murâd b. Mehemmed Hân: İzladi ve Varna Savaşları (1443–1444) Üzerinde Anonim Gazavâtnâme.* Ankara.

İnalcık, Halil, and Donald Quataert, eds. 1994. *An Economic and Social History of the Ottoman Empire, 1300–1914.* 2 vols. Cambridge.

İnbaşı, Mehmet. 2004. *Ukrayna'da Osmanlılar: Kamaniçe Seferi ve Organizasyonu (1672).* Istanbul.

Ingrao, Charles, Nikola Samardžić, and Jovan Pešalj, eds. 2011. *The Peace of Passarowitz.* West Lafayette, IN.

Iordanou, Ioanna. 2019. *Venice's Secret Service: Organizing Intelligence in the Renaissance.* Oxford.

İpçıoğlu, Mehmet. 1990. "Kanuni Süleyman'ın Estergon (Esztergom) Seferi." *OA* 10, 137–59.

İpşirli, Mehmet. 1994. "Eyalet (Taşra) Teşkilatı." In İhsanoğlu 1994, 221–45.

Irwin, Robert. 2004. "Gunpowder and Firearms in the Mamluk Sultanate Reconsidered." In Michael Winter and Amalia Levanoni, eds., *The Mamluks in Egyptian and Syrian Politics and Society.* Leiden and New York.

Işıksal, Turgut. 1969. "Arşivlerimizde Osmanlıların Süveyş Tersanesi ve Güney Denizleri Politikasına İlişkin en Eski Belgeler." *BTTD* 13, 18, 54–73.

Işıksel, Güneş. 2016. *La diplomatie ottomane sous le règne de Selîm II: Paramètres et périmètres de l'Empire ottoman dans le troisime quart du XVIe siècle.* Paris.

Isom-Verhaaren, Christine. 2013. *Allies with the Infidel: The Ottoman and French Alliance in the Sixteenth Century.* London.

Issawi, Charles. 1993. "The Ottoman-Habsburg Balance of Forces." In İnalcık and Kafadar 1993, 145–51.

Istvánffy, Miklós. 2001–9. *Istvánffy Miklós magyarok dolgairól írt históriája: Tállyai Pál XVII. századi fordításában.* Vol. 1. Parts 1–3. Edited by Péter Benits. Budapest.

Ivanics, Mária. 1994. *A Krími Kánság a tizenöt éves háborúban.* Budapest.

———. 2007. "Enslavement, Slave Labour and Treatment of Captives in the Crimean Khanate." In Dávid and Fodor 2007, 193–219.

Ivanović, Miloš. 2017. "Cyrillic Correspondence between the Commune of Ragusa and Ottomans from 1396 to 1458." In Srđan Rudić and Selim Aslantaş, eds., *State and Society in the Balkans before and after the Establishment of Ottoman Rule.* Belgrade, 43–59.

Iványi, Béla. 1941. "Buda és Pest sorsdöntő évei 1526–1541." *Tanulmányok Budapest Múltjából* 9, 32–84.

Jacobs, Martin. 2004. "Joseph ha-Kohen, Paolo Giovio, and Sixteenth-Century Historiography." In David B. Ruderman and Giuseppe Veltri, eds., *Cultural Intermediaries: Jewish Intellectuals in Early Modern Italy.* Philadelphia, PA, 67–85.

Jakó, Klára. 2009. "Adalék Constantin Şerban és III. Mihnea Radu havasalföldi vajdák portréjához." In József Bessenyei and István Draskóczy, eds., *Pénztörténet—gazdaságtörténet. Tanulmányok Buza János 70. születésnapjára.* Budapest and Miskolc, 172–81.

———. 2016. "Moldva és Havasalfölde viszonya az Erdélyi Fejedelemséghez az államközi szerződések és a külügyi levelezés tükrében." In Horn et al. 2016, 271–94.

Janos, Damien. 2005–6. "Panaiotis Nicousios and Alexander Mavrocordatos: The Rise of the Phanariots and the Office of Grand Dragoman in the Ottoman Administration in the Second Half of the Seventeenth Century." *AO* 23, 177–96.

Jászay, Magda. 1990. *Velence és Magyarország: Egy szomszédság küzdelmes története.* Budapest.

Jászay, Pál. 1846. *A magyar nemzet napjai a mohácsi vész után.* Pest.

Jefferson, John. 2012. *The Holy Wars of King Wladislas and Sultan Murad: The Ottoman-Christian Conflict from 1438–1444*. Leiden and New York.

Jenkins, Hester Donaldson. 1911. *Ibrahim Pasha, Grand Vizir of Suleiman the Magnificent*. New York.

Jennings, R. C. 1986. "Some Thoughts on the Ghazi-Thesis." *WZKM* 76, 151–61.

Kafadar, Cemal. 1995. *Between Two Worlds: The Construction of the Ottoman State*. Berkeley, CA.

———. 1997–98. "The Question of Ottoman Decline." *Harvard Middle Eastern and Islamic Review* 4, 30–75.

———. 2007. "Janissaries and Other Riffraff of Ottoman Istanbul: Rebels without a Cause?" In Baki Tezcan and Karl K. Barbir, eds., *Identity and Identity Formation in the Ottoman World: A Volume of Essays in Honor of Norman Itzkowitz*. Madison, WI, 113–34.

Kafescioğlu, Çiğdem. 2009. *Constantinopolis/Istanbul: Cultural Encounter, Imperial Vision, and the Construction of the Ottoman Capital*. University Park, PA.

Kahane, Henry, Reneé Kahane, and Andreas Tietze. 1988. *The Lingua Franca in the Levant, Turkish Nautical Terms of Italian and Greek Origin*. Istanbul.

Káldy-Nagy, Gyula. 1960. "Bevölkerungsstatistischer Quellenwert der Cizye-Defter und der Tahrir Defter." *AOH* 11, 259–69.

———. 1968. "The Administration of the Sanjāq Registrations in Hungary." *AOH* 21, 181–223.

———. 1970. *Magyarországi török adóösszeírások*. Budapest.

———. 1974a. *Szulejmán*. Budapest.

———. 1974b. "Suleimans Angriff auf Europa." *AOH* 28, 163–212.

———. 1976. "The Conscription of Müsellem and Yaya Corps in 1540." In Gyula Káldy-Nagy, ed., *Hungaro-Turcica: Studies in Honour of Julius Németh*. Budapest, 275–81.

———. 1977a. *A Budai szandzsák 1559. évi összeírása*. Budapest.

———. 1977b. "The First Centuries of the Ottoman Military Organization." *AOH* 31, 147–83.

———. 1988. "Contribution to the History of the Jews of Buda in 1526: Banishment or Resettlement?" In Róbert Dán, ed., *Occident and Orient: A Tribute to the Memory of Alexander Scheiber*. Budapest, 257–60.

———. 1990. "Budin Beylerbeyi Mustafa Paşa (1566–1578)." *Belleten* 54, 649–63.

———. 2000. *A csanádi szandszák 1567. és 1579. évi összeírása*. Szeged.

Kalous, Antonín. 2007. "Elfeledett források a mohácsi csatáról: Antonio Burgio pápai nuncius jelentései és azok hadtörténeti jelentősége." *HK* 120, 603–22.

Kappert, Petra. 1976. *Die osmanischen Prinzen und ihre Residenz Amasya im 15. und 16. Jahrhundert*. Istanbul.

Karácson, Imre. 1914. *Török-magyar oklevéltár, 1553–1789*. Budapest.

Karaman, Kıvanç, and Şevket Pamuk. 2010. "Ottoman State Finances in European Perspective, 1500–1914." *Journal of Economic History* 73, 593–629.

Karamustafa, Ahmet T. 1992. "Military, Administrative, and Scholarly Maps and Plans." In Harley and Woodward 1992, 209–27.

Kármán, Gábor, and Lovro Kunčević, eds. 2013. *The European Tributary States of the Ottoman Empire in the Sixteenth and Seventeenth Centuries*. Leiden and New York.

Károlyi, Árpád. 1879. *Adalékok a nagyváradi béke s az 1536–38. évek történetéhez*. Budapest.

———. 1880. "A Német Birodalom nagy hadi vállalata Magyarországon 1542-ben." *Századok* 14, 265–99, 357–87, 445–65, 558–89, 621–55.

————, ed. 1881. *Fráter György levelezése, 1535–1551*. Budapest.

Kárpáthy-Kravjánszky, Mór. 1933. *Rudolf uralkodásának első tíz éve (1576–1686). A velencei kir. állami levéltár császári udvarból való követjelentései alapján*. Budapest.

Kastritsis, Dimitris J. 2007a. *The Sons of Bayezid: Empire Building and Representation in the Ottoman Civil War of 1402–1413*. Leiden and New York.

————. 2007b. "Religious Affiliations and Political Alliances in the Ottoman Succession Wars of 1402–1413." *Medieval Encounters* 13, 222–42.

Kâtib Çelebi. 2008. *Tuhfetü'l–Kibâr fî Esfâri'l–Bihâr (Deniz Seferleri Hakkında Büyüklere Armağan)*. Edited by İdris Bostan. Istanbul.

Katona, Tamás. 1987. *Mohács emlékezete*. Budapest.

Kelenik, József. 2000. "The Military Revolution in Hungary." In Dávid and Fodor 2000, 117–59.

————. 2016. "The Champion of the Christian World." In Hausner 2016, 108–73.

————. 2019. "The Sieges of Szigetvar and Gyula, 1566." In Fodor 2019a, 397–410.

Kemal Paşa-zâde. 1893. "Mohácsnáme." In Thúry 1893–96, vol. 1, 191–276.

————. 1996. *Tevarih-i Âl-i Osman. X. Defter*. Edited by Şefaettin Severcan. Ankara.

Kemény, János. 2000. "Ruina exercitus Transylvanici." In *Kemény János művei*. Edited by Éva V. Windish. Budapest. http://mek.oszk.hu/06100/06166/html/kemeny0010002.html.

Kennedy, Hugh. 2006. *When Baghdad Ruled the World: The Rise and Fall of Islam's Greatest Dynasty*. Cambridge, MA.

Kenyeres, István. 2003. "Die Finanzen des Königreichs Ungarn in der zweiten Hälfte des 16. Jahrhunderts." In Edelmayer, Lanzinner, and Rauscher 2003, 84–122.

————. 2005. "Die Einkünfte und Reformen der Finanzverwaltung Ferdinands I. in Ungarn." In Fuchs, Oborni, and Újváry 2005, 111–46.

————. 2007. "A Habsburg monarchia katonai kiadásai az Udvari Pénztár és a hadi fizetőmesterek számadásai alapján, 1543–1623. Adalékok a török elleni küzdelem finanszírozásának történetéhez." *LK* 78, 85–137.

————. 2008. *Uradalmak és végvárak: A kamarai birtokok és a törökellenes határvédelem a 16. századi Magyar Királyságban*. Budapest.

————. 2010. "Die Kriegsausgaben der Habsburgermonarchie von der Mitte des 16. Jahrhunderts bis zum ersten Drittel des 17. Jahrhunderts." In Rauscher 2010, 41–80.

————. 2011. "Grundherrschaften und Grenzfestungen. Die Kammerherrschaften und die Türkenabwehr im Königreich Ungarn des 16. Jahrhunderts." In Krisztián Csaplár-Degovics and István Fazekas, eds., *Geteilt-Vereinigt: Beiträge zur Geschichte des Königreichs Ungarn in der Frühneuzeit (16.–18. Jahrhundert)*. Berlin, 98–119.

————. 2012. "Die Kosten der Türkenabwehr und des Langen Türkenkrieges (1593–1606) im Kontext der ungarischen Finanzen des 16. und 17. Jahrhunderts." In Rauscher, Serles, and Winkelbauer 2012, 19–41.

————. 2013. "A Habsburg Monarchia és a Magyar Királyság pénzügyei és hadi költségei a 16. század közepétől a 17. század első harmadáig." *TSz* 4, 541–658.

Kerekes, Dóra. 2003. "Johann Christoph von Kindsberg konstantinápolyi császári követ hagyatéki leltára 1678-ból." *Lymbus*, 129–57.

————. 2004a. "Császári tolmácsok a magyarországi visszafoglaló háborúk idején." *Századok* 5, 327–68.

———. 2004b. "Egy császári tolmács megfigyelései: Giorgio Cleronome magyarországi utazásai." *Lymbus* 71–77.

———.2010. *Diplomaták és kémek Konstantinápolyban.* Budapest.

———. 2014–15. "Transimperial Mediators of Culture: Seventeenth-Century Habsburg Interpreters in Constantinople." In Szymon Brzezinski and Áron Zarnóczki, eds., *Diplomacy, Information Flow and Cultural Exchange.* Vol. 2, *A Divided Hungary in Europe: Exchange, Networks and Representations, 1541–1699.* Newcastle upon Tyne, 51–68.

Kermeli, Eugenia, and Oktay Özel, eds. 2006. *The Ottoman Empire: Myths, Realities and "Black Holes" (Contributions in Honour of Colin Imber).* Istanbul.

Kerslake, Celia J. 1978. "The *Selim-name* of Celal-zade Mustafa Çelebi as a Historical Source." *Turcica* 9–10 (2), 39–51.

Khodarkovsky, Michael. 2002. *Russia's Steppe Frontier: The Making of a Colonial Empire, 1500–1800.* Bloomington, IN.

Khoury, Dina Rizk. 1997. *State and Provincial Society in the Ottoman Empire: Mosul 1540–1834.* Cambridge.

Khvānd Mīr, Ghiyās̱ al-Dīn ibn Humām al-Dīn. 1994. *Habibu's-Siyar.* Translated and edited by W. M. Thackston. Tome Three. *The Reign of the Mongol and the Turk.* Pt. 2: *Shahrukh Mirza-Shah Ismail.* Cambridge, MA.

Kılıç, Orhan. 1997. *XVI. ve XVII. Yüzyıllarda Van (1548–1648).* Van.

———. 2001. "Van Eyaletine Bağlı Sancaklar." *OA* 21, 189–207.

———. 2012. "Teşkilat ve İşleyiş Bakımından Doğu Hududundakı Osmanlı Kaleleri ve Mevacib Defterleri." *OTAM* 31, 87–127.

Kılıç, Remzi. 2001. *XVI. ve XVII. Yüzyıllarda Osmanlı-İran Siyasi Antlaşmaları.* Istanbul.

Kiprovska, Mariya. 2004. *The Military Organization of the Akıncıs in Ottoman Rumelia.* MA thesis, Bilkent University, Ankara.

———. 2008. "The Mihaloğlu Family: Gazi Warriors and Founders of Derwish Hospices." *OA* 32, 193222.

———. 2013. "Byzantine Renegade and Holy Warrior: Reassessing the Character of Köse Mihal, a Hero of the Byzantino-Ottoman Borderland." *JTS* 40 [*Defterology: Festschrift in Honor of Health Lowry,* ed. Selim Kuru and Baki Tezcan], 245–69.

———. 2016. "Ferocious Invasion or Smooth Incorporation? Integrating the Established Balkan Military System into the Ottoman Army." In Oliver Jens Schmitt, ed., *The Ottoman Conquest of the Balkans.* Vienna, 79–102.

Kırzıoğlu, M. Fahrettin. (1993) 1998. *Osmanlılar'ın Kafkas-Elleri'ni Fethi, 1451–1590.* 2nd ed. Ankara.

Knecht, R. J. 1982. *Francis I.* Cambridge.

Köhbach, Markus. 1992. "Çasar oder imperator? Zur Titulatur der römischen Kaiser durch die Osmanen nach dem Vertrag von Zsitvatorok." *WZKM* 82, 223–34.

Kohler, Alfred. 1999. *Karl V.: 1500–1558. Eine Biographie.* Munich.

Kohn, Sámuel. 1881. *Héber kutforrások és adatok Magyarország történetéhez.* Budapest.

Kolçak, Özgür. 2017. "Egy erdélyi fejedelem a 'héják' karmai között: II. Rákóczi György és Köprülü Mehmed pasa." *Keletkutatás* 2017 tavasz, 63–82.

Kołodziejczyk, Dariusz. 1994. *Podole pod panowaniem tureckim: Ejalet Kamieniecki 1672–1699.* Warszawa.

————. 2000. *Ottoman-Polish Diplomatic Relations (15th-18th Century): An Annotated Edition of 'Ahdnames and Other Documents*. Leiden and New York.

————. 2004. *The Ottoman Survey Register of Podolia (ca. 1681): Defter-i Mufassal-i Eyalet-i Kamaniçe*. Cambridge, MA.

————. 2006. "Slave Hunting and Slave Redemption as a Business Enterprise: The Northern Black Sea Region in the Sixteenth to Seventeenth Centuries." *Oriente Moderno* 25, 1, 149–59.

————. 2007. "Inner Lake or Frontier? The Ottoman Black Sea in the Sixteenth and Seventeenth Centuries." In F. Bilici, I. Candea, and A. Popescu, eds., *Enjeux politiques, économiques et militaires en Mer Noire XIVe-XXIe siècles. Études à la mémoire de Mahail Guboglu*. Braïla, 125–39.

————. 2011. *The Crimean Khanate and Poland-Lithuania: International Diplomacy on the European Periphery (15th-18th Century): A Study of Peace Treaties Followed by Annotated Documents*. Leiden and New York.

————. 2012a. "Between Universalistic Claims and Reality: Ottoman Frontiers in the Early Modern Period." In Woodhead 2012, 205–19.

————. 2012b. "Khan, Caliph, Tsar and Imperator: The Multiple Identities of the Ottoman Sultan." In Bang and Kołodziejczyk 2012, 175–93.

————. 2014. "Ottoman Frontiers in Eastern Europe." In Spannenberger and Varga 2014, 25–37.

Konstam, Angus. 2003. *Lepanto 1571: The Greatest Naval Battle of the Renaissance*. Oxford.

Kornrumpf, Hans-Jürgen. 1989. "Süd-Russland und die Krim um 1740." *OA* 9, 235–62.

Kottannerin, Helene. 1971. *Die Denkwürdigkeiten der Helene Kottannerin (1439–1440)*. Edited by Karl Mollay. Vienna.

Korobeinikov, Dimitri. 2010. "How Byzantine Were the Early Ottomans? Bithynia in ca. 1290–1450." In I. V. Zaitsev and S. F. Oreshkova, eds., *Osmanskii mir i osmanistika: Sbornik statei k 100-letiiu so dnia rozhdeniia A.S. Tveritinovoi (1910–1973)*. Moscow, 215–39.

————. 2014. *Byzantium and the Turks in the Thirteenth Century*. Oxford.

Kosáry, Domokos. 1978. *Magyar külpolitika Mohács előtt*. Budapest.

Kovács, József László, trans. and ed. 1986. *Ungnád Dávid konstantinápolyi utazásai*. Budapest.

Kreiser, Klaus. 1976. "Osmanische Grenzbeschreibungen." In *Studi preottomani e ottomani: atti del Convegno di Napoli 24–26 settembre 1974*. Naples, 165–72.

Kretschmayr, Henrik. 1901. *Gritti Lajos, 1480–1534*. Budapest.

Kritovoulos. 1954. *History of Mehmed the Conqueror*. Translated by Charles T. Riggs. Princeton, NJ.

Kropf, Lajos. 1896. "Malvezzi elfogattatása." *Századok* 30, 389–93.

Krstić, Tijana. 2011a. *Contested Conversions to Islam: Narratives of Religious Change in the Early Modern Ottoman Empire*. Stanford, CA.

————. 2011b. "Of Translation and Empire: Sixteenth-Century Ottoman Imperial Interpreters as Renaissance Go-Betweens." In Woodhead 2012, 130–42.

Kubinyi, András. 1990. "A Mátyás-kori államszervezet." In Gyula Rázsó and László V. Molnár, eds. *Hunyadi Mátyás: Emlékkönyv Mátyás Király halálának 500. évfordulójára*. Budapest 1990, 53–147.

————. 1991. "Két sorsdöntő esztendő (1490–1491)." *TSz* 33, 1–54.

————. 2000. "The Battle of Szávaszentdemeter-Nagyolaszi (1523): Ottoman Advance and Hungarian Defence on the Eve of Mohács." In Dávid and Fodor 2000, 71–115.

————. 2004. "A Szapolyaiak és familiárisaik (szervitoraik)." In József Bessenyei, ed., *Tanulmányok Szapolyai Jánosról és a kora újkori Erdélyről*. Miskolc, 169–94.

————. 2008. *Matthias Rex*. Translated by Andrew T. Gane. Budapest.

Kucharská, Veronika. 2014. *Ducissa. Život kňažnej Hedvigy v časoch Jagelovcov*. Bratislava.

Kunt, Metin. 1971. *The Köprülü Years: 1656–1661*. PhD dissertation, Princeton, NJ.

————. 1973. "Naima, Köprülü, and the Grand Vezirate." *Boğaziçi Üniversitesi Dergisi* 1, 57–64.

————. 1974. "Ethic-Regional (Cins) Solidarity in the Seventeenth-Century Ottoman Establishment." *IJMES* 5, 3, 233–39.

————. 1978. *Sancaktan Eyalete: 1550–1650 Arasında Osmanlı Ümerası ve İl İdaresi*. Istanbul.

————. 1983. *The Sultan's Servants: The Transformation of Ottoman Provincial Government, 1550–1650*. New York.

————. 2012. "Royal and Other Households." In Woodhead 2012, 103–15.

Kunt, Metin, and Christine Woodhead, eds. 1995. *Süleyman the Magnificent and His Age: The Ottoman Empire in the Early Modern World*. London.

Küpeli, Özer. 2014. *Osmanlı–Safevi Münasebetleri (1612–1639)*. Istanbul.

Kurat, Akdes Nimet. 1961. "The Turkish Expedition to Astrakhan' in 1569 and the Problem of the Don-Volga Canal." *Slavonic and East European Review* 40, 7–23.

————. 1966. *Türkiye ve Idil Boyu. 1569 Astarhan Seferi, Ten-İdil Kanalı ve XVI-XVII. Yüzyıl Osmanlı-Rus Münasebetleri*. Ankara.

————. 1972. *IV-XVIII. Yüzyıllarda Karadeniz Kuzeyindeki Türk Kavim ve Devletleri*. Ankara.

Kurşun, Zekeriya. 2012. "Does the Qatar Map of the Tigris and Euphrates Belong to Evliya Çelebi?" *OA* 39, 1–15.

Kütükoğlu, Bekir. 1993. *Osmanlı-Iran Siyâsi Münasebetleri, 1578–1612*. Istanbul.

Kütükoğlu, Mübahat S. 1994. *Osmanlı Belgelerinin Dili: Diplomatik*. Istanbul.

Kyriakidis, Savvas. 2011. *Warfare in Late Byzantium, 1204–1453*. Leiden and New York.

Labib, Subhi. 1979. "The Era of Suleyman the Magnificent: Crisis of Orientation." *IJMES* 10, 4, 435–51.

Laiou, Angeliki E. 2008. "The Palaiologoi and the World around Them (1261–1400)." In Jonathan Shepard, ed., *The Cambridge History of the Byzantine Empire c. 500–1492*. Cambridge, 803–33.

Łaski, Hyeronimus. *(1527–28)* 1996. "Hyeronimus Łaski tárgyalása a töröknél János király nevében." In Barta 1996, 99–172.

Leitsch, Walter. 1988. "Miért akarta Kara Musztafa meghódítani Bécset?" In Kálmán Benda and Ágnes R. Várkonyi, eds., *Bécs 1683. évi török ostroma és Magyarország*. Budapest, 65–94.

Lellouch, Benjamin. 2006. *Les Ottomans en Égypte: Historiens et conquérants au XVIe siècle*. Paris and Louvain.

Lellouch, Benjamin, and Nicolas Michel, eds. 2013. *Conquête ottoman de l'Égypte (1517)*. Leiden and New York.

Lesure, Michel. 1976. "Un document ottoman sur l'Inde portugaise et les pays de la Mer Rouge." *Mare Luso-Indicum* 3, 137–60.

————. 1983. "Michel Černović 'explorator secretus' a Constantinople (1556–1563)." *Turcica* 15, 127–54.

Leube, George. 2015a. "Uzun Hasan in Isfahan. Some Thoughts on Uzun Hasan's Inscription in the Masjidi Jami of Isfahan: Gleichzeitigkeit des Ungleichzeitigen?" *DYNTRAN Working Papers*, no.° 1, online edition, June 2015. https://dyntran.hypotheses.org/259.

———. 2015b. "Ottoman Building Inscriptions I. Some Context: Two 15th Century Ottoman Building Inscriptions from Edirne." *DYNTRAN Working Papers*, no.° 4, online edition, September 2015. https://dyntran.hypotheses.org/749.

———. 2015c. "Ottoman Building Inscriptions II. A Hierarchy of Rule? 15th Century Ottoman Building Inscriptions in Bulgaria and Thrace." *DYNTRAN Working Papers*, no.° 5, online edition, October 2015. https://dyntran.hypotheses.org/763.

Levend, Agâh Sırrı. 1956. *Gazavatnameler ve Mihaloğlu Ali Bey'in Gazavatnamesi*. Ankara.

Lewis, Bernard. 1984. *The Jews of Islam*. London.

Lindner, Rudi Paul. 1983. *Nomads and Ottomans in Medieval Anatolia*. Bloomington, IN.

———. 2007. *Explorations in Ottoman Prehistory*. Ann Arbor, MI.

Longrigg, Stephen. 1925. *Four Centuries of Modern Iraq*. Oxford.

Lorge, Peter Allan. 2008. *The Asian Military Revolution: From Gunpowder to the Bomb*. Cambridge.

Lowry, Heath W. 2002. *Fifteenth Century Ottoman Realities: Christian Peasant Life on the Aegean Island of Limnos*. Istanbul.

———. 2003. *The Nature of the Early Ottoman State*. Albany, NY.

———. 2010. *The Shaping of the Ottoman Balkans, 1350–1550: The Conquest, Settlement & Infrastructural Development of Northern Greece*. 2nd ed. Istanbul.

———. 2011. *Hersekzâde Ahmed Paşa: An Ottoman Statesman's Career & Pious Endowments*. Istanbul.

———. 2012. *Fourteenth Century Ottoman Realities: In Search of Hâcı-Gâzi Evrenos*. Istanbul.

Lowry, Heath W., and İsmail E. Erünsal. 2010. *The Evrenos Dynasty of Yenice-i Vardar: Notes & Documents*. Istanbul.

Lukinich, Imre. 1918. *Erdély területi változásai a török hódítás korában, 1541–1711*. Budapest.

Luttrel, Anthony. 1993. "Latin Responses to Ottoman Expansion before 1389." In Zachariadou 1993a, 120–23.

Lybyer, A. H. 1913. *Government of the Ottoman Empire in the Time of Suleiman the Magnificent*. Cambridge. MA, and London.

———. 1915. "The Ottoman Turks and the Routes of Oriental Trade." *English Historical Review* 30, 120 (October), 577–88.

Mack, Rosamond E. 2002. *Bazaar to Piazza: Islamic Trade and Italian Art, 1300–1600*. Berkeley, CA.

Madunić, Domagoj. 2013. "Frontier Elites of the Ottoman Empire during the War for Crete (1654–1669): The Case of Ali-Pasha Čengić." In Gábor Kármán and Radu G. Păun, eds., *Europe and the 'Ottoman World': Exchanges and Conflicts*. Istanbul, 47–82.

Mahmud, bin Abdullah. 1996. *Nagy Szulejmán udvari emberének magyar krónikája: A Tarih-i Ungurus és kritikája*. Edited by György Hazai. Budapest.

———. 2019. (Tercüman Mahmud). *Tarih-i Ungurus*. Edited by György Hazai. Ankara.

Mahmud, Muhammed es-Seyyid. 1990. *XVI. Asırda Mısır Eyaleti*. Istanbul.

Malcolm, Noel. 2015. *Agents of Empire: Knights, Corsairs, Jesuits and Spies in the Sixteenth-Century Mediterranean World*. Oxford.

————. 2019. *Useful Enemies: Islam and the Ottoman Empire in Western Political Thought, 1450–1750*. Oxford.

Mályusz, Elemér. 1984. *Zsigmond király uralma Magyarországon, 1387–1437*. Budapest.

Margalits, Ede. 1900–1902. *Horvát történelmi repertorium*. 2 vols. Budapest.

Margetić, Lujo. 1990. "Cetinski sabori u 1527." *Senj Zbornik: Prilozi za geografiju, etnologiju, gospodarstvo, povijest i kulturu* 17, 1, 35–44.

Markowicz, Marcin. 2011. *Najazd Rakoczego na Polskę, 1657*. Zabrze.

Marsili, Luigi Ferdinando. 1986. *Relazioni dei confini della Croazia e della Transilvania a Sua Maestà Cesarea*. Edited by Raffaella Gherardi. Modena.

————. 2007. *Az Oszmán Birodalom katonai állapotáról, felemelkedéséről és hanyatlásáról*. Translated by Mónika F. Molnár. Budapest.

Masters, Bruce. 2013. *The Arabs of the Ottoman Empire, 1516–1918: A Social and Cultural History*. Cambridge.

Maťa, Petr. 2006. "Landstände und Landtage in den böhmischen und österreichischen Ländern (1620–1740): Von der Niedergangsgeschichte zur Interaktionsanalyse." In Maťa and Winkelbauer 2006, 345–400.

Maťa, Petr, and Thomas Winkelbauer. 2006. *Die Habsburgermonarchie 1620 bis 1740: Leistungen und Grenzen des Absolutismusparadigmas*. Stuttgart.

Mathew, K. S. 1986. *Portuguese and the Sultanate of Gujarat, 1500–1573*. Delhi.

Matschke, Klaus-Peter. 1981. *Die Schlacht bei Ankara und das Schicksal von Byzanz: Studien zur spätbyzantinischen Geschichte zwischen 1402 und 1422*. Weimar.

Matthee, Rudi. 1996. "Unwalled Cities and Restless Nomads: Firearms and Artillery in Safavid Iran." In Charles Melville, ed., *Safavid Persia: The History and Politics of an Islamic Society*. London, 389–416.

————. 2003. "The Safavid-Ottoman Frontier: Iraq-i Arab as Seen by the Safavids." *IJTS* 9, 157–73.

————. 2014. "The Ottoman-Safavid War of 986–998/1578–90: Motives and Causes." *IJTS* 20, 1–2, 1–20.

Mattingly, Garrett. 1955. *Renaissance Diplomacy*. London.

Mattio, Erika. 2013. "L'artiglieria del nemico turco." In Carlo Beltrame and Marco Morin, eds., *I cannoni di Venezia: Artiglierie della Serenissima in Turchia, Grecia e Dalmazia*. Florence, 45–46.

Matuz, Josef. 1971. *Herrscherurkunden des Osmanensultans Süleyman des Prächtigen: Ein chronologisches Verzeichnis*. Wiesbaden.

————. 1975. "Die Pfortendolmetscher zur Herrschaftszeit Süleyman des Prächtigen." *SoF* 34, 26–60.

Mayhew, Tea. 2008. *Dalmatia between Ottoman and Venetian Rule: Contado di Zara 1645–1718*. Rome.

McNeill, John. 2000. "Ecology and Strategy in the Mediterranean: Points of Intersection." In John B. Hattendorf, ed., *Naval Policy and Strategy in the Mediterranean: Pats, Present and Future*. London and Portland, 374–91.

McNeill, William H. 1982. *The Pursuit of Power: Technology, Armed Force, and Society since A.D. 1000*. Chicago.

————. 1989. *The Age of Gunpowder Empires, 1450–1800*. Washington, DC.

Mehmed Halife. 2000. *Tarih-i Gılmanî*. Edited by Ertuğrul Oral. PhD dissertation, Marmara University, Istanbul.

Meienberger, Peter. 1973. *Johann Rudolf Schmid zum Schwarzenhorn als kaiserlicher Resident in Konstantinopel in den Jahren 1629–1643*. Bern and Frankfurt am Main.

Ménage, V.L. "Djandarlı." In *EI2*.

———. "The Mission of an Ottoman Secret Agent in France in 1486." *JRAS*, 3–4, 112–32.

Mihailović, Konstantin. 2011. *Memoirs of a Janissary*. Translated by Benjamin Stolz. Historical Commentary and Notes by Svat Soucek. Princeton, NJ.

Miljković-Bojanić, Ema. 2004. *Smederevski sandžak, 1476–1560: Zemlja, naselja, stanovništvo*. Belgrade.

Mikó, Árpád. 2000. "Imago Historiae." In Árpád Mikó and Katalin Sinkó, eds., *Történelem–Kép: Szemelvények múlt és művészet kapcsolatából Magyarországon*. Budapest, 34–47.

Miović, Vesna. 2013. "Diplomatic Relations between the Ottoman Empire and the Republic of Dubrovnik." In Kármán and Kunčević 2013, 187–208.

Modelski, George, and William R. Thompson. 1988. *Seapower in Global Politics, 1494–1993*. Seattle.

Molnár, Antal. 2009. *Egy Raguzai kereskedőtársaság a hódolt Budán: Scopione Bona és Marino Bucchia vállalkozásának története és dokumentumai (1573–1595)*. Budapest.

Monshi, Eskandar Beg. 1978. *History of Shah 'Abbas the Great*. Translated by Roger M. Savory. 2 vols. Boulder, CO.

Motyl, Alexander J. 2001. *Imperial Ends: The Decay, Collapse, and Revival of Empires*. New York.

Mughul, Muhammad Yakub. 1965. "Portekizli'lerle Kızıldeniz'de Mücadele ve Hicaz'da Osmanlı Hakimiyetinin Yerleşmesi Hakkında Bir Vesika." *Belgeler* 2, 3–4, 37–47.

———. 1973–74. "Türk Amirali Emir ibn Behram Bey'in Hindistan Seferi (1531)." *TED* 4–5, 247–62.

———. 1974. *Kanuni Devri Osmanlıların Hint Okyanusu Politikası ve Osmanlı Hint Müslümanları Münasebetleri, 1517–1538*. Istanbul.

———. 1987. *Kanuni Devri*. 2nd ed. Ankara.

Mugnai, Bruno. 2018. *The Cretan War, 1645–1671: The Venetian-Ottoman Struggle in the Mediterranean*. Warwick.

Murphey, Rhoads. 1993. "Süleyman's Eastern Policy." In İnalcık and Kafadar 1993, 229–48.

———. 1999. *Ottoman Warfare, 1500–1700*. New Brunswick, NJ.

———. 2008. *Exploring Ottoman Sovereignty: Tradition, Image and Practice in the Ottoman Imperial Household, 1400–1800*. London.

Muslu, Cihan Yüksel. 2014. *The Ottomans and the Mamluks: Imperial Diplomacy and Warfare in the Islamic world*. London.

Müteferrika, İbrahim. (1732) 1995. *Usûlü'l-Hikem fi Nizâmi'l-Ümem*. Edited by Adil Şen. Ankara.

Nagy, Lajos. 1987. "Az 1686–87. évi hadjárat." In Szita 1987a, 15–51.

Nagy, László. 1985. *"Megint fölszánt magyar világ van . . ." Társadalom és hadsereg a XVII. század első felének Habsburg-ellenes küzdelmeiben*. Budapest.

———. 1986. *Hajdúvitézek 1591–1699*. Budapest.

Naima, Mustafa Efendi. 2007. *Târih-i Na'imâ: (Ravzatü'l-Hüseyn fî hulâsati ahbâri'l-hâfikayn)*. Edited by Mehmet İpşirli. 6 vols. Ankara.

Necipoğlu, Gülru. 1989. "Süleyman the Magnificent and the Representation of Power in the Context of Ottoman-Hapsburg-Papal Rivalry." *Art Bulletin* 71, 3, 401–27.

———. 1991. *Architecture, Ceremonial, and Power: The Topkapı Palace in the Fifteenth and Sixteenth Centuries.* New York.

———. 1992. "The Life of an Imperial Monument: Hagia Sophia after Byzantium." In Robert Mark and Ahmet Ş. Çakmak, eds., *Hagia Sophia from the Age of Justinian to the Present.* Cambridge, 195–226.

———. 2005. *The Age of Sinan: Architectural Culture in the Ottoman Empire.* Princeton, NJ.

———. 2019. "The Aesthetics of Empire: Arts, Politics and Commerce in the Construction of Sultan Süleyman's Magnificence." In Fodor 2019a, 115–58.

Necipoğlu, Nevra. 2009. *Byzantium between the Ottomans and the Latins: Politics and Society in the Late Empire.* Cambridge.

Neck, Rudolf. 1950. "Andrea Negroni. (Ein Beitrag zur Geschichte der österreichisch-türkischen Beziehungen nach dem Frieden von Zsitvatorok)." *MÖStA* 3, 166–95.

Nehring, Karl. 1986. "Magyarország és a zsitvatoroki szerződés." *Századok* 120, 3–49.

Németh, István. 1996. "'Ugyan ott Jenőnél Ur Barcsai Ákos fejedelemmé tétetek' (Ismeretlen magyar nyelvű forrás Barcsay Ákos török követjárásáról")." *Keletkutatás* 1996 tavasz, 57–80.

Neumann, Tibor. 2010. "Békekötés Pozsonyban-országgyűlés Budán. A Jagelló-Habsburg kapcsolatok egy fejezete (1490–2). (Első közlemény)." *Századok* 144, 335–72.

———. 2011. Békekötés Pozsonyban-országgyűlés Budán. A Jagelló-Habsburg kapcsolatok egy fejezete (1490– 1492) (Második közlemény)." *Századok* 145, 293–346.

———. 2014. "Dózsa legyőzője: Szapolyai János erdélyi vajdasága (1510–1526)." *Székelyföld* 18, 11, 93–107.

———. "Két nádor és egy vajda, avagy a Szapolyaiak útja a királyi trónig." In Fodor and Varga 2020, 13–45.

Newman, Andrew J. 2009. *Safavid Iran: Rebirth of a Persian Empire.* London.

Nicol, Donald M. 1968. *The Byzantine Family of Kantakouzenos (Cantacuzenus) ca. 1100–1460: A Genealogical and Prosopographical Study.* Washington, DC.

———. 1988. *Byzantium and Venice: A Study of Diplomatic and Cultural Relations.* Cambridge.

———. 1993. *The Last Centuries of Byzantium, 1261–1453.* Cambridge.

———. 1994a. *The Immortal Emperor: The Life and Legend of Constantine Palaiologos, Last Emperor of the Romans.* Cambridge.

———. 1994b. *The Byzantine Lady: Ten Portraits, 1250–1500.* Cambridge.

Nicolle, David. 2005. *Nicopolis, 1396: The Last Crusade.* Westport, CT

Nowakowska, Natalia. 2004. "Poland and the Crusade in the Reign of King Jan Olbracht, 1492– 1501." In Norman Housley, ed., *Crusading in the Fifteenth Century: Message and Impact.* Houndmills, Baskingstoke, 128–47.

Nye, Joseph S., Jr. 2004. *Soft Power: The Means to Success in World Politics.* New York.

Oborni, Teréz. 2002. *Erdély pénzügyei I. Ferdinánd uralma alatt.* Budapest.

———. 2003. "Die Herrschaft Ferdinands I. in Ungarn." In Fuchs and Kohler 2003, 147–65.

———. 2004. "From Principality to Province: Continuity and Change in Transylvania in the First Half of the Sixteenth Century." In Zombori 2004, 165–79.

———. 2011. *Udvar, állam és kormányzat a kora újkori Erdélyben—tanulmányok.* Budapest.

————. 2013a. "Gábor Bethlen and the Treaty of Nagyszombat (1615)." *Hungarian Historical Review* 2, 4, 761–89.

————. 2013b. "Between Vienna and Constantinople: Notes on the Legal Status of the Principality of Transylvania." In Kármán and Kunčević 2013, 67–89.

————. 2013c. "The Artful Diplomacy of István Báthory and the Survival of the Principality of Transylvania (1571)." In Spannenberger and Strohmeyer 2013, 85–93.

————. 2015a. "Le royaume des Szapolyai, du royaume de Hongrie orientale à la principauté de Transylvanie (1541–1571)." *Histoire, Économie et Société (Époques Moderne et Contemporaine)* 34, 3, 65–77.

————, ed. 2015b. *'Várad, Erdély kapuja . . .' Nagyvárad történelmi szerepe a fejedelemség korában.* Nagyvárad.

————. 2017. *Az ördöngös Barát: Fráter György (1482–1551).* Pécs and Budapest.

————. 2020. "'Georgius Monachus contra Reginam:' Queen Isabella and Her Reign over the Eastern Kingdom of Hungary (1541–1551)." In Ágnes Máté and Teréz Oborni, eds., *Isabella Jagiellon, Queen of Hungary (1539–1559).* Budapest, 209–33.

Oikonomides, Niholas. 1993. "The Turks in Europe (1305) and the Serbs in Asia Minor (1313)." In Zachariadou 1993a, 159–63.

————. 1994. "From Soldiers of Fortune to Gazi Warriors: The Tzympe Affair." In Heywood and Imber 1994, 239–48.

Ömich, Franz. (1582) 1986. Franciscus Omichius, *A tekintetes Ungnád Dávid Úr Sonneck bárója és Bleiburg zálogbirtokosa követségének és utazásának leírása Bécsből, Ausztriából Konstantinápolyba 1572-ben . . . Anno 1582.* In Kovács 1986, 23–56.

Önalp, Ertuğrul. 2008. "Hadım Süleyman Paşa'nın 1538 Yılındaki Hindistan Seferi." *OTAM* 23, 195–239.

Orhonlu, Cengiz. 1970a. *Osmanlı Tarihine Aid Belgeler: Telhisler (1597–1607).* Istanbul.

————.1970b. "Seydi Ali Reis." *TED* 1, 39–56.

————. 1970c. "Hint Kaptanlığı ve Piri Reis." *Belleten* 34, 235–54.

————. (1974) 1996. *Osmanlı İmparatorluğu'nun Güney Siyaseti: Habeş Eyaleti.* Ankara.

Ortvay, Tivadar. 1910. *A mohácsi csata elvesztésének okai és következményei.* Budapest.

————. 1914. *Mária. II. Lajos magyar király neje (1505–1558).* Budapest.

Ostapchuk, Victor. 2001. "The Human Landscape of the Ottoman Black Sea in the Face of the Cossack Naval Raids." *Oriente Moderno,* n.s., 20, 81, 23–95.

Ostapchuk, Victor, and Svitlana Bilyayeva. 2009. "The Ottoman Northern Black Sea Frontier at Akkerman Fortress: The View from a Historical and Archeological Project." In Peacock 2009, 137–70.

Ostrogorsky, George. 1969. *History of the Byzantine State.* Translated by Joan Hussey. Revised ed. New Brunswick, NJ.

Óváry, Lipót. 1890–1901. *A Magyar Tud. Akadémia Történelmi Bizottságának oklevél-másolatai.* 3 vols. Budapest.

Özbaran, Salih. 1977. "Osmanlı İmparatorluğu ve Hindistan Yolu: Onaltıncı Yüzyılda Ticaret Yolları Üzerinde Türk-Portekiz Rekabet ve İlişkileri." *TD* 31, 66–146.

————. 1978. "A Turkish Report on the Red Sea and the Portuguese in the Indian Ocean (1525)." *Arabian Studies* 4, 81–88. Reprinted in Özbaran 1994, 99–110.

———. (1986) 1994. "The Ottomans' Role in the Diffusion of Fire-arms and Military Technology in Asia and Africa in the Sixteenth Century." *Revue International d'Historire Militaire* [Ankara] 67, 77–83. Cited here from Özbaran 1994, 61–66.

———. 1994. *The Ottoman Response to European Expansion: Studies on Ottoman-Portuguese Relations in the Indian Ocean and Ottoman Administration in the Arab Lands during the Sixteenth Century.* Istanbul.

———. 2004a. *Yemen'den Basra'ya Sınırdaki Osmanlı.* Istanbul.

———. 2004b. "Basra ve Lahsa Eyaletlerinde Mali Uygulamalar." In Özbaran 2004a, 188–94.

———. 2009. *Ottoman Expansion toward the Indian Ocean in the Sixteenth Century.* Istanbul.

———. (2011) 2013. "Bir Korsan Denizcinin Gözlemleri ve Raporu (1525): Osmanlılar ve Hint Okyanusu." *Toplumsal Tarih* 215. Cited here from Özbaran 2013a, 33–58.

———. (2012) 2013. "1538'de Preveze ile Eşzamanlı Bir Hüsran: Hindistan Kapılarında Donanma-i Hümayun." *Toplumsal Tarih* 119. Cited here from Özbaran 2013a, 195–216.

———. 2013a. *Umman'da Kapışan İmparatorluklar: Osmanlı ve Portekiz.* Istanbul.

———. 2013b. "Ottoman Expansion in the Red Sea." In Faroqhi and Fleet 2013, 173–201.

Özcan, Abdülkadir. 1980–81. "Fâtih'in Teşkilât Kanunnâmesi ve Nizam-ı Âlem İçin Kardeş Katli Meselesi." *TD* 33, 7–56.

Özel, Oktay. 2016. *The Collapse of Rural Order in Ottoman Anatolia: Amasya 1576–1643.* Leiden and New York.

Öztürk, Said. 1999. "1042–1045 (1632–1635) Yıllarına Ait Bosna Eyaleti Bütçesi." *Dumlupınar Üniversitesi Sosyal Bilimler Dergisi* 1, 325–37.

Öztürk, Yücel. 2000. *Osmanlı Hakimiyetinde Kefe, 1475–1600.* Ankara.

Özvar, Erol. 2003. *Osmanlı Maliyesinde Malikâne Uygulaması.* Istanbul.

———. 2006. "Osmanlı Devletinin Bütçe Harcamaları (1509–1788)." In Genç and Özvar 2006, vol. 1, 197–238.

Özveri, Murat. 2006. *Okçuluk Hakkında Merak Ettiğiniz Her Şey.* Istanbul.

———. 2014. "Early Islamic Turkish Archery and Thumb Release." Tirendâz, http://www .tirendaz.com/en/?page_id=580 (accessed November 26, 2014).

Pagden, Anthony. 2009. *Worlds at War: The 2,500-year Struggle between East and West.* New York.

Pálffy, Géza. 1999a. *A császárváros védelmében: A győri főkapitányság története 1526–1598.* Győr.

———. 1999b. "Hírszerzés és hírközlés a törökkori Magyarországon." Petercsák and Berecz 1999, 33–59.

———. 2000a. "The Origins and Development of the Border Defence System against the Ottoman Empire in Hungary." In Dávid and Fodor 2000, 3–69.

———. 2000b. *Európa védelmében. Haditérképészet a Habsburg Birodalom magyarországi határvidékén a 16–17. században.* 2nd rev. ed. Pápa.

———. 2003a. "Türkenabwehr, Grenzsoldatentum und die Militarisierung der Gesellschaft in Ungarn in der Frühen Neuzeit." *Historisches Jahrbuch* 123, 111–148.

———. 2003b. "Der Preis für die Verteidigung der Habsburgermonarchie. Die Kosten der Türkenabwehr in der zweiten Hälfte des 16. Jahrhunderts." In Edelmayer, Lanzinner, and Rauscher 2003, 20–44.

———. 2008. "Scorched-Earth Tactics in Ottoman Hungary: On a Controversy in Military Theory and Practice on the Habsburg-Ottoman Frontier." *AOH* 61, 181–200.

———. 2009. *The Kingdom of Hungary and the Habsburg Monarchy in the Sixteenth Century.* Translated by Thomas J. DeKornfeld and Helen D. DeKornfeld. Boulder, CO.

———. 2010. *A Magyar Királyság és a Habsburg Monarchia a 16. században.* Budapest.

———. 2011a. *Die Anfänge der Militärkartographie in der Habsburgermonarchie.* Budapest.

———. 2011b. "Egy rendkívüli forrás a magyar politikai elit 16. századi földrajzi ismereteiről. Az 1526 és 1556 között török kézre került magyarországi városok, várak és kastélyok összeírása a Német-római Birodalom rendjei számára." In Gy. Terei et al., eds., *Várak nyomában: Tanulmányok a 60 éves Feld István tiszteletére.* Budapest, 177–94.

Pálosfalvi, Tamás. 2018. *From Nicopolis to Mohács: A History of Ottoman–Hungarian Warfare, 1389–1526.* Leiden and New York.

Pamuk, Şevket. 2000. *A Monetary History of the Ottoman Empire.* Cambridge.

———. 2004. "Institutional Change and the Longevity of the Ottoman Empire, 1500–1800." *Journal of Interdisciplinary History* 35, 2, 225–47.

Panaite, Viorel. 2000. *The Ottoman Law of War and Peace: The Ottoman Empire and Tribute Payers.* Boulder, CO.

———. 2013. "The Legal and Political Status of Wallachia and Moldavia in Relation to the Ottoman Porte." In Kármán and Kunčević 2013, 9–42.

Panciera, Walter. 2006. "La frontiera dalmata nel XVI secolo: fonti e problemi." *Società e Storia* 114, 783–804.

———. 2013. "Building a Boundary: The First Venetian-Ottoman Border in Dalmatia, 1573–1576." *Radovi - Zavod za hrvatsku povijest* 45, 9–38.

Panzac, Daniel. 2009. *La marine ottomane: De l'apogée à la chute de l'Empire (1572–1923).* Paris.

Papademetriou, Tom. 2015. *Render unto the Sultan: Power, Authority, and the Greek Orthodox Church in the Early Ottoman Centuries.* Oxford.

Papp, Sándor. 2003. *Die Verleihungs-, Bekräftigungs- und Vertragsurkunden der Osmanen für Ungarn und Siebenbürgen: Eine quellenkritische Untersuchung.* Vienna.

———. 2004. "Hungary and the Ottoman Empire (from the Beginnings to 1540)." In Zombori 2004, 37–89.

———. 2011. "Bethlen Gábor, a magyar királyság és a Porta (1619–1621)." *Századok* 145, 915–73.

———. 2013. *Török szövetség—Habsburg kiegyezés. A Bocskai-felkelés történetéhez.* Akadémiai doktori disszertáció. Szeged.

———. 2016. "Tarihi Üngürüs." *DİA* Ek-2, 586–87.

———. 2018. "Az Oszmán Birodalom, a Magyar Királyság és a Habsburg Monarchia kapcsolattörténete a békekötések tükrében (vázlat és adatbázis)." *Aetas* 33, 4, 86–99.

Parker, Geoffrey. 1995. "In Defense of the Military Revolution." In Rogers 1995, 337–65.

———.1998. *The Grand Strategy of Philip II.* New Haven, CT, and London,

———.1999. *The Military Revolution: Military Innovation and the Rise of the West, 1500–1800.* Revised ed. Cambridge.

———. 2019. *Emperor: A New Life of Charles V.* New Haven, CT, and London.

Parrott, David. 2012. *The Business of War: Military Enterprise and Military Revolution in Early Modern Europe.* Cambridge.

Parry, Vernon J. 1975. "La manière de combattre." In Parry and Yapp 1975, 218–56.

Parry, Vernon J., and M. E. Yapp, eds. 1975. *War, Technology and Society in the Middle East.* London.

Pataki, József. 1976. "Radu de la Afumaţi és Zápolya János magatartása a Mohácsi csata előestéjén." In László Bányai ed., *A magyar nemzetiség története és testvéri együttműködése a román nemzettel: Tanulmányok.* Bucharest, 63–84.

Peacock, A. C. S., ed. 2009. *The Frontiers of the Ottoman World.* Oxford.

Peçevi, İbrahim. (1864–66) 1980. *Tarih-i Peçevi.* 2 vols. Reprint with index by Fahri Ç. Derin and Vahit Çabuk. Istanbul.

———. 1916. "Pecsevi Ibráhim Tárikhjából." In *Török történetírók* vol. 3. Edited by Imre Karácson and Gyula Szekfű. Budapest, 67–193.

Pécsi Kis, Péter. (1564) 1993. *Magyarázat [Exegeticon].* Translated and edited by József Bessenyei. Budapest.

Pedani, Maria Pia. 1994. *In nome del Gran Signore: Inviati ottomani a Venezia dalla caduta di Costantinopoli alla Guerra di Candia.* Venice.

———. 1996. "Ottoman Diplomats in the West: The Sultan's Ambassadors to the Republic of Venice." *TİD* 11, 187–202.

———. 1998. "Ottoman Fetihnames: The Imperial Letters Announcing a Victory." *TİD* 13, 181–92.

———. 2002. *Dalla frontiera al confine.* Rome.

———. 2005 "Some Remarks upon the Ottoman Geo-political Vision of the Mediterranean in the Period of the Cyprus War (1570–1573)." In Imber, Kiyotaki, and Murphey 2005, vol. 2, 23–35.

———. 2009. "The Sultan and the Venetian *Bailo*: Ceremonial Diplomatic Protocol in Istanbul." In Ralph Kauz, Giorgio Rota, and Jan Paul Niederkorn, eds., *Diplomatisches Zeremoniell in Europa und im Mittleren Osten in der Frühen Neuzeit.* Vienna, 287–99.

———. 2010. *Inventory of the Lettere e Scritture Turchesche in the Venetian State Archives.* Leiden and New York.

———, ed. 2013. *Il Palazzo di Venezia a Istanbul e I suoi antichi abitanti/ İstanbul'daki Venedik Sarayı ve Eski Yaşayanları.* Venice.

———. 2014. "Ottoman Ships and Venetian Craftsmen in the 16th Century." In Dejanirah Couto, Feza Günergun, and Maria Pia Pedani Fabris, eds., *Seapower, Technology and Trade: Studies in Turkish Maritime History.* Istanbul, 460–64.

Peirce, Leslie P. 1993. *The Imperial Harem: Women and Sovereignty in the Ottoman Empire.* Oxford.

Perdue, Peter C. 2005. *China Marches West: The Qing Conquest of Central Eurasia.* Cambridge, MA.

Perjés, Géza. 1979. *Mohács.* Budapest.

———. 1989. *The Fall of the Medieval Kingdom of Hungary: Mohács 1526—Buda 1541.* Boulder, CO. [English translation of Perjés 1979]

Péter, Katalin. 2002. "The Golden Age of the Principality (1606–1660)." In László Makkai and Zolán Szász, eds., *History of Transylvania II: From 1606 to 1830.* Boulder, CO, 5–228.

Petercsák, Tivadar, and Mátyás Berecz, eds. 1999. *Információáramlás a magyar és török végvári rendszerben.* Eger.

Petritsch, Ernst Dieter. 1982. "Österreich und die Türkei nach dem Ersten Weltkrieg. Zum Wandel der diplomatischen und kulturellen Beziehungen." *MÖStA* 35, 199–237.

———. 1985. "Der habsburgisch-osmanische Friedensvertrag des Jahres 1547." *MÖStA* 38, 49–80.

———. 1991. *Regesten der osmanischen Dokumente im Österreichischen Staatsarchiv.* Vienna.

———. 1993. "Tribut oder Ehrengeschenk? Ein Beitrag zu den habsburgisch-osmanischen Beziehungen in der zwieten Hälfte des 16. Jahrhunderts." In Elisabeth Springer and Leopold Kammerhofer, eds., *Archiv und Forschung. Das Haus-, Hof- und Staatsarchiv in seiner Bedeutung für die Geschichte Österreichs und Europas.* Vienna, 49–58.

———. 2005. "Abenteurer oder Diplomaten? Ein Beitrag zu den diplomatischen Beziehungen Ferdinands I. mit den Osmanen," In Fuchs, Oborni, and Ujváry 2005, 249–61.

———. 2014. "Grenz- und Raumkonzeptionen in den Friedensverträgen von Zsitvatorok und Karlowitz." In Spannenberger and Varga 2014, 39–51.

Philippides, Marios, and Walter K. Hanak. 2011. *The Siege and the Fall of Constantinople in 1453: Historiography, Topography, and Military Studies.* Farnham, UK.

Philliou, Christine May. 2009. *Biography of an Empire: Governing Ottomans in an Age of Revolution.* Berkeley.

Pinto, Karen. 2012. "Searchin' His Eyes, Lookin' for Traces: Piri Reis' World Map of 1513 and Its Islamic Iconographic Connections (A Reading Through Bağdat 334 and Proust)." *OA* 39, 63–94.

Pitcher, Donald Edgar. 1973. *An Historical Geography of the Ottoman Empire from Earliest Times to the End of the Sixteenth Century.* Leiden.

Popović, Mihailo St. 2009. "Mara Branković. Eine Frau zwischen dem christlichen und dem islamischen Kulturkreis im 15. Jahrhundert." *Ostkirchliche Studien,* 58, 2, 357–64.

———. 2010. "The Order of the Dragon and the Serbian Despot Stefan Lazarević." In Ekaterini Mitsiou et al. eds., *Emperor Sigismund and the Orthodox World.* Vienna, 2010, 103–6.

———. 2012. *Mara Branković. Eine Frau zwischen dem christlichen und dem islamischen Kulturkreis im 15. Jahrhundert.* Wiesbaden.

Pósán, László. 1998. "Zsigmond és a Német Lovagrend." *HK* 111, 3, 85–112.

Posch, Walter. 2013. *Osmanisch-safavidische Beziehungen (1545–1550): Der Fall Alkas Mirza.* Vols. 1–2. Vienna.

Preto, Paolo. 1975. *Venezia e i Turchi.* Florence.

———. 1993. "Relations between the Papacy, Venice and the Ottoman Empire." In İnalcık and Kafadar 1993, 195–202.

———. 1994. *I Servizi Segreti di Venezia.* Milan.

Prlender, Ivica. 1991. "Sporazum u Tati 1426. godine i Žigmundovi obrambeni sustavi." *Historijski zbornik,* 44, 1, 23–41.

Pryor, John H. 1992. *Geography, Technology, and War: Studies in the Maritime History of the Mediterranean, 649–1571.* Cambridge.

Pullan, Brian S. 1997. *The Jews of Europe and the Inquisition of Venice, 1550–1670.* New York.

R. Várkonyi, Ágnes. 1978. "Erdély és a német-római császárválasztás 1658-ban." In Ágnes R. Várkonyi, *Magyarország keresztútjain. Tanulányok a XVII. századról.* Budapest, 157–66.

———. 2002. "The Last Decades of the Independent Principality (1660–1711)." In László Makkai and Zolán Szász, eds. *History of Transylvania II: From 1606 to 1830.* Boulder, CO, 233–513.

———. 2016. "Zrínyi, the Statesman." In Hausner 2016, 58–107.

Raby, Julian. 1983. "Mehmed the Conqueror's Greek Scriptorium." *Dumbarton Oaks Papers* 37, 15–34.

Rácz, István. 1969. *Hajdúk a XVII. században.* Debrecen.

Rady, Martyn. 1992. "Voivode and *Regnum*: Transylvania's Place in the Medieval Kingdom of Hungary." In László Péter ed., *Historians and the History of Transylvania.* Boulder, CO, 87–101.

Râşid Mehmed Efendi, Çelebizâde İsmaîl Âsım Efendi. 2013. *Târîh-i Râşid ve Zeyli (1071– 1114/1660–1703).* Edited by Abdülkadir Özcan, Yunus Uğur, Baki Çakır, and A. Zeki İzgöer. 3 vols. Istanbul.

Rauscher, Peter. 2004. *Zwischen Ständen und Gläubigern. Die kaiserlichen Finanzen unter Ferdinand I. und Maximilian II. (1556–1576).* Vienna.

———. ed. 2010. *Kriegführung und Staatsfinanzen: Die Habsburgermonarchie und das Heilige Römische Reich vom Dreißigjährigen Krieg bis zum Ende des habsburgischen Kaisertums 1740.* Münster.

———. 2019. "Camerale, Contributionale, Creditors and Crisis: The Finances of the Habsburg Empire from the Battle of Mohács to the Thirty Years' War." In Fodor 2019a, 193–212.

Rauscher, Peter, Andrea Serles, and Thomas Winkelbauer, eds. 2012. *Das "Blut des Staatskörpers."* Munich.

Rázsó, Gyula. 1973. "A Zsigmond-kori Magyarország és a török veszély (1393–1437)." *HK* 20, 403–41.

———. 1982. "The Mercenary Army of King Matthias Corvinus." In Bak and Király 1982, 125–40.

———. 2002. "Military Reforms in the Fifteenth Century." In Veszprémy and Király 2002, 54–82.

Regele, Oskar. 1949. *Der österreichische Hofkriegsrat 1556–1848.* Vienna.

Reid, Anthony. 2014. "Turkey as Aceh's Alternative Imperium." *Archipel* 87, 81–102.

Reindl, Hedda. 1983. *Männer um Bāyezīd: Eine prosopographische Studie über die Epoche Sultan Bāyezīds II. (1481–1512).* Berlin.

Reindl-Kiel, Hedda. 2013. "Some Notes on Hersekzade Ahmed Pasha, His Family and His Books." *JTS* 40 [*Defterology: Festschrift in Honor of Health Lowry,* ed Selim Kuru and Baki Tezcan], 315–26.

Reinert, Stephen W. 1993. "From Niš to Kosovo Polje: Reflections on Murad I's Final Years." In Zachariadou 1993a, 169–211.

Reinsch, Diether Roderich. 2003. "Kritobulos of Imbros—Learned Historian, Ottoman Reaya and Byzantine Patriot." *Zbornik radova Vizantološkog instituta* 40, 297–308.

Repp, Richard C. 1986. *The Mufti of Istanbul: A Study in the Development of the Ottoman Learned Hierarchy.* London.

Reychman, Jan, and Ananiasz Zajaczkowski. 1968. *Handbook of Ottoman-Turkish Diplomatics.* The Hague.

Rodríguez-Salgado, María José. 1988. *The Changing Face of Empire: Charles V, Philip II, and Habsburg Authority, 1551–1559*. Cambridge.

———. 2015. "Eating Bread Together: Hapsburg Diplomacy and Intelligence-Gathering in Mid-sixteenth-century Istanbul." In Emilio Sola Castaño and Gennaro Varriale, eds., *Detrás de las apariencias: Información y espionaje (siglos XVI-XVII)*. Alcalá de Henares, 73–100.

Rogers, C. J., ed. 1995. *The Military Revolution Debate: Readings on the Military Transformation of Early Modern Europe*. Boulder, CO.

Rogers, J. M. 1992. "Itineraries and Town Views in Ottoman Histories." In Harley and Woodward 1992, 228–55.

Röhrborn, Klaus. 1973. *Untersuchungen zur osmanischen Verwaltungsgeschichte*. Berlin.

Roider, Karl A. 1972. *The Reluctant Ally: Austria's Policy in the Austro-Turkish War, 1737–1939*. Baton Rouge.

Römer, Claudia. 2008. "Contemporary European Translations of Ottoman Documents and Vice Versa (15th–17th Centuries)." *AOH* 61, 215–26.

Römer, Claudia, and Nicolas Vatin. 2015. "Aceh et la Porte dans les années 1560." *Turcica* 46, 63–111.

———. 2019. "The Hungarian Frontier and Süleyman's Way to Szigetvár according to Ottoman Sources." In Fodor 2019a, 341–58.

Ross, E. Dennison. 1921. "The Portuguese in India and Arabia between 1507 and 1517." *JRAS* 53, 4, 545–562.

———. 1922. "The Portuguese in India and Arabia, 1517–38." *JRAS* 54, 1, 1–18.

Roşu, Felicia. 2017. *Elective Monarchy in Transylvania and Poland-Lithuania, 1569–1587*. Oxford.

Rota, Giorgio. 2015. "Fighting with the Qızılbash: Preliminary Remarks on Safavid Warfare." In Kurt Franz and Wolfgang Holzwarth, eds., *Nomad Military Power in Iran and Adjacent Areas in the Islamic Period*. Wiesbaden, 233–45.

Rothman, E. Natalie. 2009. "Interpreting Dragomans: Boundaries and Crossings in the Early Modern Mediterranean." *Comparative Studies in Society and History* 51, 4, 771–800.

———. 2012. *Brokering Empire: Trans-Imperial Subjects between Venice and Istanbul*. Ithaca, NY.

Rouillard, Clarence Dana. 1941. *The Turk in French History, Thought, and Literature (1520–1660)*. Paris.

Rozsnyai, Dávid. 1867. *Rozsnyai Dávid az utólsó török deák történelmi maradványai*. Edited by Sándor Szilágyi. Pest.

Runciman, Steven. 1988. *The Great Church in Captivity: A Study of the Patriarchate of Constantinople from the Eve of the Turkish Conquest to the Greek War of Independence*. Cambridge.

Rúzsás, Lajos, ed. 1966. Szigetvári emlékkönyv. Szigetvár 1566. évi ostrománnak 400. évordulójára. Budapest.

Rúzsás, Lajos, and Ferenc Szakály, eds. 1986. *Mohács. Tanulmányok a mohácsi csata 450. évfordulója alkalmából*. Budapest.

Rycaut, Paul. 1686. *The History of the Present State of the Ottoman Empire*. London.

Šabanović, Hazim. 1982. *Bosanski pašaluk: Postanak i upravna podjela*. Sarajevo.

Sabev, Orlin. 2002. "The Legend of Köse Mihal: Additional Notes." *Turcica* 34, 241–52.

Sahillioğlu, Halil. 1965. "Dördüncü Marad'ın Bağdat Seferi Menzilnamesi–Bağdat Seferi Harp Jurnalı." *Belgeler* 2, 3–4, 1–35.

———. 1985. "1524–1525 Osmanlı Bütçesi." *İFM* 41, 1–4, 415–52.

————. 1990. "Osmanlı Döneminde Irak'ın İdari Taksımatı." *Belleten* 54, 211, 1233–54.

————. 2002. *Topkapı Sarayı H.951–952 Tarihli ve E-12321 Numaralı Mühimme Defteri.* Istanbul.

Şahin, İlhan. 1979. "Timar Sistemi Hakkında Bir Risale." *TD* 32, 905–35.

————. 1999. "XV. ve XVI. Asırlarda Osmanlı Taşra Teşkilati'nin Özellikleri." In Mahir Aydın ed., *XV ve XVI Asırları Türk Asrı Yapan Değerler*. Istanbul, 123–130.

Şahin, İlhan, and Feridun Emecen. 1994. *Osmanlılarda Divan–Bürokrası–Ahkam. II Bayezid Dönemine Ait 906/1501 Tarihli Ahkam Defteri*. Istanbul.

Şahin, Kaya. 2013. *Empire and Power in the Reign of Süleyman*. Cambridge.

Sahlins, Peter. 1989. *Boundaries: The Making of France and Spain in the Pyrenees*. Berkeley, CA.

Şakul, Kahraman. 2011. "General Observations on the Ottoman Military Industry, 1774–1839: Problems of Organization and Standardization." In Günergun and Raina 2011, 41–55.

————. 2019. "Siege Warfare in Verse and Prose: The Ottoman Conquest of Kamianets-Podilsky (Kamaniçe), 1672." In Anke Fischer-Kattner and Jamel Ostwald, eds., *The World of the Siege: Representations of Early Modern Positional Warfare*. Leiden and New York, 205–40.

————. 2020. "The Azadlu Gunpowder Works: Catalyst for the Military Industry Complexes of Istanbul." In Frank Castiglione, Ethan L. Menchinger, and Veysel Şimşek, eds., *Ottoman War and Peace. Studies in Honor of Virginia H. Aksan*. Leiden and Boston, 72–100.

Salamon, Ferenc. 1884. *Két magyar diplomata a tizenhetedik századból*. Budapest.

————. 1886. *Magyarország a török hódítás korában*. 2nd rev. ed. Budapest.

Salzmann, Ariel. 2004. *Tocqueville in the Ottoman Empire: Rival Paths to the Modern State*. Leiden and New York.

Sanuto, Marino. 1878. Wenzel Gusztáv, ed., *Marino Sanuto Világkrónikájának Magyarországot illető tudósításai*. III. *Magyar Történelmi Tár* 25, 1–390.

Schaendlinger, Anton C. 1978. *Die Feldzugstagebücher des ersten und zweiten ungarischen Feldzugs Süleymans I*. Vienna.

Schaendlinger, Anton C., and Claudia Römer, eds. 1983. *Die Schreiben Süleymans des Prächtigen zur Karl V., Ferdinand I. und Maximilian II. Transkriptionen und Übersetzungen*. Vienna.

————. 1986. *Die Schreiben Süleymans des Prächtigen an Vasallen, Militärbeamte, Beamte und Richter. Transkriptionen und Übersetzungen*. Vienna.

Schamiloğlu, Uli. 2004. "The Rise of the Ottoman Empire: The Black Death in Medieval Anatolia and Its Impact on Turkish Civilization." In Neguin Yavari et al., eds., *Views from the Edge: Essays in Honor of Richard W. Bulliet*. New York, 255–79.

Schmitt, Oliver Jens. 2009. *Skanderberg: Der neue Alexander auf dem Balkan*. Regensburg.

Schnerb, Bertrand. 1998. "A francia-burgundi kontingens részvétele a nikápolyi hadjáratban." *HK* 111, 35–45.

Schulze, Winfried. 1995. "The Emergence and Consolidation of the 'Tax State.' I. The Sixteenth Century." In Bonney 1995a, 261–79.

Seidel, Friedrich. 1711. *Denckwürdige Gesandtschafft an die Ottomannische Pforte, Welche ehmahls auf Röm. Kays. Maj. Rudolphi II. Hohen Befehl Herr Fridrich von Krekwitz . . . verrichtet*. Görlitz.

————. 2010. *Sultanın Zindadında. Osmanlı İmparatorluğuna Gönderilen Bir Elçilik Heyetinin İbret Verici Öyküsü (1591–1596)*. Translated by Türkis Noyan. Istanbul.

Seipel, Wilfried. 2000. *Der Kriegszug Kaiser Karls V. gegen Tunis: Kartons und Tapisserien.* Vienna.

Selânikî, Mustafa. 1999. *Tarih-i Selânikî.* 2nd ed. Edited by Mehmet İpşirli. 2 vols. Ankara.

Semendire. 1530. *MAD 506 Numaralı Semendire Livası İcmal Tahrir Defteri (937/1530).* Ankara.

Setton, Kenneth M. 1976–84. *The Papacy and the Levant, 1204–1571.* 4 vols. Philadelphia, PA.

———. 1991. *Venice, Austria, and the Turks in the Seventeenth Century.* Philadelphia, PA.

Severi, Bart. 2001. "'Denari in loco delle terre' Imperial Envoy Gerard Veltwijck and Habsburg Policy towards the Ottoman Empire, 1545–1547." *AOH* 54, 211–56.

———. 2015. "Diplomats from the Low Countries in Istanbul: Astuteness, Pragmatism and Professionalization in Habsburg-Ottoman Diplomacy of the Sixteenth Century." https://www.researchgate.net/publication/281068618.

Silahdar, Fındıklı Mehmed Ağa. 2001. *Nusretname.* (1106–1133/1695–1721). Ed. Mehmed Topal. PhD dissertation, Marmara University, Istanbul.

———. 2012. *Zeyli Fezleke (1065–22 Ca. 1106 / 1654–7 Şubat 1695).* Ed. Nazire Karaçay Türkal. PhD dissertation, Marmara University, Istanbul.

Sinkovics, István. 1968. *Magyar történeti szöveggyűjtemény II: 1526–1790.* Budapest.

———. 1985. "Az ország megosztottságának állandósulása (1541–1570)." In R. Várkonyi Ágnes, ed., *Magyarország története 1526–1686.* Vol. 1. Budapest, 223–83.

Şimşirgil, Ahmet. 2012. *Slovakya'da Osmanlılar: Türk Uyvar (1663–1685).* İstanbul.

Šišić, Ferdo. 1912. *Hrvatski saborski spisi/ Acta comitialia regni Croatie, Dalmatiae, Slavoniae. Knjiga prva. Od godine 1526 do godine 1536.* Zagreb.

Skilliter, S. A. 1971. "The Hispano-Ottoman Armistice of 1581." In C. E. Bosworth, ed., *Iran and Islam: In Memory of the Late Vladimir Minorsky.* Edinburgh, 491–515.

———. 1977. *William Harborne and the Trade with Turkey, 1578–1582: A Documentary Study of the First Anglo-Ottoman Relations.* Oxford.

Smith, Dianne L. 1993. "Muscovite Logistics, 1462–1598." *Slavonic and East European Review* 71, 1, 38–39.

Smith, Robert Douglas, and Kelly DeVries. 2001. *Rhodes Besieged: A New History.* Stroud.

Soucek, Svat. 1971. "The Rise of the Barbarossas in North Africa." *AO* 3, 238–50. Reprinted in Soucek 2009, 66–78.

———. 1975. "Certain Types of Ships in Ottoman-Turkish Terminology." *Turcica* 7, 233–49.

———. 1993. "Piri Reis and Suleyman the Magnificent." In İnalcık and Kafadar 1993, 343–52.

———. 1994. "Piri Reis and the Ottoman Discovery of the Great Discoveries." *Studia Islamica* 79, 121–42.

———. 1996. *Piri Reis & Turkish Mapmaking after Columbus: The Khalili Portolan Atlas.* London.

———. 2004. "Naval Aspects of the Ottoman Conquests of Rhodes, Cyprus and Crete." *Studia Islamica* 98/99, 219–61.

———. 2009. *Studies in Ottoman Naval History and Maritime Geography.* Istanbul.

———. 2010. "About the Ottoman Age of Exploration." *AO* 27, 313–42.

———. 2012. "Five Famous Ottoman Turks of the Sixteenth Century." *OA* 40, 325–41.

———. 2013. "The Ottoman Conquest of Egypt and Algeria." In Lellouch and Michel 2013, 79–98.

Spandounes, Theodore. 1997. *On the Origin of the Ottoman Empire*. Translated and edited by Donald Nicol. Cambridge.

Spannenberger, Norbert, and Arno Strohmeyer, eds. 2013. *Frieden und Konfliktmanagement in interkulturellen Räumen: Das Osmanische Reich und die Habsburgermonarchie in der Frühen Neuzeit*. Stuttgart.

Spannenberger, Norbert, and Szabolcs Varga. 2014. *Ein Raum im Wandel: Die osmanisch-habsburgische Grenzregion vom 16. bis zum 18. Jahrhundert*. Stuttgart.

Sperl, Karin, Martin Scheutz, and Arno Strohmeyer, eds. 2016. *Die Schlacht von Mogersdorf/St. Gotthard und der Friede von Eisenburg/Vasvár. Rahmenbedingungen, Akteure, Auswirkungen und Rezeption eines europäischen Ereignisses*. Mogersdorf.

Spremić, Momčilo. 2014. "Le despote Stefan Lazarević et 'Sieur' Djuradj Branković." *Balcanica* 45, 145–63.

Spuler, Bertold. 1935. "Die Europaeische Diplomatie in Konstantinopel bis zum Frieden von Belgrad (1739)." *Jahrbücher für Kultur und Geschichte der Slaven*, Neue Folge 11, 53–115, 171–222, 313–66.

Sroka, Stanisław A. 2005. *Jadwiga Zapolya: Piastówna śląska na Węgrzech w dobie panowania Jagiellonów*. Kraków.

Stavrides, Theoharis. 2001. *The Sultan of Vezirs: The Life and Times of the Ottoman Grand Vezir Mahmud Pasha Angelović (1453–1474)*. Leiden and New York.

———. 2016. "From Byzantine Aristocracy to Ottoman Ruling Elite: Mahmud Pasha Angelović and His Christian Circle, 1458–1474." In Christine Isom-Verhaaren and Kent F. Schull, eds., *Living in the Ottoman Realm: Empire and Identity, 13th to 20th Centuries*. Bloomington and Indianapolis, 55–65.

Stevens, Carol B. 2007. *Russia's Wars of Emergence, 1460–1730*. Harlow.

Stoye, John. 1965. *The Siege of Vienna*. New York.

———. 1994. *Marsigli's Europe, 1680–1730: The Life and Times of Luigi Ferdinando Marsigli, Soldier and Virtuoso*. New Haven, CT.

Strauss, Johann. 1992. "How Cyprus Came under Turkish Rule: A Conquest and the Historians." *WZKM* 82, 325–34.

Stripling, George William Frederick. 1942. *The Ottoman Turks and the Arabs, 1511–1574*. Urbana, IL.

Strohmeyer, Arno. 2019. "'Clash' or 'Go-Between'? Habsburg-Ottoman Relations in the Age of Süleyman (1520–1566)." In Fodor 2019a, 213–39.

Sudár, Balázs. 2009. "Tko je bio Hasan-Paša Jakovali?" *Scrinia Slavonica* 9, 398–406.

———. 2011a. "A hódoltsági pasák az oszmán belpolitika forgatagában (1657–1665)." *HK* 124, 888–909.

———. 2011b. "Iszkender és Bethlen Gábor: A pasa és a fejedelem." *Századok* 145, 975–95.

———. 2015. "A váradi török tartomány első évei (1600–1665.)" In Oborni 2015b, 110–12.

———. 2017a. "The Ottomans and the Mental Conquest of Hungary." In Pál Fodor and Pál Ács, eds., *Identity and Culture in Ottoman Hungary*. Berlin, 55–68.

———. 2017b. "Egy kisiklatott hadjárat. Fázil Ahmed pasa nagyvezír 1664. évi hadműveletei." In Tóth and Zágorhidi 2017, 275–86.

———. 2017c. "A téli hadjárat és Pécs pusztulása 1664-ben." In Varga Szabolcs, ed., *Vészterhes idők a Mecsekalján: Háborúk, járványok és természeti katasztrófák Pécsett az ókortól a második világháborúig*. Pécs, 123–30.

Sugár, István. 1979. "A mohamedán vallásról katólikusra térő török alattvalók Egerben." *Az Egri Múzeum Évkönyve* XVI-XVII. Eger, 183–216.

———. 1991. *Az egri vár históriája.* 2nd rev. ed. Budapest.

Sugar, Peter. 1978. "A Near-Perfect Military Society: The Ottoman Empire." In L. L. Farrar, ed., *War: A Historical, Political and Social Study.* Santa Barbara, CA, 95–104.

Szabó, Pál. 2010. "'Ahol Magyar Királyságunk épsége ered.' Nándorfehérvár első török ostroma (1440)." *Belvedere* 22, 2–4, 59–85.

Szakály, Ferenc. 1969. *Parasztvármegyék a XVII. és XVIII. században.* Budapest.

———. 1975. *A mohácsi csata.* Budapest.

———. 1978. "Remarques sur l'armée de Jovan Tcherni." *AHASH* 24, 41–82.

———. 1979. "Phases of Turco-Hungarian Warfare before the Battle of Mohács (1365–1526)." *AOH* 33, 65–111.

———. 1981. *Magyar adóztatás a török hódoltságban.* Budapest.

———. 1982. "The Hungarian-Croatian Border Defense System and Its Collapse." In Bak and Király 1982, 141–58.

———. 1983. "Magyar diplomaták, utazók, rabok és renegátok a 16. századi Isztambulban." In Ferenc Szakály, ed., *Szigetvári Csöbör Balázs török miniatúrái 1570.* Budapest, 5–77.

———. 1986. *Hungaria Eliberata: Budavár visszavétele és Magyarország felszabadítása a török uralom alól, 1683–1718.* Budapest.

———. 1990. "The Early Ottoman Period, including Royal Hungary, 1526–1606." In Peter F. Sugar, Péter Hanák, and Tibor Frank, eds., *A History of Hungary.* Bloomington, IN.

———. 1994. "Nándorfehérvár, 1521: The Beginning of the End of the Medieval Hungarian Kingdom." In Dávid and Fodor 1994a, 47–76.

———. 1995. *Lodovico Gritti in Hungary: 1529–1534.* Budapest.

———. 1997. *Magyar intézmények a török hódoltságban.* Budapest.

Szakály, Ferenc, and Lajos Tardy. 1989. "Nyomozás egy magyar származású szultáni tolmács után." *Keletkutatás.* Ősz. 60–67.

———. 1992. "Auf der Suche nach einem aus Ungarn stammenden Dolmetscher des Sultans." In Christa Fragner and Klaus Schwarz, eds., *Osmanistik, Turkologie, Diplomatik: Festgabe an Josef Matuz.* Berlin, 289–301.

Szalárdi, János, 1980. *Siralmas magyar krónikája.* Edited by Ferenc Szakály. Budapest.

Szalay, László. 1859. *Adalékok a magyar nemzet történetéhez a XVI-dik században.* Pest.

———. ed. 1860. *Verancsics Antal, m. kir. helytartó, esztergomi érsek összes munkái.* Vol. 5, *Második portai követség, 1567–1568.* Pest.

———. 1861. *A Magyarországi Szerb telepek jogviszonya az államhoz.* Pest.

———. 1862. *Erdély és a Porta (1567–1578).* Pest.

Szántó, Imre. 1980. *A végvári rendszer kiépítése és fénykora Magyarországon, 1541–1593.* Budapest.

———. 1985. *Küzdelem a török terjeszkedés ellen Magyarországon: Az 1551–52. évi várháborúk.* Budapest.

Székely, Ottokár. 1919–21. "Hunyadi János első török hadjáratai (1441–1444)." *HK* 22–22, 1–64.

Szerémi, György. 1857. *Epistola de perdicione Regni Hungarorum.* Edited by Gusztáv Wenzel. Pest

———. 1979. *Magyarország romlásáról.* Budapest.

Szilády, Áron, and Sándor Szilágyi, eds. 1868–73. *Török-magyarkori állam-okmánytár.* 9 vols. Budapest.

Szilágyi, Sándor. 1866. *Erdélyország története tekintettel mivelődésére*. 2 vols. Pest.

———. 1875. *II Rákóczy György és az európai diplomaczia: Okmánytár II Rákóczy György diplomacziai összeköttetéseihez (1648–1660)*. Budapest.

———. 1890–91. *Erdély és az észak-keleti háború: Levelek és okiratok*. 2 vols. Budapest.

Szita, László. 1987a. *Budától–Belgrádig. Válogatott dokumentumrészletek az 1686–1688. évi törökellenes hadjáratok történetéhez. A nagyharsányi csata 300. évfordulójának emlékére*. Pécs.

———. 1987b. "Erdély megszállása 1687 őszén. Az 1688. évi belgrádi, szlavóniai és boszniai hadjárat." In Szita 1987a, 55–69.

———. 1997. "Az 1697 évi hadjárat a források tükrében." In Szita and Seewann 1997, 11–48.

Szita, László, and Gerhard Seewann, eds. 1997. *A legnagyobb győzelem: Dokumentumok az 1697 évi török elleni hadjárat és a zentai csata történetéhez*. Pécs and Szigetvár.

Sz. Simon, Éva. 2014. *A hódoltságon kívüli "hódoltság." Oszmán terjeszkedés a Délnyugat-Dunántúlon a 16. század második felében*. Budapest.

Tabakoğlu, Ahmet. 2006. "Osmanlı Devletinin İç Hazinesi." In Genç and Özvar 2006, vol. 1, 51–56.

Takáts, Sándor. 1915–17. *Rajzok a török világból*. 3 vols. Budapest.

———. 1915a. "Magyar és török íródeákok." In Takáts 1915–17, vol. 1, 1–104.

———. 1915b. "A budai basák emlékezete." In Takáts 1915–17, vol. 1, 105–59.

———. 1916. "Kalauzok és kémek a török világban." In Takáts 1915–17, vol. 2, 133–212.

Takáts, Sándor, Ferenc Eckhart, and Gyula Szekfű, eds., 1915. *A budai basák magyar nyelvű levelezése*. Budapest.

Tansel, Selâhattin. 1966. *Sultan II. Bâyezit'in Siyasî Hayatı*. Istanbul.

———. 1969. *Yavuz Sultan Selim*. Ankara.

Tardy, Lajos. 1977. *Rabok, követek, kalmárok az oszmán birodalomról*. Budapest.

———. 1983. *Régi magyar követjárások Keleten*. 2nd ed. Budapest.

———. 1986. "Mohács és a perzsa hadba lépés elmaradása." In Rúzsás and Szakály 1986, 241–74.

Tekgul, Nil. 2016. "Cash Loans to Ottoman Timariots during Military Campaigns (Sixteenth-Seventeenth Centuries)." *Journal of the Economic and Social History of the Orient* 59, 590–617.

Tekin, Şinasi. 1989. "XIV Yüzyılda Yazılmış Gazilik Tarikası: 'Gaziliğin Yolları' Adlı bir Eski Anadolu Türkçesi Metni ve Gaza/Cihad Kavramları Hakkında." *JTS* 13, 139–204.

Tekindağ, Şehabeddin M.C. 1970. "Selimnameler." *TED* 1, 197–230.

Teleki, József. 1852a. *Hunyadiak kora Magyarországon*. vol 1. Pest.

———. 1852b. *Hunyadiak kora Magyarországon*, vol 2. Pest.

———. 1853. *Hunyadiak kora Magyarországon*, vol 3. Pest.

Teply, Karl. 1968. *Kaiserliche Gesandtschaften ans Goldene Horn*. Stuttgart.

Terbe, Lajos. 1936. "Egy európai szállóige életrajza (Magyarország a kereszténység védőbástyája)." *Egyetemes Philológiai Közlöny* 60, 297–350.

Teszelszky, Kees. 2009. *Az ismeretlen korona: Jelentések, szimbólumok és nemzeti identitás*. Pannonhalma.

———. 2014. "Crown and Kingdom in the Republic: The Cultural Construction and Literary Representation of Early Modern Hungary in the Low Countries (1588–1648)." In Kees

Teszelszky, ed., *A Divided Hungary in Europe: Exchange, Networks and Representations, 1541–1699*. Vol. 3, *The Making and Use of the Image of Hungary and Transylvania*. Newcastle upon Tyne, 145–66.

Tezcan, Baki. 2009. "Khotin 1621, or How the Poles Changed the Course of Ottoman History." *AOH* 62, 185–98.

———. 2010. *The Second Ottoman Empire: Political and Social Transformation in the Early Modern World*. Cambridge.

Thackston, W. M. 2012. *Classical Writings of the Medieval Islamic World: Persian Histories of the Mongol Dynasties*. Vol. 2, *Habibu's-Siyar: The History of the Mongols and Genghis Khan*. London.

Thallóczy, Lajos, and Antal Áldásy, eds. 1907. *A Magyarország és Szerbia közti összeköttetések oklevéltára, 1198–1526*. Budapest.

Thallóczy, Lajos, and Sándor Horváth. 1912. *Alsó-Szlavóniai okmánytár. (Dubicza, Orbász és Szana vármegyék) 1244–1710*. Budapest.

———. 1915. *Jajca (bánság, vár és város) története 1450–1527*. Budapest.

Theunissen, Hans. 1998. "Ottoman-Venetian Diplomatics: The 'Ahd-names. The Historical Background and the Development of a Category of Political-Commercial Instruments Together with an Annotated Edition of a Corpus of Relevant Documents." *Electronic Journal of Oriental Studies* 1, 2, 1–698.

Thúry, József. 1893–96. *Török történetírók*. 2 vols. Budapest.

Thys-Şenocak, Lucienne. 2006. *Ottoman Women Builders: The Architectural Patronage of Hadice Turhan Sultan*. Aldershot.

Tomkó, Viktor. 2004. "Török közigazgatás Magyarországon: A szolnoki szandzsákbégek története." *Zounuk* 19, 9–44.

Tormene, Augusto. 1903–4. "Il bailaggio a Costantinopoli di Girolamo Lippomano e la sua tragica fine." *Nuovo Archivio Veneto*, n.s. 3, 6, 375–431; n.s. 4, 7, 66–125, 288–333; n.s. 4, 8, 127–61.

Török, Pál. 1929. "A Habsburgok első sztambuli rezidense. (Malvezzi János Mária)." *Budapesti Szemle* 214, 622, 413–35; 215, 623, 88–104.

———. 1930. *I. Ferdinánd konstantinápolyi béketárgyalásai 1527–1547*. Budapest.

———. 1932. "A török birodalom pénzügyei Szolimán korában." In *Jahrbuch des Wiener Ungarischen Historischen Institutes* 2.

Török, Zsolt Győző. 2004. "Angielini Magyarország-térképe az 1570-es évekből." *CH* 8, 2–9.

———. 2015. "16th Century Fortification Atlases of the Habsburg-Ottoman Border Zone." In Gerhard Holzer, et al., eds., *A World of Innovation Cartography in the Time of Gerhard Mercator*. Newcastle upon Tyne, 63–83.

Tóth, Ferenc, and Balázs Czigány Zágorhidi, eds. 2017. *A szentgotthárdi csata és a vasvári béke/ La bataille de Saint Gotthard et la paix de Vasvár*. Budapest.

Tóth, István György. 1992. *Három ország egy haza*. Budapest.

Tóth, Sándor László. 2000. *A mezőkeresztesi csata és a tizenöt éves háború*. Szeged.

Tóth, Zoltán. 1925. *Mátyás király idegen zsoldossserege (A fekete sereg)*. Budapest.

Tracy, James D. 1996. *Erasmus of the Low Countries*. Berkeley, CA.

———. 2002. *Emperor Charles V, Impresario of War: Campaign Strategy, International Finance, and Domestic Politics*. Cambridge.

———. 2004. "War Finance and Fiscal Devolution in Charles V's Realms." In Wim Blockmans and Nicolette Mount, eds., *The World of Emperor Charles V*. Amsterdam.

———. 2013. "The Road to Szigetvár: Ferdinand's Defense of His Hungarian Frontier, 1548–1564." *Austrian History Yearbook* 44, 17–46.

———. 2015. "The Logic of *Kleinkrieg*: The 'Book of Halil Beg' and Habsburg-Ottoman Diplomacy, 1564–1576." Paper presented at a conference at the Institute für Osteuropäische Geschichte at the University of Vienna in October 2015.

———. 2016. *Balkan Wars: Habsburg Croatia, Ottoman Bosnia, and Venetian Dalmatia, 1499–1617*. Lanham, MD.

———. 2019. "Tokaj, 1565: A Habsburg Prize of War, and an Ottoman *Casus Belli*." In Fodor 2019a, 359–76.

Traljić, Seid M. 1973. "Tursko-Mletačke granice u Dalmaciji u XVI. i XVII. Stoljeću." In *Radovi Instituta JAZU u Zadru*, sv 20. Zagreb, 447–58.

Turan, Osman. 1955. "The Ideal of World Domination among the Medieval Turks." *Studia Islamica* 4, 77–90.

Turan, Şerafettin. 1997. *Kanuni Süleyman Dönemi Taht Kavgaları*. Ankara.

Turetschek, Christine. 1968. *Die Türkenpolitik Ferdinands I. von 1529 bis 1532*. Vienna.

Tursun Beg. 1977. *Târîh-i Ebü'l-Feth*. Edited by A. Mertol Tulum. Istanbul.

———. 1978. *The History of Mehmed the Conqueror*. Translated by Halil İnalcık and Rhoads Murphey. Minneapolis.

Uğur, Ahmet. 1985. *The Reign of Sultan Selim in the Light of the Selimname Literature*. Berlin.

Ünal, Uğur, İskender Türe, and Salim Kaynar, eds. 2017. *Başbakanlık Osmanlı Arşivi Rehberi*. İstanbul.

Ürekli, Muzaffer. 1989. *Kırım Hanlığının Kuruluşu ve Osmanlı Himayesinde Yükselişi*. Ankara.

Ursu, J. 1908. *La Politique Orientale de François 1er (1515–1547)*. Paris.

Uzunçarşılı, İsmail Hakkı. 1940. "Sakarya Nehrinin İzmit Körfezine Akıtılmasıyla Marmara ve Karadenizin Birleştirilmesi Hakkında." *Belleten* 4, 14–15, 149–74.

———. (1943) 1984. *Osmanlı Devleti Teşkilâtından Kapukulu Ocakları*. 2 vols, 2nd ed. Ankara.

———. (1945) 1984. *Osmanlı Develtinin Saray Teşkilâtı*. 2nd ed. Ankara.

———. (1951) 1983. *Osmanlı Tarihi*. Vol. 3, pt 1., 3rd ed. Ankara.

———. 1952. "Barcsay Akos'un Erdel Kırallığına Ait Bazı Orijinal Vesikalar." *TD* 4, 7, 55–59.

———. 1974. *Çandarlı Vezir Ailesi*. Ankara.

Valensi, Lucette. 1993. *The Birth of the Despot: Venice and the Sublime Porte*. Ithaca, NY.

Varga, J. János. 1994. "Ismeretlen adalékok az 1716 évi péterváradi ütközethez." *Századok* 3–4, 634–49.

———. 2007. *Válaszúton: Thököly Imre és Magyarország 1682–1684-ben*. Budapest.

Varga, Szabolcs. 2008. "Az 1527. évi horvát–szlavón kettős 'királyválasztás' története." *Századok* 142, 5, 1075–134.

———. 2013. "Croatia and Slavonia in the Early Modern Age." *Hungarian Studies* 27, 2, 263–76.

———. 2016. *Europe's Leonidas: Miklós Zrínyi, Defender of Szigetvár (1508–1566)*. Translated by David Robert Evans. Budapest.

Vásáry, István, and Lajos Tardy. 1974. "Andrzej Taranowskis Bericht über seine Gesandschaftreise in der Tatarei (1569)." *AOH* 28, 213–52.

Vatin, Nicolas. 1994. *L'Ordre de Saint-Jean-de Jérusalem, l'Empire ottoman et la Méditerranée orientale entre les deux sièges de Rhodes, 1480–1522*. Paris.

———. 1997. *Sultan Djem, Un prince ottoman dans l'Europe du XVe siècle d'après deux sources contemporaines*. Ankara.

———. 2011. "'Comment êtes-vous apparus, toi et ton frère?' Note sur les origines des frères Barberousse." *Studia Islamica* 106, 1, 77–101.

Veinstein, Gilles. 1986. "L'occupation ottoman d'Očakov et le problème de la frontière lituano-tatare 1538–1544." In Chantal Lemercier-Quelquejay, Gilles Veinstein, and S. Enders Wimbush, eds., *Passé turco-tatar, présent soviétique: Études offertes à Alexandre Bennigsen*. Louvain, 123–55.

———. 1990. "Les campagnes navales franco-ottomanes en Méditerranée au xve siècle." In Irad Malkin, ed., *La France et la Méditerranée: Vingt-sept siècles d'interdépendance*. Leiden and New York, 311–34.

———, ed. 1992. *Soliman le Magnifique et son temps*. Paris.

———. 2008. "Les capitulations franco-ottomanes de 1536 sont-elles encore controversables?" In Vera Costantini and Markus Koller, eds., *Living in the Ottoman Ecumenical Community. Essays in Honour of Suraiya Faroqhi*. Leiden and New York, 71–88.

———. 2013. "On the Ottoman Janissaries (Fourteenth-Nineteenth Centuries)." In Erik Jan Zürcher, ed., *A Comparative Study of Military Labour 1500–2000*. Amsterdam, 115–34.

———. 2014. "Retour sur les privilèges des Alamanoğlu: Une lignée juive ottomane à travers les siècles." In Eyal Ginio and Elie Podeh, eds., *The Ottoman Middle East: Studies in Honor of Amnon Cohen*. Leiden and New York, 131–47.

Veszprémy, László. 2001. "Some Remarks on Recent Historiography of the Crusade of Nicopolis (1396)." In Zsolt Hunyadi and József Laszlovszky, eds., *The Crusades and the Military Orders: Expanding the Frontiers of Medieval Latin Christianity*. Budapest, 223–30.

———. 2008. "Zsigmond Galambócnál 1428-ban." *HK* 283–94.

———. 2009. "Szabács ostroma (1475–1476)." *HK* 122, 36–61.

Veszprémy, László, and Béla K. Király, eds. 2003. *A Millennium of Hungarian Military History*. Boulder, CO.

Veszprémy, László, and Orsolya Sasvári, eds., 2011. *The Noon Bell in Hungary and the World*. Budapest.

Visy, Zsolt, ed. 2000. *La campana di mezzogiorno: Saggi per il Quinto Centenario della bolla*. Budapest.

Vlašić, Anđelko. 2015. "Georgius Husztthius, a Traveller from Croatia, and His Account of the Ottoman Naval Campaign in India (1538–1539)." *AOH* 68, 3, 349–62.

Warner, Jayne L. 2001. "Tribute to a Translator." In Jayne L. Warner, ed., *Cultural Horizons: A Festschrift in Honor of Talat S. Halman*. 2 vols. Syracuse, NY, 343–56.

Wawrzyniak, Krzysztof. 2003. *Ottoman-Polish Diplomatic Relations in the Sixteenth Century*. MA thesis, Bilkent University.

Wenzel, Gusztav ed. 1871. *Verancsics Antal m. kir. helytartó, esztergomi érsek összes munkái*, vol. 10. Pest.

Whaley, Joachim. 2012. *Germany and the Holy Roman Empire*. 2 vols. Oxford.

Wheatcroft, Andrew. 2009. *The Enemy at the Gate: Habsburgs, Ottomans and the Battle for Europe*. New York.

White, Sam. 2011. *The Climate of Rebellion in the Early Modern Ottoman Empire*. Cambridge.

Wilson, N. G. 1992. *From Byzantium to Italy: Greek Studies in the Italian Renaissance.* Baltimore.

Winkelbauer, Thomas. 2003. *Ständefreiheit und Fürstenmacht: Länder und Untertanen des Hauses Habsburg im konfessionellen Zeitalter.* 2 vols. Vienna.

———. 2006. "Nervus rerum Austriacarum: Zur Finanzgeschichte der Habsburgermonarchie um 1700." In Maťa and Winkelbauer 2006, 179–215.

Winter, Michael. 1992. *Egyptian Society under Ottoman Rule, 1517–1789.* London.

Wittek, Paul. 1938. *The Rise of the Ottoman Empire.* London.

———. 1955. "Devshirme and Shari'a." *BSOAS* 17, 2, 271–78.

———. 2012. *The Rise of the Ottoman Empire: Studies in the History of Turkey, Thirteenth-Fifteenth Centuries.* Edited by Colin Heywood. London.

Wolf, John B. 1969. "Commentary." In Wright and Paszek 1969, 33–43.

Woodhead, Christine. 2012. *The Ottoman World.* Milton Park.

Woods, John E. (1976) 1999. *The Aqquyunlu: Clan, Confederation, Empire.* Revised ed. Salt Lake City.

Wratislaw, A. H., ed. 1862. *Adventures of Baron Wenceslas Wratislaw of Mitrowitz.* London.

Wright, Monte D., and Lawrence J. Paszek, eds. 1969. *Science, Technology, and Warfare.* Washington, DC.

Yavuz, Hulusi. 1984. *Kabe ve Haremeyn için Yemen'de Osmanlı Hakimiyeti (1517–1571).* Istanbul.

Yekeler, Numan, et al. 2014. *Yoldaki Elçi: Osmanlı'dan Günümüze Türk–Leh İlişkileri.* Istanbul.

Yekeler, Numan, et al. 2016. *Arşiv Belgelerine Göre Osmanlı'dan Günümüze Türk Macar İlişkileri.* Istanbul.

Yılmaz, Fikret. 2018. "Selim'i Yazmak." *OA* 51, 297–390.

Yılmaz, Gülay, 2009. "Becoming a Devshirme: The Training of Conscripted Children in the Ottoman Empire." In Gwyn Campbell, Suzanne Miers, and Joseph C. Miller, eds., *Children in Slavery through the Ages.* Athens, OH, 119–34.

———. 2011. "The Economic and Social Roles of Janissaries in a Seventeenth-Century Ottoman City: The Case of Istanbul." PhD dissertation, McGill University.

Yılmaz, Hüseyin. 2018. *Caliphate Redefined: The Mystical Turn in Ottoman Political Thought.* Princeton, NJ.

Yurdaydın, Hüseyin Gazi. 1950. "Ferdi'nin Süleymannamesi'nin Yeni Bir Nüshasi." *DTCFD* 8, 201–23.

———. 1961. *Kanuni'nin Cülusu ve İlk Seferleri.* Ankara.

Yurdusev, Nuri A. 2004. "The Ottoman Attitude toward Diplomacy." In A. Nuri Yurdusev, ed., *Ottoman Diplomacy: Conventional or Unconventional.* Basingstoke, 5–35.

Zachar József. 2004. *Habsburg-uralom, állandó hadsereg és magyarság: 1683–1792.* Budapest

Zachariadou, Elizabeth A. 1970. "The Conquest of Adrianople by the Turks." *Studi Veneziani* 12, 246–71.

———, ed. 1993a. *The Ottoman Emirate (1300–1389).* Rethymnon.

———. 1993b. "The Emirate of Karasi and That of the Ottomans: Two Rival States." In Zachariadou 1993a, 225–36.

———, ed. 1996. *The Via Egnatia under Ottoman Rule, 1380–1699.* Rethymnon.

———, ed. 1999. *Natural Disasters in the Ottoman Empire.* Rethymnon.

———, ed. 2002. *The Kapudan Pasha: His Office and His Domain.* Rethymnon.

Zahirović, Nedim. 2012. "A Memibégovicsok Magyarországon, Szlavóniában és Horvátország-ban a 17. század első felében." *Korall* 48, 121–32.

Zay, Ferenc. 1980. *Az Lándorfejírvár elveszésének oka e vót, és így esött.* Edited by István Kovács. Budapest.

Ziegler, Karl-Heinz. 2004. "The Peace Treaties of the Ottoman Empire with European Christian Powers." In Randall Lesaffer, ed., *Peace Treaties and International Law in European History: From the Late Middle Ages to World War One.* Cambridge, 338–64.

Zimmermann, T. C. Price. 1995. *Paolo Giovio: The Historian and the Crisis of Sixteenth-Century Italy.* Princeton, NJ.

Zirojević, Olga. 1971. "Smederevski sancak-beg Ali-Beg Mihaloglu." *Zbornik za istoriju Matica Srpska* [Novi Sad], 9–27.

———. 1974. *Tursko vojno uređenje u Srbiji (1459–1683).* Belgrade.

———. 1976. *Carigradski drum od Beograda do Budima u XVI i XVII veku.* Novi Sad.

———. 1987. "Zur historischen Topographie der Heerstrasse nach Konstantinopel zur Zeit der osmanischen Herrschaft." *Etudes Balkaniques* 1, 81–106.

Zombori, István, ed. 2004. *Fight against the Turk in Central-Europe in the First Half of the 16th Century.* Budapest.

Žontar, Josip. 1971. "Michael Černović, Geheimagent Ferdinands I und Maixmilians II, und seine Berichterstattung." *MÖStA* 24, 169–222.

———. 1973. *Obveščevalna služba in diplomacija Avstrijskih Habsburžanov v boju proti Turkom v 16. stoletju.* (Der Kundschafterdienst und die Diplomatie der österreichischen Habsburger in Kampf gegen die Türken im 16. Jahrhundert) Ljubljana.

INDEX

Italic page numbers indicate illustrations.

A NOTE ON THE TYPE

This book has been composed in Arno, an Old-style serif typeface in the classic Venetian tradition, designed by Robert Slimbach at Adobe.